S0-BNI-324

Opening America's Market

BUSINESS, SOCIETY, & THE STATE

William H. Becker, editor

Opening

U.S. FOREIGN TRADE

America's

POLICY SINCE 1776

Market

ALFRED E. ECKES, JR.

THE UNIVERSITY OF

NORTH CAROLINA PRESS

Chapel Hill & London

© 1995 The University of North Carolina Press

All rights reserved

Manufactured in the United States of America

The paper in this book meets the guidelines for permanence and durability of the Committee on Production Guidelines for Book Longevity of the Council on Library Resources.

Library of Congress Cataloging-in-Publication Data

Eckes, Alfred E., 1942–

Opening America's market : U.S. foreign trade policy since 1776 / Alfred E. Eckes, Jr.

   p. cm.

Includes bibliographical references and index.

ISBN 0-8078-2213-2 (alk. paper)

1. United States—Commercial policy.   2. Exports—United States—History.   3. Free trade—United States—History.   4. United States—Commercial policy—Sources.   I. Title.

HF1455.E28   1995

382'.3'0973—dc20   95-2791

                CIP

An abbreviated version of Chapter 4, "Infamous Smoot-Hawley," appears as "Revisiting Smoot-Hawley" in the *Journal of Policy History* 7, no. 3 (Summer 1995).

Chapters 5, 6, and 7 include some material published first in "Trading American Interests," *Foreign Affairs* 71, no. 4 (Fall 1992): 135–54.

99 98 97 96 95   5 4 3 2 1

Contents

382.3
E19
96-0433
31970585

Tables

Illustrations

Congress shall have the power

1. To lay and collect taxes, duties, imposts, and excises . . .

3. To regulate commerce with foreign nations, and among the several

States, and with the Indian tribes. (emphasis added)—U.S. Constitution, art. 1,

sec. 8

Introduction

"We're at war," Deputy Commerce Secretary Clarence J. "Bud" Brown exclaimed as he arrived at the Capitol Hill Club for lunch.

Have the Russians bombed New York? I wondered, or has President Reagan retaliated against Japanese trade barriers?

"At war with whom?" I asked.

"With Congress, of course," Brown responded.

Brown's comment in September 1985 reflected the unique culture of Washington, D.C., where Democrats and Republicans shared the government and battled relentlessly for advantage. With one party entrenched in Congress and the other holding the White House, the real enemy often seemed only sixteen blocks away. Until the bitter 1993 debate over the North American Free Trade Agreement (NAFTA) energized ordinary Americans and fractured the two major political parties, trade struggles usually aroused only Washington insiders—a group largely composed of U.S. officials, foreign representatives, and lobbyists. Many of the lobbyists were former presidential appointees who chose to remain near the center of government power representing business interests, especially foreign corporations eager to share the giant American market. This trade policy elite lived and thrived inside the Washington beltway, distant from the farms, factories, and concerns of average Americans.[1]

Particularly in the half century after World War II pundits, editorial writers, and cartoonists portrayed inside-the-Beltway conflicts over trade policy as battles in the unceasing war between executive branch free traders and congressional protectionists. Executive officials wore white hats and supported deregulating trade, opening markets, acting as responsible creditors, and promoting economic cooperation among nations. With trade liberalization, Americans would benefit as producers, workers, and consumers.[2]

Columnists dismissed congressional opponents as troglodyte protectionists, ignorant of generally accepted economic wisdom. Depicted as wearing black hats, these supposedly parochial politicians responded to special interest appeals from local constituents, greedy labor unions, and declining industries. According to the media, the foes of trade liberalization jeopardized America's role as a world leader when they sought to restrict the president's trade negotiating authority. If Congress, or the president, took action to aid domestic industries, the press gleefully invoked memories of Smoot-Hawley protectionism, the Great Depression, trade wars, and foreign retaliation.[3]

Simplistic images, slogans, and myths—all reflecting unfamiliarity with the factual record—still shape American attitudes toward trade policy. As a historian who left academic research and teaching for more than a decade to work as a journalist and serve as a federal official, I believe it is time for scholars and public officials to revisit the historical documents. They should also examine critically the familiar stereotypes and interpretations in light of facts and consider trade policy issues in a more robust manner.

This book has four specific goals. The first is to offer an introduction to, and an interpretation of, some two centuries of American trade policy. While preparing for congressional hearings in 1981, I could find no extensive scholarly study of U.S. commercial policy based on substantial research in archival sources. This book may serve the informational needs of future government officials, opinion makers, scholars, and other interested persons.

My second related goal involves encouraging government officials to examine issues in a historical perspective, paying greater attention to archival records and to the writings of scholars. Policymakers also may find the present discussion a useful supplement to the limited institutional memory available in most government agencies. While serving as a trade decision maker, I was shocked to find that U.S. officials had little information about the origin and evolution of present policies and about the results of previous negotiations. This absence of historical memory is a distinct disadvantage in international negotiations, when frequently inexperienced U.S. officials match wits with adversaries having years of relevant experience.

While researching these issues, I discovered archival evidence and data that compelled me to reconsider key elements of the conventional trade wisdom. Thus a third objective is to correct the public record, and to question several popular myths that continue to influence thinking about international trade policy. My conclusions may spark debate and force public officials and scholars to revisit the empirical record.

Finally, this volume emphasizes, as only the study of history can, how knowledge of the past relates to present and future governance in an area of immense importance to the United States and its people. In a technology-driven world economy without national borders, residents of North America now compete for economic opportunities and jobs with the residents of developing countries around the world. For many professionals and skilled workers economic interdependence has produced new prospects; but especially for the unskilled, more dislocations, anxieties, and alienation.

My own involvement with these issues began in July 1981, when President Ronald Reagan honored me with a nine-year appointment to the U.S. International Trade Commission (ITC), the independent, quasi-judicial, and fact-finding agency responsible for assessing the impact of imports on domestic industries. A few months later, after the Senate confirmed my nomination, this former history professor and editorial page editor became a decision maker in some of the most contentious trade remedy complaints of the 1980s, cases involving many of America's traditional industries and high technology as well. Thousands of American jobs and hundreds of plants hinged on these administrative decisions. Members of Congress, foreign embassies, and lobbyists quickly discovered that the ITC, a once invisible government agency, had become a major player in the trade process.

From the daily battles over trade administration, I rediscovered the abiding wisdom of cowboy comedian Will Rogers. He compared tariff battles to arguments over religion. "[T]wenty men can enter a room as friends," Rogers said, "and someone can bring up the Tariff and you will find nineteen bodies on the floor with only one living that escaped."[4]

During my nine years as a trade fact finder and administrator from 1981 to 1990, emotions still ran strong. One angry shoemaker, dissatisfied with a decision rejecting footwear import relief, bought space in the *Washington Post* to tell Congress and the president "what stupid commissioners they have." He said that the U.S. International Trade Commission was "as useful as a pitcher of warm 'spit.'" Seymour Fabrick advised President Reagan to "get rid" of the commissioners and "give them an opportunity to go out in the job market and find some jobs for themselves."[5]

The 1980s were exciting years to serve on the ITC. Measured in terms of caseload, it was the busiest decade in the commission's history. One cold morning in January 1982 a rental truck pulled up to the docket room at the old Tariff Commission building, at 701 E Street N.W., and domestic steel producers filed ninety-four separate antidumping and countervailing duty cases against European steelmakers. The trade petition deluge had begun. Indeed, over the course of the decade I participated in hundreds of separate steel investigations as the domestic industry utilized provisions of the 1979 trade law to battle injurious imports.

Other industries joined the fray. Over the nine-year period I participated in about 1,500 separate investigations. These ranged from commodities, like pork, tobacco, and potatoes, to leading edge technologies. Machines tools, sparklers, shoes, apparel, and many other familiar items appeared on our agenda. So did brain scanners, cellular telephones, and pharmaceutical products. Even novelty items like Rubik's cubes and Pac-man video games came to the ITC for trade decisions. Moreover, the president and our congressional oversight committees requested dozens of fact-finding studies assessing changing circumstances of competition.

On the commission my voting record fit neither the free trade nor the protectionist pattern. In assessing the determinations of ITC commissioners on antidumping and countervailing duty cases, University of Wisconsin economist Robert E. Baldwin and his colleague Jeffrey W. Steagall placed me among a middle group of commissioners who voted affirmatively between 50 and 80 percent of the time. Other commissioners in this group were Democrats Paula Stern, David Rohr, and Donald Newquist; Republican Seeley Lodwick; and independent Michael Calhoun. *New York Times* reporter Clyde Farnsworth correctly concluded that my "views on trade are not easy to characterize": "clearly they do not fit into the mold of either a strict free-trader or a protectionist."[6]

Service on the ITC afforded a unique opportunity to study changing competitive conditions in America and to examine the evolving international economy. Hearings provided a window to shifting business trends and to the working conditions of average citizens. Powerful lawyers, chief executive officers, and congressmen came to testify—as did representatives of the working people and consumers. Steel workers, shoemakers, potato farmers, copper miners, and fishery workers all appeared. Many retained the assistance of high-priced Washington lawyers, most of whom previously had served in the executive branch or gained public sector experience advising key members of Congress.

During my government years, I viewed trade battles from the front lines and encountered on a daily basis the nasty dilemmas easily ignored in classroom discussions. At ITC import-remedy hearings, the victims of expanded trade had an opportunity to present their perspective. Many could demonstrate that soaring imports from cheap-labor countries had cost them high-paying factory jobs. They often testified that employers had shut domestic plants and moved capital equipment to new manufacturing facilities abroad in cheap-labor countries. On other occasions, the case record showed that foreign governments subsidized exports, or that powerful corporations headquartered in countries with protected home markets engaged in discriminatory pricing to seize market share from American competitors.

Witnesses at ITC hearings frequently presented poignant descriptions of import competition that seemed to conflict with neoclassical international trade theories found in many textbooks. Those discussions assumed away market anomalies and political barriers. Workers dislocated when imports surged rapidly found new high-paying employment or received compensation. Money moved easily within nations but not between nations, and so direct investment flows seldom swamped the gains from trade. With open markets and perfect competition, textbook writers claimed that arbitrage erased incentives to indulge in international price discrimination.[7]

During the 1980s the theories often proved inadequate for understanding policy problems, like the persistent merchandise trade deficit with Japan and the general surge in imported finished goods. Academic economists advanced a variety of fascinating explanations. Some attributed rising imports to a strong dollar. Others claimed that Americans saved too little and borrowed too much and introduced equations with accounting identities as proof. The real world was more complex than these mechanistic theories. When the U.S. government embarked on a program of exchange depreciation in 1985, the bilateral imbalance with Japan showed little improvement. Many other factors—including supply-and-demand conditions in both the exporting and importing countries for a full range of trade products—influenced merchandise trade balances, not simply the price of the dollar.[8]

To one trained in history, fashionable theories did not adequately explain developments in the marketplace or permit policymakers to anticipate future developments with confidence. Joseph Schumpeter, the prominent Austrian-born economist of the early twentieth-century, appreciated this problem: "Nobody can hope to understand the economic phenomena of any, including the present, epoch who has not an adequate command of historical *facts* and an adequate amount of historical *sense* or of what may be described as *historical experience*."[9]

To understand America's trade problems, I searched the archives of trade negotiations over the last two generations. The National Archives has primary sources and documents about all of the bilateral negotiations conducted under the Reciprocal Trade Agreements Program (RTAP), as well as ample material on developments in the General Agreement on Tariffs and Trade (GATT). For documents about trade policy and negotiations over the period since 1960, presidential libraries proved indispensable. These facilities, dispersed around the country, hold the official files of every administration since President Herbert Hoover. For the perspectives of important trading partners and allies in post–World War II efforts to reconstruct the world economy, I consulted documents in the British Public Record Office and the National Archives of Canada.

Among government officials my preoccupation with trade history was perhaps unique. Most trade policymakers have academic training in economics or law. Many on the federal fast track, leading to service on congressional committees and presidential appointments, acquired their first exposure to trade policy in the State Department where the diplomatic perspective predominates. Few had business experience outside a law firm.

In Washington I discovered that officials seldom have the time or the desire to study extensively the background of contemporary problems. Like Henry Ford, the early twentieth-century automaker, most officials behave as if they believe history is bunk. Immersed in the government process, they frequently approach problems with little specific knowledge of how the concern emerged, or how previous decision makers attempted to address similar issues. Instead, those trained in economics bring classroom theories and stereotypes to policy discussions. Those schooled in the law frequently emphasize narrow legal considerations. When asked to discuss the evolution of a problem, both groups blithely recycle the conventional wisdom.[10]

Other countries have more respect for history. Our principal economic competitors carefully review the records of prior negotiations and have a cadre of experienced negotiators with several generations of institutional memory. As a result, they frequently seem to exploit that advantage successfully in trade negotiations. During the bilateral free trade negotiations with Canada in 1986 and 1987, for instance, Canada fielded a team of veteran negotiators, led by Simon Reisman, who had negotiated the 1964 automobile pact. Not only did they have more experience than the Americans, but also the Canadians had a long institutional memory. They knew how specific commodity problems addressed in the free trade talks had been resolved in previous negotiations, particularly the unsuccessful attempt to negotiate a similar agreement in 1947–48. The American negotiators lacked a specific knowledge of this agreement or the one proposed in 1911.[11] Oblivious to historical precedents, bright young U.S. officials rely on energy and intelligence in negotiations. Not surprisingly, they sometimes end up reinventing the wheel. Former Commerce Department official Clyde Prestowitz has observed that American officials are sometimes so blind to prior events that they purchase the same horse from experienced Japanese negotiators![12]

My historical fact-finding journey, conducted over a ten-year period, resulted in this book. Overall, it is my conclusion that too often myths, and not facts, shape public discussion of commercial policy issues. For one thing, many citizens, and some public officials, believe that America rose to world economic and political leadership on the strength of its commitment to free trade policies. That familiar interpretation is incompatible with the factual record. Before the New Deal the United States prospered behind high protective tariffs and used a variety of import restrictions to shelter home market producers from competition, much the way Asian countries have done successfully since World War II.

Nonetheless, among U.S. policymakers there is a pervasive belief that "concrete historical comparisons" demonstrate the superiority of free trade to protectionism. Indeed, in 1985 the Council of Economic Advisers asserted: "The conclusions . . . from *such comparisons over the past two centuries are unambiguous*: Countries that have followed the least restrictive economic policies both at home and abroad have experienced the most rapid economic growth and have enabled the greatest proportions of their populations to rise above subsistence living standards" (emphasis added). During the Reagan administration, Under Secretary of State W. Allan Wallis, an economist, inveighed against the protectionist "fallacies." Wallis declared: "Prosperity and protection are inconsistent. . . . Prosperity is our goal; but, . . . protection is its enemy."[13]

Historical research indicates that easy generalizations do not capture the American experience. In the late nineteenth century, for example, a protectionist America and a protectionist Germany both outperformed free trade Britain. The relationship between trade policy and economic growth is thus more complex than many theorists and politicians assume. Free trade does not assure prosperity, nor does protectionism automatically produce ruin.[14]

My research does not dispute the essential elements of classical free trade theory rooted in deductive reasoning. That theory, explaining the basis for trade in terms of differences in comparative costs, is valid economically *if* certain conditions exist. For one thing, within participating nations there is internal factor mobility, perfect competition, and full employment, as well as markets that respond rationally to pecuniary signals. Also, capital and labor do *not* move easily between nations. Under such restricted conditions, free trade does maximize welfare and income—benefiting both *individuals* and *mankind*.

To explain why production costs vary among nations, two Swedish economists—Eli Hecksher and Bertil Ohlin—focused on differences in factor endowments. Nations tend to export goods making intensive use of the most abundant factors of production and to import items making intensive use of less abundant factors. A version of this model suggests why populous developing countries export goods intensive in unskilled labor, whereas advanced industrial countries export products intensive in skilled labor. Because the Hecksher-Ohlin theory concludes that free trade tends to equalize factor costs, some economists predict that globalization will narrow the gap between U.S. and foreign wages. It also may widen the gap between the wages of skilled and unskilled workers within the United States.[15]

It is important to note that free trade theory focuses on benefits to individuals and to world welfare, not to nations. Even if all the theoretical conditions prevail, nineteenth-century economists pointed out, individual *nations* may still lose. It is possible for free trade to maximize the wealth of individuals and the global community while it destroys the nation and its social stability.[16] According to John Maynard Keynes, doctrinaire free traders "overvalued the social advantage of mere market cheapness." Conceding that "protection is a dangerous and expensive method" for achieving national economic balance and security, the renown economist concluded: "there are times when we cannot safely trust ourselves to the blindness of economic forces; and when no alternative weapon as efficacious as tariffs lies ready to our hand."[17]

Since World War II economists have become more sensitive to the shortcomings of classical free trade theory for explaining actual trade patterns. John Dunning, a specialist on transnational corporations, has observed that only a minority of world trade involves arms-length transactions between buyers and sellers. The majority is intrafirm trade among units of transnational corporations. Nineteenth-century free traders simply did not contemplate a world economy in which giant corporations engaged in transfer pricing. Nor did they foresee the mobility of capital.[18]

As Chapter 1 makes clear, America's founding generation—particularly Thomas Jefferson and James Madison—did understand and draw inspiration from laissez-faire economics. The rationale for free trade had intellectual appeal. But this first generation of leaders pragmatically adopted policies that assigned priority to the nation's economic security and long-term welfare, not the immediate pecuniary interests of consumers. Chapters 2 and 3 consider protectionism and reciprocity, the principal legs of American trade policy during the seventy-year period from the Civil War to the Great Depression.

Chapter 4 questions another familiar legend, the "notorious Smoot-Hawley" Tariff of 1930. According to the popular wisdom recycled in high school and college textbooks, this act raised duties to record levels, worsened the depression, provoked extensive foreign retaliation, and destroyed world trade. However, official data and archival materials from the United States, Canada, and Great Britain, as well as the related research of other economic historians, led me to less catastrophic conclusions. Smoot-Hawley was a molehill, not a mountain. Partisans and ideologues have long exaggerated its consequences.

My investigation of the post–World War II trade record also produced unorthodox conclusions. As American leaders pursued their grand bipartisan vision for an open international economy, as part of the successful strategy for winning the Cold War, they assigned little weight to the concerns of domestic producers and workers. During the Cold War years the United States treated trade policy as an instrument of foreign policy for fulfilling hegemonic responsibilities, not as an end in itself. Time after time, U.S. diplomats and negotiators promoted trade liberalization in order to advance other immediate, albeit worthy, foreign policy objectives—stability and prosperity in Japan and Western Europe, economic opportunities for developing nations. While the United States pursued such systemic objectives, and vowed to maintain harmony and international cooperation at all costs, pragmatic adversaries, like the French, Japanese, Canadians, and British, pressed their own business interests. As a result, they gained access to the large North American trading market, while amiable U.S. leaders and strategists acquiesced to discrimination against American exports. The United States thus stripped away its tariff barriers, lowering rates on dutiable imports from some 45 percent ad valorem average in 1934 to about 3.5 percent today. Meanwhile, it allowed emerging competitors to waive parallel obligations and to maintain restrictive trade barriers, sheltering their national markets and corporate champions from U.S. competition. The United States and its allies did win a great power struggle with the Soviet Union and establish a more open international economy, but in the process America lost critical commercial battles. This theme—how U.S. officials unilaterally opened the American market without gaining commensurate advantages in foreign markets for the products of American workers and American factories—is developed in Chapters 5 and 6.

Many economic theorists note that the advantages of free trade are so overwhelming that those who gain from trade can easily compensate those temporarily dislocated from import concessions. Chapter 7 shows that shock absorbers—like the escape clause and adjustment assistance—were largely window dressing. The Cold War internationalists generally failed to aid those domestic interests harmed by trade liberalization. Often, as the case record discloses, trade administrators set aside legal obligations to trade losers in order to pursue military and international political objectives considered of greater national importance at that time.

A similar pattern applied to the administration of "unfair trade" laws, as Chapter 8 demonstrates. Because dumping and export subsidies produce distortions in the marketplace, the General Agreement on Tariffs and Trade authorizes use of antidumping and countervailing duties when such anticompetitive behavior proves injurious to import-competing industries. Until the 1970s, however, U.S. officials frequently took advantage of executive discretion to avoid enforcing such laws when trade remedies conflicted with other foreign policy objectives. For instance, predatory competitors destroyed the domestic television industry when the U.S. Treasury failed to assess and collect antidumping duties. Many other domestic industries also found officials reluctant to perform their statutory duties.

This book rests on extensive research in documentary sources and secondary materials over a ten-year period. It also has benefited from my first-hand experiences in government. In particular, Chairman Russell Long and his colleagues on the Senate Finance Committee, including the late H. J. Heinz III, first alerted me to the trade-off between foreign policy and trade policy. At my confirmation hearings in 1981, Long observed that some officials in the State Department believed that "it would be worth practically any price if we could achieve peace in the world by simply making trade concessions."[19]

Obviously, I did not write this account to engage in partisan debate, to pursue an ideological agenda, or to settle personal differences, as some memoirists may do. Indeed, I have avoided extensive comment on many individuals and developments during the 1980s until passions have cooled and more abundant documentation becomes available to supplement my own memory and records. Careful readers will note other omissions. The work does not attempt to deal systematically with bilateral trade relations with major trading partners, such as Canada, Japan, and the European Economic Community (EEC), or with East-West issues. Nor does it deal systematically with the General Agreement on Tariffs and Trade and the multilateral trade negotiating process. Moreover, the book focuses on trade in goods and avoids important international trade issues involving investments, intellectual property, and services among others. I hope to address these complex themes in a subsequent volume.

In offering a revisionist interpretation of American trade policy, I do not wish to impugn the reputations of individual officials, the vast majority of whom have worked diligently to promote the national interest. In most cases, U.S. officials have faithfully followed the policy guidance of superiors and operated within legal and political constraints. At the negotiating table trade officials, especially in recent decades, have pressed vigorously for concessions benefiting American businesses and consumers. However, as this account shows, diplomatic priorities drove American trade policy by 1938. Time after time during the Cold War years, when policymakers confronted a conflict between foreign policy and domestic interests, the diplomatic imperative prevailed.

Other disclaimers seem appropriate. I did not write this book to espouse an ideology—such as free trade or protectionism—or to proselytize. Readers also should resist any temptation to impute specific policy prescriptions from this account. An historical work can illuminate the past and help the present generation understand the development of current policies. But history cannot offer policymakers a specific road map to the future. In a decision-making context, officials often encounter unforeseen legal, political, and policy constraints.

The assessments offered in this book reflect my own thinking, and I take responsibility for any errors. A number of government officials, academic colleagues, and business professionals have supplied information and offered helpful suggestions. In particular, I want to thank Susan Aaronson, Italo Ablondi, Fred Beavers, Catherine May Bedell, Donald Bedell, Seth Bodner, Pat Choate, Bruce Clubb, Tom DeLoach, Charles Ervin, Frank Fenton, Lynn Featherstone, Bill Fry, John Gaddis, Bill Gearhart, Veronica Haggart, Alonzo Hamby, Bill Hawkins, Kent Hughes, Jeffrey Lang, Thea Lee, Bill Leonard, Seeley Lodwick, James McClure, Richard McCormack, Diane Manifold, Jock Nash, Stanley Nehmer, Don Newquist, Joan Reed, Bill Reinsch, David Rohr, Eugene Rosengarden, Lyn Schlitt, Michael Stein, Eugene Stewart, Alan Tonelson, Richard Vedder, and Thomas Zeiler. Sheppard Black and Lars Lutton of Alden Library, Ohio University, helped with editorial cartoons from *Judge*. The courteous and helpful staff of the U.S. International Trade Commission libraries—the National Library of International Trade and the General Counsel's Law Library—rendered invaluable assistance. So did archivists and librarians at the many depositories cited in the Bibliography.

Here at Ohio University, graduate students David Broscious and Doug Dziak assisted in preparing the manuscript for publication. Finally, I wish to thank all associated with the University of North Carolina Press, particularly executive editor Lewis Bateman and copyeditor Stevie Champion.

[C]ommerce is the grand panacea, which, like a beneficent medical discovery,

will serve to inoculate with the healthy and saving taste for civilization all the

nations of the world. (emphasis added)—Richard Cobden, 1835

By adopting "free trade," we give our markets and our money to foreigners; by

adhering to protection, we secure both to our own people . . . the fate of the

country depends on the result.—Representative Andrew Stewart, 1846

Free Trade and Economic Security, 1776–1860

From colonial times the "Spirit of Commerce" has inspired and shaped America's relations with the world. During the eighteenth and nineteenth centuries the founders of U.S. foreign policy pressed to open markets ("freedom to trade") and attacked mercantilistic barriers abroad in order to bolster the domestic economy and secure independence. Access to European markets for American ships and commodities, like cotton, rice, and tobacco, they considered essential to the nation's long-term prosperity and growth.[1]

While actively seeking foreign trade opportunities, the first generation of American leaders championed a set of universal principles that would become the "foundation" for American commercial policy. These included *free trade*, *equality* (either national or most-favored-nation treatment), and *reciprocity*. But the European mercantilists—especially Britain and France—repeatedly ignored American diplomatic appeals, restricted and managed trade, impressed ships and sailors, and engaged in predatory pricing to disrupt infant industries after the War of 1812.[2]

As a result, the founders reluctantly acquiesced to elements of mercantilism. Recognizing, as Adam Smith had, that "defense . . . is of much more importance than opulence," they experimented with retaliation and then adopted a policy of economic nationalism.[3] To compel respect for commercial rights, they concluded that the U.S. government must demonstrate its resolve and capacity to *retaliate* unilaterally against foreign restrictions. As a long-run strategy to *protect the national economic security*, they embraced interventionist measures similar to those of European competitors. To avoid future economic dislocations and jeopardy to American independence and living standards, early leaders—both Federalists and Jeffersonian Republicans—deliberately used the powers of government to encourage domestic manufactures. Thus industrial policy became a critical element of the nation's economic strategy. In particular, they regarded tariffs not only as effective instruments for raising government revenue but also as powerful tools for fashioning a diversified manufacturing base. In their paradigm, the so-called American system, the interests of domestic producers and workers took priority over short-term consumer interests. These policies, adopted after the War of 1812, would endure with only brief interruption for the next 120 years.

Free Trade Vision

A vision of open markets, freer trade, and economic interdependence inspired the first generation of American leaders, as it would leaders after World War II. This enthusiasm for free trade preceded publication of Adam Smith's *Wealth of Nations* on March 9, 1776. In an essay published two years earlier, colonial merchant Benjamin Franklin argued that commerce should be "as free between all the nations of the world, as it is between the several counties of England." He added: "No nation was ever ruined by trade, even, seemingly the most disadvantageous."[4]

Franklin was an ardent free trader. Others like Tom Paine and Thomas Jefferson used the slogan more loosely as an abbreviated version of "freedom to trade." They opposed mercantile restrictions and favored nondiscriminatory commercial regulations. In his January 1776 pamphlet *Common Sense*, Paine apparently took that approach: "Our plan is commerce, and that, well attended to, will secure us the peace and friendship of all Europe; because it is in the interest of all Europe to have America a free port. Her trade will always be a protection, and her barrenness of gold and silver secure her from invaders."[5]

Jefferson, a thirty-one-year-old lawyer-philosopher, boldly asserted that "free trade with all parts of the world" was a "natural right" that no law could abridge. His claim, appearing in a 1774 summary memorandum on the rights of British North America, reflected colonial dissatisfaction with British mercantile restrictions. In subsequent comments, Jefferson continued to embrace free trade in the context of his agrarian worldview. In *Notes on Virginia*, published in 1785, the author of the Declaration of Independence recommended that the independent American states specialize in agriculture and rely on Europe for manufactures. "It is better," he said, "to carry provisions and materials to workmen there, than bring them to the provisions and materials, and with them their manners and principles." Added Jefferson: "The loss by the transportation of commodities across the Atlantic will be made up in happiness and permanence of government. The mobs of great cities add just so much to the support of pure government, as sores do to the strength of the human body." In July 1785 correspondence with his Massachusetts friend, John Adams, the Virginian effused: "I think all the world would gain by setting commerce at perfect liberty."[6]

As Jefferson matured and gained experience in public service, his thinking on commercial issues became less doctrinaire. Although favoring free trade in principle, he understood that the desire for commercial interdependence with Europe might conflict with aspirations for political independence. In August 1785 he warned: "Our commerce on the ocean and in other countries must be paid for by frequent war." Privately, Jefferson preferred for the United States to "practice neither commerce nor navigation, but to stand with respect to Europe precisely on the footing of China. We should thus avoid wars, and all our citizens would be husbandmen." As a public official, he understood that he was not at liberty to pursue his hermit republic theories. Instead, he was "duty bound" to implement market-opening policies—"throwing open all the doors of commerce and knocking off it's shackles."[7]

Adams, too, held private reservations about the American enthusiasm for trade, even as this Massachusetts politician prudently spoke up for the "freedom to trade." In April 1777 he said: "I am against all shackles upon Trade. Let the Spirit of the People have its own way." However, his papers show that privately he had serious misgivings. In one April 1776 letter he criticized "the Spirit of Commerce . . . which even insinuates itself into Families, and influences holy Matrimony, and thereby corrupts the Morals of families as well as destroys their Happiness."[8]

On a practical level, Adams perceived that giving "liberty to trade" would lead to the seizure of American vessels and seamen. In October 1775 he asked rhetorically: "Can the inhabitants of North America *live* without foreign trade?" He answered the question affirmatively, suggesting that Americans might sacrifice "some of our appetites [for] coffee, wine, punch, sugar, molasses, . . . silks and velvets . . ." (and other imports). "But these are trifles," he said, "in a contest for liberty."[9] Despite his personal misgivings, Adams, like

Jefferson, supported trade liberalization. He fully understood how much New England merchants wanted to eliminate British mercantile restraints on colonial trade.

More than pecuniary interests stirred American enthusiasm for freer trade. The ideology of commerce and open markets had roots in Enlightenment thought. Among intellectuals in France and Great Britain there was growing support for an alternative to mercantilism, one based on laissez-faire government, individualism, reason, and economic internationalism. French physiocrats, for instance, believed that "all political problems would be solved if the right economic principles were followed, the right economic measures adopted." Montesquieu, the eighteenth-century French philosopher and jurist, held that "commerce cures destructive prejudices" and leads to peace. "The spirit of commerce unites nations," he said.[10]

In Britain, too, the ideology of commerce had influential friends in Parliament and among intellectuals. In 1773, according to Thomas Boswell, Samuel Johnson said that "the great increase of commerce and manufactures hurts the military spirit of a people; because it produces a competition for something else than martial honors—a competition for riches." English economists, especially David Hume and Adam Smith, shaped and benefited from American thinking. Their analysis helped transform antimercantilism into the positive cosmopolitical vision of free trade benefiting humanity. Indeed, many early American leaders, including Thomas Jefferson, James Madison, and diplomat Arthur Lee, were familiar with Scottish economist Adam Smith's powerful theoretical rationale for free trade presented in the *Wealth of Nations*. They found his reasoning impeccable, convenient, and compatible with their own instincts and desires.[11]

Smith gave the American colonists additional intellectual ammunition to oppose mercantilism. As embodied in the restrictive Navigation Acts, British mercantilism rested on the belief that the central government in London could manage trade successfully to augment national power and acquire wealth. Adam Smith observed that the mercantile system sought to enrich British producers and workers with an advantageous trade balance. But the mercantile system also depressed the manufactures of neighboring countries and discouraged colonial production. Smith said that "the interest of the consumer is almost constantly sacrificed to that of the producer."[12]

The Quest for Equality and Reciprocity

In July 1776, after declaring independence, the Continental Congress prepared to launch a trade initiative with long-term ramifications. Eager to obtain foreign diplomatic recognition and break the British stranglehold on Atlantic commerce, the Americans prepared to offer the only meaningful lure available: access to the U.S. market. They wanted free trade, meaning a freedom to trade on equal terms with other nations. They also sought reciprocal access to foreign markets.

With assistance from Benjamin Franklin and others, John Adams drafted a model plan for commercial treaties to guide U.S. negotiators; the Continental Congress approved it with only minor changes in September. As adopted, the treaty plan proposed two options: *reciprocal national treatment* in commercial matters or *unconditional most-favored-nation policy*. The first, and preferred, provision called for complete equality of treatment with foreign country nationals. In a strict sense, it was not a a call for bilateral free trade, as eighteenth-century governments still depended on tariff revenues to finance government expenditures. In a different sense, however, it would give the subjects of each country far more benefits than a narrow free trade agreement to remove customs duties would confer. Draft article 1 proposed that the subjects of either country pay only duties or imposts imposed on natives and "enjoy all other . . . rights[,] liberties, privileges, immunities and exemptions in trade, navigation and commerce" that natives or their companies enjoyed. If implemented as drafted, this would have opened European colonies to American commerce.[13]

The most-favored-nation alternative sought a different objective: nondiscriminatory trade conditions equal to those accorded most favored third parties. Because nothing was said about conditionality, it must be presumed that the drafters either envisaged unconditional most-favored-nation treatment, the prevailing practice in Europe at that time, or had not addressed the issue.

In retrospect, it appears that U.S. policymakers wanted assured access to European and colonial markets and proposed to yield European manufacturers unimpeded access to the American market in return. However, neither condition was essential to concluding a commercial agreement. Accompanying instructions told U.S. representatives to insist only on obtaining French aid to nullify the British Navigation Acts and protect American shipping.[14]

Although the treaty plan of 1776 had proposed a commitment to equality, the Franco-American Treaty of Amity and Commerce of February 1778, which was the first trade treaty actually negotiated, did not satisfy that objective. It failed to obtain either *equality* (national treatment) or *unconditional* most-favored-nation treatment, generalizing the mutual concessions to other parties. Indeed, the Treaty of Amity and Commerce contained only a *conditional* most-favored-nation clause that gave each party the right to purchase concessions provided to third countries.

Because Europeans had previously employed only the unconditional clause, this first attempt to limit the benefits of most-favored-nation treatment invites questions. Why did the parties choose to restrict the value of their concessions? Why did they insist on compensation for extending such concessions to third parties? Vernon Setser has argued that French negotiators inserted the conditional phrasing hoping to demonstrate to suspicious Europeans that French assistance to the American Revolution was disinterested.[15] The French were prepared to purchase any concessions that an independent America might later extend to third parties with equivalent compensation. I find this explanation overly altruistic and perhaps incomplete. From available records, it is apparent that French officials worried about a possible reconciliation with England, while some Americans desired to dilute and restrict British commercial influence after the conflict. Thus neither France nor America desired to confer gratuitous benefits on Britain from this bargain.

In particular, the Americans wanted Britain and other Europeans to buy access to the American market with reciprocal trading privileges in Europe and their American colonies. Thus Benjamin Franklin and his colleagues had instructions to negotiate a series of separate trade agreements. Yielding unconditional most-favored-nation treatment for the sake of consistency with abstract principles and traditions would have dissipated America's bargaining chips without gaining assured reciprocal access to European markets. Interestingly, France soon reverted, in 1783, to the unconditional most-favored-nation approach, but the United States consistently practiced the conditional form until 1923, when changed circumstances appeared to warrant a policy shift. Another feature of the 1778 Franco-American Treaty of Amity and Commerce also shaped future U.S. commercial policy. The preamble, Secretary of State John Quincy Adams asserted, was "the foundation of our commercial intercourse with the rest of mankind." He claimed that the preamble "should be the political manual for every negotiator of the United States, in every quarter of the globe." It placed "the true principles of all fair commercial negotiation between independent states" on the "diplomatic record of nations" for the first time. That preamble announced the agreement's purpose as being "the most perfect equality and reciprocity."[16]

Despite the joint statement of lofty principles, the agreement failed to achieve "perfect equality and reciprocity." It contained some anomalies. For instance, although the United States provided most-favored-nation treatment to France in all of its ports, France confined such treatment to Europe, thus restricting access to the French colonies. As a matter of practice, whereas American ports were open to French commerce and navigation, French ports sometimes discriminated against U.S. ships. In Bordeaux, American traders complained about paying higher than most-favored-nation rates on salt. French merchants sought to limit American imports and to preserve their trade monopoly with the West Indies. During the 1780s the Marquis de LaFayette lobbied the French government to remove mercantile restrictions and promote better access. And French foreign minister Vergennes assured Franklin that the United States "shall constantly experience a perfect reciprocity in France."[17]

Jefferson, while serving as minister to France, grew frustrated with difficulties in implementing the commercial treaty and diversifying commerce away from Britain. In April 1788 Foreign Affairs Secretary John Jay wrote Jefferson: "It is to be regretted that the mercantile people in France oppose a system, which, certainly, is calculated to bind the two nations together, and from which both would eventually derive commercial as well as political advantages." Another part of the problem lay in America, where the thirteen states pursued separate and discriminatory policies to raise revenues and protect local manufactures without regard for treaty obligations. Favoring a stronger central government with Congress having the authority to regulate commerce, Jefferson and his colleague John Adams in London anticipated the day when a national government could use the weapon of trade to influence the European balance of power.[18]

American diplomats had hoped to negotiate similar commercial agreements with other European countries based on the 1776 plan, but they found little interest. Consequently, the 1776 trade initiative failed to revolutionize the way European nations conducted commercial relations. The Netherlands and Sweden did sign agreements similar to the U.S. treaty with France, but only the Netherlands yielded most-favored-nation access to overseas colonies.[19] An ally of France, Spain dallied; it was not eager to encourage revolutionaries openly and determined not to admit them to colonial markets.

As the mother country and the principal trading partner, Great Britain retained a strong hand. The Americans might win independence, but they needed British markets, goods, and credit. Thus in the peace negotiations, although Britain flirted with bilateral free trade, national treatment, and reciprocity, it eventually opted to avoid any trade agreement. Although elements in the British government were sympathetic to free trade theories, Lord Sheffield rallied the opposition with a tract opposing any commercial treaty. None was necessary, he claimed, because Britain could buy American products from other sources, and the superiority of British manufactures assured their access to American markets. An embittered King George III also opposed a commercial agreement, and powerful merchants counseled restraint, believing that the prospect of a trade agreement might encourage the Americans to pay commercial debts. During the Confederation period American diplomats launched a second campaign to conclude commercial treaties. In 1784 envoys were instructed to propose treaties based on "the most perfect equality and reciprocity" and compatible with existing agreements. The last phrase indicated that diplomats were to offer conditional most-favored-nation treatment. Once again the envoys sought to exchange access to the U.S. market for equal access to European markets and in the process gain an important political plumb: diplomatic recognition of the new American nation.[20]

The American envoys had little success, however. They entered negotiations with Denmark, Portugal, Naples, Tuscany, and Prussia, as well as Britain and Spain. An agreement concluded with Prussia in 1785 resembled the 1778 French treaty. The preamble espoused the twin principles of equality and reciprocity, but the United States gained only conditional most-favored-nation treatment. One of the problems with the American campaign for most-favored-nation treatment was that no country enjoyed preferential treatment in the American market. Therefore, whereas Denmark could expect few immediate export gains from signing a reciprocity agreement with America, some feared that the Americans might use the agreement to gain nondiscriminatory access to the benefits of Denmark's existing trade agreements.[21]

Given the lack of trade organization in the United States, and the inattention to problems of actually administering the treaty structure, some American officials like John Jay and Elbridge Gerry also considered the quest for commercial treaties unrealistic. After reviewing the draft agreement with Prussia in May 1785, Jay, the Confederation's secretary of foreign affairs, wrote the American negotiators "that, in his opinion, a system for regulating the trade of the United States should be formed and adopted before they enter into further treaties of commerce." Jay thought that "such treaties should be accommodated to their system, than that their system should be accommodated to such treaties." Treaties, he said, might "embarrass" U.S. discussion of possible export duties, discriminatory duties, import prohibitions, and shipping regulations.

Jay had reservations about the use of the most-favored-nation clause. For a variety of reasons, he believed it "inexpedient" to insist on this provision. For one thing, "we may have reasons for *freely* granting to one nation what we may have no reason to grant to another." Also, he anticipated conflicts over the application of this clause to colonial areas and over the use of the conditional provision to purchase most-favored-nation benefits. Moreover, Jay recognized that the United States held a weak bargaining hand in such negotiations: "our trade is at present free to all, we have few *favors* to grant to any; whereas, their trade being charged with various duties and restrictions, they need only relax to have favors to grant." In essence, Jay favored bilateral agreements of limited duration, "without reference to or connection with any other." Over time, he anticipated that the United States would gain both experience and commercial importance and so increase its capacity to make more favorable agreements. Elbridge Gerry also preferred a strict reciprocity system: "This favored Nation system appears to me a system of Cobwebs to catch Flies. Attend to it as it respects Restrictions, prohibitions, and the carrying Trade, and it is equally distant from a Rule of Reciprocity, which is the only equitable and beneficial Rule for forming Commercial Treaties."[22]

With Spain and Britain, major European powers having colonies in America, the Confederation government enjoyed no success at all. The Jay-Gardoqui negotiations for an agreement with Spain foundered on sectional issues involving navigation of the Mississippi River. But the proposed commercial provisions, considered attractive to eastern maritime states, also contained disadvantages. Spain still refused access to its American colonies, prohibited tobacco imports, and maintained much higher duties on imports than the American states imposed on Spanish goods. Critics in Congress, like Charles C. Pinckney of South Carolina, complained that the agreement "proposes nothing more than she [Spain] will always be willing to grant . . . without a treaty, and nothing which can be termed an equivalent for the forbearance she demands."[23]

At the end of the Revolution Britain had avoided a commercial agreement with its former colonies. At first, John Adams and many of his peers remained optimistic that time and circumstances would produce a mutually beneficial treaty of commerce. But throughout the 1780s London continued to reject commercial reciprocity, perceiving that the weak American Confederation had nothing to offer and Britain nothing to gain from such negotiations. Thus London prohibited American trade with the British West Indies and feasted on export sales of manufactures to America. In effect, Britain enjoyed the commercial benefits of empire without the security costs. From his post in London, Adams experienced enormous frustration. Convinced at last that Britain would not sign a commercial treaty and concede "true reciprocity," he urged a stronger central government, one having the power to regulate commerce and conduct foreign affairs. Adams also urged retaliation to place pressure on Britain: "Patience, under all the unequal burdens they impose upon our commerce, will do us no good. . . . nothing but retaliation, reciprocal prohibitions, and imposts, and putting ourselves in a posture of defense will have any effect."[24]

The Foundations of American Trade Policy

Institutional weaknesses and the failure to protect national commercial interests under the Articles of Confederation finally produced a more effective union in 1789 under the Constitution. Indeed, Chief Justice John Marshall later observed: "it may be doubted whether any of the evils proceeding from the feebleness of the federal government, contributed more to that great revolution which introduced the present system, than the deep and general conviction that commerce ought to be regulated by Congress." He was right. Under the weak Articles of Confederation, trade problems nearly doomed the new government. Customs disputes among the newly independent states and an inability to conduct negotiations with European powers jeopardized the new government. Refusing to grant the Continental Congress taxing power, the thirteen states imposed their own revenue and protective tariffs on goods imported from other jurisdictions. For instance, Pennsylvania levied duties on New England imports; Massachusetts imposed tariffs on "foreign products," including goods from New York and Rhode Island. As a consequence of these divisions, support grew to cede Congress the power to regulate commerce and to establish what was in effect a customs union among member states. The result was a Constitution that authorized free trade among the thirteen states, established a common external tariff, and prohibited export duties.[25]

Concerned about domestic weaknesses and pernicious foreign influences, the authors of the Constitution bifurcated authority in trade matters between Congress and the executive branch. Congress, not the executive, would authorize customs duties (art. 1, sec. 8). But the executive acquired authority to make treaties (art. 2, sec. 2), execute laws, and appoint public officials with the advice and consent of Congress. In thus separating authority for trade negotiations, the Constitution effectively prevented the executive branch from trading access to the American market for export opportunities abroad. Commenting on the bifurcated treaty-making procedure in the *Federalist Papers*, Alexander Hamilton expressed concern about elected officials "being corrupted by foreign powers." As he saw it, "An avaricious man might be tempted to betray the interests of the state to the acquisition of wealth."[26] Moreover, under the Constitution the Senate would have to approve any treaty, and only Congress as a whole could adjust tariff rates to effect the terms of an agreement. Future events would show that this complex system of checks and balances guarded the nation against human error and foreign corruption, but it contributed to deadlock and delay. The slow-moving treaty implementation process gave the advantage to domestic producers and local interests, which would use their influence with Congress to amend or block ratification.

National security and trade strategies pursued during the first century after independence reflected the thoughts and experiences of President George Washington. In his famous "Farewell Address," a September 1796 statement considered the keystone of early American foreign policy, the first president summarized essential principles. "The great rule of conduct for us in regard to foreign nations is, in extending our commercial relations to have with them as little *political* connection as possible" (emphasis added). In warning against "permanent alliances," Washington effectively counseled the new nation to remain aloof from European disputes. The "Farewell Address" also addressed commercial policy. Washington embraced the general principles of equality and reciprocity and warned against exclusive preferences. "[O]ur commercial policy," he said, "should hold an equal and impartial hand, neither seeking nor granting exclusive favors or preferences." While urging government to negotiate temporary "conventional rules of intercourse" to define the rights of merchants, he warned against unrequited concessions, giving "equivalents for nominal factors" and then "being reproached with ingratitude for not giving more."[27]

Washington's successors, especially Thomas Jefferson, echoed his call for trade expansion and political isolation. In his own first inaugural message, Jefferson employed similar language, listing among the "essential principles" of government, "peace, commerce, and honest friendship with all nations, entangling alliances with none."[28]

Some years later Secretary of State John Quincy Adams summarized the foundations of American trade policies. During the 1820s he wrote lengthy instructions to new diplomats accredited to the newly independent Latin American republics. Adams emphasized the concepts of *equality* (most favored nation) and *reciprocity*. Equality with the most favored nation he deemed "the great foundation of our foreign policy," noting that this principle was adopted at "the time of" the Declaration of Independence and elaborated in the preamble to the 1778 treaty with France. "That preamble," Adams stated, "was to the foundation of our commercial intercourse with the rest of mankind, what the Declaration of Independence was to that of our internal government." For John Quincy Adams, *equality* meant "the right of the United States to be treated in every respect on the footing of the most favored." He conceded that this construction, authorized in the 1778 treaty with France, was not as liberal as national treatment—"placing the *foreigner*, in regard to all objects of navigation and commerce, upon a footing of equal favor with the *native* citizen." The latter was "congenial to the spirit of our institutions," but "the fairness of its operation depends upon its being admitted universally." Another country might attempt "to secure advantages to its own people, at the expense of both the parties to the treaty." Apparently Adams anticipated that some countries, like Britain, might attempt to ride free if the benefits of a reciprocity agreement were extended generously and unconditionally to other countries without requiring them to make equivalent concessions.[29]

What did *reciprocity* mean in this context? Adams repeatedly referred to it in general terms as "the basis of all our intercourse with foreign powers." Seemingly he construed it as a bilateral bargaining technique, one in which both parties to a negotiation sought mutually acceptable and equal concessions but left to each government the problem of weighing actual results.[30]

In the *Federalist Papers* Alexander Hamilton had advised that the federal government might employ "prohibitory regulations" obliging "foreign countries to bid against each other, for the privileges of our markets." Indeed, several officials representing the Confederation abroad—especially Adams and Jefferson—did favor such retaliation.[31] And during the first months of the new Washington administration Congressman James Madison began pushing for discriminatory restrictions against Britain.

When his friend Jefferson became secretary of state in 1790, the French Revolution was under way. Along the frontier, hostile Indians and foreign influence thwarted expansion. Britain and Spain, in particular, continued to regulate and discriminate against American trade. Jefferson wanted to retaliate, but he found Secretary of the Treasury Hamilton opposed to sanctions, eager now to maintain the flow of revenues to the new government from expanding trade with Britain. As France and Great Britain prepared for war, the conflict between their partisans in America also heated up. On the high seas, both sides infringed neutral rights, seizing American commerce and impressing sailors. The story is complex, but in essence Secretary of State Jefferson found himself without even a crowbar to pry open the markets of Europe. Because the United States had adopted a single-schedule tariff, he lacked discretionary authority to retaliate against European trade restrictions with higher duties on export sales in America. In this predicament it is not surprising that Secretary Jefferson sought to obtain authority from Congress for using reprisals to gain access to European markets and to command respect for American commercial rights.[32]

Three years later, as he prepared to leave office, Jefferson released a report to Congress recommending significant changes in U.S. commercial policy. This important document, the "Report on the Privileges and Restrictions on the Commerce of the United States in Foreign Countries," resulted from a congressional request.[33] Although American trade encountered prohibitions, discriminations, and heavy duties in Europe, especially in Britain, the Netherlands, Denmark, and Sweden, the secretary noted, trade with European colonies in the Americas was even "harder." Jefferson recommended "friendly arrangements" to open commerce along the lines of reciprocal free trade. "Instead of embarrassing commerce under piles of regulating laws, duties, and prohibitions," he called for relieving it "from all its shackles in all parts of the world," anticipating that "the greatest mass possible would then be produced of those things which contributed to human life and human happiness." He proposed bilateral free trade agreements, or reciprocity arrangements: "Would even a single nation begin with the United States this system of free commerce, it would be advisable to begin it with that nation; since it is one by one only that it can be extended to all." Jefferson thus emerges as an early advocate of negotiating bilateral free trade agreements. But he was not a doctrinaire free trader. Jefferson recognized the expedience of revenue duties.

In a warning to the mercantilists of Europe, the secretary said: "should any nation . . . suppose it may better find its advantage by continuing its system of prohibitions, duties and regulations, it behooves us to protect our citizens, their commerce and navigation, by counter prohibitions, duties and regulations." Warning against unilateral concessions, Jefferson added: "free commerce and navigations are not to be given in exchange for restrictions and vexations; nor are they likely to produce a relaxation of them." Rejecting nondiscrimination (equality) for nations "who extinguish our commerce and navigation by duties and prohibitions," Jefferson advised that "fair and equal access" to foreign markets depended not on "moderation and justice" but on "our own means of independence, and the firm will to use them."[34]

Jefferson and his allies in Congress were laying the foundation for a policy of retaliation and nonimportation directed at Great Britain. Madison, who had long favored retaliation, soon proposed a schedule of additional duties on manufactures imported from European nations having no commercial treaty with the United States. A partisan battle erupted in Congress, and to avoid retaliation President Washington sought a diplomatic solution. He authorized John Jay's diplomatic mission to London, which produced a treaty settling some territorial questions and postponing others. The British concessions confirmed Jefferson and Madison's faith in the economic weapon. They would experiment with it again in 1808. Although Jay's treaty did not achieve most-favored-nation treatment or resolve other commercial issues, it represented an important beginning. Writing in the 1820s, Theodore Lyman said that "ratification of this instrument may be considered the proper solid foundation of the commercial prosperity of the United States." It was, he asserted, "the first act of the government that provided the stability of the federal Constitution."[35]

A century later, in the 1890s, as surging exports of U.S. manufactures encountered discrimination and rising protectionism in regulated European markets, support again emerged for a flexible tariff and the powers of retaliation. This time the business community joined the State Department in seeking ways to strengthen the hands of American trade negotiators.[36]

First Tariff, 1789

"A nation cannot long exist without revenue," Alexander Hamilton observed in the *Federalist Papers*. In the eighteenth century customs duties provided the principal source of government revenues, and Hamilton warned that America must depend for a long time on import duties. He hinted at duties averaging 9 percent.[37] With Hamilton as secretary of the Treasury, the first Congress promptly turned its attention to revenue issues and completed a tariff that President Washington signed on July 4, 1789. Among its purposes was "the encouragement and protection of manufactures." However, this act was hardly a protective tariff. It contained a schedule of relatively low, specific, and ad valorem duties, ranging from 5 to 15 percent. The law imposed a 10 percent ad valorem duty on paints, glass, gunpowder, chinaware, and earthenware. On an ad valorem basis, the average rate of duty was 8.5 percent, consistent with Hamilton's prediction.[38]

The Tariff Act of 1789 contained several administrative provisions with future significance. Of seven years' duration, the act employed both specific and ad valorem duties. It authorized drawbacks, or the remittance of duties, on goods imported and subsequently exported. A related law discriminated against foreign shipping and authorized a 10 percent discount on duties imported in vessels built or owned entirely in the United States.

One feature with special significance was the single-schedule tariff. Congress authorized a single list of duties applied to imports from all countries. Outwardly this approach was consistent with the quest for equal treatment and nondiscrimination advanced in the treaty plan of 1776. In practice it left the executive branch without discretionary authority or leverage to bargain down, or retaliate against, foreign trade barriers. Given the Treasury secretary's understandable desire to collect revenue from expanding commerce in order to address the nation's fiscal needs, it is to be expected that Hamilton's followers stood firm for a single schedule. They condemned preferential commercial treaties and rejected Senator William Maclay's call for showing "gratitude" to "those nations who had given us the helping hand in time of distress." Adoption of the nondiscriminatory approach had the effect of treating old friend France the same as adversary Britain. Not surprisingly, France protested the policy of according equal tariff treatment to commercial allies and non-treaty powers.[39]

America First

How should the national government treat domestic manufactures? Should it encourage economic diversification to reduce dependence on Europe, or should the new nation focus its energies on agriculture and commerce? During the Washington administration a major battle erupted over federal support for industry. It pitted the agrarian interests of the South against commercial New England and emerging industries in the Middle Atlantic states.

Although a Virginia landowner, President Washington believed strongly that the new country needed a manufacturing base. Undoubtedly his preference reflected bitter experiences during the Revolution, when America lacked the manufacturing facilities to supply his army with cannon, clothes, and shoes. Fearful that European nations—especially Britain—would take advantage of American weakness and dependence on imported manufactures, Washington determined to send a message of resolve to foreign adversaries and a wake-up call to his compatriots. So he used his first annual message, January 8, 1790, to warn that a "free people ought not only to be armed but disciplined; . . . and their safety and interest require that they should promote such manufactories as tend to render them independent of others for essential, particularly military, supplies."[40] The Washington administration thus determined to promote domestic manufactures.

For his inaugural the first president ordered an American-made suit and through personal example established the practice of buying American goods first. At a time when fashion-conscious gentlemen wore European suits, he had one made of American cloth and expressed the hope that "it will not be a great while, before it will be unfashionable for a gentleman to appear in any other dress." In addition, Washington said: "I use no porter [ale] or cheese in my family, but such as is made in America." He pronounced them of "excellent quality." The father of American independence believed that government had a responsibility and a duty to promote and buy domestic goods. He placed the interest of American producers and American workers first in his hierarchy of priorities and bought American goods at every opportunity. Indeed, he promised the Delaware Society for Promoting Domestic Manufacturers "to demonstrate the sincerity of my opinion . . . by the uniformity of my practice, in giving a decided preference to the produce and fabrics of America, whensoever it may be done without involving unreasonable expenses, or very great inconveniences."[41]

Responding to a more nationalistic mood after the War of 1812, even agrarians like Thomas Jefferson and James Madison expressed similar thoughts. Picking up the economic nationalist mantle, Henry Clay of Kentucky soon became the ardent exponent of home manufactures.[42]

Industrial Policy

Support for domestic manufactures became a divisive political issue in Congress after Treasury secretary Alexander Hamilton filed his famous "Report on Manufactures" in December 1791. Responding to a congressional request, Hamilton prepared what tariff historian Edward Stanwood termed a "monumental treatise" in behalf of domestic industry. James G. Blaine later wrote: "The doctrine of protection . . . has never been more succinctly or more felicitously stated." Arguing for comprehensive government involvement to promote strategic economic objectives, Hamilton's report also presented in eighteenth-century language a strong case for what is now labeled "industrial policy." Then, as now, the subject aroused partisans, and President Washington quickly recognized that the recommendations were both too extreme and untimely for adoption.[43]

On one level Hamilton's report represented a nationalistic response to Adam Smith's *Wealth of Nations*. "If the system of perfect liberty to industry and commerce were the prevailing system of nations," Hamilton said, the arguments against a program of manufactures would have "great force." In the absence of equal treatment and reciprocal access, he warned that the United States could become a "victim of a system" and be exposed "to a state of impoverishment." He advocated a program of tariffs and bounties to build up domestic manufactures.[44]

In doing so, Hamilton presented arguments that would echo for decades in American political debate. He conceded that "if the system of perfect liberty to industry and commerce were the prevailing system of nations," individual nations producing agricultural products might beneficially forgo the production of manufactures. But he perceived that "the reigning policy of manufacturing nations" was to preserve "a monopoly of the domestic market to its own manufacturers." In such circumstances, "the principles of distributive justice" dictated that the United States pursue a "similar policy" to secure for its citizens "a reciprocity of advantages."[45]

Already in congressional debate some had argued that import duties would harm consumers. According to Hamilton, however, "the fact does not uniformly correspond with the theory. A reduction of prices has in several instances immediately succeeded the establishment of a domestic manufacture." Moreover, he contended, once established a domestic manufacture "invariably becomes cheaper. Being free from the heavy charges which attend the importation of foreign commodities," it "never fails to be sold cheaper, in process of time, than was the foreign article for which it is a substitute." He concluded that "a temporary enhancement of price must always be well compensated by a permanent reduction of it."[46]

Soon the Jeffersonians also came to appreciate the need for domestic manufactures. In 1793, for instance, Jefferson's *Report on Commerce* endorsed industrial policies at the state level to supplement his trade retaliation program. Because retaliatory duties had the effect of encouraging indirectly domestic manufactures, Jefferson said that it was in the "power of the State governments" to foster "*household* manufacture, by some patronage suited to the nature of its objects." Later, President Jefferson would encourage domestic manufactures when he experimented with an embargo on exports to compel respect from the warring mercantile powers of Europe.[47] Indeed, in 1810 President Madison's Treasury secretary, Albert Gallatin, issued his own "Report on Manufactures" that echoed Hamilton's recommendation. Gallatin observed that the "plan best calculated to protect and promote American manufactures . . . [involved] bounties, increased duties on importation, and loans by government." And in his own annual message President Madison commended to the "patriotic reflections" of Congress the use of tariffs to "guard the infancy" of domestic manufactures.[48]

After the War of 1812 Americans were even more sympathetic to protection for domestic industries. Political economists and journalists launched a full-scale assault on Adam Smith's *Wealth of Nations*. The most influential was Daniel Raymond, a Baltimore lawyer who in 1820 wrote *Thoughts on Political Economy*, a work that brought him recognition as "the first systematic American economist." Focusing on how to promote an individual nation's wealth, as opposed to Smith's preoccupation with the wealth of individuals and the universe of nations, Raymond urged legislators, "the vicegerents of God on earth," to adopt a long-term perspective: "consider the nation immortal, and . . . legislate for it, as though it was to exist for ever."[49] Raymond vigorously criticized Smith's doctrine of comparative advantage—buying imports when they were cheaper than domestic products—for "destroying the unity of the nation by dividing it into classes, and looking to the interests of individuals, instead of looking to the interests of the whole, as one and indivisible." Smith assumed full employment, Raymond said, but in the absence of full employment he argued that individuals "ought not to be allowed to afford patronage and support to the industry of foreigners, when his own fellow-citizens are in want." Moreover, "*it is the duty of the legislator to find employment for all the people*, and if he cannot find them employment in agriculture and commerce, he must set them to manufacturing. It is his duty to take special care that no other nation interferes with their industry. *He is not to permit one half of the nation to remain idle and hungry, in order that the other half may buy goods where they may be had the cheapest*" (emphases added).[50]

Raymond's writings inspired Adam Smith's most famous critic, German economist Friedrich List. Visiting the United States in the 1820s, List encountered the ideas of economic nationalists and developed with eloquence an alternative to free trade, one based on building a domestic manufacturing base behind tariff walls. Many other nineteenth-century economists shared List's principal conclusion.[51]

In his writings List argued that manufactures were the basis of domestic and foreign trade. He warned that a "nation which should succeed in monopolizing the entire manufacturing of the globe . . . would necessarily achieve universal dominion." A tariff system protecting domestic manufactures, he said, would secure "the manufacturing power . . . against all events, fluctuations of prices, and against all changes in the political and economical conditions of other nations." It would also help domestic manufactures achieve "ascendancy" against their foreign competitors. For national industry to prosper and succeed, List maintained, it must be provided "steadiness." He also attacked Smithian economics for its preoccupation with the wealth of the individual and the world ("cosmopolitical economy") while neglecting the wealth and power of the nation-state.[52]

Free Trade Postponed

Years earlier, in 1785, Jefferson had forecast that "our commerce on the ocean . . . must be paid for by frequent war."[53] His comment became prophetic in 1812. Under President Jefferson and his successor James Madison, the United States experimented with trade sanctions—including embargoes and nonintercourse—to remove mercantilistic discriminations. Then, unsuccessful in efforts to compel respect for neutral commercial rights, Congress declared war. As John Quincy Adams observed, the phrase " 'free trade and sailor's rights,' was repeated from one extremity of the Union to the other."[54]

For American trade policy, the War of 1812 produced a major shift away from the idealistic policy of promoting equality and reciprocal access for U.S. exports to Europe. The change came in response to continuing violations of the nation's commercial and navigation rights, and to dislocations accompanying peace in 1815. U.S. imports soared as British merchants resorted to discount pricing to liquidate inventories accumulated during the war. American business perceived that British exporters dumped goods in order to eliminate competition from start-up U.S. industries. For such fears it found confirmation in the words of Lord Brougham, a member of Parliament, who said: "It was well worth while to incur a loss upon the first exportation, in order by the glut, to stifle in the cradle, those rising manufactures in the United States, which the war had forced into existence, contrary to the natural course of things."[55]

From a series of depredations—disruptive to commerce and manufacturing, as well as an affront to the national honor—a more nationalistic consensus developed after the War of 1812. Repeated efforts to negotiate differences, retaliate against flagrant discriminations, and even embargo commerce altogether had failed to secure equal treatment and access to European markets. It appeared that short-term expedients had failed. So a diverse group of U.S. leaders turned to a long-term trade strategy: developing a strong, diversified manufacturing base to assure independence from foreign conflicts. Former

President John Adams, and his son, the future president John Quincy Adams, favored this approach, as did leading Democratic-Republicans, Presidents Jefferson, Madison, and Monroe. In Congress Speaker of the House Henry Clay of Kentucky dramatized the nationalist call for an "American System," a phrase he first employed in 1820.[56] In effect, each of these leaders concluded that free trade, although beneficial in a theoretical sense, remained an abstract and impractical ideal.[57]

In retrospect, it is striking how exacting experience, as well as the more nationalistic public mood, made economic nationalists of Jefferson, Madison, and other Democratic-Republicans. Jefferson had resisted Hamilton's plan to build up domestic manufactures in the early 1790s, but experience in the Napoleonic Wars taught him "that manufactures are now as necessary to our independence as to our comfort." He too adopted the Buy-American practice and challenged advocates of free trade to "keep pace with me in purchasing nothing foreign where an equivalent of domestic fabric can be obtained, without regard to difference of price." When some recalled his free trade views, Jefferson complained that critics were using *Notes on Virginia* "as a stalking horse, to cover their disloyal propensities to keep us in eternal vassalage to a foreign and unfriendly people."[58]

Two other former presidents, James Madison and John Adams, agreed. Madison knew that "this golden age of free trade has not yet arrived." He believed that "every prudent nation will wish to be independent of other nations for the necessary articles of food, of raiment [garments], and of defence."[59] Adams, the second president, drew the same lesson from these disruptive events: in a world with commercial predators and adversaries, America must subordinate free trade principles to practical considerations. In an 1819 letter he wrote:

> I am old enough to remember the war of 1745, and its end; the war of 1755, and its close; the war of 1775, and its termination; the war of 1812, and its pacification. Every one of these wars has been followed by a general distress; embarrassment on commerce, destruction of manufactures, fall of the price of produce and of lands, similar to those we feel at the present day, and all produced by the same causes. *I have wondered that so much experience has not taught us more caution.* The British merchants and manufacturers, immediately after the peace, disgorged upon us all their stores of merchandise and manufactures, not only without profit, but at certain loss for a time, with the express purpose of annihilating all our manufacturers, and ruining all our manufactories. The cheapness of these articles allures us into extravagance and luxury, involves us in debt, exhausts our resources, and at length produces universal complaint. (emphasis added)

Adams concluded that so long as nations with which we have trade "persevere" in their mercantilistic practices, "I know not how we can do ourselves justice without introducing . . . portions of the same system."[60]

James Monroe, the last of the Virginians to serve as president during this era, concurred with Madison and Jefferson that the United States must stimulate manufactures. He recommended tariff increases in his 1822 annual message to Congress. "Whatever may be the abstract doctrine in favor of unrestricted commerce," Monroe said, referring to free trade, that doctrine rested on twin conditions—international peace and general reciprocity—which have "never occurred and can not be expected."[61]

Out of the Napoleonic Wars thus emerged a strong nonpartisan consensus among prominent former and elected officials. They favored using tariff policy to protect and promote American manufacturing interests. Jefferson, founder of the Democratic Party, and his intellectual heirs shared it, and so did John C. Calhoun and Andrew Jackson, leaders of different factions of the party, in the 1820s. Although representing a state—South Carolina—that might benefit from selling products of the soil at high prices and buying imported manufactures cheap, Calhoun in 1816 supported a protective tariff on cotton manufactures. He declared: "We cannot . . . be indifferent to dangers from abroad, unless, . . . [Congress] is prepared to indulge in the phantom of eternal peace, which seemed to possess the dream of some of its members."[62]

Commenting on the need for a protective tariff to preserve the national defense and independence, Jackson said: "The experience of the late war ought to teach us a lesson; and one never to be forgotten. If our liberty and republican form of government, procured for us by our revolutionary fathers, are worth the blood and treasure at which they were obtained, it surely is our duty to protect and defend them." And, in a comment that some may consider applicable to trade and fiscal circumstances of the 1990s, he observed: "we have been too long subject to the policy of the British merchants. It is time we should become a little more *Americanized,* and instead of feeding the paupers and laborers of Europe, feed our own, or else in a short time, by continuing our present policy, we shall all be paupers ourselves." Moreover, "a careful Tariff is much wanted to pay our national debt, and afford us the means of that defense within ourselves on which the safety and liberty of the country depend."[63]

Clay's American System

Jackson's rival from Kentucky, Henry Clay, had pressed a nationalistic program of tariffs and internal improvements since 1816. He elaborated a comprehensive vision for an American system, based on balance among farming, industry, and commerce, behind a protective tariff.[64] Like Madison and Jefferson before him, Clay considered himself "a friend [of] free trade." He recognized that individual nations could not unilaterally pursue that policy and acquiesce to foreign discrimination. Instead, the Kentucky statesman insisted on "free trade of perfect reciprocity."[65]

In an 1820 speech he likened America to "a fine generous hearted young fellow, who has just come to the possession of a rich estate—an estate, which, however, requires careful management. He makes nothing; he buys every thing. He is surrounded by a parcel of" peddlers, "each holding out his hand with a packet of buttons or pins, or some other commodity, for sale. If he asks these" peddlers "to buy any thing which his state produces, they tell him no; it is not for our interest; it is not for yours. Take this new book, says one of them, on political economy, and you will there perceive it is for your interest to buy from us, and to let things alone in your own country." But, concluded Clay, "this maxim, according to which gentlemen would have us abandon the home industry of the country to the influence of the restrictive system of other countries, without an effort to protect and preserve it, is not itself observed by the same gentlemen, in regard to the great interests of the nation."[66]

Nor was Clay persuaded that short-term benefits to American consumers from cheap imports warranted one-sided concessions. "If the governing consideration were cheapness; if national independence were to weigh nothing; if honor nothing; why not subsidize foreign powers to defend us? why not hire Swiss or Hessian armies to protect us? Why not get our arms of all kinds, as we do, in part, the blankets and clothing of our soldiers, from abroad?"[67]

Interestingly, unlike the doctrinaire free traders, Clay considered "foreign commerce . . . the great source of foreign wars. The eagerness with which we contend for every branch of it; the temptations which it offers, operating alike upon us and on foreign competitors, produce constant collisions." For Clay, practical experience demonstrated that free trade depended on two conditions "neither of which exists." These were "perpetual peace" and respect for the maxim of free trade everywhere. But without "perfect reciprocity" Clay saw the need for employing "countervailing" restrictions to command access for American products.[68]

Clay, like Adams, Jefferson, and Madison, noted with concern how British and French manufacturers dumped textiles and other products in the American market after the War of 1812 even as they continued to discriminate against American exports. Said Clay in 1824:

> The policy of Europe is adverse to the reception of our agricultural produce, so far as it comes into collision with its own; and, under that limitation, we are absolutely forbid to enter their ports, except under circumstances which

deprive them of all value as a steady market. The policy of all Europe rejects those great staples of our country, which consist of objects of human subsistence. The policy of all Europe refuses to receive from us anything but those raw materials of smaller value, essential to their manufactures, to which they can give a higher value, with the exception of tobacco and rice, which they cannot produce.[69]

In a comment about European protectionists that is relevant to present U.S. efforts to secure access for American agricultural exports in Europe and Japan, Clay complained that the Europeans "do not guide themselves by that romantic philanthropy . . . which invokes us to continue to purchase the produce of foreign industry, without regard to the state or prosperity of our own" so that "foreigners may be pleased to purchase the few remaining articles of ours which their restrictive policy has not yet absolutely excluded from their consumption."

It was thus Henry Clay, the Kentucky Whig, who articulated the comprehensive vision for an American system. Though unsuccessful in winning the presidency, Clay left an enduring imprint on tariff and trade policy among Whigs and Republicans.[70] Among others President Millard Fillmore, also a Whig, supported Clay's concept and asserted that as "the artisan and the agriculturalist are brought together, each affords a ready market for the produce of the other, the whole country becomes prosperous, and the ability to produce every necessary of life renders us independent in war as well as in peace."[71]

For Fillmore and Abraham Lincoln, another enthusiastic Whig backer of Clay's American system, the protective tariff was not a device for taxing consumers for the benefit of manufacturers. On the contrary, they took a long-term view, consistent with Alexander Hamilton's thinking. They held that tariffs stimulated investment in the United States and "finally enable us to produce the article much cheaper than it could have been procured from abroad, thereby benefiting both the producer and the consumer at home." In the short-run tariffs provided fiscal stability, generating revenue required to operate the government.

Consequently, a second distinct phase in U.S. trade policy followed the Napoleonic Wars. It lasted 120 years—until the Great Depression. During this period, tariff policy encouraged domestic manufacturers. Even free trade Democrats embraced this consensus, conceding that a low-revenue tariff would provide incidental protection to domestic industries.

With support from Clay and Calhoun, Congress enacted the first protective tariff in 1816, establishing 30 percent duties on iron products and 25 percent on cotton and woolen goods. In 1824 Congress raised the rates again, after a vigorous exchange in which Clay spoke for the American system and Daniel

Webster of Massachusetts urged the imposition of a revenue tariff. The 1824 legislative debate presaged a century of tariff controversy, including discussion of the conflict between building a strong self-sufficient home market and relying on foreign markets despite restrictions on American exports. Clay lambasted the domestic "partisans of the foreign policy" guided by a "romantic philanthropy" that "invokes us to continue to purchase the produce of foreign industry, without regard to the state or prosperity of our own, that foreigners may be pleased to purchase the few remaining articles of ours which their restrictive policy has not yet absolutely excluded from their consumption."[72]

Daniel Webster, at this time a spokesman for New England commercial interests, rejected this distinction, claiming that national prosperity and trade were related. Clay's protectionist prescriptions Webster deemed "destructive of all commercial intercourse between nations." In particular, he ridiculed the idea that British journalists and theorists advocated free trade to the rest of the world while the English government restricted commerce. Instead, Webster noted that England was gradually abandoning trade prohibitions.[73]

Four years later Congress approved the so-called Tariff of Abominations, enacting the highest tariff rates in American history. Under the Tariff Act of 1828, the average rate on dutiable goods soared to 61.7 percent, several percentage points higher than under the much reviled Smoot-Hawley Tariff of 1930. As a result of the South Carolina nullification controversy, Clay engineered a compromise in 1833 that provided a gradual decline over the next decade to a 20 percent revenue tariff. Although accused of sacrificing the American system to preserve the Union, Clay's compromise actually contained a highly protective amendment that shifted the basis of valuing imports for duty purposes from foreign to domestic value in 1842.[74] But, in revising the 1833 tariff, a Whig Congress would raise rates and restore the traditional method of foreign valuation.

Participants in nineteenth-century tariff battles perceived the continuing contest between the forces of free trade and protection. The tariff compromise of 1833 appeared to abandon protection, but the depression of 1837 produced a Whig victory in 1840 and a more protective tariff in 1842. However, the election of James K. Polk in 1844 brought low-tariff Democrats to power and revived interest in the revenue-only formula. Yet a review of historical data suggests that in practice the high-tariff position generally carried the day. Over the forty-year period from 1821 to 1861, the ratio of duties to total imports ranged from a low of 14.21 percent in 1861 to over 57 percent in 1832 under the Tariff of Abominations. In twenty-nine of those years the average tariff on all imports exceeded 20 percent.[75] In thirty-three of those years the average duty on all imports actually exceeded the average duty on all imports under the Smoot-Hawley Tariff of 1930 (17.75 percent in 1931), which some think plunged the world into a trade war.

What effect did such tariffs have on the domestic economy? In the mid-nineteenth century the protective tariff apparently was not a significant impediment to the growth of the nation's domestic economy or foreign trade. Exports and imports soared, both rising more than 500 percent in value terms. Cotton and tobacco exports spiraled upward; the quantity of cotton exports rose nearly 1,300 percent, and tobacco doubled. Together, the two commodities accounted for 57.6 percent of exports in 1820 and 65.8 percent in 1860. As a result, the composition of imports changed. Finished manufactures fell from 56.3 percent of total imports in 1821 to 48.6 percent in 1860 as industrialization proceeded. Twenty years later the same figure would be 29.5 percent.[76]

According to one trade history. "the foreign commerce of the United States had a remarkable growth during the forty-five years prior to the Civil War." It "reached the highest stage of development ever attained up to that time." Frank Taussig, a Harvard University economist often critical of protection, concedes that "manufactures in general grew and flourished." Thus, as Taylor notes, there is little evidence that the tariff structure had much restrictive impact on the growth of total imports or exports during this period, but it attracted investments in textiles and other import-competing industries.[77]

Reacting to the high Tariff of Abominations, Democrats challenged the American system and succeeded in gradually reducing duties during the 1840s and 1850s. Particularly under Democratic presidents James K. Polk, Franklin Pierce, and James Buchanan, Congress whittled down protective tariffs, ostensibly to reduce an unwanted budget surplus. This enthusiasm for low tariffs also reflected southern sectional interests and enthusiasm for English-style free trade.

Across the Atlantic Richard Cobden touted free trade as the "grand panacea." British enthusiasts pressed initially for repeal of the Corn Laws, which restricted wheat and other agricultural imports. Pronouncing free trade "the only means of securing the peace, safety, honor, and prosperity of our common country," Cobdenites in 1843 established *The Economist* "solely for the purpose of advocating these principles." Said its founders, "we seriously believe that *free trade*, free intercourse, will do more than any other visible agent to extend civilization and morality throughout the world."[78]

Responding to low-tariff sentiment, Democrats staked out a distinctive position in the 1840s that would sustain the party into the twentieth century. They embraced a tariff for revenue only. To protectionists like Henry Clay, this approach seemed irresponsible free trade. The Democrats, he told a crowd in Dayton, Ohio, in September 1842, "are opposed to all protection. They would let your grain wither in your barns—they would let mechanics and manufacturers sink in an unequal contest with the pauper labor of Europe—they would let your country be drained of all its specie—they would let this republic revert to its ancient, colonial, and vassal condition, rather than grant protection, direct or incidental, to American industry." In pre–Civil War debates protectionists began to portray the tariff as a "poor man's law" providing employment and wages. Said Representative Andrew Stewart, of Pennsylvania, a Clay supporter, "Repeal the tariff—adopt . . . 'free trade,' and you will bring down labor here, in every department of industry, to the level of the labor of the serfs and paupers of Europe."[79]

To protectionists of that era, a revenue tariff may have resembled dangerous free trade ideas. But from the vantage point of the 1990s, a 20 percent revenue tariff smacks of unrepentant protectionism. Even rabid free trade Democrats like Robert J. Walker, President James K. Polk's secretary of the Treasury, accepted a revenue tariff approaching 20 percent. The Tariff Act of 1846, named after Walker, lowered average duties on all imports from about 29 percent in 1845 to 23 percent and converted many duties to an ad valorem basis. Underlying these reductions was Secretary Walker's revenue philosophy. In 1844 the first Democratic platform committed the party to his approach, asserting that "no more revenue ought to be raised than is required to defray the necessary expenses of the government."[80]

Support for a low-revenue tariff reflected strong free trade sentiment in the Democratic Party. In 1848 Democrats reiterated support for the revenue tariff and celebrated "the noble impulse given to the cause of free trade" with the Walker Tariff of 1846. During the Pierce administration Great Britain attempted to persuade Secretary of State William Marcy to reciprocate for repeal of the Corn Laws. London wanted the U.S. government to roll back its duties on manufactures like cotton textiles, linens, iron products, hand tools, cutlery, and coal. Marcy refused, saying that the protectionists in Congress could block "any measure tending to free trade." But the secretary of state said that the Pierce administration intended "to proceed, as long as they could gain the support of the country, in the direction of free trade."[81]

In 1856 the Democrats again embraced a revenue tariff and free trade, asserting that "the time has come for the people of the United States to declare themselves in favor of . . . progressive free trade throughout the world." The tariff bill approved in early 1857 represented a major step in that direction, lowering average duties on dutiable imports from 26 to 19 percent. Reluctant to wage war with Congress on the free trade issue, the Democrats chose instead to pursue market-opening diplomatic initiatives. First, in 1854 they negotiated a Canadian reciprocity treaty, an arrangement pact that one prominent diplomatic historian termed "the first agreement of the kind in American history for free trade in enumerated products." Democrats hailed the pact as a prelude to reciprocal free trade throughout the world. Congress eventually abrogated it because of a perception on Capitol Hill that it conferred one-sided benefits on

Canada, not reciprocal advantages to both countries. The agreement covered only raw materials, and Canada hiked its import duties on U.S. manufactures. Later, the U.S. Tariff Commission concluded that the provisions as negotiated were "undoubtedly more favorable to provincial exports than to those of the United States." In particular, U.S. fishing and lumber interests experienced an adverse impact.[82]

Expansionist Democrats also negotiated market-opening trade agreements with China and Japan. However, these departed from previous conceptions of bilateral reciprocity and equality. The understandings with Europe and Latin America had bound both parties reciprocally. In Asia, Africa, and the Middle East, Americans, like other foreigners, sought unilateral most-favored-nation clauses or one-sided agreements that ensured the United States the same privileges enjoyed by most favored nations. The 1844 treaty with China and the 1854 treaty with Japan contained the unilateral form. That is, the United States gained access to the Japanese and Chinese markets on terms equal to the most privileged foreigners, but the Japanese and the Chinese did not gain equality in the United States. Indeed, with extraterritorial privileges, the United States acquired better than national treatment in China. However, the treaty of 1844 conceded no reciprocal privileges to China in the United States. Similarly, Commodore Matthew Calbraith Perry opened the Japanese market to American commerce without having to offer reciprocal concessions in the U.S. market, although he did not obtain extraterritorial privileges.[83]

Despite some differences, then, American leaders drew important trade policy conclusions in the period from independence to the Civil War. This consensus would endure and shape attitudes and actions in the twentieth century. First, the founders concluded that the appealing doctrine of free trade was unsuited to the nation's immediate circumstances and interests. From conflicts during the Napoleonic Wars they knew that a commitment to free trade required reciprocity. Through deductive reasoning, economic theorists might argue for unilateral steps. But, in an uncertain and unstable world, the founders had ample evidence that national security and prosperity required developing a diversified home market. A protective tariff, many concluded, was essential to preserving national independence and prosperity, while providing a bountiful, and politically palatable, source of government revenue.

The founding generation exhibited continuing enthusiasm for developing a system of international commercial agreements conducive to expanding trade. These rested on certain key principles: equality, nondiscrimination, most-favored-nation treatment, and reciprocity. Rejecting special privileges, the United States sought from its trading partners tariff treatment equal to that accorded other nations. As a consequence of the 1778 commercial agreement with France, the United States adopted the following interpretation: Trade concessions involved specific compensation, and conditional most-favored-nation status conferred third parties only a right to purchase, through reciprocal negotiations, the most favorable treatment permitted other nations.[84]

For a newly independent country seeking respect for its commercial rights, the conditional most-favored-nation policy appeared rational. Had the United States negotiated on an unconditional basis—and generously extended access to the U.S. market without compensation, it would have squandered the bargaining chips later employed in attempts to pry open the British, and other third markets, to U.S. exports.

During this period, the United States also developed important administrative practices that would guide the nation. The single-schedule tariff, involving as it did the principle of equality, later proved incompatible with efforts to bargain open closed foreign markets. Madison and Jefferson realized this, and their solution was to retaliate with additional discriminatory duties on countries restricting U.S. trade. The problem of how to negotiate access to foreign markets, when Congress mandated a single-schedule domestic tariff, would trouble American policymakers until the 1930s. In 1934 Secretary of State Cordell Hull at last obtained a mandate to lower duties in reciprocal negotiations.

Access to foreign markets for U.S. manufactures was not a primary concern of pre–Civil War diplomats. Until the late nineteenth century there was a perception that U.S. consular officials stationed abroad could do little to promote American exports. Writing in the 1880s, Eugene Schuyler noted that "American manufacturers and merchants are generally careless about foreign trade." They lacked a long-term commitment to international trade, paid little attention to foreign business practices, and ignored consumer preferences abroad. "Do what he may to make an opening for American manufactures abroad, a consul cannot overcome in this respect the inertia and obstinacy of American manufacturers."[85]

Until after the Civil War, U.S. officials would pursue a traditional formula: seeking equal access to the markets of major European competitors, but offering only equal treatment in the U.S. market in exchange. In the Western Hemisphere and Asia, however, U.S. officials strove for a more aggressive policy, seeking special privileges and offering special concessions for raw materials and agricultural products in the U.S market. Through both phases, diplomacy remained an instrument of commerce, a tool for promoting the economic-security interests of the nation and its citizens. A country adhering to the tenets of American diplomacy as elaborated in Washington's "Farewell Address" did not contemplate a leadership role in global affairs.[86]

Abandonment of the protective policy by the American Government must result in the increase of both useless labour, and idleness; and so, in pro[por]tion, must produce want and ruin among our people.—Representative Abraham Lincoln, 1847

We renew and emphasize our allegiance to the policy of protection, as the bulwark of American industrial independence, and the foundation of American development and prosperity.—Republican Platform, 1896

Protection and Prosperity?

Is protectionism the enemy of prosperity or a necessary condition for preserving jobs and maintaining the American standard of living? In the late twentieth century most U.S. economists, opinion shapers, and public officials would probably argue that "prosperity and protection are inconsistent." The establishment identifies free trade with dynamic economic growth and expanding job opportunities.[1]

In the late nineteenth century many American leaders held the opposite view. They associated free trade with "ruin" and protection with prosperity. This interpretation reflected both an enduring faith in the American system and a long record of economic achievement behind high tariff barriers. From 1871 to 1913 the average U.S. tariff on dutiable imports never fell below 38 percent. Gross national product (GNP) grew 4.3 percent annually, twice the pace in free trade Britain and well above the U.S. average in the twentieth century.

This chapter reconsiders the golden era of American protectionism, that period between the Civil War and the Great Depression when partisans battled over trade issues with a religious fervor. It revisits the fascinating tariff debates, examines the arguments advanced for protection and tariff reduction, and evaluates the era in light of subsequent events and actual economic performance.

Beneath the passions and personalities two opposing perspectives competed loudly for public favor. Economic nationalists, or protectionists, argued for advancing the wealth and safety of the American nation through development of the domestic market. They associated *protectionism* with *independence* and *national prosperity*. "Protection was the policy which would spread comfort and happiness over the face of a smiling land," stated Representative Andrew Stewart.[2]

Economic internationalists, or free traders, focused on improving the economic welfare of individuals and maximizing wealth in the cosmopolitical system. According to Richard Cobden, England's leading free trade enthusiast, "the free trade principle . . . shall act on the moral world as the principle of gravitation in the universe—drawing men together, thrusting aside the antagonism of race and creed, and language, and uniting us in the bonds of eternal peace."[3] Proponents identified *free trade* with *global peace and prosperity*.

During this engrossing period, domestic politics and economic interests influenced American trade policy far more than foreign policy considerations. Congressional tariff battles focused on local and regional interests, as well as the fears and concerns of farmers, workers, and producers. For U.S. public officials these national interests took priority over the health of the international system. As late as 1930, British officials in Washington reported to London that members of Congress regarded tariff policy as exclusively a "domestic matter." The "average manufacturer" considered "the domestic market . . . still the preserve to be guarded against all hazards and the average manufacturer, supported in this case by unionized labor, is still the ruler of congressional action."[4]

Republican Protectionists

Today most respectable academics and public officials shun the protectionist label. In the nineteenth century, however, many public and elected officials thought "protectionism" an accolade, not a slur. Although late-twentieth-century Republican presidents, like Ronald Reagan and George Herbert Walker Bush, embraced "free trade" with enthusiasm, the GOP once had a different opinion. Republican presidents—from Abraham Lincoln to Theodore Roosevelt and Herbert Hoover—proudly declared themselves "protectionists" and dismissed Democratic opponents as "English free traders." Free trade, they said, led to low wages and "ruin."[5]

Abraham Lincoln, often considered the father of the Republican Party and one of the two Republicans with his head chiseled on Mount Rushmore, advocated a high tariff. Originally a Whig supporter of Henry Clay and the American system, Lincoln adhered to the view that "the abandonment of the protective policy . . . must result in the increase of both useless labour, and idleness; and so, in pro[por]tion, must produce want and ruin among our people."[6]

In the presidential election of 1892, a century before President George Bush touted his North American Free Trade Agreement and bashed protectionists, Republicans proudly raised the high-tariff banner and attacked Democratic free traders. Their chief spokesman on trade issues, Governor William McKinley of Ohio, author of the 1890 McKinley Tariff, castigated the Democratic Party's "free-trade platform" and warned that free trade "will bring widespread discontent. It will revolutionize values. It will take away more than one half of the earning capacity of brain and brawn." As McKinley saw it, "Free trade results in giving our money, our manufactures, and our markets to other nations." Protection, the policy of the Republican Party, "has made the lives of the masses of our countrymen sweeter and brighter, and has entered the homes of America carrying comfort and cheer and courage."[7]

McKinley's vice president, the ebullient Theodore Roosevelt, also expressed protectionist sympathies. In 1895 he wrote a friend: "Thank God I am not a free-trader. In this country pernicious indulgence in the doctrine of free trade seems inevitably to produce fatty degeneration of the moral fibre."[8] As president, Roosevelt trumpeted American achievements under a policy of protection. "These forty odd years have been the most prosperous years this nation has ever seen; more prosperous years than any other nation has ever seen," he said. "Every class of our people is benefitted by the protective tariff."[9]

No Republican ever defended protection more enthusiastically than Senator Jacob Gallinger of New Hampshire. In 1902 he attributed phenomenal prosperity to the protective tariff: "*it is Christmas the year round in millions of American homes. . . .* The American standard of living, American manhood and American homes are but the resultants of Republican legislation, the sequences of a *protective tariff* which *brought to us and will continue to give us an unprecedented age of luxury, an unparalleled era of prosperity*" (emphases added).[10]

In the Senate powerful Republicans vigorously defended nationalistic trade policies throughout the period from the Civil War to the Great Depression. For forty years (1858–98) Vermont's Justin Morrill, as a Whig representative and then as a Republican senator, dominated the tariff debate. In deliberations concerning revisions to the Walker Tariff in February 1857, Morrill embraced the principle of protection: "I am for ruling America for the benefit, *first*, of Americans, and for the 'rest of mankind' afterwards." Three years later, in a dispute over the 1860 tariff, he attacked free trade theories: "There is a transcendental philosophy of free trade, with devotees as ardent as any of those who preach the millennium. . . . Free trade abjures patriotism and boasts of cosmopolitism. It regards the labor of our own people with no more favor than that of the barbarian on the Danube or the cooly on the Ganges."[11]

That perspective endured until the New Deal. Near the close of the debate over the proposed Tariff Act of 1930, Senator Samuel Shortridge (R-Calif.), a member of the Senate Finance Committee and the bill conference committee, asserted: "What the American people want is a tariff that protects . . . American-raised, American-mined, American-manufactured products and American men and women from competition with like foreign products raised, mined, or manufactured by cheap foreign labor. . . . The free-trade theory has cursed America. The protective theory has blessed America. If the free-trade theory were now put into operation, it would bankrupt America." A famous colleague, Reed Smoot, chairman of the Senate Finance Committee, later said:

> This Government should have no apology to make for reserving America for Americans. That has been our traditional policy ever since the United States became a nation. We have refused to participate in the political intrigues of Europe, and we will not compromise the independence of this country for the privilege of serving as schoolmaster for the world. In economics as in politics, the policy of this Government is, "America first." The Republican Party will not stand by and see economic experimenters fritter away our national heritage.[12]

In essence, from 1860 to 1932 Republicans preached and practiced a nationalistic trade policy that was intended to develop the American market and advance the commercial interests of domestic producers and workers. According to Representative McKinley, "free trade in the United States [among the states] is founded upon a community of equalities and reciprocities. It is like the . . . obligations of a family." But, he said, the foreign producer had no "right or claim to equality with our own. He is not amenable to our laws. . . . He pays no taxes. He performs no civil duties. . . . He contributes nothing to the support, the progress, and glory of the nation. Free foreign trade . . . results in giving our money, our manufactures, and our markets to other nations, to the injury of our labor, our tradespeople, and our farmers."[13]

Preaching class harmony, Republican economic nationalists justified the protective tariff as essential for sustaining the prosperity of domestic producers and workers against cheap-labor imports. Blaine reasoned: "Protection . . . is based on the controlling principle, that competition at home will always prevent monopoly on the part of the capitalist, assure good wages to the laborer, and defend the consumer against the evils of extortion." During this period

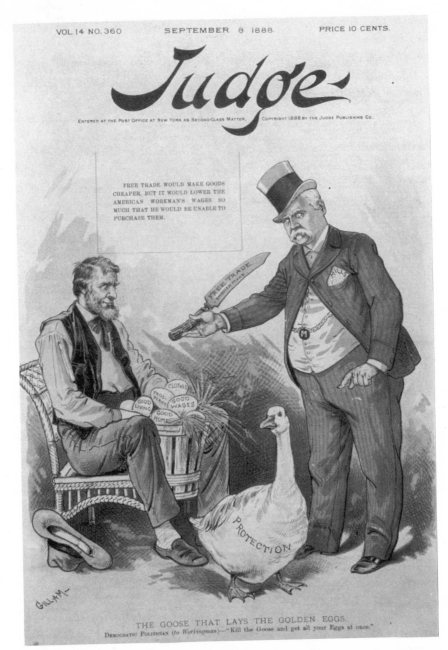

"The Goose That Lays the Golden Eggs." *Judge* (September 8, 1888) shows a Democratic politician inviting a workman to vote for free trade and thus cut American wages. (Special Collections, Alden Library, Ohio University)

Republicans emphasized the long-term employment gains from protection, not the short-term consumer gains anticipated from free trade. Responding to consumer concerns, they asserted that even with a prohibitive tariff on imports "the competition of home producers will . . . rapidly reduce the price to the consumer." Senate Finance Committee chairman Nelson Aldrich of Rhode Island described the "true theory" of protection as one stimulating domestic competition and giving "the American consumer the best possible results." He asserted that "no Senator can point out a single industry in this country subject to a protective duty that is controlled by a monopoly."[14]

In effect, Republican trade nationalists considered the tariff a fee imposed on foreign producers for participating in the U.S. market. The high tariff appeared to shift the burden of revenue collection from Americans to foreign producers and consumers of expensive imported luxuries. In particular, a tariff seemed to tax wealthy people who were determined to buy European luxuries. Said Abraham Lincoln: "those whose pride, whose abundance of means, prompt them to spurn the manufactures of our own country, and to strut in British cloaks, and coats, and pantaloons, may have to pay a few cents more on the yard for the cloth that makes them. A terrible evil, truly, to the Illinois farmer, who never wore, nor never expects to wear, a single yard of British goods in his whole life." In his public speeches, Lincoln regularly argued that "the consumer does not usually pay the tariff, but the manufacturer and importer" did.[15]

Governor McKinley's famous speech in Beatrice, Nebraska, during the 1892 campaign mirrored these themes:

Free trade gives to the foreign producer equal privileges with us. . . . It invites the product of his cheaper labor to this market to destroy the domestic product representing our higher and better-paid labor. It destroys our factories or reduces our labor to the level of his. It increases foreign production but diminishes home production. . . . it destroys the dignity and independence of American labor, diminishes its pay and employment, decreases its capacity to buy the products of the farm and the commodities of the merchant.

Among nineteenth-century Republican leaders, McKinley recognized that adherence to free trade was incompatible with high wages at home. After the party's defeat in 1892, he said: "This country will not and can not prosper under any system that does not recognize the difference of conditions in Europe and America. Open competition between high-paid American labor and poorly paid European labor will either drive out of existence American industry or lower American wages, either of which is unwise."[16]

During the late nineteenth century Republicans and their business supporters occasionally articulated an economic security argument for protection. Using vivid military metaphors to describe competition in the economic marketplace, Joseph Wharton, a Pennsylvania steel producer and chief benefactor of the Wharton School at the University of Pennsylvania, did so in 1870. He warned of "foreign legions" attacking with "missiles launched from their far-distant mines, mills, and factories." Further, "their attack has often devastated homes . . . , and broken up industries as effectually as if the conquest had been effected by warlike weapons." But, Wharton asserted, "a tariff can defeat the foreign plunderer . . . better than a fort." He also suggested that free trade for the nation, like free love for the family, "leads to ruin." Free trade, or "trade philanthropy," was a "fungus . . . a source of infection which healthy political organisms can hardly afford to tolerate."[17]

In Congress no one expressed the economic security message more forcefully than Wharton's contemporary, the influential congressman William "Pig Iron" Kelley of Philadelphia. Calling "iron and steel the muscles of our more modern civilization," Kelley warned that "a people who cannot supply their own demand for iron and steel, but purchase it from foreigners beyond seas, are not independent; . . . they are politically dependent." So long as the United States relied on England for ships, guns, and shot, it "must endure contumely and outrage with unresisting humility."[18]

Low-Tariff Democrats

During the period from 1860 to 1932 Democrats, and their muckraking allies in the press, delighted in exposing how the protective system established a corrupt relationship between import-sensitive industries and the Republican Party. The former required protection to survive; the latter needed campaign contributions to endure in public office. Investigative journalist Ida Tarbell observed that "under our operation of the protective doctrine we have developed a politician who encourages the most dangerous kind of citizenship a democracy can know—the panicky, grasping, idealless kind." In a series of articles, later published as *The Tariff in Our Times*, Tarbell traced in intimate detail connections between Republicans and high protectionists from the Civil War to the early twentieth century. Later, political scientist Elmer Schattschneider documented such ties in his prize-winning study of the 1930 tariff-writing process. Finding multiple linkages between lobbyists for domestic manufacturers and the Republican Party, Schattschneider concluded that "the dominant position of the Republican party before 1932 can be attributed largely to the successful exploitation of the tariff by this party as a means of attaching to itself a formidable array of interests dependent on the protective system and intent upon continuing it."[19]

Democratic orators spoke at length about monopolies and "robbery." During debate over the proposed Dingley Tariff in 1897, Senator Roger Q. Mills, a free trade Democrat from Texas, claimed that the bill was a "stupendous system of legislative rapine and robbery." In 1912 Democratic presidential candidate Woodrow Wilson attacked "our tariff-walled system of privilege" and asserted that "the bills of the Republican party were paid by business men who wanted a high tariff." During World War I Senator Oscar Underwood, of Alabama, who as chairman of the House Ways and Means Committee in 1913 had authored a substantial reduction in tariff rates, accused Republicans of giving "the selected few the right to monopolize and abuse the American market." And Cordell Hull of Tennessee claimed that Republican tariff policy "involves a corrupt partnership between politics and vested industrial interests, the poison of which constantly breeds national scandal."[20]

If nineteenth-century Republicans exhibited remarkable consistency in their support for the protective system, Democrats vacillated between open approval of free trade and protection for working people. Some Democrats, like Representative John R. Tucker (D-Va.), a member of the Ways and Means Committee, voiced unyielding Cobdenite views. In one 1878 speech, Tucker declared: "Free trade . . . will spread the banner of peace over the world and promote the glory of God, in 'peace on earth and good will toward men.' Free trade, the product of the divine doctrines of Christianity, would be the peacemaker of the world!" Other Democrats rationalized the quest for free trade as benefiting mankind. Said Representative W. Bourke Cockran (D-N.Y.), another member of Ways and Means, in 1894: "In seeking to find the freest markets for our products, we seek the welfare of the whole human race, we seek to establish a commercial system which will make this land the fountain of civilization—the people the trustees of humanity."[21]

When Democrats attacked protectionist "monopolies," they won grassroots applause. But rigid support for unrestricted free trade also presented political problems. It raised questions about the willingness of Democrats to collect taxes and govern responsibly. To deflect such criticisms, the Democrats endorsed a "tariff-for-revenue only." This approach, they claimed, would capture the largest revenue while providing "incidental" protection to import-competing products.

Consistent Democratic support for low tariffs exposed a second vulnerability. Freer trade appealed to individuals in their roles as consumers but not necessarily to workers. Academic economists stress that consumers gain in the short run from free trade. Indeed, nineteenth-century journalist Ambrose

Bierce joked that the purpose of a tariff was to protect a domestic producer "against the greed of his consumer."[22] But consumer greed was a fair weather argument. In hard times politicians found that workers and producers worried more about import competition endangering domestic jobs.

Unlike nineteenth-century Republicans, low-tariff Democrats waxed eloquently over the benefits of competition to the marketplace, even if that competition involved foreign firms taking sales away from domestic producers. Senator Oscar Underwood (D-Ala.) said that Democrats adopted the competitive theory: "We say that no revenue can be produced at the customhouse unless there is some competition between the products of foreign countries and domestic products."[23]

To attract business support in the 1880s, Democrats recommended the "radical reduction" of duties imposed on materials used in manufactures. President Grover Cleveland argued that this modification would give U.S. exporters "a better chance in foreign markets" when competing against countries "who cheapen their wares by free material."[24]

For individual Democratic candidates, the national party's commitment to a revenue tariff provided tactical advantages. It gave them ample room to maneuver in response to local circumstances. Democrats in the agricultural South could support only low tariffs to meet the legitimate expenses of government, whereas northern Democrats in states like Pennsylvania and New Jersey could construe the tariff-for-revenue-only pledge as providing incidental protection to import-sensitive industries.

Before the Civil War free trade sympathies ran strong among Democrats. They received encouragement from British Cobdenites, who were eager to lure the United States away from protectionism. In December 1845, during the Polk administration, Treasury secretary Robert Walker espoused free trade enthusiastically. In the 1856 presidential election Democrats boldly hoisted the free trade banner. Declaring that government should raise no more revenue than "required to defray the necessary expenses" of government, Democrats openly asserted that "the time has come for the people of the United States to declare themselves in favor of . . . progressive free trade throughout the world."[25]

Abroad, Walker's low-tariff revenue proposals received an enthusiastic reaction in England among the Cobdenites. A pragmatic British government directed its officials in North America to promote "free intercourse between the two nations," opening the U.S. market for British manufactures.[26]

For some Democrats the tariff-for-revenue-only formulation was as close as they dared go to free trade. Senator Donelson Caffery (D-La.) said: "When a Democrat plants himself upon a tariff for revenue only, he comes as near to being a free-trader as the Constitution of the United States will permit; and that is the sort of a Democrat I am. Free trade has no terrors for me."[27]

Election Year Tariff Battles

From 1860 to 1932 trade partisanship regularly enlivened presidential campaigns. In election after election the two major parties and their presidential candidates battled lustily over tariff issues. For Republicans, enthusiastic support for the American protective system regularly produced rewards at the ballot box. During this seventy-two-year-period, the party of Abraham Lincoln proudly embraced high tariffs and won fourteen out of eighteen presidential elections. The Democrats, tainted with secessionism and defeat, encountered insuperable political obstacles in the immediate postwar period. Indeed, in 1872 a still weakened Democratic Party endorsed liberal Republican editor Horace Greeley, a renown protectionist. To deflect the tariff issue, the party platform simply recognized "irreconcilable differences of opinion with regard to the respective systems of protection and free trade" and remitted "the discussion of the subject to the people in their Congressional Districts, and the decision of the Congress thereon, wholly free from Executive interference or dictation."[28]

After the 1873 economic collapse, Democratic political fortunes revived. The next year the Democrats won control of the House of Representatives. As memories of the bitter Civil War receded, a rejuvenated Democratic Party began to compete vigorously for control of the White House. To curry political favor, Democrats attempted to focus attention on the protective tariff. Tariff reform was thus a dominant issue in the elections of 1884, 1888, and 1892, and campaign rhetoric became increasingly strident.

In 1884, when the Democrats nominated New York's Governor Grover Cleveland, their platform blasted Republicans for professing "the protection of American manufactures" but subjecting workers "to an increasing flood of manufactured goods, and a hopeless competition with manufacturing nations." Urging voters to vote Democratic for change, party leaders pledged to "revise the tariff in a spirit of fairness to all interests." They promised to reduce taxes without injuring "any domestic industries" and "without depriving American labor of the ability to compete successfully with foreign labor."[29]

Although Cleveland won the election, the Democrats failed to take control of Congress. Lacking a majority on Capitol Hill, they waited patiently for an opportunity. Late in 1887 Cleveland raised the tariff reform issue in his annual message to Congress. Calling "present tariff laws, the vicious, inequitable, and illogical source of unnecessary taxation," the president devoted his entire December 1887 annual message to promoting revenue and tariff reform. The tariff imposed a "burden upon those who consume domestic products as well as those who consume imported articles," and he urged "relief from the hardships and dangers of our present tariff laws" to reduce the cost of living. As

Senator John Sherman (R-Ohio) noted, the president had drawn a line. Cleveland proposed to maintain excise taxes while lowering protection for import-competitive industries. His Republican opponents generally favored the opposite: removing excise taxes while retaining protective tariffs.[30]

In April 1888 Cleveland's ally in the House of Representatives, Ways and Means chairman Roger Q. Mills (D-Tex.), introduced a tariff reduction bill. Mills explained that "enormous taxation upon the necessaries of life has been a constant drain upon the people." Such taxation took from "the people $5 for private purposes for every dollar that it carries to the public treasury." Along with claiming that the benefits went to trusts and manufacturers, not consumers, Mills attempted to rebut Republican arguments that a lower tariff would lead to reduced wages for working people. He attributed high wages to "coal and steam and machinery" and argued that a "high rate of wages means low cost of product."[31]

Another Democratic ally, William L. Wilson of Virginia, vividly described "the fruits" of twenty-five years of protection. These included "growing antagonism between labor and capital," industrial depression, strikes, corruption, and trusts. A spirited debate ensued, with Representative William McKinley of Ohio responding to Democratic claims that consumers would gain from lower tariffs. "[I]f this bill should pass," the Ohioan said, "the effect would be . . . to destroy our domestic manufactories, the era of low prices would vanish, and the foreign manufacturer would compel the American consumer to pay higher prices than he has been accustomed to pay under the 'robber tariff.'"[32]

The partisan debate in Congress over the Mills bill set the stage for a bitter election campaign. With Republicans controlling the Senate and Democrats the House, Congress could not enact tariff reform. Both parties took their positions to the people.

In its 1888 platform the GOP declared: "We are uncompromisingly in favor of the American system of protection; we protest against its destruction as proposed by the President [Cleveland] and his party. They serve the interests of Europe; we will support the interests of America." Republican presidential nominee Benjamin Harrison of Indiana rejected the Democratic theory that consumers paid import duties. Proponents of that view, he said, were "students of maxims, not of the markets." Republicans "believe it to be one of the worthy objects of tariff legislation to preserve the American market for American producers, and to maintain the American scale of wages by adequate discriminative duties upon foreign competing products."[33]

During the 1888 campaign cartoonists had a field day. *Judge*, a humor magazine with protectionist sympathies, regularly portrayed Cleveland as a willing dupe of English free traders. One centerfold celebrated July 4, 1888, as the "Declaration of *Dependence*." It showed a kneeling Cleveland surrendering

VOL. 14 NO. 347   JUNE 9. 1888.   PRICE 10 CENTS.

ENGLAND'S CANDIDATE FOR THE AMERICAN PRESIDENCY.
"PRESIDENT CLEVELAND is the most popular American with the English people."—*London Correspondence*

"England's Candidate for the American Presidency." *Judge* (June 9, 1888) depicts free trader President Cleveland as a dupe of England's John Bull. (Special Collections, Alden Library, Ohio University)

"The Declaration of Dependence, July 4th, 1888." The Unconditional Surrender of the Anglo-Maniac President Grover Cleveland to John Bull. *Judge*, July 7, 1888. (Special Collections, Alden Library, Ohio University)

American industries to a triumphant John Bull, the symbol of England. Another issue portrayed an American workman asking England's John Bull: "Mr. Bull, if Free Trade is such a blessing, why are your agricultural interests in such a wretched condition? Why do your manufacturers cry out for 'Fair Trade,' and why does your skilled English workman come to this country instead of the American workman going to England?"[34] Free traders found support in *Puck*, another humor magazine, where cartoonist Joseph Keppler and his associates regularly depicted protectionism as a hydra monster benefiting monopolists and crushing the common person.[35]

With Republicans associating protectionism with job security, a high-tariff Republican challenger beat the low-tariff incumbent in 1888. According to historians of that election, President Cleveland's tariff position contributed significantly to the outcome. Many workers in Cleveland's home state of New York voted for Harrison. Republican protectionists successfully linked Cleveland to English free trade and foreign campaign contributions.[36]

After Harrison's inauguration, Republicans moved to revise the tariff upward. Their legislation carried the name of House Ways and Means Committee chairman William McKinley. Although some historical accounts claim that the McKinley Tariff "extended and increased [the] scope of protection," data indicate that the "infamous" McKinley Tariff may have reduced average rates.[37]

"An Old Game." Cartoonist Joseph Keppler depicts the crafty priest of protectionism receiving the people's sacrifices. *Puck*, May 23, 1888. (Author's personal copy)

The *ratio of duties calculated to all imports* fell from 30.02 percent in 1889 to 25.65 percent in 1891, the first full year under the McKinley Tariff. Duties on dutiable imports did rise slightly from 45.49 percent in 1889 to 46.5 percent in 1891. More important, the percentage of imports on the free list rose from 34 percent in 1889 to 44.8 percent in 1891.[38] Along with a bilateral reciprocity provision intended to encourage bargaining, the 1890 tariff contained a number of other noteworthy terms. It required country-of-origin markings for imports, it prohibited the importation of convict-made goods, and it liberalized the drawback requirement to encourage the importation of raw materials and the reexport of processed items. The last provision was expected to facilitate exports, creating jobs and industries along the seacoasts.

As events turned out, the battle over the McKinley Tariff represented another bitter partisan round in the prolonged post–Civil War tariff debate. It settled nothing. In the 1892 presidential campaign, the GOP gleefully "reaffirm[ed] the American doctrine of protection. . . . We maintain that the prosperous condition of our country is largely due to the wise revenue legislation of the Republican congress." Pointing to the success of Republican reciprocity policies in opening foreign markets for American exports, the platform boasted that "executed by a Republican administration, our present laws will eventually give us control of the trade of the world."[39]

The Democrats again nominated Cleveland and "denounce[d] Republican protection as fraud, a robbery of the great majority of the American people for the benefit of the few." They declared it "a fundamental principle of the Democratic party that the Federal Government has no constitutional power to impose and collect tariff duties, except for revenue only."[40]

This time the Democrats won. In March 1893, as defeated Republican incumbent Benjamin Harrison prepared to vacate the White House, he offered another glowing testimonial to the protective system. It was "a mighty instrument for the development of our national wealth and a most powerful agency in protecting the homes of our workingmen from the invasion of want."[41]

Trade Politics: Early Twentieth Century

Republican enthusiasm for protection did not ebb in the early twentieth century. "We renew our faith in the policy of Protection to American labor," asserted the GOP in 1900. Four years later Republicans claimed: "Protection, which guards and develops our industries, is a cardinal policy of the Republican party. The measure of protection should always at least equal the difference in the cost of production at home and abroad." Supporting tariff revision in 1908, Republicans nonetheless pledged to "preserve . . . that security against foreign competition to which American manufacturers, farmers and producers are entitled."[42]

Another great tariff battle occurred in 1912. In nominating New Jersey governor Woodrow Wilson, the Democrats selected a tariff reformer in the Grover Cleveland tradition. Candidate Wilson made no effort to conceal his free trade sympathies. In January 1912 he told the National Democratic Club of New York that "I wish I might hope that our grandchildren could indulge in free trade." His platform called for "the immediate downward revision of the existing high and in many cases prohibitive tariff duties." It asserted that "American wages are established by competitive conditions, and not by the tariff." Democrats also claimed that "the Federal government, under the Constitution, has no right or power to impose or collect tariff duties."[43]

In 1912 Republicans reaffirmed their belief in a protective tariff. That policy benefited the country, developed resources, diversified industries, and defended "our workmen against competition with cheaper labor abroad, thus establishing for our wage-earners the American standard of living."[44] During World War I the GOP repeated its protectionist message. The 1916 GOP platform stated: The "Republican party stands now, as always, in the fullest sense for the policy of tariff protection to American industries and American labor."[45]

In the next decade Republicans rhapsodized over the protective system. The 1920 GOP platform reaffirmed its "belief in the protective principles" and pledged tariff revision "for preservation of the home market for American labor, agriculture and industry." In a message to Congress soon after taking office, President Warren Harding stated: "I believe in the protection of American industry, and it is our purpose to prosper America first."[46] Four years later, as they nominated Calvin Coolidge, Republicans waxed that "in the history of the nation" the protective tariff system had restored confidence, promoted industrial activity and employment, and brought increased prosperity to all. "A protective tariff," the platform asserted, "is designed to support the high American economic level of life for the average family and to prevent a lowering to the levels of economic life prevailing in other lands."[47]

After World War I Democrats reiterated the tariff-for-revenue-only position in 1920 and then blasted the Fordney-McCumber Tariff in 1924. That statute was "the most unjust, unscientific and dishonest tariff tax measure ever enacted in our history," Democrats claimed. "It is class legislation which defrauds the people for the benefit of a few, . . . heavily increases the cost of living, penalizes agriculture, corrupts the government, fosters paternalism."[48]

Interestingly, four years later—in 1928—both major parties offered protectionist messages to voters. Republicans reiterated their belief in the protective tariff "as a fundamental and essential principle of the economic life of this nation." Democrats adopted a similar position. Adjusting to the campaign needs of an urban presidential candidate, Governor Alfred E. Smith of New York, Democrats abandoned the tariff-for-revenue-only formula and wrote a more protectionist trade plank, hoping to pick up electoral votes in the Northeast. They pledged Democratic tariff legislation based on "maintenance of legitimate business and a high standard of wages for American labor.... Actual difference between the cost of production at home and abroad, with adequate safeguard for the wage of the American laborer must be the extreme measure of every tariff rate."[49]

One of the last bitter trade debates between Republican protectionists and Democratic reformers occurred in 1932. This one reflected sharp partisan differences over enactment of the Smoot-Hawley Tariff and Depression-era politics. At the Republican convention, President Hoover's supporters reiterated the party's longtime position that "adequate tariff protection" was "particularly essential to the welfare of the American people." They pledged not to "surrender" the home market to "such competition as would destroy our farms, mines and factories, and lower the standard of living which we have established for our workers." But, reflecting Hoover's own enthusiasm for scientific tariff making, the Republican platform reiterated the importance of employing the impartial Tariff Commission to investigate individual rates and recommend any duty increases "necessary to equalize domestic with foreign costs of production." The GOP campaign document also reaffirmed support for the most-favored-nation principle as the only policy suitable for a country with a great variety of products, and it rejected "bargains and partnerships with foreign nations" as a "permanent policy ... unsuited to America's position."[50]

Predictably, the 1932 Democratic platform blamed the incumbent Hoover administration for having "ruined our foreign trade . . . and thrown millions more out of work." Democrats advocated "a competitive tariff for revenue with a fact-finding tariff commission free from executive interference, reciprocal tariff agreements with other nations, and an international economic conference designed to restore international trade and facilitate exchange." That language reflected the influence of Tennessee senator Cordell Hull, a reputed tariff expert.[51]

During the campaign nominee Franklin Roosevelt followed his own pragmatic instincts, attempting to satisfy both free traders and protectionists among his supporters. In a Seattle speech, Roosevelt advocated a tariff policy that rested on bilateral "barter." If another country "has something we need, and we have something it needs, a tariff agreement can and should be made that is satisfactory to both countries."[52]

Roosevelt's major speech on trade matters, presented in Sioux City, Iowa, on September 29, took a different approach. He blamed the so-called Hawley-

Smoot-Grundy Tariff of 1930 for ruining export markets for U.S. agriculture and encouraging other countries to retaliate. The candidate interpreted the Democratic platform's call for a "competitive" tariff as meaning "one that equalizes the difference in the cost of production." He distinguished this approach from the Republican commitment to a prohibitory tariff—one "looking to the total exclusion of imports." Roosevelt proposed to reduce "outrageously excessive rates" through commonsense negotiations. This would involve bartering in "our Yankee tradition of good old fashioned trading."[53]

Facing the daunting task of winning reelection in the midst of a depression, President Hoover attempted to exploit a perceived Democratic weakness—the lack of strong support for sustaining a protective tariff. Whereas Roosevelt preached reciprocity and barter, Hoover stood resolutely for tariff protection. He warned that Democratic proposals would "place our farmers and workers in competition with peasant and sweated labor products." Speaking in Des Moines, Iowa, a few days after challenger Franklin Roosevelt visited that region, Hoover warned that Democrats "will reduce agricultural tariffs if they come into power." This would mean price reductions or rotting unsold produce. Later, in Cleveland, the president warned that with a tariff-for-revenue-only American workers would compete "with laborers whose wages in their own money are only sufficient to buy from one-eighth to one-third of the amount of bread and butter which you can buy at the present rates of wages." The Democratic Party, he claimed, would surrender the American labor market to foreign countries.[54]

In response to Hoover's vigorous attacks, Roosevelt changed positions. Late in the campaign, he told a Boston crowd: "I favor . . . continued protection for American agriculture as well as American industry." During the 1932 campaign Roosevelt's real tariff policy remained an enigma, for he repeatedly adapted his words to campaign circumstances. Raymond Moley, who became disenchanted with Roosevelt's "evasion" on this issue, later asserted that FDR's "*tariff policies* contemplated . . . modified protectionism to safeguard his experiments in wage and price raising." However, in the hands of the persistent tariff reformer, Cordell Hull, this policy became "modified free-tradism." Hull generalized reciprocal concessions to all countries and embarked on a policy of tariff reduction.[55]

As the intensity of campaign rhetoric over tariff issues suggests, domestic political considerations generally drove tariff and trade policies during the years from 1860 to 1932. This debate often mirrored local concerns. Even so, one excessively candid presidential candidate, Democrat Winfield Scott Hancock, had aroused public consternation during the 1880 campaign when he frankly acknowledged that "the tariff question is a local question."[56]

Coping with a Budget Surplus

Along with parochial political concerns, other factors helped shape the debate. After the Civil War an overburdened public sought relief from the high excise taxes and customs duties imposed during the conflict. To finance the war Congress had hastily ratcheted the tariff and excise taxes ever higher. The average duties on dutiable imports soared from 18.8 percent in 1861 to 47.6 percent in 1865. Before the war customs ordinarily generated 90 percent of federal revenues, but tariff revenue could not pay for heavy wartime expenditures. Congress turned to domestic excise taxes and sales of public lands to generate supplementary income—and by 1864 the tariff supplied less than 40 percent of federal revenue.[57]

With the Union victory, commerce revived and customs revenues soared. This situation created an embarrassing fiscal dilemma for President Ulysses S. Grant and Congress. With revenues from the surplus paying down the national debt, Congress vigorously debated how best to staunch the flow of revenues. Should Congress reduce domestic excise taxes or lower tariffs on imports? Revenue reformers such as David A. Wells, commissioner of revenue, advocated making steep cuts in duty schedules and enlarging the free list. Other import-sensitive industries, like the steel industry, organized lobbying campaigns to maintain protective barriers.[58]

In 1872 Congress modified the high tariff system—changing it from one designed to tax *all* imports for revenue to a protective system intended to aid domestic industries and shelter working people from low-wage foreign competition. Accepting a 10 percent horizontal reduction in duties, Congress effectively expunged low-revenue duties, such as for tea and coffee, while retaining protective duties. In effect the United States moved toward a selective, protective system in which government admitted raw materials and noncompetitive materials duty-free but retained high tariffs on manufactured goods in order to stimulate industry and economic development.[59]

Historical statistics record this transition. Customs collections gradually shifted from a sweeping horizontal tariff, covering raw materials, intermediate goods, and manufactured products, to a selective, protective tariff sheltering value-added products. Until 1872, the average duty on all imports usually did not diverge substantially from the average duty on dutiable imports. Only 5 percent of imports entered the country duty-free, approximately the same percentage as in the early 1820s. In ten of the thirteen years from 1860 to 1872, the difference between revenue collection on dutiable products and collection on all imports was five percentage points or less. The average duty on all imports ranged from a low of 14.2 percent in 1861 to a high of 46.6 percent in 1868. Over the next thirty years, from 1872 to 1902, the gap between the two ratios always exceeded ten percentage points. Frequently, it rose to twenty percentage points. The transition is significant. In the 1890s some 45 to 52 percent of imports entered the U.S. duty-free, and high protective duties sheltered import-sensitive manufactures.[60]

Over the long span from 1860 to 1932, Congress revised the tariff every seven or eight years on the average. But, except for the Underwood Tariff reductions of 1913, average ad valorem equivalents remained high. Indeed, *in every year from 1862 to 1911, the average duty on all imports exceeded 20 percent ad valorem.* In forty-six of those fifty years the average duty on dutiable imports exceeded 40 percent ad valorem equivalent.[61] Despite periodic congressional fine tuning and experimentation with reciprocity, high protection characterized the entire period, except for a nine-year span during and after World War I when wartime economics and dislocations interfered with market conditions.

Assessing the Protective System

Did the protective system of late-nineteenth-century America promote economic development, facilitate job creation, and produce higher real incomes, as proponents claimed? Or did it merely tax consumers for the benefit of domestic monopolists?

From the written record it is apparent that the participants themselves had widely divergent interpretations. These reflected differing sectional and political perspectives. Not surprisingly, nineteenth-century protectionists claimed enormous achievements and spectacular successes. They attributed the nation's phenomenal economic achievements to the policies of Alexander Hamilton, Henry Clay, and the Lincoln Republicans. Protective duties generated abundant revenues, encouraged the development of a balanced and diversified industrial base, and produced high wages for American workers. Perhaps the 1896 Republican platform best memorialized this perspective:

We renew and emphasize our allegiance to the policy of *protection, the bulwark of American industrial independence, and the foundation of American development and prosperity.* This true American policy taxes foreign products and encourages home industry. It puts the burden of revenue on foreign goods; it secures the American market for the American producer. It upholds the American standard of wages for the American workingman; it puts the factory by the side of the farm and makes the American farmer less dependent on foreign demand and price; it diffuses general thrift, and founds the strength of all on the strength of each. In its reasonable application it is just, fair and impartial, equally opposed to foreign control and domestic monopoly[,] to sectional discrimination and individual favoritism. (emphasis added)[62]

Democrats placed a different interpretation on events. They emphasized monopolistic gains and consumer losses. Said presidential candidate Woodrow Wilson in 1912: "No frank mind can doubt that the great systems of special privilege and monopolistic advantage that have been built up have been built up upon the foundation of the tariff. The tariff question is at the heart of every other economic question."[63]

Available data suggest some interesting, and unconventional, conclusions. For one thing, the protective tariff proved to be a bountiful source of government revenue, often providing half of government tax collections in the years before 1913. During the 1880s, for instance, the federal government collected $3.64 billion in aggregate revenues (58 percent from customs duties) and reported an aggregate surplus of $1 billion. Indeed, for twenty-eight consecutive years (1866–93), the government in Washington enjoyed spectacular budget surpluses. Awash in tariff revenues, political leaders looked for ways to increase spending. They used excess revenues to reduce the national debt, which dropped from a post–Civil War high of $2.76 billion in 1866 to less than $1 billion in 1892.

Low-tariff Democrats considered the revenue bonanza an opportunity to effect tariff reform. In 1887 President Grover Cleveland devoted his entire annual message to Congress to this subject. He warned that the persistent Treasury surplus, which took money out of circulation, presaged "financial convulsion and widespread disaster. . . . The public Treasury, which should only exist as a conduit conveying the people's tribute to its legitimate objects of expenditure, becomes a hoarding place for money needlessly withdrawn from trade and the people's use, thus crippling our national energies, suspending our country's development, preventing investment in productive enterprise, threatening financial disturbance, and inviting schemes of public plunder."[64]

Until the Underwood Tariff of 1913 sharply reduced tariff levels and the federal government turned to the income tax, high tariffs generated a significant portion of federal revenues. But this source proved inadequate to Civil War military expenditures, and during the 1890s new problems emerged. Revenues declined sharply during the depression of 1893 as trade fell and lower Wilson-Gorman schedules reduced customs revenues. Then the budget deficit soared again during the Spanish-American War. Afterward, military expenditures remained high as the United States administered a large overseas empire and built up its naval forces. These developments forced Congress to find another revenue source—the personal income tax (see Table 2.1).

The nineteenth-century data suggest a second unconventional conclusion.

TABLE 2.1

U.S. Customs Duties and Federal Revenue, Selected Years from 1860 to 1992

Year	(1)	(2)	(3)	(4)
1860	15.7%	94.9%	−7.1	−12.6%
1865	38.5	25.4	−963.8	−288.8
1870	44.9	47.3	101.6	24.7
1875	29.4	54.6	13.4	4.6
1880	29.1	55.9	65.9	19.8
1885	30.8	56.1	63.5	19.6
1890	29.6	57.0	85.0	21.1
1895	20.4	46.9	−31.5	−9.7
1900	27.6	41.1	46.4	8.2
1905	23.8	48.1	−23.0	−4.2
1910	21.1	49.4	−18.1	−2.7
1915	12.5	30.7	−62.7	−9.2
1920	6.4	4.9	291.2	4.4
1925	13.2	15.0	717.0	19.7
1930	14.8	14.5	737.7	18.2
1992	3.3	1.6	−290,160.0	−26.6

Key:
(1) Average ad valorem equivalent tariff on all imports.
(2) Customs duties as a percentage of total federal revenue.
(3) Federal budget surplus (or deficit) in millions of dollars.
(4) Federal budget surplus (or deficit) as a share of federal revenue.
Sources: U.S. Bureau of the Census, *Historical Statistics of the United States*, bicentennial ed. (Washington, D.C.: GPO, 1974), 2:888, 1104, 1106, and *Statistical Abstract of the United States* (Washington, D.C.: GPO, 1993), pp. 328–29, 818. In reporting average tariff levels, I have used the ratio of average duties calculated to free and dutiable imports. On the need for caution in making ad valorem comparisons, see U.S. Tariff Commission, *The Tariff and Its History*, misc. ser. (Washington, D.C.: GPO, 1934), pp. 107–9.

TABLE 2.2

Comparative Annual Growth of Real Gross Domestic Product in Selected Countries and Western Europe, 1870–1913

Years	U.K.	Germany	France	U.S.	Western Europe
1870–80	1.9%	1.8%	2.0%	4.8%	2.9%
1880–90	2.2	2.9	0.8	4.1	2.7
1890–1900	2.1	3.4	2.1	3.8	2.2
1900–1913	1.5	3.0	1.7	3.9	2.0

Source: Sidney Pollard, *Britain's Prime and Britain's Decline: The British Economy, 1870–1914* (London: Edward Arnold, 1989), p. 5.

Although most late-twentieth-century economists argue strenuously that free trade promotes a more rapid growth of the GNP and exports than protectionism, historical statistics reveal a paradox. Before World War I, protectionism apparently did not significantly harm U.S. economic growth or retard export expansion. Between 1870 and 1913, nations pursuing more protective policies (the United States and Germany) experienced higher domestic growth rates and more rapid export expansion than did free trade Great Britain. If, as economic theorists argue, free trade is more beneficial, it is striking that the single nation pursuing a free trade policy throughout this period exhibited annual real growth far below its chief commercial rivals (see Tables 2.2–2.4).

In Tzarist Russia high-tariff policies during the 1890s also may have aided domestic growth and helped attract foreign investments. Count Sergei Witte, an enthusiastic advocate of Friedrich List's nationalistic economic policies who served as finance minister from 1892 to 1903, attributed Russia's rapid economic development to the protectionist policies pursued under Tzar Alexander III.[65]

During the late nineteenth century Great Britain and the United States pursued quite different trade strategies—a point frequently noted in congressional debates. In 1883, for example, Ways and Means Committee chairman William "Pig Iron" Kelley spent three months traveling in England and returned to report his findings. Recalling that Thomas Carlyle had warned about a race with barbarous nations for the production of the "cheap and nasty," Kelley vividly described the "desperate struggle for life imposed on British toilers by cheap goods and low wages." He found young women galvanizing bathtubs for $1.75 per week, "although the strongest of them knows

TABLE 2.3

Comparative Export Growth Rates (by Volume) in Selected Countries and the World, 1870–1913

Year	U.K.	Germany	France	U.S.A.	World
1870–80	2.9%	2.4%	3.4%	10.4%	3.4%
1880–90	1.3	2.9	2.0	1.4	3.4
1890–1900	0.6	4.1	1.5	6.1	2.4
1900–1913	4.2	6.4	3.8	2.5	4.1
1870–1913	2.8	4.1	2.8	4.9	3.4

Source: Pollard, *Britain's Prime and Britain's Decline*, p. 7.

that in less than six months the gases generated by the process will vitally impair her health." To Kelley, England seemed the "vampire of nations."[66]

Conditions in England contrasted sharply with those in the United States, Kelley said. "Our protective tariff has . . . furnished attractive and gentle employment to the feeble, the crippled, the early-orphaned, and has thus called into exercise the genius and special endowments of our people."

What were the consequences of free trade for Britain? In his biography of Joseph Chamberlain, Julian Amery lists some "bitter consequences." He says: "Ireland was ruined. . . . British agriculture collapsed; the landed interest withered away; and British industry thus lost a major sector of its home market." Amery echoes the assessment of Cambridge economic historian William Cunningham, who warned at the beginning of the twentieth-century that one-sided free trade exposed English laborers to the "malign results of cosmopolitan competition."[67]

Did Britain's unilateral free trade policies harm the domestic economy, as critics allege? Historical statistics and data available to scholars suggest a connection. Imports of finished manufactures gradually rose as a share of total British imports from 7.3 percent in 1860 to 18.8 percent in 1900.[68] Meanwhile, Britain's merchandise trade balance deteriorated. Exports and reexports in the years immediately before the American Civil War averaged 80 percent of merchandise imports. Fifty years later, exports and reexports dropped to 69.7 percent of merchandise imports, reflecting the steady rise in imports of finished goods. As these data imply, Britain's share of world manufacturing exports slipped, falling from a peak of 46 percent in 1870–72 to 39 percent in 1880 and 31 percent in 1900.

TABLE 2.4
Comparative Tariff Levels, 1913

Country/Region	Import Duties as a Percent of Total Imports	Approximate Average Duty— Manufactures
France	8.7%	20%
Germany	7.9	13
Continental Europe	10.4	19
United Kingdom	5.7	0
United States	21.4	44

Source: Paul Bairoch, "European Trade Policy, 1815–1914," in *Cambridge Economic History of Europe*, ed. Peter Mathias and Sidney Pollard (Cambridge: Cambridge University Press, 1989), 8:77, 139.

Britain's economic growth rate also lagged. Over the forty-three-year period from 1870 to 1913, industrial production rose 4.7 percent annually in the United States, 4.1 percent in Germany, but only 2.1 percent in the United Kingdom. Obviously, many other factors also contributed to the British decline—including inadequate investment and education in the new technologies. From the vantage point of the 1990s, however, it would seem that late-nineteenth-century Britain, like late-twentieth-century America, allowed commercial rivals to export from closed home markets. As a result, the latter achieved economies of scale and higher rates of return on domestic sales to finance investment in new technologies and products.[69]

Although economic theorists assert that free trade promotes more rapid growth in income and trade, some economic historians appear skeptical. In the *Cambridge Economic History of Europe*, Paul Bairoch presents data showing that in the period before World War I European countries increased domestic growth more than 100 percent and exports more than 35 percent faster after protectionist moves than before. He concludes that "protectionism does not always and necessarily hinder" the expansion of trade or domestic economic growth.[70]

U.S. data suggest a similar conclusion. Table 2.5 compares real GNP growth in two separate twenty-year periods—from 1890 to 1910 and from 1972 to 1992. During the protectionist era from 1890 to 1910, the average duty on all U.S. imports never dropped below 20 percent and the duty on dutiable imports averaged 40 percent. In the second period, after 1970, average U.S. duties on all imports never exceeded 6.5 percent or 10 percent on dutiable products. If one

TABLE 2.5

U.S. Growth in Gross National Product and Per Capita GNP, 1890–1910 and 1972–1992

Year	GNP (Billions of $)	Percent of Change	Per Capita GNP	Percent of Change
1890	$ 52.7		$ 836	
1910	120.1	4.2% increase per year	1,299	2.2% increase per year
1972	3,128.8		14,906	
1992	4,985.7	2.4% increase per year	19,515	1.40% increase per year

Sources: U.S. Bureau of the Census, *Historical Statistics of the United States,* bicentennial ed. (Washington, D.C.: GPO, 1974), 1:224, 1890 and 1910 data using 1958 prices; U.S. Bureau of Economic Analysis, *Survey of Current Business* (Washington, D.C.: GPO, December 1992), 72:30, 1972 and 1992 data using 1987 prices; U.S. President, *Economic Report of the President* (Washington, D.C.: GPO, 1995), pp. 277, 307.

compares economic growth in the protectionist period from 1890 to 1910 to the interval of relatively free trade from 1972 to 1992, a surprising picture emerges. GNP, in constant dollars, rose at a 4.2 percent rate under high tariff policies, but at a much slower rate under free trade conditions. From 1972 to 1992 it grew only 2.4 percent annually. Similarly, real per capita GNP increased at a 2.2 percent compound annual rate in the protectionist period, but it rose only 1.4 percent annually under recent free trade circumstances.

During the high-tariff period from 1869 to 1910, merchandise imports as a share of U.S. gross national product fell from 7.9 percent in 1869 to 6.0 percent in 1890 and to 4.2 percent in 1910. Under the lower Underwood Tariff, that percentage climbed slightly—from 4.5 percent in 1913 to 5.9 percent in 1920—and then receded during a period of higher tariffs. In 1929 general imports amounted to only 4.2 percent of GNP. Merchandise imports remained below 1929 levels until after 1970, then increased to 9.1 percent in 1980 and remained at about that level a decade later. These figures mask a shift in the composition of imports. In 1980 petroleum products amounted to 31.8 percent of imports; a decade later the figure had dropped to only 12.5 percent. In 1980 imports of capital goods, automotive vehicles, and consumer goods accounted for 37.7 percent of imports; in 1990 they reached 62 percent. A sharp reduction in tariff barriers during the Kennedy Round, among other factors, may have contributed to the sharp rise in manufactured imports (see Table 2.6).[71]

Over the forty years from 1889 to 1929 GNP and per capita GNP, both

TABLE 2.6

U.S. Growth in Gross National Product and Per Capita GNP 1889–1929 and 1952–1992 (in constant 1987 prices; rates compounded)

Year	GNP (Billions of $)	Percent of Change	Per Capita GNP	Percent of Change
1889	$ 199.5		$ 3,230	
1929	827.4	3.62% increase per year	6,789	1.87% increase per year
1952	1,634.3		10,413	
1992	$4,985.7	2.83% increase per year	$19,515	1.58% increase per year

Sources: U.S. Bureau of the Census, *Historical Statistics of the United States,* bicentennial ed. (Washington, D.C.: GPO, 1974), 1:224, and *Statistical Abstract of the United States* (Washington, D.C.: GPO, 1993), p. 445; U.S. Bureau of Economic Analysis, *Survey of Current Business* (Washington, D.C.: GPO, July 1994), p. 57, and *National Income and Product Accounts of the United States* (Washington, D.C.: GPO, 1993), 1:15, 190. All data have been converted to constant 1987 prices.

adjusted for inflation, rose at a higher average rate than during a recent similar period of trade liberalization. In the former period, the average customs levy on dutiable goods exceeded 20 percent in all but one year. For twenty-six of those years the average rate on dutiable imports actually exceeded 40 percent. Yet GNP climbed in real terms at a 3.62 percent annual rate, significantly higher than the 2.83 rate recorded from 1952 to 1992. Per capita gross national product also rose faster during the protectionist period—1.87 percent annually compared with 1.58 percent in the last forty years. Importantly, this occurred at a time when the U.S. population nearly doubled from 63 million to 122 million. In the next forty years population grew more slowly, rising from 151 to 247 million. Interestingly, per capita GNP grew in the United States during the peak period of protectionism at an annual rate approximately double that of Great Britain, a country that adopted free trade in 1860. However, merchandise exports and imports as a share of GNP did decline slightly, down from an estimated 12.5 percent in 1889–93 to 10.2 percent in 1907–11 to 9.5 percent in 1924–29.[72]

From 1929 to 1992 both real GNP and per capita GNP grew more slowly. Certainly the immigration rate fell, and the surge in population subsided. Slower growth in per capita GNP coincided with a steady decline in U.S. customs duties, falling from 12.7 percent as a share of dutiable imports in 1952 to 5.2 percent in 1992. In 1970 the ratio of duties to dutiable imports dropped to

10 percent, and over subsequent years the U.S. growth in per capita GNP continued to slide. Whereas foreign trade as a share of GNP averaged only 7.8 percent in the five-year period from 1966 to 1970, down from pre-depression levels, this percentage doubled afterward, reaching 15.3 percent in 1992.[73]

How did protection affect the growth of export trade? Nineteenth-century data seem to suggest a positive correlation. From 1870 to 1913 both protectionist America and Germany gained a larger share of world exports. U.S. exports rose from 7.9 to 12.9 percent and German exports from 10.7 to 13.1 percent. Free trade Britain lost five points of global export market share, declining from 18.9 to 13.9 percent. In addition, the volume of British exports rose only 2.8 percent annually from 1870 to 1913, far slower than German (4.1 percent) and U.S. exports (4.9 percent).[74]

A third data series also helps compare personal income under different tariff regimes. The Department of Labor has computed weekly earnings for production workers since 1909. During the twenty-year period from 1909 to 1929, the average tax on dutiable goods fell below 20 percent in only one year (1920) and exceeded 30 percent in fourteen years. Weekly earnings for production workers, computed in constant prices, rose at a 1.5 percent annual rate. For the twenty-two-year period from 1970 to 1992, government data show a decline in real weekly earnings.[75]

Finally, did high tariffs impact consumers negatively? Curiously, the prices of protected products, like textiles and steel, had little adverse effect on consumers. In 1900 wholesale prices for household furnishings and for textiles had fallen to 30 percent of prices a generation earlier in 1870. Metal products, also heavily protected, fell to 49 percent of 1870 values, and chemicals to 41 percent. The prices for all commodities were 42 percent of 1870 levels at the turn of the twentieth century. Thus, despite high tariffs, prices fell, reflecting both competitive circumstances and the overall macroeconomic climate.[76]

What overall conclusions do the data suggest? Was a high-tariff strategy actually more beneficial than a market-opening trade policy for promoting rising incomes? From my vantage point, the U.S. data appear to demonstrate no significant negative relationship between high tariffs and real economic growth. This may surprise, and interest, those economists who argue that openness and growth are positively related. My conclusions, however, seem consistent with the findings of Paul Bairoch. He concludes that growth promotes trade expansion, not the reverse, and finds a positive association between protectionism and faster economic growth.[77]

Based on the historical information presented here, one should not hasten to assume that home market protection necessarily promotes faster economic growth. The data presented in this chapter do not establish causal relationships. A host of other factors influenced America's economic performance in the nineteenth century—including immigration, the development of a mass market, technology transfer, high rates of domestic capital formation and foreign investment, and a legal system protecting private property rights and permitting the emergence of large oligopolistic corporations. Unfortunately, economic historians have largely ignored the protective tariff as a factor in late-nineteenth-century U.S. growth. It is apparent that this issue merits more attention from scholars.[78]

Data from different historical periods and nations may suggest a tantalizing conclusion: home market protection is not necessarily inconsistent with high domestic and export growth. The experiences of nineteenth-century America, Japan after World War II, and some newly industrialized countries in Asia point to this result. Of course, free trade also correlates with rapid internal growth and trade expansion in city-states like Singapore and Hong Kong.[79]

These international growth comparisons require cautious interpretation. The differences may reflect disparate sources and stages of growth, not divergent tariff systems. For example, in the post–World War II period the Soviet Union and some East Asian countries appeared to enjoy higher growth than the United States. Economist Paul Krugman claims that input growth distorted the comparison. Growth in the Soviet Union and some East Asian countries reflected a rapid rise in inputs, resulting from more workers entering the labor force, increased education levels, and government mobilization of resources. But he attributes growth in the United States to the more efficient use of existing inputs, such as better management.[80]

Yet, for Americans who lived in the fabled Gilded Age and could compare relative opportunities for individuals on both sides of the Atlantic, the American protective system appeared compatible with high wages, rising living standards, and rapid economic growth. Americans took comfort from the fact that during the heyday of British free trade from 1871 to 1890, about 68,000 Britons emigrated annually to the United States seeking better economic opportunities.[81]

First Industrial Policy

The late-nineteenth-century U.S. experience raises another issue of relevance to late-twentieth-century policymakers: industrial policy. The phenomenal success of Japan and other east Asian industrializing nations since 1960 may indicate that development-minded bureaucracies can manage a nation's economic growth. Among major economies, import substitution, or protection, has played a role in successful industrialization efforts.[82] Iron ically, the Asian success stories drew inspiration from the nineteenth-century U.S. example. James Fallows has observed the popularity of Friedrich List's teachings in Japan and eastern Asia. A Japanese trade negotiator in 1955 noted how tariff protection "contributed" to the development of U.S. industry and used this precedent to rationalize Japanese protection.

No intrusive bureaucracy guided American industrial policy. The policy had statutory roots. Congress and the executive branch enacted tariffs, sheltering domestic industries from competition. Politics, as well as a desire for independence, shaped this policy. In some instances, Congress even authorized subsidies and bounties to strengthen the merchant marine, to build transcontinental railroads, and to improve communications.

Interestingly, nineteenth-century Americans had no aversion to the term *industrial policy*, which apparently had its genesis in post–Civil War revenue debates. The followers of Henry Carey, the Philadelphia economist influential among Republicans and business leaders, stressed the vital importance of home production to the "harmony" of economic and social interests. They rejected the clamor for a "British industrial policy" that treated workers like paupers or slaves. Stephen Colwell, one of three revenue commissioners appointed to review the U.S. tax system after the Civil War, used the phrase "industrial policy" repeatedly in his 1866 report. Rejecting the "rigid principle of international trade" that produced "oppressive" wage competition among working people, Colwell asserted that "no nation can attain . . . its maximum wealth which does not by its national policy furnish sources of employment for its whole population."[83]

Another Carey ally, James M. Swank, the secretary of the American Iron and Steel Association, employed the phrase "industrial policy" in the title of a book published in 1876. In the *Industrial Policies of Great Britain and the United States*, Swank used the term broadly to cover both import protection for home industries and aid to export-competing industries. He noted that even countries like Great Britain, which professed free trade, utilized industrial policies when subsidizing steamship companies.

For Swank, protection was not an instrument for establishing monopolies and rewarding one class of society at the expense of others. Rather, protection developed the nation's resources, encouraged the "industry of its own people, in preference to the industry of an alien people." It diversified national employment and thus created "unbounded possibilities for a nation capable of great achievements." Protection secured independence while promoting economic advancement.[84]

In the great tariff debates between the time of the Civil War and the Great Depression, Republicans proudly defended the American protective system, while Democrats favored freer trade. This era is important for another reason.

In the Gilded Age, a high-tariff America enjoyed economic growth nearly double that of free trade Britain. The U.S. experience thus appears to have larger significance. It seems to offer a dramatic example supporting the proposition that home market protection can prove compatible with vigorous internal growth, rapidly expanding export trade, and stable or declining consumer prices. But history also suggests that the relationship between trade policy and economic performance is more complex than some theorists assume. Did the United States enjoy such rapid growth because of protection, as nineteenth-century Republicans thought, or in spite of protection, as Democrats alleged? A definitive answer to the complicated causation issues must be deferred until economic historians using regressions and computable models test these relationships.

[W]hat these other countries want is a free and open market with the United States. . . . wherever we have tried reciprocity or low duties we have always been the loser.—Representative William McKinley, 1890

A reciprocity treaty . . . is a modern invention, which, like the Trojan horse, hides in its belly all of its sinister and miscreated forces.—Senator Justin S. Morrill, 1885

✓Unreciprocal Trade

Until the 1870s a single agricultural commodity—cotton—dominated American exports, frequently generating more than half of merchandise trade earnings. Thirty years later "King Cotton" had lost its crown. In 1900 the United States was a diversified exporter of value-added manufactures as well as commodities. U.S.-built locomotives whistled across Siberia and past the Egyptian pyramids. American farm machinery gathered grain in the world's breadbaskets. American sewing machines, typewriters, phonographs, and wearing apparel sold in markets around the world. Everywhere the mark "Made in America" identified products of superior quality.[1]

That rapid transformation from a supplier of complementary raw materials to competitive manufactures aroused concern in Great Britain and Europe. In 1879 the editor of the Bristol, England, *Times and Mirror* lamented:

Where is this American competition to end? The Yankees are threatening to take the leather trade out of our hands now. American locks are superseding those of Staffordshire; American apples are taking the place of those of Somersetshire and Devon in the dye-works. American furniture is to be found in many forms in more houses than the inhabitants themselves are aware of, and many English sideboards next Christmas will probably groan under American barons of beef. You cannot go into an ironmonger's shop without finding his cases full of American notions. . . . Even the English agriculturists themselves are cultivating their fields, reaping and gathering their crops, when they can gather them at all, with implements of American invention and American manufacture.[2]

Yankee economic achievements sparked comments about the United States acquiring "supremacy" in world markets. In 1900 Secretary of State John Hay observed that the "United States is approaching . . . a position of eminence in the world's markets, due to superior quality and greater cheapness of . . . its manufactures." These "may result in shifting the center, not only of industrial, but of commercial activity and the money power of the world to our marts." Brooks Adams, the grandson of President John Quincy Adams, boldly forecast "America's economic supremacy" and Britain's continued economic decline.[3]

Across the Atlantic the American commercial challenge spurred support for import restraints. In *The American Invasion or England's Commercial Danger*, B. H. Thwaite attributed U.S. success to the "protective policy, which has enabled American industry to progress so remarkably." Listing American inventions, such as the electric streetcar, sophisticated harvesting machinery, and the telephone, Thwaite warned: "There is scarcely an operation in every-day life, in which an American device is not required." Another British writer concluded: "The most serious aspect of the American industrial invasion lies in the fact that these newcomers have acquired control of almost every new industry created during the past fifteen years."[4]

What should be done? As the "first line of trading defense," Thwaite urged a "protective or reciprocal tariff policy . . . between all the component parts of the British Empire." His solution resembled colonial secretary Joseph Chamberlain's call for "imperial free trade," an issue contested in the 1906 general election. In that campaign, free trade Liberals upset Chamberlain's Conservatives, and so England's open market policies endured for another generation. During the Great Depression London officials turned belatedly to a preferential system.[5]

On the Continent American exporters encountered vexing new trade restrictions and discrimination that were designed to limit market access. Most European nations, except Britain and the Netherlands, imposed higher protective duties on competitive imports during the last decades of the nineteenth century.[6] A majority of these nations adopted multiple-schedule tariffs, involving a higher and a lower schedule of duties, in order to penalize countries pursuing unsatisfactory policies and to favor other countries. The multiple-

"Standing Pat." Uncle Sam, the protectionist, triumphs over John Bull, the free trader. *Judge*, November 14, 1903. (Special Collections, Alden Library, Ohio University)

schedule systems varied: some systems relied on rigid statutory rates, others left discretion to government authorities.

A series of minor trade skirmishes revealed how apprehensive European governments had become about the rise of American competition. Passage of the 1894 Wilson-Gorman Tariff, repealing a reciprocity provision, provoked retaliation. "Our agricultural products are practically shut out of the markets of northern Europe," the House Ways and Means Committee reported. In 1897 the premier of Austria-Hungary, Count Goluchowski, even proposed that European nations combine to resist American trade interests.[7]

American farmers complained about export access problems. With improvements in shipping and communications, competition had increased in European markets from peripheral suppliers like Australia, Argentina, Canada, and Russia for commodity products such as wheat and flour. On the Continent, security concerns and political pressures from farmers contributed to more protective policies in the years before World War I.[8]

Reciprocity for Market Access

In such circumstances, it was predictable that export-minded U.S. business and agriculture should turn to Washington for help. Concerned about rising European trade barriers, the Agricultural Implements Association recommended a new "industrial policy" to a Senate subcommittee in 1900: "We are ready to go forth to conquer the industrial world, and we believe that the path to the freedom and equality of American commerce in the markets of the world lies through reciprocity."[9]

To gain equal access for American exports abroad, export-oriented business endorsed more flexible trade initiatives, particularly reciprocity agreements and dual-schedule tariffs. As the National Association of Manufacturers told Congress, "reciprocity commends itself as a sound and judicious business principle," one that "ought to be considered upon a strictly nonpartisan, nonpolitical basis." In place of a rigid, single-schedule tariff, written by Congress to safeguard the domestic market for home industries and workers, important business groups embraced a market-opening strategy. They proposed giving the executive branch both the carrot of reciprocity and the stick of multiple tariff schedules to facilitate bargaining. With these instruments, the United States hoped to gain access to foreign markets without sacrificing the home market or jeopardizing jobs.[10]

Other powerful export-oriented interests assessed the situation differently. In November 1908, when the House Ways and Means Committee received reactions to proposed tariff revisions, James Swank, the renown general manager of the American Iron and Steel Association, dismissed the maximum and minimum tariff as "a huckstering policy . . . that is sure to increase our imports of manufactured products to the serious injury of our own people."[11]

PRE–CIVIL WAR EXPERIENCE

To gain market access abroad, export-minded business leaders determined to press for reciprocal commercial treatment. At the State Department enthusiasm for this bargaining approach had roots in Secretary Jefferson's 1793 report on commerce. Senate Finance Committee chairman Justin Morrill (R-Vt.) quipped that State was "pregnant with unhealthy admiration of reciprocity treaties."[12]

In the generation before the Civil War the State Department had experimented with several reciprocal market-opening initiatives—with the European Zollverein, Canada, Mexico, and Hawaii. For the expansionist Democrats who directed U.S. foreign policy under Presidents Tyler, Polk, Pierce, and Buchanan, reciprocity soon became much more than a diplomatic tool for appeasing export-oriented commercial and agricultural interests. It served as an instrument for advancing foreign policy objectives. One controversial episode occurred after the House of Representatives passed a resolution in 1837 requesting information about foreign restrictions on U.S. tobacco exports. Soon the State Department directed U.S. representatives in eight European countries to focus on removing or reducing tobacco restrictions and "to prepare the way for negotiations for the promotion of the interests of the tobacco trade with those countries."[13]

Henry Wheaton, U.S. minister to Prussia and the first American recognized as an authority on international law, opened negotiations with the Zollverein, the newly created economic union among German states. Initially, he found little interest in reducing the duty on American tobacco. But when the United States raised its own tariff structure in 1842, members of the German Customs Union signaled interest in an arrangement that would lower U.S. duties on certain German manufactures in exchange for concessions on the tobacco and other American agricultural exports. President Tyler then authorized Wheaton to negotiate a treaty that "will open new advantages to the agricultural interests of the United States, and a freer and more expanded field for commercial operations, will affect injuriously no existing interests of the Union."[14]

Wheaton toiled for seven years to conclude a treaty that would reduce German duties on U.S. tobacco about one cent per pound, bind tariffs on lard and rice, and place cotton on the free list. In return, Wheaton agreed that the United States would significantly reduce its duties on a range of German-manufactured exports—including woolen and cotton apparel, musical instruments, and silk and laces. The U.S. reductions, Senator Morrill later stated, involved at least five hundred articles "some of which singly, were scarcely less, when compared in commercial magnitude, than the sum total of our Prussian tobacco trade."[15]

An enthusiastic free trader, Wheaton anticipated that the arrangement would encounter "great opposition at home." But while not upsetting the "great branches of manufacturing," he claimed that it would benefit commerce and agriculture. The low duties proposed for silk and linen imports would also promote "the general interest of the consumer" and not lead to the establishment of new industries "for which the country has no peculiar aptitude, at the expense . . . of the great body of consumers including the manufacturers themselves." In effect, Wheaton, an international lawyer with little practical business experience, assumed, as the president's agent, the delicate task of making complex decisions about what industries the United States should and should not protect from foreign competition. Living outside the United States before the telegraph and the steam ship facilitated communications, he had no opportunity to consult regularly with affected U.S. producers. Reflecting on this episode some years later, Senator Morrill observed: "the American negotiator . . . , however learned and accomplished in other respects, was sadly deficient in practical knowledge of revenue laws or of the industrial interests of the United States, and without any apprehension of the strides these interests were destined to make in the immediate future."[16]

Wheaton's correspondence shows him sensitive to broader trade policy ramifications. To incoming Secretary of State John C. Calhoun, the U.S. envoy described the commercial treaty as an "instrument of negotiation" to "obtain equivalent concessions" from other European nations for U.S. agricultural commodities. It would efface "some of the most objectionable features of our present exaggerated tariff," Wheaton said. He also considered it the "first step towards a more liberal commercial intercourse between the different nations of Europe and the United States."[17]

How did other affected nations assess the agreement? Britain complained about possible discrimination and argued that the presence of an unconditional most-favored-nation clause in the Convention of 1815 qualified it for identical tariff treatment in the U.S. market. Edward Everett, the U.S. minister to Britain, responded that Britain must pay equivalent compensation—and agree to lower its duty on tobacco to the Zollverein's level—in order to qualify for the same tariff levels offered to German exporters. Privately, he admitted to Washington "some little embarrassment" at the inconsistent U.S. position. On another occasion Washington had argued that if London should reduce the British duty on rice to a third country, "the same relaxation becomes *ipso facto* due to the United States, in virtue of our Convention."[18]

In the United States southern and western agricultural exporters hailed the

Zollverein treaty. But manufacturing interests opposed reciprocal free trade and even disputed reciprocal reductions in the treaty, Treasury secretary Robert Walker conceded later. Support for and opposition to the accord broke along party lines. Jacksonian Democrats backed it; Whigs did not. On June 14, 1844, the Senate Foreign Relations Committee released a critical report advising against ratification. It held that "the control of trade and the function of taxing belong, without abridgement or participation, to Congress." Representatives of the people "may better discern what true policy prescribes and rejects, than is within the competence of the Executive department." The appropriate function of the executive, the committee said, was "to follow, not to lead; to fulfil, not to ordain, the law . . . , not to go forward with [a] too ambitious enterprise."[19]

Counseling rejection on constitutional grounds, the Senate report criticized "the paucity of advantages" and the "inequality of the concessions." It raised concern that other parties to most-favored-nation agreements might "compel us to receive the articles of their production or manufacture of *like character* . . . on the same terms." On June 15, 1844, the Senate tabled the Zollverein treaty by a vote of 26 to 18 on a party line ballot.[20]

Secretary of State John C. Calhoun, recently a member of the Senate himself, dismissed the Senate committee report as "inconclusive." He argued that although the Constitution delegated the power of regulating commerce and laying duties to Congress, that did not "inhibit the Treaty-making power from making commerce and duties the subjects of Treaty stipulations." Most of all, Calhoun attributed the Senate's action to partisanship associated with the 1844 presidential election. Because he was a member of the executive branch, it is understandable that Calhoun also worried about the effects of the defeat on "the standing of the government abroad." He believed that implementation of the treaty would bring other "great changes in the commerce of the civilized world, and lay a solid foundation for an intimate and close commercial and political union between the United States and Germany."[21]

Viewed from the 1990s, this defeat appears to have been far more than another partisan dispute between a beleaguered president and congressional opponents. It was an important test of Congress and the executive in the long struggle to direct trade policy. In responding to the congressional request for assistance to tobacco export interests, a U.S. diplomatic representative traded off domestic manufacturing interests for perceived export and foreign policy advantages. His action angered Congress.

Certainly, the House wanted to assist tobacco exports, but in rejecting the Zollverein treaty the Senate demonstrated that it had no desire to sacrifice domestic manufacturing interests for a few more pounds of tobacco. State Department communications with Minister Everett in London show that the

Senate was correct to question the generalization of concessions. The 1815 Convention with Britain was ambiguous, and had Germany received preferential treatment for its manufactures, Britain would have demanded equal treatment. In effect, as Senator Morrill argued, Wheaton, together with his State Department superiors who had approved this initiative, sought to employ the reciprocity treaty as an instrument for amending the tariff and shackling congressional authority to regulate commerce.[22] Finally, the letter from Consul Graebe in Hesse suggests that the Senate was right to question whether the reciprocal agreement involved *real* reciprocity, an exchange of equivalent concessions.

Two other pre–Civil War reciprocity tariff treaties—one negotiated with Hawaii in 1855 and the other with Mexico in 1859—ended similarly. In each case the State Department construed reciprocity as a vehicle for binding smaller neighbors to an expanding United States, thus achieving larger political and foreign policy objectives. Both treaties failed in the Senate.[23] Eager to annex Hawaii, the expansion-minded Pierce administration attempted to write a reciprocity agreement in 1855 that would have provided for duty-free importation of certain natural products, particularly sugar, coffee, and molasses. Once again Congress exhibited concern about the need to extend similar concessions to other nations eligible for most-favored-nation treatment. Louisiana sugar growers worried about a surge in sugar imports. Moreover, some U.S. senators raised constitutional concerns about using the treaty power to alter tariffs.[24]

A few years later President James Buchanan's representative in Mexico, Robert McLane, negotiated a broad-reaching agreement with the Juarez government providing, among other things, for free trade, or perfect reciprocity, in the exchange of certain natural and manufactured products. Congress was to select the specific items from an agreed-upon list. In 1860 the Senate turned down this treaty, apparently because many lawmakers feared that the Buchanan administration intended to expand the slave system.[25]

One important exception to this pattern of Senate rejection involved Canada. Repeal of the Corn Laws in 1846 had ended Canada's preferential access to the British market and forced the provinces to find alternative trade opportunities. Nervous about annexationist sentiment in the United States, Canadian leaders nonetheless wanted secure markets for raw material and natural product exports while maintaining a political association with Great Britain. During the Polk administration, the British minister in Washington and Treasury secretary Walker, an enthusiastic free trader, negotiated a reciprocity agreement providing for free trade of agricultural and natural products but not of manufactures. When Congress debated the measure, opponents raised the familiar fear that most-favored-nation clauses in treaties with Russia, Prussia, and other nations would compel the United States to generalize the proposed concessions. In effect, America would admit the world's breadstuffs duty-free.[26]

During the Pierce administration, after Secretary of State Marcy rebuffed a British proposal for reciprocal free trade, Canada revived its reciprocity proposal—successfully. The governor general of Canada, Lord Elgin, took personal charge of negotiations in Washington and after extensive entertaining won support among Democrats. Later critics would complain that the Marcy-Elgin treaty "floated through on champagne."[27]

For Canada, the 1854 reciprocity treaty proved a bonanza. It brought about a substantial increase in trade. For the United States, the results proved controversial. The U.S. Tariff Commission (TC) later concluded that "it was in its operation undoubtedly more favorable to provincial exports than to those of the United States." Over the next eleven years (1855–66) trade between the two countries increased nearly threefold, and each became more important to the other commercially. However, U.S. figures show little increase in the value of U.S. exports to Canada. Instead, Canadian exports to the United States soared, turning a substantial U.S. merchandise trade surplus into a deficit.[28]

REPUBLICAN RESISTANCE

Skeptical of State Department motives, Republican leaders in Congress displayed little enthusiasm for more unbalanced reciprocity agreements in the late nineteenth century. "What is reciprocity?" asked Speaker of the House Thomas Reed of Maine when his longtime political rival, Secretary of State James G. Blaine, requested a reciprocity provision in 1890. It is "commerce on paper," Reed said. To wily congressional veterans like Ways and Means Committee chairman McKinley, "Pig Iron" Kelley's successor, reciprocity was a high-sounding concept that worked badly in practice. "[W]herever we have tried reciprocity or low duties," he observed, "we have always been the loser." Recalling the twelve years of reciprocity with Canada from 1854 to 1866, McKinley noted that we "bought . . . twice as much as they bought of us. Ninety-five per cent of their products came into the United States free of duty, while only 42 percent of ours went into Canada free of duty."[29]

The single most important Republican in Congress on tariff issues from the Civil War to the turn of the twentieth century was Justin Morrill of Vermont. He consistently opposed the "humbug" of reciprocity treaties. Entering the House of Representatives in 1855 as a Whig, Morrill wrote the Tariff Act of 1861 before moving to the Senate as a Republican in 1867. He served on the Senate Finance Committee for thirty-one years (1867–98), and for twenty-two of those years he chaired that key tariff-writing committee. During his tenure as Finance chairman, reciprocal tariff cutting—involving Canada, Mexico, Hawaii, and other countries—went nowhere in the Senate.[30]

Morrill staked out a negative position early in his congressional career and adhered to it. In 1858 he proposed a resolution directing the Foreign Affairs Committee to "inquire into the expediency of abrogating" Canadian reciprocity. He succeeded in 1866. His long-standing opposition to reciprocity, a biographer commented, mirrored the sentiment of frontier Vermont, where Yankee farmers remembered the Revolution and the War of 1812. "The farmer of Vermont felt himself robbed by every pound of butter, every cord of wood, and every head of cattle that came across the border to be sold in competition with his own products."[31]

Morrill's opposition also reflected longtime Whig sensitivity to the prerogatives of Congress and American economic interests. He argued, as did other members of Congress, that the reciprocity "treaty has ceased to be reciprocal." Morrill cited lost tariff revenue during the Civil War and bilateral merchandise trade imbalances. From a legal point of view, he considered reciprocity treaties "a plain and palpable violation of the Constitution which gives to the House of Representatives the sole power to originate revenue bills. If such a treaty can be made with one nation, it may be made with all, and in time the treaty-making power might absorb the entire jurisdiction of revenue questions, so far as customs duties are concerned." Morrill also thought that reciprocity treaties conflicted with congressional authority to regulate commerce. Through the conditional most-favored-nation clause other nations, like Great Britain, might successfully claim all the privileges granted in reciprocity agreements, thus undermining the protective system. As he told a friend: "I have always fought the so-called reciprocity treaties tooth and nail, as utterly unconstitutional. . . . It is a hodge-podge of free trade, undermining all stable protective Tariffs." Morrill believed that "a great and growing nation must be left free to act in any and all emergencies as its honor and interest may demand."[32]

Morrill and his Finance Committee allies in the Senate—especially Nelson Aldrich, of Rhode Island, his successor as chairman of the committee (1898–1911)—battled relentlessly against what they deemed to be "unreciprocal" treaties proposed for foreign policy reasons. During Morrill's leadership of the Finance Committee, no new reciprocity treaty cleared the Senate and was actually implemented. With Chairman Aldrich at the helm, President Theodore Roosevelt gained congressional approval for Cuban reciprocity but had to drop other pending agreements.[33]

In the State Department, where enthusiasm for foreign involvement and territorial expansion revived after the Civil War, commercial interests found renewed backing for bilateral tariff reduction agreements. Secretary of State William Seward, who served Presidents Lincoln and Andrew Johnson, and his successor Hamilton Fish were ardent expansionists. Throughout his government career Seward emphasized how commerce served as the "the chief agent of . . . advancement in civilization and enlargement of empire." Thus he argued that "political supremacy follows commercial ascendancy." Eager to settle the question of Hawaii's future and to bring the islands under U.S. influence, Seward submitted a reciprocity treaty favorable to Hawaii in 1867. Once again the Senate rejected it, with Senator Morrill leading the opposition.[34]

Secretary of State Fish had better fortune during the Grant administration. In 1875 he persuaded Congress to approve a "reciprocal agreement" with Hawaii, despite its lack of commercial balance. Believing that reciprocity would "bind these islands to the United States with hoops of steel," Fish authorized generous benefits for Hawaii. Once again, politics, defense, and global strategy—rather than a genuine concern for balance and reciprocity— drove U.S. commercial negotiations.[35]

Reviewing the record of Hawaiian trade in February 1883, Morrill's committee concluded that the Hawaiian treaty was "so obviously adverse to the interests of the United States . . . that nothing less than its abrogation affords a sufficient remedy." Noting a U.S. revenue loss of $12.8 million as a result of duty-free Hawaiian sugar, the Finance Committee asked: "Instead of throwing away this vast sum upon the temporary sojourners in remote islands of the Pacific, where by no possibility can it confer any future advantage to our own country, would it not have been wiser to have bestowed the whole of this sum as a premium on sugars produced at home?"[36]

Chairman Morrill, and future Chairmen Voorhees and Aldrich, also complained that "modern diplomatic inventions," namely reciprocity treaties, were being used to change the Constitution, infringing on the power of the House of Representatives to originate revenue bills. They pointed to "serious complications always lying in wait for all reciprocity treaties." Should any country eligible for most-favored-nation treatment "tender the same or equal terms, we must accord the same and equal favors, and any reciprocity treaty might be suddenly and wonderfully expanded," thus undermining the protective system.

During the Arthur administration the State Department made another attempt to promote reciprocity—this time in the Western Hemisphere. Along with negotiating to extend the Hawaiian treaty, Secretary of State Frederick T. Frelinghuysen authorized former president Ulysses Grant to seek a free trade agreement with Mexico and envoy John W. Foster to negotiate with Spain for reciprocity agreements affecting Puerto Rico and Cuba. Separately, the State Department concluded a reciprocity agreement with the Dominican Republic. In addition, Britain initiated discussions for reciprocity arrangements affecting its possessions in the Western Hemisphere. Only the Hawaiian extension survived the Senate. Senate Republicans and former secretary of state Blaine declined to support such arrangements.[37] Importantly, a persistent foe of reciprocity chaired the Senate Finance Committee. When the Mexican treaty arrived in the Senate, Justin Morrill swung into action. In 1884 he introduced a resolution stating: "*Resolved,* That so-called reciprocity treaties, having no possible basis of reciprocity with nations of inferior population and wealth, involving the surrender of enormously unequal sums of revenue, involving the surrender of immensely larger volumes of home trade than are offered to us in return, and involving constitutional questions of the gravest character, are untimely and should everywhere be regarded with disfavor."[38]

Defending this resolution, Morrill argued that reciprocity "with Mexico or any inferior country" providing "just and equal terms" was impossible. Mexico had a population of under 10 million people with low incomes. Three-quarters of these, he said, were "non-consumers of any foreign merchandise and contented to live almost exclusively upon corn and beans." The United States, however, had 60 million people with high wages and personal incomes. This type of reciprocity Morrill branded "international communism." It was no better than exchanging a purebred American Lexington or Morgan horse for a Mexican mustang or stump-tail mule. Morrill compared reciprocity generally to the Trojan horse. It "hides in its belly all of its sinister and miscreated forces, including its insidious and ravenous absorption of revenue." Previous agreements with Canada and Hawaii, he argued, had produced huge revenue losses for American taxpayers. Extension of "American influence" into the Pacific he dismissed as "ascendancy incapable of withstanding the slightest aggression." In essence, the Finance chairman complained that executive branch reciprocity agreements broke "the very heart-strings of the Constitution" and jeopardized the nation's revenue surplus. "I am unwilling to collect any revenue from our people for the sole purpose of giving it away to foreigners through reciprocity treaties," he declared.[39]

Morrill's position enjoyed support in Congress. In 1885 President Grover Cleveland prudently withdrew the treaties signed with Spain and Santo Domingo. In doing so, he echoed Finance Committee concerns. "These treaties," the president said, "contemplated the surrender . . . of large revenues for inadequate considerations." He noted that "embarrassing questions would have arisen under the favored-nation clauses of treaties with other nations."[40]

Blaine and Reciprocity

When the Republicans returned to power in 1889, export-oriented manufacturers found Secretary of State James G. Blaine sympathetic to reciprocity negotiations with other Western Hemisphere nations. Eager to strengthen the hand of U.S. negotiators and to promote access for U.S. manufactured exports, Blaine revived the concept of reciprocal tariff reductions when he suggested that Congress provide the executive branch with discretionary authority to negotiate higher or lower tariffs on Latin American products. Blaine urged President Benjamin Harrison to propose such a bargaining provision in the Tariff Act of 1890 as it might help gain market access in the Western Hemisphere. In particular, the secretary wanted Congress to authorize the president to pursue reciprocal free trade agreements with "any nation of the American hemisphere," a phrase that reopened the door to reciprocity negotiations with Canada.[41]

A politician experienced in congressional negotiations, Blaine proposed a bargaining strategy intended to secure access for U.S. manufactures and agricultural products to Latin American export markets. Blaine sensed that this also would improve the merchandise trade balance, and he had no intention of generalizing the benefits to all trading partners. Nor did Blaine propose to expose import-sensitive domestic industries to foreign competition. His approach rested on the tactic of first imposing a high tariff on tropical and semitropical imports—especially sugar—in order to force other nations to the bargaining table. As Representative Robert LaFollette (R-Wis.), a member of the House Ways and Means Committee, observed: "Its object is to enable the President to make a trade with foreign countries by offering to them a reduction of duties on articles which we do not care to protect, in exchange for the reduction of their duties on articles which we wish to protect but which we wish also to export."[42]

Blaine's proposal never came to a vote in Congress, where high protectionists resisted it. In the Senate, Finance Chairman Morrill and his allies—especially Nelson Aldrich (R-R.I.), William Allison (R-Iowa), and John Sherman (R-Ohio)—stood firm. During one session with the Finance Committee Blaine became so enraged that he smashed his silk hat.[43]

On reciprocity Congress remained a reluctant partner for the State Department. As always, the legislative branch proved sensitive to the concerns of domestic producers and workers, those who helped determine the outcome of elections. Anxious to safeguard domestic interests, as well as to protect their constitutional prerogatives, the senior members of Congress had no enthusiasm for radical change when they took up tariff revision in 1890. Indeed, in floor debate House Ways and Means Committee chairman William McKinley (R-Ohio) openly stated: "I am not going to discuss reciprocity or the propriety of treaties and commercial arrangements. I leave that to the illustrious man who presides over the State Department. . . . This is a domestic bill; it is not a foreign bill." Republicans applauded. A few minutes later McKinley ridiculed "much talk of foreign trade and foreign commerce, as though these were the all and only essentials to national development and prosperity, wholly disregarding our domestic commerce and our domestic trade." He reminded the House

"Our Choked Up Home Market." *Puck*, June 5, 1889. (Author's personal copy)

"A Successful Gate." *Judge* (April 13, 1901) depicts President McKinley's protectionist policies as key to American prosperity, while free trade brings ruin to John Bull's England. (Special Collections, Alden Library, Ohio University)

that "we are not legislating for any nation but our own." The purpose of the tariff bill, he said, "is to increase production here, diversify our productive enterprises, enlarge the field, and increase the demand for American workmen."[44]

Congressional leaders might view reciprocity as a threat to the protective system, but Blaine's proposal captured the popular imagination and inspired newspaper editorial writers across the country. President Harrison, along with McKinley, Morrill, and Aldrich, devised a compromise. In enacting the 1890 tariff, Congress authorized a different approach to tariff bargaining. It placed sugar and molasses on the free list and directed the president to impose penalty duties on free imports from countries producing certain tropical products—sugars, molasses, coffee, tea, and hides—that imposed unequal and unreasonable duties on U.S. exports. Subsequently, the Ways and Means Committee described this tactic as an "endeavor to apply the golden rule to commerce." It might persuade neighboring nations "to make concessions in favor of our products in return for concessions we have already made in favor of theirs."[45]

Remembering the failure of Congress to approve implementing legislation to effect reciprocity conventions negotiated with Mexico in 1883 and Spain in 1884, Secretary Blaine had obtained a unique grant of discretionary authority from Capitol Hill. Although the Constitution stated that Congress should regulate commerce, Congress delegated to the president authority to conduct negotiations and effect agreements without congressional approval. In a critical legal challenge, the Supreme Court upheld the act of Congress. In *Field v. Clark* (1892), the Court majority said: "What the President was required to do was simply in execution of the act of Congress. It was not the making of law. He was the mere agent of the law-making department to ascertain and declare the event upon which its expressed will was to take effect."[46]

Taking note of the dissent, Democrats continued to decry the "unlawful" delegation of powers. They also decried the "aggressive" approach to bargaining authorized in the McKinley Tariff. Though Congress had added sugar and molasses to the free list, they noted that other major Latin American imports—coffee, tea, and hides—had been on the free list for twenty years. Thus the bargaining approach was viewed as an unwarranted exercise of American power in both a legal and a diplomatic sense.

Until repealed in 1894, during the second Cleveland administration, this reciprocity experiment did achieve some modest successes—measured simply in terms of the number of agreements concluded. Secretary Blaine turned negotiations over to an experienced diplomat, John W. Foster, and Foster pursued executive agreements with ten hemisphere countries, including Brazil and Spain for Cuba. President Harrison concluded these agreements in accordance with authority delegated in the Tariff Act of 1890.[47] When Colombia, Venezuela, and Haiti refused to make appropriate concessions, his administration imposed penalty duties, thus demonstrating a willingness to use both the carrot and the stick.

As it turned out, Blaine's policy helped open Latin American markets to U.S. manufactured exports; it also aroused Latin resentment. Congress soon abandoned that reciprocity approach. During the presidential campaign of 1892 Democrats denounced the Blaine program as "sham reciprocity" and pledged to repeal the McKinley Tariff. In enacting the Wilson-Gorman Tariff in 1894, a Democratic Congress reimposed duties on sugar and removed the threat of further penalty duties.[48]

As a consequence, other countries soon terminated the bilateral agreements benefiting U.S. manufactured exports. In deleting the reciprocity bargaining provision, majority Democrats on the Ways and Means Committee made an important political point: "We do not believe that Congress can rightly vest in the President of the United States any authority or power to impose or release taxes on our people by proclamation or otherwise, or to suspend or dispense with the operation of a law of Congress."[49] But the Democrats had a short memory. Forty years later, when one of their own—President Franklin D. Roosevelt—sought similar discretionary authority for a reciprocal trade reduction program, a Democratic Congress authorized another experiment in executive tariff making.

The Dingley Tariff and the Kasson Treaties

Before President William McKinley took office in 1897, Capitol Hill Republicans organized to rewrite the tariff. They elected to experiment with reciprocity. Convinced that bilateral market opening merited another effort, the new president urged Congress to reenact the reciprocity principle. "The brief trial given this legislation amply justifies a further experiment and additional discretionary power in the making of commercial treaties." However, McKinley emphasized that opening export markets could not come at the expense of domestic producers and workers. He advocated the "opening up of new markets for the products of our country, by granting concessions to the products of other lands that we need and can not produce ourselves, and *which do not involve any loss of labor to our own people*, but tend to increase their employment" (emphasis added).[50]

As enacted, the Dingley Tariff of 1897 authorized reciprocal concessions, not simply penalty duties, for bargaining purposes. This time McKinley and his aides attempted to use the reciprocity provision to reduce discrimination against U.S. exports in Europe, as well as to create opportunities in the Western Hemisphere. But McKinley failed to gain the broad legislative delegation of authority that he desired.[51] As written in a Senate-House conference, the reciprocity provision authorized two distinct types of tariff negotiations. The first type came under section 3, which empowered the president to negotiate *on his own authority* reciprocity agreements covering a few items: argols, brandies, wines, champagnes, and paintings among others. This provision seemed directed at France and Germany, but other language mentioned penalties on coffee, tea, tonka, and vanilla beans imported from countries providing "unequal and unreasonable" treatment to American exports. The latter clause, which resembled bargaining language in the 1890 McKinley Tariff, had little impact on negotiations.

The second type of tariff negotiation, under section 4, empowered the president to undertake more extensive talks for two years after passage of the Dingley Act. He could cut duties on imports up to 20 percent and transfer to the free list natural products of other countries. Such treaties, of course, required Senate approval. In passing the Dingley Act, Congress apparently padded some tariff rates, anticipating that the higher rates would provide a bargaining advantage to U.S. negotiators.[52]

Pursuant to this complicated tariff-cutting authority, the McKinley and Roosevelt administrations conducted a lengthy series of bilateral trade negotiations. Sensitive to congressional prerogatives, President McKinley appointed a former Iowan congressman and diplomat, seventy-five-year-old John A. Kasson, as special commissioner for reciprocity negotiations. Using the limited authority of section 3 of the Dingley Act, Kasson soon negotiated so-called argol agreements with France, Portugal, Germany, and Italy. Subsequently, similar agreements were consummated with Switzerland, Spain, Bulgaria, the United Kingdom, and the Netherlands. These, involving foreign countries with multiple tariff schemes, aroused little controversy and had limited impact on the domestic economy. In reviewing the record, the Tariff Commission later concluded that the United States had granted limited concessions to certain European countries in order to gain suspension or repeal of discriminatory duties on U.S. exports.[53] Kasson also attempted to negotiate broader reciprocity agreements, pursuant to section 4 of the act, with France, the United Kingdom (involving the West Indies), Ecuador, Nicaragua, the Dominican Republic, Denmark (for St. Croix), and Argentina. When McKinley submitted these treaties to the Senate for ratification, the one with France produced a critical test of policy involving the executive tariff reductionists and the Senate protectionists.

Export interests, such as steel producers and manufacturers of agricultural implements, strongly supported the treaty with France. But import-competing industries lined up on the other side. These included makers of cotton goods, tiles and bricks, paper, and optical products. Makers of hosiery, cotton apparel, and knit goods claimed that the maximum 20 percent reductions would have an injurious impact on their labor-intensive industries.[54]

A fatal blow to the Kasson treaties occurred in November 1901, when a National Reciprocity Convention of diverse business interests failed to endorse their passage. Instead, the convention recommended that Congress maintain home market protection. The convention endorsed reciprocity only when "it can be done without injury to any of our home interests of manufacturing, commerce or farming." At stake, however, was a larger principle: would the executive branch breech the protective system and trade off the interests of import-sensitive domestic producers for export gains? In the Senate, Finance Committee chairman Nelson Aldrich and his colleagues bottled up the agreements, which the McKinley administration had initially submitted to the Foreign Relations Committee hoping to circumvent protectionists on the Finance Committee with established jurisdiction over tariff issues. Said Senator Francis Warren (R-Wy.): "According to the theory of the great apostle of reciprocity, James G. Blaine, and according to the contention of William McKinley and a majority of the American people we should exchange only commodities which one country or the other does not produce; but in the Argentine treaty this important principle was apparently lost sight of by its framers."[55]

In effect, the business community and Republicans divided on the value of the Kasson treaties. To succeed in fashioning bilateral trade agreements, Kasson, who operated autonomously of the State Department, had assigned higher priority to advancing and protecting American export interests in Europe and Latin America than in protecting the home market. A longtime proponent of lower tariffs, he also seemed insensitive to the McKinley administration's stated trade policy and to Republican sentiment generally. In his inaugural message, for instance, President McKinley had urged reciprocity concessions "to the products of other lands that we need and cannot produce ourselves, and which do not involve any loss of labor to our own people." The 1900 Republican platform endorsed "reciprocity so directed as to open our markets on favorable terms *for what we do not ourselves produce* in return for free foreign markets" (emphasis added).[56]

Kasson's trade-off, favoring U.S. exporters at the expense of import-competing producers and workers, foreshadowed similar trade outcomes under Secretary of State Cordell Hull's Reciprocal Trade Agreements Program after 1934. It was, moreover, a recipe for periodic conflict with Congress. Some Washington officials drew another lesson from Kasson's unsuccessful experiences. Given the power of special interest lobbies, the only feasible method for achieving reciprocal tariff reductions involved a specific delegation of negotiating authority from Congress to the executive, such as the McKinley Tariff had authorized, but not formal congressional consent to the results.

Reciprocity without Injury

At the beginning of the twentieth century, the United States had a strong and expanding industrial base capable of supplying America's needs and competing vigorously in world markets. However, trade policies still reflected the import-substitution priorities of an industrializing nation eager to establish manufacturing in a dynamic home market. President William McKinley was sensitive to changing conditions. He understood how inventions had transformed transportation and communications, making "widely separated peoples . . . better acquainted." McKinley addressed these significant trends in a September 5, 1901, speech to the Pan-American Exposition in Buffalo, New York, the day before his assassination: "God and man have linked the nations together. No nation can longer be indifferent to any other."[57]

In this last speech McKinley emerged as an internationalist. He urged the negotiation of reciprocity treaties and the reduction of unneeded tariffs to promote mutually advantageous trade with foreign countries. While looking for overseas markets as outlets for surplus domestic products, McKinley said, "we must not repose in fancied security that we can forever sell everything and buy nothing." Although favoring import expansion through reciprocity, the president adumbrated, again, what would become known as the "no-injury" doctrine: "We should take from our customers such of their products as we can use *without harm to our industries and labor*" (emphasis added).[58]

At first impression, it might seem that the presidency had changed McKinley. As a congressman in 1890 he opposed reciprocity; as president he endorsed it. During the 1890s McKinley pragmatically adapted his position to circumstances. As president he gave greater emphasis to foreign commercial opportunities than previously. To address the economic problems of Puerto Rico, acquired in the war with Spain, McKinley even recommended free trade. In his 1899 message to Congress he said: "The markets of the United States should be opened up to her products. Our plain duty is to abolish all customs tariffs between the United States and Puerto Rico and give her products free access to our markets.[59] But the McKinley of 1901 shared with the McKinley of 1890 an abiding conviction that government had a responsibility to shelter domestic industries and workers from the injurious impact of competitive imports. Until his death, McKinley assigned priority to producer and worker interests, not the consumer's freedom to buy cheap goods.

On succeeding McKinley in September 1901, Theodore Roosevelt attempted to continue the slain president's bilateral trade-negotiating policies. Like McKinley, he supported reciprocity but not at the expense of American jobs. "Reciprocity must be treated as the handmaiden of protection," Roosevelt said in his first annual message, on December 3, 1901. He emphasized a fundamental point: "Our first duty is to see that the protection granted by the tariff in every case where it is needed is maintained, and that reciprocity be sought for so far as it can safely be done without injury to our home industries." Although this might vary from industry to industry, the president firmly asserted that duties "must never be reduced below the point that will cover the difference between the labor cost here and abroad. The well-being of the wage-worker is a prime consideration of our entire policy of economic legislation." Like his predecessor, Roosevelt also recognized that foreign customers must sell in the U.S. market in order to continue buying American products. He proposed "arranging our tariff as to enable us to take from them those products which we can use without harm to our own industries and labor, or the use of which will be of marked benefit to us."[60]

The first practical test of Roosevelt's philosophy came over the Kasson treaties, awaiting Senate action. Powerful Senate Republicans led by Nelson Aldrich opposed the treaties for a variety of industry-specific reasons. After conferring with the twenty-year veteran of the Finance Committee, Roosevelt deferred to Aldrich's judgment and abandoned Kasson's reciprocity treaties.[61]

A second test came in 1902 and 1903 over reciprocity for dependencies acquired in the war with Spain, particularly Cuba and the Philippines. The U.S.

occupation forces and sugar planters promoted a preferential, reciprocal trade agreement with Cuba in order to alleviate depressed economic conditions and to avoid political instability. Roosevelt took the view that the United States had "weighty reasons of morality and of national interest" for providing market opportunities for Cuban exports. He claimed that Cuban reciprocity "stands entirely alone. The reasons for it far outweigh those for granting reciprocity with any other nation, and are entirely consistent with preserving intact the protective system." In his special message Roosevelt described Cuban reciprocity as "aid" for a struggling, newly independent nation: "I ask this aid for her because she is weak, because she needs it, because we have already aided her."[62]

Other administration officials stressed military and diplomatic reasons for reciprocity. Secretary of War Elihu Root stated that "the independence of Cuba is necessary to the safety of the United States." President Roosevelt himself related reciprocity to broader strategic issues. "Situated as Cuba is, it would not be possible for this country to permit the strategic abuse of the island by any foreign military power." During the debate it was alleged that President McKinley had promised the Cubans reciprocity in exchange for their adoption of the Platt amendment, which permitted U.S. military bases in Cuba and intervention, if necessary.[63]

Despite grumbling from protectionist trade associations and sugar beet producers, most congressional Republicans loyally backed Roosevelt's program of Cuban reciprocity as an act of party solidarity and responsibility. For Aldrich and some of his colleagues on the Senate Finance Committee, Cuban reciprocity was a difficult vote. However, they loyally supported their president in order to fulfill the McKinley legacy. In the process, they demonstrated a sympathy for reciprocity without jeopardizing domestic industries or the protective system. After all, Cuba produced natural products that were complementary, not competitive, with U.S. manufactures.[64]

As approved in December 1903, Cuban reciprocity provided a 20 percent uniform reduction in U.S. tariffs on dutiable imports from Cuba—most significantly on raw sugar. In turn, Cuba reduced duties 20 to 40 percent on manufactures imported from the United States. Interestingly, to avoid the problem of extending concessions to other most-favored-nation countries, the treaty specifically stated that the reciprocal rates of duty were "preferential in respect to all like imports from other countries."[65]

In retrospect, the supporters of Cuban reciprocity oversold the economic and commercial advantages to the United States. The House Ways and Means Committee report, written by the Republican majority, claimed that the reciprocity reductions "will result in no harm to any American industry." Domestic sugar and tobacco interests had higher levels of protection than needed to meet Cuban competition. But the committee predicted "great gains in our export trade," with U.S. import market share rising from less than 42 percent to over 80 percent.[66]

Actual results differed. Cuba gained import market share, increasing its share of U.S. sugar imports from 17.6 percent in 1900 to 60 percent in 1904. Sugar imports from the other West Indies and Europe fell sharply. "The most striking feature of the reciprocity treaty," according to the U.S. Tariff Commission, was "the price premium . . . conferred upon Cuban producers." During the first several years of the agreement this amount ranged from 10 to 14 percent of Cuba's sugar exports. Over a five-and-one-half-year period, from December 1903 to August 1909, the United States remitted $48 million on Cuban sugar, "a substantial sum" accruing to "Cuban producers at the expense of the U.S. Treasury." Altogether Cuban preferences cost the U.S. Treasury some $64 million over this period—about $11 million per year, or 3.9 percent of U.S. customs revenues.[67]

For U.S. exporters, reciprocity proved disappointing. When the Tariff Commission reviewed the workings of the treaty in 1929, it found that the reciprocal preferences had not helped the unfavorable U.S. merchandise trade balance with Cuba. When the treaty was negotiated in 1902–3, Cuba bought from the United States 65.6 percent of the value of its exports to the United States. This fell to the 49 to 53 percent range both before and after World War I, as Cuba's merchandise trade surplus with the United States widened.[68]

As expected, U.S. exporters did expand market share in Cuba, supplying nearly 66 percent of the island nation's imports in the period 1922–25. However, the TC also concluded that "the reciprocity treaty was not the major cause of the rapid increase" in exports to Cuba. During a comparable twenty-five-year period, the United States increased its import share more rapidly in eight neighboring Caribbean countries without reciprocity treaties. Exports to Cuba rose 591 percent, but they increased 669 percent to the eight Caribbean countries and 573 percent to Canada.[69] Overall the data suggest that reciprocity provided essential market access for Cuba, a country attempting to sell a commodity product at a time when a host of foreign suppliers sought shares of the U.S. sugar market. U.S. manufacturers did not, for the most part, need preferential tariffs to penetrate the Cuban market. They had superior products, as well as other transportation and distribution advantages over European competitors.

For similar strategic reasons, the United States provided the Philippines with special access to the American market. From 1909 to 1930 Philippine sugar entered the country duty-free, resulting in a remission of $190 million to Philippine producers. In effect, Washington used preferred access for sugar produced in Hawaii, Puerto Rico, Cuba, and the Philippines to bind those dependencies firmly to the U.S. market. As a result, by 1913 the United States no longer imported sugar from countries paying full duties. The principal losers were European beet sugar producers, cane sugar producers in the Dutch East Indies, and cane sugar producers in the West Indies, except Cuba and Puerto Rico.[70]

Despite these exceptions made for defense and foreign policy reasons, President Roosevelt, sensitive to domestic political currents, approached tariff revision cautiously. In public he vigorously defended the protective system and rejected the free trade theories of academic economists. During the 1904 presidential campaign he said: "The question of what tariff is best for our people is primarily one of expediency, to be determined not on abstract academic grounds, but in the light of experience." Experience, he added, had not shown "that we could afford . . . to follow those professional counsellors who have confined themselves to study in the closet; for the actual working of the tariff has emphatically contradicted their theories." Forty years of experience with the protective tariff, Roosevelt declared, "have been the most prosperous years this nation has ever seen; more prosperous years than any other nation has ever seen."[71]

Privately, the president had doubts and concerns. Appreciating the rising public demand for some tariff reduction, Roosevelt also understood that Republicans in Congress could not agree on downward revisions. "To go in and fail would be much worse than not to try at all." As a pragmatic politician, he did not want the Republican Party to split over the tariff, and so he argued that the country was not "suffering any loss from the tariff, as yet and I do not think a reduction of duties would be of any substantial benefit." Understanding the need for a predictable tariff structure, Roosevelt also thought it "far better to keep the present tariff law unaltered than to upset business by sweeping and radical alterations in it."[72]

Regarding Cuba and the Philippines, he found considerable public and congressional support for reciprocity, despite vocal opposition from domestic sugar interests. But "standpatters" in the Republican Party opposed significant change. Those who rejected his policy, Roosevelt said, were pursuing "a course of folly which threatens more than anything else the maintenance of the protective system which I deem so essential to our economic well-being." In effect, Roosevelt recognized that any sweeping tariff reform would introduce other inequities and so preferred keeping "the present tariff" unchanged for a dozen years. He thought this the "best possible thing for this country" but recognized that it might be out of the question.[73]

A believer in the value of protectionism, Roosevelt was not insensitive to the restrictions U.S. exporters encountered in world markets. After the 1904 election he told Speaker of the House Joe Cannon that it might be advantageous to consider providing for "reciprocity by a maximum and minimum scale [tariff] to be applied in the discretion of the Executive." Experience had shown, he said, that it was nearly impossible to gain Senate approval of reciprocity treaties. Nonetheless, while favoring some change himself, the politically sagacious Roosevelt resolved not to split the Republican Party over tariff reform.[74]

Payne-Aldrich and Tariff Bargaining

Roosevelt's successor, President William Howard Taft, proved more committed to tariff revision. He too saw the tariff as an instrument for achieving foreign relations objectives. But Taft was less sensitive to domestic political opinion, and this deficiency would contribute to his defeat in 1912.[75]

At the 1908 Republican National Convention Taft's supporters approved a platform commitment to summon a special session of Congress to revise the tariff. The platform also backed the "true principle of protection"—a tariff equalizing the difference between production costs at home and abroad—and a two-schedule tariff to respond to foreign discrimination against U.S. exports.

Subsequently, the Republican Congress enacted the Payne-Aldrich Tariff of 1909. It contained several important provisions to facilitate reciprocity bargaining, including a maximum and a minimum tariff. The maximum tariff would be 25 percent ad valorem above the minimum rate and would apply to nations found discriminating against U.S. exports. The president also received discretionary authority to apply the minimum rate if he found no evidence of undue discrimination. Behind the Payne-Aldrich Tariff of 1909 lay a perception that the dual-schedule tariff would enable the United States to improve market access abroad.[76]

The British embassy agreed. It advised London that the "revisionists have . . . the means they have always clamored for, of gaining reciprocal treatment abroad, and such is the strength of the American position that no nation will hardly dare to engage in a disastrous tariff war with this country." Britain worried how the Taft administration might construe colonial preferences. Would Washington view such arrangements as discriminatory?[77]

President Taft attempted to allay concerns that such a broad delegation of discretionary authority to the executive might provoke trade wars with Europe. He noted that the president had "wide" discretion in determining what was "unduly discriminatory." Furthermore, "in order that the maximum duty shall be charged against the imports from a country, it is necessary that he shall find on the part of that country not only discriminations in its laws or the practice under them against the trade of the United States, but that the discriminations found shall be *undue*; that is, without good and fair reason" (emphasis added). Taft hoped that the "maximum duties might never be applied in any case," and he promised that the president and State Department would employ "friendly negotiation to secure the elimination" of discriminatory treatment.[78]

As it turned out, Payne-Aldrich had little effect on foreign discrimination. The United States imposed no penalty duties, and it did not obtain equal treatment in major French and German markets. Although the State Department did conduct investigations and negotiate, it chose not to impose the maximum tariff schedule. State claimed that the two-schedule approach was not elastic enough: the provision did not permit the selective imposition of penalty duties. Nor did the act permit penalty duties on products assigned to the free list. Subsequently, the State Department recommended further modifications to the law in December 1911. Later the U.S. Tariff Commission concurred "that the act of 1909 did not provide a penalty method effective for the total elimination of all discrimination against American products in European markets."[79]

Taft and Canadian Reciprocity

Payne-Aldrich did have one significant result: it facilitated reciprocity negotiations with Canada. The prospect that Washington might invoke higher penalty duties against Canadian restrictions encouraged Canadian leaders to negotiate a reciprocity agreement. President Taft, who spent his summers at Murray Bay, Quebec, along the St. Lawrence River, wanted to make improved bilateral relations a hallmark of his foreign policy. Another impetus for reciprocity came from the State Department, eager to lure Canada away from the British Empire and to gain access to raw materials.[80]

In January 1911, after brief, secret negotiations, the Taft administration announced agreement to place on the free list more than 40 percent of U.S. imports from Canada and about 10 percent of Canadian imports from the United States. Canadians would gain access to the U.S. market for agricultural produce, fish, and raw materials but retain duties on manufactured imports.

With foreign policy concerns and Taft's own place in history driving the negotiations, rather than a preoccupation with U.S. economic and industrial interests, it is not surprising that congressional protectionists broke with the president. Representative Charles Dalzell, a senior Republican member of the Ways and Means Committee from the Pittsburgh area, led the opposition. He complained that the proposal threw open the "markets of 90,000,000 . . .

prosperous people to the meager markets of less than 9,000,000." Not only was this an "unwise business measure," he said, but also it was "un-Republican . . . it abandons protection and espouses free trade. It is a violation of the pledge of every Republican platform for the last 50 years of our history."[81]

In challenging the administration on Canadian reciprocity, Dalzell reiterated the constitutional and revenue arguments of earlier congressional protectionists, notably Senator Justin Morrill of Vermont. Dalzell and his colleagues believed that the bill would bring about the downfall of the protective system. In exposing the American farmer to Canadian competition, the measure represented abandonment of the Republican view that reciprocity must be confined to noncompeting articles and nothing else. In House debate President Taft had support from fellow Cincinnatian, Nicholas Longworth, who himself was destined to become Speaker. Rejecting a "hidebound and inelastic" protectionist doctrine, Longworth called for "a policy that will adapt itself at all times to changed conditions." He did not favor "an impregnable wall around this country, . . . especially across the Canadian frontier."[82]

Who was right? Taft or the congressional protectionists? A 1920 report written by the impartial U.S. Tariff Commission suggests that, as a trade agreement, the proposed concessions were indeed one-sided. Canada "obtain[ed] practically everything that she had formerly sought by way of reciprocity, while her concessions were to be little more than those which she had already extended to most countries, but not to the United States, through the operation of her conventional tariff." For instance, Canada proposed to reduce the duty on automobiles from 35 to 30 percent but retain the 20 percent rate on farm tractors and portable engines.[83]

To implement the pact, the two governments proposed to avoid the difficult treaty ratification process. Instead, they would rely on concurrent national legislation requiring a simple majority in Congress and Parliament. Determined to prevail, Taft took his case to the people with public speeches, and he did win—but only because opposition Democrats supported reciprocity.[84] In Canada the opponents of reciprocity succeeded. They played on fears of annexation, using political arguments more effectively than economic objections. In particular, Canadian critics focused on the ill-chosen words of Speaker Champ Clark of Missouri. During House debate he had proclaimed: "I am for it, because I hope to see the day when the American flag will float over every square foot of the British–North American possessions clear to the North Pole." Apparently facing a choice between the British Empire and North American continentalism, Canadians soundly rejected the incumbent Liberal Party and the reciprocity plan in the 1911 general elections. Interestingly, the Liberals who were pledged to reciprocity lost overwhelmingly in Ontario, whereas they won in Quebec, the Maritime Provinces, and the Prairie Provinces.[85]

Wilson and Unilateral Tariff Revisions

The problem of how to effectively negotiate market access for American exporters remained unsettled when Democrat Woodrow Wilson won the 1912 presidential election. Gaining control of both the presidency and Congress for the first time since 1892, the Democrats moved quickly to dismantle the protectionist system and honor platform promises. Proposing a tariff for revenue only, they asserted that farmers and laborers were the "chief sufferers" because the protective tariff "raises the cost of the necessaries of life to them, but does not protect their product or wages." Moreover, "American wages are established by competitive conditions, and not by the tariff."[86]

Summoning Congress into special session, President Wilson delivered a short address at a joint gathering on April 8, 1913. He urged Congress to revise the protective tariff and lighten the burden "as soon as possible." "[T]he object of tariff duties," he said, "must be effective competition, the whetting of American wits by contest with the wits of the rest of the world."[87]

The resulting Underwood-Simmons Tariff Act did provide sharp reductions in duties; indeed, the ratio of fees collected to dutiable and free imports dropped to 9.1 percent in 1916, far below the 25.7 peak reached under the Dingley Tariff of 1897 and the 13.7 percent imposed by the Smoot-Hawley Tariff in the last half of 1930. The new tariff reestablished a single schedule, as the House rejected a provision for continuing maximum and minimum duties. The Senate Finance Committee had wanted, and indeed the Senate approved, a program of penalty duties on specified products imported from countries that did not provide "reciprocal and equivalent" treatment to American exports. But this provision was dropped in the House-Senate conference. As enacted, the law also contained a provision authorizing the president to negotiate reciprocity agreements. However, these agreements had to be submitted to Congress for approval.[88]

In effect, the Underwood-Simmons Act, which became law on October 3, 1913, unilaterally lowered American tariffs without obtaining improved access for American exports in foreign markets. Eager to redeem domestic campaign pledges to cut duties and aid consumers, the Wilson administration and Congress responded to domestic constituencies urging tariff reform. In doing so, they ignored an opportunity to use the high protective tariff as a bargaining chip to lower foreign trade barriers and to improve U.S. export opportunities.[89]

The reduction in duties delighted British representatives. Ambassador C. Spring-Rice advised the Foreign Office that the tariff cuts offered British firms "great opportunities" for an "immediate extension of American business." But the ambassador had several concerns. "The President . . . reveals himself every day more clearly as the autocrat of his party." His plans for freeing trade, reforming banking, and revising antitrust are "too hastily undertaken and forced through Congress by men of good intentions but little business experience." In the next recession, he anticipated a political reaction. The Underwood tariff might become "the scapegoat of industrial evils for which it is not in the least responsible."[90]

Officials in the State Department responsible for conducting trade negotiations understood the significance of this legislative outcome and had concerns of their own. The Underwood act did not encourage reciprocal negotiations. Counselor Robert Lansing observed that foreign governments did not act altruistically on commercial matters. "Reductions in duty are usually refused unless some additional concession can be offered or some threat of higher duties suggested." At an interagency meeting on April 15, 1914, Lansing and other trade officials concluded that "the only practicable means of bringing to an end foreign discrimination against the United States is to confer on the President the power to retaliate." Lansing suggested that if the grant of authority were "sufficient. It would not be necessary to exercise it."[91]

The Underwood tariff achieved the aspirations of many tariff reformers—it lowered rates significantly and appeared to benefit consumers. However, it did little to secure equal treatment for American exports abroad. Because the United States retained a rigid single-schedule tariff, its negotiators had no meaningful authority to take the initiative to open foreign markets to U.S. exports.

Confronting Foreign Discrimination

In Germany, France, and Canada, as well as in Haiti and Salvador, the United States lacked most-favored-nation treatment, and its corporate citizens faced serious commercial discrimination. Even where America received most-favored-nation treatment—as in Russia, Italy, Austria-Hungary, Sweden, Spain, Portugal, and Japan—concessions accorded to other countries often provided few benefits to U.S. exporters. Other countries often conducted tariff negotiations in ways designed to benefit the specialized exports of parties to the agreement while limiting the gains to third countries, like the United States. Thus the United States found that foreign tariff reductions frequently did not create meaningful opportunities for American export products. Automobile exports, for instance, often encountered a sliding scale—higher duties on cars with the largest seating capacity and the lightest weight. Both systems discriminated against American cars, which were large in capacity and lightweight. In Europe U.S. automakers encountered rising protectionism, but they learned to adapt, investing in foreign assembly facilities to avoid high duties on finished automobiles. Other distinctly American products, like typewriter ribbons, also encountered customs classification problems because tariff schedules often did not provide specifically for some products.[92]

Officials in the U.S. government, as well as the private sector, appreciated the need for further changes in the U.S. commercial policy in order to address market access problems for American exports. One federal representative particularly concerned about foreign discrimination was Tariff Commission chairman Frank Taussig, a prominent international economist and friend of President Wilson. Taussig urged Wilson and Lansing to make a "determined and active effort" to keep the United States from being "frozen out" of postwar foreign markets. Washington should promote as a matter of principle the "international policy of the open door—the same terms for all." To achieve this goal, Taussig said, the United States needed a bargaining or retaliatory tariff. He urged the administration to support legislation that would "put the power to apply the weapon in the hands of the President." The president should also have the authority to implement a bargaining tariff without Senate confirmation.[93]

To facilitate a change in trade policy, Taussig, the first chairman of the newly created U.S. Tariff Commission, encouraged research on postwar trade problems. In December 1918 the commission completed a classic study of *Reciprocity and Commercial Treaties.* Assuming that the "United States is committed to wide participation in world politics," the TC urged a "clear and simple policy" based on the equality-of-treatment principle. However, it acknowledged the need for exceptions. One such situation occurred where nations shared common frontiers, such as Spain and Portugal or Canada and the United States. Another, the commission claimed, pertained to situations where "special political ties and political responsibilities" led to commercial relations of a "special character," such as the United States enjoyed with Cuba and Hawaii. To achieve equality of treatment, there was a need for legislative authority empowering the president either to provide concessional duties or tariff reductions to countries affording the United States equality of treatment or to impose retaliatory duties against those that failed to provide the United States satisfactory treatment. In either case, "it would seem indispensable that a considerable degree of freedom be left to the executive department." On the related issue of whether to continue the conditional most-favored-nation approach or to adopt the unconditional approach, the Tariff Commission made no recommendation.[94]

In its last years, the Wilson administration had little inclination to revisit and revise tariff policy. Overwhelmed by the immediate problems of peacemaking, as well as his incapacitating illness, President Wilson could not address such issues. Accordingly, during the 1920 election Democrats merely reiterated their longtime commitment to a tariff-for-revenue only. This gave the Republicans an opportunity. Anticipating a postwar surge in imports, as a consequence of the low Underwood tariff rates and the disruptive pricing practices of foreign cartels, the GOP reiterated its historic commitment to "protective principles" and pledged tariff revision "as soon as conditions shall make it necessary for the preservation of the home market for American labor, agriculture and industry."[95] In November 1920 an electorate weary of war and uneasy about the domestic economy voted overwhelmingly for the Republican nominee, Senator Warren G. Harding of Ohio.

Harding and Fordney-McCumber

Soon after his inauguration in 1921, President Harding asked Congress for emergency tariff legislation. "I believe in the protection of American industry," Harding said, "and it is our purpose to prosper America first." According to him, "the privileges of the American market to the foreign producer are offered too cheaply today, and the effect on much of our own productivity is the destruction of our self-reliance, which is the foundation of the independence and good fortune of our people. . . . imports should pay their fair share of our cost of government." Rebutting the argument that imports benefit consumers, the new president asserted: "One who values American prosperity and . . . American standards of wage[s] and living can have no sympathy with the proposal that easy entry and the flood of imports will cheapen our cost of living. It is more likely to destroy our capacity to buy."[96]

In May 1921 Congress approved an act (H.R. 2435) increasing temporarily certain agricultural duties and establishing a procedure for offsetting injurious dumping. The latter modified a 1916 act never successfully administered, because it required complainants to prove that importers intended to destroy or injure a U.S. industry. The following year Congress completed a comprehensive tariff revision—the Fordney-McCumber Tariff Act. This law represented a return to pre–World War I protection, for Congress feared European producers could undersell U.S. manufacturers. The Senate Finance Committee attributed foreign advantages to low wages, government subsidies, and lower taxation. Pursuant to the Underwood-Simmons Tariff, the U.S. ratio of duties collected to dutiable imports had averaged 27 percent, down from 40.8 percent under the Payne-Aldrich Tariff of 1909 and 46.5 under the Dingley Tariff Act of 1897. Under Fordney-McCumber the average dutiable rate rose back to 38.5 percent. The average duty on all imports, which had fallen to 9.1 percent under Underwood, returned to 14 percent. Under Dingley and Payne-Aldrich this rate was 25.5 percent and 19.3 percent, respectively.[97]

In drafting the Fordney-McCumber Act, U.S. officials also sought to address export access issues. Indeed, the State Department, Commerce Department, and Tariff Commission united to recommend that the Ways and Means Committee give the president discretionary authority to defend U.S. commerce: "The United States should, it is believed, stand firmly for the principle of equal rights for all and special privileges for none." To counter discriminations against America, they wanted flexible retaliatory authority, such as the amendments to the Payne-Aldrich Tariff proposed by Secretary of State Philander Chase Knox in 1911. In effect, what officials in the State Department sought was a bargaining tariff—"strictly defensive"—that gave flexibility and discretion to the executive branch. "Each case would be considered on its own merits, and obviously the penalties would not be put into force unless, after full consideration of all political and economic effects, it should be decided that more is to be gained than to be lost by the application of the penalties." One specific objective was to "make a direct attack upon British imperial tariff preferences," considered "one of the most serious dangers at the present time to American trade and to the future expansion of our trade."[98]

What emerged from the Ways and Means Committee the Harding administration considered unsatisfactory. This bill contained a bargaining provision (sec. 302) authorizing the president to impose penalty duties when foreign countries prescribed higher duties on American products. In addition, sections 301, 302, and 303 revised the reciprocity and retaliation concepts. They authorized negotiations for commercial treaties containing special favors. "Special negotiations" could lead to an exchange of "exclusive concessions" in the American tariff for "special concessions in foreign countries." Section 302 placed in the hands of the president authority to penalize the trade of any foreign country that set duties on its imports that he considered higher, reciprocally unequal, and unreasonable. Most of all, the Ways and Means Committee recommended substituting American valuation for foreign valuation as the basis for computing duties. In particular, this last provision was a highly protectionist development.[99]

At this stage, President Harding personally interceded. After meeting with key officials from the executive branch and Congress, he requested a flexible tariff, with authority to raise and lower duties according to scientific criteria. Subsequently, the Senate Finance Committee followed Harding's suggestion and deleted provisions authorizing reciprocity negotiations. Instead, it offered section 317, a provision allowing the president to retaliate unilaterally against foreign discrimination. And Congress stipulated that the independent Tariff Commission should "ascertain and at all times . . . be informed" about discrimination against U.S. commerce and bring this matter to the attention of the president, together with recommendations. Officials in the State Department noted that the new provision was in general harmony with the unconditional most-favored-nation approach and viewed it as a vehicle to encourage non-treaty nations to enter into most-favored-nation agreements. The Senate also dropped the American valuation requirement.[100]

Another important contribution to trade remedies occurred when the Senate strengthened unfair trade laws directed at infringement of intellectual property rights. Section 316 of Fordney-McCumber declared unlawful "unfair methods of competition and unfair acts in the importation of articles into the United States . . . the effect or tendency of which is to destroy or substantially injure an industry, efficiently and economically operated in the United States."[101] In effect, this provision authorized the president to impose penalty duties or exclude goods in violation of the act. Interestingly, in light of the State Department's subsequent opposition to vigorous trade law enforcement, the department's economic adviser at first lauded these provisions as "an important step toward the economic peace of the world."[102]

The Unconditional Most-Favored-Nation Policy

Following enactment of the Fordney-McCumber Act, the executive branch considered how to administer the new law. Tariff commissioner William S. Culbertson, a participant in the tariff-writing process, recommended using the retaliatory provision (sec. 317) to negotiate a new series of commercial treaties extending the principle of equality and implementing broadly the unconditional most-favored-nation policy. Within the State Department, two lower-level drafting officers, Wallace McClure and Stanley Hornbeck, also saw section 317 as a "valuable weapon of defense against discriminations affecting American commerce." Initially, however, they favored a "moderate" enforcement policy, keeping a sharp lookout for discrimination against U.S. exports, but avoiding increased duties unless circumstances left no reasonable doubt.[103] Then, as now, the State Department wanted to avoid disturbing delicate political relationships as it attempted to defend U.S. commercial interests.

Out of State's policy review emerged strong support for switching to the unconditional most-favored-nation approach. Because the historic conditional policy depended on foreign compensation, this in practice often resulted in the United States providing "special concessions to some instead of equal treatment for all." According to State Department officials, the conditional approach aroused "antagonism, promotes discord, creates a sense of unfairness and tends in general to discourage commerce." Often the special concessions gained in the past invited retaliation from third countries, and, as a result, "special concessions secured by reciprocity transactions are not generally worth their cost." The unconditional approach, it was argued, would avoid diplomatic misunderstandings, "eliminate conflict, prevent charges of unfairness, promote commerce and improve international relations."[104]

Within the State Department pressure gradually increased on Secretary Charles Evans Hughes to alter the nation's historic approach to equal commercial treatment. The bureaucracy wanted him to use the new tariff legislation to "place the commercial relations of this country on a definite and stable basis" by negotiating a new system of commercial treaties.[105] Hughes communicated with President Harding, who was also cautious and concerned about jeopardizing Cuban reciprocity.

In Congress the subtleties of most-favored-nation treatment were too complex for most elected members. Commissioner Culbertson claimed that, on such technical matters, "there is no one in Congress with a very fundamental grasp of the issues that are involved."[106] Thus, in the absence of congressional opposition, Harding responded to the recommendations of the State Department bureaucracy and authorized negotiating a new series of commercial treaties based on the unconditional most-favored-nation principle.

This momentous decision, made on February 27, 1923, was not announced until August 18, when Secretary Hughes issued a circular letter to overseas diplomatic posts. When the conditional approach was formulated in the French treaty of February 1778, Hughes said, "discrimination in commercial matters was the general rule among nations, and it was deemed advisable for the United States to adopt a policy of making concessions only to such states as granted in each case some definite and equivalent compensation." But, the secretary continued, the principle of equality had gained wider acceptance, and "it is now considered to be in the interest of the trade of the United States, in competing with the trade of other countries in the markets of the world, to endeavor to extend the acceptance of that principle." In his view, "The enlarged productive capacity of the United States developed during the World War has increased the need for assured equality of treatment of American commerce in foreign markets."[107]

Hughes indicated that U.S. diplomats were not to discuss reciprocal concessions. Instead, they should negotiate new commercial treaties that guaranteed unconditional most-favored-nation treatment. "The United States . . . will offer nothing more than a guarantee of the treatment, which, in practice, it already accords to the commerce of other countries." The Cuban situation was considered an exception, as was free importation from American dependencies. Hughes noted that the United States had already begun negotiations with Spain, Germany, Austria, Hungary, and Czechoslovakia.[108]

This significant change in U.S. trade policy coincided with a rise in European discrimination against American exports after World War I. The French situation was especially acute; according to State Department officials, France had discriminated against the United States for at least forty years. This was viewed as a "very great detriment to American export trade." Tactically, State preferred to negotiate unconditional treaties first with Central American nations and then with European countries like Germany, Finland, Poland, Austria, Czechoslovakia, Latvia, and Hungary before pressing Spain to accept this more liberal policy. If this intricate strategy succeeded, they anticipated that "France would necessarily have to modify its policy."[109]

Throughout the trade policy debate, the State Department exhibited special concern about the growth of the British Empire's preferential system and the proliferation of trade restrictions in continental Europe. Since the beginning of World War I European nations had moved away from the unconditional most-favored-nation interpretation and turned to exclusive and restrictive trading arrangements. Washington feared that as a consequence American exporters "would be excluded from or at a disadvantage in foreign countries."[110]

A RELUCTANT STATE DEPARTMENT

The State Department was reluctant to use section 317 (a forerunner of the notorious sec. 301) aggressively to pry open closed markets. Predictably, it preferred the diplomatic option—engaging in negotiations to create a new set of commercial treaties containing unconditional most-favored-nation clauses as quickly as possible. Institutionally, the department was eager to achieve successes and demonstrate that "the policy of authorizing the executive to defend American commerce against discriminations should become a permanent part of our economic policy." But, as always, State seemed reluctant to allow an aggressive trade expansion policy to disturb existing political relations.[111]

Over the next eight years the State Department approach enjoyed only paper success. By March 1930 the United States had negotiated commercial treaties with forty-three countries, and twenty-one of these contained unconditional most-favored-nation provisions. The department negotiated formal treaties with China, Germany, Honduras, Hungary, Latvia, and Estonia. Other executive agreements provided for unconditional most-favored-nation treatment with Albania, Brazil, Czechoslovakia, the Dominican Republican, Finland, Greece, Guatemala, Haiti, Lithuania, Nicaragua, Persia, Poland, Rumania, Spain, and Turkey. In addition, officials fashioned treaties with Turkey, Norway, Austria, and Salvador that had not yet taken effect.[112]

Despite its "successes," measured in individual treaties and agreements, State was unable to open the most important foreign markets, particularly Canada, Great Britain, and France. The problem, it claimed, was the rigid single-schedule tariff. Without some statutory authority to reduce U.S. tariffs, the United States had little to offer foreign governments in exchange for acceptance of the unconditional most-favored-nation principle and equal treatment for American exports. In Europe and other countries, governments wanted access to the huge U.S. market, but they had no intention of yielding concessions to aggressive American exporters without obtaining reciprocal opportunities in the U.S. market.

Notwithstanding claims of discrimination, U.S. exporters achieved substantial success in export markets immediately after World War I. Payment problems and trade restrictions proved small obstacles as exports to Europe soared, far exceeding European exports to the United States. The resulting merchandise trade gap reflected the heavy reliance of Europe on crude materials, including foodstuffs, where the United States held a 4-to-1 export advantage during the early 1920s. For semifinished and finished manufactures, the imbalance was much narrower. From 1921 to 1925 average U.S. exports of these items to Europe amounted to $710 million; average U.S. imports from Europe equaled $688.1 million.[113]

Senate delays in handling treaties negotiated with Germany and Turkey discouraged the State Department from pursuing other commercial treaties. Instead, State turned to executive agreements—that is, simply exchanging notes to enter a modus vivendi for the purpose of securing equality of treatment. Frustrated by the inability to protect U.S. export interests, some State Department officials contemplated a more comprehensive bargaining approach, one based on reciprocal tariff reductions. In effect, these strategists favored trading off high protection in the domestic market for improved access abroad for U.S. exporters, as Henry Wheaton and John Kasson had done in the nineteenth century. Cosmopolitan in outlook, State seldom viewed American interests in nationalistic terms.

RECIPROCAL TARIFF REDUCTIONS

After President Calvin Coolidge's electoral landslide in 1924, a young State Department economist from Tennessee, Wallace McClure, suggested a program of reciprocal tariff reductions, with concessions extended to third countries on an unconditional most-favored-nation basis. Such an approach, McClure believed, might facilitate bilateral negotiations with France, Spain, and the British Dominions. He thought that "there may be a chance" that Congress would authorize the president "to proclaim limited reductions in tariff duties whenever by doing so he could obtain reductions in other countries calculated to promote the commerce of the United States." As a consequence, the economist foresaw the U.S. tariff being gradually reduced to "moderation, not as a free gift to other countries but in return for corresponding advantages" that would be generalized to all nations. After a considerable number of bilateral agreements had been negotiated, he noted, the most "thorough method of achieving uniformity" would be a single commercial convention open to all countries.[114]

In essence, what was to become Secretary of State Cordell Hull's Reciprocal Trade Agreements Program emerged nearly a decade before Congress authorized the RTAP (1934). The record shows that McClure and Hull, two Tennesseeans, worked closely together, frequently exchanging ideas, to fashion what would become the reciprocal trade program. Early in 1929 Hull himself began pushing the idea of bilateral negotiations for tariff reductions to congressional colleagues. In a House speech on January 3, 1929, he advocated employing the bargaining method to lower tariff and trade barriers and to gain respect for the unconditional most-favored-nation approach. Initially, some congressional Democrats resisted, preferring the Underwood Tariff method of legislating unilateral tariff reductions rather than authorizing the Hoover administration to negotiate reductions bilaterally. Hull wrote McClure that the present time was not ideal for introducing a "temporary policy of bargaining agreements."[115]

Hull Strives to Fashion a Democratic Export Coalition

As the Ways and Means Committee considered the Hawley bill in 1929, Hull, the perceived tariff specialist among House Democrats, prepared a strong dissent. Dismissing Republican "embargo tariffs" as incompatible with the needs of American producers for export markets in which to sell excess production, Hull again recommended that the Democrats join to revise the tariff downward. McClure encouraged Hull's efforts. In May 1929, after reading Hull's dissent, he wrote the Tennessee congressman: "If your voice is that of one crying in the wilderness, it is all the more certainly the voice of the future. There may be some time yet to wait, but there can be little doubt of complete about face of sentiment in this country with reference to the kind of tariff which the Republicans are insisting upon this year."[116]

For Cordell Hull, a low-tariff Democrat and a former chairman of the Democratic National Executive Committee, tariff reduction had several other attractions. From the standpoint of national policy, Hull was dissatisfied with the Hoover administration's high-tariff approach, limited as it was by statutory protectionism. He knew that European governments engaged in bargaining to lower tariffs, while the United States sat back with nothing to offer except equal treatment. "We are seeking to get something for nothing from each country that negotiates reciprocal tariff arrangements with another," he wrote.[117] Politics also influenced Hull's thinking. He regularly lambasted Republican tariff policy for involving "a corrupt partnership between politics and vested industrial interests, the poison of which constantly breeds national scandal." For the Tennessee legislator, a tariff reduction program had other political benefits. In particular Hull envisaged tariff reduction as a device to reunite Democrats and to create a strong Democratic majority oriented to export expansion. As he told his friend Josephus Daniels in January 1929, "There is in my judgment, a real opportunity to drive a wedge between the old moss back tariff standpats and the opposing groups and elements whose judgment and whose personal interest in most instances will constrain them to favor a steady move along lines of liberal tariffs and trade policies."[118]

His friend Norman Davis complemented Hull for emphasizing exports. "The automobile industry is becoming powerful industrially and politically, and if these, and other industries which do not need to hide behind a tariff wall, can be made to realize that their interests are not with those who are seeking high protection, the Democratic Party can gather support which it has never had before." Thus it is evident that Hull, the wily veteran of tariff and political battles, viewed the tariff as a device to create a new export-led coalition, one joining efficient assembly line manufacturing in automobiles and related industries with the traditional export interests of southern agriculture. He communicated his ideas to low-tariff Democrats and to emerging party figures such as Governor Franklin Roosevelt of New York.[119]

In the late 1920s battling Democrats could not rally behind Hull's tariff reduction program. Some Democrats, like John J. Raskob, a Du Pont official, favored a commitment to higher tariffs and the use of the flexible tariff provision to make tariff adjustments. While Raskob railed about the need to maintain a tariff to protect living standards, export interests took the view that the U.S. standard of living depended on finding export markets for surplus production. As banker Norman Davis told Hull, "we can not develop our world trade without substantial readjustments in the tariff."[120]

Within the State Department Wallace McClure and other tariff cutters struggled unsuccessfully to change policy. McClure urged the department to "use its full influence with the administration to prevent the enactment into law of the [Smoot-Hawley] tariff bill." Then, assuming that the tariff increase bill was rejected, he wanted President Hoover to request from Congress authority to enter into arrangements with other countries for reducing tariffs by executive agreement. Another internal advocate of tariff reform was William S. Culbertson, the former tariff commissioner and now U.S. ambassador to Chile. Culbertson urged the Hoover administration to employ the bargaining approach to promote acceptance of unconditional most-favored-nation treatment. In June 1931 he requested authority to negotiate bilaterally with Chile a reciprocal stabilization and reduction of rates, generalized to all countries entitled to unconditional most-favored-nation treatment. This treaty, a test case, would be submitted to Congress, which Culbertson hoped could be persuaded to underwrite a broader program of bargaining to "remove discriminations, arrest the world-wide tendency toward high tariffs, and furnish adequate protection for American trade."[121]

Concerned about the deterioration of world trade, State Department officials also discussed, in August 1931, another tariff reduction proposal. They considered urging the president to request that Congress authorize a 10 percent reduction of all duties from countries with which the United States had made unconditional most-favored-nation arrangements and that accorded U.S. commerce nondiscriminatory treatment. After a number of meetings, Assistant Secretary James G. Rogers rejected the idea, arguing that the United States should adhere to its established policies—equality of treatment and the unconditional most-favored-nation principle—while making protests and representations against discrimination in cases where America had no treaty rights. Rogers specifically rejected adopting the bargaining approach, which some economists wanted. He doubted that "tariff walls are as considerable a barrier to international trade as the current school of economists assume." And he questioned whether a country with diverse and varied exports could engage in successful tariff bargaining. It would pose political problems, requiring rapidity of action and secret negotiations "to which our constitutional machinery so far as developed is little adapted." Moreover, "the present period of international confusion and hysteria is not a sound background against which to frame an altered American policy." "My instinct," Rogers said, "is to distrust the ideas of the present period and to ride out the storm without changing our rigging."[122]

Politics undoubtedly affected this decision. Senior policymakers in the Hoover administration probably knew that the president had no disposition to reopen the contentious tariff issue after the eighteen-month ordeal leading to Smoot-Hawley in June 1930. In effect, his decision ended administration efforts to alter policy until after the 1932 presidential election. This rejection did not end internal debate. In September 1931 another State Department newcomer, Harry Hawkins, later to become the principal tactician of Hull's bargaining program, circulated his own memorandum on commercial policy within the State Department. Citing European experiences with bargaining tariffs, Hawkins suggested negotiating only with major foreign suppliers in order to avoid diminishing U.S. bargaining power. Most of all, he urged the department to continue its efforts to negotiate new commercial treaties.[123]

Congressional Democrats, eager to embarrass the administration for its high-tariff stance, took the initiative. Having gained effective control of the Seventy-second Congress, elected in 1930, they assigned top priority to tariff negotiations. In October 1931, before the new Congress was seated, Senator-elect Cordell Hull circulated a plan to authorize the president to enter into reciprocal tariff reduction agreements with other countries. These would bind the United States unless Congress expressly vetoed the pacts within six months. Hull told his friend McClure that only by executive action not requiring congressional confirmation could the American tariff be reduced in exchange for reductions from U.S. trading partners on American exports.[124]

A few weeks later Senator Hull called publicly for a world economic conference to promote tariff liberalization and urged Congress to "proceed at once with the readjustment downward of rates." He proposed "a plan to reduce tariffs by commercial treaties with two or more countries, in return for reciprocal reductions, with the unconditional favored-nation doctrine made as nearly as possible the basis."[125]

To undermine Hoover and the Republicans during the 1932 presidential campaign, Democrats then passed the Collier Tariff Act (H.R. 6662) with support from insurgent Republicans. This measure requested the president to "negotiate with foreign governments reciprocal trade agreements under a policy of mutual trade concessions." But Congress stipulated that any such agreements required congressional approval. On May 11, 1932, Hoover vetoed the Collier bill. Fundamentally, the embattled president opposed congressional revisions in the tariff, preferring that the independent Tariff Commission have an opportunity to use its authority under the flexible tariff. The president said that the bill also would start "our country upon the road of a system of preferential tariffs between nations with all the trade wars, international entanglements, . . . which our country has sought to avoid by extending equal treatment to all of them."[126]

Foreign observers did not take the Collier bill seriously. The British embassy concluded that it was of "domestic rather than international interest." Democrats wanted to pass a tariff bill designed to provoke a presidential veto. It contained "sheer bunkum" in order to give "Democrat orators something to orate about."[127]

Reciprocity Again

After the 1932 presidential election, State Department officials and Democrats on Capitol Hill collaborated to develop a tariff bargaining program. Senator Hull called for the United States to offer leadership in the direction of "sanity and sound business recovery." Not surprisingly, the single-minded Hull pressed his idea for a moratorium on protectionist practices and reciprocal negotiations to expand exports, presenting it as a device to restore markets and boost employment at home. Specifically, he wanted the U.S. government to propose that other governments effect a 10 percent horizontal reduction in tariff rates. "Reciprocal commercial treaties based on mutual tariff concessions and, as nearly as possible, the unconditional favored-nation policy if other governments will agree, would greatly supplement the usual legislative method of tariff readjustment," he argued.[128]

When President Franklin Roosevelt designated Hull as his secretary of state, the State Department established an interdepartmental committee to analyze trade policy options for the incoming administration. This working group, which included representatives of State, Commerce, Treasury, Agriculture, the U.S. Tariff Commission, and other agencies, shared a consensus that "fundamental to any reciprocity policy" should be maintenance of the unconditional most-favored-nation approach and an executive agreement procedure. Wallace McClure, Hull's Tennessee friend, chaired the interagency group.[129]

Meanwhile, the Tariff Commission conducted a fact-finding investigation relating to tariff bargaining in response to Senate Resolution 325. This, too, was intended to pave the way for a negotiating policy based on reciprocal tariff reductions. Among the recommendations, if Congress should adopt a bargaining approach, the commission recommended generalizing concessions on an unconditional most-favored-nation basis to avoid retaliation against U.S. exports. It suggested bargaining reciprocally only with major suppliers, as European countries did, so as to gain maximum market-opening advantages from U.S. concessions.[130]

When President Roosevelt nominated Tennessee senator Cordell Hull in 1933 to become secretary of state, few could anticipate the revolution in U.S. trade policy that this decision foreshadowed. For Hull had a personal and political agenda. It was to gain bargaining authority from Congress to reduce tariffs and use this authority to improve market access abroad for U.S. exporters, particularly automakers, mass manufacturing, and commodity agriculture. He anticipated that this approach would create a strong coalition of financial supporters for the Democratic Party.

Hull's program had its genesis in the State Department and reflected that agency's long-standing approach to commercial policy issues. From the department's perspective, the rigid American protective system, which reflected the constitutional authority of Congress to regulate commerce, complicated relationships with foreign nations and created nasty conflicts. Such disputes handicapped State's efforts to nurture stable relationships and to pursue other political and security objectives, including continental expansion.

As the experiences of Henry Wheaton and John Kasson show, the foreign policy community had long sought to restrain Congress and to use the executive's treaty-making authority to promote stable commercial relations with other nations. To succeed with the powers of Europe, this negotiating strategy depended on trading off import-competing interests in the United States for the benefit of U.S. exporters and foreign policy interests.

During the nineteenth century, the Senate Finance Committee under the direction of Justin Morrill and Nelson Aldrich vigilantly protected congressional prerogatives and preserved the dynamic American system. Morrill and Aldrich understood that many of the proposed reciprocity treaties lacked an equivalent exchange of concessions. Too often, as in the case of the Zollverein treaty or Kasson's treaty with France, Congress perceived that the State Department consented to commercially "unreciprocal" agreements, which were potentially injurious to American workers and producers.

When the Republican Party fractured in 1912, Democrats elected Woodrow Wilson with only a plurality of the popular vote. With low-tariff Democrats finally in control of both the executive and Congress, they had a unique opportunity to fulfill campaign rhetoric and revise the tariff. World War I disrupted this initiative. Concern that the Democrats had gone too far contributed to Republican victories in the 1920s—and to higher tariff levels in the 1920s.

The Great Depression, the successful attack on Smoot-Hawley, and the election of Franklin Roosevelt in 1932 gave Democrats a third opportunity to implement their low-tariff agenda. This time officials at State had a negotiating strategy ready for implementation. It involved persuading Congress to delegate tariff making to the president—and to his executive branch agent, the State Department.

[T]he Smoot-Hawley Tariff Act ... has been probably the foremost factor in saving our industries from collapse.—Chairman Reed Smoot, 1932

We have learned the lesson of the Smoot-Hawley tariff once. It would be stupid—as well as tragic—to start down that road again.—President Harry S. Truman, 1968

Infamous Smoot-Hawley

Reed Smoot and Willis Hawley are two deceased members of Congress the world loves to hate. Their principal legislative achievement, the Smoot-Hawley Tariff of 1930, continues to evoke such epithets as "infamous" and "notorious." To most Americans, that act, which incidentally remains the fundamental tariff law of the United States, conjures up images of rising tariff barriers, beggar-thy-neighbor nationalism, and ruinous trade wars.[1]

The Enduring Metaphor

Over the course of the twentieth century, only a few other traumatic events—Munich, the German invasion of France in 1940, Pearl Harbor, Yalta, and Vietnam—have seared the public consciousness similarly and become enduring metaphors for public policy failures. Yet the latter crises emerged from military defeats or perceived diplomatic failures, not from political combat over domestic legislation.

One prominent international economist, a former undersecretary of state

Senator Reed Smoot (*right*) and Representative Willis Hawley, authors of the 1930 Tariff Act. (Library of Congress, Washington, D.C.)

for economic affairs in the Carter administration, offered this astringent assessment: "the most disastrous single mistake any American president has made in international relations was Herbert Hoover's signing of the Hawley-Smoot Tariff Act into law in June 1930." Richard Cooper explained that the sharp increase in tariffs, the apparent indifference of U.S. authorities to the external implications of their actions, and the subsequent foreign retaliation helped convert what would have been otherwise a normal economic downturn into a major world depression. In his view, the resulting sharp decline in foreign trade and economic activity undermined the position of the moderates in Japan and helped elect the Nazis in Germany. "The seeds of the Second World War, both in the Far East and in Europe, were sown by Hoover's signing of the Hawley-Smoot tariff," Cooper declared.[2]

For three generations, secondary and college students have learned to associate Smoot-Hawley with the "evil consequences" of protectionism. One widely used high school text states that in passing the Smoot-Hawley Tariff, Congress set "the highest tariff rates in history." European nations retaliated, and "[t]his hurt United States exports and brought international trade to a virtual standstill." Another claims: "In 1930 Congress raised tariff rates to the highest level in our nation's history." President Hoover signed the measure, although economists and bankers warned against it. "Within the next year," the book contends, "25 foreign nations struck back by cutting down their imports of American goods. The drop in foreign trade made the depression even worse."[3]

A popular college-level history text proclaims Smoot-Hawley "an unqualified disaster. . . . It provoked foreign governments to enact trade restrictions of their own in reprisal." Economics texts repeat all the familiar criticisms—and frequently add more biting invective. The author of a widely used book on international economics writes that under Smoot-Hawley "the average import duty in the United States reached the all-time high of 59 percent in 1932, provoking foreign retaliation" from sixty countries. He concludes: "The result was catastrophic. . . . The net result was a collapse of world trade . . . , and this contributed in a significant way to the spreading and the deepening of the depression around the world." Similar passages appear in dozens of textbooks used in history, economics, political science, and law courses.[4]

For over sixty years this bugbear interpretation dominated all discussion of trade policy. Individuals prepared to challenge the conventional wisdom received only a cursory hearing. Beginning with Franklin Roosevelt, a series of American presidents invoked the infamous Smoot-Hawley image to aid their reelection efforts, mobilize public support for further trade liberalization, or rally opinion against congressional restrictions on commerce. On the campaign trail both Presidents Franklin Roosevelt and Truman found Smoot-Hawley a convenient target. Invoking the memories of Senator Reed Smoot and Congressman Willis Hawley, they sought to portray opposition Republicans as hostile to international trade.[5]

Concerned about a protectionist backlash after the Kennedy Round, President Lyndon Johnson directed his staff to draft a speech emphasizing that "this is no time for high tariff walls or Smoot-Hawley." A few days later, while signing a trade proclamation, Johnson asked what "captain of industry or . . . union leader . . . is eager to return to the days of Smoot-Hawley? For the world of higher tariffs . . . was also the world of . . . deep depressions, rampant unemployment."[6]

In time even Republicans forgot about President Hoover and began to vilify Smoot-Hawley. In his memoirs President Dwight Eisenhower rejected any attempt to restore Smoot-Hawley Tariff rates as "ruinous." During the 1980s President Ronald Reagan regularly assailed the mistakes of 1930. "The Smoot-Hawley tariff helped bring on the Great Depression," he said in November 1987. On another occasion, he asserted that "the Smoot-Hawley tariff . . . made it virtually impossible for anyone to sell anything in America, and . . . spread the Great Depression around the world." In other remarks, Reagan chided Smoot and Hawley for coauthoring the bill that "brought about the collapse of the world trading system. . . . both of them felt that a bit of demagoging about trade was good politics. It certainly did get them in the history books. . . . they were both thrown out of office 2 years later when the voters had time to see the effects of their bill." For Reagan, one lesson gained from Smoot-Hawley was that "protectionism isn't just bad economics, it's bad politics." History, the president stated, "points in the opposite direction: more trade, not less; increasing cooperation, not isolationism and retaliation; expanding global networks of investment, production and communication, not mercantilist national economics shrinking behind tariff barriers."[7]

During the Clinton administration, Vice President Albert Gore invoked the famous image in his debate with businessman Ross Perot on the North American Free Trade Agreement. Gore presented the Texas billionaire with a framed photograph of Senator Reed Smoot and Congressman Willis Hawley. "They raised tariffs," Gore said, "and it was one of the principal causes . . . of the Great Depression." Opinion shapers jumped with joy. Claiming that the "famous tariff lives on in the annals of invincible ignorance," the *Wall Street Journal* recalled that Smoot and Hawley "represented a brand of dumb and reactionary Republicanism that consigned the party to also-ran oblivion." *Business Week* assailed the Smoot-Hawley Tariff for "triggering the Great Depression and paving the way for World War II."[8]

As presented in textbooks and political debates, the Smoot-Hawley legend generally appears to rest on six claims. First, Smoot-Hawley increased U.S. tariff rates to the highest levels in history. Second, these sky-high tariffs frightened the stock market. Third, Smoot-Hawley exacerbated the Great Depression. It did so because American consumers reduced their purchases of foreign goods and because angry foreigners stopped buying American exports. Fourth, upset at congressional protectionists, some thirty-four foreign governments protested, as did over a thousand economists. Fifth, unable to moderate the legislative process or to persuade President Hoover to sign a veto, other nations retaliated with trade restrictions of their own. The resulting trade war depressed American exports, shattered world commerce, and contributed to the coming of World War II. And sixth, dissatisfaction with the consequences of Smoot-Hawley cost its principal congressional authors, Chairmen Reed Smoot and Willis Hawley, their elective positions.

Smoot-Hawley or Hawley-Smoot?

After sixty years of one-sided commentary, it is time to review archival materials, revisit the data, and reconsider the Smoot-Hawley legend. In particular, archival evidence indicates that that legend does not comport with reality. To start with, some may ask, Is the 1930 tariff act properly called Smoot-Hawley or Hawley-Smoot? Despite a popular preference for Smoot-Hawley, purists can make a compelling case for Hawley-Smoot. Their reasoning rests on the constitutional requirement that revenue measures begin in the House of Representatives. Accordingly, protocol directs that the name of the House Ways and Means Committee chairman precede his Senate counterpart. Indeed, all of the hyphenated tariff acts of the twentieth century begin with the name of the Ways and Means chairman. This convention explains why the Tariff Act of 1909 is familiarly known as the Payne-Aldrich Tariff of 1909, in honor of Representative Sereno Payne, of New York, chairman of the House Ways and Means Committee, and Senator Nelson Aldrich, of Rhode Island, chairman of the Senate Finance Committee. Similarly, Representative Oscar Underwood, of Alabama, chairman of the House Ways and Means Committee, and Senator Furnifold M. Simmons, of North Carolina, chairman of the Senate Finance Committee, gave their names to the Underwood-Simmons Tariff of 1913. The Fordney-McCumber Act of 1922 took its hyphenated form from Representative Joseph Fordney, of Michigan, chairman of the Ways and Means Committee, and Senator Porter McCumber, of North Dakota, chairman of the Senate Finance Committee. Nineteenth-century tariffs such as the Morrill, Dingley, and McKinley acts were named for the Ways and Means Committee chairman. No senator enjoyed such exclusive recognition.

There are several exceptions to this convention. The controversial 1845 tariff revision bears the name of Robert Walker, the Treasury secretary. The 1894 Wilson-Gorman Act represents another deviation. It begins with William L. Wilson, chairman of the Ways and Means Committee, and ends with Senator Arthur P. Gorman, of Maryland, an influential friend of President Grover Cleveland who was not even a member of the Finance Committee.[9] Daniel W. Voorhees, of Indiana, the Finance Committee chairman, left no personal mark on that law.

The weight of historical precedent directs that the Tariff Act of 1930 begin with the last name of the House Ways and Means chairman, Representative Hawley of Oregon. Since 1930 many in the press and public have preferred Smoot-Hawley, while others remain loyal to Hawley-Smoot. A few persist with a third version, Smoot-Hawley-Grundy, a reference to Pennsylvania protectionist Joseph Grundy, who served briefly in the Senate.[10]

In June 1930, as Congress approved the conference report for President Hoover's signature, newspapers and wire services chose divergent forms of reference. The *Washington Post* preferred Smoot-Hawley in stories written by its own staff but allowed the Associated Press preference for Hawley-Smoot to prevail in wire service stories. The *New York Herald Tribune*'s lead story on June 15 reported: "The *Hawley-Smoot* tariff bill was passed by the House today." Similarly, the *New York Times* stated: "Carrying out the predictions of its leaders, the House this afternoon passed the *Hawley-Smoot* tariff bill."[11] *Time* magazine employed the same form.

Editors at the United Press, however, apparently adopted Smoot-Hawley. *The Wall Street Journal* used that version in a wire service account on June 14 but called it the Hawley-Smoot Tariff in front-page editorials. A third wire service, International News Service, referred to the "Grundy Tariff." In regional newspapers the form frequently varied, depending on the wire service that filed the story. The *Columbus Dispatch* used all three forms.[12]

From the beginning, the participants themselves confused the issue. President Hoover and Senator Smoot referred to Smoot-Hawley. Chairman Hawley stuck to traditional protocol.[13] I suspect that the real explanation has little to do with knowledge of convention and constitutional law. Probably it has everything to do with facility of expression. Most people simply found it easier to say Smoot-Hawley than Hawley-Smoot.

Some have suggested another possible reason—that Senator Smoot was a stronger advocate of protectionism than Congressman Hawley, or that Chairman Smoot played a more visible role in the Smoot-Hawley tariff-writing drama. It is my reading of the evidence that Hawley was every bit as protectionist as Smoot, so the first distinction seems unwarranted. A comparison of the House and Senate bills shows that the House bill, named for Chairman Hawley, had higher average schedules than the Senate Finance Committee version written at Smoot's direction.[14]

Smoot was certainly more visible during the tariff writing. For more than a year—from June 11, 1929, when the Senate Finance Committee began public hearings, to June 13, 1930, when the Senate finally approved the conference report, the public spotlight focused on the Senate's role. And many of the controversial high rates reflected changes made in the Senate. Smoot, a master of legislative detail, worked closely with President Hoover to achieve administration objectives. Among members of the Senate Smoot merits special recognition for his exceptional technical knowledge and ability.[15]

After considering such factors, I elected to avoid the less felicitous Hawley-Smoot in favor of the familiar Smoot-Hawley. In weighing the competing claims, I was influenced by two other factors. Chairman Reed Smoot kept a diary and left many records for future historians. It is apparent from these and other archival documents, as well as contemporary press accounts, that Smoot was a superior legislator. He was, in legislative parlance, a workhorse, not a showhorse. After his defeat the *New York Times* wrote: "It may be doubted if there is another Senator who has so thorough a knowledge of public affairs."[16] Unfortunately for Hawley, he left few records and his office files have disappeared. This handicaps any historian's effort to assess his legacy.

The Highest Tariff in American History?

Smoot-Hawley did not establish the highest tariff schedule in American history. Official statistics show that many writers and commentators err on this crucial point. Textbook writers who assert that the Tariff Act of 1930 enacted the highest rates in American history, or in peacetime, or in the twentieth century, have not examined the evidence carefully.

Table 4.1, which compares U.S. tariff levels from 1828 to 1992, indicates that Smoot-Hawley did not increase average tariff levels significantly. In assessing the nominal height of tariffs, specialists look at two ratios: average duties collected as a share of *dutiable and free* imports and average duties collected as a share of *dutiable* imports. With either method Smoot-Hawley established no record. The *average duty on all imports*—free and dutiable—amounted to 13.7 percent during the final six months of 1930. For ninety-four consecutive years, from 1821 to 1914, average rates surpassed 13.7 percent. During the last half of 1930, after enactment of the Tariff Act, the ratio of duties collected to total dutiable imports was 44.9 percent. But over the period from 1821 to 1930, the *average levy on dutiable goods* exceeded 44.9 percent in thirty-three other years. Stated differently, the average U.S. tariff on dutiable goods regularly exceeded tariff levels enacted in 1930. It is true, however, that Smoot-Hawley levies on dutiable goods represented a return to higher pre–World War I levels. Considered either way, Smoot-Hawley did not enact the highest tariff levels in American history or even in the twentieth century.[17]

To support their conviction that the Tariff Act of 1930 represented a high-water mark for protectionism, many authors focus on a single number—the average ad valorem equivalent rate on *dutiable imports* in 1932. This 59.1 percent average rate was one of the higher dutiable rates in American history. It was not the highest. In 1830 under the Tariff of Abominations, dutiable rates averaged 61.69 percent.[18]

In emphasizing the 59.1 percent figure, scholars overlook two critical points. First, Congress did not enact such a high average tariff in 1930. Price declines during the depression produced that result. Like predecessor tariffs, Smoot-Hawley relied on a combination of specific and ad valorem duties. Nearly half of dutiable imports carried specific rates—meaning a fixed amount per quantity, such as 20 cents per pound. When prices plunged during the Great Depression, the percentage equivalent of such specific duties soared. A 20 cent duty on an item valued at $1.00 effectively became a 40 percent duty if the good's price fell to 50 cents per unit.[19]

According to the U.S. Tariff Commission (TC), 48.6 percent of dutiable imports in 1930–31 entered at specific duty rates.[20] Among goods bearing the same specific duty in both the 1922 and 1930 acts, the TC concluded that

TABLE 4.1

U.S. Tariff Levels, Selected Years from 1828 to 1992

Year	(1)	(2)	(3)	(4)
Tariff of Abominations (1828)				
Calendar year 1830	8.0%	92.0%	61.7%	57.3%
Morrill Tariffs (Civil War)				
Calendar year 1868	4.3	95.7	48.7	46.6
McKinley Tariff (1890)				
Annual average, 1891–94	52.4	47.6	48.4	23.0
Wilson Tariff (1894)				
Annual average, 1895–97	49.4	50.6	41.3	20.9
Dingley Tariff (1897)				
Annual average, 1898–1909	45.2	54.8	46.5	25.5
Payne-Aldrich Tariff (1909)				
Annual average, 1910–13	52.6	47.4	40.8	19.3
Underwood Tariff (1913)				
Annual average, 1914–22	66.3	33.7	27.0	9.1
Fordney-McCumber (1922)				
Annual average, 1923–30	63.8	36.2	38.5	14.0
Fordney-McCumber (1922)				
January–June 17, 1930	64.6	35.4	44.6	15.8
Smoot-Hawley (1930)				
June 18–December 31, 1930	69.5	30.5	44.9	13.7
Smoot-Hawley (1930)				
Calendar year 1931	66.6	33.4	53.2	17.8
Smoot-Hawley (1930)				
Calendar year 1932	66.8	33.2	59.1	19.6
Smoot-Hawley as modified				
Calendar year 1970	34.9	65.1	10.0	6.5
Smoot-Hawley as modified				
Calendar year 1992	37.1	62.9	5.2	3.3

Key:
(1) Percentage of duty-free imports to total imports.
(2) Percentage of dutiable imports to total imports.
(3) Ratio of all duties calculated to total dutiable imports.
(4) Ratio of all duties calculated to free and dutiable imports.
    Columns 3 and 4 thus present two standard measures of tariff height— expressed as ad valorem equivalents to include both specific and ad valorem duties. Tariff specialists recognize the need for caution in interpreting average ad valorem equivalents. If higher duties cause imports to decline, the average ad valorem equivalent may also fall.
Sources: U.S. International Trade Commission, Statistical Services Division, March 1985; U.S. Bureau of the Census, *Historical Statistics of the United States*, bicentennial ed. (Washington, D.C.: GPO, 1974), 2:888, and *Statistical Abstract of the United States* (Washington, D.C.: GPO, 1993), p. 818.

declining prices had a significant impact: "For this group the average ad valorem equivalent in 1929 was 25.5 percent, and if there had been no change in prices it would probably have been about the same in 1930–31, whereas the actual figure for the later year was 33.5 percent."[21]

With specific duties the average ad valorem equivalent ratcheted upward as prices for goods fell. This was particularly true with sugar and agricultural commodities. The Tariff Commission noted that the average ad valorem equivalent for the sugar schedule was 84 percent in 1929 and 132.4 percent in 1930–31, "but when the 1929 prices are applied to the imports of 1930–31 the average falls to about 91 percent."[22] Tariff schedule 7 (agricultural products and provisions) carried a 19 percent ad valorem equivalent in 1929 and a 37.7 percent equivalent in 1930–31. Adjusting for 1929 prices, the average for 1930–31 becomes 28.3 percent.

Had 1929 price levels endured, the Tariff Commission calculated that the Smoot-Hawley rate on dutiable items would have averaged 41.6 percent—certainly not a prohibitive tariff by historical standards. Indeed, in fifty-one out of ninety-four years, from 1821 to 1914, the average rate on dutiable imports exceeded that amount.[23] This leads to an important, counterfactual observation. Senator Reed Smoot of Utah and Congressman Willis Hawley of Oregon, the two Republican legislators who acquired immortality as demons of protectionism for devising the 1930 tariff, attained that notoriety largely because of conditions beyond their own control. Had Congress and President Hoover never enacted Smoot-Hawley, falling depression-era prices would have ratcheted up effective tariff rates under the 1922 tariff. In such circumstances, textbook authors might censure Representative Joseph Fordney (R-Mich.) and Senator Porter McCumber (R-N.Dak.) for their protectionist infamies.

There is a second reason to disregard the 59.1 percent rate on dutiable imports in 1932 as a measure of Smoot-Hawley's protective effect. Subsequently, a bipartisan majority in the Seventy-second Congress enacted the Revenue Act of 1932, increasing duties on certain commodity imports: coal, copper, lumber, gasoline, and other petroleum products. This measure, approved in a Congress with Republicans controlling the flow of legislation in the Senate and Democrats in the House of Representatives, increased the 1932 average rate on dutiable imports.[24]

Official data suggest several other interpretations. Far from boosting tariff barriers, Smoot-Hawley briefly lowered the average ad valorem equivalent on all imports and made a contribution to the expansion of duty-free trade. In looking at customs revenue collected in 1930, one finds that Smoot-Hawley may actually have lowered average duties. During the last six months of 1930, when the act was first implemented, the ratio of duties collected to all imports—free and dutiable—under Smoot-Hawley was 13.7 percent, *down* from 15.8 percent in the first half of 1930. Thus Smoot-Hawley differed little from Fordney-McCumber. Arguably, based on revenue collections from actual imports, it may have reduced average tariff levels. The *Washington Post* understood this point in 1930, when it dismissed high-tariff claims as "twaddle." Congress "complied with the President's request for a limited revision."[25]

Many textbook writers and commentators overlook another key point. The peak 59.1 percent ad valorem equivalent rate applied only to one-third of total imports in 1932. Smoot-Hawley actually expanded the share of U.S. imports on the free list slightly. Two-thirds entered with no import duties whatsoever.[26] In light of this point, scholars should acknowledge that Smoot-Hawley enacted not the "highest tariff" in American history, but one conforming to nineteenth-century patterns. Column 1 in Table 4.1 notes that 69.5 percent of imports entered the country duty-free in the last half of 1930, 66.6 percent in 1931, and 66.8 percent in 1932. Except under the Underwood schedules during World War I, no tariff before or after Smoot-Hawley permitted such a large percentage of U.S. imports, by value, to enter duty-free. In 1992, for example, only 37 percent of U.S. imports entered duty-free. If one takes the percentage of duty-free imports as the standard for comparing tariffs, then Chairmen Reed Smoot and Willis Hawley, self-styled protectionists, emerge as closet free traders. They wrote a tariff schedule that effectively expanded the share of freely traded goods, as it raised rates on certain sensitive dutiable items.[27]

The Cause of the Stock Market Collapse?

Did Smoot-Hawley cause the stock market collapse? On the surface this claim seems preposterous. President Hoover and Congress completed their work on the tariff in June 1930; the stock market break had occurred in October 1929, nine months earlier. Elementary logic might suggest that an event in 1930 could not cause an event in 1929.

Economics writer Jude Wanniski perceived a connection. In his book, *The Way the World Works*, he declared: "The stock market Crash of 1929 and the Great Depression ensued because of the passage of the Smoot-Hawley Tariff Act of 1930."[28] Citing front-page headlines from the *New York Times*, Wanniski argued that the financial markets anticipated passage of higher tariffs and the prospect for protectionism spooked markets and brought about the October crash.

This is an intriguing theory. Wanniski offered little evidence, such as the testimony of contemporary observers or newspaper accounts. He even acknowledged that "not a word appeared in the press making note of this remarkable coincidence." He said that "the [*New York*] *Times* and other Wall

Street observers groped for an answer and looked to the Federal Reserve, which was also forced to deal with reaction to the tariff news without knowing it."[29] Thus this alluring idea apparently rests primarily on the author's conviction that invisible hands discerned the real reason for the October crash.

To what extent did the tariff battle in Congress affect the stock market? At first glance, newspaper accounts and stock market price fluctuations show little relationship, apparently confirming the view that the spheres of government and finance remained worlds apart. For example, on May 28, when the House of Representatives approved the Hawley bill, the Dow Jones industrial average rose over five points—to 298.87—and then lost two points the next day. The industrials remained on an upward climb, peaking at 381 on September 3 after Chairman Smoot presented an even more protectionist Finance Committee bill to the Senate. This peak came some ten days after Senator William Borah of Idaho and a maverick band of agrarian Republicans called for the measure's defeat. However, during September the Dow-Jones industrial average slowly dropped 10 percent and on October 3 plummeted nearly fifteen points. The press reported that "a drastic break in stock prices shook" the New York stock market. That morning the front page of the *New York Times* carried the following lead story: "Hoover Defeated on Flexible Tariff; Coalition in Senate, 47 to 42, Takes from President Duty-Fixing Power."[30] This was a critical test of power, revealing that insurgent Republicans and Democrats had the votes to remove the flexible tariff provision from the Finance Committee bill. A week later, however, the market had climbed back to 352.86, its monthly high, although the impasse intensified in the Senate. During the second week in October, the New York Stock Exchange recovered lost ground.

New waves of selling rocked the exchange later in the month. Hoover's allies lacked a working majority to pass a tariff bill, but the president retained sufficient votes to sustain a veto. On October 19 the insurgent Democratic coalition tacked on Senator George Norris's export debenture program of agricultural subsidies. The industrial average lost over nine points that day and fell three more points the next day. As Senator Borah and the agrarians took charge of the tariff writing, the stock market broke and reached a bottom of 198.69 on November 13. The stock market crashed after evidence of legislative gridlock, when it appeared that Congress could not approve *any* tariff revision.

It was not the fear of higher protective duties that frightened the market. Instead, the financial and business community perceived a collapse of leadership and discipline in Congress, and they feared that the Senate could not function. Wall Street and big business loathed uncertainty. More than a month before the October crash the National Association of Manufacturers had complained to Hoover: "For five months this vital economic question has been on the political operating table while the legislative physicians have haggled over a correct diagnosis and proper treatment." Meanwhile, "business has been marking time and in many instances plans for industrial extension and expansion have had to be held up."[31]

Fred Kent, a director and former vice president of Bankers Trust, made headlines in November when he blamed the Democratic insurgent coalition for contributing to the stock market collapse. He said that "industry cannot proceed, employ men, buy and process raw materials unless it can feel confident of markets. Every consideration of the tariff develops uneasiness on the part of industry." Kent told a group of bankers that "there was the fear that if this [insurgent] bloc succeeded in rewriting the tariff bill in its own way, it might come to believe that it had the power to reduce tariffs."[32] In effect, he claimed that the coalition's dilatory tactics created unrest, aroused fear that industry would be injured, and contributed to a general uneasiness that prompted stockholders to begin dumping stocks. Such Wall Street criticism did not shake the agrarian insurgents in the Senate. Their leader, William Borah, retorted: If the tariff fight for equality between agriculture and industry "shakes the Stock Exchange to the earth, let it go."[33]

After Chairman Smoot and the Republican leaders broke the coalition's back in March and April 1930, demonstrating that Congress could write a tariff bill after all, the market rebounded to 294 on April 17, near its high on Black Monday. On March 24, when the Senate voted out its version of the tariff act, the Dow-Jones industrials had climbed nearly three points and added another point the next day. Interestingly, the April 17 peak came as Senate-House conferees concluded work on the bill's tariff rates. Thus the financial markets did not fear protection; rather, they recoiled at anarchy in Congress and a further business uncertainty.

It is true, however, that the stock market dropped in June 1930, when Congress and President Hoover finally finished the tariff bill. On June 16, the day Hoover announced his intention to sign the tariff, the market fell fourteen points. It dropped another point on June 17, when the president formally signed the Tariff Act of 1930. This nervousness apparently reflected stories in leading newspapers about the possibility of foreign retaliation, rumors that caused temporary jitters. A month later, in mid-July, the market recovered much lost ground.

Given the correlation of key events in the tariff revision with Wall Street gyrations, it is doubtful that the prospect of higher tariffs spooked the stock market. The Dow-Jones industrial average reached a low point (198.69) on November 13, 1929, when an agrarian Democratic coalition controlled events, and neither side had the necessary votes to write and enact a tariff bill. Wall

Street feared stalemate and legislative deadlock, not upward tariff revisions. During the spring of 1930, after Chairman Smoot and his allies had broken the logjam, the stock market rebounded.[34]

Did Smoot-Hawley Worsen the Depression?

Many authors and public officials think that enactment of Smoot-Hawley heightened the Great Depression. Vice President Al Gore voiced this idea in his 1993 debate over NAFTA with Ross Perot. For the 1930 tariff to have exacerbated the world depression, it must have depressed U.S. imports or exports or both. Proponents of these interpretations argue that higher U.S. tariffs affected the movement of goods, and as a result production and employment declined. In this way, they contend, Smoot-Hawley spread the slump worldwide. These advocates assume a negative relationship between tariffs and either economic growth or overall trade levels.

Economic theory may suggest such relationships, but historical evidence occasionally contradicts textbook concepts. Experience from the nineteenth century shows that tariff cuts do not automatically produce expanded trade or production. In 1857 and 1872 Congress *cut* tariffs, but economic collapse followed. The 1872 revision sliced the average duty on all imports from 37.99 percent to 27.90 percent, a 26.60 percent reduction. During the crash of 1873, however, the value of total imports dropped sharply.[35]

The early twentieth century offers much more data for analyzing this complex relationship. In 1913 the Underwood-Simmons Tariff sharply reduced average duties on all imports. As a consequence, the government collected an average duty of 6.4 percent on all goods imported in 1920, down from an average 19.3 percent under Payne-Aldrich schedules. On dutiable imports, the Underwood schedules averaged 16.4 percent in 1920, as compared with 40.8 percent during implementation of Payne-Aldrich. Initially, these steep cuts had little impact because World War I conditions and controls disrupted private trading patterns. However, at the end of World War I imports surged, and domestic industries appealed for tariff relief. Congress responded with an emergency tariff supplement in 1921. In 1922 it undertook a comprehensive tariff revision, enacting the Fordney-McCumber Act. This legislation raised average duties on all imports to 15.2 percent and to 36.2 percent on dutiable imports in 1923. Effectively, Fordney-McCumber elevated the average tariff on dutiable goods 138 percent in two years.

How did higher Fordney-McCumber duties affect trade? Did sharply higher tariffs depress imports and economic growth? They did not. Congress raised

TABLE 4.2

U.S. Dutiable and Duty-Free Imports, 1920 and 1923

Year	Dutiable Imports (Millions of $)	Percent of Change	Free Imports (Millions of $)	Percent of Change
1920	$1,985.9		$3,116.0	
1923	1,566.6	(21.1)%	2,165.1	(30.5)%

Source: U.S. International Trade Commission, Statistical Services Division, March 1985.

tariffs after a post–World War I slump began. As the average tariff rose from 6.4 percent ad valorem equivalent in 1920 to 15.2 percent in 1923, an increase of 137.5 percent, the *quantity* of imports continued to rise. Experience after passage of the Fordney-McCumber Act does not confirm negative relationships between either increased tariffs and imports or increased tariffs and GNP. In fact, Table 4.2 shows that during the 1920–23 recession the value of dutiable goods fell less than duty-free imports. The data seem to suggest that macroeconomic conditions exerted a greater negative impact on trade than higher tariffs.

After passage of Smoot-Hawley in 1930, both the value and the quantity of U.S. imports declined. That is indisputable. From the cyclical peak in 1929 to the depths of the depression in 1932, the value of U.S. imports fell 69 percent. The quantity of imports fell less—40 percent. If higher Smoot-Hawley duties reduced import access to the U.S. market, one might expect to find evidence that dutiable imports fell much more rapidly than duty-free imports. Interestingly, available trade data do not show that. From 1929 to 1931, as the United States entered the depression, imports of dutiable and non-dutiable goods both declined about 52 percent. From 1929 to 1932, as demonstrated in Table 4.3, dutiable imports fell 69.8 percent and duty-free imports dropped 69.24 percent. But from 1932 to 1936, as the domestic economy began to recover, the value of dutiable imports climbed faster (136 percent) than duty-free imports (56 percent).

These data point to an important conclusion: Policymakers, and perhaps economists generally, have a tendency to overestimate the importance of tariffs on trade flows.[36] But tariffs are only one of many factors that affect trade patterns. Others involve demand and supply circumstances in both the exporting and importing nations, as well as currency rates. From 1929 to 1932, then, U.S. import declines appear to reflect macroeconomic circumstances—declining demand in the United States and falling world prices.[37]

TABLE 4.3

U.S. Dutiable and Duty-Free Imports, 1929–1936

Year	Dutiable Articles		Duty-Free Articles	
	Millions of $	Percent of Change	Millions of $	Percent of Change
1929	$1,458		$2,880	
1930	1,033	(29.1%)	2,081	(27.7%)
1931	697	(32.5)	1,392	(33.1)
1932	440	(36.9)	886	(36.4)
1929–31	(761)	(52.2)	(1,488)	(51.7)
1929–32	(1,018)	(69.8)	(1,994)	(69.2)
1934	645		991	
1935	833	29.1	1,206	21.7
1936	1,039	24.7	1,385	14.8
1932–36	599	136.1	499	56.3

Source: Calculated from data in U.S. Bureau of the Census, *Historical Statistics of the United States*, bicentennial ed. (Washington, D.C.: GPO, 1974), 2:888, 891–93.

Higher Smoot-Hawley tariffs did not necessarily reduce import competition for domestic producers. The U.S. Tariff Commission reported one hundred products in which increased Smoot-Hawley duties correlated with higher import volumes between 1929 and 1931. For instance, the duty on refined sugar (par. 501) rose from 2.39 cents per pound less 20 percent to 2.65 cents per pound less 20 percent. From 1929 to 1932 the quantity of refined sugar imports rose 64 percent. On Canadian bacon, hams, and shoulders the duty rose from 2 cents per pound to 3.25 cents, but the quantity of imports rose 44 percent from 1929 to 1932. Along with agricultural products and certain chemicals, this occurred with a variety of products—including vacuum cleaners, metal-cutting tools, cameras, musical instruments, brooms, leather gloves, hair brushes, woolen yarns and outerwear, rugs, steel products, and earthenware.[38] There are a variety of explanations for these results. Some reflect currency depreciation in the exporting country; others may indicate a disposition to shift from higher-grade domestic materials to low-quality imports; and some, like vacuum cleaners, reveal successful foreign sales promotions.[39]

Over the last decade economic historians, like Gertrud Fremling, Peter Temin, and Barry Eichengreen, have begun to attack claims that Smoot-Hawley exerted a contractionary effect on the U.S. and world economies. According to one such theory, Smoot-Hawley switched U.S. expenditures toward domestic goods and away from foreign imports, thus having a deflationary impact on foreign economies. Ultimately, the decline reduced foreign demand for U.S. exports. Another approach focuses on the balance of payments. In reducing imports and moving the United States into a stronger surplus position, the tariff supposedly sucked monetary reserves from European countries and brought about monetary contraction.

Gertrud Fremling shows that the U.S. merchandise trade surplus declined from $842 million in 1929 to $782 million in 1930 and $334 million in 1931. Using quantity indices, she finds that export quantities fell 31 percent from 1928 to 1931 while import quantities dropped 15 percent. Fremling thus concludes that "the United States cannot possibly have generated a downswing in the rest of the world through the balance of trade." She also examines and rejects the argument of Milton Friedman and Anna Schwartz that gold reserves flowed to the United States and monetary mechanisms transmitted the Great Depression to the rest of the world.[40]

The idea "that the Smoot-Hawley tariff was a major cause of the Depression is an enduring conviction," Peter Temin acknowledges. But he maintains that the contractionary argument "fails on both theoretical and historical grounds. . . . the argument has to be that the tariff reduced the demand for American exports by inducing retaliatory foreign tariffs."[41]

Barry Eichengreen agrees. The U.S. "tariff, as an expenditure-switching policy, most likely ameliorated rather than exacerbated the initial slump." Eichengreen questions whether foreign retaliation "swamped" the direct benefits of Smoot-Hawley. He claims that the "most damning indictment of the tariff is that it unleashed a tidal wave of retaliation which had undesirable repercussions on the operation of international monetary and financial institutions." That is to say, Smoot-Hawley indirectly damaged the international system while directly helping the United States. In this regard, Eichengreen argues that Smoot-Hawley may have hastened gold flows to America and, in the course of 1931 events, forced Britain off gold, initiating a cycle of competitive depreciations.[42]

Interestingly, Eichengreen questions the extent of actual retaliation, suggesting that contemporary writers proceeded "on the *assumption* that foreign tariffs were retaliatory, interpreting and selecting evidence accordingly." He asserts that "in light of the biases of earlier literature" it is appropriate to "take a skeptical view of its generality."[43]

Reassessing Protests and Retaliation

Because it is not possible to demonstrate a causal relationship between higher tariff rates and reduced U.S. imports, those who believe Smoot-Hawley harmed world trade and other economies must demonstrate that foreign protests and retaliation actually depressed U.S. exports. Joseph Jones Jr., a twenty-six-year-old graduate student at the University of Pennsylvania, set out to prove this relationship in his 1934 book, *Tariff Retaliation*. In introducing the study, Jones boldly asserted that

> never has the United States in peace time experienced such an extended and violent foreign reaction to any piece of local legislation as that attending the Tariff Act of 1930. . . . The often-quoted formal and official protests of thirty-three foreign nations to the United States Government sink into insignificance beside the general protest and indignation of the populations of the principal trading nations of the world as expressed through an outraged press, mass meetings, and resolutions of trade, industrial, and labor organizations in the various countries.[44]

Among the repercussions to Hawley-Smoot, Jones identified "*widespread retaliation and discrimination against American exports*" (emphasis added). Yet he conceded that "there were no pure cases following the Hawley-Smoot Tariff Act" where foreign governments openly proclaimed retaliation. To support his conclusion of extensive foreign retaliation, Jones defined *retaliation* more broadly—including "cases in which the psychological effect of one country's tariff action, when placed in the scales in a second country on the side of these interests which continually work for higher tariffs, causes that government to decide in favor of increased import duties."

In the preface Jones acknowledged that "this book . . . originated as a study of foreign tariff retaliation against the United States growing out of the Tariff Act of 1930." With a travel fellowship from the University of Pennsylvania for two years of research abroad, he toured European capitals, talking with representatives of foreign governments and interest groups. Jones apparently did not conduct similar research in the United States to assess how Smoot-Hawley impacted import-sensitive industries and workers. His book remains the principal academic source for the protest-and-retaliation thesis.[45]

Did the 1930 tariff deliberations actually invoke a flood of protests and a tidal wave of retaliation against American exports? A review of internal State Department records, unavailable to Jones in the early 1930s, points to a different conclusion. The evidence suggests that early accounts, including many newspaper stories, misinterpreted routine diplomatic contacts and communications, exaggerated foreign dissatisfaction, and confused press stories of possible retaliation with actual reprisals. Indeed, the historical record indicates that the U.S. executive and foreign governments raised the bogey of foreign protests and retaliation as part of a sophisticated public relations strategy to moderate congressional enthusiasm for higher tariffs.

Who protested the tariffs? Many texts claim that thirty-four countries complained to the State Department, an assertion found in Secretary of State Cordell Hull's *Memoirs*. Hull declared that he found thirty-four "formal and emphatic diplomatic protests" in the files. Official records do show that at least thirty-four countries contacted the State Department; indeed, the Senate Finance Committee published communications from thirty-six nations (counting the Bahamas, Bermuda, and the British West Indies separately).[46]

Of the 163 communications actually submitted, the Netherlands presented 22, Great Britain 14, Italy 12, Switzerland 11, France 10, Austria 10, Belgium and Spain 8, Norway 7, Canada and Sweden 5, and Egypt, Finland, and Germany 4 each. Compared with upward tariff revisions in 1897 and 1922, the number of communications had increased. In 1897 eight foreign governments sent communications; in 1922, seventeen foreign governments did.[47] Without further inquiry, the U.S. press elected to interpret all such notes as protests. A Canadian diplomat concluded that use of the diplomatic channel "has swollen the volume of foreign protest in the mind of the American public, for the United States press has not undertaken to discriminate between the kinds of representation set forth."[48]

Were all these letters and notes diplomatic protests? The vast majority were not. A diplomatic protest is a "formal communication from one State to another that objects to an act performed, or contemplated, by the latter." The protest serves to preserve rights and to indicate that the protesting government does not acquiesce in, and does not recognize, certain acts. In 1929–30 only "*three or four governments*" submitted formal protests that related to violations "of treaty rights." According to State Department economist Herbert Feis, who subsequently won a Pulitzer Prize in history, "*no other 'formal' protests against the Tariff Act of 1930 have been received.*" He noted that "in the absence of treaty provisions, tariff legislation by the United States affords no ground for formal protest by other governments" (emphases added).[49]

Great Britain, one of America's largest trading partners, did not present any formal protests. On the contrary, fearful that a British protest might fuel in Congress claims of foreign interference and encourage high-tariff enthusiasts, London avoided direct comment. Political concerns aside, the British Board of Trade doubted whether high U.S. tariffs actually restricted Britain's capacity to buy American goods. Said Sir L. Fountain, secretary of the Board of Trade: "It is . . . true that particular trades with the United States have been destroyed by excessive tariff rates, but I doubt whether trade as a whole has been so materially affected as the parties particularly injured are inclined to suppose." The British ambassador in Washington, Sir Esme Howard, told London: "official representations . . . against the proposed tariff increases . . . [would be] a mistake." He speculated that "the wide publicity given to the number of foreign protests received was possibly inspired by the Administration in order to create a public atmosphere favorable to a policy of moderation, but I think that our contribution to this should continue to be confined to the transmission of protests from individual British firms or commercial organizations."[50]

Like British submissions, most official communications transmitted to the State Department contained technical comments from foreign producers and importers about provisions of the tariff legislation working through Congress. Most were personal protests, but a few contained comments from governments. Generally, the communications resembled the comments that a U.S. interest group might present to Congress. Because congressional committees chose not to take testimony directly from foreign interests, the latter elected to use official diplomatic channels to communicate and influence the process. The State Department agreed to accept and forward communications to the appropriate congressional committees. But State did not transmit to Congress the comments of foreign organizations or individuals unless they communicated formally to the department through customary diplomatic channels under the cover of diplomatic notes.[51]

All participants soon understood the ground rules. New York and Washington law firms drafted technical tariff comments for their foreign clients, forwarded them to U.S. representatives of the appropriate foreign government, and these legations and the U.S. State Department acted as a postal service for affected alien interests. Thus the Austrian minister, Edgar Prochnik, transmitted statements from the American representative of the Austrian Glue Manufacturers in New York, as well as other American importers of Austrian hard-rubber goods. The Belgian ambassador, Prince de Ligne, sent memoranda relating to a variety of products, including window glass, bone glue, photo film, poultry wire netting, rabbit skins, and rattan furniture.[52]

Secretary of State Henry Lewis Stimson told U.S. and foreign officials that he did not want "unnecessarily provocative matter" going to the Senate. For instance, the State Department advised the Dutch minister that the typical note "comprised a discussion of the balance of trade of the particular country with the United States and a discussion of the commodities of particular interest to the respective countries." Indeed, "there was no ground for formal 'protests' and any strong argumentative tone might be, in the Spanish phrase, 'contraproducente,' and react to the disadvantage of the complaining country." When the German ambassador raised the tariff with Stimson in June 1929, the secretary informed the foreign diplomat: "I simply acted as a conduit, sending the protests of the different nations at once to the Senate Finance Committee and getting any views from the Treasury on that subject to be sent to them too; that my own Department expressed no views unless some treaty relation or international law was affected."[53]

Although Stimson employed the word *protests*, he did not use it in the formal diplomatic sense. The only legal basis for a diplomatic protest involved the violation of treaty rights. Because tariff legislation was an internal matter for every government, most foreign officials knew they that had no lawful basis to "protest" without risking interference with the internal political relations of the United States.

Stimson and his subordinates did communicate concerns to congressional committees about certain tariff provisions, like contingent duties, that appeared to contradict most-favored-nation treaty obligations. There were several such protests. For instance, the State Department agreed with the Czechoslovakian government's formal protest in May 1930 of a discriminatory provision involving lumber. Spain also attempted to argue in June 1929 and May 1930 that higher duties on agricultural products were incompatible with the spirit, if not the letter, of existing most-favored-nation commitments.[54]

Foreign businesses voiced some alarm, but sophisticated diplomats in Washington generally avoided talk of threats and retaliation. They wanted to communicate and influence congressional deliberations discretely so as to avoid any appearance of interfering with national sovereignty. Thus Italian ambassador Giacomo de Martino took pains to inform Secretary of State Stimson that, contrary to press reports, the "Italian protests contained no threat." Rather, the communications addressed technical aspects of trade involving a variety of products: travertine stone, tomatoes, filberts, olive oil, straw hats, and many other items.[55]

What impact did the foreign communications and personal complaints have on the tariff-writing process? In August 1929 Ambassador Howard reported to London that "apprehensions as regards Canada are causing the Senate Finance Committee to proceed very carefully" on tariff schedules of concern to that country. After enactment of the 1930 tariff, the British embassy reviewed the results and concluded that Britain's private representations had no effect. France, the British noted, was the only foreign country to influence the outcome successfully in the final stages before enactment—and it did so over lace. Fearful that higher duties proposed for lace products would disrupt production and employment in Calais, Caudry, and Lyon, France threatened to retaliate against American automobile exports. Congress responded, requesting the Tariff Commission to initiate an investigation under the flexible tariff provision (sec. 336) but only after the Detroit automakers lobbied the legislature to remove the offending duties. Ambassador Sir Ronald Lindsay reported that, except for lace, "I have not been able to discover any instance in which foreign representations could be said to have brought about a modification of the rates."[56]

Within the State Department officials did monitor and assess possible foreign reactions. Secretary Stimson warned the president that the most serious dangers involved "further building up of the imperial preference system in the British Empire and the possible creation of an European economic bloc against the United States." But State also knew that "no dire consequences have followed previous upward revisions of the tariff, despite the protests and threats of retaliation and reprisal which have attended them." Nonetheless, though some believed that the "protests can probably be considerably discounted," it was thought better for the department to "err on the side of over-estimation of their importance rather than under-estimation."[57]

Press frenzy and preoccupation with so-called foreign protests suggest another interpretation: that the State Department and a few foreign governments encouraged such talk in order to restrain high-tariff enthusiasts in Congress. Certainly, British ambassador Howard read events that way. He advised London that the widespread publicity given to foreign protests was "possibly inspired by the Administration" to create a "public atmosphere favorable to moderation." He noted that Canada, the foreign country most directly affected by higher U.S. duties on farm products, made no official protest. However, "There seems to be no difficulty in raising the bogey of Canadian displeasure in the daily press," Howard observed.[58]

The Canadian archives offer additional corroboration. In February 1929 Canadian minister Vincent Massey had met with outgoing secretary of state Frank Kellogg and voiced concerns about proposed tariff changes. Massey warned that the increases would arouse "deep resentment" in Canada and produce strong pressure for "retaliatory measures." Invited to submit a written communication covering the Canadian position, Massey found Ottawa disposed to wait for the incoming Hoover administration. Canadian officials apparently feared that a formal protest might constitute unwarranted interference with U.S. internal matters and thus antagonize Congress. Ottawa opted instead to influence Congress through the press. On one occasion Massey entertained Walter Lippmann, editor of the New York World, at the Canadian legation. Afterward, the diplomat wrote Ottawa prime minister Mackenzie King that the influential New York journalist thought the U.S. tariff bill "utterly indefensible." Massey said that he was "impressed" with Lippmann's emphasis "that Canada will never be taken seriously by the United States . . . until she is prepared to strike back." Criticized by political opponents for not taking more vigorous action, Mackenzie King defended his strategy publicly, contending that "by reason of our geographical position and daily exchange of opinion through the press there can be no misunderstanding on the part of the United States regarding current opinion in Canada."[59]

Other evidence that the State Department wanted to emphasize foreign criticisms to Congress comes from U.S. diplomatic reports. State Department files contain extensive reports on negative press campaigns abroad. Belgium represents a case in point. This small country, with 8 million people in 1930, purchased about 2 percent of U.S. exports, especially cotton, automobiles, copper, wheat, and fuels. Along with diamonds, Belgium's major export to the United States, it shipped a variety of import-sensitive products, including gloves, fabrics, cement, glass, steel, and furs. In 1929, according to TC estimates, 67.7 percent of Belgian exports to America, by value, encountered duties averaging 31.4 percent ad valorem. For all countries in 1929, 35.4 percent of imports paid U.S. duties, averaging 40.1 percent on dutiable products ad valorem.[60]

Consul William C. Burdett warned of a "heavy press campaign in Brussels against the proposed changes in American tariff rates." Shortly after passage of Smoot-Hawley, Minister Hugh Gibson reported that "the Belgian press has launched a campaign for reprisals against the United States." But the climate soon improved after the U.S. embassy discussed actual tariff changes and the flexible tariff provision with the Belgian Foreign Ministry. Anticipating that the Hoover administration might take steps unilaterally to reduce duties on diplomatically sensitive items, the foreign minister acted "to calm down the agitation" for reprisals. Before long Belgian newspapers exhibited a more "conciliatory tone" and "called attention to the Tariff Commission, to the President's ability to lower duties, and to Mr. Hoover's well-known friendship for the Belgian people." Another important consideration probably influenced the Belgian reaction. As a result of Smoot-Hawley, the average tariff on dutiable imports from Belgium actually fell from 31.4 percent ad valorem equivalent in 1929 to 30.7 percent in 1931.[61]

In Switzerland, a country with only 4 million people, public opinion was much agitated. Embassy officials reported vocal demonstrations in Swiss cities involving textile, embroidery, shoe, and watch workers who were concerned that the fate of world commerce stood in mortal danger. In May 1930 the Berne embassy reported consumer boycotts against American cars and typewriters. As Smoot-Hawley came up for final passage in Congress, the U.S. minister, Hugh Wilson, reported growing Swiss "resentment": "The Swiss seem to be convinced that the adoption of the proposed tariff rates will have disastrous effects on their economic life and with this conviction they seem to be intent on fighting back with every means at their disposal."[62]

As in Belgium, tempers cooled when President Hoover signed the tariff bill. The Swiss press reported that event without extensive comment. Wilson learned that the Swiss government had "requested papers not to excite further agitation because of [the] possible injurious effect upon tourist trade." In September Wilson forecast that "if the agitation is allowed to pursue its natural course it will die [a] natural death." Nonetheless, among the thrifty Swiss passage of the 1930 tariff did produce consumer boycotts against some American products—especially automobiles, tires, typewriters, business machines, household appliances, and similar consumer products.[63]

Swiss objections represented another tempest in a teapot. The average ad valorem duty equivalent on Swiss imports into the United States rose only slightly, from 44 percent in 1929 to 47.6 percent in 1931, compared with 40.1 percent in 1929 and 53.2 percent in 1931 for imports from all countries. Nor apparently did U.S. exporters experience significant retaliation. From 1929 to 1931 the value of all U.S. exports fell 53.7 percent, but exports to Switzerland dropped only 22.4 percent.[64]

In France, a major market taking 5 percent of U.S. exports, Ambassador Walter Edge helped to puncture misconceptions. He released a press statement saying that "the revised American Tariff . . . can have no serious effect on French exports to the United States." The average increase on French goods, he reported, was only 3.35 percentage points, and French exports to the United States involved quality items, noting: "It would indeed be a very small percentage of American buyers who would desist from purchasing exclusive French designs because of such a small possible increase in costs." Edge also directed French attention to the flexible tariff provision permitting the U.S. Tariff Commission to review in impartial and scientific investigations the justification for such rates. As a result, French officials avoided calls for reprisals and exhibited interest in waiting for the TC to review duties on silk, textiles, and other products.[65]

In September 1930 Ambassador Edge raised questions about French fears that a Tariff Commission investigation of lace, requested in a Senate resolution, might lead to upward revisions. The State Department assured him that the French embassy in Washington was in "confidential touch" with the Tariff Commission. State felt "hopeful" that the investigation would result "in entirely fair revisions which will satisfy French complaints of excessive tariffs. We expect the new Commission to examine these cases with a broad view and with precaution to avoid disturbing business relations with France."[66]

In the French case, as in others, President Hoover's flexible tariff (sec. 336) helped to deflect foreign pressure for retaliation. Rather than making reprisals against U.S. exports, French petitioners sought to redress grievances through the Tariff Commission's fact-finding process. As a result, although the 1930 tariff did increase the ad valorem equivalent on dutiable imports from France from 44.6 percent in 1929 to 53.6 percent in 1931, before adjustments for deflation, U.S. exports to France apparently suffered little effective discrimination. From 1929 to 1931 U.S. exports to France declined 54.1 percent, a fraction more than the 53.7 percent decline to all foreign export markets. While automobile exports suffered, for example, France bought more Hollywood films, prunes, and apples.[67]

One reason that French officials took a cautious approach related to tourism. France did not want to upset the advantageous tourist trade. Whereas the U.S. merchandise surplus with France approached $95 million, American tourists reportedly spent $180 million annually in France, more than offsetting the merchandise trade deficit.[68]

In Italy, another medium-sized market taking about 3 percent of U.S. exports, authorities also responded cautiously, despite some newspaper bluster. On June 21, 1930, an unsigned article attributed to Mussolini appeared on the front page of Italian newspapers. It threatened bilateral balancing, stating that Italy "would buy from the United States only the amount of goods equivalent" to U.S. purchases from Italy. Privately, Mussolini told foreign diplomats that it was necessary to treat the United States with "extreme circumspection," as American retaliation could severely harm Italian sales of olive oil and tomatoes. After enactment of Smoot-Hawley, the U.S. chargé d'affaires, Alexander Kirk, observed a decline in newspaper criticism. On July 24, after meeting with the minister of foreign affairs, Kirk reported that, according to Signor Grandi, Italian efforts to boycott American goods "were of no importance." Whereas, the Italians claimed, the French "were inclined to foment agitation," the foreign affairs minister assured Kirk that the Italian government was "not losing its head on this subject and that the few outbursts that appeared in the press should not be taken too seriously." In fact, from 1929 to 1931 U.S. exports to Italy declined 64.4 percent, more than the average decline for all exports. However, over a three-year period ending in 1932, exports to Italy dropped less than average. This is not evidence of a trade war or significant retaliation. As one might expect in competitive markets, some U.S. exports expanded while others declined.[69]

During the summer months, after Congress had completed its work on the tariff bill, the State Department and U.S. envoys abroad shrewdly deflected foreign criticism and encouraged dissatisfied parties to file petitions seeking review under the flexible tariff provision. Under this authority—section 336— the Tariff Commission and the president could adjust tariff rates. Indeed, Secretary Stimson told the Italian ambassador that the commission would prove to be a "new and almost revolutionary instrument of government."[70]

Most foreign governments accepted Hoover's assurances that the flexible tariff provision afforded an opportunity to adjust individual inequities away from the spotlight of full Senate consideration. Most of all, this process avoided the disruption of retaliation and ensuing strains on political relations. The British ambassador reported to London that the Hoover administration was "sincere" in its desire to use the elastic tariff provision to remedy levies shown to be excessive. He also noted that "the nations that might like to retaliate cannot afford to do so, while those that could retaliate without endangering their own interests are in no mood to do so." Ambassador Lindsay believed that any European retaliatory measures "would certainly do more harm than good. They would weave a halo of patriotism around a piece of legislation which is now widely looked upon in this country as an economic blunder of the worst kind." Moreover, retaliation might arouse Congress and the press to demand controls on capital exports.[71]

Little Real Retaliation

The conventional wisdom holds that Smoot-Hawley brought fierce retaliation and trade wars, along with a spiraling decline in U.S. trade.[72] Such an interpretation does not comport with official trade data or with State Department records. These sources suggest that Smoot-Hawley produced little meaningful retaliation in the first year after its adoption. During this period the trend toward higher tariffs did continue, but this trend had begun about 1878 and resumed after World War I. From June 1928 to June 1930, the Commerce Department reported "substantial tariff revisions" in twenty-six countries. That pattern continued and accelerated after the United Kingdom abandoned the gold standard in September 1931.[73]

By 1932, some newspaper accounts sought to link the 1930 U.S. tariff to the decline in world commerce and spread of the depression. The *New York Times* advanced this notion: "It is clear . . . that many drastic changes have been made by other nations since midsummer of 1930 and that in certain instances a direct connection apparently exists between this action and the adoption of the Hawley-Smoot act in the United States."[74]

Official data show that both the quantity and the value of U.S. imports and exports declined sharply during the depression. From 1929 to 1931 the quantity of U.S. imports dropped 25.7 percent and the value plunged 52.5 percent. The quantity of U.S. exports fell 33 percent, while the value tumbled 54 percent. Commerce Department data, based on foreign statistics, indicate that from 1929 to 1931 the United States lost market share in twenty-seven out of thirty-two leading export markets.[75]

At first glance, these data may seem consistent with claims for foreign retaliation. In instances of discrimination, one might expect to find export volume and values falling faster than similar imports. However, countries reliant on commodity exports, like the United States, generally experienced sharp declines in overall trade during 1931. Among the forty largest trading countries, Australia, British Malaya, Canada, Chile, Cuba, Hungary, and New Zealand experienced percentage total trade losses far greater than the United States.[76]

If Smoot-Hawley triggered massive foreign retaliation against U.S. exports, as the conventional wisdom holds, such discrimination should show up in bilateral trade patterns. In his much cited book, Joseph Jones claimed retaliation from seven countries—Austria, Canada, France, Italy, Spain, Switzerland, and the United Kingdom. One might thus expect to find that U.S. exports to these seven nations declined more rapidly than overall exports or sales to third countries less concerned about the tariff adjustments.[77]

According to Table 4.4, the total value of U.S. exports declined 53.7 percent from 1929 to 1931 and 69.3 percent from 1929 to 1932. But exports to Jones's seven countries decreased less than average. They fell 53.6 percent from 1929 to 1931, slightly less than the 53.7 percent decline. Over the three-year period they dropped 68.7 percent, slightly less than the 69.3 percent decline for all exports. It is true, however, that exports to Canada, Italy, and Spain did shrink more rapidly than average exports during the two-year period (1929–31). But exports to Switzerland, a country angry over higher duties on watch imports, declined far less than average (22.4 percent).

It is also evident that exports to commodity-exporting countries like Argentina, Australia, Brazil, and Cuba declined even more rapidly. Did this reflect retaliation or merely the fall in commodity prices for wheat, coffee, and sugar? Although Smoot-Hawley raised the average rate on free and dutiable imports from Argentina from 15.2 percent to 31.9 percent in 1931, the increase had little impact on Brazilian goods. The average Brazilian duty rose only slightly, from 1.2 to 2.0 percent. Yet both countries reduced their purchases of U.S. exports 74 to 75 percent between 1929 and 1931. There was considerable public agitation against the United States in Argentina, but little in Brazil.[78]

In Australia, a nationalistic government reacted to depressed commodity prices and increased revenue needs. It imposed prohibitive duties on all imports, including manufactures from the United Kingdom. As these data suggest, some of the sharpest export deterioration came in bilateral trade relationships with primary product–exporting countries.[79]

To interpret trade statistics during this turbulent period, diplomatic correspondence provides an indispensable supplement. In this record of official correspondence, one does not find the "quick," "angry" reactions and "fierce," spiraling trade wars mentioned in academic texts and some official speeches. Indeed, the State Department files contain significant evidence contradicting such claims. The most important is a survey of U.S. consular officials at ninety-

TABLE 4.4

U.S. Exports by Region and Principal Country, 1929–1932

Region/Country	1929	1931	1932
		(Millions of \$/Percent of Decline)	
Total Exports	\$5,241.0	\$2,424.3/ 53.7%	\$1,611.0/ 69.3%
Europe	2,340.8	1,186.9/ 49.3	784.3/ 66.5
Americas	1,934.4	749.5/ 61.3	461.5/ 76.1
Canada	948.4	396.4/ 58.2	241.4/ 74.5
United Kingdom	848.0	456.0/ 46.2	288.3/ 66.0
Asia	643.2	386.4/ 39.9	292.4/ 54.5
Germany	410.4	166.1/ 59.5	133.7/ 67.4
France	265.6	121.8/ 54.1	111.6/ 58.0
Japan	259.1	155.7/ 40.0	134.9/ 47.9
Argentina	210.3	52.7/ 74.9	31.1/ 85.2
Australia/Oceania	192.0	41.6/ 78.3	36.8/ 80.8
Italy	154.0	54.8/ 64.4	49.1/ 68.1
Mexico	133.9	52.4/ 60.9	31.9/ 76.2
Africa	130.5	60.0/ 54.0	36.0/ 72.4
Cuba	128.9	47.0/ 63.5	28.8/ 77.7
Netherlands	128.3	65.6/ 48.9	45.3/ 64.7
China	124.2	97.9/ 21.2	56.2/ 54.8
Belgium	114.9	59.4/ 48.3	40.3/ 64.9
Brazil	108.8	28.6/ 73.7	28.6/ 73.7
Spain	82.1	34.0/ 58.6	26.7/ 67.5
Sweden	58.7	32.2/ 45.1	17.5/ 70.2
Switzerland	12.5	9.7/ 22.4	7.3/ 41.6
Austria	5.3	2.6/ 50.9	0.8/ 84.1

Sources: Data calculated from data in U.S. Bureau of the Census, *Historical Statistics of the United States,* bicentennial ed. (Washington, D.C.: GPO, 1974), 2:903, and *Statistical Abstract of the United States* (Washington, D.C.: GPO, 1934), pp. 424–29.

six posts. In May 1931 State circulated a TC questionnaire requesting comment on foreign discrimination against U.S. exports. According to the Tariff Commission, the U.S. auto industry, the one most concerned about foreign retaliation, had requested the survey to obtain evidence supporting its claim of extensive foreign discrimination.[80]

Summarizing the responses, the State Department found that "With the exception of discriminations in France, the extent of out right discriminations against American commerce is very slight." The report concluded: "by far the largest number of countries do not discriminate against the commerce of the United States in any way." The questionnaire specifically asked for information about duties increased since enactment of the Tariff Act of 1930. Although overseas consuls reported a number of upward adjustments, the overall report cautioned that such increases were not directed against the United States. "The increases in the import duties of Canada, Argentina, Chile and Uruguay have been declared to aim at the reduction of the unfavorable trade balance, the protection of domestic economic activities and the correction of the budget situation."[81]

Reporting from Buenos Aires, Argentina, Vice Consul Theodore Cleveland noted increased duties on motor trucks, motion picture films, radio apparatus, and electric refrigerators, but he concluded that "there is in no way discrimination against American products as such." The Argentine government had resisted pleas from foreign competitors to impose duties on imported automobiles according to engine horse power ratings, a device that might have seriously disadvantaged American cars. Instead, Cleveland concluded, the Argentine government had developed a policy "to reduce all imports . . . and . . . to curtail" or exclude luxury imports until Argentina gained a favorable balance of trade. In neighboring Brazil, Consul Julian Pinkerton consulted the American business community and also found "no cases of discrimination."[82]

From Berlin, Consul General George S. Messersmith noted "numerous changes in the German tariff, since January, 1930, increasing the rates on articles which are imported to a large extent from the United States." But he found little evidence of discrimination, as Germany sought to increase revenues.[83]

From Barcelona, Consul Curtis C. Jordan acknowledged increased tariff rates on goods imported from the United States and from third countries. Spain had imposed higher duties, for instance, on bicycles and sparkling wines that came mainly from France. He attributed the increased duties on automobiles and tires to the general business depression and the low exchange value of the Spanish currency. Jordan noted: "it would appear that while the rate of increase of American automobiles is lower than before the 1930 Spanish customs tariff, the proportion of American cars to the total now being imported is greater than before."[84]

From Colombia, Consul Erick Magnuson observed that high tariffs "have admittedly been influenced by the new customs tariff of the United States," but he concluded that Colombia did not discriminate "outright against American trade." Vice Consul Lyle C. Himmel in Buenaventura took the view that "the recent rise in tariff duties has been made to protect the Colombia industries and not as a means of discrimination against any one country."[85]

From the port of Antwerp, Belgium, Walter S. Reineck reported no discrimination against American goods. Nor, he added, had the post "received any evidence or statements from businessmen indicating that American merchandise is not admitted into Belgium on precisely an equal footing with similar merchandise from any other country." Reineck indicated that "feeling ran high" against the United States on cement, glass, and textile products, and that a consensus of opinion seemed to favor retaliation. However, he could find "no evidence . . . to indicate that any tariff increases which may have been made, were ascribable to motives of retaliation." The need for government revenue was the "prime purpose" for higher import duties.[86]

In Stockholm, John Ball Osborne, the consul general, could find "no instance of retaliatory tariff action on the part of Sweden against the United States." Indeed, the Swedes had few grounds for complaint. Wood pulp and newsprint, two principal exports, remained on the free list, although tool steel faced some higher duties.[87]

From Istanbul, Consul Charles E. Allen wrote that "Turkish import duties have not been altered in retaliation against the American tariff act of 1930." From Cape Town, Cecil M. P. Cross indicated that the Union of South Africa "found its position rather improved" under the Tariff Act of 1930. He attributed the decline in U.S. exports to the economic depression, not discrimination. Leo D. Sturgeon, American consul in Tokyo, reported minor changes in Japanese tariffs subsequent to January 1930, but "none appear aimed solely at products of American manufacture and [there are] no examples of increased rates levied against articles imported solely or mainly from any other foreign country." He noted, however, that Japan had expended effort to reduce imports in general and to improve its merchandise trade balance; nonetheless, "this results from the following of the national policy of encouraging home industries rather than a tariff policy that is discriminating in character."[88]

Although Joseph Jones devotes an entire chapter to his claim that Mussolini's Italy switched imports from the United States in retaliation for Smoot-Hawley, his evidence comes primarily from newspaper accounts. Ralph A. Boernstein, the consul in Naples, informed Washington in July 1931 that "there are few if any definite discriminations against American commerce in Italy." He also stated that Italy discriminated similarly against other foreign imports. Boernstein claimed that Italian authorities sought merely to "protect the Italian automobile industry . . . which was suffering a severe decline owing to foreign competition. . . . The feeling seems to be general among better informed businessmen that the increased duties were adopted chiefly in order to bolster the declining automobile product."[89]

Elsewhere at European posts consuls did report some limited discrimination against U.S. automobile exports. Robert Murphy, in Paris, stated that French automobile tariffs, assessed according to gross weight of the vehicle, did impact U.S. exports. Britain taxed engine horsepower, a practice that adversely affected sales of U.S. cars, but the State Department did not consider this discrimination because it was imposed equally on automobile imports from other countries. In Finland, U.S. government officials related declining auto sales to the depression, not discrimination. Hungary taxed cars according to weight, a practice that discriminated against American cars, but Consul John Morgan noted that "this system of levying duties has no connection with the new American tariff as the system has been in effect since 1924." American consuls in Prague, Czechoslovakia, and in Vienna, Austria, also reported auto-related problems.[90]

Interestingly, representatives of the U.S. auto industry abroad pandered to European sensitivities, criticized the U.S. tariff, and talked up discrimination. General Motors officials visiting Belgium and Sweden scheduled addresses to attack the U.S. tariff policy. Said Walter H. Sholes, the consul in Brussels: "we find at least one great American corporation definitely engaged abroad in stimulating opposition to the American policy of high tariffs." But, he remarked, "Those familiar with the history of the American motor car industry and American motor car exporters . . . are persuaded that General Motors' advocacy of American free trade, before European audiences, is not altogether an altruistic gesture."[91]

How much did Smoot-Hawley harm the U.S. auto export industry? Certainly, the value of automobiles and parts did decline 72.6 percent over the critical two-year period, 1929 to 1931. However, automobiles were considered luxury items at that time, and higher import duties enabled authorities everywhere to tax the affluent and to encourage the establishment of local auto assembly facilities. Some European governments also wanted to develop automobile industries to strengthen national security-industrial bases. In France and Italy such duties had national policy ramifications. Finally, it is easy to generalize from the automobile situation and exaggerate the significance of foreign restrictions on U.S. exports generally.[92]

Department of Commerce data show that almost every major export industry experienced a severe drop in the total value of exports from 1929 to 1931. For the most part, these industries blamed the depression for economic problems, not retaliation against the Smoot-Hawley Tariff (see Table 4.5). On the other

TABLE 4.5

U.S. Exports by Product, 1929–1931

Product	(Millions of $)		Percent of Decline
	1929	1931	
Cotton (unmanufactured)	$770.8	$325.7	57.7%
All Machinery	606.8	316.8	47.8
Petroleum	561.2	270.5	51.8
Automobiles and parts	541.4	148.1	72.6
Packing house products	202.8	96.2	52.6
Iron and steel	200.1	63.2	68.4
Wheat	192.3	84.2	56.2
Agricultural machinery	140.8	57.4	59.2
Cotton manufactures	135.1	60.1	55.5
Leather manufactures	17.7	7.0	60.5

Source: U.S. Tariff Commission, *Economic Analysis of Foreign Trade of the United States in Relation to the Tariff* (Washington, D.C.: GPO, March 1, 1933), list 5.

hand, quantitative data indicate that many U.S. exports boosted sales and gained foreign market share during the same period. Fresh fruit exports held up—with apples, grapefruit, and pears gaining sales abroad. Exports of dried apricots rose 72 percent and prunes 31 percent. Raw cotton exports stood their ground, as did rayon. Some chemical products gained in foreign markets—particularly borax and carbon black. Film exports rose 49 percent, and false teeth increased 24 percent.[93]

How did Smoot-Hawley affect the Ottawa Conference of 1932 and Britain's imperial preference system? Some commentators and historians sought to view the Ottawa system as the "capstone" of retaliation against Smoot-Hawley. More recently, two Canadian scholars have rejected as "incorrect" the notion that imperial preference represented "simple retaliation for the American Smoot-Hawley tariff increases of 1930."[94] Barry Eichengreen agrees. Though acknowledging "some disagreement over the precise reasons for Britain's adoption of the General Tariff," he says that "there is no dispute that retaliatory motives rank low on the scale." In parliamentary debate and internal government exchanges "there is little evidence" that "retaliation played much role in British discussion."[95]

In Canada, anger over increased U.S. duties on farm products and an impending national election conspired to produce limited retaliation. Prime Minister Mackenzie King frequently criticized for his partiality to the United States, expediently authorized countervailing duties against some U.S. products in May 1930 in order to steal the political issue from his election opponent, Conservative Richard Bennett. Traditionally, the Canadian Tories had favored protection, but King anticipated that a "real crack at the [United] States" would appeal to Canadian farmers: "Switch trade from U.S. to Britain, that will be the cry and it will sweep this country I believe. We will take the flag once more out of the Tory hands." King's supporters in Parliament cheered. "No longer can the cry be raised that our Prime Minister gives more to the United States than he is willing to give to the mother country," one Liberal member effused.[96]

King's Liberals lost control in the July election. Running on a "Canada First" platform that promised to "blast a way" into world markets and to end unemployment at home, Bennett's Tories picked up twenty seats in Quebec. King blamed his "surprise" defeat on depressed dairy prices and unemployment in that French-speaking province, traditionally a Liberal stronghold. With imports of New Zealand butter soaring, the result of a Liberal trade treaty, and higher U.S. duties on milk and cream in 1929 and 1930, embittered dairy farmers voted for change.[97]

The new government called Parliament into special session to enact more tariff amendments. In 1931 Parliament undertook a more general revision, with nearly two hundred upward revisions. From the U.S. State Department's perspective, such parliamentary action did not constitute the type of discrimination required for U.S. retaliation pursuant to section 338. Because Canada and the United States lacked a most-favored-nation treaty, Canadian retaliation did not infringe any U.S. rights and thus represent discrimination within the meaning of the American tariff act.[98]

How significant was Canadian retaliation? Democrats and low-tariff newspapers in the United States played it up, with many asserting that Canada responded appropriately to Smoot-Hawley. Republicans and the *Washington Post* held that Canada was simply imitating the successful American example and enacting higher tariffs.

Bilateral trade statistics suggest that press accounts may have exaggerated the impact of Smoot-Hawley and the extent of Canadian retaliation. From 1929 to 1931 total U.S. imports fell 52.5 percent, but imports from Canada declined only 47.1 percent.[99] At first impression, Canadian import data do show some retaliation. Canadian imports from all foreign sources fell 51.6 percent, but imports from the United States dropped more—55.9 percent. Interestingly, duty-free imports from the United States declined more rapidly

(60.4 percent) than dutiable imports (53.9 percent). This surprising result may indicate that actual retaliation had a relatively minor impact on U.S.-Canadian trade patterns compared to macroeconomic factors, but it may also reflect the imposition of duties on some goods previously imported duty-free, such as certain steel products.[100]

How significant generally was foreign dissatisfaction with Smoot-Hawley to the disruption of trade patterns? Those who believe that the 1930 U.S. tariff produced fateful consequences point to statistics showing a sharp decline in U.S. foreign trade. Import market share in the United States fell as a percentage of gross national product from 4.2 percent in 1929 to 2.7 percent in 1931 and 2.3 percent in 1932. Exports as a share of gross national product also dropped— from 5.0 percent in 1929 to 3.2 percent in 1931 and 2.8 percent in 1932. Certainly, the Great Depression did disrupt international trade patterns and currency relationships. Nation after nation introduced nationalistic trade and currency controls after Smoot-Hawley, but not necessarily because of it. Particularly after Britain devalued the pound sterling in September 1931, many nations resorted to trade and currency controls.[101] In fact, by February 1932 foreign currency depreciation of 20 to 30 percent apparently had offset higher Smoot-Hawley tariffs. During the presidential campaign Herbert Hoover and some congressional Republicans urged the U.S. Tariff Commission to consider upward tariff adjustments.[102]

Spurning the Economists?

In signing the Smoot-Hawley Tariff Act, did President Hoover imprudently reject the advice of more than a thousand economists, as the conventional wisdom indicates? Many scholars apparently think that the academic economists understood the economy better than Hoover.[103]

Released on May 5, some forty days before the tariff cleared Congress, a petition signed by 1,028 economists strongly urged that "any measure which provides for a general upward revision of tariff rates be denied passage by Congress, or if passed, be vetoed by the President." Among the signatories were Paul H. Douglas, of the University of Illinois, a future U.S. senator; Frank Taussig, of Harvard University, the first chairman of the U.S. Tariff Commission; and Clair Wilcox, an associate professor at Swarthmore College, who after World War II would take charge of the multilateral trade negotiations that led to the General Agreement on Tariffs and Trade in 1947.[104]

Although most secondary accounts construe this document as an application to Hoover, it was in fact an appeal to both Congress and the executive to reject tariff increases. The statement reiterated familiar concerns among economists: "restrictive duties would . . . operate, in general, to increase the prices which domestic consumers would have to pay. . . . The vast majority of farmers . . . would lose. . . . as consumers they would have to pay still higher prices for the products, made of textiles, chemicals, iron and steel, which they buy. . . . as producers, their ability to sell their products would be further restricted by the barriers placed in the way of foreigners who wished to sell manufactured goods to us."[105]

The economists also asserted that "our export trade, in general, would suffer. Countries cannot permanently buy from us unless they are permitted to sell to us, and the more we restrict the importation of goods from them by means of ever higher tariffs, the more we reduce the possibility of our exporting to them. This applies to such exporting industries as copper, automobiles, agricultural machinery, typewriters, and the like fully as much as it does to farming."

It is noteworthy that the petition made no specific mention of provisions in the pending tariff, nor did the economists in any way address Hoover's belief that the flexible tariff would take tariff making out of politics. Furthermore, the statement criticized "a general upward revision," not the "limited" revision that the president had requested and that Republicans claimed to deliver. As a consequence, the economists' manifesto, although much discussed and later often quoted as a reflection of informed economic thinking, had little relevance for or impact on the policy-making process. Indeed, Senator Henry Hatfield of West Virginia dismissed the economists as "intellectual free traders, who seem to be more concerned with the prosperity of foreigners than they are with the well-being of our own American people."[106]

The *New York Herald Tribune* scorned the economists' protest as "largely thunder in the index. . . . The 1,028 economists dwell outside the sphere of politics and popular feeling. Otherwise they would scarcely have mailed their olympian and transcendental memorial to Washington."[107] Labor was also critical. Matthew Woll, a union official who supported the tariff bill, had this to say about economists:

With few exceptions they are free traders. They are neither producers nor creators of any commodity or article of trade. They are generally cloistered in the atmosphere of the schoolroom and their mental wares do not enter into the competition with producers where lower wage levels and longer working hours prevail and where standards of living are not only lower but in other respects much inferior to the standards built up in our own country under the American tariff policy. Briefly, these economists and college professors are consumers, not producers.[108]

The managing director of the American Trade-Mark Association, Harold Hanson, also slapped at the professors' "dramatic stunt." He observed that the "economists belong to the fixed salary gentry and have . . . the smugness that goes with a sheltered means of support. . . . these theorists in our educational institutions have never had 'to hustle a pay roll' so as to fill pay envelopes on Saturday." Many of the professors, he said, received income from large endowment funds contributed by captains of industry who benefited from the protective tariff policy.[109]

Did Hoover Fail as a Leader?

Scholars in a variety of disciplines have lambasted President Hoover's leadership during the eighteen-month tariff-making period. These criticisms vary: Hoover submitted special interest legislation, he encouraged protectionist predilections in Congress, he yielded to political opportunism and domestic politics in signing the widely criticized bill.[110]

Hoover's critics ignore a critical point. The president persistently and doggedly pressed for tariff reform, requesting a strengthened flexible tariff provision that would enable a reorganized, independent Tariff Commission to modify individual rates subject to presidential approval. He considered the flexible tariff provision "one of the most progressive steps taken in tariff making in all our history." And, when resistance flared in the Senate, Hoover told Senator Smoot: "No flexible tariff, no tariff bill." In effect, Hoover prevailed in his effort to create a permanent nonpolitical administrative process for adjusting tariffs according to statutory criteria. His obsession with the flexible tariff antagonized some members of the GOP who feared that the president wanted Congress to delegate tariff-writing authority without the specific consent of Congress. Republicans like Senator Hiram Johnson of California denounced any surrender of congressional authority. Democrats also opposed Hoover in 1930.[111]

Hoover may have been unduly optimistic—even naive—in believing that an independent U.S. Tariff Commission could adjust tariffs according to scientific principles. But as an escape valve for adjusting the excesses of congressional tariff writing, the administrative method worked reasonably well. From July 1930 to November 1931 the TC completed thirty-nine fact-finding investigations, and the process produced reductions in sixteen cases. The flexible clause did help policymakers remove tariff anomalies and ameliorate foreign discontent with the 1930 tariff schedules. Thus the fact-finding approach made a genuine contribution. It authorized specialists to decide issues according to merit rather than to political or policy imperatives. However, as the depression worsened in 1931 and currencies floated, the Tariff Commission could not calculate the costs of production and found the approach unworkable.[112]

The Tariff Commission's approach to tariff writing had several advantages. Presidential appointees, who were subject to Senate confirmation, decided sensitive cases affecting the jobs of workers and the future of industries, not legislators responsive to short-term political concerns or civil service appointees insulated from public accountability. Moreover, the Tariff commissioners conducted business in public. As Hoover said: "All proceedings were to be open to public hearings and in judicial form. The orgy of greed and privilege which surrounded constant change by Congress was at least done away with." In addition, the TC process was fairer to foreign interests. Commissioner Edgar Brossard noted that foreign producers had "a better opportunity for open, fair, equal, and public presentation of their tariff cases than is granted in any other country in the world."[113]

During the New Deal years, the Reciprocal Trade Agreements Program evolved quite differently. The Roosevelt administration effectively transferred tariff making from Congress to the State Department, where unelected and unconfirmed officials made sensitive decisions in accordance with policy agendas. "[T]he New Deal . . . sidetracked this [Tariff] Commission," Hoover said. It provided for the "secret determination of tariffs in back rooms without public hearings. . . . Men are deprived of their livelihood by secret covenants secretly arrived at."[114]

For some thirty years, until the Kennedy Round, Congress would permit State Department officials to trade off import-sensitive industries to achieve foreign policy objectives and pursue international economic theories. Gradually, however, the pendulum swung again, and during the 1970s Congress revived the independent regulatory approach. The Tariff Commission, renamed in 1974 the U.S. International Trade Commission, would not write "scientific tariffs," but it would provide a forum for resolving certain trade disputes in a quasi-judicial manner away from politics and executive policy.

Did Voters Retaliate at the Polls?

Did public dissatisfaction with Smoot-Hawley protectionism cost Chairmen Smoot and Hawley their elective offices in 1932? Such an interpretation, although appealing to free traders, does not conform to the factual record. Home state newspapers in both Oregon and Utah attributed their defeat at the polls to nontariff factors.

Congressman Willis Hawley lost the May 1932 Oregon Republican primary to a colorful state official, corporation commissioner James Mott. Both the *Salem Oregon Statesman* and the *Portland Oregonian* credited the defeat to "local issues." In obtaining a federal soldier's hospital for one town in his district, Hawley angered other localities. Noting that "democracies . . . are ungrateful . . . they are sometimes foolish," the *Portland Oregonian* stated that "Mr. Hawley lost many votes that he would have retained had he let the hospital go to the state of Washington." Both papers also cited the Prohibition controversy. Hawley was a "dry," his opponent a "wet." Above all, Chairman Hawley had served in Congress a quarter century; he had not even returned to Oregon for the primary campaign to rebuild his personal ties with voters. In such circumstances, it is not surprising that voters replaced a sixty-eight-year-old incumbent with a popular official twenty years younger. The local press attached little significance to the tariff issue. Those dissatisfied with Smoot-Hawley, according to the *Portland Oregonian*, were timber interests concerned about inadequate protection.[115]

In Utah a Democratic tidal wave toppled Senator Reed Smoot and other Republican candidates. According to a *New York Times* correspondent, Smoot was not "discredited, but the victim of a nation-wide demand for a 'new deal.' " In losing, Smoot gained more votes in Utah than either President Hoover or the Republican candidate for governor. Like Hawley, the seventy-year-old Smoot fell to an opponent some twenty years younger: Elbert Thomas, a University of Utah political scientist. Both candidates were Mormons, and some Mormons may have voted to bring Smoot home to devote more time to his responsibilities as an apostle of the Mormon Church. Dissatisfaction with the Smoot-Hawley Tariff does not seem to have influenced the outcome of the election, although Democratic candidate Thomas did pledge "protection of Utah products, including lead, copper and sugar."[116]

Was Smoot-Hawley the Wrong Tariff at the Wrong Time?

Internationalists reject Smoot-Hawley for complicating international economic relationships and inviting other nations to pursue their own beggar-thy-neighbor trade policies. Harvard University business economist Sumner Slichter asserted that "the American tariff, by restricting the ability of the world to pay us with goods instead of gold, was a major factor in forcing a large part of the world off the gold standard and in accentuating the depreciation of many foreign currencies."[117]

Foreign Affairs, a publication of the New York–based Council on Foreign Relations, carried articles that were hostile to the 1930 tariff. In one, Percy Bidwell emphasized Europe's "immediate, undisguised and unanimous" antagonism toward Hawley-Smoot and stressed that "retaliatory tariffs are the most obvious weapons to oppose the new American barriers to European trade."[118] In essence, the economic internationalists asserted that the United States should have lowered its tariffs, not raised them, in 1930. With lower tariffs, they said, other countries could have serviced debts and repaid obligations, despite the decline in private lending. After America's shortsighted protectionist moves, European nations had little recourse but to erect their own commercial restrictions in order to protect currencies and trade balances.

This line of criticism reflected a perception widespread in the State Department and among the economic foreign policy elite that the health of the international economic system should take priority over the health of individual national economies. Clearly, Chairmen Smoot and Hawley, as well as a majority of lawmakers on Capitol Hill in 1930, defined their responsibilities differently. Their loyalties lay with constituents and voters, not international bankers and shareholders. To them, the arguments of New York bankers seemed disingenuous. The financial community wanted tariff cuts to facilitate debt repayment. Concerned about financial issues, the bankers had little sensitivity for the plight of American workers who might lose employment to increased imports as a consequence.

For a Congress traditionally responsive to grassroots concerns, the parochial and the immediate took priority over abstract economic and long-term foreign policy concerns. In retrospect, it is at least arguable that in passing Smoot-Hawley Congress acted prudently. Economic historians, like Temin and Eichengreen, acknowledge that a conscious policy of switching expenditures to home producers "ameliorated rather than exacerbated the initial slump." Moreover, it is doubtful that a downward adjustment in U.S. tariffs would have done much in the short run to facilitate international adjustment. Stephen Schuker argues that "formidable non-tariff obstacles" hampered European efforts to expand the export of manufactures to the United States.[119]

Why have textbook authors, editorial writers, and public officials beat up on the bogey of Smoot-Hawley for three generations? For one thing, the image of resurgent protectionism conformed to the strongly held beliefs of economic theorists, many of whom simply chose to ignore historical evidence. British economic historian Susan Strange has accused free trade economists of propagating the myth that protectionism caused the Great Depression.[120]

Many perpetrators of the Smoot-Hawley myth also had political and policy axes to grind. Sensing public disquiet with the protracted eighteen-month tariff-writing exercise, congressional Democrats resolved to exploit the tariff issue in the 1930 election. They saw the tariff controversy as a wedge issue to recover control of Congress and possession of the White House in 1932. Although many congressional Democrats also advocated higher import duties to please constituents and obstructed the tariff-writing process with votes on minor amendments, their campaign managers successfully focused public dissatisfaction on the Republicans, who controlled both Congress and the White House.[121]

Democratic publicist Charles Michelson later admitted that he and his colleagues "helped the chorus of protest along in every way we could." He recounted gleefully how the "fertilizing processes" at the Democratic National Executive Committee "blossomed" across the country as cartoon caricature's mimicked Hoover's tariff.[122]

Foreign observers understood that the Smoot-Hawley debate was political theater. The British embassy advised London that the tariff dispute was "not a real issue between parties. Democratic campaign managers have carried on a species of guerilla warfare, asking the electorate to censure the Republicans . . . for having . . . unnecessarily and wantonly exposed the country to a wave of foreign resentment."[123]

During the 1932 presidential campaign Democratic candidate Franklin Roosevelt exploited the issue, repeatedly attacking the "Grundy," or the "Hawley-Smoot-Grundy," tariff. In Sioux City, Iowa, he asserted: "the ink on the Hawley-Smoot-Grundy tariff bill was hardly dry before foreign Nations commenced their program of retaliation. Brick for brick they built their walls against us." The Hoover administration had been warned, Roosevelt said: "our State Department received 160 protests from 33 other Nations, many of whom . . . erected their own tariffs to the detriment or destruction of much of our export trade."[124] Arthur Krock, a *New York Times* writer, alleged that the president had "personal" responsibility for the Hawley-Smoot Tariff.[125] Hoover thus remained on the defensive.

After World War II the Smoot-Hawley metaphor apparently served another purpose. Like the lessons of Munich and Pearl Harbor, it helped to rationalize a continuing U.S. commitment to international cooperation and collective security. In this task the myth of Smoot-Hawley proved a powerful weapon to discredit isolationist and protectionist sentiment, and to promote the Hullian vision of free trade and international cooperation. Committed to this goal, Wall Street, Washington, corporate America, academic economists, and the media elite found it expedient to thrash Smoot-Hawley at each opportunity.

For some sixty years the "infamous" Smoot-Hawley myth has acquired wide acceptance. But Smoot-Hawley did not live down to its reputation. In their zeal to simplify and communicate, textbook writers and advocates have strayed far from the factual record. In particular, Smoot-Hawley did not raise the average U.S. tariff to record levels. Rates on some import-sensitive products climbed upward, but Smoot-Hawley preserved unobstructed access to the U.S. markets for about two-thirds of U.S. imports.

There is no persuasive documentation that the Smoot-Hawley Tariff precipitated the stock market crash. Nor is there compelling evidence that it exacerbated the Great Depression. Foreign governments and private interests did seek to influence the U.S. tariff revision process, but few of these communications constituted formal diplomatic protests. Contrary to the conventional wisdom, Smoot-Hawley produced little retaliation or discrimination against American exports. The fury of the global depression, not the irritation of American tariff changes, forced foreign governments to restrict trade and currency flows, and to concentrate on domestic economic recovery. Nor does the archival evidence confirm claims that the 1930 tariff contributed significantly to the breakdown of international peace and the coming of World War II.

That the legend of Smoot-Hawley endures and continues to influence trade policy debate is a tribute to the public relations skills of partisans and ideologues with agendas. They successfully transformed a molehill into a mountain.

[T]oward 1916 I embraced the philosophy I carried throughout my twelve years as Secretary of State. . . . From then on, to me, unhampered trade dovetailed with peace; high tariffs, trade barriers, and unfair economic competition, with war.—Cordell Hull

[T]he Americans have put more into G.A.T.T., and got less out of it, than any of the other big trading countries. . . . by and large the Americans have kept their doors wide open to our trade (and at a time when they might have urged that we were shutting out their goods by quotas long after we were genuinely short of dollars to pay for them).—Reginald Maudling

Cordell Hull's Tariff Revolution

A revolution occurred in U.S. trade policy during the thirty years from 1930 to 1960. This country abandoned the nationalistic "American System" of protective tariffs, erected after the War of 1812, and removed the tariff levee that had sheltered a vast continental market from import competition. The average tariff on dutiable items fell from a peak near 60 percent equivalent in 1932 to 12 percent in 1960. Along with reducing rates the United States made another important concession. It *bound* existing duties against future increases.[1]

By 1960 the United States was no longer an impregnable commercial fortress but the world's largest and most inviting target of commercial opportunity for foreign producers. Most of America's trading partners had substantially higher tariff levels. More important, they maintained various quantitative and exchange restrictions on imports from the dollar bloc and Japan. In effect, the United States was the only major market open to world trade.[2] This was not accidental. From the Civil War to the 1930s, Congress guarded the domestic market, sheltering the high-wage U.S. workers and high-cost domestic producers market from cheaper foreign competitors. During the 1930s, after low-tariff

Democrats took control of both the executive branch and Congress, national leaders adopted a different trade policy strategy. Using access to the huge protected American market as a bargaining lure, they attempted to negotiate down foreign tariffs. Eager to promote the export sales of commodity agriculture and automobiles, they progressively opened the domestic market to foreign manufactures. This produced immediate and short-term benefits to domestic consumers, but over the longer term it exposed domestic producers and workers in high-wage import-competing industries to the trauma of global competition.

The Tariff Revolutionary and Reciprocal Trade

It is unusual in the modern world for a single individual to change the course of history. Cordell Hull, the silver-haired former senator and congressman from Tennessee who President Franklin D. Roosevelt named secretary of state, did so. At first impression, Hull was an unlikely revolutionary. He was, after all, a professional politician who had served in both houses of Congress. From 1921 to 1924 he chaired the Democratic National Committee. Unlike Adam Smith or Karl Marx, Hull was neither a philosopher nor an original thinker. His views on trade reflected the low-tariff outlook of his political mentor, Representative Benton McMillin (D-Tenn.), who served on the Ways and Means Committee from 1886 to 1899. After drafting the income tax amendment, Hull devoted his public career to promoting tariff reform. His opportunity came in 1933, when Roosevelt chose Hull to become secretary of state. In this cabinet post, the Tennessean mobilized congressional support for tariff liberalization.

Years later Hull summarized his trade philosophy this way: "to me, unhampered trade dovetailed with peace; high tariffs, trade barriers, and unfair economic competition, with war." Thus Hull was a low-tariff Democrat in the free trade tradition of Robert Walker and Grover Cleveland. Like English anti–Corn Law crusader Richard Cobden, he associated commerce with world peace.[3]

Reciprocal Trade

As enacted in 1934, Hull's reciprocal trade program contained no direct reference to tariff reduction as a goal. Instead, House Resolution 8687, an amendment to the Tariff Act of 1930, proposed "expanding foreign markets for the products of the United States . . . by regulating the admission of foreign goods into the United States in accordance with the characteristics and needs of various branches of American production." To attain this end, Congress granted the executive temporary authority, for three years, to *raise or lower* tariffs as much as 50 percent from 1930 levels.[4]

On Capitol Hill, Secretary Hull portrayed the plan as "an emergency measure to deal with emergency panic conditions." He emphasized that the "entire policy of this bill would rest upon trade relationships which would be *mutually and equally profitable* both to our own and other countries." Furthermore, each proposed trade agreement "would be considered with *care and caution by fully competent Government agencies* and only after the fullest consideration of all pertinent information. Nothing could be done blindly, hastily, or inconsiderately" (emphases added).[5]

In requesting this unusual delegation of authority from Congress, which after all had constitutional responsibility for regulating commerce and levying taxes, the administration emphasized what was to become known as the "no-injury concept." As President Roosevelt stated in his transmittal message: "The successful building up of trade *without injury to American producers* depends upon a cautious and gradual evolution of plans. . . . *no sound and important American interest will be injuriously disturbed*" (emphases added).[6]

Despite such assurances, Congress remained uneasy about delegating absolute power over the "life and death" of domestic industries to the executive. It insisted on inserting a provision stipulating "reasonable public notice" so that "any interested person may have an opportunity to present his views." Congress also required the president "before concluding [any] such agreement" to seek information and advice from the U.S. Tariff Commission and the Departments of State, Agriculture, and Commerce.[7]

Notwithstanding the administration's pledges and the statutory language, Hull's more enthusiastic aides interpreted the Reciprocal Trade Agreements Program (RTAP) in more ambitious terms. It was *both* an opportunity to trade off protected home markets for export benefits to the depressed automobile industry and commodity agriculture and an instrument to effect significant, permanent tariff reductions. Indeed, an early version of the reciprocal trade bill, written in the State Department, openly avowed the goal of advancing "the movement for the lowering of tariffs and trade barriers in the United States and the world over."[8]

Executive Tariff Making

To satisfy legal requirements while pursuing bilateral trade agreements in secret negotiations, Hull established two interdepartmental working committees within the executive branch. The Executive Committee on Commercial

Policy, an interagency group composed of representatives at the assistant secretary level and chaired by a representative of the State Department, had general policy supervision. At the working level, the Committee for Reciprocity Information would serve as a hearing body, without policy-making authority, to receive petitions and take testimony on proposed tariff reductions.

The real power, however, would be lodged in the Committee on Trade Agreements (CTA), a group of technicians from the State Department and other agencies who coordinated trade strategy and supervised negotiations. In order to facilitate their work, and reduce pressure from elected officials and lobbyists, the members of this committee operated secretly and anonymously. Indeed, for over twenty years State declined to reveal the identities of these technicians to Congress. Essentially, in choosing this structure, Hull sought to take congressional politics out of tariff making. In place of the relatively transparent and accountable process pursued when Congress wrote tariff legislation, he delegated tariff making to a small group of middle-level officials who were not subject to congressional confirmation. Hull relied on these specialists to implement aggressively and loyally the executive's trade expansion program.

Who sat on the Committee on Trade Agreements? According to the organization chart, a representative of the State Department chaired this committee. Other members were from cabinet departments—Agriculture, Commerce, and Treasury—as well as the U.S. Tariff Commission. On closer inspection, certain common features emerge. Like many New Dealers, the majority of CTA members were recently hired academics without significant private sector experience.[9] Many of them, including the committee's chairman, Henry F. Grady, had earned doctoral degrees in economics. In retrospect, it is plain that the members of this group had an enthusiasm for tariff reduction and construed their mission to lower the Smoot-Hawley Tariff levels.[10]

With a mandate from Hull and little daily supervision, these economic theorists turned with delight to the critical task of reducing trade barriers and in effect picking the corporate "winners and losers."[11] Members of the Committee on Trade Agreements held that the "primary object" of the RTAP "is to reduce trade barriers rather than to drive a sharp bargain." Their policy envisioned "permitting a greater increase in imports than in exports with a view to correcting the trade balance problem of the United States."[12]

What domestic industries should be sacrificed for the sake of international equilibrium and export concessions? The specialists approached this issue—one that a later generation would label "industrial policy"—through the lenses of economics, focusing on such issues as perceived comparative advantages, efficiencies, and static benefits from trade. One committee member even devised a scheme for grading all U.S. industries for commercial policy purposes. In the highest category would be export-competitive agricultural commodities—cotton, wheat, hog products, and apples—as well as mass production manufactures like automobiles, agricultural machinery, and electronics. At the other extreme would be industries with high rates of duty and low wages. Examples cited were lace and hand-labor industries as well as pineapples, sugar, and sugar beet.[13]

Discussion in CTA apparently did not consider whether the long-term national interest required maintaining a balanced and healthy industrial base as insurance against a future challenge to U.S. security interests. Instead, members evaluated issues on the basis of English classical economic theory, with its emphasis on efficiency and welfare. Assuming that competitive advantages reflected basic resource endowments and remained unchanging over time, the State Department planners focused on improving welfare through the specialization of production. Implicit, too, was their assumption that industries inefficient in the 1930s would continue to lag behind foreign competitors, and that export-competitive industries—like automobiles—would retain a comparative advantage in the future. Thus they reasoned that government could benefit society by reducing tariffs on both and concentrating negotiating efforts on obtaining foreign concessions for the latter. Given the New Deal penchant for planning and government regulation, it is not surprising that Hull's trade policymakers apparently never expressed doubts about the capacity of government officials to make such complex economic decisions prudently and more effectively than the marketplace. With the United States running a strong merchandise trade surplus, they attached no urgency to considering how U.S. government policies might encourage emerging industries with export-competing potential.

A colleague later described those running the trade agreements program as "ill-informed enthusiasts." Herbert Feis lost enthusiasm for the RTAP as he watched Hull's loosely supervised subordinates turn negotiations into unreciprocal trade concessions. A representative example involves the bilateral agreement with Belgium, the first concluded with a European industrial nation, in February 1935.[14]

UNBALANCED CONCESSIONS: BELGIUM, 1935

When Belgian negotiators arrived in late 1934 expecting to pursue a limited agreement, they found American negotiators eager to offer the maximum 50 percent reduction on a wide range of products, including basic steel, woven fabrics, cotton textiles, and building materials.[15] Anxious to cut U.S. tariffs sharply and obtain more advantageous treatment for automotive products, apples, and wheat flour and a binding of existing Belgian trade restrictions, U.S. negotiators early in the reciprocal trade program offered to make steep cuts in U.S. duties despite the no-injury pledge. Their proposals to Belgium reflected a much different negotiating philosophy. According to an internal State Department memorandum, "a reciprocity program which hurt no one could not go very far in improving the general economic welfare."[16]

During the Belgian negotiations, one participant later acknowledged, Hull's subordinates "ran wild," with maximum allowable offers on building materials, steel, and textiles. Protests from affected domestic industries ultimately forced the White House to intervene and withdraw some of the more extreme concessions, and for a time it seemed that the State Department might lose control over trade policy. According to Undersecretary of State William Phillips, "The *experts* had gone forward much too rapidly" (emphasis added).[17]

In retrospect, this bilateral agreement offered liberal concessions to the Belgo-Luxembourg Economic Union, and it proved a harbinger of the generous approach the State Department would take through the Reciprocal Trade Agreements Program. The United States provided tariff reductions on certain steel and textile items although Belgium had not requested them and was not even the major supplier of such goods. Afterward, the United States permitted Belgium to void the terms of the agreement before it was formally implemented. Despite the generous tariff reductions, the Belgians were permitted to retain quotas and to depreciate their currency (by 28 percent), which they did before the trade agreement took effect, essentially nullifying their concessions to America and giving their exports additional stimulus.[18]

How did the agreement affect bilateral trade patterns? According to the U.S. Department of Commerce, the U.S. share of Belgium's imports promptly declined from 7.29 percent in 1934 to 6.93 percent in 1936, the first full year of the agreement. In 1934 Belgium supplied 1.62 percent of U.S. imports, but this share rose to 2.42 percent in 1936. A bilateral U.S. export surplus, averaging 42 percent of exports to Belgium in the period 1931 to 1935, vanished—becoming a slight deficit in 1936. These losses proved temporary. In 1937 U.S. exports to Belgium recovered lost market share and reached 8.75 percent. Imports from Belgium remained at 2.46 percent of total U.S. imports. The United States enjoyed a healthy bilateral surplus.[19]

EXTENDING BENEFITS TO OTHERS

Hull's aides faced a far-reaching decision after completing the Belgian pact. Other nations inquired whether the United States intended to generalize concessions conferred in reciprocal agreements with Belgium and Brazil on a most-favored-nation basis to third countries. Although America had abandoned the conditional most-favored-nation approach, which characterized its policy before 1923 and required compensations, it was not clear that third countries would automatically benefit from generalization under the new unconditional approach. Would the United States generalize benefits to all foreign countries or only those eligible for unconditional most-favored-nation treatment? How would it treat countries that discriminated against America?

In authorizing the reciprocal trade program, Congress stipulated that "the proclaimed import duties . . . shall apply to articles . . . of *all* foreign countries." But the president might suspend application to the products of any country discriminating against U.S. commerce, "or because of other acts or policies which in his [the president's] opinion tend to defeat the purposes set forth."[20]

Within the Committee on Trade Agreements there was vigorous debate about the best course of action. On the one hand, George N. Peek, the president's special adviser, held that the Roosevelt administration should reverse the Harding administration's position and return to the traditional *conditional* most-favored-nation policy. Peek favored bilateral balancing and barter, if necessary, to promote domestic recovery. "If we can stage our own national recovery and build up our own national trade we shall have done much to restore world recovery and world trade," he said.[21] Peek perceived that cheap-labor nations like Japan would become free riders and take advantage of unconditional most-favored-nation-treatment to gain access to the U.S. market without providing reciprocal access at home.[22]

On the other hand, Hull's principal aides argued for continuing the unconditional approach and withholding benefits only when other countries flagrantly discriminated against U.S. exports. Using this narrow test, not a broader one that might focus on the height and magnitude of foreign trade barriers, they hoped to prevent international friction and ill feeling. Peek's approach, the State Department feared, would involve weighing each concession on an apothecary's balance. As Hull's aides construed the program, the goal was to "reduce trade barriers rather than to drive a sharp bargain" for the United States. "Such a policy," they wrote, "envisages the possibility of permitting a greater increase in imports than in exports with a view to correcting the trade balance problem of the United States." In short, Hull's assistants viewed the RTAP as a trade liberalization program designed to increase U.S. imports.[23]

Even the narrow test of flagrant discrimination presented serious problems to administrators. The State Department initially planned to extend the Belgian concessions only to foreign governments that were not discriminating against American commerce. However, the CTA found that most of America's major trading partners—including Canada, Great Britain, Germany, and France—"substantially" discriminated against American trade.[24] After agonizing over this decision, the State Department decided in a "conciliatory" move to extend trade agreement concessions to *all* countries except Germany.[25] In effect, then, those responsible for implementing the reciprocal trade program signaled to foreign nations that the United States would not vigorously enforce its commercial rights except in the most flagrant cases of discrimination. More interested in stimulating international trade than in promoting American export interests, the State Department economists would not leverage the extension of gains from bilateral trade agreements. As a result, they lost an opportunity to promote export interests.

In effect, this decision reflected a fundamental change in the Reciprocal Trade Agreements Program. As discussed in the 1932 campaign, reciprocity appeared to mean bilateral negotiations with mutual concessions confined to the two countries reaching agreement. Indeed, Roosevelt repeatedly referred to reciprocal barter arrangements and stressed late in the campaign a resolve to protect both industry and agriculture from injury. In a Baltimore speech on October 25, 1932, he said that "no tariff duty should be lowered to a point where our natural industries would be injured." A few days later in Boston he claimed to "favor . . . continued protection for American agriculture as well as American industry."[26]

Certainly, presidential adviser Raymond Moley, who was involved in the campaign and early New Deal activities, perceived that the new president desired to pursue "modified protectionism" in order to "safeguard his experiments in wage and price raising."[27] That perspective seemed secure in February 1934, when the president appointed conservative businessman George Peek as trade coordinator. But, as Moley notes and records of the interagency trade committees confirm, Hull's assistants converted the RTAP into a "modified free-trade program," one primarily intended to reduce U.S. trade barriers.[28]

BUYING SWISS "GOOD WILL," 1936

The 1936 reciprocal trade agreement with Switzerland offers a second example of how the executive branch construed the RTAP. In this case, American officials failed to protect U.S. export interests. In October 1936, a few months after signing the accord, Switzerland devalued its currency about 30 percent. Even though this move undoubtedly benefited Swiss exports, handicapped U.S. exports to Switzerland, and represented changed circumstances, the State Department declined to invoke an escape clause permitting the parties to reopen negotiations. As a result, the Swiss were permitted to manage the agreement to their own advantage.

During the first year of the bilateral agreement, U.S. exports to Switzerland declined, while Swiss exports to America rose 41 percent. When U.S. watchmakers complained that watch imports were surging, the State Department refused, despite the no-injury pledge, to make representations or try to modify the agreement.[29] By 1939, evidence had accumulated that Swiss watchmakers were evading U.S. customs duties. To avoid higher duties on 21-jewel watches, they shipped watch movements containing only 7 to 17 jewels, which entered the country at lower customs rates even though they contained casings designed for additional jewels. Once the watch movements were in the United States, workers added more jewels. Thus Swiss watchmakers, alert to customs anomalies, used a screwdriver plant to circumvent protective tariff barriers.[30]

Meanwhile, Switzerland zealously guarded its bilateral merchandise trade surplus with the United States. From 1931 to 1935, before the trade agreement, the value of Swiss exports generally was double that of imports from the United States. During 1937 and 1938 that pattern turned more favorable to Switzerland, with exports to America averaging 247 percent of imports from America. Exchange controls, clearing arrangements, and quantitative restraints all helped the Swiss bureaucracy to discourage U.S. imports. By 1938 it was apparent "that for certain typical American products, which formerly enjoyed a good reputation and wide sales in Switzerland, the market has been practically ruined." In October 1939 a U.S. diplomat reported from Switzerland that U.S. exporters had been unable during the life of the trade agreement to utilize fully allotted quotas in Switzerland. "The principal value of the Trade Agreement . . . was primarily the good will which it helped to create in the commercial relations between the two countries."[31]

The RTAP as an Instrument of Economic Appeasement

Within Cordell Hull's State Department the reciprocal trade program increasingly became an instrument of U.S. foreign and international economic policies. To ambitious economists on the Committee on Trade Agreements, the RTAP presented unanticipated opportunities to implement international economic theories. For the committee, it was far more than an emergency program to expand U.S. exports. This transformation became manifest in 1937. During congressional hearings on extending the tariff program, the administration portrayed the RTAP as both an "essential requirement of a full and balanced economic recovery" and "a powerful instrument of economic appeasement and stability . . . to strengthen the foundations of world peace." In approving a three-year extension, the legislative history suggests that many lawmakers in Congress accepted this rationale.[32]

Over the next three years, as the world teetered on the edge of World War II, diplomatic and security concerns increasingly drove trade policy. More and more, the State Department permitted noncommercial considerations to influence its evaluation of reciprocal trade agreements. The 1938 pact negotiated with Great Britain presents a case in point.

Since 1934 a primary objective of Cordell Hull's trade policy had been to force major modifications in the Ottawa preferential system. Britain and its dominions had erected this system in 1932 to counteract the Smoot-Hawley Tariff Act and to insulate the British Empire from depression forces.[33] From Hull's perspective, the preferential system encouraged trade discrimination and promoted international friction. In particular, it had sharply reduced export opportunities for American agricultural products, especially fresh and canned fruit, wheat, rice, lard, and tobacco. According to the U.S. Tariff Commission, the Ottawa preferences resulted in the proportion of British imports originating in empire countries rising from 28.7 percent in 1931 to 40.4 percent in 1938.[34]

Under pressure from agricultural interests to demonstrate that the reciprocal trade program actually could open foreign markets to U.S. farm exports, Hull and his aides approached the British negotiations with ambitious expectations. It would be a critical test. They intended to "crack the Commonwealth" system and gain wide-ranging advantages for American farmers. To achieve these objectives, the State Department proposed to reduce U.S. duties on labor-intensive manufactured goods—especially woolens, cotton goods, and dinnerware—as well as some machinery. Among significant concessions, they offered to cut more than a hundred tariff items 40 to 50 percent.[35]

Along with the "revolutionary change in the United States tariff," British officials discovered that the bait included a sharp reduction in the U.S. bilateral trade surplus. During the fifteen years since 1921, U.S. imports from Britain had averaged only 37 percent of the value of U.S. exports. Rather than seeking to preserve the bilateral advantage, Hull's CTA proposed to assist Britain. The committee determined not simply to increase U.S. imports of British goods but to *increase imports more rapidly than exports.* This reflected the belief among government economists that to increase exports, the United States must first increase its own purchases of foreign manufactures—otherwise, trading nations would discriminate against U.S. exports in order to conserve scarce foreign exchange reserves.[36]

British representatives in Washington viewed the proposed U.S. concessions on manufactured goods favorably. H. O. Chalkley, the British Board of Trade representative, thought that the allowances "would represent a *Revolutionary* change in the United States tariff." On another occasion, he said: "Tariff concessions now offered by the United States would be not only highly beneficial but essential to expansion of our export trade." Predictably, the Foreign Office and its representative, Sir Ronald Lindsay, the British ambassador, saw a trade agreement as a step toward closer cooperation on political and security issues.[37]

London remained cool to the State Department's plan so long as it required significant British concessions. The Board of Trade refused to reduce its tariffs on certain key industrials and manufactured goods, which might have exposed British manufacturers to intense German, and perhaps Japanese, competition as a consequence of most-favored-nation treatment. On automobiles, for instance, the United Kingdom's duty was 33⅓ percent compared to 10 percent in the United States. Sensitive to domestic industry pressure and to defense considerations, declined any concession except a binding of existing duties. Electrical machinery and machine tools presented other problems given the strength of German competition. Noting the "key importance of the machine tool industry," the Board of Trade determined to reject any offer.[38]

In agriculture the British dominions resisted any significant breech of the preferential system. Prime Minister Neville Chamberlain's government offered only minimal agricultural concessions. Tobacco, the single item of greatest importance to Hull, presented special problems for London in light of commitments to Rhodesia. After lengthy negotiations, the two sides agreed simply to bind the imperial preference rate and to reexamine that rate in 1942 when the preferential arrangements came up for renewal.

Such constraints defined the final agreement, concluded in November 1938. According to the U.S. Tariff Commission, Great Britain made 296 concessions amounting to $321.6 million on 1937 imports. Of this, $234.4 million involved reductions or bindings of agricultural products (73 percent of the total). Among the agricultural concessions, only $34.1 million in 1937 trade had duties reduced or removed. Regarding nonagricultural products, Britain reduced or removed duties on $25.6 million, while binding $61.6 million. Britain's total duty reductions or removals amounted to only 18.6 percent of its total concessions.[39]

In response, the United States made 621 concessions to the United Kingdom and its colonies, valued at $457.8 million in 1937. In 1937 imports of these items from all countries amounted to $813.3, or 27 percent of all U.S. imports. Interestingly, whereas over 81 percent of Britain's concessions were bindings, only 58 percent of U.S. concessions to Great Britain were bindings.[40]

In essence, the United States and Great Britain signed a bilateral agreement providing steep cuts in U.S. tariffs but offering only modest concessions for U.S. manufactured exports in the British market.[41] The U.S. auto industry gained no improved access for exports to Britain, only a binding of existing duties. Machine toolmakers gained nothing, nor did makers of electric engines. Britain lowered its duties 25 percent on office machinery, with restrictions. On typewriters the concession was limited to expensive office models, but it deliberately excluded portable and second-hand models in order to shelter the smaller British industry. The most important U.S. reductions, the

Tariff Commission observed, were on textiles (cotton, wool, and linen), leather and manufactures, metal manufactures, and ceramics. In effect, these sharp cuts represented Hull's contribution to tariff liberalization and to modification of the Smoot-Hawley system.

Overall, London successfully resisted U.S. efforts to crack the preferential system and provided relatively minor concessions on agriculture. Indeed, a decade later the United States sold less cotton and tobacco to Britain than in 1938, and lard sales disappeared—a casualty of changing tastes. Eager to gain whatever concessions the British might offer for agricultural exporters, the State Department abandoned its first major efforts to open the British market to U.S. manufactures in July 1938. Among the U.S. gains, Britain transferred wheat and lard to the free list, effectively removing the commonwealth preference on these items. It agreed to consider a subsequent reduction of the tobacco preference benefiting Rhodesia, and it bound raw cotton on the free list. But some of these concessions had limited value and were largely window dressing.[42]

A good example of such fictitious concessions involves fresh apples. During the 1938 bilateral negotiations the United States bought a reduction in Ottawa agreement duties on apples with reductions on U.S. manufactures. In 1947 it paid Britain again to bind these duties against any increase. Internal British documents show that "this was a major concession which we [the United Kingdom] had to make in order to reach agreement in our negotiations with the United States and thus obtain a wide range of further reductions in the United States' tariff for the benefit of our industrial exports."[43]

During World War II, and until 1951, the United Kingdom permitted only the government to import apples. It also encouraged domestic apple producers to invest in orchards, and British production rose from 70,000 tons to 267,000 tons in 1958. Finally, in 1951 Britain again permitted private parties to import apples, but quotas imposed for balance-of-payments reasons facilitated apple imports from Italy but not from the dollar bloc. With the Farmers' Union requesting protection, it is not surprising that the British government delayed removing balance-of-payments restrictions. As a result, in 1958, twenty years after buying a reduction in Britain's apple tariff, the United States exported only 10 percent of the fresh apples supplied in the mid-1930s, when Ottawa duties applied. A similar pattern applied to pears and other products. British officials recognized that such conduct violated their international trade agreements. In 1959 Reginald Maudling, president of the Board of Trade, told Prime Minister Harold Macmillan: "by and large the Americans have kept their doors wide open to our trade (and at a time when they might have urged that we were shutting out their goods by quotas long after we were genuinely short of dollars to pay for them)."[44]

In retrospect, the 1938 agreement had major shortcomings. For one thing, in the short run neither Britain nor the United States stood to gain much in a commercial sense. Despite 50 percent reductions in U.S. tariff levels for cotton goods, linens, woolens, and other items, British industry doubted its capacity to take advantage of these steep concessions.[45] For U.S. exporters of leading-edge manufactures and commodity agriculture, the concessions were largely cosmetic. The agreement permitted parties to impose quotas for a variety of purposes (art. 15), and the tariff schedule specifically "made reference to quantitative restrictions for pork and ham.

Would the United States and Britain permit third countries to benefit from this bargain without opening their own markets? For many British exports to the United States, third countries, like Japan, stood to gain improved market access. In 1938 the magnitude of this free-rider problem was not fully appreciated. Hull's tariff negotiators granted a number of concessions to Britain although it was not the principal supplier of that item.[46] However, where the free-rider problem was foreseen, as in cotton textiles, negotiators broke out tariff classifications to exclude low-cost suppliers, like Japan, from the benefits of the bargain.

Given the final agreement, a disinterested observer might inquire: Why did the United States and Britain invest so much time in this enterprise? Much of the answer, of course, lies outside the world of commerce and involves foreign policy. At a White House ceremony on November 17, Secretary Hull, British ambassador Sir Ronald Lindsay, and Canadian prime minister W. L. MacKenzie King also emphasized the political significance. Said MacKenzie King: "the stability of the civilization we cherish depends more than ever on the friendly association of the great English-speaking nations of the old world and the new."[47]

By late 1938 Munich and European stability influenced the negotiations. Both the British Foreign Office and the U.S. State Department deemed an agreement essential for diplomatic reasons, not for commercial considerations. Indeed, from the beginning London had adopted the perspective that negotiations should not fail. As Ambassador Lindsay wrote in July 1938, "it is we who are trying to woo the United States away from isolation[,] not the United States who desire to involve themselves [sic] in non-American entanglements. We thus stand to lose far more from a breakdown than the United States government."[48] Similarly, when Hull confronted the prospect of failing to breech the British preferential system in October, he too opted for a more limited agreement—to promote Anglo-American solidarity and to avoid political damage from failure. As Richard Kottman wrote in his study of *Reciprocity and the North Atlantic Triangle, 1932–1938*, "the Secretary thought it better to accept an agreement not wholly to his liking rather than to prolong the discussions and risk the economic and political consequences of their collapse."[49]

More recently, two Canadian historians, Ian M. Drummond and Norman Hillmer, examined archival records in Ottawa, London, Washington, and Canberra, Australia. They also conclude that in early October 1938 foreign relations considerations drove the negotiations to a "successful" conclusion. The British government, especially the Foreign Office, wanted an agreement at any price for diplomatic reasons: "to improve their political relations with the United States, and to help construct a united front against the Rome-Berlin-Tokyo alliance." President Roosevelt, concerned about global instability, wanted to improve relations with Canada. But it seems to Drummond and Hillmer that the agreement was balanced in "the rather negative sense that neither side won significant concessions of real substance."[50]

What did the United States gain? Certainly not major modifications in the British preferential system and certainly not expanded markets for agricultural surpluses in the United Kingdom. Drummond and Hillmer agree that "the Americans actually did not make much of a dent in the preferential system." The reciprocal traders, however, had fulfilled one long-term objective—a major reduction in the U.S. tariff extending across hundreds of items. In signing an agreement both countries achieved an important political objective: closer Anglo-American cooperation during a time of European instability.[51]

REWARDING FRIENDS AND ALLIES

Secretary Hull and trade-enthusiastic subordinates did not permit World War II to disrupt the trade agreements program. Instead, the global conflict presented new opportunities for them to reduce tariffs while establishing the value of the RTAP as a tool of American diplomacy. Indeed, in seeking congressional reauthorization of the program in 1940, 1943, and 1945, the State Department presented a timely new rationale. State no longer construed reciprocal trade as an "emergency" program to expand exports, or as a device to promote "economic appeasement," since that phrase had fallen into disfavor. Instead, President Roosevelt informed Congress in 1940 that reciprocal trade was "an indispensable part of the foundation of any stable and durable peace."[52]

As open conflict in Europe approached, Roosevelt and Hull increasingly used the tariff reduction program to pursue foreign policy objectives. On April 1, 1939, the United States signed an agreement with Turkey, the twenty-first concluded since 1934 and the first with a Middle Eastern country. The State Department trumpeted this as another success of the trade liberalization program at a time when Nazi Germany was extending its economic influence eastward. Evaluated in commercial terms, it is debatable whether the agreement represented a reciprocal and balanced exchange of concessions. Turkey granted concessions (tariff reductions or bindings) on $6.1 million (or 44 percent) of its total imports from the United States ($13.9 million in 1937). The United States, however, granted concessions on $12.6 million (92 percent) out of $13.7 million in imports from Turkey.[53]

During the 1939–41 period, the United States also employed reciprocal trade agreements to strengthen its position in the Western Hemisphere. Washington concluded agreements with Venezuela and Argentina and pursued trade pacts with several other nations as part of an effort to solidify support in the Western Hemisphere.[54] The State Department signed supplementary accords with Canada and Cuba. After Pearl Harbor, it reached agreement with Peru, Uruguay, and Mexico in 1942 and with Iran and Iceland in 1943.

The trade agreement with Argentina was perhaps the most controversial negotiated during Hull's tour at the State Department. With similar climates, the two countries fiercely competed for agricultural sales. They also battled for influence in the Western Hemisphere. To avoid giving the Axis a foothold, Hull considered it essential to tie Argentina economically to the inter-American system. In 1939 and 1940 the Roosevelt administration came close to an agreement when Congress was in recess but terminated negotiations in 1940, when it appeared that an Argentine pact might sink renewal of the trade liberalization program. Talks resumed in the spring of 1941, despite the strong opposition of Raymond Stevens, chairman of the U.S. Tariff Commission and a Roosevelt friend. He and fellow commissioner Oscar Ryder argued that inclusion of flaxseed in a bilateral accord could cause "violent opposition here."[55]

Hull and Undersecretary Sumner Welles persevered, eager to innoculate the Western Hemisphere against the Axis threat. Signed in October 1941, as the Atlantic war disrupted Argentina's long-standing commercial ties with Britain, the document reflected unique conditions. Argentina agreed to lower duties on 127 items, amounting to 30.2 percent of its imports from the United States. Sixty percent of these concessions involved duty reductions; the remainder, bindings. Argentina obtained lower U.S. duties on 84 tariff items and concessions affecting about 75 percent of its 1940 exports to the United States. The major items included flaxseed, wool not finer than 40s, and canned meats, particularly corned beef. Eager—for foreign policy reasons—to conclude a pact, the State Department permitted Argentina to insert a provision pledging to put into effect its full duty reductions "when Argentine customs receipts from import duties exceed 270 million pesos national currency." After World War II, when revenues increased, Argentina declined to implement its obligations, and the United States filed several protests. Moreover, Argentina invoked other provisions to justify quotas and exchange controls. Articles in the agreement permitted the use of quantitative restrictions to regulate production and prices or to maintain a currency's exchange value. Washington also consented to supplementary notes in which Argentina qualified further its acceptance of nondiscrimination. Argentina pledged to carry out the provisions of the agreement "as soon as it becomes possible for Argentina to convert its sterling balances into free currencies."[56]

In his rush to ink an agreement with the troublesome Argentines, Hull consented to a pact honeycombed with loopholes. Whereas the United States relaxed its import barriers to provide markets for Argentine flaxseed, canned meat, and other products, Argentina chose to invoke the small print to deny the United States the commercial benefits of its bargain for years after World War II.[57]

The Icelandic agreement is another excellent example of a reciprocal trade agreement fashioned to redeem a foreign policy commitment rather than to promote mutually beneficial commerce. From a trade perspective, a trade agreement with Iceland made little sense. Indeed, when Iceland approached the United States with requests for tariff reductions on herring oil, frozen fish fillets, salted cod fish, herring, canned fish, and other items, the State Department took the view that Iceland was an "unimportant supplier" of herring oil and the other products mentioned. Other countries, like Norway or Canada, were the main suppliers of most items Iceland exported before the outbreak of war and thus the proper candidates for trade negotiations.[58]

All this changed in the spring of 1941. As compensation for wartime military cooperation, President Roosevelt pledged to make "favorable commercial and trade agreements" with Iceland. To honor this commitment, State set aside the principal supplier rule and negotiated an agreement in 1943 that contradicted basic principles of Hull's program. The most ill-advised concession, in retrospect, pertained to canned fish packed in substances other than oil (par. 718[b]). The bilateral agreement provided a maximum allowable reduction from 25 percent ad valorem to 12.5 percent ad valorem. By 1950, however, the Japanese, who faced a U.S. duty of 45 percent on tuna canned in oil, had discovered this loophole, and they began to flood the U.S. market with tuna canned in brine, a development that would eventually lead to the destruction of the high-labor-cost California fish-canning industry.[59]

Like other reciprocal trade agreements signed during this period, foreign policy and strategic considerations drove the 1943 agreement with Iran. In May 1941 the State Department's Division of Near East Affairs urged the Committee on Trade Agreements to open negotiations for political reasons. Developing trade ties with the United States, it was argued, would discourage Iran from strengthening economic ties with Germany. After Britain and the Soviet Union occupied Iran, State pressed negotiations "for reasons of political expediency and in order to safeguard American trade interests in Iran during the post-war period." The State Department saw a trade agreement as a "restraining influence upon possible Russian attempts in the future to dominate the economy and foreign trade of Iran."[60]

Similarly, negotiations with Mexico and other Latin American countries in 1941 reflected war circumstances. The State Department wanted to improve relations with Western Hemisphere nations in order to facilitate national defense efforts and the purchase of raw materials. But, as congressional critics later pointed out, the administration readily set aside its own strict trade criteria to conclude these agreements. Also, for a number of products the executive branch offered concessions to minor suppliers in order to improve the terms of the bargain. Thus it ignored sanitary laws on hoof-and-mouth disease to provide Argentina a concession on meat, and it reduced the duty on beer and tuna fish in oil from Mexico although Mexico was not a leading supplier.[61] Eager to consolidate the U.S. position in Peru, Hull conceded Peru a reduction on long-staple cotton, although Egypt was the primary supplier. Previously, Peru had exported substantial quantities of cotton to Japan.[62]

In the days before Pearl Harbor, Cuba leveraged its strategic position for a guaranteed share of the U.S. sugar market, as well as another reduction in U.S. sugar duties, effectively a device for transferring revenue from the U.S. Treasury to bolster the Cuban economy. Like an earlier sugar concession provided in the 1934 reciprocal agreement, a major purpose of the trade agreement was to give the Cuban planters revenue ($6 million) from the U.S. Treasury.[63] From his post in Havana, Ambassador George Messersmith strongly backed the Cuban request on foreign policy grounds. Acknowledging that some might question the value of Cuban concessions, he said that this negotiation "can not be considered on purely a commercial give-and-take basis." In Washington, the usually assertive Department of Agriculture, which voiced policy concerns about the relationship of this concession to the overall sugar program in meetings of the CTA, chose not to oppose the supplemental or to press for access to the Cuban rice market.[64]

In presenting these agreements to Congress and the public, the Roosevelt administration and supporters preferred to emphasize Hull's belief that trade liberalization promoted international cooperation. From such a perspective, the American concessions appeared not only to assist commerce but also to advance long-term American interests. In 1943 the House Ways and Means majority declared: "It is desirable to continue in existence this tested and sound instrument of international cooperation, in the interest both of unity in the war effort, of a secure peace hereafter, and of American prosperity." The majority noted that repeatedly in congressional hearings—1934, 1937, 1940, and 1943—protectionists expressed fears of dire dislocation from tariff reductions. But these were "fears for the future," not actual injury resulting from Hull's trade agreements.[65]

It is entirely understandable that opposition Republicans on the House Ways and Means Committee interpreted the record differently. They grumbled that the administration was "surrendering the American market to the world in return for relatively small and often illusory foreign markets." Up to this point, however, their claims seemed more partisan than persuasive. Despite the major tariff concessions made, high production and employment levels, as well as wartime dislocations in private trade, postponed any significant impact.

Reshaping the Postwar World

Despite Cordell Hull's retirement after the 1944 election and Franklin Roosevelt's death in April 1945, the secretary's vision of a peaceful, prosperous world without trade barriers continued to inspire American policymakers. Hull's trade liberalization program rejuvenated as an integral component of postwar plans. When Cold War conflict with the Soviet Union disrupted world economic cooperation, the trade program soon became a powerful instrument of foreign policy as Washington struggled to contain Soviet expansionism.

With wartime allies in Western Europe exhausted—their industries outmoded, their finances weakened—and with Axis powers facing the bleak task of recovery from wartime devastation, the United States confronted a difficult choice. It could disengage from events, as it did after World War I, or use its vast power and influence to help rebuild its competitors and reconstruct the international economy. Adopting a "Marshall Plan mentality," American leaders chose the latter course. They pursued foreign economic policies designed to make overseas allies self-sustaining participants in a thriving, open international economy, even at the expense of domestic American economic interests.

As part of the overall containment strategy, U.S. economic foreign policy had three principal goals. First, it sought to facilitate the recovery and economic viability of Great Britain and other West European allies so that they might stand as a bulwark against the expanding influence of the Soviet Union. Second, it sought to integrate former enemies Germany, Italy, and Japan into a thriving international economy and thus anchor these nations to the West economically and militarily. And third, it sought to deny the Eastern bloc valuable Western technology. To achieve these ends, Washington initially provided reconstruction assistance and then sought to make Europe and Japan self-supporting. From 1946 to 1953 the United States extended some $33 billion in nonmilitary aid, an amount equal to one-fourth of all its exports.[66] This aid helped rebuild steel mills in Europe and textile mills in Japan, while off-shore defense procurement also enabled friendly countries like Japan to build up production bases. Over the longer term, however, American officials encouraged aid recipients to become self-supporting and competitive in the international economy.

Eager to promote "trade, not aid" and thus lighten the direct costs of reconstruction, officials actively encouraged U.S. imports, not exports. The State Department, Commerce Department, and Economic Cooperation Administration all promoted foreign exports to the dollar bloc, as did U.S. occupation forces. They wanted to reduce the U.S. merchandise trade surplus in order to relieve a dollar shortage abroad. The three departments approached this task with enthusiasm, unconcerned about long-term competitiveness and employment issues or the need to secure market access for U.S. exporters. Indeed, in communicating to domestic audiences, the State Department espoused the view that this country's balance of trade surplus posed a "serious" problem: "We have an unfavorable balance of trade, unfavorable to the taxpayer and unfavorable to the consumer. . . . We must become really import-minded." Americans should not fear that "someone in the United States is going to be hurt."[67]

Public officials seem to have had complete confidence in America's ability to lead during the 1940s and 1950s. At a time when imports of goods and services were less than 4 percent of gross national product, they spoke and acted as if American manufacturing would remain permanently strong, efficient, and invulnerable to foreign competition. A 1953 report, prepared by President Harry S. Truman's Public Advisory Board for Mutual Security, even called for the United States to eliminate "unnecessary" tariffs on industries producing automobiles, machinery, and consumer electronics like radios and televisions. These industries are so "highly developed and very efficient" that "this country has nothing to fear." The report also identified pottery products, flatware, textiles and apparel, and sundry items with duties of 25 percent or more. It called for tariff reductions to open the way for a "substantial increase in imports." In making these market-opening proposals, the report asserted that "decisions on trade policy be based on [the] national interest, rather than the interest of particular industries or groups."[68]

American presidents from Truman through Lyndon B. Johnson shared the conviction that foreign policy concerns should take priority over domestic economic interests. Truman observed: "Our industry dominates world markets. . . . American labor can now produce so much more than low-priced foreign labor in a given day's work that our workingmen need no longer fear, as they were justified in fearing in the past, the competition of foreign workers."[69]

It is not surprising that his successor, Dwight D. Eisenhower, a former military leader, also gave priority to strategic considerations. Indeed, he criticized protectionist U.S. businesses for "shortsightedness bordering upon tragic stupidity." In the face of aggressive communism, he considered freer trade essential to help other nations "make a living." He emphasized: "We are not talking about trying to put American people out of work or undersell an American manufacturer and drive him to the wall or anything else. We are striving to make a better world for ourselves and for our children."[70] Trade was important, Eisenhower thought, to sound political relationships. To secure allied support for strategic export controls against the Soviet Union, the United States must provide alternative markets in the West.

This emphasis on opening the huge American market to aid foreign allies and promote international economic reconstruction had surfaced in the State Department during World War II and, publicly, during the 1947 Geneva trade negotiations. Eager to construct a liberal economic order without high tariffs and exchange controls, department planners contemplated drastic—and disproportionate—cuts in U.S. tariffs to stimulate imports and assist foreign reconstruction and participation in an open trading community. To them, the statute requiring mutually balanced tariff concessions seemed overly restrictive and inappropriate to postwar circumstances. In December 1943 a special State Department committee considering the relaxation of trade barriers recommended that the United States "pursue policies which in the long run will result in greater increases in its imports than in its exports."[71]

Others in Congress and the private sector were less sensitive to the dollar shortage and problems of international economic adjustment, less enthused about textbook solutions, and more cautious about the implications of opening the U.S. market for the benefit of U.S. consumers and foreign producers. To the Republican Congress elected in 1946, further tariff reductions immediately after the war seemed highly imprudent and overly idealistic. The war had disrupted economies and created distortions. It was not clear whether previous cuts, especially the steep reductions effected in the 1938 reciprocal trade agreement with Britain, could be accommodated without injury to domestic industries and workers. But the congressional critics hesitated to vote down the RTAP and to undercut Truman's efforts to provide leadership. Instead, Senator Arthur Vandenberg, chairman of the Senate Foreign Relations Committee, and Senator Eugene D. Millikin, chairman of the Senate Finance Committee, negotiated with the administration. The Republicans would renew reciprocal trade tariff cutting if President Truman would reiterate the no-injury (to domestic industry) pledge of preceding presidents. Truman promised that "domestic interests will be safeguarded in this process of expanding trade. . . . This government does not intend, in the coming negotiations, to eliminate tariffs or to establish free trade. All that is contemplated is the reduction of tariffs, the removal of discriminations, and the achievement, not of free trade, but of freer trade."[72]

"Cracking" the British Commonwealth, 1947

Truman's commitment facilitated U.S. participation in the Geneva Round of multilateral tariff negotiations. As a result of wartime talks with Britain and several other allies, the United States published its plan for an International Trade Organization (ITO), the trade equivalent of the International Monetary Fund and the International Bank for Reconstruction and Development, both established at the Bretton Woods Conference in July 1944. The Geneva meetings pursued two parallel tasks: one was to complete work on the charter for the International Trade Organization, the other to conduct a round of multilateral tariff negotiations among participants.[73]

During the 1947 trade negotiations with fifteen countries, the primary U.S. goal remained the same as in 1938. It proposed to bargain away what remained of the Smoot-Hawley system in exchange for the elimination of foreign preferences and discriminations against American exports. Because Britain was the largest market for world imports in 1938 (18.5 percent), it was natural that the United States should focus on negotiations with the United Kingdom and its commonwealth.[74]

The United States tabled the proposed concessions, which had the effect of lowering the average ad valorem U.S. tariff from about 25 percent to below 20 percent, reducing rates on 50 percent of total imports from the United Kingdom in 1939, and offering major reductions of 36–50 percent on 70 percent of the items. In return, the United States requested what it had sought before World War II and, as part of a lend-lease settlement, the elimination of Ottawa preferences on about sixty-five items.

Britain's Labour government was no more eager to abandon the commonwealth than the Conservative government had been in 1938. It merely tabled a modest list of concessions and proposed to eliminate preferences on frozen salmon, motor bicycles, and tricycles. Britain offered concessions on only 10 percent of imports from the United States. On three principal items—tobacco, maize, and automobile accessories—London offered nothing.[75]

The long history of the Geneva tariff negotiations is complex and warrants separate, comprehensive treatment. Essentially, the British battled to protect "at all costs the empire preference system," while U.S. delegates took the view "that if the British Empire preference system is ever to be cracked, now is the time to do it." U.S. negotiators believed that the lend-lease agreement obligated Britain to dismantle the preferential system. British officials, however, insisted on a different interpretation: they were obliged only to move in the direction of dismantling the preferential system.[76]

After months of haggling over the meaning of wartime commitments, the United States faced a difficult choice. As Carl Corse, a participant in those negotiations, later wrote, "the final British offers appeared so inadequate that serious consideration was given the possibility of breaking off negotiations with the United Kingdom." But President Truman and the secretary of state decided "that a 'thin' agreement was better than no agreement."[77]

In the last analysis, foreign policy, not hard commercial calculations, produced an agreement. In October 1947 Washington wanted to paper over differences and sustain cooperation for reasons related to cooperation in the Cold War and plans for the International Trade Organization. To effect this common interest, the chief trade negotiators worked out a compromise that could justify the wide and deep U.S. tariff reductions while avoiding the appearance of failure. The British negotiators claimed to make "innocuous improvements on our offers," enabling U.S. negotiators to "dress up . . . statistics [so] as to have what appears to . . . be a chance of getting away with it with Congress."[78] Specifically, according to J. R. C. Helmore, the chief British negotiator, the key concession involved an agreement for the Americans to assure access to the U.S. market for natural rubber in exchange for an agreement to reduce colonial preferences 25 percent.

This item, Helmore said, was "of considerable window-dressing value to the Americans, but of little economic cost to us." He emphasized that "no colonial preferences are to be eliminated." And because the United States had already agreed to permit discrimination against U.S. exports from countries in balance-of-payments difficulties, Britain's own concessions were "inoperative." Thus from the British standpoint the negotiations were a huge success: Washington had provided major concessions for British textiles and manufactures; Britain had preserved the empire with only token reductions in preferences and maintained American goodwill to facilitate passage of the Marshall Plan.[79]

Convinced apparently that an unbalanced deal was better than no deal at all, the United States signed an agreement that cracked open only one market— its own. In a memorandum informing President Truman of the results at Geneva, State Department negotiators glossed over the unsatisfactory outcome. They did acknowledge that Washington had gained concessions with a trade value of $1.19 billion while yielding concessions worth $1.77 billion. American tariff reductions averaged 35 percent on dutiable items.[80] State claimed that the United Kingdom agreement must be considered "a satisfactory part of the multilateral agreement" when account is taken of "the effect that the conclusions of such agreement will have upon the success of the Charter of the International Trade Organization, which is the central element in United States economic foreign policy." In effect, the State Department told Truman that British consideration for American trade concessions at Geneva was continued British support for the ITO, not the specific elimination of preferences in the commonwealth and empire, now or in the future.[81]

Within the U.S. delegation to the Geneva negotiations, there was considerable dissatisfaction with the outcome. It was "only with the greatest difficulty that the negotiators were able to convince all U.S. agencies" to endorse the settlement. One of the most important factors in persuading the U.S. delegates to accept the agreement was the rubber-for-colonial-preferences deal (schedule 19[c]). One individual not disposed to cover up the results was John Gregg, a tariff commissioner, who had once served as executive secretary to the Committee for Reciprocity Information and who participated in the talks. He cast his vote in the CTA against the bilateral trade pact: "I do not believe the balance between the proposed schedules as submitted is in accord with the implications of the Trade Agreements Act, and the commitments made as to the way in which that Act would be employed." In a comment that may also be construed as a damning criticism of the 1938 negotiations, Commissioner Gregg conceded that the 1947 proposed agreement "represent[s] substantial improvements over the 1939 [sic] trade agreement with the United Kingdom." Nonetheless, he observed that "the major concessions obtained from the United Kingdom were expected to consist of eliminations and reductions in the preferential treatment enjoyed by British products in Dominion markets. But the concessions actually offered to the United States were "*not adequate* to warrant granting the concessions proposed to the United Kingdom" (emphasis added).[82]

As it turned out, the Geneva agreement proved more unbalanced and one-sided than even the skeptical Gregg imagined. As a result of a drafting error, the rubber-for-preferences provision included a flawed formula for calculating the share of British rubber allowed into the U.S. market. Consequently, in November 1947 London asked to suspend the formula until it was renegotiated. The U.S. ambassador in London agreed. But the British later refused to reopen the negotiations, claiming that changing circumstances made the arrangement less attractive to London. In effect, then, the 1947 Geneva agreement produced not even a 25 percent reduction in colonial preferences. For the State Department, twice thwarted in efforts to crack the British preferential system, this was an embarrassing blunder. Indeed, the British embassy in Washington reported that State had a "pathological fear" of congressional critics raising the issue in debate over the renewal of reciprocal trade–negotiating authority in 1951.[83]

FAILURE AT TORQUAY
Evidence that the one-sided Geneva bargain had established a pattern of expectations for future unbalanced concessions emerged in the next round of Anglo-American trade negotiations at Torquay, England, in 1951. According to

the U.S. negotiators, at Torquay "the British Delegation never deviated from the effort to obtain an agreement on a limited, one-sided basis." The "United Kingdom did not intend to make any reduction in duty on any competitive product large enough to have an appreciable effect on imports . . . nor did it intend to make any significant reduction in any preference." Carl Corse, acting chairman of the U.S. delegation, later said: "it was quite obvious throughout the negotiations that the United Kingdom, *remembering our position at Geneva*, . . . was confident that in the end we would accept an unbalanced agreement rather than have no agreement" (emphasis added).[84]

British records show that the United Kingdom did indeed want a one-sided agreement. Wrote Board of Trade official S. L. Holmes: "We were out to secure an agreement which was somewhat, at least unbalanced in our favor." London wanted an agreement that would give Britain a chance to increase exports to the dollar bloc more than dollar exports to Britain, "thus helping to correct the dollar-sterling dis-balance."[85] It also would not "contemplate any serious losses of preferences."[86]

This time, with renewal of the trade agreements program up before a skeptical Congress, the CTA voted to terminate negotiations with the British. The State Department declined to sign a pact "without receiving adequate reciprocal concessions." There was concern that a weak agreement with Britain and the commonwealth "might have become public just as the Senate voted upon extension of the Trade Agreements Act." Tactically, participants in the CTA reasoned that it "would help in the renewal of the . . . Act if we could say that we refused to conclude an agreement with the U.K. because we could not get adequate concessions."[87] The British embassy noted a hardening of the State Department's bargaining position after the House of Representatives dealt harshly with reciprocal trade renewal; the embassy concluded that Washington wanted to demonstrate that "United States negotiators were not suckers."[88]

In explaining to President Truman the failure to reach agreement with Britain, the Committee on Trade Agreements indicated that London wanted all the politically controversial U.S. tariff offers—involving woolen and cotton textiles, leather, china and earthenware—but offered nothing substantial in return. Of the proposed British concessions, "no one . . . offered any break in the preferential system and no one . . . offered any substantial improvement in the British treatment of United States agricultural products."[89] Thus it is evident that the failure in 1938 and 1947 to insist on an advantageous agreement had encouraged the British to press for unilateral concessions. Facing a difficult reauthorization battle in Congress, the Truman administration free traders pragmatically broke off negotiations to demonstrate their toughness as negotiators and to enhance the RTAP's prospects on Capitol Hill.

During the talks at Geneva and Torquay, American negotiators insisted, as the law required, on reciprocal concessions. They repeatedly told British officials that the United States could not legally "make unilateral concessions." Indeed, U.S. diplomats informed their British counterparts and others, "there is no reason to do so since the British can maintain import restrictions and nullify their tariff concessions for so long as they are in balance-of-payments difficulties."[90] In effect, U.S. negotiators indicated a willingness to accept promises of future foreign tariff reductions, or other concessions, as the sufficient equivalent of immediate U.S. reductions or bindings.

Such a result was possible partly because the Marshall Plan mentality encouraged altruism. But it was also possible for serious individuals—negotiators and lawmakers—to disagree honestly over what constituted an equivalent concession. "[T]he equating of reciprocal concessions is a highly subjective business," one U.S. negotiator said later.[91] Thus, given the difficulty of evaluating the results of negotiations objectively, it was possible in 1947 for State Department officials to bring home an unsatisfactory agreement from the Geneva trade conference and still place a positive spin on the results.

Out of the Marshall Plan era of helping troubled neighbors emerged a pattern of tolerance for discrimination against American exports. U.S. officials proudly embraced a policy of "trade, not aid," implying that foreign nations should earn their own way. Trade in goods would substitute effectively for direct income transfers and so promote effective recovery. To facilitate this process, the United States chose to ignore discrimination against U.S. exports and investments. In fact, the "trade, not aid" policy had its origins in London, not Washington. The British Foreign Office considered it "a most successful slogan for winning public acceptance of the need for more imports" in the United States.[92] Later the British commercial counselor in Washington proudly boasted to the Board of Trade about the success of "propaganda for freer trade policies" in restraining America's natural isolationist and protectionist sentiment.[93]

The Marshall Plan mentality surfaced regularly in trade policy decisions. In October 1948 the United States quietly waived temporarily its rights under a number of trade agreements—with Brazil, Ceylon, Cuba, and Pakistan—and acquiesced to discrimination against American exports for balance-of-payments and development reasons. In 1950 discrimination was so widespread that the U.S. Tariff Commission found that "only 4 of the 42 countries with which the United States had trade agreements in force" during the period "employed neither import licenses nor exchange controls." These were such important economic adversaries as Cuba, El Salvador, Guatemala, and Haiti.[94]

During the 1950s discrimination against American exports ran rampant. In March 1958 the U.S. Chamber of Commerce, which was sympathetic to the tariff reduction program, phoned the State Department for information of interest to its business members. The chamber wanted to know if State could "name products (1) on which the United States has received tariff concessions, (2) which were liberalized by the country concerned, and (3) which were competitive with domestic products of that country." After considering the request, State offered several examples: typewriters and office machines for Germany, vitamins for Japan. Daniel M. Lyons of the Trade Agreements Division explained to the chamber official: "there must be many more such items, but that . . . would require research which we had not so far done." As this episode demonstrates, in 1958 the State Department did not monitor the results of its negotiations and lacked specific information about the benefits of trade liberalization for American business.[95]

Promoting Imports

The "trade, not aid" policy had another astonishing result. The U.S. government enthusiastically employed taxpayer funds to promote the sale of foreign goods in the United States and third countries. In December 1946 the State Department instructed diplomatic and consular officials around the world to assist those nations exporting to America: "In general, a Foreign Service officer should give the same attention to servicing United States importers as he would give to United States exporters." This instruction, in effect, authorizing the use of American tax dollars to promote competition for domestic businesses, represented a major departure from traditional policy. American diplomatic and commercial officers serving abroad were expected to assist U.S. exporters, not work against the direct interests of U.S. producers and workers.[96]

This was not an isolated anomaly. With the slow pace of recovery and the growing Soviet military and political threat, State Department economists revived plans for unilateral U.S. tariff reductions on manufactures. Early in 1949 economist Joseph Coppock stirred European interest with his suggestion that further "feasible [tariff] reductions could give rise to an expansion of imports in the neighborhood of one billion dollars within a few years."[97] In London U.S. officials assigned to the European Cooperation Administration distributed Coppock's article and encouraged British officials to develop information that could be employed in congressional testimony to justify further reductions in U.S. tariffs.[98]

The State Department also sought to discourage U.S. industries from invoking the escape clause, a provision authorizing withdrawal of tariff concessions if domestic producers could prove that increased imports, as a consequence of duty reductions, caused serious injury. In April 1952 department officials solicited, and then apparently leaked, memoranda from Great Britain and Italy claiming that escape clause actions handicapped the efforts of foreign countries to earn needed dollars. In particular, the escape clause weakened Britain's ability to play its necessary part in defending the West against aggression.[99]

Enthusiasm for further tariff cuts to support the State Department's foreign economic policy goals appeared in several blue-ribbon reports commissioned by the Truman administration. A 1950 report, prepared under the supervision of Gordon Gray, a former secretary of the army, proposed "temporary emergency legislation" to authorize the president to eliminate duties on scarce commodities.[100] The Bell report (named for Daniel Bell, a Washington banker and former budget director in the Roosevelt administration), which the Truman administration prepared to influence the 1953 reciprocal trade debate, also called for tariff reductions to allow the "freer import of goods." It recommended a "national interest" test for trade policy decisions: "in cases where choice must be made between injury to the national interest and hardship to an industry, the industry [must] be helped to make adjustments by means other than excluding imports—such as through extension of unemployment insurance, assistance in retraining workers, diversification of production, and conversion to other lines." In effect, this proposal implied sacrificing import-competing industries for the sake of restoring balance in international trade. The Bell Commission viewed "American investment abroad" as a "supplement to, rather than a substitute for, an increase in imports."[101]

Such cosmopolitan thinking had strong support among State Department economists. Eager to promote imports and achieve "equilibrium at a high level of two-way trade," officials endorsed sharp unilateral concessions in U.S. tariffs on cotton and woolen textiles, scientific apparatus, household and office electrical appliances, chemicals, and raw materials. In offering these recommendations the State Department seemed oblivious to President Truman's no-injury commitment to Senators Vandenberg and Millikin in 1947. Their institutional concern was the state of the world and American foreign policy, not the health of the American domestic economy. Assistant Secretary for Economic Affairs Harold Linder expressed this thought succinctly: "The great question is . . . whether the country is willing to decide, in the broader national self-interest, to reduce tariffs and increase United States imports even though some domestic industry may suffer serious injury, or whether the policy shall continue to be one of maintaining tariffs and restricting imports to avoid such injury. . . .

Effective tariff reductions by the United States very largely relate to imports of finished manufactures."[102]

Eisenhower's Approach: More Import Liberalization

During the Eisenhower administration American priorities remained the same. Foreign policy considerations usually overrode the concerns of import-competing industries in White House decisions—and invariably at the State Department. Deputy Assistant Secretary for Economic Affairs Thorsten V. Kalijarvi stated the issue this way:

> In our efforts to prevent actions harmful to the free-world security system, we face the practical dilemma posed by the conflict between the special and often short-run interest of particular domestic economic groups and the more general longer-run national need for free-world strength and solidarity. *Much of the time and energy of the people concerned with foreign economic affairs is devoted to assuring that in resolving these conflicts the longer-run national interest is adequately taken into account.* (emphasis added)[103]

In 1953 the president and his secretary of state, John Foster Dulles, were preoccupied with the Cold War. As Eisenhower told congressional leaders, "all problems of local industry pale into insignificance in relation to the world crisis." In particular, they worried about the Far East. "Japan cannot live, and Japan cannot remain in the free world unless something is done to allow her to make a living," Eisenhower declared in a speech to newspaper editors in June 1954. Secretary Dulles also questioned the ability of Japan to pay its way internationally through trade. At a meeting with visiting Japanese prime minister Shigeru Yoshida in November 1954, Dulles held up a "brightly patterned flannel shirt made in Japan of cheap material copying a better quality cloth made in the United States." The secretary noted "that this is one of the reasons the Japanese have difficulty in expanding their trade."[104]

As a former military leader and not a businessman, it is perhaps understandable that Eisenhower should give priority to international political and military considerations. Unfamiliar with the details of domestic issues and commerce, he reacted negatively to calls for import protection. Such protection was "shortsightedness bordering upon tragic stupidity," he commented in his diary. Eisenhower believed that as a matter of "enlightened self-interest," the United States could not export industrial and agricultural products unless it also imported. In a world with aggressive communism, he wanted a system of global trade that allowed "backward people to make a decent living—even if only a minimum one measured by American standards—[otherwise] . . . in the long run we must fall prey to the communistic attack."[105]

REPUBLICAN DOUBTS

In his emphasis on foreign policy and international cooperation, Dwight Eisenhower diverged from traditional Republican doctrine. While the president focused on problems of international security, other Republicans worried about the competitiveness of U.S. industries in a world with reduced tariffs. In October 1953 former president Herbert Hoover voiced private concern about the impact of further tariff reductions on small industries. He recognized that pottery, ceramics, rubber goods, cotton textiles, and a host of others would be impacted negatively if the United States further reduced its tariffs. Hoover foresaw the impact of intense import competition on small-town America. "Thousands of villages and towns would be deprived of their employment. Their schools, churches and skills would be greatly decimated."[106]

Within Eisenhower's cabinet Secretary of the Treasury George Humphrey, a Cleveland businessman with experience in mining, and Secretary of Commerce Sinclair Weeks, who operated import-sensitive fastener and flatware plants in Connecticut, were responsive to the problems of high-wage U.S. industry competing with Asian products. At one cabinet meeting Humphrey went "completely Neanderthal" and "roared about the trade program." He said "that not only should there be no tariff reduction for Japan but that the existing tariffs should be raised." Behind Humphrey's outburst was recognition that "we were protectionists by history and had been living under a greatly lowered schedule of tariffs in a *false sense of security* because the world was not in competition. That has changed now and the great wave of world competition from plants we had built for other nations was going to bring vast unemployment to our country" (emphasis added).[107]

In Congress, there was even less Republican support for Eisenhower's open trade policy. One of his closest Senate supporters, the freshman senator from Connecticut, Prescott Bush (father of future president George Bush), had reservations. Bush later commented: "I never was a free trader. I never felt that we could abolish tariffs and do away with all protective devices, because we would have been flooded with imports which would have hurt our economy, hurt our defense posture, and I felt that these things had to be done gradually, selectively."[108]

TRADE CONCESSIONS FOR JAPAN

Pressure for additional tariff reductions developed soon after Eisenhower's inauguration in 1953. The British government and U.S. State Department officials floated proposals for steep and unilateral cuts in the U.S. tariff to facilitate the recuperation of international commerce.[109] The White House was not disposed to give unilateral concessions to Britain, but Japan was a different matter.

On the critical issue of assisting the Japanese recovery, the British and other Europeans differed from the Americans. Based on the intense competition of Japanese textile producers before World War II, Britain anticipated that Japanese competition would threaten one-third of British industry. As a consequence, London opposed extending most-favored-nation treatment to Japan, blocked Japanese membership in GATT, and voiced grave concern about renewed Japanese export competition. London forecast "that many American commerce interests would in due course come to feel about Japan as certain British industrial interests now felt."[110]

John Foster Dulles, who had negotiated the Japanese peace treaty, placed trade negotiations on a fast track, and his State Department lobbied allies to support Japan's membership in GATT and to provide markets for Japanese goods. State took the view that such commercial opportunities would enable the United States to "obtain Japan's cooperation in such important projects as their defense measures and export security controls." Thus once again U.S. tariff concessions were viewed as a lure to gain political and military cooperation.[111]

In August 1953 the Committee on Trade Agreements recommended temporary GATT membership for Japan, despite the Department of Commerce's sensitivity to domestic business concerns. Commerce acquiesced "in the face of the firm foreign relations judgment of the Department of State that any United States action short of support of the Japanese proposal for temporary accession to the General Agreement [GATT] would threaten fulfillment of overall United States objectives in Japan."[112]

Negotiating with Japan

After the 1954 congressional elections, the Eisenhower administration assigned bilateral trade negotiations with Japan a high priority. The State Department proposed extensive concessions on 56 percent of total imports from Japan. The negotiating list included a number of import-sensitive items: among them, handmade glassware, crabmeat, shelled walnuts, canned hams, earthenware and chinaware, optical goods, automobiles, Christmas tree ornaments, sewing machines, surgical instruments, tuna fish, cotton cloth, velveteens, toys, cameras, and rubber footwear. In addition, State recommended offering third countries concessions in the U.S. market if they in turn provided benefits to Japan.

This sweeping proposal distressed other government agencies with programs and interests to protect. The Department of Agriculture, sensitive as always to farm concerns, opposed listing hops, brined cherries, olive oil, and dried egg albumen. The Labor and Interior Departments had trouble with listings for silk handkerchiefs, wool-knit gloves, and pearl buttons, because concessions to Japan would "materially interfere and perhaps negate . . . efforts to increase the minimum wage in Puerto Rico."[113]

With White House support, the State Department played the foreign policy card to trump opponents: "the overriding interest of the United States is to strengthen our national security by taking the first step toward binding Japan to the Free World." In this context, then, as one White House aide said, "the Japanese negotiations were vastly more important than efforts to raise minimum wages in Puerto Rico."[114]

In February 1955, as Congress debated extension of the reciprocal trade program, the State Department sent President Eisenhower a supplemental list of concessions to Japan and third countries that included a number of import-sensitive concessions on textiles, footwear, and chinaware. Eager to help Japan, the interagency Committee on Trade Agreements recommended cuts on low-value countable cotton cloth, on cotton velveteens, and on cotton table damask. On velveteens the interagency group of "experts" proposed sharp cuts. As events turned out, within two years the domestic industry would demonstrate successfully to the Tariff Commission that these concessions increased imports and injured domestic producers.[115]

There can be no question that foreign policy considerations drove the administration's approach to bilateral negotiations with Japan. Secretary of Commerce Weeks wrote Eisenhower that his agency acquiesced to the cuts on a number of items, including textiles, with "mental reservation. . . . Our agreement to the listing of textile items has been based on broad foreign economic policy considerations and the realization that if textiles were excluded from the list the basis for negotiations with Japan would be severely curtailed." Weeks hoped that if the reductions in textile duties "should result in a substantial inflow of textiles from Japan" that the Eisenhower administration would give "sympathetic consideration" to "any escape clause action requested by the textile industry."[116]

AT THE NEGOTIATING TABLE

U.S. minutes of the 1955 negotiations show eager U.S. participants pressing the Japanese for concessions on leaf tobacco, soft drinks, lubricating oils, automobiles, synthetic fibers, and many other products important to political supporters of the administration's tariff reduction program. C. Thayer White, the chief of the U.S. delegation, reminded the Japanese that "some of the most powerful support for the trade agreements program comes from American agriculture and the automobile industry."[117]

U.S. officials also cited international economic justifications for Japanese concessions. Arguing for a Japanese duty reduction on automobiles, White stated:

> [T]he United States industry is the largest and most efficient in the world; (2) the industry is strongly in favor of expanding the opportunities for world trade; (3) its access to foreign markets in recent years has been limited by import controls. . . . (4) although the United States Government appreciates that it is necessary for some countries to impose import restrictions for balance of payments reasons . . . it would be in Japan's interest to import automobiles from the United States and export items in which Japan could excel.

On other occasions White referred to a statement that Japan only desired to establish industries that could compete in world markets and said that "it would be inconsistent for Japan to attempt to establish an automobile industry because its prospects were not very promising for the future." He also urged a concession on machine tool imports, doubting "that Japan could compete with the United States in world markets because of the difference in the relative efficiency of the industries in both countries." Establishment of "high cost industries behind a tariff wall does not contribute to the sound growth of national economy," White said. He encouraged the Japanese not to use tariffs, but to increase productivity, promote foreign private direct investment, utilize technical assistance, facilitate domestic capital investment through tax incentives, and pursue a sound domestic fiscal policy.[118]

The Japanese had a different vision of their future in the international economy. Said K. Otabe, a Japanese delegate: "(1) if the theory of international trade were pursued to its ultimate conclusion, the United States would specialize in the production of automobiles and Japan in the production of tuna; (2) such a division of labor does not take place . . . because each government encourages and protects those industries which it believes important for reasons of *national policy*" (emphasis added). Asked to reduce import duties on synthetic textiles, Otabe declined, stating that "the Japanese Government believes that a synthetic industry is necessary to diversify and promote the development of the Japanese economy." Otabe also refused to lower tariffs on hand tools because "the domestic industry was having difficulty competing and it was concerned over the competitive effects of increased imports." A lower duty on raisins would "interfere with the consumption of domestically produced sugar confectionery." Reductions on boots and shoes might "destroy" an industry composed of small firms.[119]

Asked to lower the Japanese duty on movie cameras, Otabe said that his government "wished to advance the development of the Japanese optical industry." When queried about reductions on radios and television sets, he demurred. The Japanese industry was at a "competitive disadvantage"; the government feared "political repercussions." The story was similar for electronic equipment: "The Japanese Government believes that an electronics industry is essential to the development of the Japanese economy, the communications industry and national defense." Much the same explanations applied to petrochemicals, tractors, and heavy machinery. Heavy machinery and machine tools were vital to the development and diversification of the Japanese economy and to a skilled labor force. Indeed, Otabe reminded the Americans "that a protective tariff had contributed to the development of new industries in the early history of the United States and that similarly a protective tariff could promote the development of the petrochemical, heavy machinery and other promising industries in Japan."

EVALUATING THE RESULTS

What did the United States gain as a result of the 1955 negotiations with Japan and third countries? In seeking Eisenhower's approval, the Committee on Trade Agreements claimed that America received "direct concessions on exports valued in 1953 at $395 million (reductions in rate of duty on $61 million; bindings of dutiable status on $139 million; free list bindings of $195 million dollars)." Among the concessions obtained were duty reductions on automobiles, business machines, raisins, antibiotics, soybeans, and corn. In return, the State Department claimed, the United States made only $123 million in concessions to Japan, of which $53 million were duty reductions and the remainder bindings of dutiable or free list items. Among the principal concessions cited were U.S. duty reductions on chinaware, monosodium glutamate, low-value countable cloths, velveteens, and tuna canned in oil.[120]

The State Department's tally did not reveal the whole story.[121] For one thing, given the political sensitivity of these negotiations, it is not surprising from a public relations perspective to find State claiming—based on 1953 trade value data—that U.S. gains exceeded Japanese gains by better than three to one. However, the use of 1953 statistics, rather than prewar trade data, tends to minimize the value of U.S. concessions and exaggerate the value of Japanese concessions. This is so because in 1953 Japan supplied only 2.4 percent of all U.S. imports for consumption, whereas the average Japanese share for 1934–36 was 7.2 percent of all U.S. imports. American exports to Japan during 1953 were exaggerated because of military expenditures related to the Korean War and agricultural commodity credits.[122]

Viewed from a different perspective, the evidence does indeed show an unbalanced agreement—but one favoring Japan. First, the Japanese concessions were largely bindings of existing tariff rates, not real tariff reductions. Although Japan made concessions on goods valued at $397 million in 1953, 84 percent of these locked in existing duties.[123] Japan reduced duties on items valued at $61.4 million in 1953, and of these major tariff reductions (over 35 percent) applied to commodities valued at only $6.4 million in 1953. In effect, the United States won *major tariff reductions* on only 1.6 percent of Japanese trade involved in all tariff concessions (including bindings and reductions). Only one major reduction—for drinking glasses—involved a manufactured product. The United States exported only $62,000 of these to Japan in 1953. Apparently, this concession was window dressing to impress Congress. In essence, Japan cut tariffs substantially on food products and raw materials (lemons, raisins, skim milk, tomato paste, cottonseed oil, and lard, as well as tetraethyl lead) but successfully retained duties on manufactures.

The Japanese press trumpeted its government's success at the talks. The *Mainichi Daily News* reported that "domestic industries in Japan will not suffer any unfavorable influence. . . . Fifty-six out of 75 tariff rates concessed [*sic*] by Japan are reduced only by less than 5 percent." The *Nippon Times* also cited Japanese government sources who "anticipated that the adverse effects the Japanese concessions would bring on the domestic industries would be negligible as compared with the benefits Japan would gain."[124]

American officials also conceded that the Japanese had maneuvered skillfully. Marshall Smith, the acting assistant secretary of commerce for international affairs, told State Department officials that the Japanese were "shrewd negotiators." Knowing that the United States considered a trade agreement "extremely important," he said, "they must have reasoned the United States cannot risk to lose an agreement because of the importance we attach to Japan. Consequently they played their hand well[,] being certain that we would not permit the negotiations to fail. In one or two instances they even threatened to break off negotiations for they could not possibly meet our request."[125]

What did America give Japan? First, according to the State Department, the United States provided concessions on $131 million in imports, using 1954 trade values. Forty-five percent, or $59 million, of these concessions were tariff reductions, and bindings applied to $72 million in 1953 trade. However, the United States agreed to major reductions—more than 35 percent—on 63 percent of the Japanese imports in 1954 ($37.2 million). Thus, when major U.S. and Japanese tariff concessions are compared, it is apparent that the United States granted far more ($37.2 million) than it gained ($6.4 million). Moreover, although the significant Japanese reductions involved raw materials and agricultural products, many of the U.S. reductions were on labor-intensive manufactures: earthenware and chinaware, glassware, textiles, apparels, tile and floor coverings, rubber manufactures, and electrical products.

Second, the United States traded immediate concessions for deferred benefits. American concessions to Japan took effect on September 10, 1955, but it was understood that "the United States will not at once enjoy the full benefit of the concessions granted by Japan" because of Japan's trade and exchange controls imposed to conserve foreign exchange. In effect, this meant that the Japanese concessions had no commercial meaning until Japan ended exchange controls and restored currency convertibility. In a conversation with Ambassador Sadao Iguchi in April 1955, State Department official Isaiah Frank emphasized "the political difficulty in the United States . . . that we are getting concessions which may mean benefits at some undefined future time in return for concessions conferring real present benefits on Japan."[126] As it turned out, Japan still imposed quantitative restrictions, or other restraints, on some of the American gains eighteen years after the State Department concluded the agreement. These involved canned fruit, items containing sugar, jewelry, coal, and aircraft engines and parts.[127]

Third, and most controversial, the so-called triangular negotiations resulted in significant American reductions without corresponding gains for U.S. exports. To help Japan expand its exports at a time when many European nations continued to discriminate, the United States made concessions to third countries, effectively purchasing market access for Japan in those countries. Such benefits went to Canada (on amorphous graphite, ferrosilicon, pig iron, and turkeys), Denmark (cork tile), Finland (sulphite wrapping paper), Italy (reptile leather articles and leather purses), Norway (dried and unsalted fish), and Sweden (tanning extracts, candles, and sulphite wrapping paper). These were not token reductions involving inconsequential trade values. Seven of the thirteen U.S. tariff paragraphs reduced in these "triangular" negotiations fell the maximum-authorized 50 percent, and this procured additional foreign concessions on traditional Japanese export specialties valued at over $2 million in 1953.

Although the State Department claimed that Japan had provided additional concessions to the United States on imports valued at over $1.1 million in 1953, it did not attempt to explain these benefits publicly in a detailed way. One reason may be that the triangular negotiations resulted in too many phony concessions. For instance, Italy provided concessions on agar and camphor imported principally from Japan, America reduced its duties on leather goods from Italy, and Japan reduced rates on tape recorders and bound the rate on parts for tape recorders but retained nontariff barriers. Certainly some members of Congress concluded that the triangular negotiations were a sham, in which U.S. tariff-cutting authority was being used not to remove impediments on U.S. exports but to acquire markets in Europe and Canada for Japanese exports.[128]

How, then, did the reciprocal agreement with Japan effect U.S. trade? From 1954 to 1960 U.S. exports to Japan rose from $684 million to $1.33 billion, about 95 percent. Japanese imports rose from $279 million to $1.12 billion, up 312 percent. But the composition of the trade changed. The United States increased its share of Japan's imports, with the major growth in crude materials, mineral fuels, and animal and vegetable products. Japan, however, more than doubled its share of America's manufactured imports—from 7.6 percent in 1955 to 15.4 percent in 1960.[129]

In essence, the 1955 trade negotiations with Japan, far more than the negotiations with Great Britain in 1938 and 1947, opened U.S. borders to imports of labor-intensive products and other manufactures. They also sparked a political reaction. Particularly negatively impacted were the textile and apparel industries. Robert Stevens, the president of textile giant J. P. Stevens and Company, voiced the concerns of this large industry, employing about 1 million workers, when he opposed RTAP renewal in 1958 and called for higher tariffs and import restrictions to "preserve our American standard of living." In pursuing "reciprocity," he said, "we have done all the giving and yielding and losing. . . . The American standard of living is under attack from overseas."[130]

Increasingly, the administration faced appeals from the cotton textile industry for relief, and out of necessity it negotiated voluntary export restraints with Japan. Besieged with lobbyists requesting quotas and special legislation, Congress deflected protectionist pressures to the U.S. Tariff Commission and reminded the executive branch that it had authority to take "emergency action to relieve distress in industries being affected by increasing imports."[131] It directed the commission to expedite textile investigation brought under the escape clause. A 1958 TC report indicated that over the preceding five years one-third of the escape clause applications involved articles imported mainly from Japan. These included velveteen fabrics, ginghams, cotton pillowcases, women's and girls' cotton blouses, Toyo cloth caps, woolen gloves, hardwood plywood, stainless steel flatware, umbrella frames, and clinical thermometers.[132]

The unbalanced agreement with Japan produced strong reactions in Congress—particularly when the RTAP came up for renewal in 1958. On this occasion, the Senate Finance Committee refused the Eisenhower administration's request for a five-year extension and authority to reduce tariffs an additional 25 percent. It noted, after hearing witnesses, that "the protection afforded domestic industries by way of tariffs is at an unprecedented low point and extreme caution must be exercised in future negotiations to mitigate possible injury to the domestic industry." The Finance Committee instructed the administrative agencies to "make some progress toward the mitigating of trade restrictions abroad."[133]

Mounting Concerns about Trade Policy

By 1959 the Eisenhower administration was aware of an emerging conflict between unilateral tariff reduction policies used to achieve foreign policy objectives and the rising demand for import restraints in Congress. An important debate occurred in the National Security Council in June. In briefing the participants, William T. Beale, the deputy assistant secretary of state for economic affairs, observed that American trade restrictions had "an increasingly serious effect upon our ability to achieve our foreign policy objectives." Such import barriers affected 28 percent (or $2.1 billion) of U.S. trade, he asserted, including $1.5 billion in oil imports. The State Department official declared that each decision to limit imports had negative foreign policy repercussions. Thus restrictions on woolen tops caused Uruguay to sell goods to the Soviet bloc, and higher duties on oil, lead, and zinc produced foreign policy problems in Peru and Venezuela.[134]

In short, the State Department claimed that import restrictions hampered the conduct of U.S. foreign policy and would "determine to an important extent" whether "we are successful in the economic contest with the Soviet Union." What the State Department advocated, in place of import restrictions to protect domestic industries from import-related injury, was a predictable panacea: adjustment assistance for dislocated workers and producers.

President Eisenhower shared the State Department's point of view. He considered it "silly" that eleven foreign nations were affected by U.S. import restrictions on clothespins, which were made by only six small companies in Maine employing 260 employees. Some kind of "adjustment policy . . . would enable us to find a solution for some of our domestic industries in the face of foreign competition," Eisenhower said. Clothespin manufacturers, he suggested, might switch to the production of baseball bats. The president also spoke of the "mental anguish" he experienced whenever he "declared a restriction on the import of a commodity from abroad." In his opinion, trade restrictions "which tend to drive away an ally as dependable as Great Britain . . . do much more harm in the long run to our security than would be done by permitting a U.S. industry to suffer from British competition."[135]

Interestingly, during the National Security Council discussion, several other senior officials voiced reservations about the administration's short-term approach to national security. Secretary of the Treasury Robert Anderson noted that the balance of payments was the "acid test" of a sound economy, and he warned that the United States would be in "real trouble" if the deficit continued. "We have bitten off rather more obligations than we can chew," he said. CIA director John McCone also predicted that "the problem of foreign competition with American business was a problem that was going to grow rapidly in the future. The costs of production abroad of competitive products were shockingly lower than costs in the U.S., mostly as a result of cheaper labor costs."[136] From this broad-ranging discussion, it is apparent that at least some members of Eisenhower's cabinet foresaw the emerging problems of competing in an international economy. Of course, Eisenhower himself continued to put foreign policy considerations first.

Cordell Hull and his associates had pulled off a revolution in U.S. trade policy. As a result of the Reciprocal Trade Agreements Program, the average tariff level fell 80 percent, effectively opening the U.S. market to international competition and helping to erase the merchandise surplus that had embarrassed U.S. officials during the 1930s. Over time foreign suppliers with new facilities and lower cost structures would enter the giant American market, bringing the heat of global competition to high-paid U.S. workers and producers. When the Eisenhower administration left office in 1960, foreign policy continued to drive U.S. trade policy. It had done so since 1937, when the State Department presented the RTAP to Congress as a vehicle for "economic appeasement and stability." During the decade after World War II executive branch officials gave priority to international cooperation, using unbalanced trade concessions as levers to promote overall diplomatic objectives. The 1947 Geneva negotiations and the 1955 bilateral agreement with Japan stand out as monuments to the strategy that assigned priority to foreign policy and to international economic cooperation.

Without a doubt it was important—and necessary—to defeat Nazi Germany and to contain, and eventually defeat, Soviet Russia. It is arguable, however, that the course selected by U.S. decision makers imposed unnecessary burdens on U.S. producers and workers, severely harmed long-term U.S. economic performance, and circumvented the authority and will of Congress. As the more recent experience of Japan suggests, the United States had another option. It might have continued to protect the home market, using tariff and nontariff barriers, while encouraging the export of U.S. goods and private capital. In President Eisenhower's cabinet, only Treasury Secretary George Humphrey and Commerce Secretary Sinclair Weeks expressed support for this traditional Republican approach. Cosmopolitan in outlook and preoccupied with security issues, Eisenhower embraced and sustained the trade liberalization program. In effect, he led Republicans from protectionism to Cobdenism.[137]

The Kennedy Round has moved the world a step closer to freer trade, which will help us all.—President Lyndon Johnson, 1967

In today's world, all major countries must pursue freer trade if each country is to do so. The principle of true reciprocity must lie at the heart of trade policy—as it lies at the heart of all foreign policy.—President Richard M. Nixon, 1970

Opening America's Market, 1960–1974

"Each generation builds a road for the next," said President John F. Kennedy in May 1962, quoting an old Chinese saying. The Trade Expansion Act (TEA), he predicted, would "build our road for the next generation."[1] The president foresaw enormous gains from freer trade benefiting American workers, producers, and consumers, while improving the nation's competitiveness internationally. Praising his TEA as the most important piece of international economic legislation since "passage of the Marshall Plan," Kennedy predicted great stimulus "from increased export opportunities as other nations agree to lower their tariffs. . . . The results can bring a dynamic new era of growth." Because "a vital expanding economy in the free world is a strong counter to the threat of the world Communist movement," Kennedy also viewed the act as "an important new weapon to advance the cause of freedom."[2]

As his rhetoric indicated, a sense of mission and a concern for global security interests continued to drive American foreign economic policy during the Kennedy administration, as it had since World War II. The United States had assisted the victors and victims of that conflict to recover and become prosperous participants in the international economy. It also provided military assistance and security guarantees to smaller powers vulnerable to Cold War pressures. Until the mid-1960s the United States had carried these hegemonic responsibilities with apparent ease. It acted as a banker to the world, as a customer for the exports of other nations, and as the major provider of military security to the Western world.[3]

Eager to promote recovery and stability abroad and to strengthen defenses against communist expansionism, the U.S. State Department dismantled tariff barriers and invited European and Asian manufacturers to sell in the huge American market. In thus acquiescing to unbalanced trade concessions, Norwegian historian Geir Lundestad has suggested that the United States was "organizing its own decline."[4]

President Kennedy saw events differently. He had an optimistic vision of the future. In removing barriers to the world's imports, he believed that the United States could act as a giant engine of economic development for developing nations. In a 1963 speech Kennedy addressed the "Atlantic responsibility" to open "our markets to the developing countries of Africa, Asia, and Latin America." Recalling an expression used on Cape Cod, the president stated that "a rising tide lifts all the boats. . . . Together we have been partners in adversity—let us also be partners in prosperity."[5]

Economic Outlook

When President Kennedy entered office in January 1961 there were some indications of trouble. U.S. exports as a share of industrial countries' exports continued to slide, falling from 32 percent in 1950 to 28 percent in 1960 to 20 percent in 1973.[6] The dollar, long the linchpin of the Bretton Woods monetary system, faced speculative pressures.

The domestic U.S. economy appeared sound, however. The Eisenhower administration had balanced the domestic budget three times in eight years—the most in two presidential terms since the 1920s—and maintained price stability. Unemployment stood at a troublesome 5.5 percent, but 54 million Americans had nonagricultural jobs—more than ever before. During the twenty years from 1947 to 1967, real gross national product rose at a 4 percent annual rate, a full point above the 3 percent average for the sixty-year period from 1910 to 1970. Output per worker in manufacturing rose 77.5 percent, nearly as fast as real hourly compensation at 79.5 percent. The number of production workers in manufacturing climbed 13 percent, from 12.7 million to 14.4 million workers. Weekly earnings for production workers increased 57 percent. And total manufacturing employment rose by 3.9 million workers.

In these circumstances, it was understandable that President Kennedy should propose to accelerate the quest for trade liberalization in order to address foreign policy problems. In 1961 the future of Western Europe remained a troublesome issue for U.S. policymakers. Since World War II the U.S. government had encouraged the movement for European unification through the Marshall Plan, the European Coal and Steel Community, the Organization for European Economic Cooperation, and in 1957 the formation of the European Economic Community (EEC). In political and strategic terms Washington favored these regional efforts to bind Germany and France together permanently.[7]

During the Kennedy years the regional integration of Europe appeared to present serious trade-diverting implications for third countries—especially in agricultural trade. The president anticipated that if Britain joined the Common Market, and smaller European Free Trade Association countries followed, the expanded European market could take 30 percent of U.S. exports. But studies also indicated that the common external tariff might negatively affect some 60 percent of U.S. exports as customers within the Common Market shifted purchases to other European suppliers.[8]

Consequently, the new administration attempted to fashion a foreign economic policy that continued to support European regional integration and unification while promoting further liberalization of the international trading system. To achieve both objectives, Kennedy's team wanted additional tariff-cutting authority for multilateral trade negotiations under the auspices of GATT. Appreciating that a dynamic regional market was emerging in Western Europe, Kennedy and his advisers considered further multilateral market-opening negotiations as a lever to pursue the historic American quest for open and nondiscriminatory trade. And over the decade Western Europe moved forward toward regional economic integration and became more competitive in world markets. The average annual growth for European exports soared from 8.2 percent in the 1950s to 10.1 percent in 1960s and to 19.3 percent in the 1970s. Europe's share of world exports rose from 33.1 percent in 1950 to 43.2 percent in 1970. Meanwhile, Japanese exports grew 15.9 percent annually during the 1950s, 17.5 percent during the 1960s, and 20.8 percent during the 1970s. Its share of world exports rose from 1.4 percent in 1950 to 6.1 percent in 1970.[9]

DILLON ROUND PROBLEMS

Public officials must respond pragmatically to a variety of inherited problems, and the Kennedy administration found several percolating on the stove in 1961 as it contemplated new GATT negotiations. One involved the Dillon

Round of trade negotiations in Geneva. Eager to encourage the European Economic Community to pursue open trade policies, State Department officials took a keen interest in these negotiations, although they had little negotiating authority. In 1958, when Congress last renewed reciprocal trade authority, it had limited the president's tariff reduction authority to 15 percent over three years. Not more than 5 percent of these cuts could take effect in any given year.[10] An increasingly skeptical Congress also strengthened safeguard provisions and retained the peril point. The latter directed the U.S. Tariff Commission to investigate and report for individual products the lowest rate of duty necessary to avoid serious injury to the domestic industry.

This peril point restriction handcuffed the executive branch. The Tariff Commission had submitted peril point findings that reduced the items listed for possible tariff concessions in 1959 to only 17.5 percent of total imports from countries with which the State Department contemplated negotiations. When this happened, Secretary of State Christian Herter informed President Eisenhower that "unless the United States is able to induce the EEC to accept a one-sided agreement," it was unlikely that America would be able to secure "the lowest possible level in the new common external tariff of the EEC as well as substantial tariff reductions by other countries." The administration had proceeded cautiously, restricting the commodities listed for actual tariff concessions to only 26.3 percent of total imports and acquiescing to the TC's high peril points on listed items.[11]

President Eisenhower's response reveals that he had revised his thinking on unreciprocated trade concessions since the 1955 bilateral negotiations with Japan. He said: "it seems to me we ought to put our own current balance of payments situation very strongly before the conferees and make unmistakably clear that *we have gotten into this situation through generous and liberal assistance and trading policies*. Now it is time for them to do their share, and a failure on their part to do so would bring into question our basic relationships and attitudes toward these problems" (emphasis added).

During the Dillon Round, the European Economic Community offered steep linear cuts—that is, as a percentage of ad valorem duties. But in 1958 Congress restricted U.S. negotiating authority and insisted on use of the traditional item-by-item approach when it authorized renewal of the trade agreements program. U.S. negotiators could offer only 20 percent cuts on existing rates, and these cuts must be negotiated, as previously, on an "item-by-item" basis. Furthermore, the peril point requirement, which required a TC determination on all items to be listed for negotiations, ensured that the negotiators would not violate the long-standing no-injury pledge to domestic producers. When tariff reductions did cause serious injury to domestic industries, the Tariff Commission had authority in an escape clause investigation to recommend withdrawal of the concession. The executive branch feared that use of the escape clause option could undercut the process of tariff liberalization and provoke European protests and retaliation. This had occurred when President Kennedy accepted an escape clause recommendation on carpets and glass.[12]

During the actual negotiations, the State Department attempted to argue that the United States was entitled to some over-payments on account of concessions . . . made in the past." Because of quantitative restrictions, the United States claimed that it "had not received reciprocal benefits." But the Europeans rejected that argument. A British official observed that "memories were short in matters of this kind." Instead, London argued that the United States needed to sweeten its offers. And so the State Department again approached the White House to complain that it lacked "bargaining authority" to successfully negotiate with Great Britain on a range of traditional export products: china, cutlery, flatware, cotton yarns and textiles, and woolen and sporting goods. This time State urged President Kennedy to breach peril point findings and to instruct the Trade Policy Committee, chaired by the Secretary of Commerce, to "resolve doubtful cases in favor of granting our negotiators the necessary increased bargaining power."[13]

Eager to salvage the Dillon Round and to cooperate with the Europeans, Kennedy agreed to waive limitations on a number of import-sensitive items. These included steel products, machine tools, tableware, ferrochromium, firearms, yarns, woven fabrics, toweling, and linen handkerchiefs among others.[14] The president also authorized a concession on agriculture with far-reaching implications. It affected Europe's new Common Agricultural Policy (CAP) as well as existing American commercial rights. In six earlier rounds of trade negotiations the United States had purchased with its own concessions foreign tariff bindings and reductions to facilitate U.S. agricultural exports to Europe. In 1960 agricultural exports to Europe ($2.2 billion) amounted to 33 percent of total U.S. exports to Europe. But to complete the Common Market, Europe unbound the national concessions and established a program of variable levies. Particularly for wheat, corn, grain sorghum, rice, and poultry, the new system jeopardized U.S. exports. In negotiations, the EEC refused to bind new common rates or to guarantee access for U.S. agricultural exports.

Once again the State Department forced a decision adverse to domestic producers. Rather than insist on new bindings and possibly jeopardize the Dillon Round's outcome, as well as the political momentum for European unification, State recommended concluding the negotiating round. As Congressman Thomas Curtis, a member of the Ways and Means Committee, noted later, in these GATT negotiations "the President and his advisers decided that the variable levy would be the price the United States would pay for the growth of the EEC and for other concessions in the Dillon round." As this episode illustrates, when foreign policy interests—in this case, support for the European Economic Community—conflicted with U.S. export interests, the State Department had no difficulty sorting out its priorities and influencing Kennedy administration policy.[15]

In December 1961 State presented "dire predictions" that "chaos will ensue in our international trade, and the entire GATT arrangements would be in danger of collapsing" if the United States did not conclude the Dillon Round. An angry Department of Agriculture complained to the White House that the results were inadequate for U.S. farmers producing tobacco, vegetable oils, prunes, and the like. The Kennedy White House listened to Foggy Bottom.[16]

State won the Dillon Round battle, but it lost the war in Washington. The decisions on agriculture and peril points left bitter feelings on Capitol Hill. The unusual determination to ignore peril point limitations on so many tariff items aroused the administration's critics in Congress—particularly Senator Prescott Bush of Connecticut—and encouraged the lawmakers to curb the State Department's role in trade negotiations when it fashioned the 1962 Trade Expansion Act.[17]

TEXTILE PROBLEMS

State Department backsliding on efforts to regulate textile imports also jeopardized the trade liberalization program. The textile firestorm had ignited during the mid-1950s, when cheap cotton and woolen imports began to hammer the domestic textile industry. It is well documented in reports of the Senate Commerce Committee. Over the decade from 1947 to 1957, the committee found declining textile production, except in the case of man-made fibers. Production of woolen and worsted goods dropped 44.2 percent. With 717 mills closed, displacing 196,875 workers, total employment in textile mills fell 24 percent, from 1.3 million workers in 1947 to about 1 million in 1957. The Senate committee also heard testimony critical of the Eisenhower administration's efforts to address the problem through voluntary textile restraints. The foreign aid program also came under attack. In 1957, for example, the International Cooperation Administration (ICA) purchased $96.3 million of textiles, but only $7.2 million (7 percent) went for American-made textile products. Senate investigators found that ICA had financed foreign textile machinery purchases—especially to France, Italy, and the United Kingdom. Subsequently, imports, particularly of woolen cloth, increased from these three countries.[18]

As part of his successful 1960 presidential campaign, Senator John F. Kennedy pledged protection for the textile industry. Early in the Kennedy administration, Senator Pastore's committee issued a supplementary report recommending a program of flexible quotas on textile products, covering cotton and woolen mill products, apparel, and man-made fibers. "To us the facts indicate an urgent need for remedial action," the report asserted.[19]

The State Department, however, attempted to block restraints and limit coverage. Undersecretary of State George Ball, an Adlai Stevenson internationalist and a former lobbyist for European and other foreign interests, took personal charge of the negotiations. Ball recalled later how he took "private and secret gratification" in appearing before U.S. textile makers "dressed in a British-made suit, a British-made shirt, shoes made for me in Hong Kong, and a French necktie." Ball and his aide Warren Christopher devised a program of cotton textile restraints that permitted importing nations to refuse imports when imports surged, threatening to disrupt the domestic market, but allowed for orderly growth. This program, Ball said, was "the least I could get away with, since I had to get the American cotton textile industry off the President's back." The cotton textile restraint program, State Department officials knew, was a necessary evil if the Kennedy administration was to win critical support for the TEA in Congress.[20]

Although President Kennedy pledged to limit cotton imports to 5.2 percent of the domestic market, the level reached in fiscal year 1961, imports continued to surge. The Johnson administration's official history of the program notes that the growth in trade resulted from several factors—including "State Department reluctance to make the necessary diplomatic approaches." In 1965 and 1966 the State Department even succeeded in liberalizing access for Japan and Hong Kong textile exporters.[21]

Whereas cotton goods producers gained some relief from imports, woolen and man-made fibers did not. The State Department succeeded in confining initial efforts to cotton textiles, despite "misgivings by the Department of Commerce and by the labor-management industry advisors." In January 1964 the Japanese told Secretary of Commerce Luther Hodges that in the course of negotiating the long-term cotton agreement, all countries, including the United States, had agreed that "no agreement would be sought on wool."

Wool imports continued to surge, rising from 13.3 percent of domestic consumption in 1961 to 20.6 percent in 1963. During the 1964 presidential campaign President Lyndon Johnson praised the Kennedy-Johnson administration efforts to prevent cotton textile imports from disrupting the domestic market. He pledged vigorous efforts to assist woolen textiles and apparel, declaring: "I consider it essential that the wool textile industry be restored to good health."[22]

Johnson was unwilling to push for a long-term agreement covering woolens when Great Britain and Japan refused to negotiate. Warren Christopher did lead a delegation of wool makers to Japan in June 1965. Both sides exchanged threats—with Christopher warning that Congress might be forced to act and the Japanese saying: "We do not like political threats. We are not North Vietnam. We hope you will make distinctions between your friends and enemies."[23]

The following year, as the economy picked up and inflation revived, White House staff assistants Francis Bator and Harry McPherson advised Johnson of ways to "get us off the hook." They said efforts to continue restricting cotton imports tightly and to add wool quotas were "*bad economics, bad foreign policy, and bad domestic politics.*" Along with citing inflation problems, they noted that "we are paying a foreign policy price in our relations with textile producing countries." Giving Singapore as an example, they noted that attempts to impose quotas on cotton goods might result in unemployment. This "is likely to lead to anti-U.S. street agitation and strikes." Assistant Secretary of State Bill Bundy also voiced concerns. Anti-Western rioting in Singapore might jeopardize the British base there. But an exception for Singapore would produce trouble with Taiwan, Japan, and Korea. "They are angry at us already about textiles."[24]

In Foggy Bottom, there was concern that the textiles dispute might impact negatively on overriding political and defense relationships. Over the next four years the Commerce, Labor, and Treasury Departments supported an effort to extend the long-term cotton agreement to man-made and woolen textiles, but the State Department, special trade negotiator, Council of Economic Advisers, and Budget Bureau opposed it.[25]

Kennedy Round Preparations

Frustrated by the statutory restraints on its freedom of action, the Kennedy administration resolved to seek a new grant of negotiating authority that would enable it to respond flexibly and fully to the European commercial challenge and to encourage Great Britain's joining the continental market. Underlying this strategy was a willingness to provide all Free World countries improved access to the U.S. market. To Washington, greater economic unification would strengthen trading partners against the communist economic offensive.

The Kennedy administration understood that an ambitious trade liberalization program to integrate the Free World must necessarily injure some domestic industries. At least in communicating with trading partners, U.S. officials openly accepted these consequences. They told British officials: "improving standards of living are reaped in the form of imports, and exports should only be looked upon as a means of obtaining imports." The United States believed that "stepped-up competition from imports" would impart new strength and vigor to the American economy. But this "necessary" structural adjustment would prove "painful."[26]

Appreciating that future tariff cuts would affect some U.S. industries and workers adversely as reciprocal concessions created new export opportunities, administration strategists chose to eviscerate the escape clause. Instead, the president would obtain authority to provide adjustment assistance to import-impacted workers and firms. Privately, they recognized that although "adjustment assistance is politically desirable," it was "not likely to be much help in practice."[27]

In his own public statements President Kennedy lauded the adjustment assistance option. He told the December 1961 AFL-CIO convention that this new program of safeguards would "provide a recognition of the national responsibility in the period of transition for those industries and people who may be adversely affected." Kennedy said that he did not intend to see those hit hard by imports "made victims for the national welfare. I do not intend to give them a medal and an empty grocery bag." However, "more absolute protection," such as higher tariffs, risked "driving potential trading partners into the arms of the Soviets, denying competitive prices to our consumers and industry, and shutting off the export markets abroad on which our own job and growth opportunities depend."[28]

In December 1961, speaking to the National Association of Manufacturers, Kennedy called for the "two great Common Markets of the Atlantic" to lead industrial nations in lowering trade barriers. At the heart of the administration's request for a "new and bold instrument of American trade policy," he said, would be a linear negotiating strategy. Instead of negotiating item by item in a laborious process, the United States would for the first time agree to chop tariffs across the board by 50 percent. The administration would seek a five-year mandate of negotiating authority to look for reciprocal concessions. As an incentive for Britain to become a Common Market member, the administration sought authority to remove tariffs entirely on items in which Europe and the United States were responsible for 80 percent or more of world production.[29]

Other objectives, Kennedy stated, were to help expand U.S. export markets—to "maintain the free flow of our agricultural commodities into the Common Market"—so as to discourage American industry from "jumping the wall in order to compete." In addition, improved export opportunities would take pressure off the U.S. balance of payments and the possible need to withdraw troops from Europe. "[O]ur imports will . . . increase," Kennedy said, "but not as much as our exports."[30]

The interests of Japan and the developing countries were important as well. "We do not want Japan left out of this great market," Kennedy told the National Association of Manufacturers. Privately, some administration officials advised that the negotiating round be used to persuade Europe to accept Japanese goods and thus take "some of the pressure off Japanese sales to the United States." Kennedy also raised the need for developed nations to open their markets to the products of developing countries.[31]

With the submission of Kennedy's trade bill in January 1962, attention turned to Congress, where the House Ways and Means Committee and the Senate Finance Committee would hold hearings and write the actual legislation. In Ways and Means Chairman Wilbur Mills generally supported the White House initiative, as did Representative Hale Boggs, (D-La.), the majority whip. With heavy public interest in the proposals, the House committee devoted an entire month to public hearings and heard from more than four hundred witnesses.

At these sessions, the administration lined up a coalition of important supporters. AFL-CIO president George Meany backed the bill, explaining that "this program, properly implemented, will offer to American private enterprise a far greater opportunity to expand its markets around the world; and it therefore holds out the prospects of more jobs for American workers, as well." But "indispensable" to labor's support, Meany said, was a provision for adjustment assistance.[32]

Other supporters included export giants like Caterpillar, importers, and foreign business groups. Nelson A. Stitt, director of the U.S.-Japan Trade Council, anticipated congressional concerns about a "flood" of Japanese imports. Noting that Japan experienced a bilateral trade deficit with the United States, he cited estimates of an increase in Japanese exports to the United States from $1.1 billion in 1961 to $2.5 to $3 billion by 1970. But, he said, it was "obvious that Japan's capacity to export is confined within relatively narrow limits. The projected increase of Japanese exports to the United States in the next 10 years is by no means a 'flood.'"[33]

In light of subsequent developments—intense foreign competition in the U.S. market for consumer, intermediate, and capital goods—it is appropriate to examine carefully the comments of several key industries during congressional hearings. The National Machine Tool Builders Association, which incidentally would lose some forty points of market share from 1968 to 1988, vigorously opposed the president's proposals. Francis J. Trecker, the association president, told the Ways and Means Committee that the industry had only "marginal technical superiority" over foreign competitors, and it faced "relatively unique problems as a high labor content industry of vital importance to our national security."[34]

Producers of antifriction bearings warned that the Trade Expansion Act "would cause upheavals in our economy and to our free enterprise system of unpredictable proportions." Said Harry Purcell, vice president of the Torrington Company, "the great danger that is inherent in a policy of uncontrolled imports can no longer be disregarded or minimized. The evidence is all around us, in chronic unemployment and underemployment, in factories going abroad, and going south, or just going out of business." He also observed that U.S. producers faced a variety of nontariff barriers selling abroad, including import licensing, cartels, currency manipulation, exchange permits, and quotas.[35]

The Electronic Industries Association approved the broad objectives of nondiscrimination and trade expansion but expressed a number of specific concerns. The industry as a whole had a $436 million trade surplus in 1961, but Japanese imports had risen rapidly—especially transistor radios. Indeed, within three or four years some expected the Japanese industry to introduce color television sets at prices one-third lower than domestic firms could offer. "Japanese electronic shipments of all types to this country rose from $250,000 in 1955 to $94 million in 1960 and an estimated $120 million in 1961." The electronics industry wanted Congress to place additional restrictions on the "extraordinary power" that House Resolution 9900 would grant the president over U.S. industry. It desired a greater emphasis on "true reciprocity" in order to knock down nontariff barriers restricting U.S. exports. Too often, said H. B. McCoy, an industry consultant, "we have in the past been trading horses for rabbits."[36]

Business equipment manufacturers complained about the "lack of reciprocity" between foreign countries and the United States. Edwin J. Graf, vice president of Smith-Corona Marchant, noted that whereas the United States had bound its typewriter duties on the free list, duties in other countries ranged from 4 to 25 percent, creating a competitive disparity. "[T]he domestic typewriter industry . . . is exposed to competition from companies sheltered by high tariffs against American made machines," he stated. The typewriter industry noted that U.S. producers had to pay prescribed minimum wages on government sales, whereas federal procurement practices exempted foreign competitors from satisfying fair labor standards.[37]

The Kennedy administration had greased the way in Congress, and the Trade Expansion Act (H.R. 11970) slid through easily after some revisions. The Ways and Means Committee version of the TEA passed 299 to 125 on June 28, 1962. The Senate bill sailed through 78 to 8.[38]

House opposition cut across party lines, with John Dent of Pennsylvania leading the Democratic protectionists. On final passage, 218 Democrats supported the president and 35 voted against him. Eight Republicans were for the TEA and 90 opposed it. The opposition included twenty-three southerners, many representing textile areas, or constituencies with labor-intensive industries. Noah M. Mason of Illinois and Jackson Betts of Ohio led McKinleyite

Republicans in the opposition.[39] They focused on the revolutionary nature of Kennedy's proposal. Previously, the Reciprocal Trade Agreements Program had provided for "gradual and selective tariff reduction, one which gives public consideration to each item before any reduction in tariffs is made, and which provides opportunity for reconsideration when serious injury occurs or is threatened." But as Betts, a Yale-educated attorney from northwestern Ohio, observed: "The vice of H.R. 11970 is that it rejects any and all regulations of imports. It throws the U.S. market open to unlimited importation of goods from every nation of every kind and description, without the possibility for adjustment in the future."[40]

Criticizing the unprecedented delegation of power to the president, the removal of effective safeguards, and continued reliance on the unconditional most-favored-nation policy, Betts forecast that it was "only a question of time" until the United States would receive imports from "every industrialized nation and every emerging nation turning to industry as a natural means of improving their standard of living."[41]

In the Senate some of the most vigorous opposition came from Senator Prescott Bush of Connecticut. He proposed an amendment to restore the peril point and lost by only two votes (40–38) on September 18. On final passage Bush and seven colleagues—Republicans Wallace Bennett (Utah), Norris Cotton (N.H.), Carl Curtis (Nebr.), Barry Goldwater (Ariz.), Len B. Jordan (Idaho), and Karl Mundt (S.Dak.) and Democrat Strom Thurmond (S.C.)— cast negative votes. Bush warned that the tariff-cutting authority would lead to unemployment for "hundreds of thousands of American workers." He rejected a measure that "would give the President the authority deliberately to vacate the no-injury policy, which has been the historic policy, and substitute for it economic hospitals and first aid stations."[42]

In retrospect, it is clear that the Kennedy TEA, as approved by Congress, marked a significant departure from previous reciprocal trade extensions. As Cordell Hull aide Harry Hawkins and his associate Janet Norwood observed: "The TEA extends to the President greater flexibility and tariff-reducing authority than any other legislation in the history of the trade-agreements program." Thus "the opportunities for significant tariff reductions . . . are unparalleled."[43] Congress authorized multilateral negotiations to reduce duties 50 percent and even to eliminate levies on some items. It provided a mandate of negotiating authority with a June 30, 1967, expiration date and consented to weakened peril point and escape clause procedures. The law did not bar concessions that might cause injury or adjustment problems for domestic industries and workers. Importantly, for the first time Congress authorized "across the board" reductions, not simply item-by-item cuts. However, Capitol Hill also exercised its prerogative to limit and structure the negotiations. It established the position of special trade negotiator and insisted that any agreements relating to nontariff barriers be submitted to Congress for implementation.[44] It also stipulated that members of Congress from both parties would participate in negotiations.

In drafting the act, State Department supporters of an Atlantic partnership—including the EEC with Great Britain and the United States—inserted a provision allowing the elimination of tariffs on items where the Common Market and the United States generated 80 percent of world production.[45] This provision proved unworkable after President Charles de Gaulle of France vetoed Britain's application for admission to the European European Community in January 1963.

Negotiating at Geneva

Lyndon Johnson, a devoted free trader, succeeded the assassinated Kennedy in November 1963. He agreed to press the trade liberalization agenda. Eager to continue the multilateral process begun in 1947, the executive branch initially sought an accommodation with the emerging European Economic Community on a broad range of outstanding trade problems—including agricultural protectionism. The Johnson administration signaled that although it was prepared to "offer our free world friends access to American markets, . . . we *expect* and we *must have access to* their markets also. That applies to our *agricultural* as well as our *industrial* exports" (emphasis added). The United States, Johnson said in April 1964, "will enter into no ultimate agreement unless progress is registered toward trade liberalization on the products of our farms as well as our factories." The administration, increasingly nervous over balance-of-payments problems, acknowledged that because of global defense commitments, U.S. "exports must substantially exceed imports, if we are to keep our currency sound."[46]

This warning apparently was directed primarily at Europe, not Japan. Regarding the latter, the special trade representative's office listed as a "most important negotiating objective" modifying "the Japanese Government's highly protective attitude toward its industries, which inevitably is translated into reduced imports, irrespective of the level of tariff or status of non-tariff barriers, because of the close working relationship between government and industry."[47]

The Commerce and Agriculture Departments were cautious about negotiating prospects. Secretary of Commerce John T. Connor reported decreased export performance during the first five months of 1965 and told the president: "accumulating evidence suggests that we must be prepared to cover a large increase in imports, and to compensate elsewhere in the balance of payments for a decline in the over-all trade surplus." Secretary of Agriculture Orville Freeman was pessimistic about the outlook for meaningful agricultural gains in the Kennedy Round, and he resisted, unsuccessfully, the administration's plan to table sweeping proposed cuts in the U.S. tariff. Freeman wanted to withhold offers until the EEC was prepared to participate in agricultural negotiations, but foreign policy advisers prevailed. Even so, National security adviser McGeorge Bundy told President Johnson: "Agriculture in the Kennedy Round is not going to be a success story. The problem is to prevent it from being a failure that is marked as our fault."[48]

A related issue involved negotiating tactics. In the Kennedy Round the United States would follow its long-established practice of tabling large offers and then withdrawing items from the table when other powers failed to match proposed concessions. From the standpoint of the special trade negotiator, this approach had succeeded in previous negotiations when the United States tabled large offers in order to maximize pressure on other participants to maximize their own offers. As a result, America chopped away its own tariff barriers, frequently in exchange for pledges from other nations to remove tariffs and nontariff restrictions in the future. According to deputy special trade representative Bill Roth, "the opposite tactic of beginning with low offers and negotiating upwards tends to lessen the total scope and substance of the negotiations."[49]

The Department of Agriculture disagreed. Anxious to gain meaningful access for U.S. farms exports to the Common Market, it proposed a different approach. Secretary Orville Freeman believed that on agriculture the EEC would make "no meaningful offer." "It appears that all the EEC is trying to do is legalize internationally its notorious variable levy and gate price system, which relegates third countries to a residual supplier position." Already, he said, U.S. industrial and agricultural offers were unbalanced and would necessitate withdrawals; yet it would be difficult to withdraw them later, particularly for developing countries that "complain bitterly about the lack of preferential access to our markets for their raw materials."[50]

For U.S. policymakers the Kennedy Round also offered an opportunity to create market opportunities for developing countries. This was a response to demands from seventy-seven developing nations participating in the first United Nations Conference on Trade and Development, held in Geneva in the spring of 1964, for a positive program to encourage their exports. In November a U.S. task force on foreign economic policy recommended to President Johnson a "war on poverty—worldwide." Focusing on North-South problems, the group—headed by economist Carl Kaysen—suggested importing more manufactures from developing countries. "The whole country would be the gainer if, over time, we could shift resources away from textiles, shoes and other unsophisticated manufactures into more advanced items where we have a real comparative advantage. These are mainly items which use resources that are higher-paid and relatively more abundant here than abroad—capital, scientific and technological research, skilled and educated labor."[51]

For the Kennedy Round multilateral trade negotiations, 1967 was the critical year. Eric Wyndham White, the director general of GATT, effused that "there is every reason to hope that, at the end of the Kennedy Round, a substantial measure of *tariff disarmament* will have been achieved and that the general level of tariffs will have been so far reduced as to set the stage for a further significant growth in international trade" (emphasis added). The Kennedy Round, he said, would be a "doorway to the future" in which a free trade arrangement would emerge among major industrialized nations and discriminatory restrictions on developing country exports would be swept away. President Kennedy had "invited the world to prepare for an era of interdependence. The full implications of this interdependence have perhaps not yet been fully envisaged nor the consequences absorbed and accepted." Within the administration the Kennedy Round negotiations also continued to generate great enthusiasm, as would the Uruguay Round a generation later. Bill Roth was already looking to the future—toward an initiative in 1969 aimed at opening markets for less developed countries. He urged the president to emphasize the Kennedy Round in his January 1967 State of the Union message as a matter of "pre-eminent economic and political significance." But President Johnson had other concerns—notably the Vietnam War and unrest in the United States—and his State of the Union message lacked any "significant mention" of the Kennedy Round. Others in Congress and Europe interpreted this omission as a positive signal to the footdraggers. Congressman Thomas Curtis, of Missouri, a Ways and Means Committee member who reported regularly on GATT developments to his colleagues, asserted: "I have to conclude that President Johnson apparently does not understand the importance of the trade program."[52]

On Capitol Hill, opposition to the Kennedy Round grew. Senator Everett Dirksen of Illinois and Representative Gerald Ford of Michigan, the Republican leaders, released critical statements in March 1967. Dirksen said that "Republicans in Congress strongly favor truly reciprocal trade" but noted that "for years the United States has not benefitted reciprocally from its trade agreements. . . . A number of basic domestic industries have suffered grievously under unwisely 'liberalized' customs and tariff practices and ineptly administered trade agreements legislation. Foreign-produced goods have prospered in our markets. But foreign markets have not reciprocally responded to our products of America's mines, farms, forests and industry." Dirksen also criticized the administration for ignoring Tariff Commission advice on the probable effects of tariff reductions and for failing to administer existing trade remedy laws—particularly the escape clause relief, antidumping, and countervailing duty statutes. The Republican leader in the Senate warned that "sweeping across-the-board reductions in duty being pursued by the United States in the Kennedy Round could have an even worse effect on the trade position of the United States in future years."[53]

Key Democrats had concerns about the trade agreements program and Kennedy Round concessions. The chairman of the Senate Finance Committee, Russell Long of Louisiana, told the press that "this nation in its trade and aid programs has played the part of Andy Gump until it is on the verge of becoming an international Barney Google." Deciding to hold oversight hearings on trade administration as a way to stiffen the U.S. negotiating position, Long announced at the opening session that "the advantages of freer trade can come only if concessions on all sides are truly reciprocal." Senator George Smathers (D-Fla.) urged trade representative Bill Roth to "stoutly defend our market, the greatest market on earth, from those who are unwilling to strike a fair bargain with us." He advised Roth to "look at the bargain closely and coldly, and agree to it only if we get as much as we give. Don't trade off a horse and accept a rabbit. Don't trade off a barrel of wheat for a biscuit. *If agriculture does not get a fair shake there should be no agreement*" (emphasis added).[54]

Other Finance Committee members also were upset. Senator Vance Hartke (D-Ind.), an ally of organized labor, called the Trade Expansion Act a "colossal failure." He declared: "Our economy cannot be dismantled to make the rest of the world happy."[55]

Senator Abraham Ribicoff (D-Conn.), the elected successor to Prescott Bush, had also become a vigorous critic of Johnson administration trade policies. In particular, Ribicoff remained dissatisfied with the 1965 bilateral U.S.-Canadian auto agreement. To forestall a U.S. Treasury countervailing duty determination that was expected to damage bilateral political relations, the State Department fashioned an automotive products market-sharing agreement with Canada. In effect, it was a one-sided "free trade agreement" opening the U.S. market to Canadian automotive products. Only original equipment manufacturers could import vehicles and parts freely into Canada; consumers could not. Other side understandings between U.S. auto producers and the Canadian government effectively transferred auto production—and jobs—to Canada. The result was a $657 million automotive products trade surplus with Canada in 1965 turned negative. Over the next twenty-five years the United States experienced automotive deficits with Canada in all but one year.

"It was a bad agreement," Senator Ribicoff said. "[S]old as free trade, it is the very antithesis of free trade, a restrictive bilateral arrangement for the benefit of Canadian industrial expansion and several U.S. auto companies." He believed that "American industry and thousands of American jobs were sacrificed for State Department policy." On another occasion, he branded the agreement "another effort by the Administration to turn our international trade program into foreign aid, and buoy the Canadian economy at the expense of our own." Johnson himself privately agreed, telling Canadian ambassador Charles Ritchie: "You screwed us on the auto pact!"[56]

Why was the Johnson administration so obliging? Senator Hartke speculated that the auto agreement compensated Canada for supporting the Vietnam War. A Canadian historian suggests that Johnson was paying a debt for peacekeeping efforts in Cyprus. Certainly, a sensitivity to the overall political-military relationship disposed the executive to treat the Pearson administration in Canada generously.[57]

Other Democrats suspected that the Johnson administration was too eager to conclude the Kennedy Round. John Pastore of Rhode Island worried that the administration would sell out the textile and shoe industry for the sake of an international trade agreement. Herman Talmadge of Georgia had reservations about agriculture as well as textiles.[58]

"SUCCESS" IN GENEVA

In 1967 Lyndon Johnson found himself consumed by foreign policy decisions. Preoccupied with managing the Vietnam War, he could not give undivided attention to the Kennedy Round negotiations. General William Westmoreland wanted another 200,000 troops, and elsewhere in the world peace was in jeopardy. In June 1967 war would break out in the Middle East. During this critical phase Johnson relied heavily on the advice of White House staff, who consulted him routinely about matters of domestic political consequence. Like other presidents, he does not seem to have engaged deeply in the substantive trade issues.[59]

In Washington, a small command group composed of National Security Council staffer Francis Bator, Secretary of Commerce Alexander Trowbridge, Deputy Secretary of Agriculture John Schnittker, and Assistant Secretary of State Anthony Solomon met regularly to work out last-minute strategy. In Geneva, trade representative Roth and his deputy Mike Blumenthal orchestrated a crisis in the spring of 1967 to force concessions and somehow save the faltering Kennedy Round. They also exhorted the White House to have President Johnson put pressure on German chancellor Kurt Kiesinger at Konrad Adenauer's funeral in April. The "Germans are in a key position," Bator told the president. The "single most important move needed in agriculture" was a significant reduction in EEC tariffs.[60]

From the standpoint of reciprocity, the prospects were not good. Trowbridge learned from his sources in Geneva that the United States faced an "industrial imbalance with Japan, Canada and the [European Economic] Community. The discrepancy with Japan amounts to a total of $500 million to $1 billion and if we reduce our offers on textiles, steel, etc., the imbalance will still amount to $150 to $200 million."[61]

Nothing budged the Europeans on substantive agricultural concessions. EEC commissioner Jean Rey, the chief European negotiator, Bill Roth reported, "refused to take seriously our position that the Kennedy Round must include agriculture if it is to succeed at all." Therefore, Roth warned that the president "will shortly be faced with having to choose between a Kennedy Round with no offers of substance in non-group agriculture (and perhaps even no grains agreement) or no Kennedy Round Agreement at all."[62]

On May 1, with key decisions immediately ahead, Roth reported in detail to Johnson on the agricultural deadlock at Geneva. "Although we cannot achieve exact reciprocity with each country—especially Japan—*overall* we would expect to have a balanced package," he said. "*Of necessity, industry would pay for some of the benefits achieved for agriculture*" (emphasis added), Roth acknowledged. Also, the United States would not expect reciprocity for trading privileges granted the less developed countries. But to achieve even this agreement, Roth proposed to abandon the quest for assured access to the European market for American grain and he requested authority to provide additional concessions to Italy—on such import-sensitive items as glassware, gloves, and woolens. The president approved these recommendations.[63]

Despite its long-standing demand for significant agricultural concessions from the Europeans, meaning assured access for American grain exports, the United States withdrew this requirement on May 9 after an all-night marathon on the cereal issue. The next day Bator summarized the situation for President Johnson and requested his approval for Ambassador Roth to initial an agreement. The United States would end up about on even terms with the EEC, Bator said, notwithstanding the agricultural failure, but we "give more than we get from Japan (the Japanese sell us so much more than we sell them in industry that arithmetic balance is practically impossible." America would give more than it got from the United Kingdom, but vis-à-vis "the rich countries *as a whole*, [would] be in appreciable deficit in industry (Japan, UK, Canada), but in considerable surplus in agriculture (counting the grains agreement)." Recognizing that the calculations were "arbitrary," Bator anticipated that the advanced countries would be "some $600 million in the red." In five years, he claimed, the export surplus "might be reduced by some $25 million on a total now running between $4–7 billion." Bator recommended to Johnson that the United States approve the Kennedy Round even if the most pessimistic assumptions about the EEC position prevailed. "In economic terms, failure of the Kennedy Round could lead to the kind of commercial warfare in which we, as a trade surplus nation, have a great deal to lose," he noted. The "central point" was "not primarily the level of tariffs. Rather, it is holding to a reasonable set of trade rules without which international trade would become jungle warfare." In addition to predicting that failure would risk "spiraling protectionism," Bator warned that the "direct political implications of Kennedy Round failure would . . . be even more serious. It would encourage strong forces now at work to make the EEC into an isolationist, anti-U.S. bloc, while, at the same time, further alienating the poor countries."[64]

When the European Economic Community refused to yield on agriculture and when Japan stonewalled on market access, U.S. negotiators reluctantly abandoned the farm export issue and recommended that Johnson accept an agreement on industrial products that left the United States in a substantial deficit with Japan. At the moment of decision, the president heard from his advisers what foreign negotiators had long suspected: America's interest in a "successful" Kennedy Round outcome required accepting a compromise that did not satisfy the major U.S. negotiating objectives.[65] Failure to achieve an agreement, a staff aide informed the president, risked "spiraling protectionism" and "even more serious" political implications. "It would encourage strong forces now at work to make the EEC into an isolationist, anti-U.S. bloc, while, at the same time, further alienating the poor countries." The Kennedy Round thus ended with a face-saving agreement intended to sustain the multilateral process and demonstrate U.S. support for European unification.[66]

At a meeting on May 11, 1967, Johnson surveyed his advisers, including Vice President Hubert H. Humphrey. They unanimously backed an agreement "even if our best efforts were not able to move the Common Market from its present position." They did so without knowing the precise details of the final Kennedy Round package.[67]

When the negotiations ended, no one seems to have known for certain—in light of complex assumptions—what the bottom line was. President Johnson proclaimed the results a great success. "General agreement has been reached on all the major issues," he said proudly. Later, while toasting British prime minister Harold Wilson at the White House, Johnson exulted: "The Kennedy Round has moved the world a step closer to freer trade, which will help us all." Trade negotiator Roth assured Treasury secretary Henry Fowler that "the reciprocal nature of the final agreements is such that there should be no harm to the U.S. balance of payments." And he told Senator Russell Long of the Finance Committee: "the package we negotiated both in industry and agriculture was a fully reciprocal one. We did not trade a barrel of wheat for a biscuit but rather, I believe, achieved a good bargain for the United States." As often happens in trade negotiations, the lawyers and technicians needed another month to scrub the agreement and work out details. During that period the United States withdrew some concessions to Japan from the table in order to make the published agreement more balanced.[68]

ASSESSING THE RESULTS

The Johnson administration proclaimed the Kennedy Round "the most successful multilateral agreement on tariff reduction ever negotiated." The pleased participants noted that Kennedy Round concessions affected some $40 billion in world trade, about a quarter of the total. The duty reductions applied mainly to semimanufactured and manufactured products. At Geneva in 1947 the United States had reduced levies on 56 percent of its dutiable imports; in the Kennedy Round it slashed duties on 64 percent. In both the depth of U.S. reductions averaged 35 percent. As in the past, a gleeful executive branch generated data to show that "those who negotiated at Geneva drove a hard bargain, . . . a fair bargain." President Johnson reported to Congress that the United States received concessions from other countries on $7.5–$8 billion in agricultural and industrial exports. "We reduced duties on about the same volume of our imports." Separately, the U.S. Tariff Commission stated that the United States granted concessions on $8.5 billion in trade (45.6 percent of its imports) but received concessions on exports worth $8.1 billion (see Table 6.1).[69]

The great success of the 1967 agreement was the breadth and depth of tariff cuts on industrial goods. Ernest Preeg, a member of the U.S. delegation, observed that average Kennedy Round reductions for all major industrial countries were 36 to 39 percent. Steeper cuts occurred in advanced technology items, including machinery, transportation equipment, and chemicals. In textiles and steel, both import-sensitive areas, the reductions were small. From the U.S. perspective, the great failure of the Kennedy Round was the inability of negotiators to liberalize agricultural trade, a chronic problem for U.S. trade negotiators since the 1930s. In this area numerous quantitative barriers and other nontariff restraints limited the gains from tariff reductions.

At the time of the Kennedy Round many economists talked openly about trade serving as the "engine of growth" for developing countries. In approving the Trade Expansion Act, Congress authorized duty reductions in excess of 50 percent on tropical and forestry products if the European Economic Community provided comparable access on a nonpreferential basis and if there was no "significant" domestic production. But the negotiators achieved little in Geneva. In particular, many developing countries chose not to participate in the Kennedy Round, and their agricultural and primary exports faced substantial nontariff barriers in developed markets. Developing countries did obtain

TABLE 6.1

U.S. Concessions in Multilateral Trade Negotiations, 1947–1967
(Millions of $)

Round	Year	Place	U.S. Granted	U.S. Received
First	1947	Geneva	$1,766	$1,192
Second	1949	Annecy	250	489
Third	1951	Torquay	477	1,100
Fourth	1956	Geneva	753	395
Fifth	1960–62	Geneva	1,755	1,564
Sixth	1964–67	Geneva	8,500	8,100

Source: U.S. Tariff Commission, Operation of the Trade Agreements Program, 1967
(Washington, D.C.: TC, 1969), p. 238.

some reductions on textile duties but found cotton goods regulated by the Long-Term Cotton Textile Arrangement. The Kennedy Round also provided an opportunity for trade negotiators to begin discussions on nontariff barriers. They considered issues involving discriminatory taxation, customs valuation, unfair practices, and quantitative import restrictions. These talks accomplished little during the Kennedy Round, although European negotiators did persuade the U.S. delegation to relinquish American selling price (ASP) valuation for certain chemical products as part of a chemicals package that lowered duties in Europe and America. Also controversial in the United States was an antidumping agreement.

The decision to proceed with such nontariff negotiations produced a critical test with Congress over presidential authority. In June 1966 the Senate passed a concurrent resolution warning against the negotiation of any agreement that could not be implemented pursuant to existing delegated authority. Executive agencies urged President Johnson to proceed. They wanted to harmonize international antidumping procedures and to aid U.S. exporters facing capricious foreign antidumping administration, especially in Canada. Some voiced concerns that "many countries may resort to antidumping laws as protectionist devices" if the Kennedy Round succeeded in reducing tariff barriers. Despite the Senate warning, the special trade negotiator informed Johnson that negotiations "clearly come within the President's Constitutional authority to conduct foreign affairs." In June 1967, after completing the Kennedy Round, aides advised the president that the antidumping agreement required no implementing legislation because it was consistent with existing domestic law. Of the nontariff issues, only one, the ASP concession, "will require Congressional action."[70]

Members of the Senate Finance Committee had a different interpretation and the determination to stand firm. Vance Hartke complained that the international dumping code altered the U.S. Antidumping Act of 1921. According to him, "such substantive changes in our law amount to unauthorized legislation by an international agreement whose execution exceeds the mandate for these negotiations and usurps the legislative responsibility of the Congress."[71]

From the executive branch perspective, the Kennedy Round produced significant political gains. It encouraged Europeans to negotiate together under the EEC umbrella, and it strengthened the European Commission in Brussels. Germany, for example, linked its support for a common farm policy with French backing for a successful Kennedy Round package. The multilateral round also produced an accommodation with the United States. Stanley Metzger, a former TC chairman and drafter of the Trade Expansion Act, observed afterward that "failure to agree upon a significant reduction in the EEC's Common External Tariff in exchange for similar reductions in American duties undoubtedly would have caused the most serious suspicions about the EEC's objectives and might even have triggered a trade war."[72]

To domestic constituents and Congress, which were more concerned about commercial gains, the Johnson administration had difficulty placing a positive spin on the outcome. Privately, the Department of Agriculture was dissatisfied, although Secretary Orville Freeman loyally attempted to put the best possible face on the disappointing outcome. "Considering the problems encountered, he said, "we emerged with far better results than we thought possible during some of the darkest days when negotiations almost broke off." The "better results" included "some modest trade liberalization" and a greater awareness of the problems U.S. agricultural exporters faced.[73]

Commerce secretary Alexander Trowbridge also offered a tepid defense. "At times, it seemed that we were supporting political integration at the expense of our economic well-being," he noted. "The Kennedy Round . . . has *reduced my fear that we are sacrificing American economic interest for a political objective*." Prudently, he alerted American business to the real meaning of Geneva. The "Kennedy Round . . . represents a very large step toward the thing we've heard so much about in the postwar years: the truly one-world market." This means that "the American domestic market—the greatest and most lucrative market in the world—*is no longer* the private preserve of the American businessman" (emphases added). Viewed from the 1990s, these words echoed with prescience.[74]

Who actually won the Kennedy Round? A quarter century later, a more detached verdict is possible. The United States achieved few of its initial goals. Although it did negotiate down European tariffs on industrial products and preserve the open global trading system, America failed to open agricultural markets or increase opportunities for exports from developing countries. The Kennedy-Johnson liberal trade policies, Thomas Zeiler writes, had the opposite effect—touching off a protectionist backlash at home. Moreover, "pursuing trade liberalization for the sake of national security and economic health, the president forged an agreement at the Kennedy Round that hurt U.S. interests." Zeiler also says that at Geneva "America met its match in international trade talks." The European Economic Community "won *its* aim of lowering industrial tariffs while maintaining agricultural barriers."[75]

It is arguable that Japan was the real winner. Keeping a low profile, as they typically do in trade talks, the Japanese negotiators allowed the Europeans and Americans to battle, knowing full well that Japan could enjoy another free ride. It obtained many export benefits with minimal reciprocal concessions. The record suggests that on tariff reductions, Japan gained a phenomenal deal. On nonagricultural imports, the United States reduced duties on Japanese goods valued at $1.44 billion. But Japan actually agreed to reduce duties on only $667 million in imports from the United States. To achieve a measure of reciprocity, the United States chose to count Japan's duty-free bindings ($932 million).[76]

Not surprisingly, the Japanese press hailed the Kennedy Round agreement as paving the way for continued export expansion. Government sources in Tokyo indicated that "Japan will gain much eventually . . . because U.S. products to be affected by the Kennedy Round include many heavy industrial and chemical products which this country [Japan] intends to emphasize in the future." Another reason for anticipating that Japanese exports would rise more than imports from the United States was that Japan excepted "almost all the strategic industrial goods" from tariff cuts.[77]

Japan made few concessions of its own, because the U.S. president had no authority to deny it most-favored-nation treatment. Perhaps learning from the experience of nineteenth-century America, wily bureaucrats in the Japanese Ministry of International Trade and Industry (MITI) knew how to gain export opportunities without yielding the home market. In effect, they dined at the world trade buffet but declined to share the bill. U.S. trade negotiators knew that the Japanese were aware of the American need to conclude negotiations before expiration of the negotiating authority delegated to the executive branch. Trade representative Carl Gilbert later told President Richard M. Nixon that "the Japanese took advantage of this situation along toward the close of the Kennedy Round." Congress understood as well and sent the Japanese a thinly veiled warning in the next trade legislation, the Trade Act of 1974. Section 126 required the president to determine after the conclusion of future negotiations whether any major industrial country (defined as Canada, the EEC, or Japan) had failed to make concessions "substantially equivalent" to U.S. concessions.[78]

Canadians also hailed the Kennedy Round as a success. The *Financial Post* reported that "the three rough years of the Kennedy Round of tariff talks produced for Canadian exporters many significant improvements in the U.S. tariff and some useful concessions by the Europeans and Japanese. In return, Canada has managed to avoid sweeping tariff cuts of the type that could spell disaster to large sections of local industry."[79]

To end the Kennedy Round on a positive note, the Johnson administration sought support from the politically powerful domestic industries—textiles, steel, and chemicals—that were likely to oppose a one-sided agreement. Indeed, in June, after announcing general agreement, the negotiators removed some proposed textile and steel concessions offered to Japan in a vain effort to achieve a defensible balance.[80]

These efforts failed to silence domestic interests. As soon as the schedules were released, the textile, steel, and chemical industries all blasted the results. Criticizing the tariff cuts, Senator Strom Thurmond (R-S.C.) noted widespread feeling that "the textile industry has been sacrificed to meet diplomatic goals." A Democratic colleague, Senator Sam Ervin of North Carolina, also expressed disappointment: "our negotiators failed to receive reciprocal concessions from foreign countries for the concessions extended by them." The American Iron and Steel Institute refused to support the steel tariff cuts; it noted that "non-tariff trade barriers which prevent fair competition in other steel markets were not dealt with effectively." The Manufacturing Chemists Association called on Congress to defeat the administration's concession on the American selling price, maintaining that the chemical deal was "not reciprocal."[81]

Dissatisfaction with the Kennedy Round concessions produced a bipartisan explosion in the House of Representatives. Labor Subcommittee chairman John Dent (D-Pa.) accused the Johnson administration of "trading away the little fellow." This "sellout" would spell death and destruction for many American industries."[82] Predicting a surge in domestic unemployment as Kennedy Round tariff cuts took effect, Dent's subcommittee held hearings. The full Education and Labor Committee marked up a bill (H.R. 478) amending the Fair Labor Standards Act of 1938. It gave the president permission to restrict imports if the secretary of labor found that imported goods from low-wage areas impaired or threatened to impair the standard of living of domestic workers or the economic welfare of communities. In effect, Dent sought to close a loophole that allowed the products of cheap foreign labor to compete with domestic goods produced in accordance with federally mandated minimum wage and overtime provisions.

Dent's bill directed the labor secretary to make findings but left intact the president's discretionary power to approve or or reject those recommendations. Permissive at the White House level, the measure thus lacked teeth. In voting for Dent's bill, members of the House could send a signal of dissatisfaction to the administration without jeopardizing existing international trade commitments. On September 28, 1967, when the vote came, House Resolution 478 enjoyed broad bipartisan support, passing 340 to 29.[83]

The vote on House Resolution 478 also allowed House members to sympathize with the plight of organized labor and import-sensitive industries. Within the union movement some contemplated more effective legislative solutions—quotas on imports. At a labor conference George Baldanzi of the United Textile Workers drew a burst of applause from labor leaders when he called for an absolute ban on goods from countries paying 12 to 26 cents per hour. "What the hell good are we doing for this country or for world peace," he asked, "by exporting jobs to Taiwan or Hong Kong?" He attributed "many of the problems" in American ghettos to U.S. trade policy, which was eliminating the need for unskilled and semiskilled workers. Reflecting the general dissatisfaction, members of Congress proposed restrictive quotas on many imports. By the end of 1967 members had introduced 729 bills in the House of Representatives to impose quotas on imports.[84]

The Impact of U.S. Concessions

How did Kennedy Round tariff concessions actually affect the U.S. balance of payments and the merchandise trade balance? Available evidence suggests that Kennedy Round reductions had, on balance, a negative effect, one that economist John Kenneth Galbraith had foreseen. Galbraith, a former ambassador to India, warned President Johnson in March 1964: "If we are screwed on tariffs this will have an enduringly adverse effect on the balance of payments. It will be a serious problem for you for years to come."[85]

This forecast proved prescient. As the United States implemented Kennedy Round tariff cuts, its merchandise trade surplus vanished. Beginning in January 1968 and each January for five years thereafter the multilateral cuts took effect. These tariff reductions coincided with a turbulent period in currency markets. The Bretton Woods monetary system, based on fixed but adjustable parities defined in gold or the U.S. dollar, broke down. The United States had to devalue the dollar twice. By March 1973 the U.S. dollar was worth only 81 cents, a factor that should have spurred U.S. exports and discouraged U.S. imports. In fact, the U.S. merchandise trade balance strengthened in 1973 and 1975, but this proved temporary. Viewed from a historical perspective, the Kennedy Round marked a watershed. In each of the seventy-four years from

1893 to 1967 the United States ran a merchandise trade surplus (exports of goods exceeded imports). During the 1968–72 implementation period for Kennedy Round concessions, the U.S. trade surplus vanished and a sizable deficit emerged. For twenty of the next twenty-two years, the United States experienced merchandise trade deficits—as much as $160 billion in 1987.[86] U.S. exports of capital goods, automotive products, and consumer goods did increase after the Kennedy Round, rising 81.3 percent in constant dollars from 1967–68 to 1973–74. But imports of the same products climbed even faster—95.6 percent.[87]

Obviously, other factors impacted U.S. competitiveness during this period. The Kennedy Round reductions represented only one of these factors—and perhaps not the most important. The Nixon administration and economists generally attributed the emerging trade deficit to Vietnam War inflation, lagging productivity gains, an overvalued dollar, and ballooning energy costs. Each factor added to the problem, as an analysis prepared for President Nixon's Commission on International Trade and Investment Policy explained.[88]

The evidence and administrative record clearly indicate that foreign trade barriers and U.S. trade concessions exacerbated the deficit. Richard Nixon himself raised the issue of foreign barriers to U.S. exports: "our major trading partners maintain barriers—in many cases both unwarranted and outmoded—which are detrimental to our exports. These have been focal points of political friction and have held back growth in employment in specific U.S. industries." These restrictions impeded U.S. exports.[89]

The U.S. Tariff Commission reported in 1974 that "innumerable practices, other than tariffs, by governments and private organizations interfere with or distort the flow of trade." Although quantitative barriers in Japan and various EEC countries hampered U.S. exports, the commission concluded that the EEC's Common Agricultural Policy "probably can be considered the most significant trade barrier which U.S. exports encounter among the major nations." For Japan, the TC obtained information from U.S. firms about a variety of nontariff barriers, including subsidies, quotas, exchange controls, licensing, government monopolies, and restrictive business practices. It heard complaints that licensing procedures enabled the Japanese government "to identify end users of imported goods with a view to dissuading them from the purchase of foreign merchandise."[90]

Other documentation showing that nontariff barriers retarded the growth of U.S. exports appeared in the report of the Williams Commission. It stated: "Despite the tariff reductions of the last two decades, U.S. industries continue to meet difficulties at home and abroad as a result of foreign policies, practices, and institutional arrangements which distort competitive conditions to our disadvantage."[91]

TABLE 6.2

*Kennedy Round Tariff Concessions on Manufactures: Average Tariff on Dutiable
Imports as a Percentage of Cost, Insurance, and Freight Value*

Country/Region	Before	After	Percent Cut
United States	14.3%	9.9%	−36%
EEC	13.5	8.6	−36
United Kingdom	17.8	10.8	−39
Japan	17.6	10.7	−39

Source: Ernest H. Preeg, *Traders and Diplomats: An Analysis of Kennedy Round Negotiations under the General Agreement on Tariffs and Trade* (Washington, D.C.: Brookings Institution, 1970), pp. 208–11.

How did U.S. tariff concessions in the Kennedy Round affect bilateral trade
patterns? In discussing the results, Washington insiders generally avoided this
issue, perhaps because it could invite questions about the competence of U.S.
negotiators and their policy guidance. Ernest Preeg, for instance, placed a
multilateralist spin on events: "the major accomplishment of the Kennedy
Round . . . was the reduction of tariff levels." He claimed that the United
States, the European Economic Community, the United Kingdom, and Japan
all cut tariff levels on manufactures almost equally (see Table 6.2).[92] Preeg's
calculations suggest essential reciprocity in the negotiations. His data, however, reflect nominal tariffs—those appearing in tariff schedules—and not effective tariffs. The latter consider the presence of *nontariff barriers*, such as
quotas, subsidies and other market imperfections, and even structural barriers
to trade.

Congressman Thomas Curtis, who monitored the negotiations, acknowledged as much. He noted that step-by-step tariff reductions from 1930 had
lowered rates "to levels where the tariff per se has ceased to be a really meaningful restriction to flows of international trade in the industrialized free
world." Curtis also observed that quotas, licenses, commodity agreements, and
other neo-mercantilist efforts could distort the results.[93]

A different perspective on this issue emerges from data that the independent U.S. Tariff Commission prepared for the Senate Finance Committee in
1974. These data suggest that although the formulaic approach, employed in
the Kennedy Round, may have facilitated negotiations to lower tariffs, it contributed to asymmetrical results. In the case of automobiles, for instance, the
United States lowered duties from 6.5 percent to 3 percent—further opening
the American market to import competition. But reductions in Canada, the

European Economic Community, the United Kingdom, and Japan left those markets all with tariff rates on automobiles from 10 to 15 percent. If one assumes, as the U.S. International Trade Commission (the successor to the Tariff Commission) does, that a tariff of 9–10 percent is somewhat restrictive, a comparison of post–Kennedy Round nominal tariff levels may indicate that the multilateral round did more to open the U.S. and EEC markets than the other major markets.[94]

The 1974 Tariff Commission report shows that it is very difficult to measure the marketplace effect of tariff changes—as these may be passed along in whole or part, or absorbed by some of the parties to transactions. Also, currency fluctuations, as well as supply-and-demand changes in each country to a transaction, may distort the effect of the tariff rate changes. In a 1983 study, the ITC concluded: "although changes in exchange rates influenced trade, other trade factors were often more important. Variation in competitors' prices, product demand, local production, and manufacturing costs also played a key role in trade fluctuations."[95]

Another method for estimating the impact of tariff reductions on U.S. producers involves the *but for* test used in legal analysis. In this formulation, the relevant question becomes, *But for* the tariff reduction, would imports have risen as they did? From 1968 to 1973, when Congress wrote a new statute modifying provisions of the 1962 Trade Expansion Act, members of the U.S. Tariff Commission regularly conducted investigations that examined the relationship between past tariff concessions and import-related injury. They did so in various escape clause and adjustment assistance recommendations to the president.

Simply stated, the statute authorized remedies if petitioners could demonstrate that injury was in major part a consequence of tariff rate concessions. A review of these administrative decisions indicates that President Nixon regularly accepted the independent TC's findings that tariff cuts were responsible for injury to domestic industries as a result of Kennedy Round concessions. In reaching such conclusions, the commissioners also heard testimony from economists and analysts that other causes existed for injury—declining productivity, ballooning energy costs, and disparate rates of inflation. The fact that the Tariff Commission made a series of legal findings linking tariff concessions to import injury, and that the president upheld these findings, offers a fact-finding record for the conclusion that some Kennedy Round tariff cuts impacted domestic producers and workers negatively. As a result of TC recommendations, Nixon provided adjustment assistance to nearly 40,000 workers producing electrical equipment, metal products, footwear, musical instruments, industrial machinery, textiles, and motor vehicles.[96]

It is appropriate to review some of these TC findings, because they show

how Kennedy Round concessions had a negative impact on domestic industries and workers and encouraged some U.S. manufacturers to move assembly plants offshore. In a January 1971 escape clause determination, Commissioners Bruce Clubb and George Moore held that a 50 percent cut in duties on women's vinyl and leather shoes during the Kennedy Round brought a surge of injurious imports. President Nixon accepted their determination, effectively affirming their legal interpretation, and provided adjustment assistance.[97]

Workers at a Whittier Mills plant in Atlanta producing cotton osnaburgs and sheeting complained about tariff concessions and petitioned for adjustment assistance in August 1971. In its investigation the U.S. Tariff Commission found that the quantity of these imports had risen 31 percent. A majority of the commission concluded that "the reduction in duties in 1968, 1969, 1970, and 1971 [Kennedy Round] served to spur increased imports and to weaken the competitive position of Whittier Mills to such an extent as to bring about the collapse of its financing and the closing of the plant."[98]

The consumer electronics industry experienced a severe jolt from import competition after Kennedy Round tariff concessions. Duties on television picture tubes fell from 30 percent ad valorem in July 1962 to 15 percent ad valorem during the Kennedy Round. For television receivers and radio-television-phonograph combinations, duties dropped from 10 to 5 percent during Kennedy Round negotiations. For transistors and semiconductors there were other steep tariff reductions. The United States lowered duties from 12.5 percent ad valorem on July 1, 1962, to 6 percent during the Kennedy Round. In an adjustment assistance investigation, the Tariff Commission found that the reduction in duties from 1930 to 1971 accounted "for more than the difference between the cost of the imported product and the cost of the domestic article." Indeed, the "50-percent reduction in duty resulting from the Kennedy Round obviously served as an incentive to . . . U.S. manufacturers to turn to imports to establish production facilities in foreign countries." President Nixon accepted this conclusion and provided adjustment assistance relief.[99]

The administrative record also reveals that the Tariff Commission believed that Kennedy Round tariff concessions prompted U.S. producers to close radio assembly plants in the United States and move overseas. The commission determined that trade agreement concessions of 24.6 percentage points for transistor radios, since 1930, had provided an important price advantage to importing radio receivers. General Electric, which began importing from foreign facilities in 1967 and brought a second overseas plant on line in 1970 "would not have moved its radio-manufacturing operations offshore nor would imports of radios have approached the present volume, had it not been for the concessions."[100]

In a February 1972 escape clause finding, a majority of the Tariff Commission held that increased imports of earthenware and dinnerware articles resulted from trade agreement concessions and recommended an increase in the rates of duty to pre–Kennedy Round levels. These commissioners found that prior to the Kennedy Round concessions imports increased at an annual rate of 2.9 percent, but after implementation of Kennedy Round cuts imports rose by 7.7 percent. For some chinaware mugs, the increase was 23.5 percent. President Nixon also accepted this recommendation and increased tariffs.[101]

One industry long considered critical to a strong military-industrial base was the antifriction ball and ball bearing industry. In 1930 Congress set duties on these items at 10 cents per pound plus 45 percent ad valorem. Under the reciprocal trade program, the executive branch lowered these rates in concessions to Sweden in 1935 and 1950. At the beginning of the Kennedy Round these rates stood at 3.4 cents per pound plus 15 percent ad valorem, estimated at a 16.3 percent ad valorem equivalent. Further, Kennedy Round linear tariff cuts reduced these rates 50 percent, to 1.7 cents per pound plus 7.5 percent ad valorem, an 8.2 percent ad valorem equivalent. Once again the administrative record indicates that Kennedy Round tariff cuts had a severe negative impact on U.S. producers. In 1973 the TC presented the president with an affirmative escape clause finding showing how Kennedy-Round concessions had injured the domestic bearings industry. Wrote the commission majority, including Catherine Bedell, Joseph Parker, and George Moore: "*The further duty reductions of 50 percent in the Kennedy Round obviously proved too great a handicap to the United States industry on top of the trade agreement concessions which had already taken place. The heavy rise in imports from 1968 to 1972 was the result*" (emphasis added). In accepting this finding, President Nixon effectively agreed that tariff concessions had harmed the domestic antifriction bearings industry.[102]

Kennedy Round tariff cuts impacted another vital component of the defense base, the machine tools industry. Machine tools are capital goods used to make other items. Product buyers, who often purchase through distributors, are less responsive to short-term price changes and more concerned about overall performance, specifications, and servicing. A 1983 ITC survey of domestic purchasers of U.S.-made machine tools revealed that the delivered price was less significant than the availability of spare parts and machines, compatibility with existing systems, and servicing. Thus it might be expected that new competitors would take some time to become established in the U.S. marketplace after tariff concessions made their products more price competitive.[103]

During the Kennedy Round the executive branch authorized a 50 percent cut in U.S. duties on machine tools as part of the effort to negotiate down EEC duties. Initially, this concession had little noticeable impact, and import market share remained near 10 percent from 1967 to 1973. However, foreign market share rose rapidly when Japanese producers of standard machine tools entered the United States in the mid-1970s. By 1980 the free-riding Japanese had captured nine percentage points of market share in America. Then further reductions made in the Tokyo Round took effect. From 1979 to 1987 duties on machine tools fell from 7.5 percent to 4.4 percent. In response, import market share rose from 23 percent to 39 percent in 1984. Japanese producers garnered most of this increase.

A similar pattern occurred in other manufacturing industries, including automobiles. In the Tariff Act of 1930 Congress had set the levy on automobiles at 10 percent. Under the reciprocal trade program, the executive branch lowered this rate to 8.5 percent in July 1956 and then to 6.5 percent after Dillon Round negotiations with Europe. Preoccupied with promoting imports and restoring international economic equilibrium, U.S. government officials exhibited little concern about auto imports. In both 1947 and 1950 interagency committees even proposed to slash the U.S. auto duty to 5 percent on the theory that "imports will ordinarily [not] be able to compete except in supplying limited and special demands in the United States."[104]

During the Kennedy Round the U.S. executive agreed to a full 50 percent reduction. Because of a rounding provision in the law, this cut the auto duty from 6.5 percent to 3 percent ad valorem. This reduction, coming as Japanese automakers prepared to mount a vigorous attack on the U.S. market, undoubtedly aided foreign penetration. In the three years before the Kennedy Round reductions took effect (1965–67), non-American suppliers captured 7.2 of the domestic market. In 1968 and 1969, as authorities began to implement reductions, non-American automobile imports nearly doubled—up from 696,980 units in 1967 to 1,155,571 units in 1969. Domestic producers quickly lost more than three percentage points of market share—most of this to European automakers. In the three calendar years after the Kennedy Round cut took effect (1972–74), auto imports soared to 15.8 percent of the domestic market.

Other factors—such as the energy crisis and the shift in consumer taste toward smaller, energy-efficient cars—obviously contributed to the phenomenal growth in automobile imports during the early 1970s. Japanese automakers knew how to produce four-cylinder cars at affordable prices. Detroit could not adapt quickly enough. Ironically, twenty years earlier U.S. government trade experts foresaw no threat to the domestic industry from small imported cars. In 1950 they had complete confidence in the American industry and its capacity to repulse the competition: "Should the United States demand for very small cars increase sharply, the major United States manufacturers would no doubt shift to the production of more of such cars in this country."[105]

Although U.S. concessions in the Kennedy Round provided some advantage to Japanese automakers eager to crack the U.S. market, parallel Japanese duty reductions did not benefit Detroit. A host of nontariff barriers, including internal taxes that discriminated against large American cars, continued to block outside competitors from Western Europe and North America.[106]

Protectionism Revives

Dissatisfaction with the Kennedy Round results and a growing unease about the import challenge to American jobs produced an important shift in public opinion. Until the mid-1950s, Gallup polling data showed that half of the people who had heard of the Reciprocal Trade Agreements Program favored lower tariffs. In August 1954, for example, 49 percent supported lower tariffs, 27 percent higher tariffs, and 16 percent existing tariffs; 8 percent were undecided. In March 1962, of those who had heard of President Kennedy's trade expansion program, 38 percent wanted lower tariffs, 15 percent higher tariffs, and 18 percent the same tariffs; 29 percent were undecided.[107]

A decade later the mood had changed. Louis Harris and Roper polling data both demonstrated that a solid majority now favored more restrictions on foreign products entering the United States. Although the nation's corporate, banking, media, and policy elite enthusiastically embraced free trade and internationalism, working Americans had more parochial interests—jobs.[108]

Despite growing public opposition, trade liberalization enthusiasts in the executive branch determined to launch another round of GATT negotiations. During the summer of 1966, the State Department devised a post–Kennedy Round strategy to address the drift toward regional trading blocs, involving the expanded European Economic Community as well as developing nations. This approach anticipated a presidential request to Congress for negotiating authority in 1969 after the general election.[109]

Responding to the United Nations Conference on Trade and Development, developed countries contemplated a program of unilateral trade preferences to address the economic problems of disadvantaged countries. At a November 1967 annual session, contracting parties to GATT organized a work program to begin preparations for another round of negotiations. They agreed that the next multilateral trade round should focus on nontariff barriers and attempt to resolve vexing agricultural trade issues.[110]

Within the beleaguered Johnson administration, trade officials ruminated about resurgent protectionism in Congress and how to deflect it. For them, further negotiations represented a device to divert calls for industry-specific legislation. With talks in progress, they could counsel parties with trade grievances and Congress not to rock the boat and to wait for developments in

Geneva. Hoping to sustain the liberal trade agenda after the 1968 presidential election, the special trade representative prepared a supportive report. It backed further liberalization of trade but came down hard on "inequitable" foreign barriers to U.S. trade. This study recommended new presidential authority to enforce U.S. interests unilaterally in GATT when foreign restrictions impaired the value of benefits in the General Agreement. Specifically, it called for amending section 252(a)(3) of the 1962 Trade Expansion Act to permit the full range of retaliatory powers against illegal foreign restrictions on either U.S. industrial or agricultural exports.[111]

Needing congressional approval to implement Kennedy Round undertakings, President Johnson submitted the TEA of 1968, House Resolution 17551. This bill proposed to eliminate the contentious American selling price system of customs valuation used for chemicals. As a sweetener for lawmakers with trade grievances, the legislation contemplated easier access to adjustment assistance for import-impacted workers and industries. Eager to fulfill the administration's commitments and to strengthen the world trading system, Johnson vowed to stand firm against protectionist quota legislation.[112]

Congressional hearings provided the Johnson administration's critics a forum. A variety of industries—including the American Loudspeaker Manufacturers Association, the Parts and Distributors Products Divisions of the Electronics Industries Association, and the American Iron and Steel Institute—asked for quotas to restrain surging imports. The National Machine Tool Builders Association favored progressive import surcharges. The Bicycle Manufacturers Association predicted that Kennedy Round reductions would bring a "further sharp increase in imports." The Synthetic Organic Chemical Manufacturers Association forecast that Japan and Europe "will take over increasing shares of the world export market, the domestic market, and our export market." With dissatisfaction running high in an election year, Chairman Wilbur Mills of Ways and Means decided to defer action.[113]

The House hearings produced a Mexican standoff, as a staff aide had predicted to Johnson. The administration obtained no trade bill to implement the Kennedy Round, but Congress did not succeed in enacting quotas on imports. The resulting stalemate awaited the outcome of the 1968 presidential election.[114]

Nixon's New Look in Trade

The 1968 election marked an important milestone in the evolution of U.S. trade policy. For a generation presidential candidates of both major parties generally had embraced trade liberalization, putting international rehabilitation over the interests of import-sensitive domestic producers and workers. In 1960, for instance, Democrats hailed trade expansion: "world trade is more than ever essential to world peace. In the tradition of Cordell Hull, *we shall expand world trade in every responsible way. . . . To sell, we must buy.* We therefore must resist the temptation to accept remedies that deny American producers and consumers access to world markets and destroy the prosperity of our friends in the non-Communist world" (emphasis added).[115]

In 1968 the presidential race revealed public dissatisfaction with one-sided trade liberalization. Each of the major candidates pledged vigorous action to aid import-sensitive industries and workers. George Wallace's American Independent Party, seeking to attract blue-collar workers, promised "reasonable quantitative limits" to stem the increasing inflow of imports from low-wage countries. Appealing to a similar constituency, Republicans pledged "hardheaded bargaining to lower the non-tariff barriers against American exports." But they also asserted that "imports should not be permitted to capture excessive portions of the American market." Regulated through international agreements, foreign nations should be "able to participate in the growth of consumption." Even incumbent Democrats adopted similar language and attempted to straddle the intraparty conflict between free trade advocates who wanted to continue market liberalization and labor unionists concerned about rising imports. They endorsed trade negotiations to free international trade and negotiate the "reciprocal removal of non-tariff barriers," while hinting at "negotiated international agreements" to remedy "unfair and destructive import competition."[116]

Richard Nixon, the victor, concentrated his presidential energies on foreign policy, attempting to end the controversial Vietnam War and to improve relations with the Soviet Union and China. For Nixon the intricacies of trade policy had little personal attraction. Trade was secondary to domestic politics and to foreign policy. It was a diplomatic bargaining chip to entice cooperation on more important foreign policy issues. Thus in pursuing "linkage" with the Soviet Union, Nixon dangled most-favored-nation treatment and other trade concessions to solicit Soviet cooperation on Vietnam, the Middle East, and Berlin. In promoting reconciliation with China, his administration set in motion a process that led to extension of most-favored-nation treatment in February 1980.[117]

Nonetheless, President Nixon revolutionized domestic trade law enforcement. To handle trade problems, he appointed a team with private sector experience and directed officials to administer existing trade remedy laws vigorously. During his presidency, the executive branch enforced U.S. trade laws more zealously than any other in the post–World War II period. This assertive approach contrasted sharply with the decisions of Kennedy and Johnson appointees, who generally declined to enforce the escape clause, to impose antidumping and countervailing duties, or even to authorize adjustment assistance for dislocated workers.

Behind the administration's more nationalistic position was a widespread belief in Congress and in the business community that State Department officials involved in previous negotiations had placed military and political objectives ahead of trade priorities. Carl Gertstacker, chairman of Dow Chemical, said: "We were out-bargained badly in the Kennedy Round and a major reason was that foreign countries used businessmen advisers." Frederick Dent, of Mayfair Mills, attributed the resurgence of protectionism to a "'Marshall Plan' psychology in the implementation of our foreign trade policy . . . which has catered almost exclusively to the interest and advantage of our trading partners overseas."[118]

In Nixon's cabinet, Secretary of Commerce Maurice Stans emerged as a vigorous defender of American business interests. Early in the administration, he advised the president that "Congress and a good part of the business community have lost confidence in the ability of our Government to conduct trade negotiations on a business-like basis." Stans, a powerful figure with considerable skills as a political fund-raiser, proposed transferring the special trade representative to the Department of Commerce. A new, "tough-minded" image was needed for trade policy, he maintained, arguing that trade reorganization might restore business confidence, attract support from agriculture, and buy time from Congress. It would also "condition foreign governments to expect a quid-pro-quo attitude from the U.S. on trade matters."[119]

Although Nixon did not approve that particular recommendation, other actions signaled a White House more responsive to domestic concerns. At the Tariff Commission the president appointed several individuals with congressional experience and thus a sensitivity to statutory construction and legislative intent. They also exhibited a determination to enforce existing trade laws. These included Chairman Catherine May Bedell, a former congresswoman from Washington State; George Moore, a former congressional staffer and Civil Service commissioner; and Joseph Parker, a Kansas lawyer who served in the Department of Agriculture and on the House Agriculture Committee. Not since the Eisenhower administration had the TC recommended affirmative escape relief or adjustment assistance to dislocated workers. These Nixon appointees brought a pro-enforcement outlook to trade remedy proceedings. So did the selection of lawyer Eugene Rossides to supervise antidumping and countervailing duty enforcement at Treasury.[120]

On GATT, President Nixon played down the prospects for further multilateral trade negotiations. In March 1969 he told reporters: "We have to realize that we cannot anticipate in the near future another big round of reductions of tariff barriers. We are going to do well if we can digest what we have on the plate." A few months later he submitted a trade bill and sought a modest grant of negotiating authority to implement Kennedy Round commitments. This included the power to eliminate the American selling price. The president stressed the need for "fair competition among all countries" and proposed new retaliatory authority so that he might retaliate against the products of nations placing unjustifiable restrictions on U.S. goods.[121]

Responding to international business interests concerned about Japanese restrictions, Nixon also requested unilateral authority to enforce U.S. rights. The White House had learned that Japanese restrictions on foreign investment effectively neutralized the value of tariff concessions on automobile parts and components gained in the Kennedy Round. A few months later the president renewed his call for reciprocal market access and fair trade. In a report to Congress, Nixon observed: "In today's world, all major countries must pursue freer trade if each country is to do so. The principle of *true reciprocity* must lie at the heart of trade policy—as it lies at the heart of all foreign policy" (emphasis added).[122]

Like his mentor, President Dwight Eisenhower, who turned to a blue-ribbon panel to construct a consensus for trade policy reforms, Nixon established a Randall-style advisory group—the U.S. Commission on International Trade and Investment Policy. Albert Williams, an IBM executive, chaired the panel. Along with representatives of export-minded firms like General Electric, Honeywell, Motorola, General Motors, Cargill, and other large businesses, the group included representatives of labor and agriculture as well as several academics.

In testimony before the Williams Commission, Commerce secretary Maurice Stans rejected the widespread notion among academic economists and State Department officials that America's emerging trade problems resulted only from U.S. inflation. He warned that America "must stop being overly generous toward others in our trade attitudes and dealings." New circumstances compel "stronger representations of our national economic interests in international affairs." With nontariff barriers, the country was "more the victim than culprit." The United States "must press for full and government-wide reciprocity in our economic dealing with other governments. . . . Most importantly, we must stop subordinating national economic interests to political interests in the international sphere."[123]

The Williams Commission issued a grim report in July 1971. A "crisis in confidence" had developed in the United States over the present multilateral trade and payments system. Among the signs of crisis were the mounting pressures for import restrictions, growing demands for retaliation against foreign trade barriers, a rising concern that America "has not received full value for the tariff concessions made over the years," and an increasing perception that "the foreign economic policy of our government has given *insufficient weight to our economic interests and too much weight to our foreign political relations.*"[124]

A number of commission members also took note of an "alarming" trend, a trend that was turning the United States into a service economy. "We cannot have a strong, growing, and viable U.S. economy unless we maintain a strong manufacturing and agricultural base. Others are making a concentrated effort to maintain a balanced manufacturing and agricultural base." To sustain a strong economy and society, they said, the nation must "be willing to give up some of the hoped for but never quite achievable benefits of freer world trade and investment."[125]

The Burke-Hartke Quota Proposals

In Congress, the Nixon team had to play vigorous defense. After the 1968 election, organized labor had turned its energies and resources to legislative solutions. Chairman Mills of Ways and Means observed the mood of desperation. In 1970 the House approved a Mills bill containing textile and footwear restraints, but it died in the Senate after a filibuster. The measure would also have strengthened provisions for safeguards in order to encourage the use of trade remedies for import-impacted industries. But it lacked support from the administration.

When the Ways and Means Committee rejected repeal of the American selling price to fulfill Kennedy Round commitments, White House aide C. Fred Bergsten advised Henry Kissinger that "the resulting bill will be wholly protectionist. The President could not possibly sign it. . . . The trade policy crisis has now become a total disaster." Separately, Paul McCracken, chairman of the Council of Economic Advisers, warned that "we may be on the verge of a trade war with Europe and Japan."[126]

Mills and his colleagues on the Ways and Means Committee said that they wanted to redress the unbalanced results of previous trade concessions. They understood that whereas the United States had lowered tariffs barriers, trading partners had raised nontariff barriers to U.S. exports. Declared Representative Phil Landrum (D-Ga.): "the Kennedy Round . . . failed to deal with two principal areas of trade relations: U.S. negotiators were unable to change the growing protectionist trend in the European agricultural policies, nor was there any success in dealing substantively with the non-tariff-barrier issues."[127]

During 1971–72 organized labor pushed aggressively, but unsuccessfully, for passage of the Burke-Hartke bill, a measure to regulate the direct investment activities of multinational corporations and to restrict the import of goods competitive with domestic products with mandatory quotas. Opponents branded it "potentially the most disastrous legislation since the Smoot-Hawley Tariff." According to Kent Hughes, "the breadth of the Burke-Hartke quota proposals was virtually unprecedented in the history of U.S. foreign trade policy." It represented a "radical departure from past practice," including Smoot-Hawley, which relied on higher tariffs, not quotas.[128]

Meanwhile, the dollar crisis forced the Nixon administration to act, and it did so with dramatic fashion in August 1971, after Great Britain attempted to convert three billion dollars into gold. The administration imposed a surcharge on imports and permitted the dollar to float, effectively bringing to a close the era in which a U.S. commitment to buy and sell gold provided the confidence for international monetary stability and expansion.[129]

In 1973, as part of the agreements negotiated with major trade and financial partners, the president agreed to move forward on a new round of trade negotiations, the so-called Tokyo Round. In April he asked Congress for a delegation of negotiating authority. His rationale linked efforts to promote peace and accommodation with the Soviet Union to trade negotiations. They would help create a "new economic order" in which America is "no longer the sole, dominating economic power." Under the new scheme, nations would share economic leadership while economic forces achieved growing levels of interdependence and dramatic change. Nixon promised to use the new delegation of authority to build a "fair and open trading system." This would employ more rules to ensure fairness to all nations and to distribute the benefits of trade fairly. Expanding trade, he argued, "should create no undue burdens for any of these groups." In a new round of multilateral negotiations, the president pledged to consider the problems of nontariff barriers, agricultural protectionism, and preferential trading arrangements and to promote domestic adjustment. To address the problems of import surges, he proposed a less restrictive test for escape clause relief and greater presidential flexibility to provide remedies. Nixon also recommended modernizing countervailing duty and antidumping laws to address unfair trade practices. He asked for extended authority to retaliate against foreign trade barriers, explaining: "I will consider using it whenever it becomes clear that our trading partners are unwilling to remove unreasonable or unjustifiable restrictions against our exports."[130]

Growing restiveness in Congress and dissatisfaction with a "soft trade policy" that "granted trade concessions to accomplish political objectives" produced the Trade Act of December 1974. During congressional hearings and debate, Chairman Russell Long and members of the Senate Finance Committee frequently vented their displeasure with recent trade policy. Their report stated: "Throughout most of the postwar era, U.S. trade policy has been the orphan of U.S. foreign policy. Too often the Executive has granted trade concessions to accomplish political objectives. Rather than conducting U.S. international economic relations on sound economic and commercial principles, the Executive has used trade and monetary policy in a foreign aid context."[131] The committee complained about the executive's "soft" response to certain unfair foreign trade practices. "By pursuing a soft trade policy, by refusing to strike swiftly and surely at foreign unfair trade practices, the Executive has actually fostered the proliferation of barriers to international commerce. The result of this misguided policy has been to permit and even to encourage discriminatory trading arrangements among trading nations." On safeguards it expressed the view that "no U.S. industry which has suffered serious injury should be cut off from relief for foreign policy reasons."[132]

The statute enacted in December 1974, after a difficult gestation period, represented a milestone in trade legislation. Like Smoot-Hawley in 1930, the Reciprocal Trade Agreements Act of 1934, and the Trade Expansion Act of 1962, it produced a major adjustment in the relationship between Congress and the executive branch. Chairman Long construed the result favorably from the congressional perspective. The conference report retained Senate amendments strengthening U.S. statutes dealing with unfair trade practices. It also established the basis for more vigorous oversight of authorities delegated to the president and a fast-track procedure to speed implementation of Tokyo Round agreements.[133]

As enacted, the Trade Act of 1974 appeared to represent a major shift away from the philosophy that had guided trade policy since 1934. With the Nixon White House paralyzed in the final stages of Watergate and President Ford eager to buy peace with his former congressional colleagues, Long and his associates seized the opportunity to reassert congressional prerogatives.

Retrospective: Dynamic New Era or Economic Decline?

President Kennedy initiated the Kennedy Round with typical enthusiasm and exuberance. He promised "increased export opportunities" and a "dynamic new era of growth." He urged his generation to "build our road for the next generation."

A generation later Kennedy's words and policies look somewhat different. The face of America has changed dramatically from that day in 1962 when Congress enacted the Trade Expansion Act. In 1962 manufacturing accounted for 29 percent of national income, whereas agriculture, forestry, and fisheries provided only about 4 percent. Services and finance added another 23 percent.

Thirty years later, in 1992, manufacturing accounted for only 18.3 percent and agriculture 2.6 percent. Services and finance amounted to 37.6 percent.

Employment figures show this economic transition. In 1962 16.4 million workers had full-time equivalent manufacturing jobs, about 28.2 percent of the work force; 2.6 million worked in finance (4.5 percent) and 8.4 million in services (14.5 percent). A generation later, there were 17.7 million full-time equivalent positions in manufacturing (17 percent), whereas 27 million (26 percent) had jobs in services and another 6.4 million (6.2 percent) worked in finance.[134]

As it turned out, the road that President Kennedy and his colleagues built for future generations was not the smooth superhighway of economic opportunity he had forecast in 1962. Before the Kennedy Round, trade liberalization had coincided with higher wages and living standards for American manufacturing workers. But in the twenty years after 1970 the opportunities Kennedy foresaw vanished for high-paid but relatively low-skilled U.S. workers. From 1972 to 1992 the United States created 44 million net jobs—particularly in services and government. However, America generated no net jobs in internationally traded industries. Japan and many of the other rapidly industrializing powers—Taiwan, South Korea, and Brazil among others—enjoyed rapid economic growth, not because they practiced free trade at home, but because they enjoyed access to the open American market. Like nineteenth-century America, they practiced protectionism at home while America's generous market-opening policies provided bountiful export opportunities. Paul Bairoch noted the lesson: "Those who don't obey the rules win."[135]

A disproportionate burden of adjustment fell on the U.S. economy, the one that absorbed more of the manufactured exports of developing nations than Japan and Europe combined. In America, the growth in manufacturing employment stalled in 1969 and then began an irregular decline. Real hourly wages in manufacturing stagnated during the 1970s and then generally fell.[136]

Open world markets intensified competition and brought disruption and dislocation to some product markets in high-income countries. U.S. steel production employment peaked in 1966 with 1,055,500 workers averaging $410.01 per week in constant 1982 dollars. This was 71 percent more than steelworkers had made twenty years earlier. But a quarter century later, in 1992, the average employed steelworker made less than twenty years earlier.[137] Over that time production employment in steel fell 50 percent, to 531,400 workers. In textiles and apparel the pattern was similar. Textile production employment dropped from 886,000 jobs averaging $261.63 per week in 1973 to 580,800 thousand jobs averaging $246.93 in 1992. Production employment in apparel peaked in 1966 and again in 1973 at 1,249,700 averaging $214.83 per week in constant dollars.

Over the next twenty years employment fell 32 percent to 852,000 in 1992. The average weekly wage also fell 16 percent, to $180.62 in 1992. Contractions in these three industries cost 1,227,000 jobs.[138]

Organized labor took a big hit. From 1979 to 1991 foreign competition decimated industrial unions representing import-sensitive workers. The United Steelworkers lost 505,000 members; electrical and electronics unions, 178,000; Machinists and Aerospace Workers, 154,000; Garment Workers, 171,000; Clothing and Textile Workers, 154,000; Oil, Chemical, and Atomic Workers, 56,000; and the list continued. From 1985 to 1991 the United Autoworkers lost 134,000 members.[139]

The Kennedy Round of multilateral tariff negotiations thus marked a milestone in American economic history. Prior to the 1960s the United States gained manufacturing jobs; afterward, the growth in manufacturing employment came to a halt and factory jobs began moving offshore. In 1967 the U.S. merchandise trade surplus in capital goods, automobiles, and consumer goods, measured in constant dollars, was about the same as in 1947. Although the nation had begun to run large import surpluses on automotive products and consumer goods, American capital goods sales still generated healthy surpluses. Twenty years later the surplus on capital goods, automotive products, and consumer goods had disappeared, and deficits averaged $110 billion over the period 1986–88.[140]

American officials saw the Kennedy Round as an opportunity to accommodate the European Common Market. Once again U.S. leaders chose not to jeopardize this complex relationship with insistence on assured access to European markets for American farm products. Focusing on the Atlantic economic relationship, Washington gave little attention to the emerging economic challenge from eastern Asia. Instead, eager to preserve alliances, the Johnson administration rewarded Canada for its diplomatic support in Indochina and Cyprus with a one-sided auto pact. Washington also turned a blind eye to Japanese protectionism. In thus treating access to the huge U.S. market as a reward to loyal allies, the Kennedy and Johnson administrations unwittingly made a series of policy decisions that contributed to the domestic economic dislocations of the 1980s and 1990s.

No nation was ever ruined by trade, even seemingly the most disadvantageous.

—Benjamin Franklin, 1774

[D]omestic interests will be safeguarded in this process of expanding trade.

—President Harry Truman, 1947

Illusive Safeguards

America's first successful trade negotiator, Benjamin Franklin, had a merchant's enthusiasm for commerce. He railed against burdensome government regulations, effused over laissez-faire teachings, and associated the activities of traders with the "common good of mankind."[1] Though favoring free trade, he nonetheless argued fervently for "fair and equitable commerce." The Philadelphia philosopher condemned unfair trading practices such as bounties, or subsidies, comparing these to the "knavish" efforts of "pickpockets." In today's parlance, the compassionate Franklin probably would stand prominent among those who advocate fair, free trade.[2]

As negotiators, Franklin and his colleagues who drafted the 1778 Treaty of Amity and Commerce with France proved wily and astute. They pragmatically sought and acquired access to the French market for U.S. exporters without yielding the American market to countries, like Britain, that persisted in discriminating against U.S. commerce. Sensitive to the nation's long-term economic interests, Franklin's generation avoided unilateral concessions to free riders and ignored the siren call of untested theories.

If this country's first negotiators could examine the way the Reciprocal

Trade Agreements Program evolved in the twentieth century, they might have several concerns. Did a generation of officials preoccupied with providing leadership after World War II assign inordinate weight to foreign policy concerns and neglect parallel obligations to domestic producers and workers? Did the governing elite allow an enthusiasm for free trade and international cooperation to overwhelm prudent concern for import-sensitive domestic workers in unskilled positions—those most vulnerable to cheap foreign competition? While opening the U.S. market, did government officials honor their commitment to provide effective cushions and safeguards to these victims?

For a generation—from the mid-1930s to the early 1960s—congressional support for the reciprocal trade program hinged on executive pledges to avoid injury to import-competing industries and workers. Congress and the executive branch effectively struck a bargain in 1934. Under certain conditions, the executive could reduce tariffs in exchange for reciprocal concessions abroad. In return, Congress gained a commitment to safeguard American producers and workers from serious import-related injury. If domestic parties could demonstrate that increased imports resulted from tariff reductions, and thus caused or threatened serious injury to U.S. producers of the like product, the executive agreed to withdraw or modify the tariff concessions. With this provision in place, a majority in Congress could vote to renew the executive's trade negotiating authority confident that adequate safeguards existed to protect import-sensitive constituents from injurious foreign competition.

In 1962 the Trade Expansion Act altered the terms of this arrangement. Congress and the executive agreed to abandon the no-injury pledge, effectively recognizing that market-opening trade concessions produced injury to some. In return, they would compensate firms and workers with adjustment assistance to help trade losers adapt to increased import competition. Only in extraordinary circumstances would escape clause action lead to the withdrawal of previous tariff concessions.

Origins of the Escape Clause

The escape clause, a circuit-breaker mechanism to protect domestic producers from import-related injury, first emerged in 1935. Under pressure from domestic industries to prevent third countries with low labor costs from reaping the principal benefits of reciprocal trade agreements, the Roosevelt administration inserted the first such provision in a trade agreement with Belgium. For the next sixty years variations of this escape clause offered hope to many distressed domestic industries and workers.

The story begins with President Franklin Roosevelt and his response to business criticism of the trade program of Secretary of State Cordell Hull. In 1934 and 1935 the White House received numerous complaints about the trade agreement negotiated with Brazil. This reciprocity pact contained a concession on manganese, even though Brazil was not the primary U.S. supplier. Domestic manganese producers anticipated, correctly, that a third country, the Soviet Union, would become the major beneficiary. Special trade adviser George Peek, a nationalist businessman, also complained to Roosevelt about the State Department practice of generalizing bilateral trade agreement reductions to other countries, even to nations discriminating against U.S. commerce.

During the Belgian negotiations in early 1935, affected U.S. industries grumbled about the steep 50 percent reductions offered on cotton textiles, steel, and building materials. Domestic industries warned that third countries—especially Japan—would gain the chief benefits and flood the American market with low-cost imports. Eager to insulate the program from critics, Roosevelt directed the State Department to prepare some type of safeguard provision.[3]

As drafted in the Belgian bilateral agreement, the provision stated: "Each of the two Governments reserves the right to withdraw the concession granted on any article under this agreement, or to impose quantitative restrictions on the importation of such article, if at any time there should be evidence that, as a result of the extension of such concession to third countries, the latter will obtain the major benefit of such concession and that, in consequence thereof, an unduly large increase of the importations of such article will take place." With this clause, Under Secretary of State William Phillips hoped to reassure Roosevelt. State anticipated that Belgian exporters would "supply a major portion of any increase in imports resulting from the reduction in duty," but "remedial measures" could be taken if "competitive strength in some other country (e.g., *Japan*)" should be "greatly in excess of expectations."[4]

Subsequently, the State Department inserted similar escape clauses in reciprocity agreements with Sweden, Canada, the Netherlands, and Switzerland. Curiously, the negotiators did not include it in early agreements with Brazil, Haiti, Colombia, and Nicaragua—perhaps because these Latin American countries did not export goods that competed with U.S. products. Rising coffee imports, for instance, did not jeopardize any domestic interest.

Weak Enforcement

Before World War II the State Department and the interagency Committee on Trade Agreements administered these third-country escape clauses. Predictably, the State Department, more concerned with negotiating trade agreements than with monitoring results, discouraged efforts to reopen the terms of agreements. For instance, it rejected a complaint from the New Haven Clock Company attributing increased watch imports to the Swiss concession. Without offering the petitioner a hearing, Assistant Secretary Francis B. Sayre responded that "our studies to date have not revealed any injury to our trade or commerce resulting from the devaluation of the Swiss currency."[5]

The executive branch rejected several other pre–World War II petitions to invoke the third-country escape clause. These petitions involved heliotropin, tapioca and sago, and edible gelatin. Interestingly, special circumstances enabled one industry to obtain some relief. In May 1937 Puerto Rico complained that imports of machine-embroidered linen handkerchiefs from China and Japan benefited from a concession to Belgium on this article. Nonetheless, an interagency country committee, responsible to the CTA for screening the complaint, upheld State's unbending position. It recommended against reopening the agreement on grounds that no evidence of substantial injury to Puerto Rico existed.

After the governor of Puerto Rico complained loudly to the Interior Department about Japanese and Chinese imports of handkerchiefs, the bureaucracy took another look. In May 1939 the CTA concluded that the handkerchief concession had misfired. In the spring of 1940 it was withdrawn—the only tariff concession nullified among the many pre–World War II reductions.

What distinguished handkerchiefs from other sensitive products? Possibly, the facts of the case were decisive; certainly, the attitude of President Roosevelt was relevant. In November 1934 Roosevelt had informed the State Department that he was anxious to avoid any tariff concessions that would "seriously hurt our difficult task in Puerto Rico, the Virgin Islands, and Hawaii."[6]

After the outbreak of war in Europe, several other domestic industries requested escape clause relief. Some reflected war-related disruptions. The Committee on Trade Agreements rejected requests on softwood lumber, zinc, cord and twine, tapioca, and petroleum. For foreign policy reasons the State Department did not wish to provide relief, and government lawyers found ample reason to dismiss the petitions. Most lacked compelling evidence, and each sought import protection from the principal beneficiary of a trade agreement. The third-country, or free-rider, escape clause sought to guard against *unanticipated surges from third countries*—not rising imports from a party to a reciprocity agreement.

One meritorious case—involving fox furs from Canada—emerged late in 1939. Lacking access to the European market, Canadian fur producers had little choice but to substantially increase exports to the United States—creating a surge situation. In this instance, the CTA negotiated a supplementary quota agreement with Canada. The complex process employed to evaluate the petition, which included public hearings and negotiations with Canada, proved time-consuming. What the episode demonstrated was the need for a unilateral remedy procedure—one not requiring international negotiations.[7]

The modern escape clause, designed to address import surges from *any* supplier country, was introduced in response to World War II circumstances. To facilitate the purchase of war materials, for example, Great Britain in 1941 requested maximum tariff reductions on its woolen and cotton exports to the United States. Tariff commissioners Raymond Stevens and Oscar Ryder opposed such drastic cuts. Once "the present emergency has passed," the reductions would "result in imports in such volume as to cause real injury to domestic producers and serious political repercussions." They agreed to support the tariff reductions only if the CTA approved a new escape clause provision permitting modification of the concession should real injury materialize. Ryder drafted such a clause for inclusion in any agreement with the United Kingdom and the British Dominions.[8]

As it turned out, the United States relied on lend-lease to finance British aid, not further tariff reductions. But in 1942 a version of Ryder's draft appeared in a reciprocal trade agreement with Mexico. Secretary of the Interior Harold Ickes insisted on an escape clause to protect independent oil producers, fearful that tariff concessions on petroleum would harm them after the war. Lead and zinc producers also wanted a safeguard provision. The clause inserted in the Mexican agreement did not permit the United States to take unilateral action except by risking denunciation of the entire agreement.[9]

During the war the State Department and the interagency trade apparatus denied several other industry requests for trade agreement modifications. In May 1945, for instance, the Schwinn Company requested restrictions on light English-type bicycles to equalize the differential in labor costs. The Committee on Trade Agreements refused this petition, noting that the domestic industry had not shown that it was suffering serious injury. In the absence of compelling evidence, the CTA refused to take any action that might conflict with its market-opening policy. It noted the importance of political and security factors in reaching this decision.

The U.S. watch industry also pressed unsuccessfully for restraints on Swiss imports. Although the 1936 reciprocal trade agreement contained a third-country escape provision, this provision did not apply to increased imports from Switzerland, the party to the concession. Within the U.S. government the U.S. Tariff Commission and particularly the Defense Department advocated quotas to protect the watch industry. Skilled watchmakers also made specialized timing devices essential to the military. But State Department representatives temporized and talked vaguely in interagency meetings of using the escape clause to demonstrate the administration's willingness to aid domestic industries.

Despite President Roosevelt's personal commitment to the no-injury concept, Congress continued to grumble about lax enforcement and the absence of effective safeguards. It demanded concrete evidence that the executive would actually use safeguards when domestic industries encountered import-related injury. In 1945 Congress insisted on further assurances as the price for renewing reciprocal trade agreements and authorizing additional tariff cuts to as much as 75 percent below 1934 rates. Eager to continue the trade liberalization program, President Harry Truman pledged not to "trade out" U.S. industry. He also promised to cut tariffs selectively only after careful study had shown that the reduction would not cause serious injury to any essential domestic industry.[10] The State Department agreed to include escape clauses in all future trade agreements. Although essential to renewal of the RTAP, this bargain did not allay all congressional concerns.

Several problems remained. Many lawmakers on Capitol Hill perceived—correctly, as the record shows—that the State Department regarded trade policy as an instrument of foreign policy. From the congressional perspective, this meant that State would continue to subordinate tariff considerations to "extraneous and overvalued diplomatic considerations." Congress simply did not trust the mysterious interdepartmental Committee on Trade Agreements, considered a group "dominated by the State Department." The legislature had much more confidence in the independent, bipartisan TC, an agency with considerable institutional experience assessing trade problems. Its six commissioners were presidential appointees subject to Senate confirmation, not obscure civil servants beyond the direct reach of Congress.[11]

Independent Fact Finder

Major changes occurred after the 1946 congressional elections, when the Republicans took control of both the Senate and House of Representatives. Officials in the State Department read the election returns and understood their meaning for trade policy. A few weeks later, in December, the U.S. government invoked the third-country escape clause again—for only the second time. On this occasion the CTA withdrew the concession on linen fire hose granted to Canada. This decision came at a politically significant moment. Reciprocal trade faced a difficult renewal battle in Congress, and the administration wanted new negotiating authority to conduct the Geneva Round of trade negotiations and proceed with plans for an International Trade Organization (ITO), a companion to the United Nations. But congressional Republicans generally opposed more cuts in tariff rates and believed that U.S. trade negotiators frequently ignored the legitimate interests of domestic producers and workers in labor-intensive industries.

Senate Republican leaders Arthur Vandenberg (chairman of the Foreign Relations Committee) and Eugene Millikin (chairman of the Finance Committee) negotiated another compromise with the Truman administration. In return for extending the Reciprocal Trade Agreements Act, the administration agreed to include an escape clause in all future trade agreements permitting the withdrawal or modification of concessions if, as a result of unforeseen developments and of the concessions, imports increased to such an extent as to cause or threaten serious injury to domestic producers. Truman also consented to issue an executive order (E.O. 9832) directing the TC to investigate these complaints either on its own motion or at the request of the president and make appropriate recommendations. A few days later, while delivering a major speech on foreign economic policy at Baylor University, Truman pledged that "domestic interests will be safeguarded in this process of expanding trade. . . . There is no intention to sacrifice one group to the benefit of another group."[12]

The negotiations with Vandenberg and Millikin, longtime critics of Hull's program, salvaged the reciprocal trade program politically. The new compromise appeared to alter fundamentally the executive's approach to trade administration. In place of the mysterious interagency review process, which State directed, the executive branch consented to more open and transparent procedures for hearing and processing complaints. It also established an independent fact-finding process for evaluating escape clause petitions. However, the record shows that the Truman administration had no intention of moderating the trade liberalization program or of permitting TC decisions to interfere with proposed tariff reductions.

To make their plans for a postwar International Trade Organization palatable to a Congress suspicious of international economic organization, State Department planners had proposed inclusion of a version of the clause inserted in the Mexican agreement. In bilateral discussions with the British in 1945, the United States at first proposed a steep tariff cut in combination with a temporary escape clause. But when British officials expressed "apprehension" that the clause might be used to "nullify or substantially impair the reduction of tariffs by the United States," Hull's chief trade planner, Harry Hawkins, made a telling observation: the United States had invoked the escape clause only once out of some 1,200 cases. Hawkins noted that "our failure to make full use of the escape clauses in trade agreements was not for lack of pressure, which domestic producers had brought to bear in numerous cases, but primarily because the Administration, and particularly the interdepartmental organization handling these matters, was fully conscious of the vital need for enlarging the volume of United States imports."[13]

Congress did not approve U.S. membership in the ITO, but an interim version, known as the General Agreement on Tariffs and Trade, contained an escape clause. Article 19 provided:

> If, as a result of unforeseen developments and of the effect of obligations incurred by a contracting party under this Agreement, including tariff concessions, any product is being imported into the territory of that contracting party in such increased quantities and under such conditions as to cause or threaten serious injury to domestic producers in that territory of like or directly competitive products, the contracting party shall be free, in respect of such product and to the extent and for such time as may be necessary to prevent or remedy such injury, to suspend the obligation in whole or in part to withdraw or modify the concession.[14]

This article requires that a nation wishing to nullify or withdraw concessions must compensate trading partners for the privilege.

INFLUENCING THE TARIFF COMMISSION

After the 1947 compromise establishing an independent procedure for evaluating escape clause petitions, the selection of presidential appointees to the six-member TC became critical to the State Department. As early as 1934 Secretary Hull had recognized that an uncooperative Tariff Commission could jeopardize his tariff-cutting program. Consequently, State began to intervene in the appointments process. In 1937, for instance, Assistant Secretary Sayre recruited Henry Grady, a former chairman of the CTA to accept a TC appointment. He wrote: "I need not point out to you how vitally important the work of the USTC is to the success of our trade agreements program. As you well know, a USTC which did not see eye to eye with us, or which should swing away from our program, would be fatal to the success of our undertaking."[15] There was no reason to doubt Grady's loyalty to the president or to Hull's trade liberalization program. He had demonstrated his enthusiasm for tariff cutting, and both Grady and his wife Lucretia, a Democratic national committeewoman from California, were Roosevelt activists.[16]

In 1942 Hull pressed the candidacy of Oscar Ryder for TC chairman. He noted that as a commissioner Ryder "has been cooperating well with the State Department, especially as it relates to . . . trade agreement undertakings."[17] After the independent TC acquired new responsibilities in 1948, the State Department looked for "a strong and independent supporter of the program." The chairman of the trade agreements program described the "ideal appointee" as an individual not dependent on confirmation in his post by the next Congress or on continuous federal service. In other words, "the appointee needed is a man who would act vigorously in the interests of trade-barrier reduction and independently of future reappointment possibilities."[18]

Protecting Open Markets

During this period the State Department generally succeeded in placing loyal reciprocal trade enthusiasts on the TC. Indeed, from 1945 to 1951, when Congress amended the trade act to limit the commission's discretion in escape clause proceedings, the TC regularly rejected domestic industry petitions for relief. It dismissed fourteen out of twenty-one petitions without initiating an investigation and without affording the parties a formal hearing or an explanation. Pursuant to Truman's order in 1947, the commission enjoyed wide discretion. It could institute an investigation only when, in its judgment, "there is good and sufficient reason therefore."[19]

A review of voting by members of the TC shows an identifiable pattern. Three Democratic commissioners (Oscar Ryder; Lynn Edminster, a former aide to Secretary Hull; and Dana Durand, an economist with nominal Republican connections known to support Hull's program) frequently combined to dismiss applications for relief or to make negative determinations after a full investigation. This pro-reciprocal trade majority provided the votes necessary to reject a substantial number of petitions in 1949, 1950, and 1951. In the instances where the commission did conduct a full investigation, it usually rendered negative findings along partisan lines.

Commissioner Edminster expressed the majority's philosophy in a 1948 speech to cigar manufacturers. Noting that the Trade Agreements Act was intended to promote increased U.S. exports by "enabling foreign countries to sell more of their products to us," Edminster said: "If . . . a very substantial increase occurs in our imports as a result of the concessions we have granted, that will be only what the Act itself contemplates. If these very substantial increases in total imports should occur with but a few cases in which the increases are so great and so injurious as to require action, or perhaps even investigation, under the escape clause, then I suppose nearly everyone should be happy."[20]

One commissioner who frequently dissented from the TC's majority was Edgar Brossard, a protégé of Finance Committee chairman Reed Smoot, appointed in the Coolidge administration. Privately, Brossard criticized the majority's disposition to prejudge in secret without a public hearing.[21]

During the Truman administration the Tariff Commission continued to deflect and bury petitions for import relief. It did, however, make several timely, and token, affirmative determinations. In two instances, in 1950 and 1951, President Truman upheld the commission's recommendation to provide relief in the form of modified concessions. As a result, both the president and Congress could claim that the escape clause worked in genuinely deserving cases.

The first involved women's fur felt hats. In September 1950 the commission rendered a unanimous affirmative determination, and in November 1951, under the provisions of a revised law, it made a second unanimous finding for hatters' fur.[22] In both cases President Truman accepted the Tariff Commission's findings for import relief. Eager to win renewal of its trade program in 1951, the State Department supported Truman's decision.[23] Because the process was new, executive agencies apparently did not review the commission's findings. In the second case, however, President Truman warned Chairman Ryder that modifications in tariff concessions "for a period longer than is necessary to prevent or remedy the injury" could adversely affect the domestic economy, "injure American consumers," and "impede American foreign policy objectives."[24]

These two early escape clause findings in favor of domestic producers, and the subsequent modifications in tariff concessions, represented a conciliatory signal to congressional critics. Gradually, the Truman administration came to recognize that a credible, impartial escape clause process was required to maintain support for the tariff program on Capitol Hill.

Even so, in 1951 Republican members of the House Ways and Means Committee decried the escape clause's "patent looseness and ambiguity" and the resulting "complete ineffectiveness." They noted that the TC would not order an investigation unless imports increased relative to domestic production, thus ignoring the threat or imminence of increased imports.[25] In response to criticism from the business community, Congress provided more specific statutory direction as it revised the escape clause in 1951. The lawmakers set a time limit on escape clause proceedings, directing the commission to complete its investigation in one year. The 1951 law also provided for public hearings that afforded opportunity for interested parties to testify and introduce evidence. It ordered the TC to consider a variety of factors—including trends in production, prices, employment, imports, and inventories. Once the commission submitted its findings to the president, the law directed him to take action within sixty days or report to Congress.[26]

Before Congress made its procedural changes, few escape clause proceedings led to import remedies. In January 1952 Chairman Ryder told the House Appropriations Committee that the president had taken action in two out of about twenty cases. Congressman John Phillips (R-Calif.) retorted: "You have a .100 batting average."[27]

Viewed retrospectively, that statistic probably skewed the record. Although a number of domestic industries did seek relief from 1947 to 1951, the available evidence suggests that most of those applications lacked persuasive factual support. In the period from 1947 to 1951 it is difficult to find an industry important to the national interest that suffered irreparable harm.

The success ratio improved after the Trade Agreements Extension Act took effect in June 1951. Six industries soon filed escape clause petitions in order to test the new provisions and deadlines.[28] These filings initiated a pattern that would continue for over forty years. Before presidential elections, domestic industries filed import remedy petitions in a way calculated to force the president and his appointees to make difficult decisions during the campaign, when domestic issues could override foreign policy concerns. When a negative determination might offend blocs of voters, domestic producers calculated that they could exert maximum political leverage on the president.

An important test of the Truman administration's attitude toward the 1951 law took place when the California garlic producers filed an escape clause petition with the Tariff Commission in October 1951. Following a hearing in February 1952, the commission voted 4 to 2, with Democrats Ryder and Edminster dissenting, recommending that the president modify the existing tariff concession and impose a quota on imports.[29] In this instance, one the State Department considered a "test case," the Tariff Commission for the first time submitted a split decision to the White House. Truman rejected that recommendation, setting a pattern for presidents to ignore findings when the TC divided evenly or lacked unanimity.

At the presidential review level, the State Department and other agencies registered strong dissents. They established another important precedent: after the TC made a recommendation, executive agencies would review, then reverse, the Tariff Commission's findings of fact for policy reasons. In the garlic case, the State Department argued that the "dissenting minority opinion" of Commissioners Ryder and Edminster, two Democrats strongly supportive of the tariff reduction, was "much more closely in accord with the facts and far more persuasive than that of the majority." State openly played the foreign affairs card, determined to save Mexico and Italy from the impact of trade restrictions on garlic. It advised President Truman that "the Tariff Commission's recommended action would set a highly restrictive precedent. From the standpoint of United States foreign relations, the action would be contrary to overriding interests of the country and would be inconsistent with our international undertakings."[30]

In letters to Congress, Truman sided with his foreign policy advisers. The president even adopted the State Department's language and rationale as his own. The TC was "flooded" with escape clause actions. If "the standards employed by the [TC] majority were to be applied generally to American imports, I am confident that our trade agreements program would soon be impaired beyond all possible remedy, and gains of the negotiated tariffs completely nullified," he asserted. Truman ignored the fact that foreign quantitative restraints and exchange controls already nullified the "benefits" supposedly gained for U.S. exporters in such negotiations. As he saw it, "A way must be found for these countries to carry their share of defense costs without continued reliance on our aid. It is to their own benefit—and to the benefit of the American taxpayer—that we find ways and continue to improve them, as quickly as possible, to the end that *substantial foreign imports may become a substitute for direct foreign aid*" (emphasis added).[31]

The garlic case demonstrated that where Truman's obligation to enforce the escape clause conflicted with foreign policy concerns, he would not hesitate to dismiss the claims of domestic industry. In effect, he directed the California garlic industry to help reconstruct Italy.

Truman thus delivered a strong free trade message. Those who wanted to modify trade concessions must sustain the burden of proof. He could afford to strong-arm domestic industries and give priority to foreign policy. Truman was not a candidate for reelection. During the remainder of 1952, he, as a retiring officeholder, used other opportunities to vote his free trade convictions.

He did so in the high-visibility Swiss watch case. In this proceeding, a four-member TC majority found a "threat of serious injury" and recommended modification of the tariff concession.[32] From 1936 to 1940 imports took 20 percent of the domestic market for jeweled-lever and pin-lever watches and then increased rapidly after World War II, capturing 83 percent in the 1946–50 period.

The president's rejection letter again relied heavily on State Department analysis. In a "top secret" memorandum, State reminded Truman that on December 11, 1951, he had approved a policy regarding Switzerland "designed to attempt to draw that country away from its relatively neutral position in world affairs. It was determined that Swiss military, economic and democratic strength is such that closer relationship between Switzerland and the common defense effort of the free European community would be advantageous to the security interests of the United States." In particular, State noted how Switzerland had cooperated with the United States in July 1951 to impose export controls on Soviet trade.[33]

A pattern thus emerged. During the early Cold War years President Truman relied heavily on State Department advice for decisions in trade remedy cases.

In approving the dissenting opinions of Commissioners Ryder and Edminster, and rejecting the majority opinion, he stated: "I have examined the evidence . . . and I am unable to agree with their conclusion. Rather, I am of the opinion that the weight of evidence does not support the claim that our domestic watch industry has been seriously injured, or that there is a threat of serious injury."[34]

In effect, the president retried the evidence without a public hearing and substituted his own judgment for that of the tariff commissioners. This result had significant long-term procedural implications. Hereafter parties dissatisfied with the TC's affirmative determinations would seek to persuade the president and executive agencies to review and reverse the commission on the record. Truman's decision in the watch case helped establish several important precedents. The White House would become more involved in each escape clause case, reviewing the evidence in a detailed way but not making the opportunity to hear the testimony and question the witnesses in a formal hearing. This approach had at least one pernicious consequence. It removed the layer of political insulation that an independent, nonpartisan decision-making process afforded executive decision makers and gave a green light to the lobbyists and lawyers eager to involve the president in each import remedy decision.

President Truman also cited international considerations, including "apprehension abroad concerning the course of United States trade policy," for not accepting the TC finding. "These events," he said, "do not mean we must never use the escape clause again. They do mean . . . that if we wish to avoid a serious loss of confidence in our leadership, any new restrictive action on our part must be clearly justified." With regard to the specific Swiss circumstances, Truman noted that any U.S. action would "adversely" affect "an industry tailored in large part to the United States market and employing one out of every ten industrial workers in the country." Thus "we would be striking a heavy blow at our whole effort to increase international trade and permit friendly nations to earn their own dollars and pay their own way in the world."

Truman's criticism of the Tariff Commission angered one member who signed the majority opinion. Commissioner Brossard said: "For the President to set himself up as a tariff expert in opposition to the fact-finding, bipartisan, TC, its staff of technical tariff experts, in finding injury to the domestic industry is a bit far-fetched and just another way the President has of showing his contempt for laws he does not like, as in the case of the Taft-Hartley-Act and the Steel Strike case."[35]

In retrospect, it is apparent that the president's negative decisions in the garlic and watch cases sent clear signals to the TC. Soon afterward, in another escape clause case relating to spring clothespins, Commission Democrats

Ryder, Edminster, and McGill all voted against relief, whereas the only two Republican commissioners—Brossard and John P. Gregg—made affirmative findings. Privately, Brossard expressed his outrage, believing the outcome to be incompatible with the evidence developed in the investigation:

> It looks like the stage is now set for future findings of no relief for domestic industries by the Democratic members of the USTC who have now been given their public "spanking" and policy direction. . . . Apparently, . . . relief to domestic farmers, industries, and laborers is to be denied by President Truman and his party henchmen in the State Department and on the Tariff Commission in most "escape clause" cases. The law [is] . . . to be interpreted and executed by this administration as a political party measure to uphold and confirm what the President does irrespective of its clear intent and clearly stated Congressional objective of relief where serious injury is found.[36]

The facts of other cases support Brossard's claim of political interference. In 1930 Congress had established a duty on spring clothespins of 20 cents per gross, but in trade agreements with Sweden and Mexico the Roosevelt administration reduced that duty 50 percent to 10 cents per gross. After World War II clothespin imports surged from Sweden and Denmark. In two years (1949–51) the ratio of imports to domestic shipments rose from 24 percent to 43 percent. Meanwhile, the domestic industry's economic health deteriorated, and several leading domestic producers began to import clothespins. A similar arrangement appeared in other TC decisions during this period. Voting along partisan lines, Truman's Democratic supporters on the commission rejected escape clause relief for the Massachusetts fisheries industry, the maraschino cherry association, and the California fish canners.[37] On the other hand, in unanimous decisions the Tariff Commission opposed relief to bicycle manufacturers but determined that fig producers should receive it.[38]

In 1951 and 1952 President Truman set a pattern for his successors. Despite his promises to Congress in 1945 and 1947 not to trade off domestic interests, Truman's actions and words show that he had little sympathy for domestic industries battling foreign competition. On each key decision he sided with the State Department and other foreign affairs agencies that wished to pursue international political and economic objectives at the expense of U.S. industry. Later, in material prepared for but not included in his *Memoirs*, Truman explained his position: "I felt that in certain lines of manufacture, American producers should have no real difficulty in competing with foreign-made goods." The president rejected some petitions because "to have done otherwise would have been to invite unemployment in other countries—such as Italy and

France—where Communism adds to its ranks from persons thrown out of work."[39]

In this regard, Truman's attitude mirrored the larger public confidence in America's competitive advantage. It reflected his philosophy that to restore a healthy world economy, the United States must extend a helping hand to foreign business. During these years no critical U.S. industry, except perhaps watches, engaged in a war of survival with foreign competitors.

Eisenhower: Helping Other Nations Earn a Living

Domestic industries hoped that the election of General Dwight Eisenhower would bring a significant change in the executive's approach to import remedies. Republican commissioner Edgar Brossard wanted the new president to administer "laws as they are passed by Congress" and to discontinue "having their clear intent and meaning ignored . . . and . . . altered to suit the pleasure of the executive by their subsequent personal interpretation."[40]

Eisenhower would disappoint Brossard and many import-sensitive domestic industries. The new president's position resembled Truman's. Although Eisenhower approached individual decisions with "a great deal of judiciousness," he believed that "the burden of proof was on those whose views were against the established policy of expanding trade." He would impose escape clause relief only when it was unavoidable. This attitude appeared to contradict the promise Eisenhower gave Representative Joseph Martin (R-Mass.) in 1955, when reciprocal trade was up for renewal: "No American industry will be placed in jeopardy by the administration of this measure."[41]

As a military leader who had spent much of his adult life outside the United States, Eisenhower was sensitive to foreign concerns. The new president shared the view of eastern corporate and banking elites that other nations needed expanded trade to make a living. Privately, he criticized protectionist Republicans and business leaders for "shortsightedness bordering upon tragic stupidity. . . . by and large, the case for lowered American tariffs is so generally valid." In a world threatened by aggressive communism, Eisenhower favored a system of world trade that allowed "backward people to make a decent living— even if only a minimum one measured by American standards—then [otherwise] in the long run we must fall prey to the communistic attack."[42]

Domestic industries sensed that Eisenhower, far more than Truman, was receptive to national defense arguments for escape clause relief. Watchmakers dissatisfied with the Truman decision in the Swiss case decided to test Eisenhower. They filed another escape clause petition in September 1953. When an affirmative TC determination reached the president's desk in May 1954, he predictably focused on its defense ramifications. "It is difficult for me to believe that we have any room for complacency as we look at our demands in war for people skilled in the handling of miniature gears, bearings and appliances, and in dealing with minute tolerances." This time the Defense Department strongly endorsed increased duties, as did Commerce, Treasury, and other agencies.[43] As it turned out, Eisenhower considered the watch industry a special case having national security significance. Whereas Truman had approved three out of the five recommendations that reached his desk, Eisenhower rejected twice as many as he granted.[44]

The 1953 brier tobacco pipe case, the first to come up for review on Eisenhower's watch, proved an early, and more accurate, barometer of the new president's priorities. This example involved on one side a small domestic industry, with a dozen producers and a few thousand workers, and on the other side three major European allies: Great Britain, France, and Italy. Data developed in the investigation showed imports rising from 6 percent of domestic consumption in 1939 to over 18 percent in 1951 and 1952. Domestic sales had declined, as had the number of domestic producers and their profits. In 1952 twelve U.S. producers represented 89 percent of domestic production, and eight of these firms experienced losses. The average number of production workers fell from 3,000 in 1946 to 1,300 in 1952. Viewed retrospectively, the brier pipe case seems to be a classic example of trade concession–related injury to a domestic industry. Obviously, the tariff commissioners thought so, for a unanimous Tariff Commission recommended relief to President Truman in December 1952.[45]

On January 20, 1953, when Dwight Eisenhower took office, he found the brier pipe case awaiting a presidential decision. Executive agencies offered the White House contradictory advice. The foreign affairs agencies implored him to reject the finding. France, Britain, West Germany, and Japan—the State Department warned—looked at this decision for signs of coming administration policy. In Italy "communist agents" would cite a determination to follow the TC as an "example of the unwillingness of the United States to make economic self-help a reality" and so "undermine confidence in United States leadership."[46]

Sensing a difficult decision, Eisenhower asked the TC for more information while the administration pondered options and gained familiarity with its statutory responsibilities. On the one hand, the president understood that "to decline to grant the [tariff] increase, when the case is so clear-cut as to comply with legal conditions, would probably provoke the Congress and might result in a failure to reenact the law." On the other hand, "approval would hurt the morale of our allies far more than it will hurt them economically."[47]

In November 1953 Eisenhower decided to reject the brier pipe recommendation. Privately, he wrote Finance Committee chairman Eugene Millikin and Ways and Means chairman Dan Reed that "good" possibilities existed for displaced pipe makers to transfer to furniture and other woodworking establishments.[48] In a public statement the president avoided any emphasis on foreign policy considerations. Despite the unanimous TC recommendation, he chose to dispute the fact finders' conclusions—saying that the "primary cause of the industry's difficulty [was] . . . a shift in consumer preference."[49]

BICYCLES

The bicycle case in 1954 also tested Eisenhower's resolve. Here the administration faced a decision to either protect a domestic consumer goods industry that was rapidly losing market share to imports or yield to pressures from powerful allies—Great Britain, West Germany, and France among others.

The record appeared to favor the domestic industry. In June 1954 the Bicycle Manufacturers Association of America had filed an escape clause petition, and the TC voted 4 to 1 in favor of withdrawing the tariff concession, originally granted to the United Kingdom in 1938.[50] The commission found that imports of bicycles as a share of domestic production had risen from 3.5 percent in 1950 to 28.5 percent in 1953 and 62.0 percent in 1954. Although consumption had expanded with the postwar baby boom, the domestic bicycle industry lost 32 percentage points of market share in four years (1951–54). For domestic producers, the ratio of net operating profit to sales of bicycles and parts dropped precipitously from 7.6 percent in 1951–52 to a loss of 1.0 percent in 1954. Employment of production workers fell from 3,437 in 1951 to 2,901 in 1954.

The Tariff Commission's findings excited the foreign affairs community and prompted foreign representations at the White House. According to British records, the State Department encouraged this lobbying. It provided British officials with a copy of the TC report "in strict confidence and with the request that we should not admit publicly to having received it."[51]

From his post in London U.S. ambassador Winthrop Aldrich cabled that "bicycles are . . . a crucial test of the whole idea of 'trade not aid.'" With U.S. encouragement to help close the so-called dollar gap, British manufacturers had created a "new market in the U.S. by making and selling at reasonable price an item of high-quality standards." If the United States now imposed tariffs, the effort to encourage British exports and to expand world trade would be seen as a program of "words not deeds."[52]

Secretary of State John Foster Dulles took a personal interest in the outcome, telling Eisenhower that "acceptance of the Tariff Commission's recommendation could stimulate adverse political and psychological effects among our Allies, far out of proportion to the grievances claimed by the United States industry." Dulles wanted the president to turn down the bicycle petition in a way not prejudicial to enactment of new trade-negotiating authority. Elsewhere in the administration officials were divided. Treasury, Labor, and Commerce supported the TC recommendation. But State, Interior, Agriculture, Defense, the Council of Economic Advisers, and the International Cooperation Administration opposed it.[53]

Sensitive to the issues, Eisenhower authorized a compromise. He agreed to raise duties on balloon tire bicycles from 15 to 22.5 percent, as the TC majority suggested, but he asserted the president's prerogative and provided only a small increase on lightweight bicycles, increasing the duty from 7.5 to 11.25 percent, not 22.5 percent as the commission majority recommended. With this compromise, Eisenhower claimed that the domestic industry could "strengthen its position," while assuring producers in "friendly foreign lands an excellent competitive chance to share handsomely in our large and growing market for bicycles." The decision, he said, "helps strengthen the economies of our allies and their ability to buy our products."[54] This outcome pleased British officials, who considered Eisenhower personally sympathetic to their economic position. However, his "legal approach" raised concern that the president's "powers of discretion would be less valuable to us than we had once thought."[55]

As it turned out, the bicycle remedy not only bought time for the administration in Congress, it facilitated adjustment in the domestic industry. The increased rates of duty, as well as investment in new plants, development of new models, and use of imported parts, enabled the bicycle industry to recapture market share. Imports declined from 41.2 percent of the U.S. market in 1955 to 16.1 percent in 1966. Later the U.S. International Trade Commission would cite bicycle manufacturing as a shining example of an industry that "modernized, improving its performance and becoming more competitive with imports following escape-clause relief."[56]

Throughout his eight years in the White House, Eisenhower remained sensitive to the foreign repercussions of escape clause decisions. Understanding his orientation, executive agencies gave him ample reasons for rejecting protectionist moves at home. Records of the Eisenhower administration show that in one escape clause investigation after another, the State Department counseled the president to withhold relief to U.S. industries and workers. For instance, in the 1953 handblown glassware case, State warned that import restrictions would have "grave political repercussions in the Federal Republic of Germany . . . and would provide the Soviet Union with unanswerable material for propaganda."[57] In 1954 the State and Defense Departments argued against relief to U.S. producers of scissors and shears. State emphasized that West German production came from areas near the Ruhr where "Soviet propaganda has already had considerable effect." Defense warned that a hike in duties could have an adverse effect on Germany, Italy, Japan, and the United Kingdom. "The increase would affect the morale of such countries as well as their economic welfare and stability."[58]

LEAD AND ZINC, 1954

In a 1954 investigation affecting the domestic mining industry and relations with several important Western Hemisphere nations (Canada, Mexico, Bolivia, and Peru), the State Department proved especially insistent. Although all six tariff commissioners found that U.S. lead and zinc producers had been seriously injured as a consequence of tariff concessions, Secretary of State Dulles advised Eisenhower to reject that recommendation on foreign policy grounds. A decision to provide import relief would have "grave consequences" for hemispheric solidarity against communist influences. "There would be strong popular resentment in Canada and Mexico, which will make our borders much less secure," Dulles said. "The great opportunity to combat Communism in this hemisphere won by the success of Guatemala, would be more than canceled out." Moreover, "Soviet Communist leaders would be elated and would redouble their efforts to divide the free world."[59]

FISH AND COLD WAR CONCERNS

During the Eisenhower years diplomatic and military considerations prompted the executive branch to dismiss trade remedy complaints against a number of Cold War allies. The Nordic countries and Iceland benefited from their strategic locations. In 1954 the president approved a national security policy memorandum regarding U.S. efforts to maintain Iceland "as an independent and economically viable nation with a stable government friendly to the United States and actively cooperating in NATO defense efforts." That document specifically asserted that the United States should "avoid trade actions which would adversely affect Iceland" and "seek to increase free world markets for Icelandic fish . . . in order to reduce Iceland's dependence on trade with the Soviet bloc."[60]

Given the importance that the administration assigned to Iceland as a "base for offensive operations in conjunction with NATO," it is not surprising that President Eisenhower twice rejected escape clause recommendations to provide relief to New England fish producers claiming that imports from Canada, Norway, and Iceland injured the domestic industry. After a 1954 TC finding, the Defense Department warned that trade restrictions benefiting New England fishermen would have effects "adverse to the security interests of the United States."[61]

In 1956 the TC again recommended escape clause relief for the New England fishermen—this time, unanimously. But once more the foreign affairs agencies scuttled import remedies. The State Department emphasized the "adverse effects on vital United States political, economic and security interests in Canada, Iceland, and Norway." Acting Secretary of State Herbert Hoover Jr. wrote the president that negotiations would soon begin about the future of U.S. military bases in Iceland. "Public and governmental reaction . . . against the restrictions might well be so strong as to constitute a decisive blow to our prospects for retaining satisfactory defense arrangements with Iceland." Said the International Cooperation Administration, a 50 percent duty on fish would strengthen "those elements in Iceland which wish to drive out U.S. NATO troops. As fish goes so goes Iceland."[62]

Without a doubt, Iceland and Norway held strategic importance during the Cold War. Consequently, two countries that sold virtually no groundfish fillets to the United States before World War II gained, with U.S. economic assistance, 20 percent of the U.S. market for fresh and frozen groundfish fillets in 1952. Canada, which held 9 percent of the U.S. market in 1939, obtained another 25 percent. Thirty years later, Canada and Iceland held over 80 percent of the U.S. market for frozen groundfish fillets.[63]

ASSISTING JAPAN

Eisenhower treated Japan with special sensitivity, reflecting a policy commitment to promote that country's economic recovery and find market opportunities for its exports. An early test came in April 1953, when the TC reported a unanimous finding in favor of import relief for domestic producers of screen-printed silk scarves. Like brier pipes, this was a small industry concentrated in the New York City area. President Eisenhower rejected the recommendation in December 1954, saying that "a stronger and more stable Japanese economy is of major importance to Japan and to the free world. . . . Restrictive action which would affect mainly a Japanese product would be warranted at this time . . . only if it were clearly and unmistakably required."[64]

During the interagency review, the Mutual Security Agency, which was responsible for foreign aid, rationalized inaction on industrial policy grounds. "The industry is unsuited to the United States," where "labor costs form a high percentage of the production cost." Japan was better suited "since it has the natural advantage of its own native raw material, and a large supply of cottage workers to whom the hand-rolling is farmed out." The foreign aid agency also claimed that higher tariffs on Japanese scarves "will place certain operations of the Mutual Security Program in manifold jeopardy." In other words, "we would be inviting discord within Japan . . . we *would be playing into the hands of the Kremlin*" (emphasis added).[65]

Throughout Eisenhower's two presidential terms, his administration looked for ways to avoid imposing trade restrictions on Japanese products while maintaining congressional support for additional tariff liberalization. This became a delicate problem in the late 1950s, when U.S. textile and apparel producers filed a number of escape clause petitions on products imported primarily from Japan. Sensitive to Japanese concerns about *formal* escape clause findings, the White House reluctantly turned to voluntary restraint agreements in an effort to address the textile problem without further antagonizing Congress. Thus a unanimous TC recommendation for higher duties on cotton velveteen in 1956 prompted the administration to negotiate a restraint arrangement with Japan. When Japan consented to a more comprehensive program of textile restraints, U.S. producers withdrew other petitions.[66]

In 1958 more escape clause rulings—on flatware and umbrella frames—as well as other investigations of tuna and plywood created anxiety and even panic in Tokyo business circles. Japanese ambassador Koichiro Asakai reported "apprehension that even a single blow to any minor industry will be enough to create social unrest and political issues in Japan." From Tokyo U.S. ambassador Douglas MacArthur II declared that "Japan must trade or die." An "inevitable consequence" of U.S. trade restrictions, he warned, was a "gradual but inevitable shift of Japanese policy away from present close ties with the U.S. I need not rpt [repeat] not elaborate on what this could mean in terms of our most vital interests in Japan, the Far East, and Asia."[67]

After a unanimous TC recommendation in January 1958 to withdraw tariff concessions on stainless steel flatware, the president deferred action when Japan agreed to limit exports voluntarily. But as in the velveteen situation, the Eisenhower administration discovered that Japanese exporters were transshipping goods to the United States through Hong Kong.

Interestingly, in flatware Senator Prescott Bush (R-Conn.) persuaded the White House to replace the voluntary agreement with a tariff quota in 1959. He succeeded even though the State Department protested that "the Japanese people and their political leaders would view restrictive action on flatware . . . as evidence of a basic lack of good-will on the part of the United States toward Japan."[68]

Despite its wish to preserve alliances and open markets, the Eisenhower administration could not ignore pressure from the domestic textile industry and some others. In winning a congressional extension in 1954, the administration found it necessary to aid the watch and mining industries. Clarence Randall confided in his diary that the White House had decided something "must be done for watches and for lead-zinc. . . . the political pressures are too great and must be faced. If we deny these two, we may wreck our entire program in Congress next year and, conversely, if we grant them, we may by appeasement gain a softening of the opposition."[69] The same was true for textiles. Political pressures from Congress and constituents forced the executive branch to fashion a textile restraint program in 1957.

Protectionist Bush

One enthusiastic Eisenhower supporter in the Senate enjoyed particular success in winning escape clause relief. He was Prescott Bush, the junior Republican senator from Connecticut. Bush had many import-sensitive, labor-intensive industries to represent, and he proved unusually persuasive. He cultivated a close working relationship with a fellow New Englander, the president's chief of staff, former New Hampshire governor Sherman Adams. As Bush recalled, "if you worked with him and were sympathetic with their objectives down there at the White House, . . . you could get what you needed to have, when things came along affecting your state or anything else. So having adopted that attitude from the start . . . I got along very well with Sherm Adams."[70]

One example of Bush's clout in obtaining protection for Connecticut industries involved safety pin producers. Safety pins had little significance for the global balance of power, but Connecticut workers had a direct stake in the industry's health. In 1957, after the Tariff Commission submitted a 4-to-2 affirmative finding recommending relief for domestic producers, Bush visited his friends in the White House.[71] Ten executive agencies opposed the relief, all except the Commerce Department, headed by another New Englander, Sinclair Weeks. But after meeting with Bush, "our friend from Connecticut," Eisenhower's staff recommended that the president provide relief. Gabriel Hauge, the White House official responsible for trade decisions, suggested, mysteriously, to Chief of Staff Adams that "this aspect of the basis for the recommendation will probably have to be explained to the President."[72]

Despite occasional victories for domestic interests, Congress and import-sensitive industries remained dissatisfied with the administration's approach to escape clause cases. Congress believed that the TC and the White House looked for ways to avoid enforcing the law. The record was open to that interpretation. During the eleven years (1951–62) that the 1951 act governed escape clause proceedings, the Tariff Commission conducted 112 investigations. It made affirmative findings in only 33 cases (29.5 percent). On 8 other occasions the commission divided equally, leaving the president with the discretion to accept either set of recommendations. Thus, out of 41 opportunities to grant relief, the president did so in only 15 cases (36.6 percent). In effect, domestic petitioners obtained some type of relief only 13.4 percent of the time, or in baseball parlance they batted .134.[73]

In 1958, when Eisenhower's aides approached Congress about a five-year extension of reciprocal trade, congressional committees devoted weeks to evaluating the escape clause. The House Ways and Means Committee proposed amendments, including an override procedure. When the president disapproved a TC recommendation, Congress might pass a concurrent resolution, requiring a two-thirds vote in each chamber, to implement the TC remedy. However, the Senate Finance Committee modified this procedure to permit overriding the president when a simple majority of Congress concurred.[74]

The Trade Expansion Act

Domestic industry and labor continued to demand effective safeguards against import surges, but the State Department and the foreign affairs community remained apprehensive. They feared that more vigorous escape clause enforcement would nullify existing concessions and invited resurgent protectionism.

Consequently, while writing President John F. Kennedy's Trade Expansion Act, internationalists pressed to dilute the escape clause. As enacted, the 1962 act tightened causation requirements so that the Tariff Commission would have to find more than a loose connection between a trade agreement concession and an increase in imports. The revision stipulated that increased imports must result "in major part" from such tariff concessions. In addition, they had to be "the major factor" causing or threatening serious injury. In an effort to avoid foreign retaliation or the need for the United States to pay compensation for withdrawing a concession, Congress also approved adjustment assistance as an alternative remedy to tariffs or quotas.

One trade expert delighted with the new provisions was Georgetown University law professor Stanley Metzger, a longtime critic of the escape clause. "[T]he result," he said, "is to make escape clause tariff relief more difficult to secure in consequence of the general tightening of requirements for such relief." Republicans on the Ways and Means Committee reached a similar, but less enthusiastic, conclusion: "The bill abandons the philosophy underlying our trade negotiations in the past—that our negotiators refrain from agreeing to a reduction in duties which will bring about serious injury to the domestic industry."[75]

Metzger and the Republicans both were right. The Trade Expansion Act effectively killed the escape clause. Until December 1969 the U.S. Tariff Commission made no affirmative determinations under the Trade Expansion Act provision—rejecting thirteen successive complaints. TCers blamed restrictive statutory language for the results. The commission also repeatedly rejected adjustment assistance petitions, angering organized labor and undercutting union support for the trade liberalization program. Congress had not anticipated that outcome.[76] But President Lyndon B. Johnson's appointees to the commission, a diverse group that included the doctrinaire Metzger, were not disposed to interpret the escape clause in a way that produced protectionist results.

Not until June 1967, when Bruce Clubb, a Johnson Republican from Minnesota, joined the commission, did legal interpretations begin to change. Clubb introduced a more expansive construction involving *but for* analysis, and this gradually became the basis for a number of import remedy decisions during the Nixon administration—especially those involving adjustment assistance. With the confirmation of Bill Leonard, a former staff assistant to Finance Committee chairman Russell Long, in October 1968 and George Moore, a Nixon appointee, in 1969, there began to surface a TC majority that was sympathetic to vigorous enforcement of the escape clause.[77]

With Metzger's free trade brigade blocking escape clause relief at the TC, import-sensitive industries turned up the heat on Congress for quotas and voluntary restraint agreements after the Kennedy Round. Eugene Stewart, a distinguished Washington trade attorney who represented domestic industries over five decades, told a presidential commission: "the escape clause as administered collectively by the USTC and the President has proven to be extremely ineffective and of such slight interest to domestic industries that it fails signally to act as a safety valve in relation to the impact of imports on the domestic economy." He noted that basic industries with deep-seated problems, such as textiles, apparel, footwear, steel, and electronics, chose not to pursue escape clause relief, and that smaller industries "rarely are rewarded for their efforts, however meritorious."[78]

The irrepressible Metzger, who was partly responsible for lax enforcement while a member of the TC, was not satisfied either. He complained that major industries like textiles and steel made "no effort to prove injury publicly," as the escape clause procedure required. They preferred to lobby for voluntary restraint agreements.[79]

Rejuvenating the Escape Clause

The incoming Nixon administration faced a foreign trade problem. To continue the bipartisan quest for trade liberalization, the new president needed a fresh mandate from Congress extending negotiating authority. This would allay concerns among foreign allies about incipient protectionism, allow the new administration to address the demands of developing countries for more aid or export opportunities, and satisfy the desire of multinational corporations for more effective government support in obtaining access to foreign markets.

Congress was in a rebellious mood. Herman Schneebeli, a Republican member of the Ways and Means Committee, told Nixon aides that Congress was fed up with previous administrations' practice of trading U.S. industries away.[80] The Nixon team thus learned that to win an extension of trade-negotiating authority for proposed multilateral trade negotiations, it must support procedural changes in safeguard provisions and exhibit a determination to administer existing escape clause provisions in accordance with congressional intentions.

Having heard about textile and other import problems while on the campaign trail, Richard Nixon entered office determined to strengthen trade remedies. More than any other president in the post–World War II period, Nixon responded to the pleas of domestic producers and workers. In a November 1969 special message to Congress, he acknowledged that free trade "caused hardships for parts of the community." Criticizing the escape clause provisions of the 1962 act as "so stringent, so rigid, and so technical that in not a single case has the USTC been able to justify a recommendation for relief," the president recommended a simpler test. "Relief should be available," he said, "whenever increased imports are the primary cause of actual or potential serious injury." He emphasized that an "industry provided with temporary escape-clause relief must assume responsibility for improving its competitive position." With encouragement from Chairman Wilbur Mills of the House Ways and Means Committee and Chairman Russell Long of the Senate Finance Committee, Nixon acted in accord with his rhetoric.[81]

Early in previous administrations, the foreign policy bureaucracy had successfully lobbied presidents—like Truman, Eisenhower, and Kennedy—not to approve trade-restrictive escape clause actions that might send a protectionist signal to foreign nations. Nixon did not succumb to such importuning on the part of State Department operatives.

In late 1969 President Nixon faced his first escape clause action, a case reviewing relief for the domestic carpet industry. Responding to a TC finding, President Kennedy had authorized escape clause relief for the carpet industry in 1962, raising import duties from 21 percent to 40 percent. President Johnson extended that relief in 1967 for two years, despite a TC finding that elimination of the additional duties would not affect the domestic industry. In 1969 the Tariff Commission unanimously reported that termination of the higher escape clause duties would have little affect.

Within the administration both the State Department and National Security Adviser Henry Kissinger urged Nixon to let the duties lapse. Said Kissinger, protecting the carpet industry without a TC recommendation to do so "would make the Administration appear fundamentally protectionist and thus seriously hurt our overall trade and foreign policies." Nixon rejected that advice and accepted the most restrictive option presented to him, one retaining higher duties on nonoriental carpets for three years.[82]

Not hesitant to put domestic interests first, President Nixon soon accepted three other escape clause recommendations. During his terms Nixon granted relief in seven out of nine escape clause cases. These involved pianos, sheet glass, barbers' chairs, nonrubber footwear, marble, ceramic tableware, and ball bearings. He even provided adjustment assistance when the TC was evenly divided. These actions spoke loudly to Congress and the world. In the eyes of the thirty-seventh president, the era of Marshall Plan unilateralism had ended. The State Department and its White House allies no longer directed foreign trade policy.

Over the next three years the Nixon administration and Congress labored to revise the trade law and to revitalize the escape clause. A prestigious panel of outsiders—the Williams Commission—recommended "more realistic" eligibility requirements for adjustment assistance and escape clause relief in 1971, as part of "an industrial and manpower policy" to assist "adjustments to change arising from international trade and investment."[83]

The 1974 Trade Act transformed the escape clause, making it a more powerful instrument for helping American industries and corporations adapt to intense import competition. As revised, the escape clause no longer provided for nullifying tariff concessions and so causing a prolonged interruption of import competition. Instead, section 201 aimed to facilitate orderly domestic adjustment to increased import competition. Industries that qualified for relief could obtain as much as a five-year breathing space. The act authorized a variety of remedies, including tariffs, quotas, and adjustment assistance. To qualify, a petitioner had to demonstrate to the U.S. International Trade Commission that increased imports were "a substantial cause of serious injury, or the threat thereof," to a domestic industry. The new act, like older statutory provisions, gave the ITC some flexibility to take into account "all economic factors which it considers relevant." It also attempted to provide administrators with some workable terminology. It defined the critical term *substantial cause* as a "cause which is important and not less than any other cause." In essence, the law marked another congressional attempt to make trade law responsive to the needs of American workers and producers.[84]

Finance Committee chairman Russell Long left a big imprint on the legislation. He believed that the executive branch should not sacrifice domestic

TABLE 7.1
Section 201: Escape Clause Filings and Results, 1975–1993

President	Number of Cases Filed	ITC Recommends Relief	President Provides Some Remedy	Percent of Cases Gaining Remedy
Ford 1975–77	15	9	6	40%
Carter 1977–81	29	18	9	31
Reagan 1981–85	10	5	3[a]	30
Reagan 1985–89	7	2	1	14
Bush 1989–93	2	1	0	0

[a] Affirmatives include motorcycles, specialty steel, and carbon steel. In the last case the Reagan administration provided relief in the form of restraint agreements, even as it publicly rejected the ITC solution.

industries for foreign policy advantages. The Senate Finance Committee report reflected this perspective: "the Committee feels that no U.S. industry which has suffered serious injury should be cut off from relief for foreign policy reasons."[85]

The procedural changes failed to effect the transformation that some sponsors envisioned, however. Foreign policy, economic considerations, and even domestic politics continued to impact the escape clause process. Nevertheless, more industries obtained relief than ever before.

In the first decade of experience with the 1974 act, from January 1975 to December 1984, eighteen out of fifty-four petitioners obtained some type of remedy. During this period, then, the domestic industry batted .333, a significant improvement over the success ratio under the previous acts. At the U.S. International Trade Commission thirty-two petitioners obtained affirmative determinations, and presidents from Richard Nixon to Ronald Reagan approved over half of these (see Table 7.1).

Interestingly, averages did not vary much among presidential administrations. Gerald Ford provided relief in 40 percent of the cases filed, Jimmy Carter in 31 percent, and Ronald Reagan in 30 percent during his first term. Of ITC recommendations sent to the White House, Ford and Nixon provided relief 67 percent of the time, Reagan 57 percent, and Carter 50 percent.

These statistics require cautious interpretation. The Nixon and Ford administrations offered protection on the cheap, as the ITC frequently recommended adjustment assistance. And in two cases—footwear and flatware—the

Ford administration actually selected the latter remedy when it was supported by fewer than a majority of the commissioners. Generally, the Carter White House provided more relief to politically powerful groups—specialty steel, footwear, color televisions, fasteners, and ferrochrome—although it turned down copper and flatware producers.

During this period foreign policy considerations continued to influence escape clause relief, especially at the presidential review level. The revised statute conceded the president discretionary authority to consider the larger national economic interest. President Nixon did so, and so did his successors. The labor-intensive nonrubber footwear industry offers an excellent example. Domestic producers repeatedly filed petitions for escape clause relief in the Nixon, Ford, Carter, and Reagan administrations. Although the shoe industry usually persuaded the independent U.S. International Trade Commission on the merits of the case to find injury and recommend a global import restraint program, it never succeeded in obtaining comprehensive relief at the presidential review level, particularly as it pertained to Spain.[86]

That story began in 1970, as a 50 percent cut in nonrubber footwear duties granted in the Kennedy Round took effect. Shoe imports soared—especially from Italy, Japan, and Spain. Indeed, the quantity of imports rose from 18 percent of domestic consumption in 1967 to 30 percent in 1970, whereas the number of production workers fell from 202,000 to 185,000. The shoe industry took two steps. It joined the textile industry in seeking quotas, and it filed an escape clause provision.

But domestic shoemakers had underestimated the executive's preoccupation with foreign policy considerations. Preparing for President Nixon's visits to Italy and Spain in October 1970, National Security Council staff aide C. Fred Bergsten warned that the shoe issue *"could lead to very serious problems."* The quota bill pending in Congress could reduce Spanish shoe sales to the U.S. by $30 million and from Italy by $100 million. He also noted that the U.S. embassy in Rome had estimated that five thousand Italian shoeworkers, "mainly in the 'red Belt,' would lose their jobs as a result." To satisfy Italy and Spain, Bergsten recommended that the president reiterate his intention to block shoe quotas. Indeed, when Nixon stopped in Madrid for a one-day visit on October 3, 1970, Spain's aging dictator General Francisco Franco reportedly raised the footwear issue and extracted from Nixon a quid pro quo: a promise that the United States would exempt Spain from any shoe restraints. It is noteworthy that the Nixon administration had recently negotiated a five-year base extension agreement for U.S. facilities in Spain.[87]

In January 1971 Nixon had an opportunity to assist Franco. An evenly divided TC sent the White House an escape clause finding that recommended higher duties on women's and men's leather footwear. Swiftly, the State Department swung into action. Secretary William Rogers warned the president that a decision to impose restraints on nonrubber footwear might invite retaliation against U.S. exports in the European Economic Community and against military bases in Spain. Also, he said, formal restraints would arouse opposition to U.S. goals in Japan. Import restrictions would "undermine" the efforts of Mexico, India, Brazil, and other developing countries to diversify economies. Given the intensity of State Department opposition, as well as Nixon's own sensitivity to diplomatic considerations, it is not surprising that he disapproved trade restrictions and instead authorized only adjustment assistance payments to domestic producers.[88]

Shoe imports continued to hammer the domestic industry. It lost another eleven points of the market share and laid off nearly 50,000 workers. The shoemakers again pursued escape clause relief, hopeful this time because to win Senate approval of the 1974 Trade Act, special trade representative William Eberle praised the escape clause procedures as "ideally suited" for use by the footwear industry. Eberle pledged that the administration would move "expeditiously" to provide relief if the industry prevailed during administrative proceedings. The shoemakers filed a petition, and in February 1976 the U.S. International Trade Commission made a unanimous injury determination, the first unanimous recommendation for relief under the 1974 Trade Act. Five commissioners proposed import restraints.[89]

As I. M. Destler has noted, however, Eberle's promise "was not kept." Once again foreign policy concerns doomed the footwear petition. National security adviser Brent Scowcroft told President Ford that the "Communists would seize on any U.S. import action against shoes . . . to argue that the U.S. was harming Italy during a time of economic crisis." He warned of similar negative reactions from Brazil, Korea, and Taiwan, as well as protectionist sentiment in France and Spain.[90] In a joint memorandum for the president, Secretary of State Henry Kissinger and Secretary of the Treasury William Simon urged a program of adjustment assistance for domestic industry and workers, not a tariff quota. Among the advantages, they listed first: "There will be no disruption in our relationships with our foreign suppliers. (For several of them, notably Spain and Italy, our decision to damage their important shoe exports could be politically destabilizing. For developing countries like Brazil, new restrictions would undermine our efforts to build up an atmosphere of confidence and cooperation.)"[91] Soon President Ford concluded that shoe restraints were not in the "national economic interest," and he too authorized only adjustment assistance to dislocated shoe workers.[92]

The shoe import surge continued. Nonrubber footwear producers filed another escape clause petition, hoping that the administration under newly elected Jimmy Carter might be more sympathetic. In February 1977 a unanimous ITC again found injury, and five commissioners recommended import restraints, including a global tariff quota. Once again, the foreign affairs agencies weighed in against any import restrictions. National Security Adviser Zbigniew Brzezinski opposed assistance to the shoe industry as harmful to the administration's overall foreign economic policy. He warned that trading partners "see shoes as a test case" and that import restraints could sour the atmosphere for the London Economic Summit. Weaker European economies, such as those of Italy, Britain, and France, might "erect trade barriers of their own." Moreover, implementing the ITC remedies would hit developing countries "hardest" and "raise serious doubts about our commitment to the economic well-being of the Third World." The State Department added that restraints "could damage our objectives in the North-South dialogue, encouraging radical LDC [less developed countries] polemic." Moreover, Spain and Greece, "countries whose friendship and economic health are of importance to us," declared that footwear exports were "vital" to our "bilateral relationship."[93]

Under enormous pressure from domestic as well as foreign interests, President Carter sought a compromise. Rejecting the ITC recommendation on the ground that it "does not provide a balance among the various interests involved," Carter authorized more adjustment assistance and directed his trade negotiators to conclude orderly marketing agreements (OMAs) with major foreign suppliers. The administration successfully concluded such pacts with only Taiwan and Korea—not with Italy, Spain, or Brazil.[94]

The OMAs helped restrain Asian competition, but not competition from Brazil. The domestic industry continued to lose market share when the OMAs were removed in 1981. Over the next three years, the nonrubber footwear industry lost another twenty points of market share and 28,000 jobs. In 1984, a presidential election year, the shoe industry filed another escape clause complaint, but this time a unanimous ITC rejected the petition.[95]

One year later, after Congress requested another investigation, the U.S. International Trade Commission unanimously found injury. But in 1985, when a unanimous commission again found injury and recommended restraints, the domestic industry no longer had the election-year advantage. President Ronald Reagan declined to use trade restraints. In his public statement Reagan criticized "protectionism . . . [as] a crippling cure, far more dangerous than any economic illness." And so the shoe industry continued to move offshore and to lay off domestic workers. In 1993 imports captured 88 percent of the U.S. market, and domestic manufacturers employed only 47,000 production workers, signifying a loss of 158,000 production jobs since the Kennedy Round tariff concessions.[96]

A leather wearing apparel case during the Carter presidency also elevated the conflict between foreign policy considerations and the employment needs of low-skilled domestic workers in labor-intensive industries. In early 1980 a unanimous ITC recommended escape clause relief for the leather wearing apparel industry. Although the U.S. trade representative, Commerce, and Labor urged the president to impose import restraints, the foreign affairs agencies insisted that relief "would damage our political and economic relationship with Taiwan, Mexico, Argentina, Hong Kong, Brazil, Canada, and especially Korea." In particular, they were concerned that economic problems would jeopardize Korea's "difficult transition to a more democratic system of government. . . . Any action to restrain leather apparel exports from Korea would run counter to US policy."[97]

During the Ford and Carter years, archival evidence shows that foreign policy considerations continued to affect the president's evaluation of escape clause recommendations. The Ford and Carter administrations rejected trade remedy petitions from U.S. industries to avoid unsettling allies and disrupting multilateral negotiations during the Tokyo Round GATT talks. At the November 1975 Rambouillet Economic Summit, President Ford specifically pledged to deal with bilateral trade problems on a "common sense basis. . . . Where flexibility exists under our domestic law and procedures, I am prepared to exercise it."[98]

True to his word, Ford proceeded to reject import restraints in five of the next six escape clause cases. The exception was specialty steel, where the White House anticipated a certain congressional override. The record shows that Secretary of State Henry Kissinger and Secretary of the Treasury William Simon lobbied hard to end relief speedily, claiming that "announcement of steps toward rapid termination of specialty steel restraints would demonstrate conclusively our commitment to an open world trading system on the eve of the San Juan Summit" in 1976.[99]

Similar episodes occurred in the Carter and Reagan years. In 1978 and again in 1984, when the ITC recommended import restraints to restrict surging copper imports, the two presidents faced difficult decisions. In the first instance special trade representative Robert Strauss endorsed a tariff rate quota as a way to head off efforts in Congress to limit presidential discretion in administering trade laws and to increase congressional receptivity to Tokyo Round agreements. He lost. President Carter sided with the State Department, the National Security Council, and other agencies opposing protection. They warned that import restrictions would damage relations with Canada, Peru, Chile, Zambia, and other copper exporters, while violating commitments made at the Bonn and London Economic Summits to resist protectionism.[100]

President Reagan also rejected import restraints on copper. Political instability in Chile reportedly intensified opposition—at the State Department and the National Security Council—to relief for the domestic producers. Like his predecessors, Ronald Reagan assigned priority to free trade pledges made at economic summits, and his decision pleased manufacturers who consumed large quantities of copper.[101]

From time to time, however, the State Department and the Council of Economic Advisers, the two agencies most critical of relief to domestic industries, did recommend a relief finding—but always for pragmatic bureaucratic reasons. The 1978–79 fastener cases provide examples. In December 1977 the U.S. International Trade Commission determined by a 3-to-1 vote that increased imports of bolts, nuts, and screws were seriously injuring the U.S. industry.[102] President Carter rejected the commission's recommendation and one from the Trade Policy Staff Committee recommending a three-year system of tariff rate quotas based on 1976 import quantities. The latter would not have provided relief to the industry but would have restrained any increase in imports. Members of the White House Economic Policy Group apparently overrode the Trade Policy Staff Committee recommendation.[103]

The fastener industry had powerful friends in Congress, most notably Representative Charles Vanik (D-Ohio), the chairman of the Ways and Means Subcommittee on International Trade. Special trade representative Bob Strauss succeeded in preventing a successful override, but the Ways and Means Committee requested another ITC investigation. This time the commission voted 2 to 1 in favor of a five-year program of duty increases.[104]

During the presidential review phase, all agencies now endorsed some relief. Commerce, Labor, Treasury, Interior, Defense, Agriculture, Justice, and the special trade representative joined to support a three-year program of tariffs on screws, nuts, and bolts, less than the ITC recommended. State and the Council of Economic Advisers sought to dilute the relief even more—confining it to large screws and bolts. In a separate note to President Carter, Strauss warned that the more comprehensive program of relief was needed to satisfy the domestic industry and Congress. "I believe this is a critical case for our trade policy. . . . a number of your strongest free trade supporters . . . think relief in this case . . . is absolutely necessary to manage our trade program in Congress in 1979." The fastener industry won, because Chairman Vanik told the White House that "substantial relief must be granted in this case to maintain the proper climate" for legislation implementing Tokyo Round multilateral trade commitments.[105]

From its inception the escape clause attracted petitions from small industries but seldom from major ones. In the 1950s the Eisenhower administration and Congress initially deflected textile industry pressure for quotas on Japanese imports to the escape clause procedure. They used TC findings as the basis for negotiating voluntary restraint agreements with Japan. In the 1960s the problems of textiles and apparel were so large, and the TC's interpretation of the 1962 act so narrow, that the affected industries looked for political solutions and gained a long-term cotton agreement. The State Department, incidentally, successfully opposed efforts to extend bilateral restraints to woolen and man-made fibers. But the Nixon administration would insist on completing a more comprehensive multifiber agreement.[106]

An important test for the regulatory approach to import relief came in 1980, when U.S. automakers filed a massive petition covering all automobile imports.[107] This investigation involved nearly $83 billion in domestic shipments and imports, including both passenger cars and light trucks. Data showed imports taking 22.5 percent of the domestic market in the first six months of 1980, up from 16.7 percent in the previous year. With the surge in imports domestic net operating profit slumped, falling from 5.4 percent in the first six months of 1979 to negative 8.4 percent in the same period of 1980.

In July of this presidential election year President Jimmy Carter attempted to expedite the ITC investigation. Claiming that this probe "has become a matter of great national and international importance," the president wrote ITC chairman Bill Alberger urging the commission to "conduct your work as expeditiously as is practicable . . . , so that all of those involved will not be burdened for a period of 6 to 8 months with the uncertainty such a case creates."[108] Internal administration records suggest that Carter hoped for an affirmative ITC decision before the November election. Certainly, at senior levels of the executive branch his appointees took steps to facilitate review and implementation of an auto relief program.

The ITC declined to make a ruling before the presidential election, however. And when the commission voted on November 10, the president had an unpleasant surprise. In a 3-to-2 decision the Trade Commission dismissed the petition. Casting the decisive votes were Carter's three appointees—Chairman Bill Alberger, Vice Chairman Michael Calhoun, and Commissioner Paula Stern. The only Republicans—Catherine Bedell and George Moore—voted in favor of relief to the domestic industry. All five commissioners had prior congressional experience—Bedell as a twelve-year elected member from Yakima, Washington, the others as congressional staffers. But they represented different generations. The Republicans were over sixty-five and drove U.S.-made cars. The three Carter Democrats were all thirty-five or younger and drove imports.

In effect, three yuppie commissioners appointed by President Carter turned down America's largest domestic industry. They claimed that other factors—such as general recessionary conditions and a shift in consumer preferences to fuel-efficient light cars—were a greater cause of serious injury than increased imports. Their pro-import judgments convinced many in corporate America that the government sector lacked sufficient experience to evaluate complex industrial problems. As a result, section 201 of the 1974 Trade Act lost credibility for major industries.[109]

Jimmy Carter had hoped for a different outcome, and he directed his administration to respond promptly and decisively. Detroit then turned to Congress and persuaded the Reagan administration to negotiate voluntary import restraints with Japan in 1981. A few years later, the three yuppie commissioners left the ITC through the revolving door to continue their professional careers as interest group advocates. Within several years of their departure, all three appeared before the Trade Commission representing foreign or import interests.[110]

In 1984 the U.S. steel industry obtained a more favorable judgment after it filed a massive escape clause petition. The five-member Trade Commission determined 3 to 2 that the domestic industry was indeed seriously injured as a consequence of increased imports.[111] Commission data showed that the ten integrated steelmakers had negative operating margins in 1982 and 1983. Also, domestic shipments and employment had declined sharply. The U.S. industry shipped 98.8 million short tons in 1979 but only 66.3 million in 1983. In 1979 average steel employment was 342,000 workers; by 1983 the number had dropped to 169,000. Imports increased their market share from 15.2 percent in 1979 to 20.5 percent in 1983. Twenty years earlier, in the 1964–68 period, steel imports had averaged 11.7 percent of consumption.

At the presidential review level, special interests and government agencies waged a vigorous battle. According to William Niskanen, a member of the Council of Economic Advisers, the Trade Policy Committee rejected the ITC recommendation, but domestic politics disposed the White House to fashion a program of steel restraint agreements. Niskanen, who was dismissed as chief economist of the Ford Motor Company for opposing the automobile petition in 1980, failed to block the restraint program, but he later claimed that the "Reagan administration subordinated its own economic policy for a few votes in a landslide election."[112]

Niskanen overstates the pernicious consequences of steel restraints in the 1980s. It is doubtful whether the voluntary restraint agreements (VRAs) harmed domestic consumers or hampered the national economy during this period. Although the VRAs apparently increased the price of imported steel by less than 10 percent between 1984 and 1989, this did not offset consumer gains from the strong dollar and the global oversupply of steel, which reduced the price of imported steel 17 percent between 1981 and 1983.[113]

The most successful escape clause case during the 1980s—perhaps in the entire history of the escape clause provision—involved Harley-Davidson motorcycles. This proved to be a successful example of Reagan administration industrial policy. In September 1982 Harley filed its petition, and in February 1983 the ITC ruled 2 to 1 that increased imports were a substantial cause of the threat of serious injury. Although Harley sought a higher tariff on both finished motorcycles and subassemblies, the commission remedy proposed a five-year program of higher tariffs only on finished cycles.[114] This impacted negatively the Japanese firms that had not established assembly facilities in the United States—namely Yamaha and Suzuki. The remedy was intended to encourage Harley, as well as the Japanese assemblers who had invested in U.S. facilities—Honda and Kawasaki. The Reagan administration approved the commission's remedy.

Harley roared back. Within five years the president could point with pride to this successful instance of a company using import relief to recapture its competitive advantage. After Harley announced its recovery and relinquished the final months of import relief, President Reagan traveled to York, Pennsylvania. At the Harley plant, he effused: "Like America, Harley is back and standing tall." He noted that "where U.S. firms have suffered from temporary surges in foreign competition, we haven't been shy about using our import laws to produce temporary relief. . . . You here at Harley-Davidson are living proof that our laws are working."[115]

Why were there not more Harley success stories? The record tells us that some of the industries seeking import relief wanted permanent protection. Among them were a number of smaller industries, such as clothespins, flatware, mushrooms, and shakes and shingles. Once protected from foreign competition, these industries led a hand-to-mouth existence during the 1980s, apparently using periods of tariff relief to generate enough additional revenue to pay the legal fees needed to obtain protection. Whereas Harley-Davidson had a credible plan to become export competitive, many other firms did not.

Other reasons why the escape clause did not produce more Harley-style outcomes related to unpredictable and capricious trade administration, costly and time-consuming procedures, and statutory shortcomings. The law emphasized past performance as a critical test for trade relief. Administrators seldom found claims of prospective injury tangible enough to justify remedies. Moreover, except in the Harley case, where the Reagan administration provided the requested tariff relief, presidents often failed to offer the adequate and timely aid necessary for domestic industries to adjust to import competition. Eager to deflect recommendations for relief in order to avoid antagonizing trading partners, executive officials continued to provide trade remedies only in unavoidable circumstances (carbon steel) or for window dressing (clothespins, shakes and shingles). During the 1980s the clothespin industry gained an extension, and Reagan granted restraints for motorcycles and shingle producers. In the latter two cases, the White House could point to its escape clause actions as evidence that the statute worked in meritorious cases. In occasionally granting relief, the administration thus deflected protectionist pressures and preserved the trade liberalization consensus.

Another observation seems warranted. At the ITC, some commissioners viewed the escape clause as a protectionist statute and declined to implement it as Congress intended in 1974. Beginning about 1984, the White House appointed several commissioners who were philosophically hostile to the escape clause statute. Several staff aides proved even more doctrinaire than their bosses.[116]

Throughout Ronald Reagan's first term, the ITC escape clause record resembled that for the Ford and Carter administrations. The pattern changed in 1984, and within a few years the escape clause effectively became a dead statute, as Senator John Danforth of Missouri observed. New appointees to the Trade Commission, especially Susan Liebeler and Anne E. Brunsdale, were less sympathetic to use of the escape clause than any nominee since the Johnson administration. These two ardent free traders, appointed to the ITC in 1984 and 1985 respectively, refused to recommend escape clause relief to the president, apparently because they disagreed with the purposes of the statute as they understood it.

In my view, the turning point came in 1985, when the Reagan White House chose to reject a unanimous ITC finding of injury in the nonrubber footwear investigation. At high levels of the administration a perception had emerged that section 201 of the Trade Act was a protectionist law. In his public statement, the president noted that the quotas proposed to limit shoe imports "could invite retaliation." He warned of a "trade war, a war we fought in 1930 with the infamous Smoot-Hawley tariffs and lost." Stating that the United States "must live according to our principles" and ensure that "the world trading system remains open, free, and, above all, fair," Reagan signaled a determination not to provide remedies except in cases of little consequence.[117]

At the ITC the president's message regarding nonrubber footwear resonated. Some commissioners and their staff members visibly lobbied for free trade solutions irrespective of the factual record, and the spirit of collegiality and inquiry that had characterized the early 1980s broke down. Among the ideological appointees, a perception emerged that the real world must be made to correspond to economic theory rather than the reverse.

Another factor contributing to the escape clause's decline was increased reliance on countervailing duty and antidumping cases. These so-called unfair trade cases, involving practices incompatible with the GATT system, could be distinguished from the so-called fair trade circumstances of escape clause proceedings. Moreover, because Congress mandated judicial review for antidumping and countervailing duty decisions, commissioners had less discretion, and so did White House policymakers. If commissioners voted their ideological convictions, both the Court of International Trade and the Court of Appeals for the Federal Circuit had the authority to remand or reverse such decisions. This occurred.[118]

In place of the independent fact-finding process, the Reagan administration pragmatically turned to export restraint agreements to address the problems of several major industries—especially machine tools and automobiles. Other restraints, covered in the multifiber agreement, contributed to the modernization of U.S. textile and apparel companies.[119]

As administered from 1975 to 1993, the escape clause authorized in the 1974 Trade Act produced only slightly better results for domestic workers and industries than did similar provisions enacted in 1951 and 1962. During the first eighteen years of its existence, from January 1975 to December 1992, parties filed sixty-three cases. Of these, the ITC made affirmative determinations in thirty-four (54 percent); the president provided some relief in only ten (16 percent). Under the 1974 act the domestic industry thus batted .158, approximately the same as under the 1951 act. Presidents offered relief as recommended by the ITC in only nine cases.[120]

Although some petitioners were repeaters, like the clothespin and shingle industries, with limited prospects for becoming competitive in the global market place, others could, and did, use a period of escape clause relief to restructure and reinvest. Along with Harley-Davidson, one might also list the domestic carbon steel industry in 1984. In this instance the escape clause led to a program of import restraints that produced a major transformation in the domestic steel industry. Not only did the integrated majors restructure, but also emerging minimills used the period of relief to expand market share. In restrospect, it appears that if the U.S. government had been more concerned about maintaining a healthy industrial base in North America, the escape clause might have enabled more industries to rejuvenate and become competitive again in foreign markets.

Benjamin Franklin may have been right in the eighteenth century to conclude that "no nation was ever ruined by trade." Many Americans living outside Washington, D.C., would probably reach a different conclusion in the late twentieth century. Since the mid-1960s, the forces of global competition have restructured the domestic market and dislocated large numbers of American workers and their families. Certainly, the record of escape clause enforcement indicates that at the presidential level officials have seldom assigned a high priority to helping domestic workers and producers adapt to the injurious impact of foreign competition. Instead, as the history of presidential decisions shows, the White House deferred time and time again to those who placed international economic and foreign policy considerations ahead of domestic economic interests. In the years after World War II America's leaders identified the broad national interest with the health of the international economic system. To preserve that open system, they frequently traded off the economic interests of domestic farmers, manufacturers, and workers in negotiations and trade remedy decisions.

[I]f this law is carried out . . . I am afraid that it may break down our whole

international trade program.—Cordell Hull, 1936

[T]he Antidumping and Countervailing Duty Laws are two great liberal trade

laws of the United States and indeed, of the international community! They are

instruments for freer trade.—Eugene T. Rossides, 1972

Curbing Executive Discretion
in Unfair Trade Cases

Along with the escape clause, trade administrators emasculated other trade remedy statutes. Until the 1970s the executive branch avoided enforcement of "unfair" trade laws. Then an angry and frustrated Congress rewrote the statute and established a quasi-judicial process for adjudicating antidumping and countervailing duty petitions. The architects of this revolution were Russell Long (D-La.), chairman of the Senate Finance Committee, and Charles Vanik (D-Ohio), chairman of the House Ways and Means Subcommittee on International Trade. Determined to level the playing field for American business, they encouraged Congress to reassert its constitutional prerogative to regulate commerce while implementing the Tokyo Round multilateral trade agreements.

Dumping

The congressional attack on ineffective trade law enforcement focused on dumping and government export subsidies—two related unfair competitive practices. The first occurs when a firm sells goods more cheaply in the export market than at home. Often sales take place at less than the cost of production.[1] The International Antidumping Code, drafted in GATT negotiations, provides the following legal definition: "[a product] . . . introduced into the commerce of another country at less than its normal value, if the export price of the product exported from one country to another is less than the comparable price, in the ordinary course of trade, for the like product when destined for consumption in the exporting country."[2]

In accordance with the GATT code, only *injurious dumping* is remediable. Dumped goods must materially injure, or threaten, the domestic industry producing a like product in the importing country. An administrative decision to impose antidumping duties, neutralizing the dumping margin, thus depends on both a finding of price discrimination ("less than fair value" pricing) and an injury determination. Each of these decisions hinges on a series of calculations, accounting decisions, and individual judgments.

Dumping occurs because some producers have protected home markets and can take advantage of imperfections in the world economy. In the absence of border barriers and transportation costs, a single price would tend to prevail throughout the world. Under textbook free trade conditions, arbitrage would eliminate dumping. If a firm sought to dump, a buyer in the importing country could resell the dumped merchandise to consumers in the exporting country and enforce the single price.

The Antidumping Code addresses product dumping and does not apply to exchange rate or social dumping. The latter problem might occur when a low-cost nation exports substantial quantities of labor-intensive goods into high-cost markets. In prosperous countries, laws often regulate working conditions—including the use of child labor, prison workers, maximum hours, and minimum wages. In the 1930s officials often used the term *social dumping* to explain Japan's phenomenal export successes. In the 1990s the same term reappeared to explain the export gains of mainland China and other low-wage countries.

Motives for dumping vary in the modern world. Some cases involve the sporadic sale of surplus agricultural products, like raspberries, but many others involve capital-intensive, oligopolistic industries. Firms in such industries frequently indulge in excess-capacity dumping, when supply exceeds demand, because they need to make regular payments on heavy fixed costs. These producers may dispose of surplus production in foreign markets at discount prices without regard to the impact of dumping on competition or on other firms. And where the foreign producer is state subsidized, as many European steel companies were in the early 1980s, political factors may drive excess-capacity dumping. Such firms may experience pressure to preserve home market employment in a cyclical downturn.

In cases involving new technologies, trade regulators sometimes encounter preemptive dumping. This may arise where products have short life cycles and the development of new items depends on experience with previous products or the use of acquired skills. Japanese management consultant Kenichi Ohmae has suggested that the globalization of competition may invite a proliferation of dumping. He notes that to compete successfully in the global economy, corporations must automate and expand capacity. As a result, global corporations, whatever their ownership or nationality, face increasing pressure to boost sales—at any price—to maximize marginal contributions to rising fixed costs. Discussing Japanese practice, Ohmae observes that when capacity exceeded growth in demand for semiconductors, Japanese producers cut prices to keep their factories growing. "This rapid erosion of prices knocked many American and European producers out of the industry entirely." This pattern, he says, occurred with facsimile machines, photocopiers, products related to office automation, watches, color televisions, automobiles, semiconductors, and shipbuilding where Japanese firms sought to beat competitors "by ruining industries." Management expert Peter Drucker has also observed the trend toward "adversarial" trade in which Asian competitors with closed home markets attack foreign markets for the purpose of driving out competitors.[3]

Reports from U.S. International Trade Commission investigations confirm that dumping is common in the marketplace. These findings seem to corroborate Ohmae's observation that Japanese firms, in particular, have employed discount pricing in order to conquer new markets and to destroy or weaken competitors. In some ITC investigations, the motive for dumping apparently was to obtain a strategic advantage from future economies of scale or from handicapping a rival's efforts to invest in new technologies.[4]

In markets with custom-made products sold through competitive bids, Japanese producers sometimes offer significant discounts to preempt the competition and to acquire market share. In a 1982 space amplifier case, for example, Nippon Electric significantly underbid Aydin, the U.S. petitioner, in an effort to control the market for future products. The ITC majority concluded that loss of the amplifier contract "which represents the latest in technology for such amplifiers means that the domestic industry has been precluded from obtaining vital practical and developmental experience."[5] Similarly, in the cell-site transceiver case, involving base stations for cellular radio communications systems, respondent Kokusai Electric significantly underbid the U.S. petitioner—apparently to grab a lucrative emerging technology market.[6]

The 1986 semiconductor cases presented classic examples of predatory import competition. Taking a long-term view of the demand for chips, Japanese firms rapidly added MOS memory production capacity, doubling their investments from $1.6 billion in 1983 to $3.2 billion in 1984. According to Japanese sources, the production of MOS memories nearly quadrupled from 311 million units in 1982 to 1.2 billion units in 1984. But during 1984 supply far exceeded demand, and prices for 64K DRAMs fell sharply, as the overextended Japanese producers pushed exports at less-than-fair-value prices. Hitachi told its distributors: "Win with the 10% rule. . . . Find AMD and Intel sockets. . . . Quote 10 percent below their price. . . . If they requote, go 10 percent again. . . . Don't quit till you win. . . . 25% distributor profit guaranteed." To maintain market share, domestic producers had to cut prices, and they experienced reduced profitability. This hampered investments in research for subsequent generations of DRAMs. The ITC majority concluded that Japanese underselling of 64K DRAMs had the effect of materially injuring a highly capital-intensive industry in which producers must continually invest large sums in research to develop the next generation of products.[7]

ANTIDUMPING REGULATION

Dumping first became a disruptive factor in import trade before the American Revolution. After each war with France, British merchants unloaded inventories of unsold goods at bargain basement prices. Late in the nineteenth century large American steel and German chemical companies engaged in differential pricing to penetrate world markets.[8] Early in the twentieth century governments began to counter this challenge with antidumping laws. Canada enacted the first statute in 1904, responding to the aggressive pricing practices of European and American trusts.[9] Finance minister W. S. Fielding explained "slaughtering," or "dumping," to Parliament: A trust or a combine, "having obtained control of its own market and finding that it will have a surplus of goods, sets out to obtain command of a neighboring market." To gain "control of a neighboring market," he said, "it will put aside all reasonable considerations with regard to the cost or fair price of the goods; the only principle recognized is that the goods must be sold and the market obtained."[10]

In proposing the antidumping measure, Minister Fielding rebutted arguments of laissez-faire economists. He noted that the "theoretical free trader . . . who attaches more importance to a theory than to the practical things of this life may ask: 'Why should we care about that; do we not get the benefit of cheap goods?'" To that question, Fielding replied: "if we could be guaranteed for ever or for a long period that we would obtain cheap goods under that system, . . . it would probably be wise for us to close up some of our industries and turn the energies of our people to other branches. But surely none of us imagine that when these high tariff trusts and combines send goods into Canada at sacrifice prices they do it for any benevolent purpose. . . . They send the goods here with the hope and the expectation that they will crush out the native Canadian industries."

During and after World War I U.S. industries worried about the increased prevalence of dumping. Secretary of Commerce William Redfield warned President Woodrow Wilson about reports that German manufacturers might dump products in the U.S. market after the war. He requested legislation to "forbid unfair foreign competition deliberately intended to destroy some of our industries." The Wilson administration also heard reports that Republicans would run a "fear" campaign in 1916 alleging that the Underwood Tariff of 1913 had exposed the United States to a "possible invasion" of its domestic market. Although there was apprehension about German chemical, steel, and newsprint sales in the American market, the concern was not confined to German trade practices. The U.S. Tariff Commission found that dumping had become "a familiar development of the private promotion of the foreign trade of many industrially advanced countries." The commission heard complaints about "unfair" Japanese competition in leather, hosiery and knitwear, and toys.[11]

Congress passed two antidumping laws in the World War I period. The first, appended to the Revenue Act of 1916, sought to eliminate predatory dumping. It provided for both criminal and civil penalties, including treble damages. This law proved impossible to enforce, however, because it was necessary to show that importers had "intent" and "conspired" to destroy or injure an industry in the United States.[12]

Responding to a TC recommendation that "administrative remedies to prevent dumping are superior to criminal laws," Congress passed a second statute, the 1921 Antidumping Act. This law endured, with only minor modifications, until 1979. It gave the Treasury secretary broad discretionary power to conduct investigations and to impose duties offsetting the injurious effects of dumping. The 1921 act did not address the issue of intent, nor did it treat dumping as a crime. Rather, the law focused on import pricing. It provided that

whenever the Secretary of the Treasury . . . , after such investigation as he deems necessary, finds that an industry in the United States is being or is likely to be injured, or is prevented from being established, by reason of the importation into the United States of a class or kind of foreign merchandise, and that merchandise of such class or kind is being sold or is likely to be sold in the United States or elsewhere at less than its fair value, then he shall make such finding public to the extent he deems necessary, together with a description of the class or kind of merchandise to which it applies in such detail as may be necessary for the guidance of the appraising officers.

Under this act, Treasury gained responsibility for administering antidumping laws, and apparently Congress intended for the secretary of the Treasury personally to take an active interest in applying the laws to individual cases. Indeed, it has been argued that the Antidumping Act of 1921 "contemplated that a Cabinet-level official would conduct an inquiry to determine whether, as a matter of *policy*, merchandise was being sold in the United States at less than its 'fair' value and that such sales were injuring or threatening the injury of a U.S. industry."[13]

The 1921 law, however, left certain key terms undefined—particularly *fair value* and *injury*. It imposed no statutory deadlines or other requirements for transparency and due process. Nor did the law provide for court review of most Treasury decisions. Congress only authorized judicial review of price discrimination, essentially an arithmetic exercise in which Treasury engaged to compute foreign values, prices, and costs. The law did not permit judicial review of *injury* findings, so Treasury retained latitude to define the term and to invoke a determination of no injury whenever convenient. With so much discretion, Treasury could weigh the interests of enforcing the Antidumping Act against other government priorities and policies.[14]

One former Treasury official responsible for administering the 1921 act revealed the significance of this discretionary authority when he compared it favorably to the more restrictive Trade Agreements Act of 1979. The 1979 act "overlook[ed] political relations with affected foreign governments." It provided "no scope" for "considering the consistency of the foreign government's behavior with the programs of the U.S. government or U.S. producers." He noted that a trade remedy decision might affect a foreign election, or the negotiation of leases for U.S. military bases, or export sales for U.S. producers.[15]

From 1921 to 1979, then, the secretary of the Treasury enjoyed broad discretionary powers. The 1921 Antidumping Act provided no standards for determining injury, imposed no deadlines, and authorized no outside review of injury findings. In effect, Congress made administration of the antidumping law an executive function and thus subordinated legal considerations to policy concerns. The Treasury secretary could consider such factors as how enforcement might affect a foreign government's decision to renew leases for U.S. military bases or impact political-military relationships.

Countervailing against Subsidies

Whereas dumping concerns the pricing actions of a business—including state-owned firms—the second type of unfair trade practice involves the use of government subsidies or bounties to facilitate exports. To offset the margin of unfairness, governments may impose countervailing duties, like antidumping duties.

From the writings of Alexander Hamilton and Adam Smith, it is apparent that industrial nations employed subsidies and bounties in eighteenth-century trade to "undersell and supplant all competitors." Not until the McKinley Tariff of 1890, however, did the U.S. enact special provisions permitting the use of a countervailing duty to counteract European bounties on beet sugar exports. In 1897 the Dingley Tariff gave the secretary of the Treasury the authority to impose countervailing duties on all dutiable items.[16]

Under section 303 of the Tariff Act of 1930, a provision that endured until 1974, the Treasury secretary acquired authority to levy countervailing duties whenever an article or merchandise was imported on which a foreign government or a private source had bestowed "any bounty or grant, directly or indirectly, upon the manufacture or production or export." Without an injury test, the statute appeared to limit discretion and to mandate Treasury action. But imaginative government lawyers found two clauses that allowed the secretary considerable enforcement discretion: "The Secretary of the Treasury shall *from time to time* ascertain and determine, or estimate, the net amount of each such bounty or grant, and shall declare the net amount so determined or estimated. The Secretary of the Treasury shall make all regulations *he may deem necessary* for the identification of such articles and merchandise and for the assessment and collection of such additional duties" (emphases added). In essence, the secretary had broad discretion to define bounties and subsidies and to develop implementing regulations.[17]

Former Commerce Department official Gary Horlick later observed that trade administrators in the "Executive Branch . . . sought to use every loophole in the countervailing duty laws to avoid the imposition of such duties." Their main instrument, he said, "was delay."[18] Because the countervailing duty law established no time deadlines, and because domestic petitioners had no right to judicial review of a negative determination, Treasury "simply let complaints gather dust."[19]

Lax Enforcement Patterns

The vagaries of administrative discretion hampered enforcement of both unfair trade laws. The countervailing duty law had a slightly higher success ratio. From January 1934 to May 1968, Treasury processed 191 cases and imposed 30 countervailing duty orders, a success rate of 16 percent. The most "sweeping use" of this statute involved assessment of countervailing duties on ten classes of goods imported from Germany in June 1936. In 1939 Treasury applied countervailing duties on all dutiable imports from Germany.[20]

Under the 1921 Antidumping Act, the most active enforcement occurred in the first full year; Treasury issued twenty-one orders in 1922. Ten of these cases affected Canada, and five involved the United Kingdom. None applied to German or Japanese imports. Interestingly, under Republican presidents in the 1920s—Warren Harding, Calvin Coolidge, and Herbert Hoover—the U.S. government imposed forty separate antidumping orders.[21]

During the New Deal a different enforcement philosophy took hold. Washington applied antidumping orders only thirteen times during Franklin Roosevelt's twelve years in the White House, and six of these occurred in 1934. Five of the findings pertained to German goods, and three involved Japanese products.

The pattern continued after World War II. The Truman administration issued no antidumping orders, and the Eisenhower White House only 3. Over the twenty-year period from January 1934 to December 31, 1954, the federal government processed 125 dumping cases but made only 7 dumping findings, a success rate for domestic industries of under 6 percent. During the twelve-year period from 1946 to 1958, the Treasury Department collected only $370 in antidumping duties, an average of $31 per year.[22]

In the 1960s foreign firms increasingly employed discount pricing to penetrate the U.S. market, and pressure for more vigorous enforcement mounted. The Kennedy administration issued four antidumping orders—all involving portland cement—against Sweden, Belgium, Portugal, and the Dominican Republic. During Lyndon Johnson's presidency, the pace of enforcement picked up; Treasury made five findings from 1964 to October 1966.[23]

Viewed in historical perspective, the enforcement rhythm reflected both cyclical conditions and policy priorities. The Treasury Department made twenty-eight antidumping findings during the 1921–23 recession and another nineteen during the 1930–34 period of the Great Depression. As one researcher observed in 1939, antidumping enforcement "varies with the phase of the business cycle, antidumping cases being much more frequent in years of depression than in years of prosperity."[24]

How much did foreign policy considerations influence administrative decision making in countervailing and antidumping proceedings? Records in the National Archives show that from 1934, when President Roosevelt designated the Executive Committee on Commercial Policy—an interagency group chaired by the Department of State—to "coordinate" U.S. trade policies, the Treasury Department deferred regularly to the State Department. Repeatedly this committee took the view that antidumping and countervailing duty orders undercut the administration's reciprocal tariff reduction program and jeopardized efforts to promote exports, particularly agricultural products.[25]

With the State Department coordinating trade policy, it is not surprising that foreign policy concerns drove administrative decisions. Treasury submitted its proposed rulings for interagency comment, and this assured "touch between the two Departments on matters of international importance arising in connection with antidumping action and the like." These procedures allowed other executive branch agencies and affected foreign governments to comment before final action.[26]

Several representative examples reveal how the diplomatic perspective prevailed. In November 1935, when the Treasury Department concluded that the facts warranted assessing countervailing duties on imported Emmenthaler cheese from Switzerland, the interagency coordinating committee objected. Such action "would be practically certain to preclude the possibility of a successful conclusion of [a reciprocal trade] agreement." Subsequently, Treasury reversed course and announced to the interdepartmental group that "no further action should be taken in the case at this time."[27]

Another illustration involved Polish rye. When the Polish ambassador complained to the State Department that the imposition of antidumping duties would bring retaliation against American exports to Poland, both State and Agriculture sought to influence Treasury decision making. After consulting with the Department of Agriculture, which was primarily interested in promoting U.S. agricultural exports to Poland, Treasury concluded that Polish imports did not injure American producers. Similarly, it determined that alleged Polish bounties "do not constitute a bounty within the meaning of the Tariff Act."[28]

On other occasions, in the absence of statutory deadlines, Treasury simply delayed inconvenient determinations. For instance, in 1935 it received a complaint about the dumping of flycatchers from Japan, Germany, the United Kingdom, and Belgium. Most such imports came from Japan. Despite the growing number of complaints about Japanese dumping in the 1930s, the U.S. government always sought to negotiate "gentlemen's agreements," voluntary restraints that did not stigmatize Japan as a dumper.[29] As a result, Treasury took no formal action. Not until December 1939, after the outbreak of World War II in Europe, did Treasury choose to complete the investigation and to impose antidumping orders.[30]

Repeatedly, the executive branch treated claims of Canadian dumping deferentially. In September 1939 Treasury concluded that dumped wood pulp from British Colombia injured the domestic industry, but it yielded to Canadian representations and State Department concern about the world situation to justify no dumping actions.[31]

Although Treasury ordinarily avoided orders that might upset political relationships, Secretary Henry Morgenthau took advantage of his discretionary authority to pursue an assertive anti-Nazi policy in the mid-1930s. Morgenthau, a vigorous anti-Nazi sensitive to the persecution of fellow Jews, saw the countervailing duty law as a weapon in the internationalist arsenal. President Roosevelt agreed. He told Morgenthau: "If it is a borderline case . . . I feel so keenly about Germany that I would enforce the countervailing duties." Secretary of State Cordell Hull demurred: "if this law is carried out it is difficult to see where it will end and I am afraid that it will break down our whole international trade program."[32]

After Munich Morgenthau directed Treasury lawyers "to establish legal reasons compelling him to impose countervailing duties against German exports to the United States." Morgenthau plunged ahead, telling State that "I am not at liberty to disregard [the law] for reasons of policy convenience." But scholars have noted that Treasury's blanket application of countervailing duties to German trade represented a departure from that department's previous policy.[33]

Morgenthau's actions indicated that a determined secretary of the Treasury Department could rationalize vigorous administration of the countervailing duty laws when he desired. But, in moving against Nazi Germany and Japan in 1939 while turning a blind eye to friendly dumpers and subsidizers in Canada and elsewhere, Treasury confirmed that policy caprice, not legal consistency, guided executive administration of these unfair trade laws.

ENFORCEMENT AFTER WORLD WAR II

After the outbreak of World War II, Treasury gave little attention to the administration of countervailing and antidumping laws. Indeed, the executive branch continued to view the presence of such laws as an embarrassment and an impediment to trade liberalization under the Reciprocal Trade Agreements Program and the General Agreement on Tariffs and Trade. Consequently, at each opportunity State maneuvered to retain executive flexibility and discretion, while resisting congressional efforts to limit executive flexibility and rejuvenate enforcement. In negotiating GATT, State inserted a formal injury requirement—"material injury"—and extended this to countervailing duty investigations as well. But the GATT provisions, as it turned out, were too general and did not bind many of America's key trading partners, such as

Canada, which, like the United States, had antidumping laws that predated GATT and thus were grandfathered.[34]

Even so, the presence of more restrictive provisions in GATT gave the State Department internationalists ammunition in their efforts to enhance executive branch discretion. As the United States approached the Kennedy Round of multilateral trade negotiations in the mid-1960s, government lawyers sought to negotiate an effective International Antidumping Code that would better protect American exporters, assuring them procedural rights, determination of fair value on an individual producer basis, and an injury test. In particular, because Canada continued to avoid an injury test and to use valuation procedures considered unnecessarily nationalistic, the United States sought to commit Canada to a material injury test.[35]

Several factors explain this emphasis. First, few U.S. industries experienced significant competition from unfair imports until the 1960s. There were some exceptions—textiles, gloves, bicycles, and certain other specialty items—but for the most part they chose to seek relief through the escape clause process. Those industries that did file antidumping and countervailing duty complaints experienced little success—largely because Treasury enjoyed sufficient discretion to delay action and weigh policy ramifications.

Second, pursuant to the Marshall Plan and overall U.S. international economic policy to reduce trade barriers and promote import-led growth, U.S. officials backed efforts to facilitate imports from friendly nations. They feared that vigorous enforcement of unfair trade laws would "obstruct cheap imports" and arouse fears of incipient protectionism. For a generation after inauguration of the reciprocal trade program, the State Department and the interagency trade apparatus regarded countervailing duty and antidumping laws as an "embarrassment to the trade agreements program." Vigorous enforcement conflicted with the goal of tariff liberalization. State took the view that "the political interests of the United States are usually of more importance than increased protection to United States industry." Imposing import restrictions inflicted a blow on "United States prestige" and "on the economy" of friendly nations.[36]

Criticism in Congress

During the 1950s Congress heard a chorus of complaints from domestic industries that trade law administrators were neglecting their statutory responsibilities to enforce unfair trade laws. Said O. R. Strackbein, of the Nationwide Committee of Industry, Agriculture, and Labor on Import-Export Policy: "the Antidumping Act is about as near extinction as the whooping cranes:

its life hangs by a narrow thread. . . . Some 4 percent of the cases since 1934 have resulted in actual findings of dumping." He claimed that "the Treasury Department has bowed to the trend in Executive policy and without legislative direction has changed the whole meaning of the Antidumping Act of 1921."[37]

Robert N. Hawes, counsel for the Hardwood Plywood Institute, and Robert C. Keck, counsel for the Hardboard Association, offered specific examples involving Finland and Sweden. On November 30, 1953, the Hardwood Plywood Institute filed an antidumping complaint against Finland. Fifteen months later, in April 1955, Hawes learned from a legal brief filed by counsel to the Finnish producers that the Treasury Department had issued a finding that the Finns had in fact dumped plywood in violation of the 1921 Antidumping Act. In October 1955, however, Treasury officially informed Hawes that it had decided to make no finding pursuant to administrative discretion.[38] In the parallel hardboard case involving Sweden, Treasury did make an antidumping finding, but imports continued to rise—more than doubling after the department's order in August 1954. Keck complained that Treasury had not collected duties on imported Swedish hardboard and that it had removed individual foreign firms from the scope of an antidumping order. "In my own judgment," he declared, "the enforcers of this act have been out of sympathy with this law since 1933."[39]

Historical records confirm what the counsel for petitioners could only suspect. Foreign policy considerations lay behind Treasury's refusal to enforce the trade laws. During the Eisenhower administration, the State Department and the National Security Council assigned high priority to disentangling Finland from the Soviet bloc and to integrating it into the world economy. A classic conflict between trade administration and foreign policy thus emerged in 1954, when the Treasury Department investigated claims, as required by law, that Finnish exporters of plywood and hardboard had dumped or sold subsidized products in the U.S. market. The State Department advised Treasury that action to implement U.S. unfair trade laws would be "particularly unfortunate from the standpoint of our political relations with Finland, as well as from the point of view of our economic defense program."[40] Sensitive to foreign policy and national security considerations, Treasury modified its bonding procedures and methods of computing less-than-fair value in order not to reach affirmative determinations. Despite finding evidence of subsidies and dumping, Treasury concluded that no countervailing or antidumping duties were warranted on Finnish plywood or hardboard. It issued an antidumping order against Sweden but failed to collect the duties.[41]

Complaints about Treasury's arbitrary procedures and "star-chamber" practices came from importers as well as domestic producers. Importers objected to withholding appraisement and to suspension of liquidation when a

Customs appraiser suspected that a foreign product was being dumped in the U.S. market. Uncertain what the tariff liability would be and without time limitations for the conduct of such investigations, the "practical effect of such action . . . is to stop importation of the commodity in question." Speaking on behalf of an American Bar Association (ABA) committee of customs lawyers, James D. Williams called for greater transparency in the form of public notices, transcripts, and published reports explaining findings. The ABA report also asked for more extensive judicial review.[42]

In 1954 Congress approved two significant procedural changes in the antidumping practice. First, it transferred the assessment of injury from the Treasury Department to the Tariff Commission. Supporters believed that the commission was better equipped to evaluate import-related injury. And second, Congress limited the retroactive application of antidumping duties to 120 days prior to the time dumping was alleged to Treasury. In 1958 Congress made other procedural changes requiring greater transparency. Thereafter Treasury and the TC had to report the reasons for their findings.[43]

These changes did not silence critics. Domestic industries continued to focus on a fundamental issue: ineffective enforcement. From 1955 to 1969 Treasury received 376 antidumping complaints. It dismissed 230 of these on the ground that there were no sales at less than fair value. In another 89 cases the department terminated the investigations after it negotiated with the foreign exporter and gained consent to increase export prices. Of the remaining 57 cases sent to the Tariff Commission with Treasury's less-than-fair value finding, only 17, or less than 5 percent of all complaints, led to antidumping orders.[44]

What explains the low percentage of affirmative determinations at the independent Tariff Commission? For one thing, the law provided no specific definition of such key terms as *injury*. In the absence of clear direction from the statute and court review, commissioners enjoyed discretion to vote their instincts, and until about 1969 a free trade majority held sway. Supporting overall administration trade policy, they took the view that injury had to be material and that dumped imports had to be a significant cause of material injury, not merely one of the causes.[45] Some appointees to the TC also questioned the basic purpose of the antidumping law and imposed high standards of injury and causation to discourage private parties from filing claims. Stanley Metzger later wrote: "The basic assumption that dumping is, on balance harmful to the economy or other national interests of the country being dumped in is *highly doubtful*" (emphasis added). Another Johnson appointee, economist Penelope Hartland Thunberg, exhibited her profession's sympathy for consumer interests and voted consistently against antidumping findings.[46]

Behind the scenes the State Department worked assiduously to allay foreign concerns. When British prime minister Edward Heath personally intervened in a 1964 steel antidumping complaint to plead for "justice" to British producers Stewarts and Lloyds, State took up Britain's case. At an interagency meeting on April 1, 1964, the department "pressed for ways the case could be resolved favorably to [the British producer], or, failing that, for the best presentation in defense of an adverse finding." According to a memorandum written by a participant from the special trade negotiator's office, "the meeting ended with State going back to look for new arguments, or for a way to get Mr. [Roger] Blough [of U.S. Steel] to drop the case."[47]

Other efforts to dilute the "embarrassing" antidumping law led in the Kennedy Round to a draft GATT Antidumping Code. It contained a provision for weighing injury to the domestic industry caused by imports against other causes of injury. Such an approach would have significantly altered existing practice and enhanced the prospects for negative injury determinations. This initiative failed when Chairman Russell Long of the Senate Finance Committee agreed with critics that the code "would weaken an already inadequate law."[48]

When President Richard Nixon took office in 1969, the White House assigned high priority to dumping and subsidies. Assistant Secretary Eugene T. Rossides, a lawyer, rejuvenated enforcement activities at Treasury. "I am *not* prepared to concede that anyone, whether it be a foreign government or a foreign firm, has a vested right in lax enforcement of our international fair trade statutes." Believing that subsidies and dumping constituted distortions harmful to the interests of efficient American producers, Rossides proclaimed antidumping and countervailing duty laws "instruments for freer trade." To achieve more vigorous enforcement, he obtained more staff for investigations. Both at Treasury and the Tariff Commission, which separately examined the issue of injury to the domestic industry, Nixon's appointees gave new life to injury investigations.[49]

Antidumping and countervailing duty orders became more frequent. From 1969, when Treasury issued five dumping and three countervailing duty orders, a peak was reached in 1972 with eighteen dumping and two countervailing duty orders. But Treasury's enthusiasm for vigorous enforcement proved short-lived. During the 1973–74 Watergate period observers noted "a shift in Treasury policy away from aggressive enforcement of the Antidumping Act."[50]

Congress Responds

During the Tokyo Round of multilateral trade negotiations, domestic industries continued to criticize antidumping and countervailing duty enforcement. In Chairman Charles Vanik of the House Ways and Means Subcommittee on

International Trade they found a sympathetic ally. Branding the antidumping laws "extremely ineffective" because of "nonenforcement" of the law, Vanik held a series of hearings that enabled the domestic steel industry and other import-sensitive industries an opportunity to build a record critical of the executive's administration of trade laws.[51]

The steel industry used the hearings to present a case for legislative reform. Cyclops Corporation complained that the Antidumping Act was administered "more like a Spanish Inquisition. The antidumping procedures provide for secret evidence, secret witnesses, no cross-examination, no discovery of evidence, no depositions or interrogatories, no adversary hearings, no trial." After receiving a complaint, "the government has total control of the investigation. All doors are closed. The complaining industry has no rights whatsoever. The scope of the so-called investigation can be broadened or narrowed according to the whims of Treasury, often motivated by extraneous political factors."[52] Steel spokesmen objected especially to Treasury's practice of permitting foreign producers to lower home market prices, thus wiping out dumping margins and avoiding antidumping duties. One witness told the Ways and Means Committee that the foreign dumper "can be almost certain Treasury will never check on the accuracy of his claims."[53]

In 1978 Richard Simmons, president of Allegheny Ludlum, complained that "antidumping statutes did not provide relief from unfair competition even when we won." He pointed to the "weakness of existing statutes, the lack of the most elementary enforcement procedures, and the lack of commitment on the part of those charged with the administration of the law."[54]

Particularly disturbing to Congress was testimony that Customs failed to collect antidumping duties. The most controversial case involved television imports from Japan. In March 1968 the Electronic Industries Association filed an antidumping complaint concerning monochrome and color television sets. According to domestic producers, imports rose from 715,000 units in 1964 to 2.7 million in 1968, an increase of 279.2 percent. Moreover, Japanese imports had increased market share from 7.3 percent to 20.5 percent in 1968. At Treasury there were inexplicable delays in obtaining information from the Japanese respondents. Not until December 1970, some thirty-three months after the complaint was filed, did Treasury publish its determination of sales at less than fair value.

Then in March 1971 the TC rendered a unanimous decision that imports of Japanese television sets injured domestic producers. The commissioners found that dumped imports had gained a "substantial share of the U.S. market," had "for the most part undersold U.S. manufacturers . . . in the domestic market," and had "contributed substantially to declining prices for domestically produced television receivers." The commission also concluded that the Japanese manufacturers targeted small monochrome and color sets and concentrated discount pricing to buy market share in the middle sizes (sets having screens larger than 9 inches but less than 20 inches), where competition with domestic producers was most intense.[55]

For technical reasons Treasury delayed assessing duties. It also refused to conduct a parallel countervailing duty investigation, fearful that it might have no choice but to assess duties. "Such a determination would have far reaching international implications with respect to many industries in Japan and industries of our other major trading partners." As a result, seven years later John Nevin, chairman of Zenith Radio Corporation, testified before a congressional committee that Treasury still had taken "no effective action" to collect antidumping duties. "The dumping of Japanese television sets in the United States is as flagrant today as it was in 1971," he stated. From this experience Zenith concluded: "Policy-level officials of the U.S. Government have regarded the American television industry to be a pawn that might readily be sacrificed in order to avoid a diplomatic confrontation with Japan."[56]

The television case was not a conspicuous but isolated example. The General Accounting Office (GAO) told Congress that Treasury generally had failed to collect antidumping duties. In June 1978 the GAO said that the United States had seventy-four findings of dumping in effect, but importers owed an estimated $700 million in back dumping duties.[57] After Congress transferred antidumping responsibilities to the Commerce Department in 1979, it agreed to settle the uncollected television duties for $77 million, an amount considerably below the government's estimate of $138.7 million.[58]

Other firms and industries complained about nonenforcement. The Diamond Chain Company claimed that a 1973 finding against Japanese producers was not being effectively enforced. Westinghouse pointed to circumvention of an antidumping order covering power transformers. Simmons of the Allegheny Ludlum Steel Corporation cited nonenforcement as the reason that imports of French and Swedish specialty steel had increased after duties were imposed: "The amount of dumping duties assessed was minimal; we have every reason to believe that the amount actually collected was even less. In point of fact, the Customs Service has been unable to tell us how much has been collected, despite requests under the Freedom of Information Act." Some of these problems continued into the 1990s. In 1991 domestic industries complained that Customs still could not provide accurate information about the actual collection of antidumping and countervailing duties.[59]

Archival records add another dimension of understanding. They show that during the 1970s Treasury strained to avoid imposing countervailing and antidumping duties on foreign producers of automobiles, steel, and canned hams. Documents at the Gerald Ford presidential library indicate that policy considerations continued to influence the trade administration process. For example, in telling Treasury Secretary William Simon that he had decided to terminate a U.S. steel complaint that the European Economic Community used value-added taxes to subsidize steel exports, Assistant Secretary David Macdonald noted communications from Secretary of State Henry Kissinger and special trade representative Fred Dent. Both were "extremely concerned," believing that the "wrong signals in this matter could easily destroy the multilateral trade negotiations in Geneva." Because the suit challenged about seventy years of Treasury Department practice, in which the administering authority had taken the view that a rebate of indirect taxes was not a bounty or a grant, Macdonald found it convenient to reject the domestic complaint. As he told Simon, "our rapid and clear decision in this matter will go a long way toward calming current foreign fears of a protectionist swing in U.S. trade policy."[60]

Congressional anger with the state of executive enforcement of these unfair trade laws surfaced in hearings to authorize U.S. participation in the Tokyo Round of multilateral trade negotiations. In 1974 Congress made some procedural changes and authorized the administration to negotiate Antidumping and Countervailing Duty Codes. These revisions chipped away at executive discretion. As a result, during ensuing GATT negotiations the White House consulted Congress regularly, and the Carter administration successfully concluded agreements creating a number of international codes addressing specific nontariff barrier problems. The most important were an Antidumping Code and a Countervailing Duty Code, both of which contained provisions compatible with vigorous enforcement of antidumping and countervailing duty petitions. In exchange for gaining international acceptance of new rules governing antidumping and countervailing duties, the United States formally agreed to impose an injury test in its countervailing duty investigations.

On Capitol Hill, decades of frustration with high-handed and arbitrary Treasury decision making produced a revolution in the implementing legislation. Finally, Congress addressed the long-simmering problem of maladministration in the 1979 legislation. First, at the suggestion of Chairman Vanik and Bill Frenzel (R-Minn.), it moved less-than-fair value determinations from the Treasury Department to the Commerce Department and made Commerce the administering authority.[61] Congress also imposed tight deadlines and more specific definitions and standards, as well as providing for court review of affirmative and negative final determinations to ensure timeliness, transparency, and consistency.[62] In the course of writing implementing legislation, the lawmakers, sensitive to the debate over how to implement the 1967 Antidumping Code, instructed trade officials to administer U.S. law in ways that the United States considered in accordance with its GATT obligations.

Underlying congressional action was the perception that past laws had not been enforced. The Ways and Means Committee put it this way: "The Committee feels very strongly that both the countervailing and antidumping duty laws have been inadequately enforced in the past, including the lack of resources devoted to this important area of law."[63]

Golden Era of Enforcement

The 1980s thus witnessed a revolution in unfair trade law enforcement. For the first time the U.S. government vigorously implemented its unfair trade laws (see Table 8.1). The result was a significant increase in both antidumping and countervailing duty orders. On September 30, 1994, the United States had 290 antidumping findings in place, up from 85 in 1979. Out of the total, 49 dated from before 1980. Interestingly, at the end of September 1994, 50 of the 290 antidumping orders affected Japanese products; 25 orders involved items from China, 18 concerned Taiwanese products and 17 goods from Korea.[64]

Responsive to the congressional mood, both Presidents Carter and Reagan appointed a number of individuals to the U.S. International Trade Commission and to the Commerce Department who were committed to enforcing the 1979 law consistent with legislative intent. The combination of mandatory provisions, specific legislation language, and energetic regulators helped produce a golden era of antidumping enforcement.

In politics, as in physics, actions invite reactions. This occurred at the ITC, where ideological enthusiasm for free trade produced creative interpretations of the 1979 statute. Several doctrinaire commissioners appointed in the 1984–85 period desired to eviscerate enforcement provisions. Believing that unfair trade laws were bad because they appeared to conflict with free trade principles, these ardent deregulators devised novel and imaginative analytic methodologies. These, they claimed, were more faithful to the language of GATT rules.

Attempts to subvert the unfair trade laws failed. For one thing, the U.S. Court of International Trade (CIT) struck down strained statutory interpretations and thus demonstrated the wisdom of judicial review. In one case the CIT bluntly rejected the views of ideological commissioners as "legally flawed and not based on substantial evidence."[65]

With strong direction from the judiciary and vigorous oversight from congressional authorizing committees, trade administrators had no recourse under the 1979 act but to perform their duties. The public record exhibited these results. During the 1960s some commissioners had refused to make affirmative determinations in dumping cases. As a result, ITC injury investigations produced few dumping orders. Before 1970 less than 5 percent of all such dumping

TABLE 8.1

U.S. Introduction of Antidumping and Countervailing Duty Orders, 1960–1990

Years	Number of Antidumping Orders	Years	Number of Countervailing Duty Orders
1960–70	4		
1971–75	18		
1976–80	21	1975–80	9
1981–85	34	1981–85	25
1986–90	118	1986–90	37

Source: GATT, *Trade Policy Review: United States, 1992* (Geneva: April 1992), 1:99–106.

complaints led to antidumping orders. Under the 1979 act, the success rate rose dramatically. Of 613 complaints, 259 (42 percent) produced offsetting duties from 1980 to 1993.[66]

Asian dumpers experienced the impact. The success rate was highest against the major Asian dumpers, Japan and China, and lowest against Canada and Western Europe. Forty-five (58 percent) of 78 cases filed against Japanese firms led to antidumping duties. Sixty-six percent (25 of 38) involving China produced affirmatives. For Korea and Taiwan, the rate stood above average. More than half (53.6 percent) of 41 Korean cases led to duties. So did 18 of 41 (44 percent) investigations involving Taiwanese firms. For Canada and European trading nations, a different pattern emerged. Thirty-six percent of 36 Canadian cases led to duties, as did 33 percent of 30 French cases and 29 percent of 35 filings against Italy.

In light of the vigorous enforcement, it is not surprising that a public campaign to dilute "unfair" trade laws flowered in Washington during the Uruguay Round negotiations. ITC director of economics John Suomela supported this effort. Suomela not only disliked the 1979 law, he distrusted politicians and lawyers. "Having lawyers write laws," he later wrote, "is . . . a conflict of interest." Claiming that Commerce bureaucrats and ITC commissioners had misapplied U.S. antidumping and countervailing duty laws "according to the intent of the Congress, not according to broader obligations that were agreed to by U.S. negotiators under the GATT," Suomela and a group of young economists worked for statutory changes that would elevate technical economic analysis. In essence, they wanted to discourage enforcement of the antidumping and countervailing duty laws. "No country alone ought to be able to impose countervailing duties," Suomela asserted. "Otherwise the countervailing duty laws will continue to be used as a protectionist tool." Antidumping laws "have been most frequently used to restrain increases in imports and they have never been used to remedy what any reasonable person would consider unfair behavior."[67]

Eager to influence Uruguay Round deliberations, the economic theorists traveled at public expense to Ottawa, Tokyo, Brussels, Geneva, and other locations to criticize U.S. procedures and to proselytize for more flexible rules. The counsel for transnational corporations and for foreign interests, who were strongly motivated to weaken U.S. unfair trade laws, aided these initiatives.[68]

Several commissioners—among them, Chairman Anne Brunsdale and Vice Chairman Ronald A. Cass—also lobbied publicly for modifications to GATT rules. Their efforts produced an unusual reprimand from Senate Finance Committee chairman Lloyd Bentsen and his House counterpart, Ways and Means Committee chairman Dan Rostenkowski. The congressional leaders warned: "There is no mandate for the ITC to negotiate with foreign officials."[69]

This debate continued in Geneva during final phases of the Uruguay Round and in Washington over statutory language to implement these agreements. Following the examples of Australia, Canada, the European Union, and the United States, more countries began to enforce antidumping laws. Free traders alleged that "anti-dumping laws have become the world's preferred method of trade protection." They advocated a return to escape clause procedures that allow "the President to take foreign policy and other considerations into account, which gives the foreign country greater leeway to try to influence the decision."[70]

Defenders of antidumping and countervailing duty laws, on the other hand, viewed these statutes as a necessary adjunct to the trade liberalization process. As globalization moved forward, national antidumping and countervailing duty enforcement would have an integral place in an international economy lacking harmonized competition policies. Some nations, like China, relied more on state control and planning than others. Others had economies in transition; these nations lacked established market mechanisms and proven legal systems for adjudicating commercial disputes. Moreover, some governments limited import competition and pursued competitive policies conducive to export dumping. In a global economy of disparate national regulatory regimes, trade distorting practices remained an important problem. Indeed, GATT scholar John Jackson has observed that such laws may serve a "useful function in world trade . . . as an 'interface' or buffer mechanism to ameliorate difficulties . . . caused by interdependence among different economic systems." For the United States and the EEC, in particular, antidumping and countervailing duty laws remain perhaps the only viable policy tools for addressing such anomalies.[71]

The 1979 Trade Agreements Act initiated a dramatic change in U.S. unfair trade enforcement. Establishing a quasi-judicial procedure for resolving trade disputes outside the policy process, it sharply reduced the opportunity for the executive branch to subordinate trade enforcement to other policy considerations or ideological caprice. This process had some disadvantages. It produced costly and time-consuming procedures. It transferred revenue to lawyers and economic consultants that domestic industries and foreign producers might have beneficially invested otherwise.

When viewed in historical perspective, however, the unfair trade laws had a compelling rationale. They placed critical decisions affecting the allocation of business resources and jobs in the hands of experienced, independent decision makers and judges responsible for applying laws impartially in a timely manner. That represented a big change from previous practice. Until the Trade Agreements Act of 1979, executive branch officials with responsibilities for foreign economic policy had administered unfair trade laws in a manner generally consistent with executive foreign policy goals. In this hierarchy of priorities, domestic interests ranked low.

[I]f we trade away American jobs and farmers' incomes for some vague concept of a "new international order," the American people will demand from their elected representatives a new order of their own, which puts their jobs, their security, and their incomes above the priorities of those who dealt them a bad deal.—Chairman Russell Long, 1976

Epilogue

What a difference three centuries make!

Improvements in communications and technology have transformed commerce and international economic relationships. At the end of the twentieth century exporters and importers enjoy instant access to a global market through paperless electronic data interchanges. Using Internet and interactive video technology, even small and medium-sized firms can display products, solicit customers, shop for supplies, and make other arrangements for credit, insurance, and transportation. Cellular communications permit instantaneous contact among geographically diverse individuals, corporations, and governments. Jet freighters and global parcel services move high-priority shipments from Asia to America by air in a day or less. Even low-value commodity shipments cross the Atlantic or Pacific in a few weeks' time, making use of other transportation improvements such as container ships and automated port facilities. Technology has shrunk the world, making trade more efficient and peoples more interdependent. Single markets have emerged for money, services, labor, and commodities.

The eighteenth-century world of George Washington was a more fragmented and forbidding place. Merchants, like Thomas Hancock of Boston, wrote out orders in longhand and waited months for shipments to arrive from England. It took several months to move goods across the Atlantic to customers in the North American colonies. Often the goods arrived damaged or defective.

In such circumstances it is not surprising that the nation's first president assigned priority to building a self-reliant national economy with manufacturing capacity to support military needs. George Washington understood the importance of trade and the need for access to European export markets, but, for him, domestic manufactures and a diversified industrial base came first. Warning against "the insidious wiles of foreign influence" peddlers, President Washington recommended an isolationist foreign policy designed to preserve the nation's hard-won independence. On trade policy the first president had similar counsel. He advised against nonreciprocal trade concessions, giving "equivalents for nominal factors" and then "being reproached with ingratitude for not giving more." His secretary of the Treasury, Alexander Hamilton, recommended a program of tariffs and subsidies to foster national economic independence.[1]

A century later Washington's basic approach remained the cornerstone of American commercial policy. In a farewell address presented in December 1892, President Benjamin Harrison celebrated the protective system as a "mighty instrument for the development of our national wealth and a most powerful agency in protecting the homes of our workingmen from the invasion of want." Like other Gilded Age Republicans, Harrison worried that trade liberalization would bring wage reductions and distress for American working people and their families: "A general process of wage reduction can not be contemplated by any patriotic citizen without the gravest apprehension. It may be . . . possible for the American manufacturer to compete successfully with his foreign rival in many branches of production without the defense of protective duties if the pay rolls are equalized; but . . . the distress of our working people when it is attained . . . [is] not pleasant to contemplate."[2]

Influential Republicans in Congress—especially Justin Morrill and Nelson Aldrich who both chaired the Senate Finance Committee—shared Harrison's concern. Jealously defending congressional prerogatives, they rejected any significant weakening of the high-tariff system. They expressed apprehension that free trade would harmonize wage levels downward to lower European levels and cause joblessness and chaos at home.

During the post–Civil War era, congressional protectionists did not mince words when discussing free trade and open markets. As noted in Chapter 2, Senator Justin Morrill warned that free trade "regards the labor of our own people with no more favor than that of the barbarian on the Danube or the coolie on the Ganges." Other prominent Republicans, such as William McKinley and William "Pig Iron" Kelley, concurred. As late as 1932, another Republican Finance Committee chairman, Reed Smoot of Utah, predicted that removal of the protective tariff barrier would force Americans "to slide back down to the economic level of the rest of the world."[3]

In the late twentieth century, some two hundred years after Washington spoke out, a different set of ideas and values prevail. Among the new internationalist American elite—*Fortune* "500" business executives and bankers, elected federal officials, and public opinion shapers in the media and universities—free trade is "in" and protectionism is "out." Like Richard Cobden, the nineteenth-century anti-Corn Law crusader, they view free trade as the "grand panacea" to heal the world's ills. Leaders now glorify the musings of Adam Smith and other English classical economists, not the nationalistic scribblings of native economists like Daniel Raymond and Henry Carey. The latter, influential in nineteenth-century America, have faded from memory. So have the writings of Friedrich List, the German economist who inspired U.S. officials in the 1820s. Free traders celebrate another visionary, President Woodrow Wilson. He, too, advocated free trade, international cooperation, and rule by law.[4]

America's forty-first president, George Bush, mirrored Cobdenism and Wilsonism. In a remarkable farewell address, one that offered a dramatic contrast to the thoughts of Washington and Harrison, Bush related the collapse of the Soviet Union to America's internationalist leadership and its steadfast commitment to democracy and open markets. He associated "nationalism" with disruption to global markets, trade wars, and economic decline, whereas free markets and democracy "enrich every region. . . . A retreat from American leadership, from American involvement, would be a mistake for which future generations, indeed our own children, would pay dearly." He called on American officials to reject isolationism and to "win the peace." Free trade inspired Bush, as it did his successor Bill Clinton. "I think protectionism is just 180 degrees wrong," Bush said on another occasion. "We're in a global economy. It's no longer just the U.S. We can't live behind those borders." Instead, he articulated a vision of universal free trade and U.S. economic leadership. Both Bush and Clinton accepted the need for America to lead and sustain the open global economy.[5]

Without a doubt, present-day enthusiasm for international cooperation and open markets represents a pragmatic response of business leaders and elected officials to changing opportunities. Rapidly improving technology and communications, as well as dramatic improvements in transportation and shipping, have spanned the continents and integrated markets, shrinking time and space. With the end of the Cold War attentions have turned from national rivalries to commercial competition.[6]

As this account shows, it would be simplistic to attribute the "triumph" of market internationalism solely to inexorable technological change and impersonal economic forces. Also influencing both timing and outcome was a tectonic shift in government regulatory policy. This change began during the New Deal years and represented both a response to the Great Depression and a reaction to the Smoot-Hawley Tariff of 1930. Before these events Republicans generally associated protection with prosperity. Indeed, faith that protection preserved jobs helped the GOP win control of the executive branch in fourteen out of eighteen presidential elections held from 1860 to 1928. During the 1930s political fortunes changed. Democrats won five successive presidential elections beginning in 1932. Over the twenty years low-tariff enthusiasts and economic internationalists in the Democratic tradition of Grover Cleveland and Woodrow Wilson held power and effected a policy revolution.

Secretary of State Cordell Hull directed the reorientation of trade philosophy and policy. He genuinely believed Smoot-Hawley to be a disastrous mistake, and as a former chairman of the Democratic National Executive Committee Hull shrewdly exploited the situation for partisan advantage. He and his associates linked Smoot-Hawley to the collapse of world trade and domestic production, to foreign protests and retaliation, and to beggar-thy-neighbor economic nationalism. The bogey of Smoot-Hawley thus became a powerful symbol for discrediting Republicans and protectionism. In the public mind Smoot-Hawley, like Munich, became an indelible metaphor for public policy failure.

However appropriate their Cobdenite vision of commerce as a remedy for the world's ills, the present work shows that Hull and his followers misinterpreted the record. Eager to score partisan points, they blamed the Republicans for Smoot-Hawley, conveniently overlooking the complicity of the many congressional Democrats who voted for amendments increasing tariffs but opposed Smoot-Hawley on final passage. In their zeal Hull and his followers misstated critical facts. Archival documents now available, as noted in Chapter 4, indicate that the "notorious" 1930 tariff-writing exercise actually provoked only three or four formal protests, not the "thirty-four formal and emphatic diplomatic protests" that Hull claimed in his memoirs.[7] Few, not many, trading partners retaliated, and this retaliation impacted selected products, such as automobiles, not all exports. Even the unbridled frenzy of the congressional logrolling associated with Smoot-Hawley ignominy pales over time. To obtain passage of the North American Free Trade Agreement, and the Uruguay Round implementing legislation, President Bill Clinton engaged in presidential vote buying on a grand scale.[8]

Hull's reciprocal trade program, introduced in 1934 as an emergency measure, evolved in the hands of his State Department successors as a powerful instrument for reshaping the post–World War II international order. In retrospect, Hull's initiative marks a turning point in U.S. and global economic relationships, one analogous in significance to Britain's repeal of the Corn Laws in 1846. The program's longevity is a tribute both to Hull's persistence and to the revolution in thinking that accompanied the Great Depression and involvement in World War II. Every president from Franklin Roosevelt to Bill Clinton chose to endorse Hull's import liberalization agenda. In effect, they all appropriated the secretary's Cobdenite philosophy that "unhampered trade dovetailed with peace; high tariffs, trade barriers, and unfair economic competition, with war."[9]

As it turned out, Hull and his executive branch successors dominated the trade liberalization process for a generation—until after the Kennedy Round. They succeeded in effecting their tariff reduction agenda: lowering U.S. tariff walls from 45 percent average ad valorem equivalent on dutiable imports in 1930 to 8.5 percent in 1973.[10] With the executive, not Congress, managing trade policy in the years from 1934 to 1974, tariff policy became another instrument of Cold War foreign relations, as well as overall foreign economic policy. Anxious to speed the economic recovery of allies and former enemies, American leaders ignored prudent George Washington. They generously opened America's market to the world without obtaining equivalent access abroad. In doing so, they redefined the national interest to include the health of the cosmopolitical economic system.

Especially after World War II, the reciprocity program failed to obtain real reciprocity. U.S. officials exchanged access to the U.S. market for cosmetic concessions from friends and former enemies. Repeatedly in negotiations held at Geneva (1947, 1955, 1961, and 1967) the United States placed support for the open system over the tangible interests of import-sensitive American producers and workers. Meanwhile, major allies—including even Great Britain—clung tenaciously to protectionist devices. The United Kingdom, for example, employed imperial preferences and controls, ostensibly for balance-of-payments purposes, to discriminate against American apples, pears, grapefruit, and other products, while protecting domestic producers. Thus, it is not surprising to find a cabinet-level British trade official admitting that "by and large the Americans have kept their doors wide open to our trade (and at a time when they might have urged that we were shutting out their goods by quotas long after we were genuinely short of dollars to pay for them)."[11]

In the 1955 bilateral negotiations with Japan, U.S. negotiators encountered an adversary that openly shunned free trade preachings and aggressively pursued industrial policies intended to build up domestic manufacturing at the expense of foreign competitors. Despite this information, foreign policy priorities drove American generosity—a generosity that even extended to purchasing market opportunities for Japanese exports in third markets with U.S. concessions.

Archival sources also indicate that through much of the period the executive branch chose not to vigorously enforce trade remedy laws. In effect, President Franklin Roosevelt and his successors placed a higher priority on achieving trade liberalization than on softening dislocations to domestic producers and workers.[12] To a large extent, this reflected preoccupation with foreign policy priorities both before and after World War II as well as the allure of the free trade vision. U.S. officials elected to ignore unfair trade laws until an exasperated Congress asserted its constitutional prerogatives and mandated more vigorous enforcement in the 1970s.

Among congressional leaders, Senate Finance Committee chairman Russell Long, the son of Louisiana's famed Senator Huey "Kingfish" Long, perceived that the executive branch was squandering the nation's patrimony in pursuit of foreign policy goals and economic ideals. He repeatedly spoke out, telling Secretary of State Henry Kissinger in 1976: "if we trade away American jobs and farmers' incomes for some vague concept of a 'new international order,' the American people will demand from their elected representatives a new order of their own, which puts their jobs, their security, and their incomes above the priorities of those who dealt them a bad deal."[13]

United Nations trade data show that American leaders succeeded in their efforts to promote imports. Over the forty-two-year period from 1950 to 1992, world exports rose at a 11.3 percent annual average rate; world imports rose 11.2 percent. But in each decade U.S. import growth exceeded export growth. Over the entire period U.S. exports climbed 9.8 percent annually, compared to 12 percent for U.S. imports. No other major developed market economy experienced such a wide gap between export and import performance or sustained such persistent merchandise trade deficits. Canada, the European Economic Community, and Japan all enjoyed export growth greater than import growth.[14]

When the Clinton administration entered office in 1993, it seemed sensitive to the lessons of past trade policy mistakes. Trade representative Mickey Kantor admitted that "past administrations have often neglected U.S. economic and trading interests because of foreign policy and defense considerations." He conceded that "American jobs and economic interests continued to take a back seat to foreign policy concerns." Kantor observed that for many years trade policy "failed to enforce our laws at home or open markets abroad." President Clinton also empathized with domestic workers and producers and seemed aware that globalization jeopardized the jobs and incomes of many workers while it created opportunities for others. In his first major speech on foreign trade policy, Clinton acknowledged that "the global village we have worked so hard to create" has produced "higher unemployment and lower wages for some of our people. . . . This is a powerful testament to the painful difficulty of trying to maintain a high-wage economy in a global economy where production is mobile and can quickly fly to a place with low wages."[15]

During his first year, however, Bill Clinton proved himself a trade liberalizer in the Hull tradition. His administration dedicated itself to extending free trade. The president pushed through Congress the North American Free Trade Agreement despite the strong opposition of his political supporters in organized labor. Eager to achieve "success" in the Uruguay Round and to preserve the open international system, Clinton consented to a multilateral agreement that appeared to provide only modest gains in terms of improved market access for exporters of agriculture, manufactures, or services. The European Union's common agricultural policy remained a major barrier to U.S. farmers, and so did many markets in developing areas to U.S. service providers and intellectual property holders.[16]

To skeptical reporters, Stuart Eisenstat, the U.S. ambassador to the EEC, explained why U.S. negotiators accepted the Uruguay Round outcome. "We have a second consideration," he said. "[A]s the only remaining superpower, as the strongest economy in the world and the world economic leader, we also have to take into account the potential impact of a failure."[17]

Understanding the U.S. government's commitment to the open global trading system, America's pragmatic trading partners aggressively pursued national objectives. France, for example, perceived "that the United States wanted a trade agreement more badly than Europe did" and forced the United States to renegotiate the Blair House accord providing for reduced European agricultural subsidies. It succeeded in protecting French culture against Jack Valenti's assertive Hollywood moviemakers.[18]

In another way the Uruguay Round agreements represented a significant departure from America's historic national policies. The pact contained provisions that appeared to encroach on national sovereignty and domestic laws. For example, article 6 of the World Trade Organization (WTO) stipulated: "Each Member shall ensure the conformity of its laws, regulations and administrative procedures with its obligations as provided in the annexed Agreements." Also, the WTO established dispute settlement panels composed of trade officials, not independent jurists, to adjudicate disputes. Previously, GATT procedures had permitted individual members to veto panel findings. But the Uruguay Round negotiations, conducted under three U.S. presidents, produced mandatory dispute settlement. Hereafter, the losing party must implement the panel's decision or pay heavy fines.[19]

During the Uruguay Round, the free trade philosophy seemed triumphant in both government ministries and corporate board rooms. In Washington,

D.C., a massive free trade lobby, composed of former legislators and trade officials, labored to preserve the open world economy on behalf of foreign and U.S.-based multinational corporations. In testimony and publications, this elite emphasized how consumers benefited from lower prices on imported goods. It decried Smoot-Hawley protectionism as threatening disruptive trade wars. Within the Washington establishment, the lobbyists, diplomats, academic soothsayers, and former trade officials had no difficulty in convincing themselves and other professionals that expanding trade benefited mankind while comporting with America's post–World War II leadership responsibilities.

Outside the Beltway, ordinary Americans saw trade policy differently. Kevin Phillips has observed that the vested interest in behalf of free trade was "obviously beneficial to perhaps 10 to 15 percent of the population, detrimental to some 30 to 50 percent." Joe Sixpack, the blue-collar worker with a high school education or less, worried about the destructive impact of low-cost import competition on jobs and living standards.[20]

Concern about the future was widespread—even in the business community. *Business Week* asserted that "global competition is dragging down pay for lower-skilled workers—widening the gulf between rich and poor." Noting the "emergence of a truly global work force," *Fortune* asked: "Will there be enough jobs to go around?" It quoted one chief executive officer of a global corporation forecasting that "Western European and American employment will just shrink and shrink in an orderly way. Like farming at the turn of the century." The *Economist*, an advocate of free trade since 1843, conceded that "low-skilled workers . . . are right to be worried." It warned that "some occupations higher up the earnings ladder will also feel the force" of third-world competition.[21]

One prominent businessman who dared challenge the conventional wisdom was Sir James Goldsmith, a corporate raider and member of the European Parliament. Predicting that the Uruguay Round agreements would speed the movement of factories and jobs to low-wage countries, Goldsmith forecast that the world trade deal would "impoverish and destabilize the industrialized world while . . . cruelly ravaging the third world." The "poor in the rich countries" would subsidize "the rich in the poor countries." He also estimated that the GATT agreement would drive two billion people off the land worldwide and make it difficult for democracy to remain the dominant structure. Goldsmith did not urge a return to nineteenth-century protectionism. Instead, he proposed regional free trade groupings, as distinguished from global free trade. Regional groupings among countries with similar levels of development would permit some international specialization without jeopardizing employment and social stability in high-income nations, he stated.[22]

Economists joined the debate. Paul Krugman of Stanford and Robert Lawrence of Harvard claimed that "international trade has had little net impact on the size of the manufacturing sector." They blamed the country's economic difficulties on technological change. President Clinton's 1994 economic report presented a similar interpretation, claiming that "the primary sources of growing wage inequality are domestic rather than foreign."[23]

But other studies associated increased imports with declining earnings and employment opportunities for American workers—particularly those with low skills and education levels. Harvard's Jeffrey Sachs and Howard Shatz conceded that imports from developing countries have reduced manufacturing sector production workers 5 percent over the last fifteen years. Ravi Batra and Daniel J. Slottje of Southern Methodist University found "that trade liberalization is correlated with an increase in poverty in the United States." Looking to the future, Edward Leamer of the University of California, Los Angeles, predicted that "our low-skilled workers face a sea of low-paid, low-skilled competitors around the world."[24]

In tone the latter writings resemble the apocalyptic warnings of forgotten nineteenth-century public officials—like Benjamin Harrison, William McKinley, and Justin Morrill—and economists such as Henry Sidgwick and Karl Marx. Sidgwick, a prominent political economist at Cambridge University, voiced concern in the 1880s that under a system of free trade dislocated manufacturing workers might experience difficulty finding employment at home "nearly as remunerative as that in which they were previously engaged." Concern about free trade–related dislocations revived interest in a speech Karl Marx presented in 1848. He openly endorsed free trade because it would hasten the global social revolution. Said Marx: "the protective system of our day is conservative, while the free trade system is destructive. It breaks up old nationalities and pushes the antagonism of the proletariat and the bourgeoisie to the extreme point. In a word, the free trade system hastens the social revolution. It is in this revolutionary sense alone, . . . that I vote in favor of free trade."[25]

Despite the heated discussion, most economists, business leaders, and government officials remained loyal to conventional free trade theories. For most of them the apocalyptic warnings had no standing and economic history little relevance. Accepting the inevitability of a global economy, instant communication, and the rapid movement of capital, goods, and people, leaders stressed the importance of investing in training and skills at home to improve the quality of the labor force. The elite exhorted ordinary workers to adapt and to accept the need for lifelong learning. President Clinton himself urged Americans "to embrace the world." He declared that the "purpose of my presidency" was to "ensure that our people have the confidence and skills" to reap rewards in a growing world economy.[26]

Among ordinary citizens vociferous opposition to further trade liberalization surfaced in the mid-1990s. During final phases of the Uruguay Round GATT negotiations militant farmers in France, India, and Korea, among many countries, had pressured their own governments to resist further concessions and to preserve protected home markets. In the Northern Hemisphere alienation soared in public debates over the European treaty of Maastricht and the North American Free Trade Agreement. Europeans worried about low-cost competition from the former Soviet empire and loss of sovereignty to supranational authority. Many North Americans feared competition from Mexico. NAFTA, the first free trade agreement between developed countries and a low-income industrializing nation, revived a nineteenth-century apprehension that free trade meant downward harmonization of wage rates. In an open world economy with no common standards governing working and environmental conditions, many believed that the transfer of high-paying factory jobs to developing countries would bring about the downward harmonization of wages and incomes that nineteenth-century Republicans had foreseen. Regional and multinational trade liberalization might benefit business, but it appeared to expose low-skilled and high-wage American workers to the consequences of global wage harmonization. Even middle managers and some professionals, like engineers, began to worry about job security.

In Canada and the United States economic insecurity produced revolutions at the ballot box. Angry over NAFTA and perceived job losses, Canadian voters slaughtered the ruling Conservative Party in 1993 parliamentary elections. A year later, in November 1994, angry American voters vented their frustrations at Democrats in Washington. Public opinion exit polls showed that large numbers of unskilled workers, long a source of strength to the Democratic Party, bolted to the GOP. This protest vote gave Republicans control of Congress for the first time in forty years. Economic insecurity, including anxiety over globalization, job losses, and declining living standards, contributed importantly to this outcome.

Concern about the implications of open markets and change were not confined to residents of wealthy nations. Similar fears surfaced among the least-developed countries belonging to the United National Conference on Trade and Development (UNCTAD). At the Columbus, Ohio, Symposium on Trade Efficiency in October 1994, UNCTAD delegates previewed twenty-first-century trade technologies. Many representatives of the poorest African countries openly worried about their own capacity to enter the world of electronic data interchange. Others, like Armenia, a former member of the Soviet Union, foresaw unique opportunities for its many skilled scientists and engineers. Using the information superhighway, Armenia hoped to export its greatest wealth, a renewable commodity known as gray matter.[27]

How would the global economy that visionaries like Cobden and Hull helped design impact the United States and the rest of the world in the twenty-first century? Would the new market internationalism produce global peace, prosperity, and democracy, as enthusiasts faithful to the Cobdenite vision insisted? Or would it accelerate the pace of change, accentuating economic dislocation and political alienation, particularly among unskilled workers in developed countries, those most vulnerable to global competition? Would the instantaneous interchange of electronic information through global networks facilitate the flow of international business transactions while promoting global welfare? Or would it also exacerbate social and political conflict within nations and jeopardize the nation-state system?

Opinions varied. History may suggest reasons for uncertainty. In the past Utopian visions of free trade and technological change, pacifying nations while promoting global prosperity have regularly fascinated the press, as well as business and political leaders. In the 1840s, for example, the London *Economist* asserted that "free trade, free intercourse, will do more than any other visible agent to extend civilization and morality throughout the world." Corn Law reformer Richard Cobden proclaimed free trade as significant to the moral world as the principle of gravitation was to science. He envisioned free trade "drawing men together, thrusting aside the antagonism of race and creed, and language, and uniting us in the bonds of eternal peace." In the United States, even President McKinley, a Republican with impeccable protectionist credentials, observed in September 1901 how improvements in transportation and communications—steam power and the interoceanic cable—brought people and nations closer together. "[I]solation is no longer possible or desirable," McKinley asserted. "God and man have linked the nations together. No nation can longer be indifferent to any other."[28]

Nearly a century later, after two bloody world wars and a costly Cold War, events again seem to be fulfilling the Cobdenite faith. With international contacts proliferating and transnational corporations allocating resources on a world scale, the "global village" had become an operational reality. Indeed, market internationalism gained another important convert in October 1994, when United Nations secretary general Boutros Boutros-Ghali, an Egyptian, effused: "A world brought together by the ties of trade will be inclined to peace rather than war, to cooperation rather than confrontation."[29]

Richard Cobden and other exponents of commercial internationalism had long envisioned a world where the centripetal forces of global communications and commerce succeeded in restraining and pacifying the centrifugal pressures of nationalism. But it was also possible that free trade among nations at vastly different income levels would exacerbate internal economic and political tensions and thus jeopardize future world peace and stability. As the twentieth century moved to a close, it was not clear whether Cobden's millennium had finally arrived or was another mirage. Historians of the future would have the perspective to decide.

Frank Taussig, the renown international economist and first chairman of the Tariff Commission, apparently understood the difficulties of prognostication. Writing a conclusion to his *Tariff History of the United States* after passage of Smoot-Hawley, Taussig ventured only the sage observation that the future lies "in the lap of the gods."[30] His caution has stood the test of time better than specific forecasts.

Notes

ABBREVIATIONS

BC	Bureau of the Census, U.S. Department of Commerce
BEA	Bureau of Economic Analysis, U.S. Department of Commerce
BOB	Bureau of the Budget
BT	Board of Trade
CEA	U.S. Council of Economic Advisers
CITIP	U.S. Commission on International Trade and Investment Policy
CRI	Committee for Reciprocity Information
DDC	*Declassified Documents Catalog*
DDE	Dwight D. Eisenhower Library, Abilene, Kans.
FDR	Franklin D. Roosevelt Library, Hyde Park, N.Y.
FO	Foreign Office
FRUS	U.S. Department of State, *Foreign Relations of the United States*
GRF	Gerald R. Ford Library, Ann Arbor, Mich.
HCH	Herbert C. Hoover Library, West Branch, Iowa
HRAC	U.S. House of Representatives, Appropriations Committee
HRE&L	U.S. House of Representatives, Education and Labor Committee
HRW&M	U.S. House of Representatives, Ways and Means Committee
HST	Harry S. Truman Library, Independence, Mo.
ITC	U.S. International Trade Commission (1975–)
ITF	International Trade Files, Department of State, Record Group 43, National Archives
JC	Jimmy Carter Library, Atlanta, Ga.
JEC	Joint Economic Committee, U.S. Congress
JFK	John F. Kennedy Library, Boston, Mass.
LBJ	Lyndon B. Johnson Library, Austin, Tex.
MD	Morgenthau Diaries, Henry Morgenthau Papers, Franklin D. Roosevelt Library, Hyde Park, N.Y.
MD/LC	Manuscript Division, Library of Congress
NA	National Archives, Washington, D.C.
NAC	National Archives of Canada, Ottawa
NFTC	National Foreign Trade Council
NSF	National Security File
OF	Official File
OTA	Office of Technology Assessment, U.S. Congress
OTAP	U.S. Tariff Commission, *Operation of the Trade Agreements Program*
PHF	President's Handwriting File
PPF	President's Personal File
PRO	Public Record Office, Kew, England
Randall	U.S. Commission on Foreign Economic Policy, Clarence B. Randall, chairman
RG	Record Group
RMN	Richard M. Nixon Collection, National Archives, College Park, Md.
SHC	Southern Historical Collection, University of North Carolina at Chapel Hill

SNFN	U.S. Senate, Committee on Finance
SNFR	U.S. Senate, Committee on Foreign Relations
SNIFC	U.S. Senate, Committee on Interstate and Foreign Commerce SOS Secretary of State
SOT	Secretary of the Treasury
STR	Special Trade Representative (1962–79)
TAD	Trade Agreements Division, U.S. Department of State
TC	U.S. Tariff Commission (1917–74)
UNCTAD	United Nations Conference on Trade and Development
USC	U.S. Code
USDC	U.S. Department of Commerce
USDL	U.S. Department of Labor
USDOD	U.S. Department of Defense
USDS	U.S. Department of State
UST	U.S. Department of the Treasury
USTR	U.S. Trade Representative (1980–)
USU	Utah State University
WHCF	White House Central File

INTRODUCTION

1. On the revolving-door syndrome, see Choate, *Agents of Influence*; Lewis, *Frontline Trade Officials* and *Trading Game*.

2. Schwab, *Trade-Offs*, p. 58; Niskanen, *Reaganomics*, pp. 146–53.

3. *New York Times*, September 17, 1985; *Wall Street Journal*, September 19, 1985; May 4, 1988.

4. Gragert, *Will Rogers' Weekly Articles*, 4:62.

5. Seymour Fabrick, Vogue Shoe, Inc., to author, June 11, 1984.

6. Baldwin and Steagall, *Factors Influencing ITC Decisions*; Madison, "Alfred Who?," p. 527; *New York Times*, May 13, 1984.

7. ITC, *Economy-Wide Modeling*, May 1992.

8. Lee and Belman, "Trade Liberalization," p. 2.

9. Schumpeter, *History of Economic Analysis*, pp. 12–13.

10. Henry Ford interview, *Chicago Tribune*, May 25, 1916.

11. Thomas M. T. Niles, U.S. ambassador to Canada, to author, September 17, 1986.

12. Prestowitz, *Trading Places*, p. 259.

13. U.S. President, *Economic Report*, 1985, p. 115; Wallis, "Protecting Prosperity from Protectionism," p. 36.

14. Economic historians have reached similar conclusions. See Bairoch, *Economics and World History*, pp. 16–55; Milward, *European Rescue*, p. 121. Milward writes that "until the early 1950s historical experience seemed to offer no solid guarantees that freer foreign trade would make national economies prosper."

15. Sachs and Shatz, "Trade and Jobs in U.S. Manufacturing," p. 1; Dunning, *International Production*, p. 14.

16. For the nationalistic perspective, see List, *National System*; Henry Carey, *Harmony of Interests*. For the dominant free trade position, see among the classics Adam Smith's *Wealth of Nations* and Mill's *Principles*, 2:99–100, 423–25. Mill disputes Carey's defense of protectionism and associates trade expansion with world peace and the "uninterrupted progress of the ideas, the institutions, and the character of the human race" (p. 100).

17. Moggridge, *Writings of John Maynard Keynes*, 21:205–10.

18. Dicken, *Global Shift*, pp. 91–96; Hill, *International Business*, pp. 115–45; Dunning, *International Production*, pp. 13–18, 119–39; Porter, *Competitive Advantage*, pp. 1–21; Tyson, *Who's Bashing Whom?*, pp. 9–14. Dunning's presidential address to the International Trade and Finance Association, July 15, 1994, University of Reading, England, will appear in the *International Trade Journal*.

19. SNFN, *Nomination of . . . Eckes*, p. 7. See also *Nomination of . . . Haggart*, pp. 5–7.

CHAPTER ONE

1. Robert J. Taylor, *John Adams*, 4:124–25. Historians emphasizing the connection between trade and foreign policy include Lyman, *Diplomacy*; Schuyler, *American Diplomacy*; Beard, *National Interest*; Gilbert, *To the Farewell Address*; William A. Williams, *From Colony to Empire*; Varg, *Foreign Policies*.

2. *Free trade* involves the unrestricted exchange of goods without any customs duties or nontariff barriers. If one country opens its border to imports, it practices *unilateral* free trade. If two countries agree to remove duties and restraints on each other's products, they practice *reciprocal* free trade. *Reciprocity* means the exchange of commercial privileges and favors through bargaining. In a reciprocity agreement, benefits are not extended automatically, generally, and freely to other governments. *Equality* means *nondiscrimination*. Nondiscrimination between nationals and foreigners involves *national treatment*. Discrimination between nationals and foreigners, but equal treatment accorded to foreigners, would be *most-favored-nation treatment*. In the *unconditional* form, nondiscrimination is provided gratuitously to nations eligible for most-favored-nation treatment. In the *conditional* form, third parties must bargain and provide *equivalent compensation* for most-favored-nation treatment.

3. Adam Smith, *Wealth of Nations*, p. 431.

4. Willcox, *Franklin*, 21:175. See generally Dorfman, *Economic Mind*, 1:78–92, 178–95. Franklin understood that trade was mutually advantageous, and his analysis may have influenced Adam Smith. Wright, *Franklin of Philadelphia*, pp. 180–81. Rae (*Life of Adam Smith*, pp. 264–65) speculates that Smith may have read each chapter in the *Wealth of Nations* to Franklin for comment. After the Revolution Franklin remained a devotee of free trade. Smyth, *Franklin*, 9:63.

5. Conway, *Writings of Thomas Paine*, 1:88. The term *free trade* has enjoyed many meanings. In late-eighteenth-century Britain *free traders* were smugglers who successfully avoided customs duties on wine and brandy. William Cunningham, "Free Trade," 11:88–89.

6. Foley, *Jefferson Cyclopedia*, p. 361 (first and last quotations); Jefferson, *Notes on . . . Virginia*, p. 165 (second quotation); Paul L. Ford, *Jefferson*, 2:68; Merrill Peterson, *Jefferson and the New Nation*, pp. 69–75.

7. Boyd, *Jefferson*, 8:427, 633; Paul L. Ford, *Jefferson*, 4:99.

8. Robert J. Taylor, *Adams*, 5:125 (quotations), 145; Bemis (*Diplomatic History*, p. 292) notes the distinction between *freedom of trade* and *free trade*.

9. Robert J. Taylor, *Adams*, 3:216.

10. Stourzh, *Franklin and American Foreign Policy*, p. 238; Montesquieu, *Spirit of the Laws*, p. 338. According to Merrill Peterson (*Jefferson and the New Nation*, p. 61), Jefferson read Montesquieu's work about 1770.

11. George B. Hill, *Life of Johnson*, 2:218. On Franklin, see Stourzh, *Franklin and American Foreign Policy*, pp. 106–7. Franklin's papers contain correspondence with David Hume, who persuaded Franklin that trade was mutually advantageous. Labaree, *Franklin*, 9:227–29. See also Morris, *Forging of the Union*, pp. 349–50; Varg, *Foreign Policies*, p. 29. See also Grampp, "Adam Smith."

12. Adam Smith, *Wealth of Nations*, p. 625.

13. Robert J. Taylor, *Adams*, 4:260–64, 290; Charles F. Adams, *John Adams*, 2:516–17.

14. This treaty plan was drafted by John Adams, John Dickinson, Benjamin Harrison, Robert Morris, and Benjamin Franklin. Adams, who prepared the first draft, adopted language contained in earlier European treaties between Britain and the smaller maritime nations. For background, see Hugh O. Davis, *Trade Equality*, pp. 2–3; Setser, *Commercial Reciprocity*, pp. 13–15. Setser interprets the treaty plan as a "bid for French aid." See also Charles F. Adams, *John Adams*, 2:516–17; Robert J. Taylor, *Adams*, 4:279–81, 290–302.

15. Setser, "Did Americans Originate . . . ?"

16. Worthington C. Ford, *Adams*, 7:460; Willcox, *Franklin*, 25:596. For French concerns about a reconciliation, see Willcox, *Franklin*, 25:440–52. In 1783 France sought to reinterpret the most-favored-nation clause in an unconditional manner, and Americans resisted, intent on pursuing a program of bilateral reciprocal market-opening negotiations with other European nations. Hugh O. Davis, *Trade Equality*, pp. 8–9; Boyd, *Jefferson*, 6:393–94; Setser, *Commercial Reciprocity*, pp. 41–42.

17. U.S. Continental Congress, *Diplomatic Correspondence*, 1:387–403, 2:36 (quotation), 3:57–66, 317–20, 332–35, 354–58, 375, 396; Worthington C. Ford, *John Quincy Adams*, 7:437, 460–61; Willcox, *Franklin*, 25:596, 28:625–26; Boyd, *Jefferson*, 10:541. "[T]he two Parties desire to establish . . . the most perfect Equality and Reciprocity . . . leaving also each party at Liberty to make, respecting Commerce and Navigation, those interior regulations which it shall find most convenient to itself; and by founding the Advantage of Commerce solely upon reciprocal Utility, and the just Rules of free Intercourse; reserving withal to each Party the Liberty of admitting at its pleasure other Nations to a Participation of the same advantages." Willcox, *Franklin*, 25:596. For a discussion of trade problems with France, see Setser, *Commercial Reciprocity*, pp. 86–87; "Commerce between France and the United States; Stover, "French-American Trade"; Merrill Peterson, *Jefferson*, pp. 314–30.

18. Merrill Peterson, *Jefferson*, pp. 304–13; Emory R. Johnson et al., *History of . . . Commerce*, 1:132–44. France also complained about discrimination in America. Boyd, *Jefferson*, 9:50–51; Manning, *Diplomatic Correspondence*, 1:234–39, 2:457–87; Boyd, *Jefferson*, 10:293–94; Peterson, "Jefferson and Commercial Policy."

19. Peterson, "Jefferson and Commercial Policy"; Setser, *Commercial Reciprocity*, pp. 53–65; U.S. Continental Congress, *Diplomatic Correspondence*, 6:489–97. The 1782 treaty with the Netherlands contained no language specifically qualifying most-favored-nation treatment, as the French treaty did. In 1787 John Jay held that when U.S. treaties lacked an express requirement for compensation, others could only reasonably demand "the favor . . . of being admitted to make a *similar* bargain" (emphasis added). Crandall, "American Construction of the Most-Favored-Nation Clause"; TC, *Reciprocity . . . and Commercial Treaties*, p. 405 (quotation).

20. Morris, *Peacemakers*, pp. 287–88, 347–50, 429–33; Setser, *Commercial Reciprocity*, pp. 40–51; Sheffield, *Observations*; Boyd, *Jefferson*, 6:393, 7:265, 463, 8:54–55, 266–67, 9:402, 404.

21. Setser, *Commercial Reciprocity*, pp. 53–98.

22. U.S. Continental Congress, *Diplomatic Correspondence*, 1:529–31. James Monroe and Jefferson also discussed the difficulties of implementing such clauses in 1784. Stanislaus M.

Hamilton, *Monroe*, 1:35–36; Paul L. Ford, *Jefferson*, 4:385–86; Boyd, *Jefferson*, 7:652, 8:605; Setser, *Commercial Reciprocity*, p. 70.

23. *American Historical Review* 10 (July 1905): 823. See also James Monroe to Jefferson, October 12, 1786, in Boyd, *Jefferson*, 10:456–58.

24. U.S. Continental Congress, *Diplomatic Correspondence*, 4:348 (quotation); Page Smith, *John Adams*, 2:636; Marks, *Independence on Trial*, pp. 52–70; Varg, *Foreign Policies*, pp. 60–61. Adams favored excluding British ships from the carrying trade, enacting navigation acts, and developing domestic manufactures. U.S. Continental Congress, *Diplomatic Correspondence*, 4:345–49, 376, 500.

25. *Brown v. Maryland*, 25 U.S. 420 (1827) (John Marshall); Marks, *Independence on Trial*, p. 52; Nettels, *National Economy*, pp. 44–88; Emory R. Johnson et al., *History of . . . Commerce*, 1:122–44.

26. Cooke, *Federalist*, p. 505.

27. Richardson, *Messages*, 1:214–15. President Washington said that

our commercial policy should hold an equal and impartial hand, neither seeking nor granting exclusive favors or preferences; consulting the natural course of things; diffusing and diversifying by gentle means the streams of commerce, but forcing nothing; establishing with powers so disposed, in order to give trade a stable course, to define the rights of our merchants, and to enable the Government to support them, conventional rules of intercourse, the best that present circumstances and mutual opinion will permit, but temporary and liable to be from time to time abandoned or varied as experience and circumstances shall dictate; constantly keeping in view that it is folly in one nation to look for disinterested favors from another; that it must pay with a portion of its independence for whatever it may accept under that character; that by such acceptance it may place itself in the condition of having given equivalents for nominal factors, and yet of being reproached within gratitude for not giving more. (pp. 214–15)

Joseph A. Fry notes that Alexander Hamilton suggested this passage. The language reflects his desire to avoid discriminating against British commerce in a way that might jeopardize Anglo-American trade and resulting tariff revenues for the Treasury. Fry, "Washington's Farewell Address." See also Syrett, *Hamilton*, p. xx.

28. Richardson, *Messages*, 1:311.

29. Worthington C. Ford, *John Quincy Adams*, 7:432–33, 437, 460–61.

30. Ibid., 7:102, 432–33.

31. Cooke, *Federalist*, p. 66. From his post in London Adams pressed for a "commercial war upon the mother country." Setser, *Commercial Reciprocity*, p. 98. Madison and Jefferson favored discrimination to break Britain's commercial monopoly. Setser, p. 105; Boyd, *Jefferson*, 16:513–23.

32. Merrill Peterson, *Jefferson*, pp. 308–9.

33. Released December 16, 1793. Paul L. Ford, *Jefferson*, 8:114–18 (all quotations in this paragraph); Merrill Peterson, *Jefferson*, pp. 512–15. Modern observers may view Jefferson's report as a predecessor of USTR reports on foreign barriers to U.S. exports of goods and services.

34. Paul L. Ford, *Jefferson*, 8:98–119.

35. Mason, *Madison*, 15:167–71. See also Brant, *Fourth President*, pp. 225, 270–71; McCoy, "Republicanism"; Malone, *Jefferson*, p. 475. In June 1794 Congress authorized the president to retaliate when Congress was not in session. *Field v. Clark*, 143 U.S. 649 (1892). Precedent

for retaliation to protect American commercial rights was established during this critical period. Lyman, *Diplomacy*, 1:208; Bemis, *Jay's Treaty*.

36. Becker, *Business-Government Relations*, pp. 69–90.

37. Cooke, *Federalist*, pp. 78–79.

38. Emphasizing the preamble, protectionists would later describe this tariff as "a second Declaration of Independence." It established "the principle of protecting the manufactures and encouraging the navigation of America." Blaine, *Twenty Years*, 1:185–86; Stanwood, *Tariff Controversies*, 1:63–71. Taussig (*Tariff History*, p. 15) also conceded that "the intention to protect was there." See also E. A. J. Johnson, *Foundations*, pp. 227–41; Elkins and McKitrick, *Age of Federalism*, pp. 65–72; TC, *Tariff and Its History*, pp. 70–71; Thompson, *Protective Tariff*, pp. 38–68.

39. Setser, *Commercial Reciprocity*, pp. 105–9; Merrill Peterson, *Jefferson*, pp. 423–29. France protested tonnage duties on shipping. See *American State Papers* (Class 1), 1:109–12. For an account of this debate, see Bowling and Veit, *William Maclay*, p. 54.

40. Flexner, *Indispensable Man*, pp. 129–30; Richardson, *Messages*, 1:57.

41. Abbott, *Washington*, 1:261–64, 2:78–79. Washington signaled his support for domestic manufactures to Jefferson on February 13, 1791. Boyd, *Jefferson*, 14:546. Freeman (*Washington*, 6:188) notes that his inaugural attire was selected to "advertise American industry."

42. Remini, *Clay*, pp. 53, 61–62.

43. Stanwood, *Tariff Controversies*, 1:77; Blaine, *Twenty Years*, 1:187. Elkins and McKitrick (*Age of Federalism*, pp. 270–71) attribute the reluctance of Congress to undertake this program to Indian unrest and the money panic of 1792.

44. Syrett, *Hamilton*, 10:262–63. For Jefferson's disagreement, see Paul L. Ford, *Jefferson*, 7:136–39. But Jefferson conceded that European discrimination might compel the United States to encourage manufactures. Boyd, *Jefferson*, 20:565–66. Hamilton's aide, Tenche Coxe, contributed to the "Report on Manufactures" and, as an economic nationalist, pressed for retaliatory duties on imported manufactures. Cooke, *Tenche Coxe*, pp. 182–205. See generally E. A. J. Johnson, *Foundations*, pp. 194–225; Cooke, *Hamilton*, pp. 100–102.

45. Syrett, *Hamilton*, 10:262, 297.

46. Ibid., 10:285–86.

47. Merrill Peterson, *Jefferson*, pp. 910–11; Syrett, *Hamilton*, 10:5–6.

48. Paul L. Ford, *Jefferson*, 8:115; *American State Papers* (Class 3), 2:430. Gallatin noted that "vastly superior capital" enabled British merchants to "give very long credits, to sell on small profits, and to make occasional sacrifices." Richardson, *Messages*, 1:470.

49. Raymond, *Political Economy*, 1:222–24. See also MacGarvey, "Daniel Raymond, Esquire."

50. Raymond, *Political Economy*, 2:230–33. Regarding tariff policy, Raymond took the position that as a general rule "a tariff ought not to be reduced, although it may frequently require to be raised." Smith's concept of buying cheaper imports Raymond considered a "most absurd and unprovident doctrine" that "leads to utter ruin. . . . It is a miserable, short-sighted, beggarly policy, calculated to prevent all improvement in the capacity of either individuals or nations, for acquiring the necessaries and comforts of life" (pp. 241–47). Raymond urged a long-term view, one relying on the government to promote industry, full employment, and a strong home market.

Early U.S. and British economists were frequently trained in law, philosophy, or religion. For a discussion of early American economics, see Teilhac, *Pioneers of American Economic Thought*; Michael J. L. O'Connor, *Origins of Academic Economics*; Dorfman, *Economic Mind*.

51. Dorfman, *Economic Mind*, 2:566–97. Especially influential was Henry Charles Carey

of Philadelphia. See Conkin, *Prophets of Prosperity*, pp. 261–307; Huston, "Political Response," pp. 35–57. Along with Raymond and Alexander Hamilton, Philadelphia publicist Matthew Carey and Baltimore publisher Hezekiah Niles also influenced List's thinking. See Hirst, *List*, pp. 109–17; Stanwood, *Tariff Controversies*, 1:246–49; Conkin, *Prophets of Prosperity*; Kaiser, *Protectionist–Free Trade Controversy*, p. 41.

52. Taussig, *Selected Readings*, p. 277 (first quotation); Hirst, *List*, pp. 229–40 (other quotations); List, *National System*, pp. 119–32.

53. Boyd, *Jefferson*, 8:426–27.

54. According to Monroe, Madison chose war reluctantly, realizing that the alternative was to lose the presidency. Monroe noted the dilemma of a war for commerce or political defeat. Stanislaus M. Hamilton, *Monroe*, 5:209. See also John Quincy Adams, *Lives*, p. 133. Representative John C. Calhoun also used the phrase. Meriwether, *Calhoun*, 1:243. Frankel ("The 1807–1809 Embargo," pp. 291–308) argues that the embargo was effective, but that the United States lacked the necessary political will.

55. Matthew Carey, *Autobiographical Sketches*, pp. 33–46; cited in Emory R. Johnson et al., *History of . . . Commerce*, 2:35. Viner (*Dumping*, pp. 41–43) notes that this quotation was widely cited as evidence of dumping. In March 1816 Victor DuPont complained to Congressman Henry Clay about the predatory pricing practices of British exporters. Hopkins, *Clay*, 2:173–74. Other relevant "memorials" to Congress from import-sensitive businesses appear in *American State Papers* (Class 3), 3:32, 454, 463. John Quincy Adams (*Lives*, p. 281) also noted that foreign competition "aided by bounties and other encouragements from their own governments, would have crushed in their infancy all such establishments here."

56. Remini, *Clay*, p. 174.

57. Clay's support for the protection of domestic industries and internal improvements, the American system, apparently developed from his diplomatic experiences as well as his nationalistic feelings. Ibid., p. 791.

58. Paul L. Ford, *Jefferson*, 11:504–5.

59. Madison, *Letters and Other Writings*, 3:43, 649. In his December 1815 message to Congress, Madison noted "exceptions" to laissez-faire theories. Richardson, *Messages*, 2:552.

60. Charles F. Adams, *John Adams*, 10:384.

61. Richardson, *Messages*, 2:760–61.

62. Meriwether, *Calhoun*, 1:348–49. In the 1820s Calhoun switched sides on the tariff to stay in step with South Carolina thinking.

63. Bassett, *Jackson*, 3:249–51. For Jackson's trade policies, see Belohlavek, *Let the Eagle Soar*.

64. Remini, *Clay*, pp. 134–39.

65. Hopkins, *Clay*, 2:828.

66. Ibid., 2:838–39.

67. Ibid.

68. Ibid., 2:828–35.

69. Ibid., 3:688–89.

70. Editor Horace Greeley, a Clay supporter, vigorously pushed the protective tariff and influenced the Republican platform of 1860. Isely, *Greeley*. Lincoln attributed his support for a high tariff to Clay. Basler, *Lincoln*, 3:486–87, 4:49.

71. Richardson, *Messages*, 6:2620.

72. Hopkins, *Clay*, 3:688–89. In Clay's rhetoric, and in nineteenth-century American protectionism generally, runs a strong fear of British influence and economic dominance. See Blaine, *Twenty Years*, 1:214.

73. Taussig, *State Papers*, p. 344. Marian M. Miller, *Great Debates*, 12:42–48. Webster maintained close personal associations with English bankers. According to Ziegler's *The Sixth Great Power*, a history of the House of Barings, he received gifts and payments (pp. 59, 146, 155). See also Bartlett, *Daniel Webster*, p. 209; Dalzell, *Daniel Webster*, p. 79.

74. Stanwood, *Tariff Controversies*, pp. 349–410; Remini, *Clay*, pp. 412–35; TC, *Methods of Valuation*, pp. 66–67.

75. In 23 of the 29 years the United States experienced a budget surplus. In only 3 of the 11 years in which duties averaged less than 20 percent did the country have a budget surplus. BC, *Historical Statistics*, 2:888, 1104; George R. Taylor, *Transportation Revolution*, pp. 352–83.

76. BC, *Historical Statistics*, 2:890, 899.

77. Emory R. Johnson et al., *History of . . . Commerce*, 2:51–52; Taussig, *Tariff History*, p. 154. Taussig subsequently became the first chairman of the TC. George R. Taylor, *Transportation Revolution*, pp. 190–95, 237, 366.

78. Naomi C. Miller, *Cobden*, 1:36; *Economist*, August 1843, pp. 14–15; Hinde, *Cobden*.

79. Hopkins, *Clay*, 9:774–75; Andrew Stewart, *American System*, p. 116. The *Economist* hailed President Polk's "free trade policy" as the American counterpart of Corn Law repeal. The former would create opportunities for British manufactures; the latter would benefit American agricultural exports. *Economist*, December 27, 1845, pp. 1319–20. Clay warned of "pauper labor" invoking an image that would become a staple of protectionist oratory. See also Huston, "Political Response," pp. 35–57.

80. On Walker, see Stanwood, *Tariff Controversies*, 2:41–45. The Treasury secretary recommended that no duty be imposed "above the lowest rate which will yield the largest amount of revenue." In his opinion "experience proves that, as a general rule, a duty of twenty per cent ad valorem will yield the largest revenue." UST, *Annual Report*, December 3, 1845. Walker favored a reciprocal free trade policy and no countervailing duties for retaliation. See also Shenton, *Walker*; Blaine, *Twenty Years*, 1:194–95.

81. Bourne, *British Documents*, 4:122, 148, 151. As late as 1930, Eric Cable, a British consular official assigned to Portland, Oreg., offered a similar assessment of U.K. interests: "Nothing could be more profitable for the United Kingdom than that the United States should be a free trade country. If there were no import duties in the United States it would be flooded with British goods, which in most cases are superior to the local article." Cable also outraged his superiors with the forecast that "a real free trade policy would not merely cause vast unemployment in the United States as it has done in Great Britain, but . . . it would for a certainty spell revolution." Cable to FO, "Memorandum on American Economic Methods," July 16, 1930, FO 371/14279, PRO.

82. Johnson and Porter, *National Party Platforms*, p. 26; Bemis, *Diplomatic History*, p. 301; TC, *Reciprocity . . . and Commercial Treaties*, p. 87. To Whigs like Representative Justin Morrill of Vermont, the Tariff Act of 1857, which proposed to lower or remove duties on raw materials like wool, jeopardized U.S. economic security and independence. "Without the production and control of the primary necessities of life," he said, "we must remain the vassals of those who are the arbiters of our supplies." *Congressional Globe*, February 5, 1857, app., p. 226. On the Canadian agreement, see Stanwood, *Tariff Controversies*, p. 136; Stuart, *Expansionism and British North America*, pp. 194–214; TC, *Reciprocity . . . and Commercial Treaties*, pp. 77–92.

83. In the 1894 treaty with Japan and the 1903 treaty with China, however, the unilateral version evolved to contain reciprocal privileges for Japanese and Chinese in the U.S. market equal to citizens of the most favored foreign nation. TC, *Reciprocity . . . and Commercial*

Treaties, pp. 400–401; William S. Culbertson, *International Economic Policies*, p. 58; Bemis, *Diplomatic History*, pp. 341–63.

84. TC, *Reciprocity . . . and Commercial Treaties*, pp. 17–39. However, the United States reserved the right to determine whether proffered compensation was sufficient to purchase most favored treatment (p. 417).

85. Schuyler, *American Diplomacy*, pp. 103–4.

86. See generally Brauer, "Economics"; Pletcher, "Economic Growth." David Lake offers another view in his *Power, Protection, and Free Trade*, pp. 91–118.

CHAPTER TWO

1. Wallis, "Protecting Prosperity," pp. 33–36.

2. Andrew Stewart, *American System*, p. 17.

3. Cobden, *Speeches*, January 15, 1846, p. 187.

4. Ambassador Sir E. Howard to FO, May 31, 1929, FO 371/13536, and J. J. Broderick memo, "Factors Affecting American Industrial Exports," April 18, 1930, FO 371/164431, both in PRO.

5. Morgan, *Hayes to McKinley*, p. 278. *The Judge*, a humor magazine with protectionist sympathies, regularly identified free trade with low English wages and ruin.

6. Theodore Roosevelt, the other Republican featured on Mount Rushmore, also endorsed protectionism. Basler, *Lincoln*, 1:407–16; Luthin, "Lincoln and the Tariff."

7. McKinley, *Speeches*, August 2, 1892, pp. 589–605 (quotations, pp. 592, 595, 605). McKinley feared that free trade would spark a revolution. That prospect led Karl Marx to endorse free trade. See his speech, "On the Question of Free Trade," Brussels, Belgium, January 9, 1848, in Marx, *Poverty of Philosophy*, p. 227.

8. Morison, *Theodore Roosevelt*, 1:504.

9. Ibid., 4:934. Later in his career Roosevelt supported reciprocity with Cuba and Canada and tariff "amendments." He favored maximum and minimum tariff rates, a two-schedule tariff, "so that the Executive could get a measure of reciprocity with foreign countries without having to submit treaties to the Senate." Ibid., 4:1056.

10. *Congressional Record*, June 25, 1902, pp. 7366–76.

11. *Congressional Globe*, February 5, 1857 (app., p. 226), April 23, 1860 (p. 1832). Morrill chaired the House Ways and Means Committee for two years (1865–67) and the Senate Finance Committee for twenty-two (1867–98).

12. *Congressional Record*, June 12, 1930 (p. 10560), July 15, 1932 (p. 15441). Until 1936, Republican conventions embraced protectionism. Johnson and Porter, *National Party Platforms*, pp. 343, 368.

13. *Congressional Record*, May 18, 1888, p. 4401.

14. Blaine, *Twenty Years*, 1:211–12. Nicholas Longworth, a future Speaker, held similar views. *Congressional Record*, August 5, 1909 (p. 4947), April 13, 1910 (A-84).

15. Basler, *Lincoln*, 1:313, 381–82. Daniel Raymond, America's first systematic economist, argued that foreign producers paid "a large proportion of the duties." Raymond, *Political Economy*, p. 452. High-tariff Republicans offered this view throughout the late nineteenth century.

16. McKinley, *Speeches*, p. 595, cited in speech of Representative Simeon D. Fess (R-Ohio), in *Congressional Record*, February 1, 1916, app. 230. During the 1888 presidential

campaign Republican candidate Harrison also warned that with free trade domestic "mills and factories must reduce wages here to the level with wages abroad, or they must shut down." Hedges, *Speeches*, August 21, 1988, p. 96.

17. Wharton, *Industrial Competition*, pp. 19–28 (quotations, pp. 16, 28), and *National Self-Protection*, p. 8; Yates, *Wharton*, pp. 181–82.

18. *Congressional Globe*, January 11, 1870, p. 369. An ardent protectionist, Kelley dismissed free trade as "sheer quackery, charlatanism" and described the "protective system . . . as the crowning glory" of the last quarter century. *Congressional Globe*, March 25, 1870, app., p. 210; *Congressional Record*, May 9, 1878, p. 3340. From 1881 to 1883 he chaired the Ways and Means Committee.

19. Tarbell, "Moral Aspects of Tariff-Making," p. 7; Schattschneider, *Politics, Pressures, and the Tariff*, p. 283. In her autobiography, *All in a Day's Work* (pp. 268–70), Tarbell noted encouragement from former president Grover Cleveland, who shared her indignation with high tariffs. Her perspective inspired Woodrow Wilson, and he offered Tarbell an appointment to the TC in 1916. Link, *Wilson*, 40:343, 372, 384.

20. Marian M. Miller, *Great Debates*, p. 353 (Mills); Link, *Wilson*, 23:611, 639; *Congressional Record*, August 23, 1916, p. 13046; Evans C. Johnson, *Underwood*; Cordell Hull, "American Tariff and Trade Policies," press release, December 21, 1928, Norman Davis Papers, MD/LC.

21. *Congressional Record*, May 8, 1878 (app., p. 145) and January 13, 1894 (app., p. 19). Representative James Garfield (R-Ohio) responded to Tucker's "grand conception." He considered it "too remote to be made the basis of the practical legislation of today. . . . For the present, the world is divided into separate nationalities." *Congressional Record*, June 4, 1878, app., p. 292.

22. Bierce, *Devil's Dictionary*, p. 277.

23. *Congressional Record*, August 23, 1916, p. 13045. This argument appeared regularly in tariff debates.

24. Richardson, *Messages*, 11:5174.

25. Johnson and Porter, *National Party Platforms*, pp. 24, 26. During the 1850s British free traders sought to encourage sympathizers in the United States. James and Lake, "Second Face of Hegemony."

26. Cobden, *Speeches*, p. 184; McKinley, "The Tariff," 10:17–18; Bourne, *British Documents*, 4:122, 140.

27. *Congressional Record*, June 8, 1897, p. 1586.

28. Johnson and Porter, *National Party Platforms*, pp. 33–54 (quotations, p. 42).

29. Ibid., pp. 65–66. During the campaign Republicans claimed that Cleveland's supporters obtained funding from English free traders. *New York Times*, October 12, 1884.

30. Richardson, *Messages*, pp. 5165–76 (quotations, pp. 5169–70); Sherman, *Recollections*, 2:1004–9.

31. *Congressional Record*, April 17, 1888, pp. 3058–61. See also Reitano, *Tariff Question*, pp. 17–39.

32. Ibid., May 18, 1888, p. 4407; app., p. 49.

33. Johnson and Porter, *National Party Platforms*, p. 80; Hedges, *Speeches*, p. 109.

34. *Judge*, June 30, July 14, 21 (long quotation), 1888.

35. *Puck*, March 7, May 23, August 1, 1888.

36. Morgan, *Hayes to McKinley*, pp. 313–17. See also Volwiler, "Tariff Strategy"; Roseboom and Eckes, *Presidential Elections*, pp. 108–10.

37. Dobson, *Two Centuries of Tariffs*, p. 143. Taussig (*Tariff History*, p. 283) claims that the act of 1890 represented a "radical extension of the protective system."

38. BC, *Historical Statistics*, 2:888. Using duties calculated to estimate the tariff may underestimate the protective effect if higher rates bar imports. Taussig (*Tariff History*, p. 251) claims that the act brought a "marked increase of duties." But see Hawke, "Tariff and Industrial Protection."

39. Hawke, "Tariff and Industrial Protection," p. 93.

40. Ibid., p. 87.

41. Richardson, *Messages*, 12:5746.

42. Johnson and Porter, *National Party Platforms*, pp. 123, 138, 158.

43. Ibid., p. 168; Link, *Wilson*, 23:647–49.

44. Johnson and Porter, *National Party Platforms*, p. 184.

45. Ibid., p. 205.

46. Ibid., p. 235; Special address to Congress, April 12, 1921, in Richardson, *Messages*, 18:8939.

47. Johnson and Porter, *National Party Platforms*, p. 260.

48. Ibid., p. 245.

49. Ibid., pp. 271–82.

50. Ibid., pp. 343–45.

51. Ibid., p. 331.

52. Rosenman, *Roosevelt*, September 20, 1932, 1:724–25.

53. Ibid., 1:766–67; Moley, *After Seven Years*, pp. 46–51. Roosevelt told Moley that he saw the speech as a "compromise between the free traders and the protectionists." Moley, *After Seven Years*, p. 51.

54. Hoover, *Memoirs*, 3:289–92.

55. Moley, *After Seven Years*, pp. 51, 369; Rosenman, *Roosevelt*, 1:853.

56. Morgan, *Hayes to McKinley*, pp. 117–18; Jordan, *Winfield Scott Hancock*, pp. 301–2. Until World War II shifted American priorities, domestic political considerations constrained tariff and trade policies. Thus in the 1920s President Calvin Coolidge defended the protective system: "Those who wish to benefit foreign producers are much more likely to secure that result by continuing the present enormous purchasing power which comes from our prosperity that has increased our imports over 70 per cent in four years than from any advantages that are likely to accrue from a general tariff reduction." Israel, *State of the Union Messages*, 3:2693.

57. BC, *Historical Statistics*, 2:888.

58. UST, *Report of the Special Commissioner of Revenue*, pp. 1372–80. On steel lobbying, see Tedesco, *Patriotism, Protection*.

59. Taussig, *Tariff History*, pp. 185–87.

60. The same pattern applied from 1821 to 1831 and from 1847 to 1860. See BC, *Historical Statistics*, 2:888.

61. Ibid. The major tariff revisions were the Morrill Tariff of 1861, Tariff Act of 1872, Tariff Act of 1883 ("Mongrel Tariff"), McKinley Tariff of 1890, Wilson-Gorman Tariff of 1894, Dingley Tariff of 1897, Payne-Aldrich Tariff of 1909, Underwood Tariff of 1913, Fordney-McCumber Tariff of 1922, and Smoot-Hawley Tariff of 1930.

62. Johnson and Porter, *National Party Platforms*, p. 107.

63. Link, *Wilson*, 23:611.

64. Richardson, *Messages*, 11:5166.

65. Harcave, *Memoirs of Count Witte*, pp. 182–88, 321; Von Laue, *Sergei Witte*, p. 56. However, Kahan (*Russian Economic History*, pp. 41, 99–103) takes the view that the Russian tariff had high consumption costs and thus represented a "mixed blessing."

66. *Congressional Record*, May 5, 1882 (app., p. 197), April 15, 1884 (pp. 2979–81, quotations).

67. Amery, *Joseph Chamberlain*, p. 208; Cunningham, *Rise and Decline*, pp. 162–63. For another economic history critical of Britain's free trade policies, see Crouzet, *Victorian Economy*, pp. 121–28.

68. Mitchell, *British Historical Statistics*, pp. 520–21.

69. Calculated from ibid., p. 453. But overseas investment earnings and a strong surplus on invisible trade left Britain with a strong current account surplus. Even so, with a growing merchandise trade deficit it was beginning to export manufacturing jobs abroad (p. 334). On Britain's export market shares, see ibid., p. 524. On industrial growth, see Aldcroft, *Development of British Industry*, p. 13. For insights, see Chandler, *Scale and Scope*. Chandler may underestimate the significance of closed home markets. See also Porter, *Competitive Advantage*.

70. Milward, *European Rescue*, p. 121; Bairoch, "European Trade Policy," 8:88–90. But see Capie, *Tariffs*, pp. 39–40.

71. It may also be significant that the U.S. population rose at an annual rate of 1.9 percent from 1890 to 1910, but at a 1.0 percent rate from 1970 to 1990. Trade statistics are from BC, *Historical Statistics*, 2:887; BEA, *Survey of Current Business*, December 1992, 12:27.

72. BC, *Historical Statistics*, pp. 224–25, 887–88. Per capita GNP is in constant 1987 dollars.

73. GNP and per capita GNP are in constant dollars. Recent data are from BC, *Statistical Abstract*, 1993, pp. 443, 811–18.

74. Statistics cited in Sidney Pollard, *Britain's Prime*, pp. 6–7.

75. USDL, *Employment, Hours, and Earnings*; BC, *Statistical Abstract*, 1993, p. 424.

76. BC, *Historical Statistics*, 1:200–201.

77. Bairoch, *Economics and World History*, pp. 30–55, 136–38, 164. For a discussion based on experience in the 1980s, see World Bank, *World Development Report*, 1991, pp. 98–102; Thomas and Nash, *Best Practices*.

78. One recent economic history does not even consider the tariff or foreign trade. See Weiss and Schaefer, *American Economic Development*.

79. World Bank, *East Asian Miracle*; Wade, *Governing the Market*.

80. Krugman, "Asia's Miracle," pp. 62–78.

81. BC, *Historical Statistics*, 1:106. See Dinerstein, Nichols, and Reimers, *Natives and Strangers*, p. 104; Philip Taylor, *Distant Magnet*.

82. World Bank, *East Asian Miracle*; Wade, *Governing the Market*. See ITC, *Foreign Industrial Targeting*, pp. 37–47, 75–89, 128–42, 181–92, 236–41.

83. UST, Stephen Colwell, *Report*. On Carey, see Dorfman, *Economic Mind*, 3:6–8.

84. Swank, *Industrial Policies*, p. 59; Tedesco, *Patriotism, Protection*.

CHAPTER THREE

1. In 1900 cotton accounted for 17.7 percent of exports, down from 60.2 percent in 1870. The composition of American trade had changed dramatically. Semimanufactures and finished manufactures rose from 18.6 percent of total U.S. exports in 1870 to 35.4 percent in 1900. BC, *Historical Statistics*, 2:885–90.

2. USDS, *Commercial Relations*, 1879, 2:277.

3. Vanderlip, *American "Commercial Invasion"*; USDS, *Commercial Relations*, 1900, 1:16;

Brooks Adams, *Economic Supremacy*. On U.S. economic expansionism, see LaFeber, *New Empire*; McCormick, *China Market*; Terrill, *Tariff, Politics*.

4. Thwaite, *American Invasion*, pp. 21–29 (quotations, pp. 21, 25); McKenzie, *American Invaders*, p. 31. See also Stead, *Americanization of the World*; Ernest E. Williams, *Made in Germany*, pp. 140–44. Williams concluded that protectionism gave Germany an advantage over England.

5. Thwaite, *American Invasion*, p. 29; Friedberg, *Weary Titan*, pp. 45–88.

6. Bairoch, "European Trade Policy"; Sidney Pollard, *Peaceful Conquest*, pp. 252–77; TC, *Reciprocity*, pp. 203–5, 461–510; Novack and Simon, "American Export Invasion."

7. Summers, *Wilson and Tariff Reform*; HRW&M, *Reciprocity and Commercial Treaties*, p. 23.

8. Emory R. Johnson, *History of . . . Commerce*, 2:90–91; HRW&M, *Tariff Negotiations*.

9. SNFR, *Reports*, 8:570–71. In 1900 James Deering, a spokesman for the Agricultural Implements Association, urged Americans "to unite on an industrial policy that will conquer the world." Ibid.

10. HRW&M, *Reciprocity and Commercial Treaties*, p. 299 (quotations); Wolman, *Most Favored Nation*, pp. 19–54; Becker, *Business-Government Relations*, pp. 69–90.

11. HRW&M, *Tariff Hearings*, pp. 1882–90 (quotation, pp. 1884).

12. Reciprocity usually involves the exchange of equivalent concessions. But it is not possible to balance such concessions on an apothecary's scale. Trade data are often incomplete, and they provide only a historical perspective. For instance, these data may not capture changing competitive conditions in the marketplace. When agreements involve different industries—and touch other political and security issues—negotiators simply may not know the costs and benefits. Also, short-term effects and long-term consequences may vary. Paul L. Ford, *Jefferson*, 8:98–119; *Congressional Record*, January 7, 1885, p. 509.

13. Richardson, *Messages*, 4:1588.

14. Baker, *Wheaton*, pp. 230–31; Richardson, *Messages*, 4:2113.

15. Wilson, *Calhoun*, 18:100–107; *Congressional Globe*, January 14, 1869, pp. 349–53 (quotation, pp. 351–52).

16. *Congressional Globe*, January 14, 1869, p. 352 (quotation); Wheaton to SOS, March 25, 1844, Dispatches from U.S. Minister to the German States and Germany, USDS, RG 59, M-44, roll 4; Baker, *Wheaton*, pp. 235–53. Wheaton stressed the "great" advantages for U.S. exporters of staple commodities. But Charles Graebe, the U.S. consul in Hesse, Cassel, had a pessimistic view. The small reduction in tobacco duties was "insufficient of producing any increase in the consumption" and the lard restriction was a "sham concession." Graebe argued: "The advantages which the United States could have gained by the treaty would according to my humble opinion, have been mere nothing, and the disadvantages very large." Wilson, *Calhoun*, 18:194, 19:724–25 (quotation). Morrill noted that U.S. concessions would have seriously injured the growth of northern industry, while leaving the "slave power of the country . . . in undisputed ascendancy. Never was John C. Calhoun so nearly victorious." *Congressional Globe*, January 14, 1869, pp. 349–53. For Wheaton's instructions, see Diplomatic Instructions of the Department of State, 1801–1906, USDS, RG 59, M-77, roll 65.

17. Wilson, *Calhoun*, 18:193–95, 19:189.

18. Baker, *Wheaton*, p. 246; Wilson, *Calhoun*, 18:141, 326–28, 393, 410 (quotation). During the early years the United States signed a number of commercial agreements, including one with Great Britain in 1815, that did not specifically provide for conditional most-favored-nation treatment. This approach led to disputes with the Netherlands and France over the Louisiana Purchase. TC, *Reciprocity . . . and Commercial Treaties*, pp. 404–8.

19. UST, *Report*, 1845, p. 12; Senate, *Journal*, 28th Cong., 1st sess., p. 446.

20. Twenty-two Whigs voted to table the treaty, as did two Democrats and one Independent. Seventeen Democrats and one Whig opposed tabling it. Norma Lois Peterson, *Harrison and . . . Tyler*, pp. 230–33. An angry Andrew Jackson said that "there never was such treachery to the laborer of the South and West." Cutler, *Polk*, pp. 3–4.

21. Wilson, *Calhoun*, 19:209–14, 315–16.

22. *Congressional Record*, January 14, 1869, pp. 349–53.

23. Holt, *Treaties Defeated*, pp. 90–95.

24. Schuyler, *American Diplomacy*, pp. 434–36; Hooley, "Hawaiian Negotiation"; Tate, *Hawaii*, pp. 27–39; Kuykendall, *Hawaiian Kingdom, 1778–1854* (pp. 416–25), *1854–74* (pp. 39–47).

25. Laughlin and Willis, *Reciprocity*, pp. 10–11; Rippy, *United States and Mexico*, pp. 212–29; Manning, *Diplomatic Correspondence*, 9:1139–41; Berbusse, "McLane-Ocampo Treaty"; Holt, *Treaties Defeated*, pp. 92–95.

26. TC, *Reciprocity . . . and Commercial Treaties*, pp. 63–67; McDiarmid, *Commercial Policy*, pp. 61–92; Spencer, *Victor and the Spoils*, pp. 300–308. See also Shippee, *Canadian-American Relations*; Tansill, *Canadian-American Relations*, pp. 412–66; Warner, *Continental Union*.

27. Oliphant, *Episodes*, pp. 27 (quotation), 36–48. U.S. officials increasingly criticized the deal for being one-sided, or "jug-handled," in favor of Canada. Gordon T. Stewart, *American Response to Canada*, pp. 64–83. British documentation appears in Bourne, *British Documents*, vol. 4.

28. BC, *Historical Statistics*, 2:904–96. These data should be treated cautiously. During the Civil War U.S. imports rose in response to war conditions, and war priorities may have diverted exports. Export statistics relating to Canada have frequently understated U.S. exports. The Tariff Commission concluded that "Canadian figures of imports into Canada are more accurate than the American statistics of exports thereto." TC, *Reciprocity . . . and Commercial Treaties*, p. 85. Two scholars challenge the conventional wisdom that Canada benefited. See Officer and Smith, "Canadian-American Reciprocity Treaty."

29. Robinson, *Reed*, p. 240; Merrill and Merrill, *Republican Command*, p. 91; *Congressional Record*, May 7, 1890, p. 4249 (quotations).

30. Parker, *Morrill*, p. 320. In 1896 Ways and Means backed reciprocity enthusiastically but acknowledged Senate opposition. HRW&M, *Reciprocity and Commercial Treaties*, p. 51.

31. Parker, *Morrill*, p. 97. Morrill's intense opposition to Canadian reciprocity discouraged Secretary of State Hamilton Fish from renegotiating the 1854 agreement in 1874. For Britain's efforts, see Bourne, *British Documents*, 8:284–90.

32. *Congressional Globe*, January 12, 1865, p. 229 (first quotation), and January 14, 1869, p. 352 (last quotation); Sumner, *Works*, 12:48–59; Parker, *Morrill*, pp. 254–56, 320 (second and third quotations).

33. Daniel Voorhees (D-Ind.), who chaired the Finance Committee from 1893 to 1895, shared this opposition to reciprocity. In February 1883 Morrill, Voorhees, and Aldrich signed a "minority report" asserting that "in every instance where a reciprocity treaty has been tried . . . immense American interests have been sacrificed." SNFN, *Report to Accompany S.R. 122*, p. 8.

Morrill chaired the Finance Committee from October 1877 to July 1898, except for four years when Democrats controlled the Senate. Congress did extend Hawaiian reciprocity, and the Senate approved President Arthur's reciprocity treaty with Mexico. But legislation implementing the Mexican treaty never passed Congress.

34. Paolino, *Foundations*, pp. 26–27 (quotations); John Patterson, "United States and Hawaiian Reciprocity"; Van Deusen, *Seward*, pp. 332–34; Tate, *Hawaii*, pp. 52–77.

35. Dozer, "Opposition to Hawaiian Reciprocity"; Chapin, "Fish," p. 247 (quotations); Tate, *United States and the Hawaiian Kingdom*, p. 42. Morrill spoke out against the reciprocity treaty in executive session. *Congressional Record*, March 18, 1875, app., pp. 157–60. He again referred to "the unconstitutional character of reciprocity agreements." Although opposed to Canadian reciprocity, he said that "the arguments in its favor were tenfold stronger than any which can be brought to the support of the reciprocity with the Sandwich Islands [Hawaii]." Military factors influenced the outcome, as General J. M. Schofield told the Ways and Means Committee that Hawaii was vital to the defense of the Pacific Coast. Pletcher, *Awkward Years*, p. 173.

36. SNFN, *Report to Accompany S.R. 122*, pp. 5, 3, 7. On efforts to abrogate the treaty, see Dozer, "Opposition to Hawaiian Reciprocity."

37. Pletcher, *Awkward Years*, pp. 139–89; Reeves, *Gentleman Boss*, pp. 390–411; Foster, *Memoirs*, 1:111, 239–60.

38. *Congressional Record*, January 7, 1885, p. 506.

39. Ibid., pp. 506–13. Morrill associated reciprocity with war. "Three-fourths of all wars arise directly or indirectly from the eagerness of foreign trade, its frictions, accidents, and complications," he said (p. 513).

40. Richardson, *Messages*, 10:4922.

41. TC, *Reciprocity . . . and Commercial Treaties*, p. 145; Gail Hamilton, *Blaine*, pp. 680–90; Muzzey, *Blaine*, pp. 426–58 (quotation, pp. 448–49); Socolofsky and Spetter, *Harrison*, pp. 118–23; Pletcher, "Reciprocity and Latin America." McGann (*Argentina*, pp. 153–57) shows that Argentina led the opposition to a customs union for the Western Hemisphere. As it turned out, the Harrison administration elected not to negotiate with Canada. Reciprocity with Latin America involved complementary trade, but reciprocity with Canada raised the issue of competition with home industries. It jeopardized the Republican approach to home market protection. Gordon T. Stewart, *American Response to Canada*, pp. 92–93.

42. William S. Culbertson, *Reciprocity*, p. 156; TC, *Reciprocity . . . and Commercial Treaties*, pp. 146–48; La Follette, *Autobiography*, pp. 112–13.

43. Stephenson, *Aldrich*, p. 84; Sage, *Allison*, pp. 243–44.

44. *Congressional Record*, May 7, 1890, pp. 4250–53.

45. Hamilton, *Blaine*, pp. 680–90; HRW&M, *Reciprocity and Commercial Treaties*, p. 47. Harrison looked for a compromise with Congress. Volwiler, *Correspondence between . . . Harrison and . . . Blaine*, 109, 113, 126.

46. *Field v. Clark*, 143 U.S. 649 (1892). Stanwood (*Tariff Controversies*, pp. 281–83) notes that the reciprocity issue came up late in the Senate tariff debate. Republicans contended that the provision did not involve delegation of legislative power to the president, whereas Democrats held otherwise.
Justice John Marshall Harlan, a Republican appointee, wrote the majority opinion. The Court's two Democrats, Chief Justice Melville W. Fuller and Justice Lucius Quintus Cincinnatus Lamar, dissented. Lamar held that the section unlawfully delegated legislative power to the executive department when it authorized the president to impose discretionary tariffs. Paul, "Lamar," pp. 1447–49; King, *Fuller*.

47. Foster, *Memoirs*, 2:1–19; Devine, *Foster*, pp. 41–42.

48. Benjamin H. Williams, *Economic Foreign Policy*, pp. 270–72; TC, *Reciprocity . . . and Commercial Treaties*, pp. 145–94. The TC concluded that the reciprocity provision "exerted a

favorable influence upon the export trade of the United States" (p. 194). Reciprocity, it maintained, had "no great effect upon [U.S.] imports" (p. 163). However, because the concessions were in effect for only three years during a period of depression, it is doubtful that the data permit reliable conclusions about the merits of this program.

49. Benjamin H. Williams, *Economic Foreign Policy*, p. 271; TC, *Reciprocity . . . and Commercial Treaties*, pp. 157–59 (quotation, p. 158).

50. Gould, "Diplomats in the Lobby"; Richardson, *Messages*, 13:6238–39. For 1897 reciprocity provisions, see TC, *Reciprocity . . . and Commercial Treaties*, pp. 197–227.

51. In the Senate William Allison (R-Iowa) successfully tacked on an amendment requiring congressional approval of treaties negotiated, and in modified form this became part of the law.

52. TC, *Reciprocity . . . and Commercial Treaties*, pp. 202–3; Gould, "Diplomats in the Lobby," pp. 659–80. The Dingley Tariff authorized reciprocity negotiations, but section 4 provided the president with no new authority. Using existing treaty power, he might have negotiated tariff reductions. What the act did establish was a negotiating process. It barred Congress from challenging presidential authority to negotiate trade agreements, as occurred during the Zollverein treaty controversy.

53. A former member of the Ways and Means Committee, Kasson knew tariff issues. Not a protectionist, he favored downward tariff revision. See Younger, *Kasson*, p. 365. Protectionists regarded Kasson with suspicion because he had counseled the Free Trade League. Tarbell, *Tariff in Our Times*, p. 38; TC, *Reciprocity . . . and Commercial Treaties*, pp. 205–14.

54. SNFR, *Reports*, pp. 474–625; *New York Times* and *Washington Post*, November 21, 1901.

55. *New York Times* and *Washington Post*, November 21, 1901; TC, *Reciprocity . . . and Commercial Treaties*, p. 224. In the Argentine treaty the U.S. negotiator, a State Department official, consented to a 20 percent duty reduction on wool. Younger, *Kasson*, pp. 361–81.

56. Becker, *Business-Government Relations*, pp. 69–78; Wolman, *Most Favored Nation*, pp. 19–38; Richardson, *Messages*, 13:623 (McKinley); Johnson and Porter, *National Party Platforms*, p. 123.

57. Younger, *Kasson*, p. 377; Richardson, *Messages*, 14:6621.

58. Richardson, *Messages*, 14:6621. Apparently McKinley foresaw ultimate approval of reciprocity agreements but chose not to force the issue with recalcitrant senators like Chairman Aldrich. Olcott (*McKinley*, 2:298–300) claims that McKinley intended to press hard for reciprocity agreements during his second term.

59. Richardson, *Messages*, 13:6403.

60. Ibid., 14:6652–53, 6713–14; Morison, *Roosevelt*, 3:152. In his December 1902 annual message Roosevelt endorsed reciprocity while stressing the need to maintain protection: "There must never be any change which will jeopardize the standard of comfort, the standard of wages of the American wage-worker." Richardson, *Messages*, 13:6714.

61. Stephenson, *Aldrich*, pp. 177–81. For a State Department eager to negotiate reciprocity agreements, congressional protectionism appeared shortsighted. See Dennett, *Hay*, pp. 416–22; Cullom, *Fifty Years*, pp. 368–75.

62. Healy, *United States in Cuba*, pp. 193–200; Benjamin, *United States and Cuba*, p. 10; Morison, *Roosevelt*, pp. 228, 265–66, 296–97, 432–34, 603; TC, *Effects of the Cuban Reciprocity Treaty*, pp. 433–34 (contains copy of Roosevelt's special message on reciprocity with Cuba, June 13, 1902); Richardson, *Messages*, 14:6682–84 (quotations, p. 6682). On Puerto Rico, see Morison, *Roosevelt*, p. 1183.

63. TC, *Effects of the Cuban Reciprocity Treaty*, p. 387; Richardson, *Messages*, 14:6742 (Roosevelt); TC, *Reciprocity . . . and Commercial Treaties*, pp. 317–18 (Root, p. 318), 427–31.

64. Stephenson (*Aldrich*, p. 185) suggests that Aldrich and Allison found it convenient to support the president's desire for trade preferences for Cuba and the Philippines while opposing reciprocity for France and other Western Hemisphere nations.

65. TC, *Effects of the Cuban Reciprocity Treaty*, p. 174.

66. *Congressional Record*, November 16, 1903, p. 274.

67. TC, *Reciprocity . . . and Commercial Treaties*, pp. 328–35, 338. Reciprocity had little effect on the tobacco trade. Stephenson, *Aldrich*, pp. 186–87; TC, *Effects of the Cuban Reciprocity Treaty*, pp. 9–10, 55–57.

68. TC, *Effects of the Cuban Reciprocity Treaty*, pp. 40–41.

69. Computed from ibid., pp. 100, 164.

70. TC, *United States–Philippine Tariff*, p. 19; Richardson, *Messages*, 14:6737; Taussig, *Tariff History*, pp. 396–400; TC, *Effects of the Cuban Reciprocity Treaty*, pp. 67–69. Dalton (*Sugar*, p. 204) notes that the United States used sugar protection to maintain living standards in insular areas. In effect, the sugar program provided aid to Cuba and other dependencies.

71. Morison, *Roosevelt*, 4:932–34.

72. Ibid., 3:267, 4:899, 1052–53.

73. Ibid., 3:494. Roosevelt favored reciprocity with Canada but feared that it would split the Republican Party (4:912–13).

74. Ibid., 4:1052–53, 1055–56.

75. On Taft's trade policies, see Wolman, *Most Favored Nation*.

76. Johnson and Porter, *National Party Platforms*, p. 158. On the tariff battle in Congress, see Stephenson, *Aldrich*, pp. 341–61; Merrill, *Smoot*, 289–97. During debate Nelson Aldrich elaborated his protective theory: "if we permit American industries to live by the imposition of protective duties, competition in this country will so affect prices that it will give the American consumer the best possible results." *Congressional Record*, August 5, 1909, p. 4947.

77. Bourne, *British Documents*, 12:285.

78. Richardson, *Messages*, 16:7426–27. For application of the maximum-minimum approach, see Wolman, *Most Favored Nation*, pp. 164–76.

79. Richardson, *Messages*, 16:7673, 7777–78; Wolman, *Most Favored Nation*, pp. 193–94; TC, *Reciprocity . . . and Commercial Treaties*, pp. 32 (quotation), 265–76; HRW&M, *Tariff Negotiations*.

80. Gordon T. Stewart, *American Response to Canada*, pp. 103–10. On Taft's special affection for Canada, see Martin, *The Presidents and the Prime Ministers*, pp. 68–69. See generally, Hannigan, "Reciprocity 1911," pp. 1–18.

81. *Congressional Record*, February 14, 1911, pp. 2509–14 (quotations, pp. 2511, 2513); HRW&M, *Reciprocity with Canada*, 1911. In floor debate Dalzell asserted that "newspaper greed for free paper is behind this free-trade movement." *Congressional Record*, February 14, 1911, p. 2510. The proposed pact did place newsprint on the free list.

82. *Congressional Record*, February 14, 1911, p. 2529.

83. TC, *Reciprocity . . . and Commercial Treaties*, p. 375 (quotation); TC, *Reciprocity with Canada*, pp. 55–58. Canada reduced duties on articles covered in the agreement from an average 15.5 to 10.3 percent ad valorem. The United States proposed to reduce its duties on articles covered from 12 percent to 1.7 percent. On the basis of 1910 imports, America would have remitted $4.85 million in revenue; Canada, $2.65 million. Had the preferential agreement taken effect, the United States would not have extended benefits to third countries without compensatory reductions. But Canada, as a member of the British Empire, might have extended benefits to Britain and other members of the empire. France also would have qualified for some reductions.

During the negotiations, the British embassy lost no opportunity to remind the Canadians not to prejudice British manufacturing interests. Ambassador Bryce assured London that a freer exchange of products in North America was not likely to lead to closer political relations. Bourne, *British Documents*, 14:316.

84. Coletta, *Taft*, pp. 141–52. In the House 84 out of 162 Republicans opposed Canadian reciprocity. With 17 Republicans absent, the vote was 77 against Taft's agreement and 67 for it. Memo to Taft, April 21, 1911, William Howard Taft Papers, MD/LC.

85. *Congressional Record*, February 14, 1911, p. 2520. See also Tansill, *Canadian-American Relations*, pp. 461–63; TC, *Reciprocity with Canada*, pp. 84–85. Lord Bryce reported to London that Speaker Clark's remarks were an "outburst of that stupid and arrogant 'spread-eagleism' which still lingers among the less educated sort of politicians." Bourne, *British Documents*, 14:316–40.

86. Johnson and Porter, *National Party Platforms*, p. 168.

87. Richardson, *Messages*, 16:7871–73 (quotation, p. 7872); Underwood, *Drifting Sands*, pp. 166–84; Evans C. Johnson, *Underwood*.

88. According to the Finance Committee, the maximum schedule approach had proven "embarrassing, clumsy, and inadequate" to the task of protecting U.S. citizens from "harsh and discriminating tariff treatment abroad." The committee proposed to give the president "retaliatory power" to "bring about equitable arrangements with those countries which do not now afford us fair treatment." SNFN, *Report to Accompany H.R. 3321*, p. 32 (quotation). See also BC, *Historical Statistics*, 2:888; ITC, Statistical Services Division, March 1985, in author's possession.

89. TC, *Reciprocity . . . and Commercial Treaties*, pp. 279–82. Senator Smoot predicted disaster as European goods inundated the American market. Merrill, *Smoot*, pp. 298–99.

90. Bourne, *British Documents*, 15:249–55.

91. Lansing memo, April 15, 1914, 611.0031/70, RG 59, NA.

92. On automobile investments, see Wilkins, *Maturing of Multinational Enterprise*, pp. 72–75; Southard, *American Industry in Europe*, pp. 115–19; USDC, *American Branch Factories Abroad*, p. 12.

93. Wilson to SOS, May 29, 1916, 611.0031/70, and Frank Taussig to Wilson and Secretary Lansing, November 8, 1917, 611.0031/102, RG 59, NA. The National Foreign Trade Council endorsed bargaining tariffs. NFTC, June 1917, 611.003/665, ibid.

94. TC, *Reciprocity . . . and Commercial Treaties*, pp. 9–15. Taussig's own views shaped the final document. William S. Culbertson, "Journal," July 16, 1918, p. 241, and "Ventures in Time and Space," memoir, Culbertson Papers, pp. 55–60, MD/LC.

95. Johnson and Porter, *National Party Platforms*, p. 235.

96. Richardson, *Messages*, 18:8939.

97. Neville, "Antidumping Act"; Viner, *Dumping*, pp. 242–51; TC, *Information concerning Dumping and Unfair Foreign Competition*; SNFN, *Report to Accompany H.R. 7456*.

98. William McClure memo, May 27, 1921, 611.003/841, and W. W. Cumberland memo to Assistant Secretary Fred M. Dearing, June 18, 1921, 611.003/842, RG 59, NA.

99. Cumberland memo, July 14, 1921, 611.003/843, ibid.

100. TC, *Annual Report*, 1922, p. 63; Cumberland memo, April 26, 1922, 611.003/1156, RG 59, NA.

101. *New York Times*, December 7, 1921.

102. Cumberland memo, April 26, 1922, 611.003/1156, RG 59, NA.

103. Culbertson to SOS Hughes, May 31, September 29, 1922, 611.003/1141, and McClure

to Hughes, October 20, 1922, 611.003/1188 (quotations), ibid.; *FRUS*, 1923, 1:121; Snyder, *Culbertson*, pp. 59–64.

104. McClure to Hughes, October 20, 1922, 611.003/1188, RG 59, NA.

105. Young to Hughes, October 21, 1979, 611.0031/179, RG 59, NA.

106. Arthur Young memo, August 29, 1922, 611.0031/177, ibid.

107. Hughes letter, August 18, 1923, 611.0031/197a, ibid.

108. *FRUS*, 1923, 1:131–33.

109. Cumberland comments on TC report on trade discrimination and Cumberland memo, July 17, 1923, 611.0031/188, RG 59, NA.

110. Allyn Young to Leland Harrison, August 22, 1923, 611.0031/200, RG 59, NA.

111. Ibid.

112. Charles M. Barnes to Hiram Motherwell, March 1, 1930, 611.0031/324, ibid.

113. BC, *Statistical Abstract*, 1940.

114. McClure memo, November 10, 1924, 611.0031/233, RG 59, NA. McClure, a Tennessee native, obtained a Ph.D. in economics from Columbia University in 1924; his dissertation was entitled "A New American Commercial Policy as Evidenced by Section 317 of the Tariff Act of 1922."

115. *Congressional Record*, January 3, 1929, pp. 1071–73; Hull to McClure, March 25, April 5, 1929, Hull Papers, MD/LC.

116. HRW&M, *Tariff Readjustment—1929*, "Minority Views," pp. 1–3; McClure to Hull, May 28, 1929, Hull Papers, MD/LC.

117. Hull to Thomas W. Page, TC, April 2, 1929, ibid.

118. Hull to Norman Davis, December 31, 1928, Davis Papers, MD/LC; Hull to Josephus Daniels, January 2, 1929, and Hull to Davis, December 29, 1928, Hull Papers, MD/LC.

119. Davis to Hull, January 2, 1929, Hull Papers and Davis Papers; Hull to Roosevelt, March 16, 1929, Hull Papers—all in MD/LC. Hull expressed concern about the "permanent partnership" between tariff beneficiaries and a single political party.

120. *Congressional Record*, February 16, 24, March 3, 1931; Davis to Hull, November 7, 1930, Davis Papers, MD/LC.

121. McClure to Joseph Cotton, May 22, 1930, 611.003/2264; Culbertson memo, June 11, 1931, 611.0031/394; Culbertson memo, June 16, 1931, 611.0031/337—all in RG 59, NA.

122. Rogers to Secretary Stimson, September 11, 1931, 611.0031/374, ibid.

123. Hawkins, "Commercial Policy of the United States," September 19, 1931, 611.0031/403, ibid.

124. McClure memo, October 31, 1931, 611.0031/375, ibid.

125. Hull, "Call Off the Tariff War!"

126. *Congressional Record*, April 28, 1932, pp. 9147–49; *Public Papers . . . Hoover*, May 11, 1932, pp. 204–10. In the 1930 congressional elections, Democrats gained control of the House, although Republicans nominally retained the Senate by one vote. In fact, insurgent Republicans worked closely with Democrats on tariff issues. Herbert Feis, State Department economist, to French Strother, administrative assistant to Hoover, May 3, 1932, 611.0031/385B, RG 59, NA. This letter contains State comments on the Collier bill. Hull's own suggestions for the Collier bill parallel the eventual reciprocal trade program. Hull envisioned a grant of tariff-bargaining authority to the executive, the use of technical specialists to develop an overall negotiating strategy, and bilateral negotiations to effect a general lowering of the U.S. tariff. According to this approach, "The object of reciprocity treaties or agreements is, as a result, not preferential treatment so much as lower duties. If the duties are lowered the main

objective is obtained. The fact that they are lowered to all countries should not and usually does not interfere with the bargain." "Reciprocity within the Most-Favored-Nation Clause," memo, n.d., Hull Papers, MD/LC.

127. Ambassador R. Lindsay to FO, January 7, 1932, FO 371/15860, PRO.

128. *Congressional Record*, December 6, 1932, p. 66.

129. Minutes of Inter-Departmental Reciprocity Group, March 6, 1933, 611.0031/428, RG 59, NA. The group prepared a proposal for a 10 percent horizontal reduction and reciprocity negotiations. The document called for presidential authority to negotiate a customs union with any country north of the Panama Canal.

130. TC, *Tariff Bargaining*.

CHAPTER FOUR

1. Reed Smoot (R-Utah) chaired the Senate Finance Committee. Born in January 1862, Smoot was first elected to the Senate in 1902. He served five six-year terms before defeat in the 1932 general election. Joining the Finance Committee in 1909, when Nelson Aldrich held the chair, Smoot became chairman in 1923. Willis Hawley (R-Oreg.) chaired the Ways and Means Committee. Born in May 1864, he won election to the House of Representatives in 1906. Hawley became a Ways and Means Committee member in 1917 and chairman in 1929.

2. Cooper, "Trade Policy as Foreign Policy," pp. 291–92.

3. DiBacco, Mason, and Appy, *History of the United States*, p. 540; O'Connor, Schwartz, and Wheeler, *Exploring United States History*, p. 579.

4. Brinkley et al., *American History*, p. 740; Salvatore, *International Economics*, p. 270.

5. Briggs, "Myth of the Hawley-Smoot Tariff"; Bedell, "Myth of Smoot-Hawley"; Love, "Real Lesson"; Rosenman, *Roosevelt*, pp. 626, 637, 724; *New York Times*, October 2, 1932, p. 33; *Public Papers . . . Truman*, September 27, 1948, pp. 592–96.

6. Johnson note, December 11, 1967, WHCF, LBJ; *Public Papers . . . Johnson*, December 16, 1967, pp. 1148–50.

7. Eisenhower, *Mandate for Change*, p. 195; *Public Papers . . . Reagan*, 1987 (2:1348), 1988 (1:61, 238, 395); Reagan, *American Life*, pp. 241–42.

8. *Boston Globe*, November 10, 1993; *Wall Street Journal*, November 11, 1992; *Business Week*, November 22, 1993, p. 146.

9. Gorman did serve on the Senate Finance Committee from 1903 to 1906.

10. Charlie Michelson (*Ghost Talks*, p. 24) at the Democratic National Committee proudly claimed that the "Grundy Bill" was "of our christening."

11. *Washington Post*, May 30, 1930; *New York Herald Tribune* and *New York Times*, June 15, 1930.

12. *Baltimore Sun*, June 16, 1930; *Wall Street Journal*, June 14, 17, 21, 1930; *Columbus Dispatch*, June 13, 1930.

13. Hoover, *Memoirs*, 2:291; Smoot, "Our Tariff and the Depression"; *New York Times*, October 2, 1932; Hawley, "New Tariff: A Defense."

14. *Congressional Record*, March 24, 1930, pp. 6012–13.

15. Dennis, "Diligent Senator Smoot."

16. *New York Times*, November 10, 1932.

17. It is arguable that the average ad valorem equivalent may not capture the full protective effect. If higher duties effectively blocked some imports, the average ad valorem equivalent might prove to be an unreliable measure.

18. BC, *Historical Statistics*, 2:888.

19. For a discussion of the relative merits of both specific and ad valorem duties, see TC, *Tariff and Its History*, pp. 5–8. With rising prices, specific duties become less protective, but with declining price levels the opposite occurs. Specific duties are easier to collect, whereas ad valorem duties require a determination of values. Thus the latter encourages efforts to undervalue merchandise. "Under ad valorem duties there is great provocation to dishonesty of officials," the Tariff Commission wrote. Hayford and Pasurka ("Effective Rates of Protection," p. 1389) also note that deflation has an upward bias on items carrying specific rates of duty.

20. According to the TC, imports dutiable with specific rates fell 53.6 percent from 1929 to September 30, 1931, while imports dutiable with ad valorem rates declined 47.6 percent. See TC, *Relation of Duties to Value of Imports*, pp. 7–12.

21. Ibid., p. 3.

22. Ibid., p. 16. The TC did not attempt to assess the impact on *free and dutiable imports.*

23. BC, *Historical Statistics*, 2:888.

24. A tax on coal helped raise the ad valorem equivalent from 12 percent in 1931 to 29.4 percent in 1932. Petroleum products, previously on the free list, received a 33 percent equivalent duty in 1932. USDC, *Foreign Commerce and Navigation*, 1932, p. s-8. The 4 cent per pound tax on copper amounted to about 65 percent ad valorem in 1932. The $3 duty per thousand board feet of lumber established a 24 percent ad valorem equivalent duty in 1932. TC, *Economic Analysis of Foreign Trade*, 1:98, 101.

25. *Washington Post*, May 30, 1930. Tariff experts do not overemphasize data during a period of transition. Importers may accelerate, or delay, shipments to take advantage of changing tariff rates or classifications. Hayford and Pasurka ("Effective Rates of Protection") note that the nominal Smoot-Hawley average rate fell below Fordney-McCumber if data for the first half of 1930 are compared with those of the second half. They say Smoot-Hawley had "at most a minor effect on the average effective rate of protection."

26. In writing the tariff, Congress shifted 75 items from the dutiable to the free list and 48 items from the free list to the dutiable list. In 68 percent (2,170 items) of all tariff clauses and categories, Congress made no change whatsoever. Congress increased 888 duties and decreased 235. *Congressional Record*, May 27, 1930, p. 9639.

27. In 1944 free imports constituted 69.9 percent of total imports. This reflected abnormal wartime conditions, when the economy imported large quantities of war materials and Congress suspended some duties. BC, *Historical Statistics*, 2:888; *Statistical Abstract*, 1993, p. 818.

28. Wanniski, *Way the World Works*, p. 125.

29. Ibid., pp. 131–34.

30. *New York Times*, October 3–4, 1929.

31. J. E. Edgerton, National Association of Manufacturers, to Hoover, September 20, 1929, President's Subject File, HCH.

32. *New York Times*, November 12, 21, 23, 1929.

33. Ibid., November 13, 1929. Analyst Roger Babson agreed.

34. The data on Wall Street activity are from Pierce, *The Dow Jones Averages*. Others disputing Jude Wanniski include Bierman, *Great Myths of 1929*, p. 120; Eichengreen, "Did International Economic Forces Cause the Great Depression?," p. 94; Kindleberger, *Financial History*, p. 366.

35. Scholars have differed over the impact of tariff changes. Taussig (*Tariff History*, p. 121) tended to discount the effect on business activity, but Stanwood (*Tariff Controversies*, 2:113) blamed reduced import duties for a severe loss of government revenue after 1857. Blaine

(*Twenty Years*, pp. 197–98, 204) agreed, as did McKinley ("The Tariff," 10:24–25). For more views, see Huston, *Panic of 1857*, p. 12; Van Vleck, *Panic of 1857*, p. 95.

36. Joseph S. Davis, *World between Wars*, pp. 240–41. Officials at the British Board of Trade held this view in 1929. When Britain considered representations against higher U.S. tariffs in 1929, a senior Board of Trade official told the Foreign Office: "It is doubtful whether progressive increases in the United States tariff have materially restricted the power of this country [the United Kingdom] to purchase United States goods." Sir H. Fountain comment, FO 371/13537, PRO.

37. Love, "Real Lesson." More recently, the ITC (*Effect of Changes in the Value of the U.S. Dollar Trade*) concluded that exchange rate adjustments have little correlation with trade balances.

38. TC, *Economic Analysis of Foreign Trade*, pp. 413–59. This list contains about one hundred items with higher duties and increased imports.

39. Ibid., p. 413.

40. Fremling, "Did the United States Transmit the Great Depression . . .?"

41. Temin, *Lessons from the Great Depression*, p. 46. See also Temin, "Great Depression," p. 8; Kindleberger, *Financial History*, pp. 367–69.

42. Eichengreen, "Did International Economic Forces Cause the Great Depression?," p. 112; Eichengreen, "Political Economy." Joseph S. Davis (*World between Wars*, p. 241) notes that some business economists questioned whether tariffs actually hindered war debt transfers.

43. Eichengreen, "Political Economy," p. 32.

44. Jones, *Tariff Retaliation*, p. 1.

45. Ibid., pp. 6–11, 303. Jones was an unabashed crusader for Hull's reciprocal trade program.

46. Hull, *Memoirs*, 1:355; SNFC, *Tariff Act of 1929, Hearings on H.R. 2667*, vol. 18.

47. Frederick Livesey memo, October 29, 1932, 611.003/2693, and economic adviser memo, July 15, 1930, 611.003/2242, RG 59, NA. The governments sending communications in 1897 included Argentina, Austria, Germany, Great Britain, Japan, the Netherlands, Switzerland, and Turkey. In 1922 correspondence came from Argentina, Belgium, Canada, Cuba, Denmark, Egypt, France, Great Britain, Haiti, Mexico, Netherlands, Nicaragua, Norway, Peru, Spain, Sweden, and Switzerland.

During 1929–30 the Department of State received communications from Australia (3), Austria (10), Bahamas (2), Belgium (8), Bermuda (3), Canada (5), Czechoslovakia (3), Denmark (2), Dominican Republic (3), Egypt (4), Finland (4), France (10), Germany (4), Great Britain (14), Greece (2), Guatemala (1), Honduras (1), Hungary (1), Irish Free State (2), Italy (12), Japan (1), Latvia (2), Mexico (1), Netherlands (22), Newfoundland (1), Norway (7), Paraguay (1), Persia (3), Portugal (3), Rumania (1), Spain (8), Sweden (5), Switzerland (11), Turkey (1), and Uruguay (1).

48. M. M. Mahoney to SOS, July 11, 1929, RG 20, NAC.

49. Parry et al., *Encyclopaedic Dictionary of International Law*, p. 301; Feis to Joseph B. Wood, May 26, 1932, 611.003/2592, and Livesey memo, October 29, 1932, 611.003/2693, RG 59, NA. Both Feis and Livesey say that the United States received only 3 or 4 formal protests among 163 communications.

50. Sir H. Fountain (BT) comment, August 10, 1929, and Sir E. Howard to Mr. R. L. Craigie, FO, July 26, 1929, FO 371/13537, PRO. Britain chose not to protest Smoot-Hawley. It did object in 1932 when Congress imposed a $2 per ton duty on coal. This seemed to be a "direct breach" of the 1815 Anglo-American Commercial Treaty, as it contained a proviso

exempting coal imported from countries that bought more coal from the United States than it sold to them. See FO 371/15860, PRO.

51. Economic adviser memo, October 29, 1932, 611.003/2693, RG 59, NA. Tariff commissioner Edgar Brossard also said that there was "nothing unusual" about the contacts. Brossard, speech to the American Academy of Political and Social Science, May 3, 1930, in Hoover Papers, President's Subject File, HCH; SOS to American Embassy, Paris, France, 611.003/2034, April 2, 1930, RG 59, NA.

52. SNFN, *Tariff Act of 1929*, 18:1–9. State learned that some countries, such as Belgium, encouraged businesses to prepare such memoranda. "Summary of Reports on Foreign Reactions to Tariff Revision in the United States," n.d., PPS-File, Tariff Commission, HCH.

53. Memo, June 6, 1929, 611.003/1741; Livesey meeting with Netherlands minister, June 19, 1929, 611.003/1641; conversation between Secretary Stimson and German ambassador, June 6, 1929, 611.003/1577—all in RG 59, NA.

54. Undersecretary Joseph Cotton to Chairmen Smoot and Hawley, April 11, 1930, 611.003/2244; Smoot to Cotton, May 2, 1930, 611.003/2080; Cotton to SOS, May 6, 1930, 611.003/2248; Harry Hawkins memo, March 7, 1934, 611.0031/651-1/4—all in RG 59, NA. Hawkins mentions objections to contingent duty provisos from Czechoslovakia, Finland, Germany, Great Britain, Italy, and Poland.

55. Conversation between SOS and Italian ambassador, July 11, 1929, 611.003/1701, RG 59, NA.

56. Howard to FO, August 8, 1929, FO 371/13537, and R. Lindsay to FO, July 25, 1930, FO 371/14280, PRO. For the British ambassador's assessment, see R. Lindsay to FO, July 25, 1930, FO 371/14280, PRO.

57. SOS to President, June 8, 1929, 611.003/1916, and FBF [Frost] memo to J.F.C. [Cotton], November 1, 1929, 611.003/1915, RG 59, NA. Brossard, a friend of Chairman Smoot, remained sanguine: "There appears to be little ground for anxiety about the peace between the United States and other countries being upset by the new U.S. tariff rates. The mutual advantages of trade between this and other countries are too great to be entirely thrown away." Brossard speech to American Academy of Political and Social Science, May 3, 1930, in Hoover Papers, President's Subject File, HCH.

58. Howard to FO, July 26, 1929, FO 371/13537, PRO.

59. Massey to SOS for External Affairs, February 8, 1929, C-2311, and Massey to Prime Minister, April 14, 1930, C-2320, Mackenzie King Papers, MG 26, NAC; Mackenzie King speech in Winnipeg, November 1, 1929, RG 25, vol. 2153, NAC.

60. TC, *Computed Duties*, pp. 4–5.

61. William C. Burdett, April 15, 1930, to USDS, 611.003/2090; Gibson to SOS, June 18, 1930, 611.003/2212; Warden McK. Wilson, First Secretary, Brussels, to SOS, July 1, 1930, 611.003/2276—all in RG 59, NA. The flexible tariff provision did lead to a reduction in duties on Belgian window glass. TC, *Cylinder, Crown, and Sheet Glass*. Not anticipating that deflation would increase the ad valorem equivalent of specific duties, the Smoot-Hawley schedules should have appeared even more favorable to Belgians in July 1930. TC, *Computed Duties*, pp. 4–5.

62. Berne to USDS, May 1, 1930 (611.003/2079), May 5, 1930 (611.003/2089); Calvin M. Hitch, Consul, Basel, to Hugh R. Wilson, Minister, Berne, May 13, 1930, 611.003/2140; Wilson to USDS, June 10, 1930, 611.003/2156—all in RG 59, NA.

63. Berne to Washington, June 17, 1930, 611.003/2177; Wilson to SOS, September 13, 1930, 611.003/2385; Calvin M. Hitch, Basel, to SOS, September 16, 1930, 611.003/2386—all in NA, RG 59.

64. TC, *Computed Duties*, pp. 4–5. See also Table 4.4.

65. Edge to SOS, June 20, 1930 (611.003/2214), June 27, 1930 (611.003/2231), RG 59, NA.

66. Edge, Paris, to SOS, September 2, 1930, 611.003/2351, ibid.

67. Ambassador P. Claudel to SOS, December 15, 1930, 611.003/2410, ibid.

68. Klein, Commerce, to Cotton, USDS, July 17, 1930, 611.003/2289, ibid.

69. Kirk to USDS, June 20, 1930 (611.003/2233), July 24, 1930 (611.003/2329), ibid. See also Table 4.4. The flexible tariff mechanism did lead to TC recommendations for reductions in U.S. duties on straw hats, wool-felt hats, and olive oil. Meanwhile, U.S. auto exports to Italy plummeted, but sales of prunes, asphalt, and calculating machines rose sharply.

70. SOS conversation with Italian ambassador, June 26, 1930, 611.003/2208, RG 59, NA.

71. Lindsay to FO, July 18, 1930, FO 371/14280, PRO.

72. Some authors claim quick foreign retaliation. Others, like Joseph M. Jones Jr., admit that "there were no pure cases" of retaliation. A fair test of the retaliation hypothesis would involve any discriminatory actions taken during the year after enactment of Smoot-Hawley. During the autumn of 1931, currency problems and intensification of the global deflation prompted most nations to erect tariff, quantitative, and currency controls. In late 1931 and early 1932, a number of governments depreciated their currencies—20 to 30 percent—in actions unrelated to passage of Smoot-Hawley. As a result, import-sensitive U.S. manufacturers began to seek even higher tariffs.

73. Chalmers, USDC, to Klein, May 5, 1931, Hoover Papers, President's Subject File, HCH; Chalmers, *World Trade Policies*, pp. 53–73. On rising tariffs, see TC, *Reciprocity . . . and Commercial Treaties Reciprocity*, p. 465.

74. *New York Times*, March 27, 1932. But see *Washington Post*, April 24, October 14, 16, 24, 1932.

75. U.S. market share increased in Chile, China, the Soviet Union, British India, and Ceylon. Only 6 of the 32 U.S. trading partners increased their share of exports to the U.S. market: Mexico, Brazil, Colombia, Peru, Sweden, and Netherland India. USDC, *Foreign Trade of the United States*, 1932, p. 7. But market share estimates involve a series of currency conversions, and in light of the general pattern currency adjustments late in 1931 may not accurately capture changing trade flows during this period.

76. BC, *Historical Statistics*, 2:888, 891–93; USDC, *Commerce Yearbook, 1932*, 2:716–18.

77. Jones, *Tariff Retaliation*, p. xii.

78. TC, *Computed Duties*; Julian L. Pinkerton, Rio de Janeiro, to SOS, July 3, 1931, 611.0031/335/767, RG 59, NA.

79. Albert M. Coyle, Sydney, Australia, to USDS, July 15, 1931, 611.0031/335, RG 59, NA. Australian data show that that country's exports fell 35.2 percent from 1929 to 1931—with exports to both France (55 percent) and the United States decreasing (50 percent) faster. Australian imports declined 52.3 percent, with purchases from the United Kingdom (53.9 percent), France (55.9 percent), and the United States (63.6 percent) dropping more rapidly than the average. Vamplew, *Australians Historical Statistics*, pp. 193–97.

80. Livesey memo, 611.003/335, April 22, 1931, RG 59, NA. Under section 338 of the Tariff Act of 1930, the president had authority to proclaim new or additional duties, not to exceed 50 percent ad valorem equivalent, in circumstances where foreign countries discriminated against U.S. exports.

81. Harry R. Turkel memo, August 17, 1931, 611.0031/396, and "Study on Discrimination against American Commerce," November 15, 1931, 611.0031/377-1/2, RG 59, NA. The following countries did not discriminate: United Kingdom, Irish Free State, Malta, Nova Scotia, Ceylon, Iraq, Aden (Arabia), Nigeria, Colony of Kenya, Italy, Spain, Portugal, Madeira,

Portuguese East Africa, Belgium, the Netherlands, Sweden, Denmark, Norway, Finland, Estonia, Latvia, Lithuania, Poland, Switzerland, Hungary, Rumania, Bulgaria, Greece, Cuba, Haiti, Santa Domingo, Mexico, Costa Rica, Nicaragua, El Salvador, Honduras, Guatemala, Panama, Argentina, Brazil, Chile, Peru, Colombia, Venezuela, Uruguay, Bolivia, Paraguay, Ecuador, China, Chosen (Korea), Siam, Persia, Turkey, Egypt, Ethiopia, and Liberia. It is, of course, arguable that State's institutional perspective colored reports from the field. Had diplomats and consuls reported widespread discrimination, President Hoover would have faced pressure to invoke the retaliatory provisions of section 338.

82. Cleveland response, August 20, 1931, and Pinkerton, Rio de Janeiro, to USDS, July 3, 1931, 611.0031/335/245, RG 59, NA.

83. Messersmith, August 27, 1931, 611.0031/335, ibid.

84. Jordan response, July 15, 1931, 611.0031/335/165, ibid.

85. Magnuson response, July 10, 1931, and Himmel, July 14, 1931, 611.0031/335/173, ibid.

86. Reineck, Antwerp, August 17, 1931, 611.0031/335/143, ibid.

87. Osborne memo, June 17, 1931, 611.0031/335/883, and John M. Morehead, Minister, to SOS, June 26, 1930, 611.003/2236, ibid.

88. Allen, Istanbul, to USDS, June 23, 1931, 611.0031/335; Cross, Cape Town, to USDS, July 30, 1931, 611.0031/335; Sturgeon, Tokyo, to USDS, September 26, 1931, 611.0031/335/939—all in ibid.

89. Boernstein memo, July 15, 1931, 611.0031/335/647, ibid.

90. Murphy to USDS, August 11, 1931, 611.0031/335/697; Morgan to USDS, June 16, 1931, 611.0031/335; Albert Halstead, London, to USDS, June 30, 1931, 611.0031/335; John W. Bailey Jr. memo, August 5, 1931, 611.0031/335/733; Ernest L. Harris memo, September 29, 1931, 611.0031/335/975—all in ibid.

91. Sholes to USDS, October 29, 1931, 611.0031/2520, ibid.

92. Although U.S. auto exports dropped from 339,447 units in 1929 to 82,457 in 1931 (75.7 percent), it is interesting to note that automobile exports from neighboring Canada fell even more sharply, from 64,863 to 9,282 units, a decline of 85.7 percent.

93. TC, *Economic Analysis of Foreign Trade*.

94. Kottman, *Reciprocity*, pp. 14–16, 36; Drummond and Hillmer, *Negotiating Free Trade*, p. 16.

95. Eichengreen, "Political Economy," p. 34. See also Rowland, *Commercial Conflict*; Kreider, *Anglo-American Trade Agreement*. In his study of Britain's turn to protectionism, *British Protectionism and the International Economy*, Rooth devotes little attention to Smoot-Hawley.

96. King, April 9, 1930, *Diaries*; Dominion of Canada, *Official Report of Debates, House of Commons*, p. 1973.

97. King to William Phillips, August 20, 1930, King Papers, MG 26, NAC. For an analysis of the election, see Glassford, *Reaction and Reform*.

98. Irving N. Linnell memo, June 22, 1931, 611.0031/335/683, RG 59, NA; Dexter and Stevenson, "Canada's Tariff Reprisals against America," pp. 208–13; McDiarmid, *Commercial Policy*, pp. 273–76.

99. BC, *Historical Statistics*, 2:906. Canadian historical statistics indicate that exports to the United States fell 51.5 percent, whereas exports to the United Kingdom dropped only 41.2 percent. Exports to all other countries declined slightly more rapidly than to either major trading partner (52 percent), suggesting that other factors, in addition to Smoot-Hawley, depressed Canada's export trade. Urquhart, *Historical Statistics of Canada*, p. 183.

100. Urquhart, *Historical Statistics of Canada*, p. 183; Leacy, *Historical Statistics of Canada*, ser. G473–87.

101. BC, *Historical Statistics*, 2:887.

102. TC, *Depreciated Exchange; Public Papers . . . Hoover*, 1932-33, pp. 621, 977; Hoover to Robert L. O'Brien, Chairman, TC, October 24, 1932, Hoover Papers, President's Subject File, HCH.

103. Blum et al., *National Experience*, p. 658; Clarfield, *United States Diplomatic History*, 2:385; Kindleberger, *World in Depression*, pp. 194, 294; Page Smith, *Redeeming the Time*, p. 287.

104. In his memoirs, *In the Fullness of Time*, p. 71, Douglas states that he and Wilcox drafted the petition.

105. A copy of the petition can be found in the George Norris Papers, MD/LC.

106. *Congressional Record*, May 28, 1930, p. 9703.

107. Quoted in *Washington Post*, May 7, 1930.

108. Edgar E. Robinson, *Hoover*, p. 141 (quotation); *Congressional Record*, May 28, 1930, pp. 9703–4.

109. Letter to editor of *Boston Transcript*, reprinted in *Congressional Record*, May 29, 1930, pp. 9774–75.

110. Schattschneider, *Politics, Pressures, and the Tariff*, p. 283; Pastor, *Politics of U.S. Foreign Economic Policy*, p. 346.

111. *Public Papers . . . Hoover*, 1929, pp. 301–3; Hoover, *Memoirs*, 2:294–96; Snyder, "Hoover and the Hawley-Smoot Tariff," pp. 1172–89; Representative Edward E. Denison (R-Ill.), *Congressional Record*, May 28, 1929, p. 2101; Burke, *Diary and Letters of Hiram Johnson*, vol. 5, June 2, 1934.

112. Ryder, "United States Tariff Commission," p. 121. Free traders have long criticized the "scientific" approach to tariff making. William B. Kelly Jr., later a senior GATT official, wrote: "equalization of foreign and domestic production costs is the antithesis of international trade. . . . Unflinching application of cost equalization would encourage the domestic production of everything, no matter how costly such production might be." Kelly, *Studies in United States Commercial Policy*, p. 17.

Such arguments appear to ignore the nonprice aspects of competition. They also assume that tariff commissioners would apply the standard in an "unflinching" manner to exclude imports in those circumstances where domestic producers lacked competitive advantages. Certainly, the cost-of-production standard did present serious administrative difficulties, as production costs vary widely over time and among producers in an industry. Moreover, some foreign governments declined to provide necessary data during the 1920s. To address such problems, the House Ways and Means Committee proposed in 1929 a different standard calling for equalization of the conditions of competition in principal markets. Over time, section 336 might have evolved into a quasi-judicial mechanism for balancing the claims of domestic producers and workers against the market-driven competitive advantages of foreign producers.

113. Hoover, *Addresses upon the American Road*, pp. 154–55; Brossard, "Commercial Policies and Tariffs," May 3, 1930, in Hoover Papers, President's Subject File, HCH.

114. Hoover, *Addresses upon the American Road*, p. 155.

115. *Salem Oregon Statesman*, May 23, 1932; *Portland Oregonian*, May 22–24, 1932.

116. *New York Times*, May 24, November 20, 1932; *Salt Lake City Tribune*, November 10, 13, 1932. In an editorial on November 10, the *New York Times* lauded the Utah senator: "The defeat of Reed Smoot is a loss to the Senate and the country." It called Smoot's defeat "a state

and national loss." He was a "statesman of the highest type." On Thomas's pledge, see *The Deseret News*, November 7, 1932. According to Merrill (*Smoot*, p. 232), "The Smoot-Hawley Tariff Act was not considered to be the frightful bugaboo in Utah that it was in the East."

117. Slichter ("Is the Tariff a Cause of Depression?," pp. 519–24) also blamed "the high and ever-rising American tariff" for preventing the development of an import surplus to facilitate debt repayment.

118. Bidwell, "New American Tariff."

119. Temin, *Lessons from the Great Depression*; Eichengreen, "Did International Economic Forces Cause the Great Depression?"; Kindleberger, *Financial History*, pp. 367–69; Schuker, *American "Reparations" to Germany*, pp. 100–101.

120. Strange, "Protectionism and World Politics," pp. 239–40.

121. Timmons, *Garner of Texas*, pp. 124–27. Without Democratic votes Smoot-Hawley would not have passed. The Senate passed the conference report on June 13, 1930, by a 44-to-42 vote. Thirty-nine Republicans voted in the affirmative, as did 5 Democrats. But 30 Democrats and 11 Republicans (progressives like William Borah of Idaho and Robert LaFollette of Wisconsin) voted against the measure. *New York Times*, June 14, 17, 1930.

To please constituents, many Democrats supported protectionist amendments but voted against the bill on final passage. Senator Tom Connally of Texas voted twenty-one times for tariff increases and twelve times against decreases before ultimately turning it down. According to Republican majority leader James E. Watson, Democrats "cast an aggregate of one thousand and ten votes either for increased tariff rates or against proposed decreases." *Congressional Record*, March 24, 1930, p. 5994; Senator Watson press statement, April 2, 1930, copy in Hugo Black Papers, MD/LC.

122. Michelson, *Ghost Talks*, pp. 23–24.

123. Ambassador R. Lindsay to FO, October 30, 1930, FO 371/14280, PRO. Canadian diplomats also reported that Democrats and low-tariff newspapers sought to exploit the Smoot-Hawley issue for political advantage. H. H. Wrong to SOS for Foreign Affairs, September 26, 1930, RG 25, vol. 2153, NAC.

124. Rosenman, *Roosevelt* (September 29, 1932), p. 764; Hoover, *Memoirs*, pp. 287–301.

125. Krock, "President Hoover's Two Years."

CHAPTER FIVE

1. Approximately half of the decline reflected negotiations, the remainder the effects of price inflation on a tariff schedule that contained many specific duties. TC, *OTAP*, 1949, 1:19.

2. The United States had 8 percent average duties ad valorem on agricultural imports. For Japan, the comparable figure was 54 percent; Italy, 29 percent; Germany, 23 percent; France, 22 percent; Switzerland, 19 percent; Canada, 12 percent; and the United Kingdom, 10 percent. U.S. duties on manufactures averaged 11 percent ad valorem. The comparable numbers were Japan, 19 percent; United Kingdom, 17 percent; Italy, 16 percent; Canada, 16 percent; France, 15 percent; Germany, 9 percent; and Switzerland, 8 percent. JEC, *Trade Restraints in the Western Community*.

Many countries discriminated against Japan. They imposed substantially higher duties on Japanese imports, denying that country the full benefits of membership in GATT. The United States maintained some restrictions on imports, pursuant to the escape clause and section 22 of the Agricultural Adjustment Act. A number of voluntary export restraints applied to Japanese products—particularly textiles. See, generally, TC, *OTAP*.

3. Hull, *Memoirs*, 1:81.

4. SNFN, *Hearings on H.R. 8687*, p. 1. In 1934 Republicans and Democrats switched sides on the issue of delegating constitutional authority to the president. In 1890 and 1930, when Republicans proposed to delegate tariff-making powers to the executive, Democrats had protested loudly. During 1930 debate Representative Robert Doughton (D-N.C.), a member of the Ways and Means Committee, complained that the flexible tariff provision transferred "the levying of taxes from the Legislative to the Executive Department of the Government. If this is to be done, our Constitution should be changed." Doughton to A. J. L. Moritz, vice president, American Enka, Enka, N.C., May 5, 1930, Doughton Papers, SHC.

Four years later, a Democrat was in the White House and Doughton chaired Ways and Means. This time Doughton loyally supported the president's request. Republicans raised constitutional objections. Senator Hiram Johnson of California noted the inconsistencies: "I can't fathom this sort of thing in a man in politics. I can understand . . . that one would change his mind upon a question of rates, . . . but upon a fundamental principle overnight to recant their most determined stand is beyond me." Burke, *Diary and Letters of Hiram Johnson*, vol. 5, June 2, 1934.

5. Hull testimony before the Senate Finance Committee, April 26, 1934, SNFN, *Hearings on H.R. 8687*, p. 7. For a similar pledge to Ways and Means, see HRWM, *Hearings on H.R. 8687* and *Report to Accompany H.R. 8687*, p. 13. The British embassy suspected that members of Congress would attribute opposition to "lofty constitutional grounds," but their "more material objection" would be that the measure removed from Congress "the opportunity to indulge in the sport of log-rolling." Lindsay to FO, March 8, 1934, FO 371/17558, PRO.

6. Edgar B. Nixon, *Roosevelt and Foreign Affairs*, 2:1–3. Roosevelt and Hull did not say that reciprocal trade would not injure any American producers and workers. From Hull's papers it is apparent that the secretary's chief goal was to lower the tariff. "[T]he object of reciprocity treaties or agreements," he said, "is . . . lower duties." In another memo he summarized his tariff philosophy succinctly: "Take the tariff out of politics and operate it as an economic instrument national and international to secure the maximum of world commerce *with a minimum of domestic disturbance*" (emphasis added). Hull memos, n.d., Hull Papers, MD/LC. Representative Allen Treadway, the ranking Republican on Ways and Means, claimed to understand Hull's motives. Treadway wanted to name the bill, "Surrender America's interests to foreign competitors." *Congressional Record*, March 23, 1934, p. 5265.

7. HRWM, *Report to Accompany H.R. 8687*, p. 22; SNFN, *Hearings on H.R. 8687*. On March 29 the House passed the bill 274 to 111. Eleven Democrats voted against the measure, and two Republicans voted for it. In the Senate, reciprocal trade passed 57 to 33 on June 4. Five Democrats, including Carter Glass of Virginia and Huey P. Long of Louisiana, opposed it. Five Republicans from the Midwest supported it.

8. Chalmers, "Essential Principles . . . for Reciprocal Tariff Program," memo, February 1, 1933, Chalmers Papers, University of Oregon.

9. From time to time other agencies participated in the CTA, including the Agricultural Adjustment Administration and the War Department. Assistant Secretary of State Francis B. Sayre (*The Way Forward*, p. 88) later said: "Its members, mature men of tested judgment and expert knowledge, have been studying foreign and domestic trade problems for years."

Unable during the depression to find teaching jobs, academics entered the federal service in large numbers, bringing their theories and enthusiasm to public policy deliberations. For background, see Richard S. Kirkendall, "Roosevelt and the Service Intellectuals," pp. 456–71; Eckes, *A Search for Solvency*, pp. xi, 2–6. Many involved with RTAP had studied at Harvard University with Frank Taussig, the most prominent international economist of his generation. Those familiar with the writings of Adam Smith, David Ricardo, and John Stuart Mill had a disposition for tariff reduction.

10. Comprising the core group were Chairman Grady, Harry Hawkins, William Fowler, Harry Dexter White, Henry Chalmers, and Leslie Wheeler. Initially, State Department economist Herbert Feis participated. Also involved was Professor Alvin Hansen, a prominent Keynesian. Grady, the first CTA chairman, reported to Assistant Secretary Francis Sayre, a Harvard-educated lawyer once married to President Woodrow Wilson's daughter. Like some officials who have served in more recent administrations, Sayre gained his trade experience and contacts abroad representing foreign interests. He did so as a consultant to the government of Siam. In 1925 that government appointed Sayre an ambassador, and in that capacity he negotiated commercial treaties with France, Great Britain, the Netherlands, Spain, Portugal, and other European countries.

11. Willard L. Thorp of the Commerce Department recalled how trade officials attempted to evaluate industries: "industries should be judged according to their efficiency, and inefficient industries should have no protection." Louchheim, *Making of the New Deal*, p. 276. Thorp's comment appears to conflict with State's testimony to the Senate Finance Committee in May 1945 that "the State Department has never construed the Trade Agreements Act as a license to remake the industrial or agricultural pattern of America." SNFN, *1945 Extension, . . . Hearings*, p. 7.

12. Fowler and Hawkins memo, February 13, 1935, CTA, RG 353, NA. On March 12, 1935, Grady told a Detroit audience that the reciprocity program "assumes that we must make possible the increased sale of products of other countries in this market if we are to increase or maintain the present volume of our export sales." The inability of foreign customers to secure dollars to buy American goods "constitutes the present log-jam in the world's trade." USDS, 611.0031/1505, March 12, 1935, RG 59, NA. The Department of Agriculture argued for unilateral tariff reductions: "it is of primary importance that the trade agreements should result in a large increase in the imports of industrial products." USDS, 611.0031/Executive Committee/799, January 28, 1935, RG 59, NA. Sayre (*The Way Forward*, pp. 169–74) claimed that increased imports would facilitate foreign debt repayment.

13. Feis "Some Observations . . . ," February 17, 1934, Feis Papers, box 124, MD/LC. See also Feis memo, November 20, 1933, 611.0031/Executive Committee/50, RG 59, NA. At the request of the Senate, the Tariff Commission assembled data to help the new administration begin a program of tariff bargaining. TC, *Economic Analysis of Foreign Trade*.

14. Feis notes, April 8, 1953, Feis Papers, MD/LC. From 1934 to 1947 the United States concluded thirty-two reciprocal trade agreements. The countries (and dates of signing) were Cuba (August 24, 1934), Brazil (February 2, 1935), Belgium-Luxembourg (February 27, 1935), Haiti (March 28, 1935), Sweden (May 25, 1935), Colombia (September 13, 1935), Canada (November 15, 1935), Honduras (December 18, 1935), Netherlands (December 20, 1935), Switzerland (January 9, 1936), Nicaragua (March 11, 1936), Guatemala (April 24, 1936), France (May 6, 1936), Finland (May 18, 1936), Costa Rica (November 28, 1936), El Salvador (February 19, 1937), Czechoslovakia (March 7, 1938), Ecuador (August 6, 1938), United Kingdom (November 17, 1938), Canada (November 17, 1938), Turkey (April 1, 1939), Venezuela (November 6, 1939), Cuba (1 supp.) (December 18, 1939), Canada (1 supp.) (December 13, 1940), Argentina (October 14, 1941), Cuba (2 supp.) (December 23, 1941), Peru (May 7, 1942), Uruguay (July 21, 1942), Mexico (December 23, 1942, Iran (April 8, 1943), Iceland (August 27, 1943), and Paraguay (September 12, 1946).

A number of these were shadow agreements without real substance. They contained duplicative or inconsequential concessions and lacked immediate commercial significance. Such documents constituted window dressing for Hull's program, allowing State to claim momentum for the program. Pacts with Central America, Ecuador, Paraguay, and Uruguay, as well as Turkey, Iran, and Finland, were shadow commercial understandings. The United States, for instance, padded its concessions by binding coffee duty-free (par. 1654) in separate agreements with eleven countries: Brazil, Colombia, Costa Rica, Ecuador, El Salvador, Guatemala, Haiti, Honduras, Mexico, Nicaragua, and Venezuela. For another scholar's discussion of such an agreement, see Grieb, "Negotiating a Reciprocal Trade Agreement with . . . Guatemala." Wartime agreements with Iran and Turkey had important political objectives.

15. Representatives of all three industries opposed the tariff cuts. The American Iron and Steel Institute warned that "low labor costs" enabled European steel producers to penetrate interior markets "at delivered prices close to or below the cost of production of similar products made by American steel producers." "Report of the Committee on Reciprocity Information," November 6, 1934, 611.5531/150, RG 59, NA. Economists Alvin Hansen and Harry Dexter White, who served on the CTA, voted for the full 50 percent reduction in steel duties, not because a steep cut could be undertaken without injury to the domestic industry. Rather, they believed that import competition would cause a substantial decline in domestic steel prices and so aid the general recovery. Lauderbaugh (*American Steel Makers*, pp. 151–55) writes that the Roosevelt administration invited foreign steel companies to compete "unfairly."

16. Hawkins memo, January 27, 1934, 611.5531/25, RG 59, NA.

17. Feis Memoranda, February 15, 26, 1935, Feis Papers, MD/LC; William Phillips, *Ventures in Diplomacy*, p. 161.

18. State Department economist Feis noted that "the Secretary [Hull] has permitted the Committee on Trade Agreements to enter into negotiations without any careful check exercised by himself." Feis believed that the proposed concessions on steel and cotton were "not sufficient to permit us to put up a successful defensive fight" from critics. He reiterated opposition to the steel tariff cuts in the Belgian agreement as "uneconomic and unwise and furthermore, calculated to so add to the political opposition that will arise from the agreement as to threaten the future development of the whole trade agreements program." Feis "diaries," February 15–16, 26, 1935, Feis Papers, MD/LC.

19. USDC, *Foreign Trade of the United States*, 1938, p. 487; USDC, *Foreign Commerce and Navigation*, 1939, p. xiv.

20. USDS, *Statutes at Large*, 48:1, pp. 943-45.

21. Peek speech, January 19, 1935, 611.0031/1541, RG 59, NA.

22. Special Adviser's Report to President on Foreign Trade, December 31, 1934, OF, FDR; Peek to Francis Sayre, USDS, December 4, 1934, FW611.0031/1246, RG 59, NA.

23. CTA, February 13, 1935, RG 353, NA.

24. CTA recommendations, 611.0031/1681, RG 59, NA. See reports on trade discrimination, February 15, 1935, Hull Papers, MD/LC.

25. CTA recommendations, March 6, 1935, 611.0031/1681, and Hull to SOT Morgenthau, April 1, 1935, 611.0031/1545A, RG 59, NA.

26. Rosenman, *Roosevelt*, pp. 835, 853.

27. Moley, *After Seven Years*, p. 369.

28. In Congress the RTAP soon became a target. Democratic Representative James Scrugham of Nevada claimed that "the United States is being handsomely trimmed in these multilateral agreements being negotiated by the State Department." *Congressional Record*, August 6, 1935, pp. 12600–5.

29. State Department response to New Haven Clock Co., June 12, 1937, 611.5431/590, RG 59, NA.

30. Sayre to Hull, March 16, 1939, 611.5431/750A, ibid.

31. USDC, *Foreign Commerce and Navigation*, 1939, p. xiv; USDS, September 24, 1938, 611.5431/722, and October 17, 1939, 611.5431/791, both RG 59, NA.

32. Roosevelt to Chairman Doughton, January 17, 1937, in HRW&M, *Report to Accompany H.J. Res. 96*, pp. 1–2. Greeting British negotiators on February 21, Hull said that he regarded these talks as a step "in the direction of world economic appeasement" and peace. Lindsay to Halifax, March 8, 1938, BT 11/971, PRO.

Seven Republicans signed the minority report (pp. 26–27) criticizing Hull's efforts to "purchase either the friendship or the peace of the world" by "lowering our trade barriers and thus throwing our markets open to foreign producers." HRW&M, *Report to Accompany H.J. Res. 96*, p. 2. The Senate Finance Committee also praised Hull's view that the RTAP program improved prospects for peace. SNFN, *Report to Accompany H.J. Res. 96*, p. 8.

33. On the evolution of the preferential system, see generally Rowland, *Commercial Conflict*. For a Canadian view, see McDiarmid, *Commercial Policy*, pp. 278–90.

34. TC, "Effect of British Imperial Preference."

35. Preliminary summary of U.S. concessions presented to the British on June 4, 1937, *FRUS*, 1937, 2:37–38. This was more than six months before the U.S. government informed the public on November 18, 1937, of its intention to negotiate a trade agreement with Great Britain. *FRUS*, 1937, 2:87; 1938, 2:2. The United States did reduce its tariffs 41 to 50 percent on 144 separate classifications with imports valued at $16.4 million from Great Britain and its colonies.

36. On September 8, 1937, the CTA approved a recommendation for negotiations with the United Kingdom. It accepted the rationale that "even more significant [than enhanced export opportunities for U.S. products] is the fact that the program provides a practical means of reducing unnecessarily high import duties and permitting a larger flow of imports into the United States. It is important, both for the general welfare and for the interests of agriculture in particular, not only that we receive larger imports but that imports be increased more rapidly than exports." CTA, September 8, 1937, RG 353, NA. A similar view appears in a November 12, 1934, memo on "Trade Agreement with the United Kingdom" submitted by the British Empire Committee to the CTA, ITF, RG 43, NA.

37. Notes of meeting with H. O. Chalkley, August 20, 1937, BT 11/806; Chalkley to BT, October 9, 1938, BT11/971; and U.K. Delegation to BT, June 26, 1938, BT11/934—all in PRO.

38. BT 11/962, November 1937, and BT11/921, January 15, 1938, PRO.

39. TC, *Trade Agreement . . . United Kingdom*, 1:46. See also estimates of the American Tariff League, *Monthly Bulletin*, November–December 1938. British colonies and Newfoundland made another $26 million in concessions to the United States. Analyzing the negotiations, a British scholar concludes that "British protection stood virtually intact at the end of 1938" and that "little was achieved at the expense of British farmers." Also, "the major American exports of machine tools, iron and steel and of cars gained practically nothing." Rooth, *British Protectionism*, pp. 304–6.

40. Of U.S. concessions to Britain's colonies, 99 percent represented bindings. The largest involved crude rubber and proved controversial. As it turned out, the U.S. decision to bind rubber on the free list had far-reaching national security implications. Because of the commitment to Britain, Congress could not impose duties to encourage the development of a synthetic rubber industry. Consequently, after Japan attacked Pearl Harbor taxpayers had to pay out some $700 million to construct synthetic rubber plants. HRW&M,

Extension of Reciprocal Trade Agreements Act, Minority Views, H. Rept. 409, pt. 2, p. 7, 611.4131/1834, September 7, 1938, RG 59, NA.

41. Scholars note that average U.S. ad valorem duties exceeded average British duties. This comparison is misleading, as methods of customs valuation differed. The British tariff was higher and more protective than generally realized. The United Kingdom valued goods on the basis of landed value, whereas the United States employed foreign value. This produced quite different results. For example, valued by the American method, lumber encountered a 10 percent British duty. In fact, it was much higher. Calculated on a landed value basis, this duty became the equivalent of 19 percent. See "Memorandum on United Kingdom Trade Agreement," December 17, 1936, ITF, box 62, RG 43, NA. Other significant differences also complicate comparisons. America had a much more comprehensive free list. U.S. officials in London reported that the complex British tariff produced uncertainty: "it is often impossible for an importer to know in advance of actual importation what duty will be chargeable on his products." For a discussion, see Lynn Meekins to Alexander Dye, USDC, November 13, 1936, ITF, RG 43, NA.

42. On October 25, 1938, British ambassador Sir Ronald Lindsay told Cordell Hull that he "must be prepared to see Empire Preference maintained in all the future." Hull responded that "if the Empire and especially Great Britain could stand it, the United States could well stand it." In effect, Hull conceded his inability to break the preferential system in the 1938 negotiations. *FRUS*, 1938, 2:67–68. Britain, as promised, did reduce the margin of preference on tobacco imported from the empire in 1943, but this did not prevent successive increases in the rate of duty on tobacco imported from imperial sources. In 1947 the duty stood at $11 per pound on nonempire tobacco. See, TC, *OTAP*, 4:47. For pork products, Britain bound the duty-free status of hams but reserved the right to impose quantitative restraints. On items, like wheat, where the U.S. government subsidized exports, Britain retained the right to impose a countervailing duty to compensate for the bounty or subsidy (art. 9). In its press advisory the Board of Trade emphasized that the interests of British farmers were "safeguarded by means other than tariffs." BT 11/952, PRO.

43. "Draft Report on Apples and Pears," October 1959, BT 11/5737, PRO.

44. Ibid.; President, BT, to Prime Minister, October 27, 1959, BT 11/5771, PRO.

45. Minutes of meeting between Sir Owen Chalkley and Federation of British Industries, January 23, 1939, BT 11/1090, PRO.

46. For a list, see American Tariff League, *Monthly Bulletin*, November–December 1938.

47. Transcript, November 17, 1938, RG 43, NA.

48. Lindsay to FO, July 25, 1938, BT11-971, PRO.

49. Kottman, *Reciprocity*, p. 263. Rowland (*Commercial Conflict*, pp. 341–61) also acknowledges the importance of foreign policy to the final settlement. In his article, "The Anglo-American Trade Agreement" (pp. 99–103), Schatz observes that "political factors increasingly dominated the thinking of both Neville Chamberlain and Hull." Reynolds (*Creation of the Anglo-American Alliance*, pp. 17–18) concurs.

50. Drummond and Hillmer, *Negotiating Freer Trade*, pp. 147–66. These authors deemphasize the value of U.S. concessions to Britain on manufactures, claiming that the steep cuts on British textile products left the United States with 50 percent ad valorem duties on English specialties. Moreover, both countries segmented and differentiated concessions to avoid generalizing concessions to emerging competitors. U.S. cuts had greater long-term significance. After World War II, nations with lower labor costs, including Germany, Italy, and Japan, increasingly attacked the U.S. market, taking advantage of reductions negotiated in 1938.

51. In 1939 lard sales to Europe did increase and so did those of milled rice, but tobacco, corn, barley, apples, and wheat sales declined. Drummond and Hillmer, *Negotiating Freer Trade*, p. 157. According to the American Tariff League (*Monthly Bulletin*, March 1939), U.S. negotiators desired not simply to roll back 1930 rates but to lower tariffs. Of 391 rates in the 1938 U.K. agreement comparable to classifications in the 1922 tariff schedules, the tariff league found that 339 were lowered below 1922 rates.

It is arguable that Canada was the "main gainer" from these negotiations. See Drummond and Hillmer *Negotiating Freer Trade*, p. 162; Neatby, *MacKenzie King*, pp. 283–86; Granatstein, *Norman A. Robertson*, p. 78. On Australia, see Megaw, "Australia and the Anglo-American Trade Agreement."

52. HRW&M, *Extending the Authority . . . Report to Accompany H.R. 407* (1940), pp. 1–2.

53. TC, *Trade Agreement . . . Turkey*; Trask, *United States Response to Turkish Nationalism*, pp. 115–22.

54. Steward, *Trade and Hemisphere*; Harold F. Peterson, *Argentina and the United States*, pp. 363–65, 409–13.

55. *FRUS*, 1939, 5:227–302; Stevens to Roosevelt, December 26, 1940, OF, Argentina, FDR.

56. Quotations are from USDS, *Reciprocal Trade . . . Argentina*, pp. 22, 82. Data are from TC, *Economic Controls and Commercial Policy in Argentina*, p. 34; USDS, *Bulletin*, October 18, 1941, supp. Harold F. Peterson (*Argentina and the United States*, p. 412) offers slightly different data. The State Department acknowledged that the figures at the beginning of this paragraph came from U.S. export data. Although the best available, U.S. export data often distort actual trade patterns. Governments tend to monitor imports more effectively because imports are subject to duties. Exports usually are not.

57. Durand, "The Trade Agreements Program," p. 123; TC, OTAP, 2:40, 67–68, 3:121, 143. For U.S. protests in 1948 and 1949, see *FRUS*, 1951, 2:1125. An agreement with Uruguay contained similar loopholes. In a headnote Uruguay said that its concessions did not include a transfer tax, an analysis tax, and a surtax of 1 percent of import duties. TC, *Trade Agreement . . . Uruguay*.

58. Constance Southworth to Henry F. Grady, August 21, 1940, 611.59A31/5, RG 59, NA. For U.S. relations with Iceland, see Nuechterlein, *Iceland: Reluctant Ally*.

59. *FRUS*, 1941, 2:786–87; Hull to Roosevelt, April 21, 1943, OF, FDR; HRW&M, *Trade Agreements Extension Act of 1958*, p. 2125. The 12.5 percent rate was bound in the 1955 bilateral agreement with Japan.

60. *FRUS*, 1941, 3:373–74. The agreement signed with Iran had few long-term trade consequences for the United States. The CTA understood that this agreement had "little economic value" and offered no objections to negotiating a bilateral pact "if political considerations are believed by higher authorities to render this desirable." CTA, May 26, 1941, RG 353, NA.

61. In the bilateral agreement with Mexico, that country provided concessions on $23.4 million (29 percent) of imports from the United States in 1939 ($80.3 million). The United States provided concessions on $35.2 million (64.7 percent) of imports from Mexico in 1939 ($54.4 million). See TC, *Trade Agreement . . . Mexico*; *FRUS*, 1942, 6:489–525.

62. *FRUS*, 1941, 7:542–47; 1942, 6:690–91. The CTA found "no abundant basis for an agreement" but proceeded at the request of higher political authorities. The United States granted concessions on 29 percent of Peru's imports into America in 1939. TC, *Trade Agreement . . . Peru*. Because World War II had disrupted sugar imports from the Philippines and forced suspension of the sugar quota system, the reduction in tariff rates on sugar imports represented in effect a transfer of revenue from the U.S. Treasury to Peruvian sugar exporters.

63. In August 1934 a reciprocal trade agreement with Cuba reduced the duty on Cuban sugar from $1.50 to $0.90 per hundred pounds. This "valuable concession" cost the U.S. Treasury $23 million in revenue but was expected to stimulate business and employment in Cuba. Laurence Duggan memo, July 21, 1934, 611.3731/925, RG 59, NA.

64. *FRUS*, 1941, 7:220.

65. HRW&M, *Extension of Reciprocal Trade Agreements Act*, 1943, 2:25–26.

66. Randall, *Report to the President and Congress*, p. 3.

67. USDS, *United States Balance of Payments Problem*, pp. 8–14.

68. U.S. Public Advisory Board for Mutual Security, *Trade and Tariff Policy*, pp. 1, 18–21.

69. Unpublished pages from memoirs, HST. Truman was a low-tariff Democrat. As a senator from Missouri, he once wrote a constituent that trade barriers were "un-American and not in line with the Constitution of the United States." Alonzo Hamby called my attention to this letter: Truman to C. E. Garner, May 5, 1941, Senate Papers, HST.

70. Ferrell, *Eisenhower Diaries*, p. 242; *Public Papers . . . Eisenhower*, 1957, pp. 460–62.

71. USDS, "Interim Report of Special Committee on Relaxation of Trade Barriers," December 8, 1943, ITF, RG 43, NA.

72. *Public Papers . . . Truman*, 1947, pp. 167–72. Vandenberg and New England businessman Sinclair Weeks, later President Eisenhower's secretary of commerce, communicated on these matters. See Weeks to Vandenberg, December 30, 1946, and Vandenberg to Weeks, January 3, 1947, Vandenberg Papers, University of Michigan.

73. Although the conference at Geneva, and the one in Havana in 1948, completed an ITO charter, the document failed to win approval in Congress. U.S. business considered the charter too ambitious and bureaucratic. As a consequence, the interim GATT, a transitional mechanism, became a de facto ITO. A former GATT staff member has published a sympathetic account. See Low, *Trading Free*. For a more critical assessment, see Prestowitz, Tonelson, and Jerome, "The Last Gasp of Gattism."

74. United Nations, *Yearbook of International Trade Statistics*, 1956, pp. 12–16.

75. Meeting of U.S. and U.K. delegations, July 12, 1947, ITF, RG 43, NA.

76. Comments of U.S. delegate Clair Wilcox at delegation meeting, July 14, 1947, and minutes of U.S. delegation meeting, August 4, 1947, ITF, ibid.

77. Corse memo at end of Torquay Conference, April 21, 1951, ITF, ibid.

78. U.K. delegation to FO, October 2, 1947, BT 11/3648, PRO.

79. U.K. Delegation to FO, October 12, 1947, Helmore to FO, BT11/3648, PRO.

80. The 1934 Reciprocal Trade Agreements Act authorized a 50 percent cut in existing rates. In 1945 the State Department gained authority from Congress to cut duties an additional 50 percent—that is, 75 percent below the original rate—on items where the maximum permissible cut had been effected. TC, *OTAP*, 1:22–23, discusses the extent of tariff cutting before and after Geneva. Pre-Geneva agreements reduced duties on 63.9 percent of U.S. dutiable imports and bound rates on 4.7 percent of total dutiable imports. The average reduction was 44 percent (of a maximum 50 percent authorized in 1934). Calculated on the basis of 1939 trade statistics, duties were reduced one-third from 1934 to 1947, cutting the average rate on dutiable imports from 48.2 to 32.2 percent ad valorem before Geneva.

At Geneva the average rate on dutiable imports was cut from 32.2 to 25.4 percent ad valorem. On items cut at Geneva the average reduction was 35 percent (of a maximum 50 percent authorized in 1945). Interestingly, as a result of all trade negotiations, including the Geneva Round, the average rate on agricultural products had been cut 47 percent and on nonagricultural products 48 percent.

81. Winthrop Brown to Truman, October 17, 1947, WHCF, HST. A "tired" and discouraged Clair Wilcox told the Canadian ambassador on October 10, 1947, that the United States had decided to conclude the Geneva trade negotiations without a British commitment to eliminate preferences. The Canadian official reported that top-level State Department decision makers, including Secretary Marshall, "felt . . . that it was vital to get an agreement at almost any cost." Department of External Relations, *Documents on Canadian External Relations*, 13:1197.

82. Gregg to Ryder, October 11, 1947, ITF, RG 43, NA; October 17, 1947 memo of conversation, 560.AL/10-1747, RG 59, NA. BT 11/4679 contains British analysis of the rubber-for-preferences deal. Gregg's dissent troubled State Department representatives, and they approached Tariff Commission chairman Oscar Ryder hoping to change Gregg's vote. Ryder declined to intercede, noting that "there are probably many other instances in the CTA minutes which would be susceptible to use by opponents of the trade program if the minutes were to become available as a result of a subpoena or otherwise."

State Department negotiators privately acknowledged that they had consented to an unfavorable deal lacking "substantially equivalent concessions." Despite what American officials perceived to be firm wartime commitments to eliminate preferences, the United States accepted Britain's refusal to end preferences "for the sake of reaching an agreement." Carl D. Corse Report on Torquay Conference, April 21, 1951, ITF, RG 43, NA.

83. Washington Embassy to BT, Burns to Holmes, February 3, 1951, BT 11/4679, PRO. For other documentation, see Colonial Office to Senior Government Trade Commission, Australia, December 17, 1952, CO 1016/35, PRO; U.S. Delegation to U.K. Delegation, Torquay, January 16, 1951, FO 371/91903, PRO; Harold Wilson to Prime Minister, December 15, 1947, PREM 8/490, PRO.

84. Corse memo assessing Torquay, April 21, 1951, ITF, RG 43, NA.

85. S. L. Holmes, minute, March 10, 1951, and T.N. (5)(51)14, February 8, 1951, BT 11/4738, PRO.

86. Y. Loval Williams to Percival, May 1954, BT 205/2, and Clark memo on Torquay failure, September 6, 1955, BT 205/4, PRO.

87. Memo, April 21, 1951, WHCF, Confidential, HST; Corse memo and James H. Lewis to Charles F. Baldwin, January 3, 1951, RG 43, NA; *FRUS*, 1951, 1:1255.

88. J. Leckie to T. G. A. Muntz, n.d., FO 371/91903, and Sir O. Franks to FO, April 2, 1951, FO 371/91903, PRO.

89. *FRUS*, 1951, 1:1253.

90. James H. Lewis to Henry R. Labouisse Jr., USDS, November 29, 1950, ITF, RG 43, NA. Benjamin Moore of the U.S. embassy in London told British officials that America could not make an agreement that is "heavily unbalanced," but it would not insist on exact arithmetical balance. S. L. Holmes, minute, March 10, 1951, BT 11/4738, PRO.

91. E. V. Siracusa to R. R. Rubottom, June 18, 1958, 394.41/6-1858, RG 59, NA.

92. FO Intel, "United States Economic Policy," January 1954, FO 371-110148, PRO. "If the worst prognostications come true, all our efforts in this field may be required to help prevent a retreat by the liberal forces in the U.S."

93. "[T]he campaign for freer trade policies has in practice been 'sold' to people here (not so much by us as by the domestic protagonists) as something which was going to help the American economy." Geoffrey Parker, Commercial Counselor, British Embassy, Washington, D.C., July 21, 1954, to Edgar A. Cohen, BT, FO 371/111050, PRO.

94. TC, *OTAP*, 3:140, offers an account of discrimination against U.S. exports during this

period. Economist Gardner Patterson, subsequently a GATT official, notes that discrimination was widespread for twenty years after World War II. Patterson, *Discrimination in International Trade.*

95. Memo of conversation, Lyons of TAD with Mrs. Vest of Chamber of Commerce, March 10, 1958, 394.41/3-1058, RG 59, NA.

96. Memo to American diplomatic and counselor offices on "Promotion of United States Import Trade," September 11, 1946, ITF, RG 43, NA.

97. Coppock, "Government Assistance in Developing Imports," p. 139.

98. BT to U.K. Delegation, Annecy, April 26, 1949, BT 11/4229, PRO.

99. *New York Times*, April 19, 1952. For British reaction to this unexpected leak, see PREM 11/285, PRO.

100. Gray, *Report to the President*, November 10, 1950, p. 80.

101. U.S. Public Advisory Board for Mutual Security, *A Trade and Tariff Policy in the National Interest*, pp. 1, 3. This report (called the "Bell report" because Daniel W. Bell was acting chairman of the advisory board) proposed increasing imports of manufactured goods $500 to $700 million annually and estimated that this would displace as many as 60,000 to 90,000 workers (p. 66). See also Thorp, "Economic Basis of Our Foreign Policy," p. 175.

102. Linder to Winthrop Aldrich, October 31, 1952, WHCF, HST. See also John Leddy memo, December 11, 1952, *FRUS*, 1952–54, 1:46–49.

103. Kalijarvi, "Foreign Economic Policy and the National Security," p. 411. For other USDS statements on foreign economic policy, see Asher, "The Economics of U.S. Foreign Policy"; Waugh, "Problems of Foreign Economic Policy."

104. Conversation with congressional leaders, February 8, 1955, Ann Whitman File—Legislative, DDE; Speech to National Editorial Association, June 22, 1954, *Public Papers . . . Eisenhower*, 1954, pp. 585–90; *FRUS*, 1952–54, 14:1782. See generally Borden, *Pacific Alliance*, pp. 168–80.

105. Ferrell, *Eisenhower Diaries*, pp. 244–45. The British loved Eisenhower's internationalist outlook. Geoffrey Parker, the commercial counselor in Washington, reported: "The President's own record is consistent and impressive. He has far more appreciation of the economic needs of other countries and far more instinctive sympathy with the ideal of international economic cooperation than any of his lieutenants." Parker to BT, July 21, 1954, FO 371/111050, PRO.

106. Herbert Hoover, October 24, 1953, Post-Presidential Papers, HCH.

107. Cabinet meeting on August 6, 1954, Ann Whitman File: Cabinet Series, DDE. For Weeks (who earlier served as president of the Boston Home Market Club, a protectionist organization), see interview, April 14, 1967, Columbia University Oral History Project, Weeks Oral History, DDE. On Humphrey's views, see "Clarence Randall Diary," Randall Papers, June 25, July 7, 15, 1954, DDE. Humphrey's "Texas jingoist" mood frightened the British. He did not accept the internationalist "trade, not aid" philosophy, which advocated increasing U.S. imports to close the dollar gap. Instead, Humphrey proposed to address the merchandise imbalance, much as Japan did in the 1980s, with increased capital exports. Notes from Ottawa, September 28, 1955, FO 371/114924, PRO.

108. Interview, September 26, 1966, Columbia University Oral History Project, Bush Oral History, DDE.

109. Memo of U.S.-U.K. Economical Talks, March 5, 1953, vol. 12, document 3234, *DDC*. This is a variation of the bargaining strategy Britain pursued during the Torquay negotiations. Within the State Department the idea had supporters. Lawyer Stanley Metzger, an enthusiastic free trader whom President Lyndon Johnson would name chairman of the TC,

embraced unilateral tariff concessions and abandonment of the no-injury concept on February 25, 1953. *FRUS*, 1952, 1:138–15. On October 20 Winthrop Brown, the U.S. delegate to GATT, recommended a "forward looking program" in which the United States would abandon the emphasis on "strict reciprocity" in tariff negotiations. As part of a "unilateral contribution . . . to the solution of the great world trade imbalance" he favored removing all tariffs over 50 percent ad valorem and barring resort to the escape clause three years after a tariff reduction. *FRUS*, 1953, 1:163–64.

110. November 1948 meeting with U.K. BT, Far East Commission, RG 43, NA.

111. July 13, 1953, *FRUS*, 1952–54, 1:156–58.

112. August 20, 1953, WHCF, Confidential, DDE.

113. Comment of John Stambaugh, the White House, in Memo of conversation, October 22, 1954, WHCF, Confidential, DDE.

114. "Japanese Tariff Negotiations—A Summary," memo, n.d., and Comment of John Stambaugh, October 22, 1954, WHCF, Confidential, DDE.

115. Carl D. Corse to Eisenhower, February 15, 1955, WHCF, Confidential, DDE.

116. Weeks to Eisenhower, February 16, 1955, WHCF, Confidential, DDE.

117. Minutes of first meeting, February 22, 1955, ITF, RG 43, NA.

118. Minutes of meetings, March 26–27, April 18, 1955, ITF, ibid.

119. The quotations in this and the next paragraph are from various meetings, February 22–April 18, 1955, Japanese negotiations, ITF, RG 43, NA. In 1970 a senior official of MITI confirmed the existence of a long-term Japanese strategy to emphasize capital- and technology-intensive industries in order to break the Asian pattern of reliance on labor-intensive industries. "From a short-run viewpoint, encouragement of such industries would seem to conflict with economic rationalism. But from a long-range viewpoint, these are precisely the industries of which income elasticity of demand is high, technological progress rapid, and labor productivity rises fast." U.S. General Accounting Office, *United States–Japan Trade: Issues and Problems*, pp. 176–77.

120. Woodrow Willoughby to Eisenhower, 1955, "Request for Approval of Results of Tariff Negotiations," WHCF, Confidential, DDE.

121. During trade negotiations with Japan in 1956, the chief U.S. negotiator, Carl Corse, told the Japanese that "in the 1955 negotiations with Japan the United States on political grounds felt that an agreement was important and that some compromises may have been made with economic factors due to the over-riding political considerations." Francis F. Lincoln notes, March 28, 1956, ITF, RG 43, NA.

122. TC, *Postwar Developments in Japan's Foreign Trade*, pp. 124–26.

123. In reporting this agreement, the State Department evaluated Japanese concessions in terms of 1953 Japanese import values, but U.S. concessions in terms of 1954 U.S. import values.

124. *Mainichi Daily News* and *Nippon Times*, June 10, 1955.

125. Marshall M. Smith to Samuel C. Waugh, June 23, 1955, 394.41/6-2355, RG 59, NA.

126. Memo of meeting between Frank and Iguichi, April 25, 1955, 394.41/4-2555, ibid. The same point emerges in the minutes of the bilateral negotiations, including the sixteenth meeting on April 18, 1955. See ITF, RG 43, NA.

127. USDS, *Analysis of Protocol . . . for Accession of Japan*, p. 8. Japan removed exchange controls in 1963, but some items on which the United States obtained tariff concessions were still restricted with licenses or quotas eighteen years later when the Senate Finance Committee looked at quantitative import restrictions of major trading countries prior to the Tokyo Round of GATT negotiations. SNFN, *Executive Branch GATT Studies*, 6:106–7.

128. U.S. delegation report, May 26, 1955, 394.41-5-2655, RG 59, NA. Six Republican members of the House Ways and Means Committee later criticized these third-country concessions as incompatible with the concept of reciprocity. HRW&M, *Trade Agreements Extension Act of 1958*, pp. 73–74. For a critique of the bilateral agreement, see the remarks of Senator George Malone (R-Nev.), *Congressional Record*, June 15, 1955, pp. 8253–57.

129. USDC, *Trade of the United States with Japan*.

130. The White House chief of staff, Sherman Adams, sent Stevens's speech to Secretary Weeks on May 13, 1958. Sinclair Weeks Papers, Dartmouth College. These also contain a July 24, 1956, report on conversations with cotton textile producers in New England. The industry was worried about growing Japanese competition and wanted import restraints.

131. SNFN, *Domestic Industries Affected by Foreign Imports*, July 2, 1956. On the declining competitiveness of the textile industry (including cotton, manmade fabrics, and woolens), see SNIFC, *Problems of the Domestic Textile Industry* and *Supplementary Report*. On trade-related textile problems, see *FRUS*, 1955–57, 9:179–82, 192–96, 253–58.

132. TC, *Postwar Developments in Japan's Foreign Trade*, p. 137.

133. SNFN, *Trade Agreements Extension Act of 1958*, pp. 2–5. In a stinging dissent, Senator Paul Douglas (D-Ill.), an economist, blasted the Finance Committee report as meaning "the virtual abandonment of the reciprocal trade program . . . started by Cordell Hull in 1934" (p. 16). Two other members of the committee, Malone (R-Nev.) and William E. Jenner (R-Ind.), recommended terminating the program. They said: "Today more nations impose more barriers to imports of American products than at any time in our history" (p. 29).

134. Discussion of 409th Meeting of the National Security Council, June 4, 1959, vol. 16 (1990), document 971, *DDC*.

135. Ibid. Prime Minister Harold Macmillan had complained about American protectionism during a visit in March. Macmillan to Eisenhower, March 23, 1959, PREM 11/4021, PRO.

136. Discussion of 409th Meeting of the National Security Council, June 4, 1959, vol. 16 (1990), document 971, *DDC*.

137. Bauer, Pool, and Dexter (*American Business and Public Policy*) show that business embraced trade liberalization after World War II.

CHAPTER SIX

1. *Public Papers . . . Kennedy*, 1962, p. 412.

2. Ibid., 1962, pp. 759–60.

3. Kindleberger, "U.S. Foreign Economic Policy," pp. 395–417. See also Ikenberry, Lake, and Mastanduno, *Foreign Economic Policy*, pp. 1–14; Gilpin, *Political Economy*, pp. 343–48.

4. Lundestad, *American "Empire,"* pp. 70–72.

5. *Public Papers . . . Kennedy*, 1963, pp. 516–21; TC, *OTAP*, 1967, p. 164.

6. Kenwood and Lougheed, *International Economy*, p. 289.

7. *FRUS*, 1955–57, 4:549–53; Marjolin, *Architect of European Unity*, pp. 212–35.

8. TC, *OTAP*, 1967, pp. 158–61.

9. UNCTAD, *Handbook*, 1991, pp. 16, 28.

10. According to the Senate Finance Committee, the "protection afforded domestic industries by way of tariffs is at an unprecedented low point and extreme caution must be exercised in future negotiations to mitigate possible injury to the domestic economy." SNFN, *Trade Agreements Extension Act of 1958*, p. 2.

11. *FRUS*, 1958–60, 4:283–84.

12. Zeiler, *American Trade and Power*, pp. 123–25. Kennedy told Prime Minister Macmillan that relief for the carpet and glass industries was needed to win passage of the TEA in Congress. Record of White House meeting, April 28, 1962, PREM 11/4014, and D. Ormsby Gore to FO, March 21, 1962, BT 11/5911, PRO. Eager to protest, the British government invited its carpet manufacturers to express dissatisfaction in letters to the *London Times* and the *Financial Times*. In organizing the protest the Board of Trade thought it "useful if we could point to public criticism of the very large increase in the [U.S.] tariff." J. L. May memo, March 23, 1962, BT 11/5911, PRO.

13. H. F. Heinemann, minute, July 10, 1961, and U.K. delegation in Geneva to FO, October 3, 1961, BT 11/5791, PRO; Rusk to Kennedy, September 11, 1961, vol. 15, document 298, *DDC*. Pushing the matter outside the State Department was Myer Rashish, a House Ways and Means staffer and an aide to Howard Petersen (Petersen, a Republican, was a Philadelphia banker helping the administration with trade legislation). Rashish to Petersen, September 8, 1961, Petersen Papers, JFK.

14. *Public Papers . . . Kennedy*, 1962, pp. 204–6. Senator Carl Curtis (R-Neb.) reported that Kennedy, acting on State Department advice, ignored the peril point findings seventy times. By contrast, President Eisenhower did so only two or three times; President Truman did so not at all. *Congressional Record*, September 18, 1962, pp. 19765–68; Ball to Kennedy, September 22, 1961, vol. 15, document 298, *DDC*; U.S. President, *Trade Agreements with EEC . . .*, 1962.

15. *Congressional Record*, April 10, 1967, p. 8800 (Curtis); Curtis and Vastine, *Kennedy Round*, pp. 23–24; Zeiler, *American Trade and Power*, pp. 62–63; SOS to President, September 11, 1961, and Ball to Kennedy, September 22, 1961, vol. 15, documents 296–98, *DDC*; TC, *OTAP*, 1960–June 1962, p. 21. On farm issues, see Curtis and Vastine, *Kennedy Round*, p. 25.

16. Myer Feldman memo to Kennedy, December 12, 1961, WHCF, JFK. Zeiler (*American Trade and Power*, pp. 59–64) reviews archival information on the Dillon Round and the decision not to challenge Europe.

17. House Republicans criticized the "error" of U.S. negotiators in accepting a disadvantageous averaging formula from the EEC. HRW&M, *Trade Expansion Act of 1962: Report*, pp. 88–89. For Bush's comment, see *Congressional Record*, March 8, 1962, p. 3619. In passing the TEA, Congress demonstrated dissatisfaction with the State Department's use of previous tariff-cutting authority. The Ways and Means Committee established the position of special representative for trade negotiations to serve as chief trade negotiator and as chairman of the interagency trade policy committee. In presenting the conference report, Chairman Wilbur Mills noted that State had previously supervised negotiations and chaired the interagency committee. "It was not our intention that this group [State] would continue its past dominant role." *Congressional Record*, October 4, 1962, p. 21097.

18. SNIFC, *Problems of the Domestic Textile Industry*, pp. 1–17. Senator John Pastore (D-R.I.) chaired this investigation.

19. Ibid., pp. 19–22.

20. Ball, *The Past Has Another Pattern*, pp. 191–92. Ball, a partner in the law firm of Cleary, Gottlieb, Friendly, and Ball, had represented the European Common Market and international petroleum interests. Bauer, De Sola Pool, and Dexter, *American Business and Public Policy*, pp. 74, 377–79. State also attempted to scuttle President Nixon's commitment to restrain textile imports. Dent, *Prodigal South Returns*, pp. 198–207; Zeiler, *American Trade and Power*, pp. 85–87.

21. Johnson Administration, State Department history of "Textile Program, 1964–1968,"

in vol. 10, document 1459, *DDC*; Conversations between Hodges and Fukuda, January 28, 1964, Herter Papers, JFK.

22. Johnson comment, September 28, 1964, as cited in State Department history of textiles program, vol. 10, document 1459, *DDC*.

23. Quoted in Aggarwal, *Liberal Protectionism*, pp. 87–88.

24. McPherson and Bator to Johnson, February 12, 1966, and Bator to Johnson, February 21, 1966, WHCF, LBJ.

25. DeVier Pierson and Harry McPherson to Johnson, September 22, October 2, 1967, and Pierson to Johnson, February 9, 1968, Pierson Papers, LBJ. In 1968 Agriculture supported restraints.

26. H. H. N. Geoghegan memo containing a report from U.S. Mission, Brussels, May 7, 1963, in FO 371/172336, PRO.

27. Memo of Howard Petersen conversation with Walter Heller, Kermit Gordon, and Carl Kaysen, October 11, 1961, Petersen Papers, JFK.

28. *Public Papers . . . Kennedy*, 1961, pp. 790–91. Further indication that the Kennedy administration planned to abandon escape clause relief appeared in Ball's speech to the German Society for Foreign Affairs. See HRW&M, *Trade Expansion Act: Report*, pp. 85–86.

29. *Public Papers . . . Kennedy*, 1961, pp. 781–83.

30. Ibid., pp. 763–64.

31. Ibid., pp. 779–81; 1962, pp. 357–61; 1963, pp. 516–21; Myer Rashish to Theodore C. Sorensen, November 25, 1961, Petersen Papers, JFK. In May 1963 GATT ministers pledged that "every effort shall be made to reduce barriers to exports of less-developed countries." They also agreed that "developed countries cannot expect to receive reciprocity from the less developed countries." TC, *OTAP*, 1967, p. 164.

32. HRW&M, *Trade Expansion Act: Hearings*, pp. 1146–48.

33. Stitt underestimated Japan's export performance. A $800 million bilateral deficit in 1961 became a $1.2 billion surplus in 1970 on exports of $5.9 billion. Ibid., p. 213.

34. Ibid., pp. 1286–87. According to the ITC, imports amounted to 46 percent of domestic consumption for metal-working machine tools in 1988, up from 7 percent in 1970.

35. Ibid., pp. 1611–17. The Antifriction Bearing Manufacturers Association warned about a Japanese cartel supported by the Japanese Ministry of International Trade and Industry.

36. Ibid., pp. 2741–60.

37. Ibid., pp. 2769–73.

38. *Congressional Record*, June 28, 1962, p. 12090. On final passage, October 4, 1962, Chairman Mills had support from several Ways and Means Republicans: Howard Baker, John Byrnes, Thomas Curtis, and Herman Schneebeli. Minority leader Charles Halleck supported the bill, as did future Republican leaders Gerald Ford of Michigan and Robert Michel of Illinois. John J. Rhodes of Arizona opposed it. Among Democrats, impassioned opposition came from veteran congressman John Dent, who represented a depressed district in northeastern Pennsylvania and articulated traditional protectionism. *Congressional Record*, September 19, 1962, p. 19876, October 4, 1962, p. 21110. Fourteen senators did not vote.

39. Among Republican state delegations, 12 out of 16 Ohioans voted against the measure, as did 8 out of 16 Republicans from Pennsylvania, 9 out of 21 from New York, 8 out of 14 from California, and 6 out of 11 from Illinois.

40. *Congressional Record*, June 28, 1962, pp. 12008–12.

41. Ibid.

42. Ibid., September 18, 1962, pp. 19762–75. After his retirement, Bush told an interviewer: "I never was a free trader. I never felt that we could abolish tariffs and do away with

all protective devices, because we would have been flooded with imports." The father of future president George Bush described himself as "skeptical" of the Trade Agreements Act. September 1966, Columbia University Oral History Project, Bush Oral History, DDE.

43. Kelly, *Studies in United States Commercial Policy*, pp. 122–23.

44. At the suggestion of George Ball, Kennedy appointed Christian Herter, a secretary of state in the Eisenhower administration, rather than an experienced businessman, as STR. Ball, *The Past Has Another Pattern*, pp. 198–99.

45. Ibid., pp. 208–22.

46. *Public Papers . . . Johnson, 1964*, pp. 505–6. Ernest Preeg, a member of the U.S. delegation in the Kennedy Round negotiations, later wrote that "concessions in agriculture were the *sine qua non* for the United States in the Kennedy Round. . . . The Americans repeatedly and unequivocally stated that no agreement would be signed unless adequate concessions on farm products were forthcoming." Preeg, *Traders and Diplomats*, p. 144.

47. Bernard Norwood to Herter, October 27, 1964, Herter Papers, JFK. State Department trade policy toward Japan emphasized keeping open the American market for Japanese exports: this "will require firm Executive Branch resistance of American industry demands for curtailment of Japanese imports." "Department of State Policy on the Future of Japan," June 26, 1964, vol. 3, document 63C, *DDC*.

48. Connor to Johnson, July 9, 1965, and Bundy to Johnson, August 17, 1965, WHCF, LBJ.

49. Roth to Johnson, August 2, 1966, NSF, LBJ.

50. Freeman to Johnson, August 1, 1966, WHCF, LBJ.

51. "Task Force on Foreign Economic Policy," November 25, 1964, ibid.

52. Wyndham White speech, October 27, 1966, *Congressional Record*, January 12, 1967, pp. 411–14; Roth to McPherson, January 13, 1967, Pierson Files, LBJ (concerns about State of the Union address); Curtis speech, *Congressional Record*, January 19, 1967, pp. 1052–54.

53. *Congressional Record*, March 20, 1967, pp. 7213–16. See also SNFN, *Compendium of Papers*, pp. 911–20.

54. *Journal of Commerce*, February 2, 1967; *Congressional Record*, April 24, 1967, p. 10588.

55. Hartke wanted trade negotiations to focus on foreign subsidies as well as tariffs. He called for vigorous antitrust enforcement to deal with foreign cartels. *Journal of Commerce*, February 2, 1967.

56. *Congressional Record*, September 29, 1965, pp. 2512–16, September 30, 1965, pp. 25627–28. Hartke saw the agreement as another example of the State Department playing international politics with U.S. jobs and industries. SNFN, *Automotive Products Trade Act*, September 27, 1965; "U.S.-Canadian Automotive Agreement Is in Default," speech, n.d., Fowler Papers, LBJ. See also *Congressional Record*, December 13, 1974, p. 39838. Johnson's comment is in Martin, *The Presidents and the Prime Ministers*, p. 219. Subsequently, other authorities also concluded that the auto pact benefited Canada more than the United States. On January 22, 1976, the U.S. International Trade Commission reported to Chairman Long that "Canada has not fully complied with the agreement." Moreover, "the agreement as implemented by Canada is not a free-trade agreement, and it has primarily benefited the Canadian economy." SNFC, *Canadian Automobile Agreement*. The ITC study contains the side agreements that U.S. auto companies provided to Canadian authorities. See also two Canadian accounts: Keeley, "Cast in Concrete for All Time?," and Winham, "Canadian Automobile Industry."

57. Bothwell, *Canada and the United States*, p. 93.

58. John B. Rehm to Ted Van Dyk, May 15, 1967, and "Congressional Briefings on Kennedy Round," May 16, 1967, both in NSF, LBJ.

59. Because Johnson frequently dictated instructions to his staff and left few written comments on documents, it is more difficult to assess his personal involvement in policy issues than, for example, President Eisenhower's role in similar decisions.

60. Roth to Bator, April 20, 1967, Roth Papers, LBJ; Bator to Johnson, April 21, 24, 1967, NSF, LBJ (quotations).

61. Trowbridge memo, April 21, 1967, ibid.

62. Roth to Bator, April 26, 1967, ibid.

63. Bator to Johnson and Roth to Johnson (quotation), May 1, 1967, Bator to Johnson, May 4, 1967—all in ibid.

64. Roth to Bator, May 9, 1967, and Bator to Johnson, May 10, 1967, ibid.

65. Zeiler, *American Trade and Power*, pp. 234–37. Briefing materials prepared for President Ford at the 1975 economic summit in Chateau de Rambouillet, France, concede that "major differences" between the United States and the EEC over agriculture "resulted in disappointing results for agriculture in the Kennedy Round. Faced with a choice of either accepting liberalization of industrial trade or failure of the whole Kennedy Round, the U.S. government chose to accept the former." "US-EC Differences over Agricultural Trade," memo, n.d., PHF, GRF.

66. Francis Bator to Johnson, May 10, 1967, NSF, LBJ.

67. Edward K. Hamilton memo, May 11, 1967, NSF, LBJ. Commerce and Labor acknowledged that the agreement would present "some political problems." The secretary of agriculture loyally voted his approval without first talking to Deputy Secretary Schnittker on his return from Geneva.

68. *Public Papers . . . Johnson*, 1967, pp. 592–93; Roth to Fowler and Long, May 16, 1967, Roth Papers, LBJ; Preeg, *Traders and Diplomats*, pp. 196–200; Evans, *Kennedy Round*, pp. 273–76.

69. *Public Papers . . . Johnson*, 1968, p. 199, 1967, pp. 1073, 1148; TC, *OTAP*, 1967, pp. 236–41. The commission noted that its comparison lacked parallelism. It compared concessions granted on imports from all sources with concessions obtained from negotiating countries. The figures also did not take into account the consequences of Britain's devaluation in the fall of 1967. A number of other countries followed, reducing the value of their concessions.

70. Herter to Johnson, October 11, 1966, and Roth to Johnson, June 26, 1967, NSF, LBJ (quotations); SNFN, *Expressing the Sense of Congress*. The Finance Committee declared that broadening the Kennedy Round negotiations to include matters not covered in the congressional delegation of authority "would violate the principles which have made our reciprocal trade program so successful for more than three decades."

71. Hartke to Johnson, August 1, 1967, WHCF, Legislation, LBJ. For more complete information on the antidumping code dispute, see SNFN, *International Antidumping Code*. These concessions made as part of a deal to liberalize European tariffs on chemicals required congressional approval, as Congress had confined executive negotiating authority to tariffs. The STR and Treasury claimed that the antidumping code did not conflict with domestic law. A majority of the TC thought differently. Pierson to Johnson, June 29, 1968, WHCF, LBJ. Ultimately, the Finance Committee attached an amendment to a bill relating to Defense Department procurement procedures. It stipulated that the Tariff Commission should resolve any conflict between the International Antidumping Code and U.S. domestic law in favor of the latter. Public Law 90–634, October 24, 1968.

72. Metzger, "Book Reviews."

73. USDS, *Bulletin*, July 31, 1967, pp. 132–33. In an oral history memoir, Undersecretary

John A. Schnittker called the negotiations "a moderate success—not a big roaring success, but a moderate success." Schnittker Oral History, LBJ.

74. USDS, *Bulletin*, July 31, 1967, pp. 127–29.

75. Zeiler, *American Trade and Power*, pp. 236–60.

76. Norwood, "The Kennedy Round." This bilateral calculation ignores something more important. As a GATT member eligible for unconditional most-favored-nation treatment, Japan automatically benefited from all U.S. concessions on manufactured products.

77. *Mainichi Daily News*, May 17, 1967.

78. Komiya and Itoh, "Japan's International Trade"; Gilbert to Nixon, June 15, 1969, WHCF, RMN; Public Law 93–618, 93d Cong., H.R. 10710, January 3, 1975. Careful not to mention Japan by name, the Senate Finance Committee reported that "very small reductions in tariffs of some industrialized countries in the Kennedy Round may be attributable to the realization by certain countries that they could automatically receive all the benefits of the trade agreement without paying any of the costs." SNFN, *Trade Reform Act of 1974*, pp. 94–95.

79. *Financial Post*, July 8, 1967.

80. Evans, *Kennedy Round*, pp. 273–75.

81. *Congressional Record*, June 27, 1967, p. 17500 (Thurmond); Ervin to Charles A. Sledge, General Aniline and Film Corp., Charlotte, July 7, 1967, Ervin Papers, SHC; *Journal of Commerce*, July 28, 1967 (American Iron and Steel Institute), August 24, 1967 (Manufacturing Chemists). The governors of thirteen southern states called for new restraints on man-made fibers, woolen, and silk goods, and for effective enforcement of existing arrangements covering cotton textiles. They recommended that Congress reject the proposed repeal of the American selling price method of customs valuation for benzenoid chemical products. *Congressional Record*, September 28, 1967, pp. 27215–16.

82. Dent quoted in *Journal of Commerce*, July 28, 1967, and *Congressional Record*, June 20, 1967, pp. 16526–27.

83. *Congressional Record*, September 28, 1967, pp. 27186–215; HRE&L, *Establishing Procedures to Relieve Domestic Industries and Workers*.

84. *Journal of Commerce*, September 20, 1967 (Baldanzi); Zeiler, *American Trade and Power*, p. 240.

85. Galbraith to Johnson, March 11, 1964, WHCF, LBJ.

86. Because of substantial net earnings on foreign investments, the U.S. current account, a broader measure of international transactions that also considers merchandise, services, and investments, did not swing into a chronic deficit position until 1982. U.S. President, *Economic Report*, 1993, p. 462.

87. Calculated from BEA, *National Income and Product Accounts*, 2:169.

88. CITIP, *Interdependent World*.

89. *Public Papers . . . Nixon*, 1972, p. 244.

90. TC, *Trade Barriers*, 1:8–26. Most complaints about EEC practices concerned Italy, France, and West Germany.

91. CITIP, *Interdependent World*, 1:13. For restrictions on U.S. exports to the EEC, Japan, and Canada, see pp. 199–233.

92. Preeg, *Traders and Diplomats*, pp. 204–11 (quotation, p. 204).

93. *Congressional Record*, July 19, 1967, p. 19502.

94. TC, *Trade Barriers*, 8:113. Auto imports from Canada entered free of duty, pursuant to the bilateral U.S.-Canadian Automotive Products Agreement of January 1965. For other

products—including nonelectrical machinery and office machinery—see ibid., 8:12, 51, 9:68–71.

95. ITC, *Effect of Changes in the Value of the U.S. Dollar Trade,* September 1983, p. 2.

96. U.S. President, *Annual Report under the Trade Agreements Program,* 1974, p. 47.

97. TC, *OTAP,* 1971, pp. 7–8.

98. TC, *Cotton Osnaburgs.* For a similar affirmative finding involving textiles, see TC, *Certain Woven Fabrics* and *Broadwoven Polyester-Cotton Fabrics.*

99. TC, *Transistors and Diodes.*

100. TC, *Audio Receivers, Phonographs, and Tape Recorders.*

101. TC, *Annual Report,* 1972, p. 7.

102. TC, *Antifriction Balls and Ball Bearings.*

103. ITC, *Competitive Assessment,* p. 104.

104. Tariff Par. 369 discussion for 1947 Geneva Round, box 195, ITF, RG 43, NA. For attitudes of the CTA in 1947 and 1950, see discussions pertaining to Tariff Par. 369 in ITF, RG 43, and the Committee on Reciprocity Information, RG 364, NA. In 1960 the TC recommended further cuts. But in 1973 it found that trade agreement concessions on passenger automobiles had led to increased imports that caused unemployment for a significant number of workers at a Chrysler assembly plant in Commerce, Calif. See TC, *New Passenger Automobiles.*

105. The Automobile Manufacturers Association praised Kennedy Round results but warned about "the many nontariff barriers to the export of automobiles." SNFN, *Compendium of Papers,* p. 563.

106. Duncan (*U.S.-Japan Automobile Diplomacy*) discusses efforts to persuade Japan to reduce barriers after the Kennedy Round.

107. Hansen and Israel, *Gallup Poll,* pp. 1267, 1761.

108. Harris and Associates, *Harris Survey Yearbook of Public Opinion, 1973,* p. 261; Kevin Phillips, "Politics of Protectionism," pp. 41–46.

109. USDS, "Post-Kennedy Round US/EC Agricultural Problems," Administrative History, LBJ; Ball to Johnson, August 15, 1966, and Rusk to Johnson, February 11, 1967, WHCF, LBJ; USDS, "Trade Preferences for Developing Countries," vol. 11, document 2864, *DDC.*

110. "Twenty Years of GATT," *Journal of World Trade Law* 2 (January–February 1968): 107–17; *Public Papers . . . Johnson,* 1968, pp. 8–13.

111. Rehm to Pierson, December 20, 1968, WHCF, LBJ. Rehm thought that industry would support a liberal trade policy, except for organized labor, steel, and textiles. The latter criticized the report as unnecessarily doctrinaire, ideological, and unrealistic. U.S. Office of the Special Trade Representative for Trade Negotiations, *Future United States Foreign Trade Policy,* 1969, pp. 97–98.

112. *Public Papers . . . Johnson,* 1968, pp. 648–52.

113. HRW&M, *Foreign Trade and Tariff Proposals,* pp. 5667–5740.

114. Pierson to Johnson, June 8, 1968, WHCF, LBJ; Pastor, *Politics of U.S. Foreign Economic Policy,* pp. 121–22; Destler, *American Trade Politics,* p. 27.

115. Johnson and Porter, *National Party Platforms,* p. 577.

116. Congressional Quarterly, *Almanac . . . 1968,* pp. 993, 1032, 1051.

117. Nixon, *Memoirs,* pp. 346, 545–80; Kissinger, *White House Years,* pp. 152–55. For reports on the growth of trade with communist bloc countries, see ITC, *East-West Trade* (quarterly report), beginning in 1975.

118. Gertstacker to Peterson, January 4, 1972, and Dent memo, January 7, 1972, WHCF, RMN.

119. Stans to Nixon, February 14, 1969, WHCF, RMN.

120. For more on escape clause, antidumping, and countervailing duty enforcement in the Nixon administration, see Chapters 7 and 8.

121. *Public Papers . . . Nixon*, 1969, pp. 187–88, 940–46.

122. U.S. President, *U.S. Foreign Policy for the 1970s*, p. 162; Donald Kendall, memo to Nixon, May 19, 1969, WHCF, RMN. Stans agreed with the proposal, June 20, 1969.

123. Stans to Nixon, August 25, 1970, WHCF, RMN. The State Department told the Williams Commission that the decline in the merchandise trade surplus was due "largely to our inflation." It noted "hopeful signs of improvement"—among them, "Japan is reducing its barriers to trade. . . . In our view, pessimism about the future position of the United States in world trade is unjustified by historical trends, recent developments, or abstract reasoning." CITIP, *Interdependent World*, 1:7.

124. CITIP, *Interdependent World*, 1:2.

125. Ibid., 1:316–17. Charles H. Sommer, chairman of chemical giant Monsanto, made this comment.

126. Bergsten to Kissinger, July 13, 1970, and McCracken to Nixon, July 2, 1970, WHCF, RMN.

127. *Congressional Record*, November 18, 1970, pp. 37858, 38147–57. Complaints came from large industries such as steel, textiles, shoes, dairy, meat, oil, electronics, and chemicals—many of which had supported the TEA five years earlier.

128. *Congressional Record*, November 16, 1971; Hughes, *Trade, Taxes, and Transnationals*, pp. 31–32. For a legal analysis, see Colvin and deKieffer, "Legal and Economic Analysis," p. 771.

129. Volcker and Gyohten, *Changing Fortunes*, pp. 59–90.

130. *Public Papers . . . Nixon*, 1973, pp. 258–70. Nixon also requested authority to establish a program of generalized preferences for the manufactures of developing countries. For internal discussion of the president's program relating to safeguards and adjustment assistance, see Bill Pearce, Deputy STR, to Peter Flanigan, February 26, 1973, WHCF, RMN.

131. Destler, *Making Foreign Economic Policy*, p. 170; SNFN, *Trade Reform Act of 1974*, p. 11.

132. SNFN, *Trade Reform Act of 1974*, pp. 11, 124.

133. *Congressional Record*, December 12, 1974, pp. 39503–4, December 20, 1974, p. 41637. On these events, see also Pastor, *Politics of U.S. Foreign Economic Policy*; Stern, *Water's Edge*; Winham, *Tokyo Round*, pp. 128–37.

134. BEA, *Survey of Current Business*, August 1993, pp. 87–89; BEA, *National Income and Product Accounts*, 2:207–21.

135. Charles W. McMillion, President, MBG Information Services, Testimony to U.S. Senate Committee on Commerce, Science, and Transportation, October 13, 1994, copy provided to author; Bairoch, *Economics and World History*, p. 168.

136. BC, *Historical Statistics*, 1:137, 162, 226; USDL, *Handbook of Labor Statistics*, Bulletin 2340, August 1989, p. 349; U.S. President, *Economic Report*, 1993, p. 396. For production workers, see USDL, *Employment, Hours, and Earnings* and *Employment and Earnings*, various monthly issues.

137. In constant dollars the average steel worker earned $498.21 per week in 1973; the worker earned $16 less per week in 1992.

138. Data are from USDL, *Employment, Hours, and Earnings* and *Employment and Earnings*, various issues. See also BEA, *Survey of Current Business*, August 1993; BEA, *National Income and Product Accounts*.

139. BC, *Statistical Abstract*, 1993, p. 435.

140. Computed from BC, *Historical Statistics*, 2:895; BEA, *Survey of Current Business*, June 1992, pp. 92–95. Three-year averages were assessed: 1946, 1947, 1948, compared with 1966, 1967, 1968, and 1986, 1987, 1988. Prices were adjusted with the producer price index. U.S. President, *Economic Report*, 1993, p. 417; BEA, *National Income and Product Accounts*, *1959–88*, vol. 2.

CHAPTER SEVEN

1. Sparks, *Franklin*, p. 386.

2. Smyth, *Franklin*, 7:176. According to Franklin, "Commerce among nations, as well as between private persons, should be fair and equitable, by equivalent exchanges and mutual supplies. . . . To lay duties on a commodity, which our neighbors want, is a knavish attempt to get something for nothing. The statesman who first invented it had the genius of a pickpocket, and would have been a pickpocket if fortune had suitably placed him."

3. CRI report, November 6, 1934, 611.5531/1950, RG 59, NA. Producers of glassware, textiles, and matches complained about low-cost Japanese competition.

4. Phillips to Roosevelt, February 16, 1935, 611.0031/1524A, RG 59, NA, and February 25, 1935, OF, FDR; William Phillips, *Ventures in Diplomacy*, pp. 161–62. State Department economist Herbert Feis also had concern about Japanese competition. "Diary," April 18, 1935, Feis Papers, MD/LC.

5. Richard Whitehead correspondence with Sayre, June 12, 1937, 611.5431/590, RG 59, NA.

6. Roosevelt to Sumner Welles, November 5, 1934, OF, FDR; Acting Secretary of the Interior to SOS, October 25, 1938, 611.5431/729, RG 59, Deimel memo, May 2, 1939, 611.5431/768, RG 59, and Swiss Handkerchief File, ITF, RG 43—all in NA.

7. In 1945 House Republicans disputed the claim that "no serious injury has been done to essential domestic industry during the 11 years in which the trade agreements have been in operation." The "yardsticks" and "definitions" of that terminology, they noted, were all "determined solely by executive fiat." HRW&M, *Foreign Trade Agreements*, p. 9.

8. For a modified version of the Ryder draft, see "Proposed Revised Draft of Standard General Provisions, Dec. 13, 1941," ITF, RG 43, NA. Harry Hawkins reported to Secretary Hull on TC objections on November 7, 1941, ITF, RG 43, NA.

9. On Ickes's concern, see Roosevelt to Cordell Hull, September 26, 1942, OF, FDR; John Leddy note, June 30, 1945, and attached memo on implementing art. 7, RG 43, NA.

10. SNFC, *1945 Extension . . . Hearings*, p. 7. On May 25 Truman wrote Speaker Sam Rayburn: "I have had drawn to my attention statements . . . that this increased authority might be used . . . to endanger or 'trade out' segments of American industry, American agriculture, or American labor. No such action was taken under President Roosevelt and Cordell Hull, and no such action will take place under my Presidency."

11. Leddy note, June 30, 1945, RG 43, NA; Vandenberg-Millikin joint statement, February 7, 1947, Brossard Papers, USU.

12. Vandenberg-Millikin joint statement, February 7, 1947, Brossard Papers, USU. Truman released Executive Order 9832 prescribing procedures for the trade program. These included inserting an escape clause in each trade agreement entered under the act of 1934 and establishing an independent escape clause hearing procedure involving the TC. It would present recommendations to the president. Senator Robert A. Taft, the second ranking Republican, did not agree with the Vandenberg-Millikin proposal. Taft to Harry H.

Cook, American Flint Glass Workers Union of North America, February 17, 1947, Robert A. Taft Papers, MD/LC; *Public Papers . . . Truman*, 1947, pp. 167–72.

13. Memo, April 12, 1945, Chalmers Papers, University of Oregon.

14. This language was a slightly modified version of art. 11 in the December 23, 1942, agreement with Mexico. USDS, *Reciprocal Trade Agreement . . . Mexico.*

15. Sayre to Grady, January 6, 1937, Sayre Papers, MD/LC.

16. Grady to Edwin Watson, May 6, 1940, PPF, FDR.

17. Hull to Roosevelt, May 21, 1942, OF, FDR. Hull favored a former staff assistant, Lynn Edminster, for a vacant position. In choosing Republicans, as required by law, Hull looked for proven supporters of the program, such as John Gregg, a former secretary of the interagency Committee for Reciprocity Information. Wilcox to Clayton, May 9, 1946, ITF, RG 43, NA.

18. W. Brown to Robert Lovett, July 20, 1948, ITF, RG 43, NA.

19. TC, *Annual Report*, 1947, p. 63. According to ITC assistant general counsel Bill Gearhart, the TC dismissed 14 out of 21 applications for relief brought between 1947 and 1951. Only one—involving women's fur felt hats—led to escape clause relief. Gearhart, "U.S. Escape Clause Law."

20. Lynn R. Edminster, "The 'Escape Clause' in Trade Agreements," January 20, 1948, ITF, RG 43, NA.

21. Memo, August 22, 1951, Brossard Papers, USU. Brossard served for thirty-four years—longer than any other tariff commissioner.

22. TC, *Women's Fur Felt Hats* and *Hatters' Fur.*

23. James E. Webb, Acting SOS, to John R. Steelman, White House, October 6, 1950, and Webb to Truman, November 26, 1951, WHCF, HST.

24. Truman to Ryder, January 7, 1952, 411.003/1-752, RG 59, NA.

25. HRW&M, *Extension of the Reciprocal Trade Agreements Act*, 1951, pp. 23–24.

26. Public Law 50, 82d Cong., 1st sess.

27. HRAC, *Independent Offices Appropriations*, 1:237.

28. Producers of screws, spring clothespins, groundfish fillets, garlic, bicycles, and cherries submitted petitions.

29. TC, *Garlic.* Average imports rose 182 percent in the five years from 1946 to 1951 as compared to the average for the period from 1935 to 1939. Imports averaged 84 percent of domestic production after World War II, but 33 percent before it.

30. Ben Brown Jr, USDS, to Frederick Lawton, BOB, July 11, 1952, and Roger Jones, BOB, to Steelman, White House, July 14, 1952, WHCF, HST. Agriculture had "no objection" to the TC's recommendation and Defense abstained. The Mutual Security Agency strongly favored rejection. Other cabinet agencies—including Interior, Labor, and Commerce—offered adverse comments.

31. USDS, *Bulletin*, August 25, 1952, pp. 303–5.

32. TC, *Watches, Watch Movements.* Brossard, Durand, Gregg, and Edminster composed the majority. Chairman Ryder and George McGill, both Democrats, voted in the negative. The original 1936 bilateral trade agreement contained only a third-country escape clause. In 1950, after the United States threatened to abrogate that agreement, Switzerland agreed to include the standard escape clause language.

33. David Bruce, Undersecretary of State, to Truman, August 1, 1952, WHCF, HST. The Bureau of the Budget surveyed executive agencies and found that only Labor supported the TC recommendation. Roger W. Jones, BOB, to John Steelman, White House, August 1, 1952, OF, HST. Most other agencies "strongly opposed" it. The Defense Department initially

offered no objection but, under pressure, switched course, saying that its interests "are so remote it defers to the view of the other departments more directly concerned." The Mutual Security Agency opposed relief on the grounds that "if we are to reduce our taxes for foreign aid, and still maintain our present export markets, we must largely increase imports from abroad and not further restrict them." Truman's letters to Congress rejecting relief appear in USDS, *Bulletin*, August 25, 1952, p. 305.

34. Truman to chairmen of SNFC and HRW&M, August 14, 1952, WHCF, HST.

35. "Comments on President Truman's Refusal to Use 'Escape Clause' in Trade Agreements," Brossard Papers, USU.

36. "Notes," n.d., Brossard Papers, USU.

37. TC, *Spring Clothespins* (1952), *Groundfish Fillets* (1952), *Glace Cherries*, and *Bonito, Canned in Oil*. As in the spring clothespins case (August 21, 1952), Democrats Ryder, Edminster, and McGill voted against relief and Republicans Brossard and Gregg voted for it in the investigations concerning groundfish fillets (September 4, 1952), cherries (October 17, 1952), and tuna (November 26, 1952).

38. TC, *Bicycles and Parts* and *Figs, Dried*. In the politically sensitive California fig case, Truman did provide temporary relief, modifying a concession made to Turkey in 1951. He suspended the fig tariff concession until June 30, 1953, when a new administration might inherit the problem.

39. "The Reasons for Foreign Aid and Reciprocal Trade," n.d., Post-Presidential Memoirs, HST.

40. Brossard, "Comments on President Truman's Refusal to Use 'Escape Clause' in Trade Agreements," Brossard Papers, USU.

41. Gabriel Hauge Oral History, DDE; Eisenhower to Martin, in USDS, *Bulletin*, March 7, 1955, p. 388.

42. Ferrell, *Eisenhower Diaries*, pp. 242–45.

43. Interdepartmental Committee on the Jeweled Watch Industry to Office of Defense Mobilization, June 30, 1954, WHCF, OF, Confidential, DDE. The Treasury, Foreign Operations Administration, and Departments of Commerce, Defense, and Labor supported the TC's recommendation. CEA offered no comment. In 1982 the ITC (*Effectiveness of Escape Clause Relief*) claimed that this period of escape clause relief had had a "positive effect" in facilitating adjustment.

44. Truman approved escape clause relief in the case of fur hats (Oct. 1950), hatters' fur (Jan. 1952), and figs (Aug. 1952); he rejected it for watches (Aug. 1952) and garlic (July 1952). Eisenhower provided some relief for watches (July 1954), alsike clover seed (June 1954), bicycles (Aug. 1955), linen toweling (June 1956), safety pins (Nov. 1957), spring clothespins (Dec. 1957), stainless steel flatware (Mar. 1958), clinical thermometers (Apr. 1958), lead and zinc (June 1958), and typewriter ribbon cloth (Aug. 1960). He declined relief for brier pipes (Nov. 1953), silk scarves (Aug. 1954), handblown glassware (Sept. 1954), scissors (May 1954), groundfish fillets (July 1954), lead and zinc (Aug. 1954), spring clothespins (Nov. 1954), woodscrews (Dec. 1954), fluorspar (May 1956), para-aminosalicylic salts (Aug. 1956), groundfish fillets (Dec. 1956), velveteen fabrics (Jan. 1957), straight pins (Mar. 1957), umbrella frames (Sept. 1958), tartaric acid (Mar. 1959), and cream of tartar (Mar. 1959).

45. TC, *Tobacco Pipes of Wood*.

46. *FRUS*, 1953, 1:1, 135. The Departments of State, Defense, Treasury, and Interior and the director for Mutual Security advised that the president not approve the TC recommendation. Only Labor supported it. Agriculture took no position. To delay a decision and to obtain more information, Eisenhower established a precedent. He referred a TC recom-

mendation back for more information. See Minnich memo, March 12, 1953, Sherman Adams Papers, Dartmouth College. State emphasized the adverse effect on southern France and Italy. And Defense claimed that the negative impact on foreign military and economic assistance programs would outweigh advantages to the domestic tobacco pipe industry from tariff increases. BOB to Gabriel Hauge, October 13, 1953, WHCF, DDE.

47. Ferrell, *Eisenhower Diaries*, pp. 228–29.

48. Eisenhower to Millikin, November 10, 1953, WHCF, DDE.

49. USDS, *Bulletin*, November 30, 1953, pp. 754–55.

50. TC, *Bicycles*, 1955. Republicans Brossard, Talbot, and Schreiber voted in the affirmative. Democrat Edminster joined the majority in part. Democrat Sutton dissented.

51. "Economic Committee," Washington Embassy, March 15, 23, 1955, FO 371/114922, PRO.

52. *FRUS*, 1955–57, 9:110–11.

53. Ibid., 9:112, 142–43. Secretary of Agriculture Ezra Taft Benson said that his aides thought higher bicycle tariffs would "seriously impede our efforts to obtain liberalization of existing restrictions against import of agricultural products into the United Kingdom, West Germany, and France." Ibid., 9:126–27. For agency responses, see BOB, April 20, 1955, to Gabriel Hauge, WHCF, DDE.

54. USDS, *Bulletin*, September 5, 1955, pp. 401–2. Importers challenged the president's decision in the U.S. Customs Court, claiming that he lacked the authority to modify the commission's recommendation. After the Court of Customs and Patent Appeals sustained the lower court's ruling in behalf of importers, President Kennedy proclaimed new tariff levels pursuant to U.S. obligations under GATT. *Schmidt Pritchard & Co., Mangano Cycles Co. v. United States*, C.D. 2029, October 6, 1958.

55. "Economic Committee," Washington Embassy, August 23, 1955, FO 371/114923, PRO.

56. HRW&M, *Foreign Trade and Tariff Proposals Hearings*, p. 5667; ITC, *Effectiveness of Escape Clause Relief*, p. vi.

57. USDS to BOB, November 2, 1953, WHCF, DDE; TC, *Hand-blown Glassware*.

58. Thorsten V. Kalijarvi, USDS, to Rowland Hughes, BOB, April 20, 1954, and Richard Buddeke, USDOD, to Hughes, April 21, 1954, WHCF, DDE. See also TC, *Scissors and Shears*.

59. Dulles to Eisenhower, August 12, 1954, 411.003/8-1254, RG 59, NA; TC, *Lead and Zinc*. Within the administration State, Defense, and the Foreign Operations Administration opposed an increase in tariff rates. Interior, the agency most familiar with mining problems, strongly endorsed the TC plan; Labor did not oppose it. Roger Jones, BOB, to Gabriel Hauge, White House, June 8, 1954, WHCF, DDE. Secretary of Commerce Weeks favored seeking further information from the TC; Treasury preferred offering subsidies to producers so as to avoid diplomatic repercussions.

60. *FRUS*, 1952–54, 6:1537–44.

61. TC, *Groundfish Fillets*, 1954. According to the TC report, the share of the domestic markets supplied by U.S. processors of fillets had declined from 95 percent in 1939 to 70 percent in 1947 and about 50 percent in 1953. Richard Buddeke, USDOD, to Rowland Hughes, BOB, June 7, 1954, OF, DDE.

62. TC, *Groundfish Fillets*, 1956; Hoover to Eisenhower, November 12, 1956, 411.006/11-956, RG 59, NA; Edwin A. Arnold, ICA, to Phillip S. Hughes, BOB, November 8, 1956, WHCF, DDE. Three departments supported the TC remedy: Interior, Labor, and Agriculture. Six opposed it: State, Defense, Treasury, Commerce, the Council of Economic Advisers, and ICA. See also Gabriel Hauge to Eisenhower, December 6, 1956, Ann Whitman File: Administration, DDE.

63. TC, *Groundfish Fillets*, 1954; ITC, *Conditions of Competition.*

64. TC, *Screen-printed Silk Scarves.* At the interagency review level, only Labor supported the unanimous TC recommendation. USDS, *Bulletin*, January 10, 1955, pp. 52–53.

65. Director of Mutual Security to BOB, May 26, 1953, WHCF, DDE.

66. TC, *Cotton Velveteen Fabrics.* In the 1955 bilateral agreement with Japan, the United States had lowered the duty on velveteens despite opposition from the Commerce Department. Soon, surging Japanese imports captured 67.3 percent of domestic consumption. *FRUS*, 1955–57, 23:247–48; USDS, *Bulletin*, February 11, 1957, p. 219; William S. Kilborne to Secretary Weeks, "Japanese Cotton Textiles," February 17, 1956, Weeks Papers, Dartmouth College.

67. Koichiro Asakai, Embassy of Japan, to Secretary Dulles, February 21, 1958, 411.944/2-2158, and MacArthur to SOS, January 20, 1958, 411.944/1-2058, RG 59, NA; *FRUS*, 1955–57, 23:330.

68. Hauge to Eisenhower, March 6, 1958; Hauge to Adams, September 10, 1957; Bush to Eisenhower, September 12, 1959, and Eisenhower to Bush, September 23, 1959—all in WHCF, DDE.

69. Diary, Randall Papers, June 21, 1954, DDE.

70. Interview, September 1966, Columbia University Oral History Project, Bush Oral History, DDE.

71. TC, *Safety Pins.*

72. Hauge to Adams, November 27, 1957, WHCF, DDE.

73. Ris, " 'Escape Clause' Relief," p. 302.

74. HRW&M, *Trade Agreements Extension Act of 1958*, pp. 8–13, 79–81. Senior Republicans, including former chairman Dan Reed, issued a stinging minority report rejecting the administration's voluntary restraint agreements.

75. Metzger, "Trade Expansion Act of 1962," pp. 442–47; HRW&M, *Trade Expansion Act of 1962: Hearings*, pp. 1147, 1166. One of the House critics, Congressman Jackson Betts of Ohio, later recalled his prophetic opposition to "the absence of effective safeguards." In 1971 he cited a list of industries "severely injured by excessive import competition." These included ceramic tile; electronic products such as radios, televisions, and components; and china and earthenware, flat glass, textiles and apparel, basic steel, specialty and tool steel, footwear, motor vehicles, motorcycles and bicycles, toys, and sporting goods. *Congressional Record*, July 29, 1971, H-7432.

76. General Counsel to TC, "Causal Relationship between Increased Imports and Trade Agreement Concessions," memo, December 14, 1962, TC, pp. 10–11, ITC Law Library; Fulda, "Adjustment to Hardship Caused by Imports." According to the Senate Finance Committee, provisions of the Trade Expansion Act "have proven to be an inadequate mechanism for providing relief to domestic industries injured by import competition." SNFC, *Trade Reform Act of 1974*, p. 119.

77. Clubb, *United States Foreign Trade Law*, 1:731.

78. Stewart, "Import Competition and Governmental Relief," in CITIP, *Interdependent World* (compendium), 1:225–27.

79. Metzger, in CITIP, *Interdependent World*, 1:189.

80. Bill Timmons to Bryce N. Harlow, December 19, 1969, WHCF, RMN.

81. Harry S. Dent discusses Nixon's campaign commitment to the textile industry in *Prodigal South Returns*, pp. 198–207. See also *Public Papers . . . Nixon*, 1969, pp. 940–45; Harlow to Peter Flanigan, February 21, 1970, WHCF, RMN.

82. Kissinger to Peter Flanigan and Flanigan to Nixon, December 30, 1969, WHCF,

RMN. Economist C. Fred Bergsten handled the carpet issue for Kissinger. He argued: "Maintenance of any protection for carpets would . . . be completely inconsistent with the basic principles of U.S. trade policy. In my judgment, it would be folly to override them in this first escape clause case of this Administration." Bergsten to Kissinger, December 29, 1969, ibid.

83. CITIP, *Interdependent World*, pp. 49–50.

84. Quoted in 19 USC 2251(b)(2)–(4); Levinson, "Title II of the Trade Act of 1974," pp. 197–232.

85. SNFN, *Trade Reform Act of 1974*, p. 124.

86. For a study of Carter administration efforts to promote adjustment, see Cohen and Meltzer, *United States International Economic Policy in Action*, pp. 91–122. In 1984 the domestic nonrubber footwear industry lost a unanimous decision at the ITC; it prevailed on the basis of a new record in 1985.

87. Author interview with a former Commerce official; Bergsten to Kissinger, September 16, 1970, WHCF, RMN.

88. Rogers to Nixon, February 24, 1971, WHCF, RMN.

89. ITC, *Footwear*; Destler, *Making Foreign Economic Policy*, p. 187.

90. Scowcroft to Ford, April 12, 1976, Seidman Papers, GRF.

91. Kissinger-Simon memo, April 7, 1976, Seidman Papers, GRF. Secretary of Agriculture Earl L. Butz agreed, saying that shoe restrictions would "adversely affect" up to $2 billion in soybean and corn exports to the EEC and Spain. Butz to Ford, April 8, 1976, PHF, GRF. The adjustment assistance option, which Ford approved, also had support from the Council of Economic Advisers, Justice Department, National Security Council, Domestic Council, and Office of Management and Budget. However, adjustment assistance combined with a tariff rate quota had the endorsement of the STR, Commerce, Labor, Defense, and Council on International Economic Policy. See Seidman to Ford, April 12, 1976, PHF, GRF.

92. *Public Papers . . . Ford*, 1976, pp. 346–48.

93. ITC, *Footwear*; Brzezinski to Carter, drafted by Robert Hormats, March 16, 1977, and Wolff, STR, to Vice President and other members of the Economic Policy Group, February 4, 1977, WHCF, JC. The Wolff memo contains a State Department assessment of foreign policy aspects.

94. *Public Papers . . . Carter*, 1977, pp. 550–52; Wolff to Carter, February 4, 1977, WHCF, JC.

95. ITC, *Nonrubber Footwear*.

96. *Public Papers . . . Reagan*, 1985, p. 1015; ITC, *Footwear*.

97. ITC, *Leather Wearing Apparel*; Tim Deal to Christine Dodson, March 20, 1980, National Security Council, WHCF, JC.

98. Hormats notes, Rambouillet Summit, November 16, 1975, Seidman Papers, GRF.

99. Kissinger and Simon to Ford, June 5, 1976, PHF, GRF. Clayton Yeutter, then a deputy USTR, accused Kissinger and Simon of an "absence of domestic political sensitivity." Showing his own political sensitivity, Yeutter contended: "their proposal is a real loser in domestic political terms. It certainly will not gain the President one additional delegate between now and Convention time, and it could lose him some." Yeutter to Seidman, June 7, 1976, Seidman Papers, GRF.

100. Strauss to Carter, n.d.; TPSC Task Force on Copper, October 10, 1978; Owen to Carter, October 18, 1978; Tim Deal to Christine Dodson, October 18, 1978—all in WHCF, JC.

101. Richard O. Cunningham, "The Copper Problem," p. 14.

102. ITC, *Bolts, Nuts, and Large Screws*.

103. Bob Ginsburg to Stu Eizenstat, February 15, 1978, WHCF, JC.

104. ITC, *Bolts, Nuts, and Large Screws.*

105. Strauss to Carter, December 20, 1978, and Stu Eizenstat and Howard Gruenspecht to Carter, December 22, 1978, WHCF, JC. Carter issued a proclamation raising duties on January 4, 1979, the day he sent Congress information about agreements in the multilateral trade negotiations. *Public Papers . . . Carter,* 1979, pp. 3–7.

106. For an official history of textile restraints during the Johnson administration, see vol. 10, document 1459, *DDC.*

107. ITC, *Certain Motor Vehicles.*

108. Carter to Alberger, July 9, 1980, WHCF, JC.

109. Had the commission voted before the presidential election, or had Carter won, the domestic auto industry probably would have prevailed. One commissioner construed Carter's defeat at the polls as providing freedom to vote against protection for the U.S. industry. A second probably would have shifted sides, producing at least a 4-to-1 vote for escape clause relief.

110. Eizenstat, Hormats, and Owen to Carter, October 16, 1980, WHCF, JC. For a partial list of clients of the three former commissioners, see Choate, *Agents of Influence,* pp. 208–45.

111. ITC, *Carbon and Certain Alloy Steel Products.* Voting in the affirmative were Commissioners Alfred Eckes, Seeley Lodwick, and David B. Rohr; in the negative, Commissioners Paula Stern and Susan Liebeler. Of the three who voted against the U.S. auto industry in 1980, only Stern remained.

112. Niskanen, *Reaganomics,* pp. 139–44.

113. Blecker, Lee, and Scott, "Trade Protection and Industrial Revitalization"; ITC, *Economic Effects of Significant U.S. Import Restraints, Phase 1: Manufacturing,* 1989.

114. The Harley Davidson case illustrates a firm's successful use of a period of relief to become export competitive. It is noteworthy that the ITC voted 2 to 1 to provide relief to domestic producers of finished motorcycles, with Veronica Haggart and Alfred Eckes, both Reagan Republican appointees, providing the affirmative votes, and Paula Stern, a Carter-appointed Democrat, casting a negative ballot. The decision split conservatives. Columnist William F. Buckley decried President Reagan for accepting the *unanimous* ITC recommendation: "he has given away the free-trade banner." *New York Daily News,* April 12, 1983. Stern set Buckley's facts straight. "Having voted against protection, I plead innocent," Stern said. "[I]t was my two Republican colleagues appointed by President Reagan who voted for the sharp tariff hike on imported motorcycles."

115. *Public Papers . . . Reagan,* 1987, pp. 476–78. For a more general discussion, see Reid, *Well Made in America.*

116. Tom Wasinger, "Fashioning an Industrial Relief Act," *Wall Street Journal,* June 21, 1984.

117. *Public Papers . . . Reagan,* 1985, p. 1015.

118. *USX Corp. v. U.S.,* 682 F. Supp. 60 (CIT 1988).

119. Tonelson ("Beating Back Predatory Trade") shows that import relief succeeded in facilitating adjustment in five major industries—automobiles, steel, machine tools, semiconductors, and textiles.

120. Other statutes, administered in the Labor Department, to provide adjustment assistance to import-impacted firms, industries, and workers also operated poorly. Aho and Bayard, "Costs and Benefits of Trade Adjustment Assistance." See also Destler, *American Trade Politics,* pp. 140–42; Hufbauer and Rosen, *Trade Policy for Troubled Industries.*

CHAPTER EIGHT

1. Economists frequently cite Jacob Viner's definition of dumping as "price-discrimination between national markets." Viner, *Dumping*, p. 3. Many academic economists defend dumping, claiming that it benefits consumers. Congress has taken a different view. In writing the 1979 act, the Finance Committee labeled dumping and subsidies "pernicious practices" that "distort international trade to the disadvantage of United States commerce." SNFN, *Trade Agreements Act of 1979*, p. 37.

2. HRW&M, *Agreements Reached in the Tokyo Round*, p. 312.

3. Ohmae, *Borderless World*, pp. 51–52; Drucker, *New Realities*. See also Abegglen and Stalk, *Kaisha*, p. 37; James, *Trojan Horse*, pp. 27–28. For a trade lawyer's perspective, see Stewart, "Administration of the Antidumping Law," pp. 288–330.

4. For a discussion of the static and dynamic effects of dumping in a contemporary context, see Labor-Industry Coalition for International Trade, *Antidumping Reform*, pp. 39–48.

5. ITC, *Certain Amplifier Assemblies*.

6. ITC, *Cell-Site Transceivers and Subassemblies*.

7. ITC, *64-K Dynamic Random Access Memory Components, Erasable Programmable Read Only Memories* and *Dynamic Random Access Memory Semiconductors*. For background, see Finan and LaMond, "Sustaining U.S. Competitiveness in Microelectronics"; Prestowitz, *Trading Places*, pp. 147–78; Tyson, *Who's Bashing Whom?*, pp. 137–38.

8. On steel dumping, see Hogan, *Economic History of the Iron and Steel Industry*, 2:783–89.

9. Canada approved an antidumping law in 1904, followed by Australia in 1906, South Africa in 1914, and the United States in 1916. Viner, *Dumping*, p. 86.

10. TC, *Information concerning Dumping*, pp. 22–23,

11. Redfield to Wilson, February 4, 1916, 36:127; William Gibbs McAdoo to Wilson, January 14, 1916, pp. 35:475; Joseph P. Tumulty to Wilson, August 10, 1916, 38:21—all in Link, *Wilson*. U.S. manufacturers of toy trains complained that Japanese sold toy train sets "at a price that is not sufficient for the American manufacturer to purchase the box in which they are packed." TC, *Information concerning Dumping*, pp. 10–17.

12. Almstedt, "International Price Discrimination."

13. Clubb, *Foreign Trade Law*, 2:719; Ehrenhaft, "Antidumping and Countervailing Duty Provisions," p. 1365.

14. Bidwell, *Invisible Tariff*, p. 105.

15. Ehrenhaft, "Antidumping and Countervailing Duty Provisions," p. 1398.

16. Adam Smith, *Wealth of Nations*, pp. 472–89. For Hamilton's comment, see Syrett, *Hamilton*, 10:268–69.

17. Feller, "Mutiny against the Bounty"; Mangan, "Trade Agreements Act of 1979."

18. Horlick, "Current Issues in the Definition and Measurement of Subsidies." Horlick, a former deputy assistant secretary of commerce for import administration, had responsibilities for administering antidumping and countervailing duty law from 1981 to 1983.

19. For parties involved in such a proceeding, Treasury procedures resembled those of the Star Chamber. Until 1967 Treasury provided no public notice of an investigation. It did not publish negative determinations until 1974, and it did not publish explanations for its determinations.

20. UST, *Annual Report*, p. 416; General Counsel to SOT, March 17, 1939, and Attorney General to SOT, March 18, 1939, MD 200, FDR; Hawkins, *Commercial Treaties*, p. 133.

21. Canadian products included chair seats, rugs, sheathing paper, wheat flour, fountain syringes, raspberries, iron oxide, sole leather, plastic brick, and roofing. The British goods were tissue paper, cut glassware, photo plates, high-pressure tube gage glass, and canvas. There were also three Czechoslovakian products: earthenware cereal sets, decorated china-ware jugs, and chinaware cereal sets, as well as one item each from Austria (hamburgs), Italy (peeled tomatoes in tins), and Switzerland (hamburgs). During the 1921–March 1933 period fifteen orders applied to Canadian goods, eight to German products, and seven to English items. SNFN, *Compendium of Papers*, 1:187.

22. One against Sweden (hardboard), the United Kingdom (cast iron soil pipe), and Czechoslovakia (bicycles). Calculated from UST, *Annual Report*, FY 1968, p. 416. See also SNFN, *Antidumping: Hearings*, pp. 48–56.

23. Three affected Canada (steel items); one involved Japan (azobisformamide) and one Australia (chromic acid). SNFN, *Compendium of Papers*, 1:187.

24. Bidwell, *Invisible Tariff*, pp. 100–101.

25. USDS, 611.0031/Executive Committee/799, April 10, 1935, RG 59, NA.

26. USDS, 611.0031/Executive Committee/799, February 6, 1934, ibid.

27. USDS, 611.0031/Executive Committee/799, November 1936–January 1937, ibid.

28. USDS, 611.0031/Executive Committee/799, February 6, March 20, April 6, 10, 1934, ibid. Treasury also reversed its initial decision to impose countervailing duties on British refined sugar after State and Agriculture entered objections. USDS, 611.0031/Executive Committee/799, September 12, 19, 1934, ibid.

29. Editorial, "Dumping by Japan," *Washington Post*, August 6, 1932.

30. USDS, 611.006 Fly Paper/1, 14, 16, August 1939–January 1940, RG 59, NA.

31. USDS, 611.423 Pulp/37, December 11, 1939, ibid.

32. Conversation with Roosevelt, April 14, 1936, MD 21, and Minutes of Meeting, May 29, 1936, MD 25, FDR. State sought to discourage Treasury action against foreign multiple currency systems. SOS to SOT, April 2, 1936, MD 20; Francis Sayre memo, May 4, 1936, MD 23; SOS to SOT, November 19, 1938, MD 151—all in FDR.

33. Blum discusses Treasury countervailing duty enforcement against Nazi Germany in MD 1 (pp. 149–52) and MD 2 (pp. 78–81). See also Bidwell, *Invisible Tariff*, pp. 96–97.

34. Minutes of meeting, January 7, 1938, USDS, 611.0031/Executive Committee/799, RG 59, NA. In July 1939 an interagency committee proposed adding an injury test to U.S. countervailing duty law. Drafting Committee to Committee on Trade Barriers, September 23, 1944, RG 43, NA.

35. Roth to Trade Executive Committee regarding Special Study of Antidumping Field, September 27, 1963, TEC-D-13/63; TSC Subcommittee on Antidumping Laws, Report, April 3, 1964, box 5, Herter Papers; Robert Hudec to Ambassador William Roth, April 1, 1964, box 5, Herter Papers—all in JFK.

36. Hawkins, *Commercial Treaties*, pp. 135–36; Hawkins to Francis Sayre, December 23, 1937 (RG 43), memo, "Some Considerations of Policy," December 21, 1937 (RG 43), Minutes of meeting, January 7, 1938, 611.0031/Executive Committee/799 (RG 59), and G. Hayden Raynor to Livingston Merchant, January 3, 1955 411.60E6/1-355 (RG 59)—all in NA.

37. HRW&M, *Amendments to Antidumping Act of 1921*, pp. 134–37.

38. Ibid., pp. 148–49.

39. SNFN, *Hearings on H.R. 6006*, pp. 48–56.

40. Samuel C. Waugh to Secretary Humphrey, September 11, 1953, 411.60E6/9-1153, RG 59, NA. State also complained about a Treasury antidumping investigation involving rayon staple fibers from ten European countries. Thorsten V. Kalijarvi, USDS, to H. Chapman

Rose, Treasury, February 2, 1954, 411.006/2-254, ibid. On April 13, 1954, the Operations Coordinating Board of the National Security Council requested Treasury to delay a formal order withholding appraisement of Finnish hardboard. The order would have disrupted hardboard shipments to the United States. Walter B. Smith, to Secretary Humphrey, April 13, 1954, 411.60E6/4-1354, ibid. State held that other agencies should subordinate actions to foreign economic policy priorities. *FRUS*, 1952–54, 1:80.

41. The complainant, the American Hardwood Plywood Institute, discussed its problems dealing with Treasury in HRW&M, *Hearings on H.R. 6006*, pp. 141–58.

42. HRW&M, *Customs Simplification Act of 1954: Hearings on H.R. 10009*, p. 49, and *Hearings on H.R. 6006*, pp. 98–102.

43. Customs Simplification Act of 1954, Public Law 83–768, September 1, 1954; Public Law 85–630, August 14, 1958.

44. UST, *Annual Report*, 1968–69; Customs Commissioner to Assistant Secretary True Davis, April 6, 1967; and Davis to SOT, April 28, 1967, Fowler Papers, LBJ.

45. TC, *Hot-Rolled Carbon Steel Wire Rods*; Metzger, *Lowering Nontariff Barriers*, pp. 69–98; Shannon and Marx, "International Antidumping Code."

46. Metzger, *Lowering Nontariff Barriers*, pp. 65–66; Hartland-Thunberg, "Tales of a Onetime Tariff Commissioner." During this period State continued to influence the choice of tariff commissioners. Three individuals chaired the commission during the Kennedy-Johnson administrations. Each was a Washington insider who supported the trade liberalization program. Ben Dorfman, formerly TC's chief economist, was a delegate to four GATT negotiations. Paul Kaplowitz, formerly TC's general counsel, drafted the GATT in 1947. Stanley Metzger, a former State Department legal adviser and Georgetown University law professor, was generally known as a "fundamentalist free trader." Metzger file, John W. Macy personnel files, LBJ.

47. Hudec to Roth, April 5, 1964, Herter Papers, JFK.

48. SNFC, *International Antidumping Code: Hearings*, pp. 142, 152.

49. For Rossides' speech on June 28, 1972, see "Antidumping and Countervailing Duty Laws: Instruments for Freer Trade," WHCF, RMN. Tariff commissioner Bruce Clubb, a Republican lawyer from Minnesota appointed by President Johnson, initiated the trend to more vigorous enforcement in injury investigations.

50. HRW&M, *Administration of the Antidumping Act of 1921*, pp. 55–65, 108–13; David Gunning to Robert Miller, May 8, 1972, and Peter Flanigan to Rossides, March 29, 1972, WHCF, RMN. On shifting enforcement during the Nixon years, see annual "Administrative Survey" in *Law and Policy in International Business*.

51. HRW&M, *Oversight of the Antidumping Act of 1921*, pp. 2, 6, 19.

52. Ibid., p. 88.

53. Ibid.

54. HRW&M, *Administration of the Antidumping Act of 1921*, p. 111.

55. TC, *Television Receiving Sets from Japan*.

56. Robert W. Miller to Peter Flanigan, May 11, 1972, and Dave Gunning to Miller, May 8, 1972 (quotation), WHCF, RMN; HRW&M, *Administration of the Antidumping Act of 1921*, pp. 61–65; John J. Nevin, "Enforcing the Antidumping Laws"; Kennedy, "*Zenith Radio Corp. v. United States.*"

57. HRW&M, *Administration of the Antidumping Act of 1921*, p. 57. Chairman Vanik's subcommittee heard testimony from a variety of industries that Treasury did not adequately enforce existing laws.

58. Former deputy U.S. trade representative Alan Wolff ("International Competitiveness

of American Industry," p. 322) describes this episode as "an appalling display of governmental ineptitude. . . . the case demonstrated nothing more than bureaucratic incompetency in calculating and applying dumping duties."

59. Ibid., pp. 98–110; *American Metal Market,* July 23, 1991; HRW&M, *Administration of the Antidumping Act of 1921,* p. 113 (Simmons).

60. MacDonald to Simon, June 14, 1976, MacDonald Papers, GRF.

61. David Rohr, former HRW&M trade subcommittee staff director, interview with author, August 9, 1994.

62. Jerome, *U.S. Senate Decision-Making.* See generally Destler, *American Trade Politics;* Nivola, *Regulating Unfair Trade.*

63. HRW&M, *Trade Agreements Extension Act of 1979,* p. 48.

64. Of the 290 orders, 15 involved members of the former Soviet Union. Commerce extended a 1968 antidumping code on titanium sponge to 15 successor nations, including Russia and the Ukraine. Data obtained on October 4, 1994, from ITC Office of Investigations. During 1984–85 the number of outstanding countervailing duty orders surged from 56 to 86. GATT, *Trade Policy Review,* 1:104. On September 30, 1994, the U.S. government had 100 countervailing duty orders in place. Of these orders, 12 concerned imports from Argentina, 10 products of Brazil, and 8 imports from Thailand. None involved Japan or China. Three orders applied to products from Korea and 1 to items from Taiwan. U.S. President, *Annual Report . . . on the Trade Agreements Program,* 1981, pp. 173–74.

65. *USX Corporation v. U.S.,* 682 F. Supp. 60 (1988). Reviewing courts instructed Commerce and the ITC to administer U.S. law, not the GATT rules. *Algoma Steel Corp., LTD. v. United States,* 688 F. Supp. 639 (CIT 1988), *aff'd* 865 F.2d 240, 242 (Fed. Cir. 1989). See also *Timken Co. v. United States,* 673 F. Supp. 495, 520–21.

66. ITC Office of Investigations to author, October 4, 1994.

67. Suomela, *Free Trade versus Fair Trade,* pp. 44–48, 142.

68. Boltuck and Litan's *Down in the Dumps* presents a critical look at unfair trade laws. The editors—and many contributors to this volume—represented foreign interests opposed to these laws. Free-lance journalist James Bovard offers a polemical critique in *Fair Trade Fraud.*

69. *Financial Times,* June 16, 1989; Bentsen and Rostenkowski to Brunsdale and Cass, June 22, 1989.

70. "Dumping on Importers," *Journal of Commerce,* June 30, 1994; Bruce Arnold, "U.S. Antidumping and Countervailing-Duty Law: A Policy Untethered from Its Rationale," Congressional Budget Office draft, May 2, 1994, p. 141.

71. Jackson, *World Trading System,* pp. 217–20, 244–45. OTA (*Multinationals and the National Interest*) notes that the interests of multinationals "do not always conform to those of the United States" (p. iii).

EPILOGUE

1. Richardson, *Messages,* 1:214–15.

2. Ibid., 12:5746.

3. *Congressional Globe,* April 23, 1860, p. 1832; Allen, "Great Protectionist," p. 341 (Smoot).

4. On Cobden's "grand panacea," see Hinde, *Cobden,* pp. 28–29, 170–71. Ironically, in Asian countries List still inspires policymakers. James Fallows, "How the World Works," p.

61. Officials in Korea and Japan often read List for inspiration. Long ago, economist Thorstein Veblen anticipated that Japan might successfully implement German economic theories. Veblen, *Imperial Germany and the Industrial Revolution*. In his *MITI and the Japanese Miracle* (pp. 15–17), Chalmers Johnson notes the influence of German nationalists.

5. *Public Papers . . . Bush*, 1992, pp. 1930, 2350–65.

6. For general discussion, see Dicken, *Global Shift*, pp. 97–119.

7. Hull, *Memoirs*, 1:355. Feis to Joseph B. Wood, May 26, 1932, 611.003/2592, RG 59, NA.

8. Estimates of Clinton's vote buying for NAFTA range from $300 million to $50 billion. Charles Lewis, "The NAFTA-Math: Clinton Got His Trade Deal, but How Many Millions Did it Cost the Nation?," *Washington Post*, December 26, 1993. For a discussion of twenty-one congressional deals, see Boyer, Wallach, and Watzman, *NAFTA'S Bizarre Bazaar*. On Uruguay Round deals, see *Journal of Commerce*, December 2, 1994.

9. Hull, *Memoirs*, 1:81.

10. Reagan, *American Life*, pp. 240–41.

11. Reginald Maudling to Prime Minister Macmillan, October 27, 1959, BT 11/5771, PRO.

12. As noted earlier, the Nixon administration did attempt to enforce trade laws.

13. SNFN, *Oversight Hearings on U.S. Foreign Trade Policy*, p. 105.

14. UNCTAD, *Handbook*, 1993, pp. 16–18.

15. *Public Papers . . . Clinton*, 1993, p. 323; Kantor, "U.S. Trade Policy."

16. The National Association of Manufacturers (NAM) had a number of "serious concerns" about the final accords. NAM statement, Draft No. 4, January 21, 1994, copy in possession of author.

17. *International Herald Tribune*, December 16, 1993.

18. Ibid.; *Financial Times*, December 16, 1993.

19. A source familiar with the conduct of the Uruguay Round indicates that Reagan administration officials agreed to mandatory dispute settlement early in the negotiations. Bush and Clinton negotiators did not reopen the issue. Although Congress listed "more effective and expeditious dispute settlement mechanisms" among the U.S. negotiating objectives in the Omnibus Trade and Competitiveness Act of 1988, it did not stipulate mandatory dispute resolution. HRW&M, *Omnibus Trade and Competitiveness Act of 1988*, p. 16.

20. Phillips, *Arrogant Capital*, p. 71.

21. *Business Week*, August 10, 1992, p. 1, August 15, 1994, p. 78; *Fortune*, December 14, 1992, pp. 6, 52; *Economist*, October 1, 1994, p. 70+. Sociologists Stanley Aronowitz and William DiFazio (*Jobless Future*) forecast massive displacement of American employees at all levels in the technology-driven economic order.

22. Goldsmith, *The Trap*, pp. 25–51 (quotations, 25, 37).

23. Krugman and Lawrence, *Trade, Jobs, and Wages*, pp. 1–2, 18; U.S. President, *Economic Report*, 1994, pp. 118, 213. See also Lawrence and Slaughter, *Trade and U.S. Wages*. But see Mishel and Bernstein's *Is the Technology Black Box Empty?*, p. 3. They contend that "technology was not the dominant force driving wage inequality."

24. Borjas, Freeman, and Katz, "Labor Market Effects of Immigration and Trade." They estimated that 30 to 50 percent of the approximately ten percentage point decline in relative weekly wages of high school dropouts between 1980 and 1988 resulted from trade and immigration flows. See also Batra and Slottje, "Trade Policy and Poverty," p. 204; Sachs and Shatz, "Trade and Jobs in U.S. Manufacturing," p. 2; Leamer, "Wage Effects of a U.S. Mexican Free Trade Agreement," p. 1.

25. Sidgwick, *Principles of Political Economy*, pp. 495–96; Marx, *Poverty of Philosophy*, p. 227.

26. President Clinton, remarks before departing for Naples G-7 Summit in July 1994.

27. *Journal of Commerce*, October 21, 1994, p. 12A.

28. *Economist*, August 1843, preliminary no., p. 15; Cobden, *Speeches*, p. 187; Richardson, *Messages*, 14:6619–20.

29. *Columbus Dispatch*, October 20, 1994.

30. Taussig, *Tariff History*, p. 526.

Bibliography

This bibliography is organized as follows:
  Manuscript Sources
  Published Official Documents
  Statistics
  Newspapers and Periodicals
  Books
  Articles, Papers, and Dissertations

MANUSCRIPT SOURCES

Official Documents

CANADA
Ottawa
  National Archives of Canada
    Manuscript Group 26
    Richard Bedford Bennett Papers
    William Lyon Mackenzie King Papers
    Record Group 20: Department of Trade and Commerce
    Record Group 25: Department of External Affairs

UNITED KINGDOM
Kew, England
  Public Record Office
    BT 11, BT 205: Board of Trade
    CAB 32: Cabinet
    CO 1016: Colonial Office
    FO 371: Foreign Office
    PREM 1, PREM 4, PREM 8, PREM 11: Prime Minister's Papers

UNITED STATES
Abilene, Kansas
  Dwight D. Eisenhower Library
    Sherman Adams Papers
    Philip Areeda Papers
    Prescott Bush Oral History
    Dwight D. Eisenhower Papers
      Cabinet Series
      DDE Diaries Series
      Legislative Meetings Series
      Ann Whitman Diary Series
    Bryce Harlow Oral History and Papers
    Gabriel Hauge Oral History and Papers

George Humphrey Papers
David W. Kendall Oral History and Papers
Gerald Morgan Papers
Don Paarlberg Oral History and Papers
Clarence Randall Papers
Glenn Sutton Oral History
Samuel Waugh Papers
Sinclair Weeks Oral History
U.S. Commission on Foreign Economic Policy
White House Central Files
White House, Office of Special Assistant for Executive Appointments
Ann Arbor, Michigan
Gerald R. Ford Library
Philip Buchen Papers
James Cannon Papers
Gerald R. Ford Papers
President's Handwriting File
White House Central File
David MacDonald Papers
William Seidman Papers
Atlanta, Georgia
Jimmy Carter Library
Jimmy Carter Papers
Domestic Policy File (Stuart Eizenstat)
President's Handwriting File
White House Central Files
Austin, Texas
Lyndon B. Johnson Library
George Ball Papers
Henry Fowler Papers
Lawrence Fox Oral History
E. Ernest Goldstein Oral History
Lyndon B. Johnson Papers
Administrative Histories (State, Agriculture)
Cabinet Papers
National Security File
Office Files of White House Aides: E. Ernest Goldstein, Harry C. McPherson,
John W. Macy Jr., DeVier Pierson
White House Central Files
White House Personnel Office
W. DeVier Pierson Oral History
William Roth Papers
John A. Schnittker Oral History
U.S. Department of Agriculture
Boston, Massachusetts
John F. Kennedy Library
Myer Feldman Papers

Christian Herter Papers
John F. Kennedy Papers
White House Central Files
Howard Petersen Papers
College Park, Maryland
Richard Nixon Collection, National Archives
Arthur Burns Papers
Peter Flanigan Papers
Richard Nixon Papers
President's Handwriting File
White House Central File
Herbert Stein Papers
Hyde Park, New York
Franklin D. Roosevelt Library
Adolf A. Berle Papers
Mordecai Ezekiel Papers
Herbert Gaston Papers
Henry Morgenthau Papers
Franklin D. Roosevelt Papers
Official File
President's Personal File
Charles Taussig Papers
Independence, Missouri
Harry S. Truman Library
Winthrop G. Brown Oral History
Thomas C. Blaisdell Jr. Papers
Honore Catudal Oral History and Papers
Clark M. Clifford Papers
Emilio Collado Oral History
Joseph F. Coppock Oral History and Papers
John Dickey Oral History
George M. Elsey Papers
Lynn R. Edminster Papers
John Leddy Oral History
Edward Mason Oral History
LeRoy Stinebower Oral History
Harry S. Truman Papers
Post-Presidential Papers
Senate Papers
White House Central Files
Raymond Vernon Oral History
Washington, D.C.
Manuscript Division, Library of Congress
Nelson Aldrich Papers
Henry J. Allen Papers
Hugo Black Papers
William Borah Papers

Tom J. Connally Papers
James Couzens Papers
William S. Culbertson Papers
Bronson Cutting Papers
Norman Davis Papers
Herbert Feis Papers
Henry Fletcher Papers
Frank L. Greene Papers
Averell Harriman Papers
Cordell Hull Papers
Philander Knox Papers
Robert La Follette Jr. Papers
Charles McNary Papers
Ogden L. Mills Papers
Justin Morrill Papers
George Norris Papers
Key Pittman Papers
Francis Sayre Papers
Charles P. Taft Papers
Robert A. Taft Papers
William Howard Taft Papers
Thomas J. Walsh Papers
David A. Wells Papers
National Archives
Record Group 20: Office of Special Adviser to President on Foreign Trade
Record Group 43: Department of State, International Trade Files
Record Group 46: U.S. Senate
Record Group 59: Department of State (including microfilm)
Record Group 81: U.S. Tariff Commission
Record Group 233: U.S. House of Representatives
Record Group 353: Records of Interdepartmental Committees
Record Group 364: Records of Special Representative for Trade Negotiations,
Committee for Reciprocity Information
U.S. International Trade Commission Law Library
General Counsel's Memoranda to the Commission, 1930–85
Russell Shewmaker Papers
West Branch, Iowa
Herbert C. Hoover Library
E. Dana Durand Papers
Herbert Hoover Papers
Commerce Papers
Post-Presidential Papers
Presidential Papers

Private Collections
Ann Arbor, Michigan
University of Michigan
Arthur Vandenberg Papers

Boulder, Colorado
    University of Colorado
        Edward P. Costigan Papers
        Eugene Millikin Papers
Cambridge, Massachusetts
    Harvard University
        Frank Taussig Papers
Chapel Hill, North Carolina
    Southern Historical Collection, University of North Carolina
        Robert L. Doughton Papers
        Samuel J. Ervin Papers
        Henry Glassie Papers
        Claude Kitchin Papers
        Lee S. Overman Papers
Durham, North Carolina
    Duke University
        Furnifold Simmons Papers
Eugene, Oregon
    University of Oregon
        Henry Chalmers Papers
Hanover, New Hampshire
    Dartmouth College
        Sherman Adams Papers
        Sinclair Weeks Papers
Logan, Utah
    Utah State University
        Edgar Brossard Papers
Princeton, New Jersey
    Princeton University
        William Burgess Papers
        Jacob Viner Papers
Provo, Utah
    Brigham Young University
        Reed Smoot Papers

PUBLISHED OFFICIAL DOCUMENTS

Canada
Department of External Affairs. *Documents on Canadian External Relations*. Ottawa: Information Canada, various dates.
Dominion of Canada. *Official Report of Debates, House of Commons*, vol. 185, 1930.
King, William L. MacKenzie. *Diaries*. Ottawa: Public Archives of Canada, 1981.

General Agreement on Tariffs and Trade
GATT. *Trade Policy Review: United States, 1992*. Geneva: April 1992.

United States

Declassified Documents Catalog. Woodbridge, Conn.: Research Publications International, 1975 to present.

Gray, Gordon. *Report to the President on Foreign Economic Policy.* Washington, D.C.: GPO, 1950.

Public Papers of the Presidents [*Herbert C. Hoover, Harry S. Truman, Dwight D. Eisenhower, John F. Kennedy, Lyndon B. Johnson, Richard M. Nixon, Gerald R. Ford, Jimmy Carter, Ronald W. Reagan, George H. W. Bush, William J. Clinton*]. Washington, D.C.: GPO.

U.S. Commission on Foreign Economic Policy. *Report to the President and Congress.* Washington, D.C.: GPO, January 23, 1954.

U.S. Commission on International Trade and Investment Policy. *United States International Economic Policy in an Interdependent World.* Washington, D.C.: GPO, July 1971.

U.S. Congress. *Annals of the Congress of the United States.* Washington, D.C.

———. *Congressional Globe.* Washington, D.C.

———. *Congressional Record.* Washington, D.C.

———. House of Representatives. Committee on Appropriations. *Independent Offices Appropriations for 1953: Hearings.* 82d Cong., 2d sess., January 15, 1952, pt. 1.

———. Committee on Education and Labor. *Establishing Procedures to Relieve Domestic Industries and Workers Injured by Increased Imports from Low-Wage Areas.* 90th Cong., 1st sess., H. Rept. 638, September 13, 1967.

———. Committee on Energy and Commerce. *Unfair Foreign Trade Practices.* 99th Cong., 2d sess., Committee Print 99-BB, May 1986.

———. Committee on Ways and Means. *Report concerning Reciprocity and Commercial Treaties.* 54th Cong., 1st sess., H. Rept. 2263, June 6, 1896.

———. *Tariff Hearings, 1908–9.* 60th Cong., 2d sess., H. Doc. 1505, 1909.

———. *Tariff Negotiations between the United States and Foreign Governments.* 61st Cong., 2d sess., H. Doc. 956, 1910.

———. *Reciprocity with Canada.* 61st Cong., 1st sess., H. Rept. 3, 1911.

———. *Reciprocity with Canada.* 61st Cong., 3d sess., H. Rept. 2150:2, 1911.

———. *Emergency Tariff Legislation.* 66th Cong., 3d sess., H. Rept. 1139, December 20, 1920.

———. *Emergency Tariff Bill: Report to Accompany H.R. 2435.* 67th Cong., 1st sess., H. Rept. 1, 1921.

———. *Emergency Tariff Bill: Conference Report.* 67th Cong., 1st sess., H. Rept. 79, May 20, 1921.

———. *Tariff Readjustment—1929.* 71st Cong., 1st sess., May 9, 1929.

———. *Hearings on H.R. 8430.* 73d Cong., 2d sess., March 8–14, 1934.

———. *Amend Tariff Act of 1930: Reciprocal Trade Agreements.* 73d Cong., 2d sess., H. Rept. 1000, March 17, 1934.

———. *To Extend the Authority of the President under Section 350 of the Tariff Act of 1930, as Amended: Report.* 75th Cong., 1st sess., H. Rept. 166, February 1, 1937.

———. *Extending the Authority of the President under Section 350 of the Tariff Act of 1930, as Amended: Report.* 76th Cong., 3d sess., H. Rept. 1594, February 14, 1940.

———. *Extension of the Reciprocal Trade Agreements Act.* 78th Cong., 1st sess., H. Rept. 409, May 6, 1943.

———. *Foreign Trade Agreements: Report.* 79th Cong., 1st sess., H. Rept. 594, May 18, 1945.

——. *Extending the Authority of the President under Section 350 of the Tariff Act of 1930, as Amended, and for Other Purposes.* 80th Cong., 2d sess., H. Rept. 2009, May 24, 1948.

——. *Extension of the Reciprocal Trade Agreements Act: Report.* 81st Cong., 1st sess., H. Rept. 19, February 4, 1949.

——. *Extension of the Reciprocal Trade Agreements Act: Report.* 82d Cong., 1st sess., H. Rept. 14, January 29, 1951.

——. *Trade Agreements Extension Act of 1955.* 84th Cong., 1st sess., H. Rept. 50, February 14, 1955.

——. *Amendments to the Antidumping Act of 1921, as Amended.* 85th Cong., 1st sess., July 29–31, 1957.

——. *Hearings on H.R. 6006.* 85th Cong., 2d sess., 1958.

——. *Trade Agreements Extension Act of 1958: Report to Accompany H.R. 12591.* 85th Cong., 2d sess., H. Rept. 1761, May 21, 1958.

——. *Trade Expansion Act of 1962: Hearings on H.R. 11970.* 87th Cong., 2d sess., May 1962.

——. *Trade Expansion Act of 1962,* Report to Accompany H.R. 11970. 87th Cong., 2d sess., H. Rept. 1818, June 12, 1962.

——. *Foreign Trade and Tariff Proposals: Hearings.* 90th Cong., 2d sess., 1969.

——. *Tariff Treatment of and Trade in Selected Commodities.* 92d Cong., 1st sess., Committee Print, December 1971.

——. *Oversight of the Antidumping Act of 1921.* 95th Cong., 1st sess., November 8, 1977. Washington, D.C.: GPO, 1977.

——. *Administration of the Antidumping Act of 1921: Hearing.* 95th Cong., 2d sess., September 21, 1978.

——. *Agreements Reached in the Tokyo Round of the Multilateral Trade Negotiations: Message from the President.* 96th Cong., 1st sess., H. Doc. 96-153. Washington, D.C.: GPO, 1979.

——. *Trade Agreements Extension Act of 1979: Report to Accompany H.R. 4537.* 96th Cong., 1st sess., H. Rept. 96-317, July 3, 1979.

——. *Omnibus Trade and Competitiveness Act of 1988: Conference Report to Accompany H.R. 3.* 100th Cong., 2d sess., April 20, 1988. Washington, D.C.: GPO, 1988.

——. Joint Economic Committee. *Trade Restraints in the Western Community.* 87th Cong., 1st sess. Washington, D.C.: GPO, 1961.

——. Office of Technology Assessment. *Multinationals and the National Interest: Playing by Different Rules.* Washington, D.C.: GPO, 1993.

——. *Register of Debate.* Washington, D.C.

——. Senate. Committee on Finance. *Report to Accompany S.R. 122.* 47th Cong., 2d sess., S. Rept. 1013, February 27, 1883.

——. *Report to Accompany H.R. 3321.* 63d Cong., 1st sess., S. Rept. 80., 1913.

——. *Report to Accompany H.R. 7456.* 67th Cong., 2d sess., S. Rept. 595, 1922.

——. *Tariff Bill: Report.* 67th Cong., 2d sess., S. Rept. 595, April 11, 1922.

——. *Tariff Act of 1929: Hearings on H.R. 2667.* 71st Cong., 1st sess. Washington, D.C.: GPO, 1929.

——. *Hearings on H.R. 8687.* 73d Cong., 2d sess., April–May, 1934.

——. *Reciprocal Trade Agreements: Report.* 73d Cong., 2d sess., S. Rept. 871, April 26, 1934.

——. *Report to Accompany House Joint Res. 96.* 75th Cong., 1st sess., 1937.

———. *Extending the Authority of the President under Section 350 of the Tariff Act of 1930, as Amended.* 76th Cong., 3d sess., S. Rept. 1297, March 8, 1940.

———. *1945 Extension of the Reciprocal Trade Agreements Act: Hearings.* 79th Cong., 1st sess., May 30, 1945.

———. *Extending the Authority of the President under Section 350 of the Tariff Act of 1930, as Amended: Report.* 80th Cong., 2d sess., S. Rept. 1558, June 8, 1948.

———. *Trade Agreements Extension Act of 1951: Hearings.* 82d Cong., 1st sess., March 16–April 6, 1951.

———. *Trade Agreements Extension Act of 1955.* 84th Cong., 1st sess., S. Rept. 232, April 28, 1955.

———. *Domestic Industries Affected by Foreign Imports.* 84th Cong., 2d sess, S. Rept. 2401, July 2, 1956.

———. *Antidumping: Hearings on H.R. 6006.* 85th Cong., 2d sess., March 26–27, 1958.

———. *Trade Agreements Extension Act of 1958: Report to Accompany H.R. 12591.* 85th Cong., 2d sess., S. Rept. 1838, July 15, 1958.

———. *Trade Expansion Act of 1962: Report,* 87th Cong., 2d sess., S. Rept. 2059, September 14, 1962.

———. *Automotive Products Trade Act of 1965: Report on H.R. 9042.* 89th Cong., 1st sess., S. Rept. 782, September 27, 1965.

———. *Expressing the Sense of Congress with Respect to Certain Trade Agreements.* 89th Cong., 2d. sess., S. Rept. 1341, June 28, 1966.

———. *Compendium of Papers on Legislative Oversight Review of U.S. Trade Policies.* 90th Cong., 2d sess., Committee Print, February 7, 1968.

———. *International Antidumping Code,* Hearings. 90th Cong., 2d sess., June 27, 1968.

———. *Trade Reform Act of 1974.* 93d Cong., 2d sess., S. Rept. 93-1298, 1974.

———. *Executive Branch GATT Studies.* 93d Cong., 2d sess., Committee Print, March 1974.

———. *Canadian Automobile Agreement,* 94th Cong., 1st sess., 1976.

———. *Oversight Hearings on U.S. Foreign Trade Policy.* 94th Cong., 2d sess., January 30, 1976.

———. *Trade Agreements Act of 1979: Report to Accompany H.R. 4537.* 96th Cong., 1st sess., July 21, 1979.

———. *Nomination of Alfred E. Eckes Jr.* 97th Cong., 1st sess., September 15, 1981.

———. *Nomination of Veronica Haggart.* 97th Cong., 2d sess., March 2, 1982.

———. Committee on Foreign Relations. *Reports of the Committee on Foreign Relations, 1789–1901.* 56th Cong., 2d sess., S. Doc. 231, 1901.

———. Committee on Interstate and Foreign Commerce. *Problems of the Domestic Textile Industry.* 86th Cong., 1st sess., S. Rept. 42, February 4, 1959.

———. *Supplementary Report.* 87th Cong., 1st sess., S. Rept. 173, April 19, 1961.

U.S. Continental Congress. *Diplomatic Correspondence of the United States of America, 1783–1789.* Washington, D.C.: Blair, 1833.

U.S. Department of Commerce. Bureau of Foreign and Domestic Commerce. *Foreign Commerce and Navigation of the United States.* Washington, D.C.: GPO, annually.

———. *Foreign Trade of the United States in the Calendar Year.* Trade Promotion Series. Washington, D.C.: GPO, annually.

———. *American Branch Factories Abroad.* 71st Cong., 3d sess., S. Doc. 258, January 22, 1931.

——. *Trade of the United States with Japan, 1956–1960.* Washington, D.C.: GPO, 1961.

——. *U.S. Foreign Trade Highlights, 1989.* Washington, D.C.: GPO, September 1990.

U.S. Department of State. *Foreign Relations of the United States.* Washington, D.C.: GPO, annually.

——. *The Statutes at Large of the United States of America.* Washington, D.C.: GPO, annually.

——. *Commercial Relations of the United States.* Washington, D.C.: GPO, 1879–1900.

——. *Reciprocal Trade Agreement between the United States of America and the Belgo-Luxemburg Economic Union.* Executive Agreement Series 75. Washington, D.C.: GPO, 1935.

——. *Reciprocal Trade Agreement between the United States of America and Switzerland.* Executive Agreement Series 90. Washington, D.C.: GPO, 1936.

——. *Text of Trade Agreement between the United States and the United Kingdom.* Department of State Publication 1256. Washington, D.C.: GPO, 1938.

——. *Reciprocal Trade Agreement between the United States of America and France.* Executive Agreement Series 146. Washington, D.C.: GPO, 1939.

——. *Reciprocal Trade Agreement and Supplementary Exchange of Notes between the United States of America and Turkey.* Executive Agreement Series 163. Washington, D.C.: GPO, 1940.

——. *Reciprocal Trade Agreement between the United States of America and Mexico.* Washington, D.C.: GPO, 1943.

——. *Reciprocal Trade Agreement and Supplemental Exchanges of Notes between the United States of America and Argentina.* Executive Agreement Series 277. Washington, D.C.: GPO, 1943.

——. *Reciprocal Trade Agreement between the United States of America and Iceland.* Washington, D.C.: GPO, 1944.

——. *The United States Balance of Payments Problem.* Commercial Policy Series 423. Washington, D.C.: Department of State, December 1949.

——. *Analysis of Protocol (including Schedules) for Accession of Japan.* Washington, D.C.: GPO, 1955.

U.S. Department of the Treasury. *Annual Report.* Washington, D.C.: GPO.

——. *Report of the Special Commissioner of Revenue for the Year 1868.* 40th Cong., 3d sess., Exec. Doc. 16.

——. Office of U.S. Revenue Commission. Stephen Colwell, *Report upon the Relations of Foreign Trade to Domestic Industry and Internal Revenue.* Special Report 10. 39th Cong., 1st sess., Exec. Doc. 68, February 1866.

U.S. General Accounting Office. *United States–Japan Trade: Issues and Problems.* ID-79-53, September 21, 1979. Washington, D.C.: GPO, 1979.

U.S. International Trade Commission. *Annual Report.* 1975 to present.

——. *Operation of the Trade Agreements Program.* Washington, D.C.: GPO, 1975 to present.

——. *Footwear.* Inv. TA-201-7. ITC Publication 758. February 1976.

——. *Bolts, Nuts, and Large Screws of Iron or Steel.* Investigation (Inv.) TA-201-37. ITC Publication 924. November 1978.

——. *Leather Wearing Apparel.* Inv. 201-40. ITC Publication 1030. 1980.

——. *Certain Motor Vehicles and Certain Chassis and Bodies Therefor.* Inv. TA-201-44. ITC Publication 1110. December 1980.

——. *The Effectiveness of Escape Clause Relief in Promoting Adjustment to Import Competition.* Inv. 332-115. ITC Publication 1229. March 1982.

——. *Certain Amplifier Assemblies and Parts Thereof from Japan.* Inv. 731-TA-48(F). ITC Publication 1270. July 1982.

——. *Competitive Assessment of the U.S. Metalworking Machine Tool Industry.* Inv. 332-149. ITC Publication 1428. September 1983.

——. *The Effect of Changes in the Value of the U.S. Dollar Trade in Selected Commodities.* Inv. 332-150. ITC Publication 1423. September 1983.

——. *Foreign Industrial Targeting.* Inv. 332-162. ITC Publications 1437 (1983, Japan), 1517 (1984, European Community), and 1632 (1985, Brazil, Canada, Korea, Mexico, and Taiwan).

——. *Nonrubber Footwear.* Inv. TA-201-50. ITC Publication 1545. July 1984.

——. *Carbon and Certain Alloy Steel Products.* Inv. TA-201-51. ITC Publication 1553. July 1984.

——. *Cell-Site Transceivers and Subassemblies Thereof from Japan.* Inv. 731-TA-163 (F). ITC Publication 1618. December 1984.

——. *Conditions of Competition Affecting the Northeastern U.S. Groundfish and Scallop Industries in Selected Markets.* Inv. 332-173. ITC Publication 1622. December 1984.

——. *Dynamic Random Access Memory Semiconductors (DRAM's) of 256 Kilobits and Above from Japan.* Inv. 731-TA-300(P). ITC Publication 1803. January 1986.

——. *Wood Shakes and Shingles.* Inv. TA-201-56. ITC Publication 1826. March 1986.

——. *64-K Dynamic Random Access Memory Components from Japan.* Inv. 731-TA-270(F). ITC Publication 1682. June 1986.

——. *Erasable Programmable Read Only Memories from Japan.* Inv. 731-TA-288(F). ITC Publication 1927. December 1986.

——. *The Economic Effects of Significant U.S. Import Restraints.* Inv. 332-262. ITC Publications 2222 (October 1989) and 2699 (November 1993).

——. *Economy-Wide Modeling of the Economic Implications of a FTA with Mexico and a NAFTA with Canada and Mexico.* Inv. 332-317. ITC Publication 2516. May 1992.

U.S. Office of the Special Representatives for Trade Negotiations. *Report to the President: Future United States Foreign Trade Policy.* Washington, D.C.: GPO, January 14, 1969.

U.S. Office of Technology Assessment. *Competing Economies: America, Europe, and the Pacific Rim.* OTA-ITE-498. Washington, D.C.: GPO, October 1991.

U.S. President. *Annual Report of the President of the United States on the Trade Agreements Program.* Washington, D.C.: GPO.

——. *Economic Report of the President.* Washington, D.C.: GPO, annually.

——. *Trade Agreements with the European Economic Community, the United Kingdom, Norway, and Sweden.* Washington, D.C.: GPO, 1962.

——. *U.S. Foreign Policy for the 1970s: First Annual Report to Congress, February 18, 1970.* Washington, D.C.: GPO, 1970.

U.S. Public Advisory Board for Mutual Security. *A Trade and Tariff Policy in the National Interest.* Washington, D.C.: GPO, 1953.

U.S. Tariff Commission. *Annual Report.* Washington, D.C.: GPO, 1917–74.

——. *Information concerning Dumping and Other Unfair Foreign Competition in the United States and Canada's Anti-Dumping Law.* Washington, D.C.: GPO, 1919.

——. *Reciprocity and Commercial Treaties.* Washington, D.C.: GPO, 1919.

——. *Reciprocity with Canada.* Washington, D.C.: GPO, 1920.

——. *The Effects of the Cuban Reciprocity Treaty of 1902.* Washington, D.C.: GPO, 1929.

——. *United States–Philippine Tariff and Trade Relations.* Report 18. Washington, D.C.: GPO, 1931.

——. *Cylinder, Crown, and Sheet Glass.* Report 33, 2d ser. Washington, D.C.: GPO, 1932.

——. *Depreciated Exchange.* Report 44, 2d ser. Washington, D.C.: GPO, 1932.

——. *Relation of Duties to Value of Imports.* Washington, D.C.: GPO, 1932.

——. *Computed Duties and Equivalent ad Valorem Rates on Imports into the United States from Principal Countries, 1929 and 1931.* Washington, D.C.: GPO, 1933.

——. *Methods of Valuation.* Report 70, 2d ser. Washington, D.C.: GPO, 1933.

——. *Economic Analysis of Foreign Trade of the United States in Relation to the Tariff.* Washington, D.C.: GPO, March 1, 1933.

——. *Tariff Bargaining under Most-Favored-Nation Treaties.* Report 65, 2d ser. March 29, 1933.

——. *The Tariff: A Bibliography.* Washington, D.C.: GPO, 1934.

——. *The Tariff and Its History.* Miscellaneous ser. Washington, D.C.: GPO, 1934.

——. *Trade Agreement between the United States and the United Kingdom.* Washington, D.C.: Tariff Commission, 1938.

——. *Trade Agreement between the United States and the Republic of Turkey.* Washington, D.C.: Tariff Commission, 1939.

——. "Effect of British Imperial Preference on Selected United States Exports." Report, 1942.

——. *Trade Agreement between the United States and Mexico.* Washington, D.C.: Tariff Commission, 1943.

——. *Trade Agreement between the United States and Peru.* Washington, D.C.: Tariff Commission, 1943.

——. *Trade Agreement between the United States and Uruguay.* Washington, D.C.: Tariff Commission, 1943.

——. *Economic Controls and Commercial Policy in Argentina.* Washington, D.C.: Tariff Commission, 1945.

——. *Operation of the Trade Agreements Program.* Washington, D.C.: GPO, 1948–74.

——. *Women's Fur Felt Hats and Hat Bodies.* Sec. 7. Inv. EO. 2d ser., 170. 1951.

——. *Motorcycles and Parts.* Sec. 7, Inv. 1. 2d ser., 180. 1952.

——. *Hatters' Fur.* Sec. 7. Inv. 3. 2d ser., 178. 1952.

——. *Spring Clothespins.* Sec. 7. Inv. 4. Washington, D.C., August 1952.

——. *Watches, Watch Movements, Watch Parts, and Watchcases.* Sec. 7. Inv. 4. 2d ser., 176. 1952.

——. *Groundfish Fillets.* Sec. 7. Inv. 5. 2d ser. 192. 1952.

——. *Garlic.* Sec. 7. Inv. 6. 2d ser., 177. 1952.

——. *Glace Cherries.* Sec. 7. Inv. 8. 2d ser., 185. 1952.

——. *Bonito, Canned in Oil; and Tuna and Bonito Canned Not in Oil.* Sec. 7. Inv. 9. 2d ser., 187. November 1952.

——. *Tobacco Pipes of Wood,* Sec. 7. Inv. 10. Publication 7-10. 1952.

——. *Bicycles and Parts.* Sec. 7. Inv. 7. 2d ser., 184. 1953.

——. *Household China Tableware.* Sec. 7. Inv. 11. 2d ser., 186. 1953.

——. *Figs, Dried.* Sec. 7. Inv. 12. 2d ser., 188. 1953.

——. *Cotton Carding Machinery and Parts Thereof.* Sec. 7. Inv. 18. Publication 7-18. July 1953.

——. *Screen-printed Silk Scarves.* Sec. 7. Inv. 19. Publication 7-19. April 1953.

——. *Hand-Blown Glassware.* Sec. 7. Inv. 22. Publication 7-22. September 1953.

——. *Scissors and Shears, and Manicure and Pedicure Nippers, and Parts thereof.* Sec. 7. Inv. 24. Publication 7-24. March 1954.

——. *Groundfish Fillets.* Sec. 7. Inv. 25. Publication 7-25. Washington, D.C., May 1954.

——. *Lead and Zinc.* Sec. 7, Inv. 27. Publication 7-27. May 1954.

——. *Spring Clothespins.* Sec. 7. Inv. 32. Publication 7-32. October 1954.

——. *Wood Screws of Iron or Steel.* Sec. 7. Inv. 34. Publication 7-34. October 1954.

——. *Bicycles.* Sec. 7. Inv. 37. Publication 7-37. March 1955.

——. *Groundfish Fillets.* Sec. 7. Inv. 47. Publication 7-47. Washington, D.C., October 1956.

——. *Cotton Velveteen Fabrics,* Sec. 7. Inv. 49. Publication 7-49. October 1956.

——. *Cotton Pillowcases.* Sec. 7. Inv. 51. Publication 7-51. November 1956.

——. *Safety Pins.* Sec. 7. Inv. 53. Publication 7-53. January 1957.

——. *Postwar Developments in Japan's Foreign Trade.* 2d ser. 201. 1958.

——. *Report to the President of "Peril-Point" Findings on Articles in the List Received from the President on May 27, 1960.* Washington, D.C.: Tariff Commission, November 1960.

——. *Hot-Rolled Carbon Steel Wire Rods from Belgium, Luxembourg, France, and West Germany.* Inv. AA1921-27–30. TC Publications 93–95, 99. June 1963.

——. *Television Receiving Sets from Japan.* Inv. AA1921-66. TC Publication 367. March 1971.

——. *Certain Woven Fabrics: Workers of Arista Mills Company, Winston-Salem, N.C.* Inv. TEA-W-57. TC Publication 37, March 1971.

——. *Cotton Osnaburgs and Sheetings: Whittier Mills Company, Atlanta, Ga.* Inv.s TEA-F-29, TEA-W-103. TC Publication 426. October 1971.

——. *Broadwoven Polyester-Cotton Fabrics: Workers of the Birmingham Plant of Avondale Mills.* Inv. TEA-W-116. TC Publication 434. November 1971.

——. *Audio Receivers, Phonographs, and Tape Recorders.* Inv. TEA-W-142. TC Publication 495, June 1972.

——. *New Passenger Automobiles,* Inv. TEA-W-165. TC Publication 545. February 1973.

——. *Transistors and Diodes.* Inv. TEA-W-196. TC Publication 588. June 1973.

——. *Antifriction Balls and Ball Bearings, including Ball Bearings with Integral Shifts and Parts Thereof.* Inv. TEA-I-27. TC Publication 597. July 1973.

——. *Trade Barriers.* Inv. 332-66, 332-67. TC Publication 665. April 1974.

U.S. Trade Representative. *Foreign Trade Barriers.* Annually.

STATISTICS

American Tariff League. *Monthly Bulletin.* 1933–38.

Leacy, F. H., ed. *Historical Statistics of Canada.* 2d ed. Ottawa: Ministry of Supply, 1983.

Liesner, Thelma, comp. *One Hundred Years of Economic Statistics.* New York: Facts on File, 1989.

Mitchell, B. R. *Abstract of British Historical Statistics.* Cambridge: Cambridge University Press, 1962.

——. *British Historical Statistics.* Cambridge: Cambridge University Press, 1988.

——. *International Historical Statistics: Europe, 1750–1988.* New York: Stockton Press, 1992.

Organization for Economic Cooperation and Development. *Historical Statistics, 1960–1990.* Paris: OECD, 1992.

——. *Main Economic Indicators: Historical Statistics—Prices, Labor, and Wages, 1962–1991.* Paris: OECD, 1993.

Pierce, Phyllis S., ed. *The Dow Jones Averages, 1885–1990.* Homewood, Ill.: Business One Irvin, 1991.

United Nations. *Yearbook of International Trade Statistics.* New York: United Nations, annually.

United Nations Conference on Trade and Development. *Handbook of International Trade and Development Statistics.* New York: United Nations, annually.

Urquhart, M. C., ed. *Historical Statistics of Canada.* Toronto: Macmillan, 1965.

U.S. Department of Commerce. Bureau of the Census. *Historical Statistics of the United States.* Bicentennial ed. Washington, D.C.: GPO, 1974.

——. *Statistical Abstract of the United States.* Washington, D.C.: GPO, annually.

——. Bureau of Economic Analysis. *Survey of Current Business.* Washington, D.C.: GPO, monthly.

——. *Business Statistics, 1963–1991.* Washington, D.C.: GPO, 1992.

——. *National Income and Product Accounts of the United States.* Washington, D.C.: GPO, 1993.

——. International Trade Administration. *U.S. Industrial Outlook.* Washington, D.C.: GPO, annually.

U.S. Department of Labor. *Employment, Hours, and Earnings, United States, 1909–1990.* Bulletin 2370. Washington, D.C.: GPO, 1991.

——. Bureau of Labor Statistics. *Handbook of Labor Statistics.* Bulletin 2340. Washington, D.C.: GPO, August 1989.

Vamplew, Wray, ed. *Australians Historical Statistics.* Broadway, New South Wales: Fairfax, Syme and Weldon, 1987.

——. *World Development Report.* New York: Oxford University Press, annually.

NEWSPAPERS AND PERIODICALS

American Metal Market
Business Week
Chicago Tribune
Cleveland Plain Dealer
Columbus Dispatch
Deseret News (Salt Lake City, Utah), 1930–32
Des Moines Register, 1929–30
Economist (London)
Financial Post (Toronto)
Financial Times (London)
Fortune
International Herald Tribune (Paris), 1993
Journal of Commerce (New York)
Judge
Los Angeles Times
Mainichi Daily News (Tokyo)
New York Times
Nippon Times (Tokyo)

Portland Oregonian, 1930–32
Puck
Salem Statesman (Oregon), 1930–32
Salt Lake City Tribune, 1930–32
Wall Street Journal
Washington Post
Washington Star

BOOKS

Abbott, W. W., ed. *The Papers of George Washington: Presidential Series*. Charlottesville: University Press of Virginia, 1987.

Abegglen, James C., and George Stalk Jr. *Kaisha: The Japanese Corporation*. New York: Basic Books, 1985.

Adams, Brooks. *America's Economic Supremacy*. New York: Harper, 1947, reprint of 1900 ed.

Adams, Charles F. *Works of John Adams*. Boston: Little, Brown, 1850–56.

Adams, John. *Works*. Boston.: Little, Brown, 1850.

Adams, John Quincy. *Lives of James Madison and James Monroe*. Buffalo, N.Y.: Geo. H. Derby, 1850.

Aggarwal, Vinod K. *Liberal Protectionism: The International Politics of Organized Textile Trade*. Berkeley: University of California Press, 1985.

Aldcroft, Derek H. *The Development of British Industry and Foreign Competition, 1875– 1914*. Toronto: University of Toronto Press, 1968.

American State Papers: Documents Legislative and Executive of the Congresses of the United States, 1789–1838. Washington, D.C.: Gales and Seaton, 1832–61.

American Tariff League. *The United States in World Trade*. New York: American Tariff League, February 1958.

Amery, Julian. *Joseph Chamberlain and the Tariff Reform Campaign*. New York: St. Martin's, 1969.

Annett, Douglas R. *British Preference in Canadian Commercial Policy*. Toronto: Ryerson, 1948.

Aronowitz, Stanley, and William DiFazio. *The Jobless Future: Sci-Tech and the Dogma of Work*. Minneapolis: University of Minnesota Press, 1994.

Bairoch, Paul. *Economics and World History: Myths and Paradoxes*. Chicago: University of Chicago Press, 1993.

Baker, Elizabeth Feaster. *Henry Wheaton, 1785–1848*. 1937. Reprint, New York: Da Capo Press, 1971.

Baldwin, Robert E. *The Political Economy of U.S. Import Policy*. Cambridge: MIT Press, 1985.

Baldwin, Robert E., and Jeffrey W. Steagall. *An Analysis of Factors Influencing ITC Decisions in Antidumping, Countervailing Duty, and Safeguard Cases*. Working Paper 4282. Cambridge, Mass.: National Bureau of Economic Research, February 1993.

Ball, George. *The Past Has Another Pattern: Memoirs*. New York: Norton, 1982.

Barnes, John, and David Nicholson, eds. *The Empire at Bay: The Leo Amery Diaries, 1929– 1945*. London: Hutchinson, 1988.

Bartlett, Irving H. *Daniel Webster*. New York: Norton, 1978.

Basler, Roy, ed. *Collected Works of Abraham Lincoln*. New Brunswick, N.J.: Rutgers
University Press, 1953–55.

Bassett, John Spencer, ed. *Correspondence of Andrew Jackson*. Washington, D.C.: Carnegie
Institute, 1928.

Batra, Ravi. *The Myth of Free Trade*. New York: Scribner's, 1993.

Bauer, Raymond A., Ithiel De Sola Pool, and Lewis A. Dexter. *American Business and Public
Policy*. 2d ed. Chicago: Aldine-Atherton, 1972.

Beard, Charles A. *Idea of National Interest*. New York: Macmillan, 1934.

Becker, William H. *The Dynamics of Business-Government Relations: Industry and Exports,
1893–1921*. Chicago: University of Chicago Press, 1982.

Becker, William H., and Samuel F. Wells, eds. *Economics and World Power: An Assessment of
American Diplomacy since 1789*. New York: Columbia University Press, 1984.

Belohlavek, John M. *Let the Eagle Soar!: The Foreign Policy of Andrew Jackson*. Lincoln:
University of Nebraska Press, 1985.

Bemis, Samuel Flagg. *Diplomatic History of the American People*. 5th ed. New York: Holt,
Rinehart, and Winston, 1965.

———. *Jay's Treaty: A Study in Commerce and Diplomacy*. 1923. Rev. ed., New Haven, Conn.:
Yale University Press, 1962.

Benjamin, Jules R. *The United States and Cuba*. Pittsburgh: University of Pittsburgh Press,
1974.

Bhagwati, Jagdish. *Protectionism*. Cambridge: MIT Press, 1988.

Bidwell, Percy W. *The Invisible Tariff: A Study of the Control of Imports into the United
States*. New York: Council on Foreign Relations, 1939.

Bierce, Ambrose. *Enlarged Devil's Dictionary*. New York: Doubleday, 1967.

Bierman, Harold, Jr. *Great Myths of 1929 and the Lessons to Be Learned*. New York:
Greenwood, 1991.

Blaine, James G. *Twenty Years in Congress*. Norwich, Conn.: Henry Bill, 1884.

Blum, John M. *From the Morgenthau Diaries*. 3 vols. Boston: Houghton Mifflin: 1959–67.

Blum, John M., Edmund S. Morgan, Willie Lee Rose, Arthur M. Schlesinger Jr., Kenneth
M. Stampp, and C. Van Woodward. *The National Experience*. 6th ed. New York:
Harcourt, Brace, Jovanovich, 1985.

Boltuck, Richard, and Robert E. Litan, eds. *Down in the Dumps: Administration of Unfair
Trade Laws*. Washington, D.C.: Brookings Institution, 1991.

Borden, William S. *The Pacific Alliance: United States Foreign Economic Policy and Japanese
Trade Recovery, 1947–1955*. Madison: University of Wisconsin Press, 1984.

Bothwell, Robert. *Canada and the United States: The Politics of Partnership*. New York:
Twayne, 1992.

Bourne, Kenneth, ed. *British Documents on Foreign Affairs*. Pt. 1, ser. C: *North America,
1837–14*. Frederick, Md.: University Publications of America, 1986.

Bovard, James. *The Fair Trade Fraud*. New York: St. Martin's, 1991.

Bowers, Claude G. *Beveridge and the Progressive Era*. Cambridge: Houghton Mifflin, 1932.

Bowling, Kenneth R., and Helen E. Veit. *The Diary of William Maclay and Other Notes on
Senate Debates*. Baltimore: Johns Hopkins University Press, 1988.

Boyce, Robert W. D. *British Capitalism at the Crossroads, 1919–1932*. Cambridge:
Cambridge University Press, 1987.

Boyd, Julian P. *Papers of Thomas Jefferson*. Princeton, N.J.: Princeton University Press, 1953.

Boyer, Gabriela, Lori Wallach, and Nancy Watzman. *NAFTA'S Bizarre Bazaar: The Deal

Making that Bought Congressional Votes on the North American Free Trade Agreement. Washington, D.C.: Public Citizen, December 1993.

Brant, Irving. *The Fourth President.* London: Eyre and Spottiswoode, 1970.

Brinkley, Alan, Richard N. Current, Frank Freidel, and T. Harry Williams. *American History.* 8th ed. New York: McGraw-Hill, 1991.

Brown, Benjamin H. *The Tariff Reform Movement in Great Britain, 1881–1895.* New York: Columbia University Press, 1943.

Brown, Lucy. *The Board of Trade and the Free-Trade Movement, 1830–42.* Oxford: Clarendon Press, 1958.

Brown, William Adams, Jr. *The United States and the Restoration of World Trade.* Washington, D.C.: Brookings Institution, 1950.

Burke, Robert, ed. *Diary and Letters of Hiram Johnson, 1917–45.* New York: Garland, 1983.

Burner, David. *Herbert Hoover: A Public Life.* New York: Knopf, 1979.

Capie, Forrest. *Tariffs and Growth: Some Insights from the World Economy, 1850–1940.* New York: Manchester University Press, 1994.

Cappon, Lester J., ed. *The Adams-Jefferson Letters: The Complete Correspondence between Thomas Jefferson and Abigail and John Adams.* Chapel Hill: University of North Carolina Press, 1988.

Carey, Henry. *The Harmony of Interests: Agricultural, Manufacturing, and Commercial.* 1851. Reprint, New York: Augustus M. Kelley, 1967.

Carey, Matthew. *Autobiographical Sketches.* New York: Arno, 1970.

Chalmers, Henry. *World Trade Policies.* Berkeley: University of California Press, 1953.

Chandler, Alfred D., Jr. *Scale and Scope: The Dynamics of Industrial Capitalism.* Cambridge: Harvard University Press, 1990.

Chandler, Lester V. *America's Great Depression, 1929–1941.* New York: Harper, 1970.

Choate, Pat. *Agents of Influence.* New York: Knopf, 1990.

Clarfield, Gerard. *United States Diplomatic History: The Age of Ascendancy.* Englewood Cliffs, N.J.: Prentice-Hall, 1992.

Clarke, John. *British Diplomacy and Foreign Policy, 1782–1865.* London: Unwin Hyman, 1989.

Clubb, Bruce. *United States Foreign Trade Law.* Boston: Little, Brown, 1991.

Cobden, Richard. *Speeches on Questions of Public Policy.* London: Macmillan, 1880.

Cohen, Stephen D., and Ronald I. Meltzer. *United States International Economic Policy in Action.* New York: Praeger, 1982.

Cole, Wayne S. *Roosevelt and the Isolationists.* Lincoln: University of Nebraska Press, 1983.

Coletta, Paolo E. *Presidency of William Howard Taft.* Lawrence: University of Kansas Press, 1973.

Congressional Quarterly. *Almanac: 90th Cong., 2d Sess. . . . 1968.* Washington, D.C.: Congressional Quarterly. 1968.

Conkin, Paul K. *Prophets of Prosperity: America's First Political Economists.* Bloomington: Indiana University Press, 1980.

Conway, Moncure Daniel, ed. *The Writings of Thomas Paine.* 1902. Reprint, New York: Burt Franklin, 1969.

Conybeare, John A. C. *Trade Wars: The Theory and Practice of International Commercial Rivalry.* New York: Columbia University Press, 1987.

Cooke, Jacob E. *Tenche Coxe and the Early Republic.* Chapel Hill: University of North Carolina Press, 1978.

———. *Alexander Hamilton.* New York: Scribner's, 1982.

——., ed. *The Federalist.* Middletown, Conn.: Wesleyan University Press, 1961.

Crouzet, Francois. *The Victorian Economy.* New York: Columbia University Press, 1982.

Culbertson, John M. *The Dangers of "Free Trade."* Madison, Wis.: Twenty-first–Century Press, 1985.

Culbertson, William S. *International Economic Policies.* New York: Appleton, 1925.

——. *Reciprocity: A National Policy for Foreign Trade.* New York: Whittlesey House, 1937.

Cullom, Shelby M. *Fifty Years of Public Service.* Chicago: A. C. McClurg, 1911.

Cunningham, W. C. *The Growth of English Industry and Commerce in Modern Times.* Cambridge: Cambridge University Press, 1892.

——. *The Rise and Decline of the Free Trade Movement.* London: C. J. Clay, 1904.

Curtis, Thomas B., and John R. Vastine Jr. *The Kennedy Round and the Future of American Trade.* New York: Praeger, 1971.

Curzon, Gerard. *Multilateral Commercial Diplomacy.* London: Michael Joseph, 1965.

Cutler, Wayne, ed. *Correspondence of James K. Polk.* Knoxville: University of Tennessee Press, 1993.

Dalton, John E. *Sugar: A Case Study of Government Control.* New York: Macmillan, 1937.

Dalzell, Robert F. *Daniel Webster and the Trend of Nationalism, 1843–52.* Boston: Houghton-Mifflin, 1973.

Dam, Kenneth W. *The GATT: Law and International Economic Organization.* Chicago: University of Chicago Press, 1970.

Davis, Hugh O. *America's Trade Equality Policy.* Washington, D.C.: American Council on Public Affairs, 1942.

Davis, Joseph S. *The World between Wars, 1919–39: An Economist's View.* Baltimore: Johns Hopkins University Press, 1975.

Dennett, Tyler. *John Hay: From Poetry to Politics.* New York: Dodd, 1933.

Dent, Harry S. *The Prodigal South Returns to Power.* New York: John Wiley, 1978.

Destler, I. M. *Making Foreign Economic Policy.* Washington, D.C.: Brookings Institution, 1980.

——. *American Trade Politics: System Under Stress.* New York: Twentieth-Century Fund, 1986.

Destler, I. M., and John S. Odell. *Anti-Protection: Changing Forces in United States Trade Politics.* Washington, D.C.: Institute for International Economics, September 1987.

Devine, Michael J. *John W. Foster: Politics and Diplomacy in the Imperial Era, 1873–1917.* Athens: Ohio University Press, 1981.

DiBacco, Thomas V., Lorna C. Mason, and Christian G. Appy. *History of the United States.* Boston: Houghton Mifflin, 1991.

Dicken, Peter. *Global Shift: The Internationalization of Economic Activity.* London: Paul Chapman, 1992.

Dinerstein, Leonard, Roger L. Nichols, and David Reimers. *Natives and Strangers.* New York: Oxford University Press, 1979.

Dobson, John M. *Two Centuries of Tariffs.* Washington, D.C.: ITC, 1976.

Dorfman, Joseph. *The Economic Mind in American Civilization.* New York: Viking, 1946–49.

Douglas, Paul. *In the Fullness of Time.* New York: Harcourt, Brace, Jovanovich, 1971.

Drucker, Peter F. *The New Realities.* New York: Harper and Row, 1989.

Drummond, Ian M. *British Economic Policy and the Empire, 1919–1939.* London: G. Allen and Unwin, 1972.

——. *Imperial Economic Policy, 1917–1939.* London: G. Allen and Unwin, 1974.

Drummond, Ian M., and Norman Hillmer. *Negotiating Free Trade*. Waterloo, Ontario, Canada: Wilfrid Laurier University Press, 1989.

Duncan, William Chandler. *U.S.-Japan Automobile Diplomacy: A Study in Economic Confrontation*. Cambridge, Mass.: Lippincott, 1973.

Dunning, John H. *Explaining International Production*. London: HarperCollins, 1988.

Eckes, Alfred E., Jr. *A Search for Solvency: Bretton Woods and the International Monetary System, 1941–1971*. Austin: University of Texas Press, 1975.

———. *The U.S. and the Global Struggle for Minerals*. Austin: University of Texas Press, 1979.

Edsall, Nicholas C. *Richard Cobden: Independent Radical*. Cambridge: Harvard University Press, 1986.

Eichengreen, Barry. *Sterling and the Tariff, 1929–1932*. Princeton Studies in International Finance, no. 48. Princeton, N.J.: Department of Economics, Princeton University, 1981.

Eisenhower, Dwight. *Mandate for Change, 1953–1956: The White House Years*. New York: Doubleday, 1963.

Ekelund, Robert B., Jr., and Robert D. Tollison. *Economics*. Boston: Little, Brown, 1986.

Elkins, Stanley, and Eric McKitrick. *The Age of Federalism: The Early-American Republic, 1788–1800*. New York: Oxford University Press, 1993.

Evans, John W. *The Kennedy Round in American Trade Policy*. New York: Harvard University Press, 1971.

Feis, Herbert. *Diplomacy of the Dollar, 1919–1932*. Baltimore: Johns Hopkins University Press, 1950.

———. *1933: Characters in Crisis*. New York: Little, Brown, 1966.

Ferrell, Robert, ed. *The Eisenhower Diaries*. New York: Norton, 1981.

Fletcher, William Miles, III. *The Japanese Business Community and National Trade Policy, 1920–1942*. Chapel Hill: University of North Carolina Press, 1989.

Flexner, James Thomas. *Washington: The Indispensable Man*. Boston: Little, Brown, 1969.

Floud, Roderick, and Donald McCloskey, ed. *The Economic History of Britain since 1700*. Cambridge: Cambridge University Press, 1981.

Foley, John P., ed. *The Jefferson Cyclopedia*. New York: Russell and Russell, 1900.

Ford, Paul Leicester, ed. *Works of Thomas Jefferson*. New York: Putnam's, 1904.

Ford, Worthington C., *Writings of John Quincy Adams*. New York: Macmillan, 1917.

Forster, Jakob Johann Benjamin. *A Conjunction of Interests: Business, Politics, and Tariffs, 1825–1879*. Toronto: University of Toronto Press, 1986.

Foster, John W. *Diplomatic Memoirs*. Boston: Houghton Mifflin, 1909.

Freeman, Douglas Southall. *George Washington*. New York: Scribner's, 1954.

Friedberg, Aaron L. *The Weary Titan: Britain and the Experience of Relative Decline, 1895–1905*. Princeton, N.J.: Princeton University Press, 1988.

Gaddis, John. *Strategies of Containment*. New York: Oxford University Press, 1982.

Gardner, Lloyd C. *Economic Aspects of New Deal Diplomacy*. Madison: University of Wisconsin Press, 1964.

Gilbert, Felix. *The Beginnings of American Foreign Policy: To the Farewell Address*. Princeton, N.J.: Princeton University Press, 1961.

Gilpin, Robert. *The Political Economy of International Relations*. Princeton, N.J.: Princeton University Press, 1987.

Glassford, Larry A. *Reaction and Reform: The Politics of the Conservative Party under R. B. Bennett, 1927–1938*. Toronto: University of Toronto Press, 1992.

Glick, Leslie Alan. *Multilateral Trade Negotiations: World Trade after the Tokyo Round*. Totowa, N.J.: Rowman and Allanheld, 1984.

Goldsmith, James. *The Trap*. New York: Carroll and Graf, 1994.

Goldstein, Judith. *Ideas, Interests, and American Trade Policy*. Ithaca, N.Y.: Cornell University Press, 1993.

Gomes, Leonard. *Foreign Trade and the National Economy: Mercantilist and Classical Perspectives*. New York: St. Martin's, 1987.

Gragert, Steven K., ed. *Will Rogers' Weekly Articles*. Stillwater: Oklahoma State University Press, 1981.

Granatstein, J. L. *A Man of Influence: Norman A. Robertson and Canadian Statecraft, 1929–1968*. Ottawa: Deneau Publishers, 1981.

——. *Canada, 1957–1967*. Toronto: McClelland and Stewart, 1986.

Haight, Frank Arnold. *A History of French Commercial Policies*. New York: Macmillan, 1941.

Hamilton, Gail [Mary Abigail Dodge]. *Biography of James G. Blaine*. Norwich, Conn.: Henry Bill Publishing Co., 1895.

Hamilton, Stanislaus Murray, ed. *Writings of James Monroe*. 1898. Reprint, New York: AMS, 1969.

Hancock, W. K. *Survey of British Commonwealth Affairs*. Vol. 2, *Problems of Economic Policy, 1918–1939*. London: Oxford University Press, 1940.

Hansen, William P., and Fred L. Israel, ed. *The Gallup Poll: Public Opinion, 1935–1971*. New York: Random House, 1972.

Harcave, Sidney, ed. *The Memoirs of Count Witte*. London: M. E. Sharpe, 1990.

Harris, Louis. *Harris Survey Yearbook of Public Opinion*. New York: Louis Harris and Associates, annually.

Hawkins, Harry C. *Commercial Treaties and Agreements: Principles and Practice*. New York: Rinehart, 1951.

Healy, David F. *The United States in Cuba, 1898–1902*. Madison: University of Wisconsin Press, 1963.

Hedges, Charles, comp. *Speeches of Benjamin Harrison*. 1882. Reprint, Port Washington, N.Y.: Kennikat Press, 1971.

Henry, William Wirt. *Patrick Henry: Life, Correspondence, and Speeches*. New York: Scribner's, 1891.

Hill, Charles W. L. *International Business: Competing in the Global Market Place*. Burr Ridge, Ill.: Irwin, 1994.

Hill, George Birbeck, ed. *Boswell's Life of Johnson* Oxford: Clarendon Press, 1934.

Hill, O. Mary. *Canada's Salesman to the World: The Department of Trade and Commerce, 1892–1939*. Montreal: McGill-Queen's University Press, 1977.

Hinde, Wendy. *Richard Cobden*. New Haven, Conn.: Yale University Press, 1987.

Hinton, Harold B. *Cordell Hull: A Biography*. Garden City, N.Y.: Doubleday, 1942.

Hirst, Margaret, *Life of Friedrich List*. 1909. Reprint, New York: Augustus M. Kelley, 1965.

Hogan, William T. *Economic History of the Iron and Steel Industry in the United States*. Lexington, Mass.: D. C. Heath, 1971.

Holt, W. Stull. *Treaties Defeated by the Senate*. 1933. Reprint, Gloucester, Mass.: Peter Smith, 1964.

Hoover, Herbert. *Addresses upon the American Road, 1933–38*. New York: Scribner's, 1938.

——. *Memoirs of Herbert Hoover*. New York: Macmillan, 1952.

Hopkins, James F., ed. *Papers of Henry Clay*. Lexington: University of Kentucky Press, 1961.

Houston, David F. *Eight Years with Wilson's Cabinet*. New York: Doubleday, 1926.

Hudec, Robert. *The GATT Legal System and World Trade Diplomacy*. New York: Praeger, 1975.

Hufbauer, Gary, and Howard F. Rosen. *Trade Policy for Troubled Industries.* Washington, D.C.: Institute for International Economics, March 1986.

Hughes, Kent Higgon. *Trade, Taxes, and Transnationals: International Economic Decision-Making in Congress.* New York: Praeger, 1979.

Hull, Cordell. *The Memoirs of Cordell Hull.* New York: Macmillan, 1948.

Humphrey, Don D. *American Imports.* New York: Twentieth-Century Fund, 1955.

Huston, James L. *The Panic of 1857 and the Coming of the Civil War.* Baton Rouge: Louisiana State University Press, 1987.

Ikenberry, G. John, David A. Lake, and Michael Mastanduno. *The State and American Foreign Economic Policy.* Ithaca: Cornell University Press, 1988.

Isely, Jeter Allen. *Horace Greeley and the Republican Party, 1853–1861.* Princeton, N.J.: Princeton University Press, 1947.

Israel, Fred, ed. *State of the Union Messages.* New York: Chelsea House, 1967.

Jackson, John H. *World Trade and the Law of GATT.* Charlottesville, Va.: Michie Co., 1969.

——. *The World Trading System.* Cambridge: MIT Press, 1989.

Jackson, John H., and William J. Davey. *Legal Problems of International Economic Relations.* St. Paul, Minn.: West Publishing Co., 1986.

James, Barrie G. *Trojan Horse: The Ultimate Japanese Challenge to Western Industry.* London: W. H. Allen, 1989.

Jefferson, Thomas. *Notes on the State of Virginia.* 1787. Reprint, Chapel Hill: University of North Carolina Press, 1955.

Jerome, Robert W. *U.S. Senate Decision-Making: The Trade Agreements Act of 1979.* Westport, Conn.: Greenwood Press, 1990.

Johnson, Chalmers. *MITI and the Japanese Miracle.* Stanford, Calif.: Stanford University Press, 1982.

Johnson, Donald Bruce, and Porter, Kirk H. *National Party Platforms, 1840–1972.* Urbana: University of Chicago, 1973.

Johnson, E. A. J. *The Foundations of American Economic Freedom: Government and Enterprise in the Age of Washington.* Minneapolis: University of Minnesota Press, 1973.

Johnson, Emory R., T. W. Van Metre, G. G. Huebner, and D. S. Hanchett. *History of Domestic and Foreign Commerce of the United States.* Washington, D.C.: Carnegie Institute, 1915.

Johnson, Evans C. *Oscar W. Underwood: A Political Biography.* Baton Rouge: Louisiana State University Press, 1980.

Johnson, U. Alexis. *The Right Hand of Power: The Memoirs of an American Diplomat.* Englewood Cliffs, N.J.: Prentice-Hall, 1984.

Jones, Joseph M., Jr. *Tariff Retaliation.* Philadelphia: University of Pennsylvania Press, 1934.

Jordan, David M. *Winfield Scott Hancock.* Bloomington: Indiana University Press, 1988.

Kahan, Arcadius. *Russian Economic History: The Nineteenth Century.* Chicago: University of Chicago Press, 1989.

Kaiser, Carl William, Jr., *History of the Academic Protectionist–Free Trade Controversy in America before 1860.* Philadelphia: University of Pennsylvania Press, 1939.

Kaplan, Edward S., and Thomas W. Ryley. *Prelude to Trade Wars: American Tariff Policy, 1890–1922.* Westport, Conn.: Greenwood Press, 1994.

Kaufman, Burton I. *Efficiency and Expansion: Foreign Trade Organization in the Wilson Administration, 1913–1921.* Westport, Conn.: Greenwood Press, 1974.

——. *Trade and Aid: Eisenhower's Foreign Economic Policy, 1953–1961.* Baltimore: Johns Hopkins University Press, 1982.

Kaye, Harvey, Paul Plaia, Jr., and Michael A. Hertzberg. *International Trade Practice*. Colorado Springs: McGraw-Hill, 1986 ed.

Kelly, William B., ed. *Studies in United States Commercial Policy*. Chapel Hill: University of North Carolina Press, 1963.

Kenen, Peter B. *International Economics*. 3d ed. Englewood Cliffs, N.J.: Prenctice-Hall, 1971.

Kennedy, Paul. *The Rise and Fall of the Great Powers*. New York: Random House, 1987.

Kenwood, A. G., and A. L. Lougheed. *The Growth of the International Economy, 1820–1990*. New York: Routledge, 1992.

Kindleberger, Charles P. *The World in Depression, 1929–1939*. Berkeley: University of California Press, 1973.

———. *A Financial History of Western Europe*. London: G. Allen and Unwin, 1984.

King, Willard L. *Melville Weston Fuller: Chief Justice of the United States, 1888–1910*. New York: Macmillan, 1950.

Kissinger, Henry. *White House Years*. Boston: Little, Brown, 1979.

Kottman, Richard N. *Reciprocity and the North Atlantic Triangle, 1932–1938*. Ithaca, N.Y.: Cornell University Press, 1968.

Kreider, Carl Jonas. *The Anglo-American Trade Agreement*. Princeton, N.J.: Princeton University Press, 1943.

Krugman, Paul. *The Age of Diminished Expectations*. Cambridge: MIT Press, 1990.

Kuykendall, Ralph. *Hawaiian Kingdom, 1778–1854*. Honolulu: University of Hawaii Press, 1947.

———. *Hawaiian Kingdom, 1854–1874*. Honolulu: University of Hawaii Press, 1953.

———. *Hawaiian Kingdom, 1874–1893*. Honolulu: University of Hawaii Press, 1967.

Labaree, Leonard, ed. *Papers of Benjamin Franklin*. New Haven, Conn.: Yale University Press, 1959–.

Labor-Industry Coalition for International Trade. *Antidumping Reform*. Washington, D.C.: Labor-Industry Coalition, February 1990.

LaFeber, Walter. *The New Empire*. Ithaca: Cornell University Press, 1963.

La Follette, Robert M. *La Follette's Autobiography*. Madison, Wis.: La Follette Co., 1913.

Lake, David A. *Power, Protection, and Free Trade: International Sources of U.S. Commercial Strategy, 1887–1939*. Ithaca, N.Y.: Cornell University Press, 1988.

Larkin, John Day. *Trade Agreements: A Study in Democratic Methods*. New York: Columbia University Press, 1940.

Lauderbaugh, Richard A. *American Steel Makers and the Coming of the Second World War*. Ann Arbor, Mich.: UMI Research Press, 1980.

Laughlin, J. Laurence, and H. Parker Willis. *Reciprocity*. New York: Baker and Taylor, 1903.

Lewis, Charles. *America's Frontline Trade Officials*. Washington, D.C.: Center for Public Integrity, 1990.

———. *The Trading Game: Inside Lobbying for the North American Free Trade Agreement*. Washington, D.C.: Center for Public Integrity, 1993.

Liepmann, H. *Tariff Levels and the Economic Unity of Europe*. New York: Macmillan, 1938.

Link, Arthur. *Papers of Woodrow Wilson*. Princeton, N.J.: Princeton University Press, 1982.

List, Friedrich. *The National System of Political Economy*. 1885. Reprint, New York: Augustus M. Kelley 1991.

Louchheim, Katie, ed., *The Making of the New Deal*. Cambridge: Harvard University Press, 1983.

Low, Patrick. *Trading Free: The GATT and U.S. Trade Policy*. New York: Twentieth-Century Fund, 1993.

Lundestad, Geir. *The American "Empire."* New York: Oxford University Press, 1990.

Lyman, Theodore, Jr. *The Diplomacy of the United States.* Boston: Wells and Lilly, 1828.

Madison, James. *Letters and Other Writings of James Madison.* Philadelphia: Lippincott, 1865.

Malone, Dumas, *Jefferson the President: Second Term, 1805–1809.* Boston: Little, Brown, 1974.

Manning, William R. *Diplomatic Correspondence of the United States: Inter-American Affairs, 1831–1860.* Washington, D.C.: Carnegie Institute, 1937.

Marjolin, Robert. *Architect of European Unity: Memoirs, 1911–1986.* London: Weidenfeld, 1989.

Marks, Frederick W., III. *Independence on Trial: Foreign Affairs and the Making of the Constitution.* Baton Rouge: Louisiana State University Press, 1973.

Marshall, Thomas R. *Recollections of Thomas R. Marshall: A Hoosier Salad.* Indianapolis: Bobbs-Merrill, 1925.

Mason, Thomas, ed. *Papers of James Madison.* Charlottesville: University of Virginia Press, 1985.

Martin, Lawrence. *The Presidents and the Prime Ministers.* Toronto: Doubleday, 1982.

Marx, Karl. *The Poverty of Philosophy.* Chicago: Charles H. Kerr, 1913.

Mastanduno, Michael. *Economic Containment: CoCom and the Politics of East-West Trade.* Ithaca, N.Y.: Cornell University Press, 1992.

May, Glenn Anthony. *Social Engineering in the Philippines.* Westport, Conn.: Greenwood, 1980.

McCormick, Thomas J. *China Market: America's Quest for Informal Empire, 1893–1901.* Chicago: Quadrangle, 1967.

McDiarmid, Orville John. *Commercial Policy in the Canadian Economy.* Cambridge: Harvard University Press, 1946.

McGann, Thomas. *Argentina, the United States, and the Inter-American System, 1880–1914.* Cambridge: Harvard University Press, 1957.

McGovern, Edmond. *International Trade Regulation: GATT, the United States, and the European Community.* Exeter, England: Globefield Press, 1986.

McKenzie, Fred A. *The American Invaders.* 1901. Reprint, New York: Arno, 1976.

McKinley, William. *Speeches and Addresses of William McKinley.* New York: D. Appleton, 1893.

Meriwether, Robert, ed. *Papers of John C. Calhoun.* Columbia: University of South Carolina Press, 1959.

Merrill, H. Samuel, and Marion Galbraith Merrill. *Republican Command, 1897–1913.* Lexington: University of Kentucky Press, 1971

Merrill, Milton R. *Reed Smoot: Apostle in Politics.* Logan: Utah State University, 1990.

Metzger, Stanley D. *Lowering Nontariff Barriers.* Washington, D.C.: Brookings Institution, 1974.

Michelson, Charles. *The Ghost Talks.* New York: Putnam's, 1944.

Mill, John Stuart. *Principles of Political Economy.* London: Colonial Press, 1900.

Miller, Marian Mills, comp. *Great Debates in American History.* New York: Current Literature Publishing Co., 1913.

Miller, Naomi Churgin, ed. *The Political Writings of Richard Cobden.* 1903. Reprint, New York: Garland, 1973.

Milner, Helen V. *Resisting Protectionism: Global Industries and the Politics of International Trade.* Princeton, N.J.: Princeton University Press, 1988.

Milward, Alan S. *The European Rescue of the Nation-State.* London: Routledge, 1992.

Mishel, Lawrence, and Jared Bernstein. *Is the Technology Black Box Empty? An Empirical Examination of the Impact of Technology on Wage Inequality and the Employment Structure.* Washington, D.C.: Economic Policy Institute, April 1994.

Moggridge, Donald, ed. *The Collected Writings of John Maynard Keynes.* Cambridge: Cambridge University Press, 1982.

Moley, Raymond. *After Seven Years.* New York: Harper, 1939.

Montesquieu, Charles Louis. *The Spirit of the Laws.* 1750. Reprint, New York: Cambridge University Press, 1989.

Morgan, H. Wayne. *From Hayes to McKinley: National Party Politics, 1877 to 1896.* Syracuse, N.Y.: Syracuse University Press, 1969.

Morison, Elting E., ed. *Letters of Theodore Roosevelt.* Cambridge: Harvard University Press, 1951.

Morris, Richard B. *The Peacemakers.* New York: Harper, 1965.

———. *The Forging of the Union, 1781–1789.* New York: Harper, 1987.

Mossner, Ernest Campbell, and Ian Simpson Ross, eds. *Correspondence of Adam Smith.* Oxford: Clarendon Press, 1987.

Muzzey, David S. *James G. Blaine.* New York: Dodd, Mead, 1934.

Nau, Henry. *The Myth of America's Decline.* New York: Oxford University Press, 1990.

Neatby, H. Blair. *William Lyon MacKenzie King: The Prism of Unity, 1932–1939.* Toronto: University of Toronto Press, 1976.

Nettels, Curtis P. *The Emergence of a National Economy.* New York: Holt, Rinehart, and Winston, 1962.

Niskanen, William. *Reaganomics.* New York: Oxford University Press, 1988.

Nivola, Pietro S. *Regulating Unfair Trade.* Washington, D.C.: Brookings Institution, 1993.

Nixon, Edgar B., ed. *Franklin D. Roosevelt and Foreign Affairs.* Cambridge: Harvard University Press, 1969.

Nixon, Richard M. *The Memoirs of Richard Nixon.* New York: Grosset and Dunlap, 1978.

Nuechterlein, Donald E. *Iceland: Reluctant Ally.* Ithaca, N.Y.: Cornell University Press, 1961.

Nussbaum, Frederick L. *Commercial Policy in the French Revolution: A Study of the Career of G. J. A. Ducher.* 1923. Reprint, New York: AMS, 1970.

O'Connor, John R., Sidney Schwartz, and Leslie A. Wheeler. *Exploring United States History.* New York: Globe Book Co. 1984.

O'Connor, Michael Joseph L. *Origins of Academic Economics in the United States.* 1944. Reprint, New York: Garland, 1974.

Ohmae, Kenichi. *The Borderless World: Power and Strategy in the Interlinked Economy.* New York: Harper Business, 1990.

Olcott, Charles S. *The Life of William McKinley.* Boston: Houghton Mifflin, 1916.

Oliphant, Laurence. *Episodes in a Life of Adventure.* New York: Harper, 1887.

Oye, Kenneth. *Economic Discrimination and Political Exchange.* Princeton, N.J.: Princeton University Press, 1992.

Paolino, Ernest N. *The Foundations of American Empire: William Henry Seward and U.S. Foreign Policy.* Ithaca, N.Y.: Cornell University Press, 1973.

Parker, William Belmont. *Life and Public Services of Justin Smith Morrill.* Boston: Houghton Mifflin, 1924.

Parrini, Carl P. *Heir to Empire: United States Economic Diplomacy, 1916–1923.* Pittsburgh: University of Pittsburgh Press, 1969.

Parry, Clive, John P. Grant, Anthony Parry, and Arthur D. Watts. *Encyclopaedic Dictionary of International Law.* New York: Oceana Publishing, 1986.

Pastor, Robert A. *Congress and the Politics of U.S. Foreign Economic Policy, 1929–76.* Berkeley: University of California Press, 1980.

Patterson, Gardner. *Discrimination in International Trade: The Policy Issues.* Princeton, N.J.: Princeton University Press, 1966.

Peterson, Harold F. *Argentina and the United States, 1810–1960.* New York: State University of New York, 1964.

Peterson, Merrill. *Thomas Jefferson and the New Nation.* New York: Oxford University Press, 1970.

Peterson, Norma Lois. *The Presidencies of William Henry Harrison and John Tyler.* Lawrence: University of Kansas Press, 1989.

Phillips, Kevin. *Boiling Point: Democrats, Republicans, and the Decline of Middle-Class Prosperity.* New York: Random House, 1993.

———.*Arrogant Capital: Washington, Wall Street, and the Frustration of American Politics.* Boston: Little, Brown, 1994.

Phillips, William. *Ventures in Diplomacy.* Boston: Beacon Press, 1952.

Pintner, Walter McKenzie. *Russian Economic Policy under Nicholas I.* Ithaca, N.Y.: Cornell University Press, 1967.

Platt, D. C. M. *Finance, Trade, and Politics in British Foreign Policy, 1815–1914.* Oxford: Clarendon Press, 1968.

Pletcher, David. *The Awkward Years: American Foreign Relations under Garfield and Arthur.* Columbia: University of Missouri Press, 1962.

Pollard, Robert. *Economic Security and the Origins of the Cold War, 1945–1950.* New York: Columbia University Press, 1985.

Pollard, Sidney. *Peaceful Conquest: The Industrialization of Europe, 1760–1970.* London: Oxford University Press, 1981.

———. *Britain's Prime and Britain's Decline: The British Economy, 1870–1914.* London: Edward Arnold, 1989.

Porter, Michael E. *The Competitive Advantage of Nations.* New York: Free Press, 1990.

Preeg, Ernest H. *Traders and Diplomats: An Analysis of the Kennedy Round of Negotiations under the General Agreement on Tariffs and Trade.* Washington, D.C.: Brookings Institution, 1970.

Prestowitz, Clyde. *Trading Places.* New York: Basic Books, 1988.

Prestowitz, Clyde, Larry Chimerine, and Paul Willen. *Closing the Trade Gap with Japan.* Washington, D.C.: Economic Strategy Institute, November 1993.

Rae, John. *Life of Adam Smith.* 1895. Reprint, New York: Augustus Taylor, 1965.

Raymond, Daniel. *The Elements of Political Economy.* Baltimore: F. Lucas, 1823.

Reagan, Ronald. *An American Life.* New York: Simon and Schuster, 1990.

Reeves, Thomas C. *Gentleman Boss: Life of Chester A. Arthur.* New York: Knopf, 1975.

Reich, Robert. *The Work of Nations.* New York: Knopf, 1991.

Reid, Peter C. *Well Made in America: Lessons from Harley Davidson on Being the Best.* New York: McGraw-Hill, 1990.

Reitano, Joanne. *The Tariff Question in the Gilded Age: The Great Debate of 1888.* University Park: Pennsylvania State University Press, 1994.

Remini, Robert V. *Henry Clay: Statesman for the Union.* New York: Norton, 1991.

Reynolds, David. *Creation of the Anglo-American Alliance, 1937–1941.* Chapel Hill: University of North Carolina Press, 1982.

Rhodes, Carolyn. *Reciprocity, U.S. Trade Policy, and the GATT Regime.* Ithaca, N.Y.: Cornell University Press, 1993.

Rhodes, Robert James. *Lord Randolph Churchill.* New York: A. S. Barnes and Co., 1960.

Richardson, James D., comp. *A Compilation of the Messages and Papers of the Presidents.* 20 vols. New York: Bureau of National Literature, 1917.

Rippy, J. Fred. *The United States and Mexico.* New York: Knopf, 1926.

Rooth, Tim. *British Protectionism and the International Economy: Overseas Commercial Policy in the 1930s.* Cambridge: Cambridge University Press, 1993.

Robinson, Edgar Eugene. *Herbert Hoover: President of the United States.* Stanford, Calif.: Hoover Institution Press, 1975.

Robinson, William A. *Thomas B. Reed: Parliamentarian.* New York: Dodd, Mead, 1930.

Roseboom, Eugene H., and Alfred Eckes. 3d ed. *A History of Presidential Elections.* New York: Macmillan, 1979.

Rosenman, Samuel, comp. *Public Papers and Addresses of Franklin D. Roosevelt.* New York: Random House, 1938.

Rowland, Benjamin M. *Commercial Conflict and Foreign Policy: A Study in Anglo-American Relations, 1932–1938.* New York: Garland, 1987.

Russell, Ronald. *Imperial Preference.* London: Empire Economic Union, 1947.

Sage, Leland L. *William Boyd Allison: A Study in Practical Politics.* Iowa City: State Historical Society of Iowa, 1956.

Salvatore, Dominick. *International Economics.* 4th ed. New York: Macmillan, 1993.

Samuelson, Paul A., and William D. Nordhaus. *Economics.* 14th ed. New York: McGraw-Hill, 1992.

Sayre, Francis B. *The Way Forward.* New York: Macmillan, 1939.

Schattschneider, Elmer Eric. *Politics, Pressures, and the Tariff.* New York: Prentice-Hall, 1935.

Schroeder, John H. *Shaping a Maritime Empire: The Commercial and Diplomatic Role of the American Navy, 1829–1861.* Westport, Conn.: Greenwood Press, 1985.

Schuker, Stephen A. *American "Reparations" to Germany, 1919–1933: Implications for the Third-World Debt Crisis.* Princeton: Department of Economics, International Finance Session, July 1988.

Schumpeter, Joseph A. *History of Economic Analysis.* New York: Oxford University Press, 1954.

Schuyler, Eugene. *American Diplomacy and the Furtherance of Commerce.* London: Sampson Low, 1886.

Schwab, Susan C. *Trade-Offs: Negotiating the Omnibus Trade and Competitions Act.* Boston: Harvard Business School Press, 1994.

Selfridge, H. Gordon. *The Romance of Commerce.* London: John Lane, The Bodley Head, 1918.

Setser, Vernon G. *The Commercial Reciprocity Policy of the United States, 1774–1829.* Philadelphia: University of Pennsylvania Press, 1937.

Sheffield, John Lord. *Observations on the Commerce of the American States.* 1784. Reprint, New York: Augustus M. Kelley, 1970.

Shenton, James P. *Robert John Walker: A Politician from Jackson to Lincoln.* New York: Columbia University Press, 1961.

Sherman, John. *Recollections of Forty Years in the House, Senate, and Cabinet.* New York: Werner, 1895.

Shippee, Lester B. *Canadian-American Relations, 1849–1874.* New Haven: Yale University Press, 1939.

Sidgwick, Henry. *The Principles of Political Economy.* London: Macmillan, 1883.

Smith, Adam. *Wealth of Nations.* 1776. Reprint, New York: Modern Library, 1937.

Smith, Page. *John Adams.* Garden City, N.Y.: Doubleday, 1962.

———. *Redeeming the Time: A People's History of the 1920s and the New Deal.* New York: McGraw-Hill, 1987.

Smyth, Albert Henry, ed. *The Writings of Benjamin Franklin.* New York: Macmillan, 1905–7.

Snider, Delbert. *Introduction to International Economics.* Homewood, Ill.: Richard D. Irwin, Inc.

Snyder, J. Richard. *William S. Culbertson.* Washington, D.C.: University Press of America, 1980.

Sobel, Robert, Roger LaRaus, Linda Ann De Leon, and Harry P. Morris. *The Challenge of Freedom.* River Forest, Ill.: Laidlaw, a division of Doubleday, 1981.

Socolofsky, Homer, and Allan B. Spetter. *The Presidency of Benjamin Harrison.* Lawrence: University of Kansas Press, 1987.

Southard, Frank A., Jr. *American Industry in Europe.* 1931. Reprint, New York: Arno Press, 1976.

Sparks, Jared, ed. *The Works of Benjamin Franklin: Essays on General Politics, Commerce, and Political Economy.* 1836. Reprint, New York: Augustus M. Kelley, 1971.

Spencer, Ivor Debenham. *The Victor and the Spoils: A Life of William L. Marcy.* Providence, R.I.: Brown University Press, 1959.

Stanwood, Edward. *American Tariff Controversies in the Nineteenth Century.* New York: Russell and Russell, 1903.

Stead, W. T. *The Americanization of the World.* 1902. Reprint, New York: Garland, 1972.

Stephenson, Nathaniel W. *Nelson W. Aldrich.* New York: Scribner's, 1930.

Stern, Paula. *Water's Edge—Domestic Politics and the Making of American Foreign Policy.* Westport, Conn.: Greenwood, 1979.

Stevens, S. K. *American Expansion in Hawaii, 1842–1898.* Harrisburg, Pa.: Archives Publishing, 1945.

Steward, Dick. *Trade and Hemisphere: The Good Neighbor Policy and Reciprocal Trade.* Columbia: University of Missouri Press, 1975.

Stewart, Andrew. *The American System.* Philadelphia: H. C. Baird, 1872.

Stewart, Gordon T. *The American Response to Canada since 1776.* East Lansing: Michigan State University Press, 1992.

Stourzh, Gerald. *Benjamin Franklin and American Foreign Policy.* Chicago: University of Chicago Press, 1954.

Strackbein, O. R. *American Enterprise and Foreign Trade.* Washington, D.C.: Public Affairs Press, 1965.

Stuart, Reginald C. *United States Expansionism and British North America, 1775–1871.* Chapel Hill: University of North Carolina Press, 1988.

Summers, Festus P. *William L. Wilson and Tariff Reform.* New Brunswick, N.J.: Rutgers University Press, 1953.

Sumner, Charles. *Charles Sumner: His Complete Works.* 1900. Reprint, New York: Negro University Press, 1969.

Suomela, John W. *Free Trade versus Fair Trade: The Making of American Trade Policy in a Political Environment.* Turku, Finland: Institute for European Studies, 1993.

Swank, James M. *The Industrial Policies of Great Britain and the United States.* Philadelphia: Lippincott, 1876.

Syrett, Harold C., ed. *The Papers of Alexander Hamilton.* New York: Columbia University Press, 1961–.

Tansill, Charles Callan. *Canadian-American Relations, 1875–1911*. New Haven: Yale University Press, 1943.

Tarbell, Ida M. *The Tariff in Our Times*. New York: Macmillan, 1911.

——. *All in a Day's Work*. New York: Macmillan, 1939.

Tasca, Henry J. *The Reciprocal Trade Policy of the United States*. Philadelphia: University of Pennsylvania Press, 1938.

Tate, Merze. *The United States and the Hawaiian Kingdom*. New Haven: Yale University Press, 1965.

——. *Hawaii: Reciprocity or Annexation*. East Lansing: Michigan State University Press, 1968.

Taussig, Frank, ed. *Selected Readings in International Trade and Tariff Problems*. New York: Ginn, 1921.

——, ed. *Tariff History of the United States*. 8th ed. 1931. Reprint, New York: Augustus M. Kelley, 1967.

——. *State Papers and Speeches on the Tariff*. 1892. Reprint, Clifton, N.J.: Augustus M. Kelley, 1972.

Taylor, George Rogers. *The Transportation Revolution, 1815–1860*. New York: Holt, Rinehart, and Winston, 1966.

Taylor, Philip. *The Distant Magnet*. London: Eyre and Spottiswoode, 1971.

Taylor, Robert J., ed. *The Papers of John Adams*. Cambridge: Harvard University Press, 1977–.

Tedesco, Paul H. *Patriotism, Protection, and Prosperity: James Moore Swank, the American Iron and Steel Association, and the Tariff, 1873–1913*. New York: Garland, 1985.

Teilhac, Ernest. *Pioneers of American Economic Thought in the Nineteenth Century*. New York: Macmillan, 1936.

Temin, Peter. *Lessons from the Great Depression: The Lionel Robbins Lectures for 1989*. Cambridge: MIT Press, 1989.

Terrill, Tom E. *The Tariff, Politics, and American Foreign Policy, 1874–1901*. Westport, Conn.: Greenwood, 1973.

Thomas, Vinod, and John Nash. *Best Practices in Trade Policy Reform*. Washington, D.C.: World Bank, 1991.

Thompson, Richard W. *The History of Protective Tariff Laws*. 1888. Reprint, New York: Garland, 1974.

Thwaite, Benjamin Howarth. *The American Invasion or England's Commercial Danger*. Wilmington, N.C.: Hugh MacRae, 1902.

Timmons, Bascom N. *Garner of Texas*. New York: Harper, 1948.

Trask, Roger R. *The United States Response to Turkish Nationalism and Reform, 1914–1939*. Minneapolis: University of Minnesota Press, 1971.

Tyson, Laura D'Andrea. *Who's Bashing Whom? Trade Conflict in High-Technology Industries*. Washington, D.C.: Institute for International Economics, 1992.

Underwood, Oscar. *Drifting Sands of Party Politics*. New York: Century, 1928.

United States Code Annotated. St. Paul, Minn.: West Publishing Co., 1980.

Vanderlip, Frank A. *The American "Commercial Invasion" of Europe*. 1902. Reprint, New York: Arno Press, 1976.

Van Deusen, Glyndon G. *William Henry Seward*. New York: Oxford University Press, 1967.

Van Vleck, George W. *The Panic of 1857*. New York: AMS Press, 1967.

Varg, Paul. *Foreign Policies of the Founding Fathers*. Baltimore: Penguin Books, 1970.

Veblen, Thorstein. *Imperial Germany and the Industrial Revolution*. New York: Macmillan, 1915.

Viner, Jacob. *Dumping: A Problem in International Trade.* 1923. Reprint, New York: Augustus M. Kelley, 1966.

Volcker, Paul, and Toyoo Gyohten. *Changing Fortunes: The World's Money and the Threat to American Leadership.* New York: Random House, Times Books, 1992.

Volwiler, Albert T., ed. *Correspondence between Benjamin Harrison and James G. Blaine.* Philadelphia: American Philosophical Society, 1940.

Von Laue, Theodore H. *Sergei Witte and the Industrialization of Russia.* New York: Columbia University Press, 1963.

Wade, Robert. *Governing the Market: Economic Theory and the Role of Government in East Asian Industrialization.* Princeton: Princeton University Press, 1990.

Wanniski, Jude. *The Way the World Works.* New York: Basic Books, 1978.

Warner, Donald F. *The Idea of Continental Union.* Lexington: University of Kentucky Press, 1960.

Warren, Harris Gaylord. *Herbert Hoover and the Great Depression.* New York: Oxford University Press, 1959.

Weiss, Thomas, and Donald Schaefer, eds. *American Economic Development in Historical Perspective.* Stanford, Calif.: Stanford University Press, 1994.

Wharton, Joseph. *International Industrial Competition.* Philadelphia: Henry Carey Baird, 1870.

——. *National Self-Protection.* Philadelphia: American Iron and Steel Association, 1875.

Wilcox, Clair. *A Charter for World Trade.* New York: Macmillan, 1949.

Wilgress, Dana. *Memoirs.* Toronto: Ryerson Press, 1967.

Wilkins, Mira. *The Emergence of Multinational Enterprise: American Business Abroad from the Colonial Era to 1914.* Cambridge: Harvard University Press, 1970.

——. *The Maturing of Multinational Enterprise: American Business Abroad from 1914 to 1970.* Cambridge: Harvard University Press, 1974.

Willcox, William B., ed. *The Papers of Benjamin Franklin.* New Haven: Yale University Press, 1959.

Williams, Benjamin H. *Economic Foreign Policy of the United States.* 1929. Reprint, New York: Howard Fertig, 1967.

Williams, Ernest E. *Made in Germany.* 1896. Reprint, Brighton, England, 1973.

Williams, Judith Blow. *British Commercial Policy and Trade Expansion, 1750–1850.* Oxford: Clarendon Press, 1972.

Wilson, Clyde N., ed. *Papers of John C. Calhoun.* Columbia: University of South Carolina Press, 1988.

Winham, Gilbert R. *International Trade and the Tokyo Round Negotiation.* Princeton, N.J.: Princeton University Press, 1986.

Wolman, Paul. *Most Favored Nation: The Republican Revisionists and U.S. Tariff Policy, 1897–1912.* Chapel Hill: University of North Carolina Press, 1992.

Wood, John Cunningham. *Adam Smith: Critical Assessments.* 4 vols. London: Croom Helm, 1983.

World Bank. *The East Asian Miracle: Economic Growth and Public Policy.* New York: Oxford University Press, 1993.

Wright, Esmond. *Franklin of Philadelphia.* Cambridge, Mass.: Belknap Press, 1986.

Yates, W. Ross. *Joseph Wharton: Quaker Industrial Pioneer.* Bethlehem, Pa.: Lehigh University Press, 1987.

Younger, Edward A. *John A. Kasson: Politics and Diplomacy from Lincoln to McKinley.* Iowa City: State Historical Society of Iowa, 1955.

Zeiler, Thomas W. *American Trade and Power in the 1960s.* New York: Columbia University Press, 1992.
Ziegler, Philip. *The Sixth Great Power: A History of One of the Greatest of All Banking Families: The House of Barings, 1762–1929.* New York: Knopf, 1988.

ARTICLES, PAPERS, AND DISSERTATIONS

Aho, C. Michael, and Thomas O. Bayard. "Costs and Benefits of Trade Adjustment Assistance." In *The Structure and Evolution of Recent U.S. Trade Policy,* edited by Robert E. Baldwin and Anne O. Krueger, pp. 153–93. Chicago: University of Chicago Press, 1984.
Allen, James B. "The Great Protectionist: Sen. Reed Smoot of Utah." *Utah Historical Quarterly* 45 (1977): 325–45.
Almstedt, Kermit W. "International Price Discrimination and the 1916 Antidumping Act—Are Amendments in Order?" *Law and Policy in International Business* 13, no. 3 (1981): 747–81.
Anderson, James E. "Effective Protection in the U.S.: A Historical Comparison." *Journal of International Economics* 2 (1972): 57–76.
Arnold, Bruce. "U.S. Antidumping and Countervailing-Duty Law: A Policy Untethered from Its Rationale." U.S. Congressional Budget Office draft, May 2, 1994.
Asher, Robert E. "The Economics of U.S. Foreign Policy." U.S. Department of State *Bulletin* 29, July 6, 1953, pp. 3–8.
Bairoch, Paul. "European Trade Policy, 1815–1914." In *Cambridge Economic History of Europe,* edited by Peter Mathias and Sidney Pollard, 8:1–160. Cambridge: Cambridge University Press, 1989.
Batra, Ravi, and Daniel J. Slottje. "Trade Policy and Poverty in the United States: Theory and Evidence, 1947–1990." *Review of International Economics* 1, no. 3 (1993): 189–208.
Bedell, Donald W. "The Myth of Smoot-Hawley." *Congressional Record,* 98th Cong., 1st sess., May 9, 1983, S6341.
Berbusse, Edward, J. "The Origins of the McLane-Ocampo Treaty of 1859." *Americas* 14 (January 1958): 223–45.
Bidwell, Percy Wells. "The New American Tariff: Europe's Answer." *Foreign Affairs* 9 (October 1930): 13–26.
Blecker, Robert A., Thea M. Lee, and Robert E. Scott. "Trade Protection and Industrial Revitalization: American Steel in the 1980s." Working Paper 104, Economic Policy Institute, Washington, D.C., February 1993.
Borjas, George J., Richard B. Freeman, and Lawrence F. Katz. "On the Labor Market Effects of Immigration and Trade." Working Paper 3761, National Bureau of Economic Research, Cambridge, Mass., June 1991.
Brauer, Kinley J. "Economics and the Diplomacy of American Expansionism." In *Economics and World Power: An Assessment of American Diplomacy since 1789,* edited by William Becker and Samuel F. Wells Jr., pp. 55–115. New York: Columbia University Press, 1984.
Briggs, B. Bruce. "The Myth of the Hawley-Smoot Tariff." *Congressional Record,* 100th Cong., 1st sess., July 14, 1987, S9873.
Castle, William. "America and the Dictatorships." *Vital Speeches,* January 1, 1939, pp. 162–66.
Chapin, James B. "Hamilton Fish." In *Makers of American Diplomacy,* edited by Frank J. Merli and Theodore A. Wilson, pp. 223–51. New York: Scribner's, 1974.

Chu, Power Yung-Chao. "A History of the Hull Trade Program, 1934–1939." Ph.D. diss., Columbia University, 1957.

Colvin, Terrence R., and Donald E. deKieffer. "A Legal and Economic Analysis of the Quota Provisions of the Proposed Foreign Trade and Investment Act of 1972." *International Lawyer* 6 (October 1972): 771.

Cooper, Richard N. "Trade Policy as Foreign Policy." In *U.S. Trade Policies in a Changing World Economy*, edited by Robert M. Stern, pp. 291–92. Cambridge: MIT Press, 1987.

Coppock, Joseph. "Government Assistance in Developing Imports into the United States." U.S. Department of State *Bulletin* 20, January 30, 1949, 139.

Crandall, Samuel B. "The American Construction of the Most-Favored-Nation Clause." *American Journal of International Law* 7 (October 1913): 708–9.

Cunningham, Richard O. "The Copper Problem: The Inadequacy of U.S. Trade Laws and the Administration's Failure to Provide Meaningful Solutions for Injury Caused by Artificial Distortions in World Commodity Trade." Paper presented at the Western National Mining Conference and Exhibition, February 13, 1986.

Cunningham, William. "Free Trade." In *Encyclopedia Britannica*, 11 ed. New York: Macmillan, 1911.

Daly, Herman E. "The Perils of Free Trade." *Scientific American* 269 (November 1993): 50–52.

Dennis, Alfred Pearce. "The Diligent Senator Smoot." *World's Work* 59 (May 1930): 62–64.

Dexter, Grant, and J. A. Stevenson. "Canada's Tariff Reprisals against America." *Current History* 34 (May 1931): 208–13.

Dorfman, Ben. "Japan's Competitive Position in International Trade, Part II." Draft, May 1935, ITC Library.

Dozer, Donald Marquand. "The Opposition to Hawaiian Reciprocity, 1876–1888." *Pacific Historical Review* 14 (1945): 157–83.

Durand, E. Dana. "The Trade Agreements Program." Manuscript, December 195?, ITC Library.

Eckes, Alfred E. "Trading American Interests." *Foreign Affairs* 71 (Fall 1992): 135–54.

——. "Antidumping after the Uruguay Round: A Former Administrator's Perspective." In *International Commercial Policy*, edited by Mordechai E. Kreinin, pp. 29–35. London: Taylor and Francis, 1993.

——. "Epitaph for the Escape Clause?" In *International Trade: Regional and Global Issues*, edited by Michael Landeck, pp. 138–46. New York: St. Martin's Press, 1994.

Ehrenhaft, Peter D. "What the Antidumping and Countervailing Duty Provisions of the Trade Agreements Act [Can][Will][Should] Mean for U.S. Trade Policy." *Law and Policy in International Business* 11 (1979): 1361–1404.

Eichengreen, Barry. "Did International Economic Forces Cause the Great Depression?" *Contemporary Policy Issues* 6 (April 1988): 90–113.

——. "The Political Economy of the Smoot-Hawley Tariff." In *Research in Economic History*, edited by Roger L. Ransom, 12:25–29. Greenwich, Conn.: JAI Press, 1989.

Fallows, James. "How the World Works." *Atlantic Monthly*, December 1993.

Feller, Peter Buck. "Mutiny against the Bounty: An Examination of Subsidies, Border Tax Adjustments, and the Resurgence of the Countervailing Duty Law." *Law and Policy in International Business* 1 (Winter 1969): 17–76.

Finan, William, and Annette M. LaMond. "Sustaining U.S. Competitiveness in Microelectronics." in *U.S. Competitiveness in the World Economy*, edited by Bruce R. Scott and George C. Lodge, pp. 172–80. Cambridge: Harvard Business School Press, 1985.

Frankel, Jeffrey A. "The 1807–1809 Embargo against Great Britain." *Journal of Economic History* 42 (1982): 291–308.

Fremling, Gertrud M. "Did the United States Transmit the Great Depression to the Rest of the World?" *American Economic Review* 75 (December 1985): 1181–85.

Fry, Joseph A. "Washington's Farewell Address and American Commerce." *West Virginia History* 37 (October 1975): 281–90.

Fulda, Carl H. "Adjustment to Hardship Caused by Imports: The New Decisions of the Tariff Commission and the Need for Legislative Clarification." *Michigan Law Review* 70, no. 5 (April 1972): 795–96.

Gearhart, William W. "The U.S. Escape Clause Law—Its Origin, Evolution, and Present Form." Paper, June 1990 version, ITC General Counsel's Office.

Gould, Lewis L. "Diplomats in the Lobby: Franco-American Relations and the Dingley Tariff of 1897." *Historian* 39 (November 1976): 659–80.

Grampp, W. D. "Adam Smith and the American Revolutionists." In *Adam Smith: Critical Assessments*, edited by John Cunningham Wood, 4:306–15. London: Croom Helm, 1983.

Grieb, Kenneth. "Negotiating a Reciprocal Trade Agreement with an Underdeveloped Country: Guatemala." *Prologue* 5 (Spring 1973): 22–29.

Hannigan, Robert E. "Reciprocity 1911: Continentalism and American Weltpolitik." *Diplomatic History* 4 (Winter 1980): 1–18.

Hartland-Thunberg, Penelope. "Tales of a Onetime Tariff Commissioner." *Challenge* 20 (July–August 1977): 6–12.

Hawke, G. R. "The United States Tariff and Industrial Protection in the Late Nineteenth Century." *Economic History Review* 28 (1975): 84–99.

Hawley, Willis. "The New Tariff: A Defense." *Review of Reviews* (July 1930): 52–55.

Hayford, Marc D., and Carl A. Pasurka Jr. "Effective Rates of Protection and the Fordney-McCumber and Smoot-Hawley Tariff Acts." *Applied Economics* 23 (1991): 1385–92.

Hooley, Osborne E. "Hawaiian Negotiation for Reciprocity, 1855–1857." *Pacific Historical Review* 7 (1938): 128–46.

Horlick, Gary. "Current Issues in the Definition and Measurement of Subsidies under U.S. Countervailing Duty Law." Paper presented at the First Annual Judicial Conference of the U.S. Court of International Trade, New York City, February 15, 1984, p. 9.

Hull, Cordell, "Call Off the Tariff War!" *Nation*, December 16, 1931, pp. 667–69.

Huston, James L., "A Political Response to Industrialism: The Republican Embrace of Protectionist Labor Doctrines." *Journal of American History* (1983): 35–57.

James, Scott C., and David A. Lake. "The Second Face of Hegemony: Britain's Repeal of the Corn Laws and the American Walker Tariff of 1846." *International Organization* 43, no. 1 (Winter 1989): 1–15.

Kalijarvi, Thorsten V. "Foreign Economic Policy and the National Security." U.S. Department of State *Bulletin* 31, September 20, 1954, pp. 409–17.

Kantor, Mickey. "U.S. Trade Policy and the Post–Cold War World." U.S. Department of State *Dispatch* 4, no. 11, March 15, 1993, pp. 143–48.

Keeley, James F. "Cast in Concrete for All Time? The Negotiation of the Auto Pact." *Canadian Journal of Political Science* 16, no. 2 (June 1983): 281–98.

Kennedy, Kevin C. "*Zenith Radio Corp. v. United States*: The Nadir of the U.S. Trade Relief Process." *North Carolina Journal of International Law and Commercial Regulation* 13 (1988): 225–49.

Kindleberger, C. P. "The Rise of Free Trade in Western Europe, 1820–1875." *Journal of Economic History* 35 (March 1975): 20–55.

——. "U.S. Foreign Economic Policy, 1776–1976." *Foreign Affairs* 55 (January 1977): 395–417.

Kirkendall, Richard S. "Franklin D. Roosevelt and the Service Intellectuals." *Mississippi Valley Historical Review* 49 (December 1962): 456–71.

Komiya, Ryutaro, and Motoshige Itoh. "Japan's International Trade and Trade Policy, 1955–1984." In *Political Economy of Japan*, edited by Takashi Inoguchi and Daniel I. Okomoto, 2:181. Stanford, Calif.: Stanford University Press, 1988.

Krock, Arthur. "President Hoover's Two Years." *Current History* 34 (1931): 490.

Krugman, Paul. "The Myth of Asia's Miracle." *Foreign Affairs* 73 (November–December 1994): 62–78.

Krugman, Paul, and Robert Lawrence. "Trade, Jobs, and Wages." Working Paper 4478, National Bureau of Economic Research, Cambridge, Mass., September 1993.

Lawrence, Robert Z., and Matthew J. Slaughter. "Trade and U.S. Wages: Great Sucking Sound or Small Hiccup?" Paper presented at the MICRO-BPEA meeting, Washington, D.C., June 10–11, 1993.

Leamer, Edward E. "Wage Effects of a U.S. Mexican Free Trade Agreement." Working Paper 3991, National Bureau of Economic Research, Cambridge, Mass., February 1992.

Lee, Thea, and Dale Belman. "Trade Liberalization, Jobs, and Wages." Paper, Economic Policy Institute, Washington, D.C., March 21, 1994.

Leffler, Melvyn P. "1921–1932: Expansionist Impulses and Domestic Constraints." In *Economics and World Power: An Assessment of American Diplomacy since 1789*, edited by William H. Becker and Samuel F. Wells Jr. New York: Columbia University Press, 1984.

Levinson, Kenneth S. "Title II of the Trade Act of 1974: What Changes Hath Congress Wrought to Relief from Injury Caused by Import Competition." *Journal of International Law and Economics* 10 (April 1975): 197–232.

Long, Russell B. "United States Law and the International Anti-Dumping Code." *International Lawyer* 3, no. 3 (April 1969): 464–89.

Love, Mark. "The Real Lesson of the Smoot-Hawley Act." *Journal of Commerce*, October 8, 1985.

Luthin, Reinhard H. "Abraham Lincoln and the Tariff." *American Historical Review* 49 (July 1944): 609–29.

MacGarvey, Charles J. "Daniel Raymond, Esquire: Founder of American Economic Thought." *Maryland Historical Magazine* 44 (June 1949): 111–22.

Madison, Christopher. "Alfred Who?" *National Journal*, 11 (March 17, 1984): 527.

Mangan, John J. "Trade Agreements Act of 1979: A Steel Industry Perspective." *Law and Policy in International Business* 18, no. 24 (1986): 241–77.

Marks, Matthew J. "Evolving Law of Unfair Practices in International Trade." *Antitrust Law Journal* 43, no. 3 (1974): 583–88.

McCloskey, Donald N. "Magnanimous Albion: Free Trade and British National Income, 1841–1881." *Explorations in Economic History* 17 (1980): 303–20.

McCoy, Drew R. "Republicanism and American Foreign Policy: James Madison and the Political Economy of Commercial Discrimination, 1789 to 1794." *William and Mary Quarterly*, 3d ser., 31 (October 1974): 633–46.

McKinley, William. "The Tariff: A History of Tariff Legislation from 1812 to 1896." In *The Works of Henry Clay*, edited by Calvin Colton, vol. 10. New York: Putnam's, 1904.

Megaw, M. Ruth. "Australia and the Anglo-American Trade Agreement, 1938." *Journal of Imperial and Commonwealth History* 3 (January 1975): 191–211.

Metzger, Stanley D. "The Trade Expansion Act of 1962." *Georgetown Law Journal* 51, no. 3 (Spring 1963): 442–47.

——. "Book Reviews." *Law and Policy in International Business* 4 (1972): 483–89.

Neville, Mark K., Jr. "The Antidumping Act of 1916: A War-Time Legacy." *New York Law School Law Review* 26 (1981): 535–75.

Nevin, John J. "Enforcing the Antidumping Laws: The Television Dumping Case." *Journal of Legislation* 6 (May 1979): 1–20.

Norwood, Bernard. "The Kennedy Round: A Try at Linear Trade Negotiations." *Journal of Law and Economics* 12, no. 2 (October 1969): 314, 319.

Novack, David F., and Matthew Simon. "Commercial Responses to the American Export Invasion, 1871–1914: An Essay in Attitudinal History." *Explorations in Economic History* 3 (Winter 1966): 120–17.

Nye, John Vincent. "The Myth of Free-Trade Britain and Fortress France: Tariffs and Trade in the Nineteenth Century." *Journal of Economic History* 51 (March 1991): 23–46.

Officer, Laurence H., and Lawrence B. Smith. "The Canadian-American Reciprocity Treaty of 1855 to 1866." *Journal of Economic History* 28 (December 1968): 598–623.

O'Reilly, Brian. "Your New Global Work Force." *Fortune*, December 14, 1992.

Patterson, James T. *America in the Twentieth Century: A History*. New York: Harcourt, Brace, Jovanovich, 1976.

Patterson, John. "The United States and Hawaiian Reciprocity, 1867–1870." *Pacific Historical Review* 7 (1938): 14–26.

Paul, Arnold M. "Lucius Quintus Cincinnatus Lamar." In *Justices of the U.S. Supreme Court*, edited by Leon Friedman and Fred Israel. Vol. 2, pp. 1431–51. New York: Chelsea House, 1980.

Peterson, Merrill D. "Thomas Jefferson and Commercial Policy, 1783–1793." *William and Mary Quarterly* 22 (October 1965): 592–93.

Phillips, Kevin. "The Politics of Protectionism." *Public Opinion* (April–May 1985): 41–46.

Pletcher, David. "Reciprocity and Latin America in the Early 1890s: A Foretaste of Dollar Diplomacy." *Pacific Historical Review* 47 (February 1978): 53–89.

——. "Economic Growth and Diplomatic Adjustment." In *Economics and World Power: An Assessment of American Diplomacy since 1789*, edited by William Becker and Samuel F. Wells Jr., 119–71. New York: Columbia University Press, 1984.

Preeg, Ernest R. "The U.S. Leadership Role in World Trade: Past, Present, and Future." *Washington Quarterly* 15, no. 2 (1992): 81–92.

Prestowitz, Clyde, Alan Tonelson, and Robert W. Jerome. "The Last Gasp of Gattism." *Harvard Business Review* (March–April 1991): 130–38.

Ris, William K., Jr. " 'Escape Clause' Relief under the Trade Act of 1974: New Standards, Same Results." *Columbia Journal of Transnational Law* 16 (1977): 297–325.

Ryder, Oscar. "United States Tariff Commission: Its Background and History." Manuscript, 196?, ITC Library.

Sachs, Jeffrey D., and Howard J. Shatz. "Trade and Jobs in U.S. Manufacturing." Paper prepared for the Brookings Panel on Economic Activity, Washington, D.C., April 7–8, 1994.

Schatz, Arthur W. "Cordell Hull and the Struggle for the Reciprocal Trade Agreements Program, 1932–1940." Ph.D. diss., University of Oregon, 1965.

——. "The Anglo-American Trade Agreement and Cordell Hull's Search for Peace, 1936–1938." *Journal of American History* 57 (June 1970): 99–103.

See, Henri. "Commerce between France and the United States, 1783–1784." *American Historical Review* 31 (1926): 732–52.

Setser, Vernon G. "Did Americans Originate the Conditional Most-Favored-Nation Clause?" *Journal of Modern History* 3 (September 1933): 319–23.

Shannon, Thomas F., and William F. Marx. "The International Anti-Dumping Code and United States Antidumping Law—An Appraisal." *Columbia Journal of Transnational Law* 7 (1968): 171–202.

Slichter, Sumner. "Is the Tariff a Cause of Depression?" *Current History* (January 1932): 519–24.

Smoot, Reed. "Our Tariff and the Depression." *Current History* 35 (November 1931): 173–81.

Snyder, J. Richard. "Hoover and the Hawley-Smoot Tariff: A View of Executive Leadership." *Annals of Iowa* 41, no. 7 (Winter 1973): 1172–89.

Stewart, Terence P. "Administration of the Antidumping Law: A Different Perspective." In *Down in the Dumps: Administration of the Unfair Trade Laws*, edited by Richard Boltuck and Robert E. Litan, pp. 288–330. Washington, D.C.: Brookings Institution, 1991.

Stover, John F. "French-American Trade during the Confederation, 1781–1789." *North Carolina Historical Review* 35 (October 1958): 399–414.

Strange, Susan. "Protectionism and World Politics." *International Organization* 39, no. 2 (Spring 1985): 233–59.

Tarbell, Ida M. "Some Moral Aspects of Tariff-Making." *Great Debates in American History*, compiled by Marian Mills Miller, pp. 1–7. New York: Current Literature Publishing Co., 1913.

Tarullo, Daniel K. "Law and Politics in Twentieth-Century Tariff History." *UCLA Law Review* 34 (December 1986): 285–370.

Temin, Peter. "The Great Depression." Historical Paper no. 62, National Bureau of Economic Research, Cambridge, Mass., 1994.

Thorp, Willard L. "The Economic Basis of Our Foreign Policy." U.S. Department of State *Bulletin* 27, August 4, 1952.

Tonelson, Alan. "Beating Back Predatory Trade." *Foreign Affairs* (July/August 1994): 123–35.

Volwiler, A. T. "Tariff Strategy and Propaganda in the United States, 1887–1888." *American History Review* 36 (October 1930): 76–96.

Wallis, W. Allen. "Protecting Prosperity from Protectionism." U.S. Department of State *Bulletin*, no. 86, March 1986, pp. 33–36.

Waugh, Samuel C. "Problems of Foreign Economic Policy." U.S. Department of State *Bulletin* 30, March 1, 1954, pp. 321–26.

Winham, Gilbert R. "The Canadian Automobile Industry and Trade-related Performance Requirements." *Journal of World Trade Law* 18 (1984): 471–96.

Wolff, Alan W. "International Competitiveness of American Industry." In *U.S. Competitiveness in the World Economy*, edited by Bruce R. Scott and George C. Lodge, pp. 315–38. Cambridge: Harvard Business School Press, 1985.

Zebel, Sydney H. "Fair Trade: An English Reaction to the Breakdown of the Cobden Treaty System." *Journal of Modern History* 12, no. 2 (June 1940): 161–85.

Index

Adams, Brooks, 60

Adams, John, 3–6, 12, 19–21; on commerce, 3; embraces mercantilism, 19–20

Adams, John Quincy, 6, 11, 18–19

Adams, Sherman, 240

Adjustment assistance, xix, 176, 186–87, 205–8, 242–48, 342 (n. 120)

Agar, 174

Agriculture, U.S. Department of, 142, 143, 156, 170, 190, 194, 236, 250, 265, 319 (n. 12), 329 (n. 17), 330 (n. 25), 339 (n. 53); and Kennedy Round, 183–86, 190–96, 199, 332 (n. 65)

Agricultural exports, 3, 24, 62, 64, 83, 141, 302 (n. 1); to Europe, 21–22, 182, 186, 190, 203; F. D. Roosevelt on, 45; and U.K. imperial preferences, 149–53, 321 (n. 39); and Japan, 171; in Kennedy Round, 190–91, 197, 200, 331 (n. 46); in Uruguay Round, 284, 286

Agricultural implements, 59, 62, 76, 84, 130, 133, 144, 172

Agricultural Implements Association, 62

Aircraft engines and parts, 174

Albania, 92

Alberger, Bill, 251

Alcoholic beverages, 15, 75

Aldrich, Nelson, 68, 71, 73, 76, 78, 79, 99, 104, 307 (n. 64); protective theory of, 33, 307 (n. 76)

Aldrich, Winthrop, 235

Allegheny Ludlum Steel Corporation, 271–72

Allen, Charles E., 128

Allison, William, 71, 307 (n. 64)

America first, 14–15, 30–31

American Bar Association, 269

American Independent Party, 211

American Iron and Steel Association, 57, 62

American Iron and Steel Institute, 201, 210, 320 (n. 15)

American Loudspeaker Manufacturers Association, 210

American selling price (ASP), 198–99, 210, 212, 333 (n. 81)

American System, 2, 19–25, 140

Amery, Julian, 51

Anderson, Robert, 176

Antibiotics, 172

Antidumping, xix–xx, 88; in Kennedy Round, 198–99, 270, 332 (n. 71); history of, 260–63; and 1979 act, 262, 271; enforcement of, 264–66, 269–77, 346 (n. 64); and GATT, 266–67, 274–76; 1954 statutory change, 269

Antidumping Act of 1921, 88, 199, 261–63, 267, 269; enforcement of, 264–66, 269–70

Apparel, xiv, 15, 18, 33, 59, 63, 114, 158, 174–75, 223, 242, 255; Washington on, 15; Lincoln on, 25

Apples, 59, 123, 130, 144, 151, 282

Apricots, 130

Argentina, 62, 125–27, 249; Kasson treaty with, 76, 306 (n. 55); 1941 agreement with, 154–56

Argols, 75–76

Armaments, 15, 34

Armenia, 287

Articles of Confederation, 8–10

Asakai, Koichiro, 239

Asphalt, 314 (n. 69)

Associated Press, 104

Australia, 62, 125, 276, 314 (n. 79)

Austria, 86, 91, 92, 117, 125, 129

Austrian Glue Manufacturers, 118

Automobiles, 84, 86–87, 140, 144, 150, 158, 255, 258, 272, 321 (n. 39), 340 (n. 75); Canadian agreement on, xvi, 193–94, 331 (n. 56), 333 (n. 94), 334 (n. 104); and Smoot-Hawley Tariff, 119, 121–23, 127–30, 133, 315 (n. 92); and parts, 130, 144, 160; U.K. duty on, 150; and Japan, 170–72; after Kennedy Round, 204–5, 208; escape clause case on, 251, 342 (n. 109)

Aydin Corporation, 259

Common Agricultural Policy (CAP), 182, 191, 203

Congress, U.S.: and authority to regulate commerce, 10; and foundations of trade policy, 12–13; first tariff, 13–14; and industrial policy, 15–17, 57; and tariff protection, 22–23, 24; and reciprocity program, 25–26, 62–74, 75, 77–84, 93–98; British view of, 29; Harding and, 43; modifies high-tariff system, 46–47, 85–86; and revenue surplus, 46–48; and Smoot-Hawley Tariff, 100–39, 208; and Hull, 141; and RTAP, 141–42, 146, 156; Republican (1946), 159; doubts about Eisenhower's open trade policy, 168; reacts to Japanese agreement, 175–76; concern about Dillon Round, 181–83; and Trade Expansion Act (TEA), 184, 188–89; and Kennedy Round, 192–94, 210, 214; and escape clause enforcement, 224–25, 242–43; and antidumping, 257, 261–62, 267–74. See also House of Representatives, U.S.; Senate, U.S.

Connally, Tom, 317 (n. 121)

Connor, John T., 190

Constitution: and bifurcated trade authority, xi, 9–10; and Zollverein treaty, 65; and reciprocity, 68–70, 73–74, 318 (n. 4); Field v. Clark (1892), 74; and revenue measures, 104; and Kennedy Round, 198–99; Truman on, 324 (n. 69)

Consumer electronics, 59, 144, 158, 166, 188, 205–7, 242, 340 (n. 75)

Containment, 157–79, 185

Continental Congress, U.S., 4–5

Coolidge, Calvin, 43, 264, 301 (n. 56)

Cooper, Richard, 101

Copper, xiv, 108, 121, 133, 136, 249, 311 (n. 24)

Coppock, Joseph, 165

Cord, 222

Corn, 172, 182

Corned beef, 154

Corn Laws, 25, 66, 282

Corse, Carl, 160–61, 163, 327 (n. 121)

Cotton, Norris, 189

Cotton: raw, 1, 59, 63, 121, 130, 144, 151, 156, 302 (n. 1); textiles, 20, 24–25, 130, 151–52,

168, 184, 223, 320 (n. 18), 328 (nn. 130, 131), 333 (n. 81); apparel, 63, 76, 151–52, 184, 223

Cottonseed oil, 173

Council of Economic Advisers, U.S., xvii, 185, 236, 250, 252, 286

Countervailing duties, xix, 131; and Treasury discretion, 263–64; enforcement of, 264–67, 270, 274–76, 346 (n. 64); and 1979 law, 273, 277; record in 1994, 346 (n. 64). See also Antidumping

Court of Appeals for the Federal Circuit, U.S., 255

Court of International Trade, U.S., 255

Coxe, Tenche, 296 (n. 44)

Crabmeat, 169

Cross, Cecil M., 128

Cuba, 68, 69, 74, 78–81, 91, 125, 154, 156, 164, 324 (n. 63)

Culbertson, William, 90, 95

Cunningham, William, 51

Curtis, Carl, 189

Curtis, Thomas, 182, 192, 204

Customs, U.S. Bureau of, 271–72

Cutlery. See Flatware

Cyclops Corporation, 271

Cyprus, 194, 218

Czechoslovakia, 91, 92, 119, 129

Dalzell, Charles, 83–84

Danforth, John, 254

Daniels, Josephus, 95

Davis, Norman, 95

Debt, federal, 48–49

Defense, U.S. Department of, 223, 234, 236–37, 250

DeGaulle, Charles, 190

Delaware Society for Promoting Domestic Manufacturers, 15

Democratic National Executive Committee, 94, 138, 141

Democratic Party, 20, 281, 287; and low-tariff Democrats, 22–24, 34–45 passim; opposition to executive tariff cutting, 74, 318 (n. 4); and Smoot-Hawley Tariff, 137–38; and trade liberalization, 141

Democratic platform: of 1844, 1848, 1856, 25; of 1872, 1884, 1892, 37; of 1892, 42; of

1920, 1924, 43; of 1928, 43–44; of 1932, 44; of 1960, 1968, 211
Democratic-Republicans, 19
Denmark, 8, 76, 174, 232
Dent, Frederick, 212, 273
Dent, John, 201–2, 330 (n. 38)
Destler, I. M., 247
Diamond Chain Company, 272
Diamonds, 121
Dillon Round (GATT), 180–83, 208, 329 (nn. 14–17)
Dingley, Nelson, 104
Dingley Tariff Act (1897), 35, 75–77, 85, 88, 263, 306 (n. 52), 312 (n. 47)
Dinnerware. *See* Chinaware
Dirksen, Everett, 192–93
Discrimination against Japanese exports, 167, 174, 317 (n. 2)
Discrimination against U.S. exports, xix, 21–22, 24; after American Revolution, 6; during French Revolution, 12–13; in nineteenth century, 60–62; before World War I, 82–86; after World War I, 86–92; Smoot-Hawley Tariff, 124–32, 314 (n. 81); after World War II, 164–65, 326 (n. 94); after Kennedy Round, 203
Dominican Republic, 69, 76, 92, 262
Dorfman, Ben, 345 (n. 46)
Doughton, Robert, 318 (n. 4)
Douglas, Paul H., 132, 316 (n. 104), 328 (n. 133)
Dow Chemical Company, 212
Drucker, Peter, 259
Drummond, Ian, 153, 322 (n. 50)
Dulles, John Foster, 167–69, 235–37
Dumping, xv; after war of 1812, 18–19, 21–22, 297 (n. 55); defined, 258–59. *See also* Antidumping; Antidumping Act of 1921; Countervailing duties
Dunning, John, xviii
Durand, Dana, 227

Earthenware. *See* Chinaware
East Asia, 56–57
East Indies, Netherlands, 81
Eberle, William, 247
Economic appeasement, 148–53, 177, 321 (n. 32). *See also* Trading interests

Economic conditions: in late nineteenth century, 47–56, 59–60; during Great Depression, 109–15; before Kennedy Round, 177–80; after Kennedy Round, 216–18; in 1990s, 278–89
Economic Cooperation Administration, U.S., 158
Economic internationalism, xix, 1–4, and Cobdenism, 1, 24, 28–29, 192, 280–81, 288–89; and State Department, 136–37; Hull and, 141, 156–57, 281–82; after World War II, 157–77, 326 (n. 105); and International Trade Organization, 161; in Kennedy administration, 178–79, 185–86; after Kennedy Round, 209, 211, 256; George Bush and, 280; Clinton and, 280, 284. *See also* State, U.S. Department of
Economic nationalism, 14–20, 29–34, 285–87, 292 (n. 15). *See also* Mercantilism; Protectionism
Economic Policy Group, White House, 250
Economic security, 2, 14–22, 26–27, 34; and G. Washington, 10–11; and Eisenhower, 167–68, 176–77, 233–34
Economist, The, 24, 285, 288
Economists: theories of, xv–xviii, 26; early American, 16, 17, 57, 296 (n. 50); petition against Smoot-Hawley Tariff, 132–33, 137; debate impact of imports on domestic jobs, 285–86. *See also* Carey, Henry; List, Friedrich; Raymond, Daniel; Smith, Adam
Edge, Walter, 122
Ecuador, 76
Edminster, Lynn R., 227–32, 336 (n. 17)
Egg albumen, dried, 170
Egypt, 117
Eichengreen, Barry, 115, 130, 137
Eisenhower, Dwight D.: on Smoot-Hawley Tariff, 102; trade philosophy, 105; on expanded imports, 159, 167–77; on Japan, 167–70; opposes import restraints, 176; and Cobdenism, 177; and Dillon Round, 180–83; escape clause actions, 233–41, 243; antidumping record, 264; British view of, 326 (n. 105)
Eisenstat, Stuart, 284

Electronic data interchange, 278, 287
Electronic Industries Association, 188, 210, 271
Elgin, Lord, 66
Equality, 4–11, 26–27, 293 (n. 2). *See also* Most-favored-nation policy
Ervin, Sam, 201
Escape clause, xix, 166, 176, 186; and 1958 extension, 175–76, 181, 241; and Nixon, 215, 242–46, 251; origins of, 220–21, 223; enforcement of, 221–24; case record, 225, 227, 240–42, 245, 255; Truman on, 225, 227–34, 336 (nn. 10, 12); and Tariff Commission, 225–44, 246, 337 (n. 19); and 1951 reciprocal trade renewal, 228–29; and Eisenhower, 233–41, 250; and Kennedy, 241–42, 329 (n. 12); and Trade Act of 1974, 244–45, 252; and International Trade Commission, 244–55; and Carter, 245, 247–52; and Reagan, 245, 248–49, 252–54; and Ford, 245, 249
Estonia, 92
European Coal and Steel Community, 180
European Cooperation Administration, U.S., 165
European Economic Community (EEC), xx, 180, 181, 190, 208–9, 218, 276, 283; and trade diversion, 180; in Dillon Round, 181; and agricultural trade, 182, 191–92, 194–96, 200, 203; and Kennedy Round, 185–201, 331 (n. 46), 332 (n. 65); and escape clause, 247; and steel, 273
European Free Trade Association, 180
Everett, Edward, 64
Exchange rates, 203, 312 (n. 37)
Executive branch, U.S. *See names of specific Presidents and Cabinet departments, especially Agriculture, Commerce, State, and Treasury*
Executive Committee on Commercial Policy, 142–43, 265
Executive tariff making, 142–48
Exports: nineteenth-century growth in, 51; decline after Smoot-Hawley Tariff, 126, 129–30; U.S. share of world, 179; in 1965, 190–91; European, 180; world vs. U.S., 283

Fabrick, Seymour, xiii
Fair Labor Standards Act, 201
Fallows, James, 57
False teeth, 130
Farnsworth, Clyde, xiv
Fasteners, 239, 246, 250, 342 (n. 105)
Federalist Papers, 10–11, 13
Federal Reserve, 110
Feis, Herbert, 117, 144, 319 (n. 110), 320 (n. 18), 336 (n. 4)
Ferrochrome, 182, 246
Ferrosilicon, 174
Fielding, W. S., 260–61
Field v. Clark (1892), 74, 295 (n. 35), 305 (n. 46)
Filberts, 119
Fillmore, Millard, 22
Film, 118, 123, 127, 130, 284
Financial Post (Toronto), 201
Finland, 92, 117, 129, 174, 268
Firearms, 182
Fire hose, linen, 224
Fish, Hamilton, 68–69
Fish, xiv, 26, 83, 155, 174, 232, 237–38, 339 (n. 61); and California canning, 155, 232
Flannel shirt, 167
Flatware, 25, 158, 168, 175, 182, 239, 245–46, 253
Flaxseed, 154–55
Flexible tariff: Section 315, 89–90; Section 336, 95–97, 122–24, 134, 313 (n. 61), 314 (n. 69), 316 (n. 112). *See also* Tariff
Flycatchers, 265
Footwear, xiv, 15, 121, 169–71, 205–6, 242, 244–48, 254, 340 (n. 75)
Ford, Gerald, 216, 245, 247, 249, 272
Ford, Henry, xvi
Ford Motor Company, 252
Fordney, Joseph, 104, 108
Fordney-McCumber Tariff (1922), 88–90, 104, 109, 112–13, 312 (n. 47)
Foreign Affairs, 136
Foreign policy and trade: before Civil War, 4–13, 18–22, 27, 63–67; post–Civil War, 68–78; in early twentieth century, 78–87, 90–93; drives trade policy after 1937, 148–77, 282; and escape clause enforce-

ment, 221–56; and unfair trade administration, 264–74

Fortune, 285

Foster, John W., 69, 74

Fountain, L., 117

Fowler, Henry, 196

Fox furs, 222

France, xix, 1, 86, 146, 183, 272, 294 (n. 18); and Treaty of Amity and Commerce (1778), 5–6, 26–27, 219; and Tariff of 1789, 14; and Kasson treaty with, 75–76; discrimination against U.S. exports, 92–93, 146; and Smoot-Hawley Tariff, 117, 119, 122–23, 125–27, 129; vetoes U.K. bid to join EEC, 190; in Kennedy Round, 199; and escape clause, 233–34, 235, 247–48; and Uruguay Round, 284, 287

Franco, Francisco, 246

Frank, Isaiah, 174

Franklin, Benjamin: as free trader, 2–3; and treaty plan, 5; and subsidies, 219; views as trade negotiator, 219, 255, 336 (n. 2); and Adam Smith, 293 (n. 4)

Freedom to trade, 1–3, 5

Freeman, Orville, 191, 199

Free-rider problem, 152, 208, 222

Free trade: theory of, xvii–xviii; vision of, 2–4, 29; Raymond's critique of, 16; postponed after War of 1812, 18–20, 26; Monroe on, 20; Clay's criticism of, 21; and Democrats, 25; and ruin, 28–30, 34; T. Roosevelt on, 30; McKinley on, 30–33; Shortridge on, 31; Morrill on, 31, 279–80; Joseph Wharton on, 34; W. Wilson on, 43; Puerto Rico and, 78; and reciprocal trade program, 146; Truman on, 159; Nixon on, 243; favored by American elite, 280, 285; Karl Marx supports, 286, 299 (n. 7); and prosperity, 292 (nn. 14, 16); defined, 293 (nn. 2, 5); Kelley on, 300 (n. 18). *See also* Cobden, Richard; Cobdenism; Economic internationalism; Mill, John Stuart; Smith, Adam

"Free trade and sailor's rights," 18, 297 (n. 54)

Frelinghuysen, Frederick T., 69

Fremling, Gertrud, 115

Frenzel, Bill, 273

Friedman, Milton, 115

Fruit, fresh and canned, 149, 174. *See also* Apples

Fur, 121, 222; hatters', 228

Galbraith, John Kenneth, 202

Gallatin, Albert, 17

Gallinger, Jacob: attributes prosperity to protection, 30

Gallup Poll, 209

Garlic, 229–30

Gasoline, 108

Gelatin, edible, 222

General Accounting Office, U.S., 272

General Agreement on Tariffs and Trade (GATT), xv, xix, xx, 132, 192, 209, 212, 254, 266–67, 282, 285–86, 324 (n. 73); and Japan, 169; Kennedy Round, 180; and escape clause (Article 19), 226; and antidumping code (1967), 258, 270, 332 (nn. 70, 71); and Tokyo Round codes, 273 and Uruguay Round, 275–76, 284–86

General Electric Company, 206, 213

Generalized System of Preferences (GSP), 335 (n. 130)

General Motors Corporation, 129, 213

Geneva Round (1947), 160–64, 177, 196, 224, 282, 324–25 (nn. 80–82)

George III (king of England), 7

Germany, xvii, 50, 54, 75–76, 86, 91–93, 146, 150, 157, 165, 303 (n. 4); Zollverein treaty with, 63–66; and Smoot-Hawley Tariff, 117–19, 127; and Kennedy Round, 194, 199; and escape clause, 234–37; and antidumping, 260–61, 264–65; and countervailing duties, 264–66

Gerry, Elbridge, 8

Gerstacker, Carl, 212

Gibson, Hugh, 121

Gilbert, Carl, 200

Ginghams, 175

Glass, 14, 118, 121, 127, 182, 236, 244, 329 (n. 12), 334 (n. 75)

Glassware, 169, 172, 174

Global village, 278, 288

Gloves, 114, 121, 170, 175, 267

Glue, 118

Democrats, 34–36, 94–95; and nine-teenth-century tariff battles, 37–42; and reciprocity, 59–98 passim; presses tobacco exports, 63–65; and Kennedy Round, 185–90. *See also* Congress, U.S.; House Appropriations Committee; House Education Committee; House Ways and Means Committee

House Ways and Means Committee, U.S., 62, 71, 73–74, 321 (n. 32); on executive delegation, 74, 318 (n. 4); and Cuban reciprocity, 79–80; Dalzell on Canadian reciprocity, 83–84; and Fordney-Mc-Cumber Act, 89; and Hull's dissent to Hawley bill, 94; originates tariff bills, 104; on reciprocal trade (1943), 156–57; hearings on Kennedy Round results, 210; Mills bill, 214; Republican criticisms of escape clause, 228; and Republican views on escape clause, 228; in 1958, 241; and fastener industry, 250; and unfair trade enforcement, 270–74, 345 (n. 57). *See also* Dalzell, Charles; Dingley, Nelson; Doughton, Robert; Fordney, Joseph; Frenzel, Bill; Hawley, Willis; Kelley, William D.; McKinley, William; Madison, James; Mills, Roger Q.; Mills, Wilbur; Morrill, Justin; Payne, Sereno; Reed, Daniel; Rostenkowski, Dan; Schneebeli, Herman; Tucker, John R.; Underwood, Oscar; Vanik, Charles; Wilson, William L.

Howard, Esme, 118–20

Hughes, Charles Evans, 91

Hughes, Kent, 214

Hull, Cordell, 27, 35, 44–45, 77, 94, 152–53, 157, 177, 211; supports bargaining tariff, 94–98, 309 (n. 126); and Smoot-Hawley Tariff, 117, 281; trade philosophy of, 140, 141, 318 (n. 6); as tariff revolutionary, 141, 281–82; favors reciprocity for economic appeasement, 148, 321 (n. 32); and Tariff Commission, 226–27; on countervailing duty enforcement, 257, 266

Hume, David, 4

Humphrey, George, 168, 177, 326 (n. 107)

Humphrey, Hubert, 196

Hungary, 91, 92, 125, 129

Iceland, 155, 237–38

Ickes, Harold, 223

Iguchi, Sadao, 174

Immigration, 56

Imports: agricultural, 108; composition of U.S., 24, 53. *See also* Exports; Trade balance

India, 247, 287

Industrial policy, 2, 14–18, 56–58, 62, 143–44, 244, 303 (n. 9), 319 (n. 11); and Japan, 171–72, 177, 327 (n. 119); and Harley-Davidson case, 253

Injury: reciprocity without, 77–78, 220, 306 (n. 60), 318 (n. 6); F. Roosevelt's pledge, 142; State Department assumes, 144–45; Truman's pledge, 159, 336 (n. 10); Kennedy and adjustment aid for, 185–86, 220, 241–42; Nixon seeks to remedy, 215, 242–44; Eisenhower on, 233; antidumping, 262, 266–69. *See also* Dumping; Escape clause; International Trade Commission; Safeguards; Tariff Commission, U.S.

Intellectual property, 90

Interior, U.S. Department of, 170, 236, 250

International Antidumping Code (1967), 198–99, 258, 267, 270, 273

International Cooperation Administration, U.S., 183, 236, 238

International News Service, 105

International Trade Commission, U.S. (ITC), xiii–xv, 135; on exchange rates, 203, 312 (n. 37); on machine tools, 207; on bicycles, 236; escape clause record of, 245, 255; and footwear, 246–47; and fasteners, 250; and automobiles, 251–52, 342 (nn. 109, 111); appointments to, 254; and dumping, 259; and semiconductors, 260; and unfair trade enforcement, 274–76; on automobile agreement results, 331 (n. 56)

International Trade Organization (ITO), 160–61, 224–26, 324 (n. 73)

Internet, 278

Iran, 155–56, 323 (n. 60)

Iron products, 25, 34, 60, 174

Italy, 76, 86, 117, 119, 123, 125, 128–29, 157,

166, 174, 183; in Kennedy Round, 195; and escape clause, 229, 233–37, 246–48

Jackson, Andrew, 20
Jackson, John, 276
Japan, xv–xix, 56, 86, 128, 140, 146, 157, 165, 184–85, 190, 222, 283; 1854 treaty with, 26; as free rider, 152, 208, 221; and tuna fish, 155; Eisenhower and Dulles on, 167; George Humphrey on, 168; membership in GATT, 169; negotiations with U.S., 169–76, 282, 327 (nn. 119–27), 328 (n. 128), 331 (n. 47); and automobiles, 171, 207–9; and Trade Expansion Act, 187; Kennedy Round, 195–96, 200–201; Ministry of International Trade and Industry (MITI), 200, 327 (n. 119); protectionism in, 203, 327 (n. 127); and televisions, 206, 271; and machine tools, 207–8; escape clause actions, 221, 234, 238–40, 246; social dumping of, 258; and semiconductors, 260; and antidumping cases, 264, 275; and fly catchers, 265
Jay, John, 7–9, 294 (n. 19)
Jay-Gardoqui agreement, 9
Jay Treaty (1794), 13
Jefferson, Thomas, xviii, 15, 27; on free trade, 2–4; *Notes on Virginia*, 3, 19; as minister to France, 7; trade principles of, 11–12; supports bilateral free trade, 12; favors retaliation, 12–13; "Report on Commerce," 12–13, 16, 63, 295 (n. 33); and embargo, 16–19; endorses domestic manufactures, 16–17, 19–20, 296 (n. 44); and dumping, 21
Jenner, William E., 328 (n. 133)
Jewelry, 174
Johnson, Hiram, 134, 318 (n. 4)
Johnson, Lyndon, 190, 243, 332 (n. 59); on Smoot-Hawley Tariff, 102; on Kennedy Round, 178, 184–202 passim; and textiles, 184–85, 201; on agriculture, 190; on automobile pact, 194; Tariff Commission appointments of, 242; and antidumping, 264
Johnson, Samuel, 4
Jones, M. Joseph, Jr.: *Tariff Retaliation*, 116, 125, 128, 314 (n. 72)

Jordan, Curtis C., 127
Jordan, Len B., 189
Judge, 32, 38–39, 40, 61, 73
Justice, U.S. Department of, 250

Kalijarvi, Thorsten V., 167
Kantor, Mickey, 283
Kaplowitz, Paul, 345 (n. 46)
Kasson, John J., 75–78, 93, 98–99, 306 (n. 53)
Kawasaki Company, 253
Kaysen, Carl, 191
Keck, Robert C., 268
Kelley, William D., 34, 50–51, 280; on England, 51; on free trade, 300 (n. 18)
Kellogg, Frank, 120
Kelly, William B., 316 (n. 112)
Kennedy, John F.: on Trade Expansion Act, 178; on U.S. imports, 179; and Dillon Round, 180–83; carpets, 182, 243; on textiles, 183–85; on adjustment assistance, 185; on Trade Expansion Act, 186–87, 241–42
Kennedy Round (1967), 53, 282; Geneva negotiations, 190–97; and nontariff barriers, 197–99, 202–3; results of, 197–210, 332 (n. 65); and antidumping, 198–99, 264, 270, 332 (n. 71); criticisms of, 201–2; retrospective on, 216–18
Kent, Fred, 111
Keppler, Joseph, 40
Keynes, John Mayard, xviii
Kiesinger, Kurt, 194
King, William L. MacKenzie, 120–21, 131, 152
Kirk, Alexander, 123
Kissinger, Henry, 214, 244, 247–49, 273
Knox, Philander Chase, 89
Kokusai Electronic Corporation, 260
Korea, South, 185, 247–49, 275, 287
Kottman, Richard, 152–53
Krock, Arthur, 138
Krugman, Paul, 56, 285

Labor, U.S. Department of, 170, 185, 201, 236, 249–50, 342 (n. 120)
Labor unions, 218; and Trade Expansion Act, 186–87; after Kennedy Round, 201–2

Meany, George, 187
Mercantilism, 1–4, 12–13, 14, 56–57. *See also*
  Economic nationalism; Protectionism
Messersmith, George S., 127, 156
Metzger, Stanley, 199, 241–42, 269, 326
  (n. 109), 345 (n. 46)
Mexico, 66–67, 69–70, 73, 156, 305 (n. 33),
  323 (n. 60); and escape clause, 223, 225,
  229, 232, 247, 249, 287
Michelson, Charles, 138
Milk, skim, 173
Mill, John Stuart, 292 (n. 16)
Millikin, Eugene D., 159, 166, 225, 235, 336
  (n. 12)
Mills, Roger Q., 35, 38
Mills, Wilbur, 187, 210, 214, 243, 329 (n. 17)
Molasses, 3, 66, 73–74
Moley, Raymond, 45, 147
Monosodium glutamate, 172
Monroe, James, 19–20, 297 (n. 54)
Montesquieu, 4
Moore, George, 206–7, 212, 242, 251
Morgan, John, 129
Morgenthau, Henry, 266
Morrill, Justin, 84, 99, 104, 286; on free
  trade, 30–31, 279–80; and reciprocity,
  59, 62–63, 67–73, 304 (nn. 31, 33), 305
  (nn. 35, 39); says State Department
  "pregnant" with admiration for reci-
  procity, 63; and Zollverein, 64, 66, 303
  (n. 16); and Hawaii, 70
Morrill Tariff (1861), 67
Most-favored-nation policy: in 1776 treaty
  plan, 5; and 1778 treaty with France, 5–6,
  26–27, 294 (nn. 16, 17, 19); and treaties
  with China and Japan, 26; 1815 British
  agreement, 64, 66, 303 (n. 18); unconditional clause (1923) in, 90–93; reciprocal
  trade and, 145–47; defined, 293 (n. 2);
  and Hull, 309 (n. 126)
Motorcycles, 252–53, 340 (n. 75)
Motorola, Inc., 213
Mott, James, 135
Mundt, Karl, 189
Munich, 100, 281
Murphy, Robert, 129
Murray Bay, Quebec, 83
Mushrooms, 253

Musical instruments, 63, 114, 205
Mussolini, Benito, 123
Mutual Security Agency, U.S., 238

Naples, 8
National Association of Manufacturers, 62,
  110, 186
National Machine Tool Builders Associa-
  tion, 187, 210
National Reciprocity Convention, 76
Navigation Acts, 5
National Security Council, U.S., 176, 194,
  244, 246–49, 345 (n. 40)
Nationwide Committee of Industry, Agri-
  culture, and Labor on Import-Export
  Policy, 267–68
Netherlands, 76, 117–18, 221; and 1782
  treaty, 7, 294 (n. 19)
Nevin, John, 272
New England, 4, 10, 14, 237, 240
New Haven Clock Company, 222
New Jersey, 36
Newquist, Donald, xiv
Newsprint, 128, 261, 307 (n. 81)
New York, 10
New York Herald Tribune, 104, 133
New York Times, xiv, 105, 109–10, 124, 136
New York World, 120
New Zealand, 125, 131
Nicaragua, 76, 92, 221
Nippon Electric, Inc., 259
Nippon Times, 173
Niskanen, William, 252
Nixon, Richard M., 200, 203; on true reci-
  procity, 178, 213; provides adjustment
  assistance, 205–8, 247; on future negoti-
  ations, 211–12; emphasizes enforcement
  of trade laws, 211–12, 270; and anti-
  dumping enforcement, 211–13; initiates
  Tokyo Round, 215; and escape clause,
  242–47; and footwear, 246–48
Nontariff barriers. *See* Kennedy Round
Norris, George, 110
North American Free Trade Agreement
  (NAFTA), 30, 281, 287, 347 (n. 8)
North Atlantic Treaty Organization
  (NATO), 237–38
Norway, 92, 117, 155, 174, 237–38

Norwood, Janet, 189
Nuts. *See* Fasteners

Ohlin, Bertil, xvii–xviii
Ohmae, Kenichi, 259
Oil, lubricating, 170
Olive oil, 119, 170, 123, 314 (n. 69)
Optical products, 76, 169
Orderly Marketing Agreements (OMAs),
    248. *See also* Voluntary restraint agree-
    ments
Osborne, John Ball, 128
Otabe, K., 171–75
Ottawa agreements, 130, 149, 151, 160

Packing house products, 130
Pac-man video game, xiv
Paine, Thomas: *Common Sense*, 2
Paint, 14
Pakistan, 164
Paper, 76
Parker, Joseph, 207, 212
Pastore, John, 183, 194
Pauper labor. *See* Cheap labor
Payne, Sereno, 104
Payne-Aldrich Tariff (1909), 82–83, 88–89,
    104, 112
Pearl Harbor, 100
Pears, 130
Pearson, Lester, 194
Peek, George N., 146–47, 221
Pennsylvania, 10, 36
Peril points, 181–83, 189, 329 (n. 14)
Perot, Ross, 103, 112
Perry, Matthew C., 26
Persia, 92
Peru, 176, 237, 249, 323 (n. 62)
Petersen, Howard, 329 (n. 13)
Petroleum, 108, 130, 176, 222–23, 311 (n. 24)
Pharmaceuticals, xiv
Philippines, 78–82
Phillips, John, 229
Phillips, Kevin, 285
Phillips, William, 145, 221
Physiocrats, 4
Pianos, 244
Pierce, Franklin, 24, 25, 66, 73
Pillowcases, cotton, 175

Pinckney, Charles C., 9
Pinkerton, Julian, 127
Pipes, brier tobacco, 234–35, 238, 338
    (n. 46)
Platt amendment, 79
Plywood, 175, 239, 268
Poland, 92, 265
Polk, James K., 23–25, 36, 66, 73; and free
    trade, 298 (n. 79)
Pork, xiv, 144, 152, 322 (n. 42)
Portland Oregonian, 135–36
Portugal, 8, 76, 86, 263
Potatoes, xiv
Pottery, 158, 168
Poultry, 182
Preeg, Ernest, 196, 204, 331 (n. 46)
Prestowitz, Clyde, xvi
Prochnik, Edgar, 118
Protectionism: xvii, 56–57; and Tariff of
    1789, 13–14, 296 (n. 38); Jackson on, 20;
    and American System, 20–25; and pros-
    perity, 28–58; and revenue surplus,
    46–48; and economic growth, 50–56;
    for equalizing costs of production, 82;
    Eisenhower opposes, 167; conservative
    Republicans on, 168; Japanese recall
    American, 172; after Kennedy Round,
    201–2, 209–10; Reagan on, 248; Bush
    on, 280; in Russia, 301 (n. 65); in Ger-
    many, 303 (n. 4). *See also* Economic
    nationalism
Prunes, 123, 183, 314 (n. 69)
Prussia, 8, 63
Public Advisory Board for Mutual Secu-
    rity, 158, 326 (n. 101)
Public opinion, 209
Puck, 40, 41, 72
Puerto Rico, 69, 78, 80, 170, 222
Purcell, Harry, 187–88

Quotas: after Kennedy Round, 202, 209–
    10; and Burke-Hartke, 214–15

Rabbit skins, 118
Radio, 127, 158, 172, 188, 206; cellular, 260
Raisins, 171–73
Rambouillet Economic Summit (1975),
    249

Randall, Clarence, 239

Rashish, Myer, 329 (n. 13)

Raskob, John J., 95

Raspberries, 258

Rattan furniture, 118

Rayburn, Sam, 336 (n. 10)

Raymond, Daniel, 280; on duty of legislator, 17; *Thoughts on Political Economy*, 17, 299 (n. 15); favors high tariffs, 296 (n. 50)

Rayon staple fiber, 344 (n. 40)

Reagan, Ronald, xiii, 29; on Smoot-Hawley Tariff, 102–3; on escape clause, 245, 248–50, 254; and Harley-Davidson, 253

Reciprocal Trade Agreements Program (RTAP), xv, 135, 146, 177, 189, 214, 266, 318 (nn. 4, 6), 336 (nn. 7, 10); enacted, 141–42, 318 (n. 7); administered, 143–44; and Belgium, 144–45; and most-favored-nation policy, 145–46; and Switzerland, 146–47; and economic appeasement, 148–53; and U.K., 148–53, 321–22 (nn. 35–42); and Canada, 152–54; and Turkey, 153–54; as instrument of foreign policy, 153–57, 224; and Iceland, 154; and Venezuela, 154; and Cuba, 154, 156; and Mexico, 154, 156, 323 (n. 61); and Peru, 154, 156, 323 (n. 62); and Uruguay, 154, 323 (n. 57); and Iran, 154–55, 323 (n. 60); and Argentina, 154–56; and Geneva Conference (1947), 160–62; and Torquay Conference, 162–64; and discrimination, 164–65; and Japan, 168–75; renewal of, 175–76, 181, 224, 228–29, 241, 321 (n. 32), 328 (n. 10); and domestic opinion, 209; agreements concluded, 319 (n. 14); tariff cuts realized, 324 (n. 80)

Reciprocity, 4–9, 11, 62–63, 279; and Canada, 25–26, 66–68, 70–71, 83–84, 304 (nn. 27, 28, 31), 305 (n. 41), 307 (n. 8); in 1890 Tariff, 42; Morrill on, 59, 70; and Zollverein treaty, 63–66; and Hawaii, 66, 69; and Mexico, 66, 69–70; Congressional resistance to, 67–70, 304 (n. 33); Blaine's bargaining approach, 70–74, 93–94; and Dingley Tariff, 75–77, 306 (n. 52); and Puerto Rico, 78; and Cuba, 79–80; and Philippines, 80–81; U.S. Tar-

iff Commission study on, 87; and Hull program, 141–77 passim; and balanced concessions, 163, 303 (n. 12); and unilateral U.S. concessions, 165–67, 326 (n. 109); in Kennedy Round, 194–96, 204; Stans on, 213; defined, 293 (n. 2)

Redfield, William, 261

Reed, Daniel, 235

Reed, Thomas, 67

Refrigerators, 127

Rehm, John, 334 (n. 111)

Reineck, Walter S., 128

Reisman, Simon, xvi

Republican Party, 35; embraces protectionism, 29–34, 38–45, 281; resistance to tariff reduction, 67–81, 168; conversion to Cobdenism, 177. *See also* House of Representatives, U.S.; Senate, U.S.

Republican platform: in 1888, 38; in 1892, 42; in 1896, 28, 47; in 1900, 42, 77; in 1904, 42; in 1908, 43, 82; in 1912, 43; in 1916, 43; in 1920, 43, 88; in 1924, 43; in 1928, 43; in 1932, 44; in 1936, 299 (n. 12); in 1968, 211

Retaliation, 11–13, 21, 27, 82–83, 86–87, 89; Fordney-McCumber Act, Section 317, 90, 92, 210, 215, 295 (nn. 31, 35), 308 (n. 88); Smoot-Hawley Act, Section 338, 314 (nn. 80, 81)

Revenue Act of 1916, 261

Revenue Act of 1932, 108, 311 (n. 24)

Rey, Jean, 195

Rhode Island, 10

Rhodesia, 150–51

Ribicoff, Abraham, 193

Rice, 1, 22, 63–64, 149, 156, 182

Ritchie, Charles, 194

Rogers, James G., 96,

Rogers, Will, xiii

Rogers, William, 247

Rohr, David, xiv, 342 (n. 111)

Roosevelt, Franklin D., 74, 95, 99, 142, 157, 282–83; attacks Smoot-Hawley Tariff, 44–45, 102; in 1932 campaign, 44–45, 138, 147, 301 (n. 53); favors protection, 45, 147; and RTAP, 142; and United Kingdom agreement, 153; and escape clause, 221–22, 224, 235–37; and antidumping,

264; and countervailing duties on German imports, 266; and Iceland, 303
Roosevelt, Theodore: supports protection, 29–30, 299 (nn. 6, 9), 306 (n. 60); and Cuba, 68; and Kasson treaties, 77; and reciprocity, 78–81; and tariff reforms, 81
Root, Elihu, 79
Roper poll, 209
Rossides, Eugene, 212, 257, 270
Rostenkowski, Dan, 276
Roth, William, 191–96
Rubber: goods, 118, 168, 172; natural, 161–62, 321 (n. 40), 325 (n. 82)
Rubik's cube, xiv
Rugs, 114
Rumania, 92
Russia, 50, 62, 86; protectionism in, 301 (n. 65)
Ryder, Oscar, 154, 223, 226–32,
Rye, 265

Sachs, Jeffrey, 286
Safeguards, 215–16. *See also* Injury
Safety pins, 240
Sago, 222
St. Croix, 76
Salem Oregon Statesman, 135–36
Salmon, 160
Salt, 6
Salvador, 86, 92, 164
San Juan Economic Summit (1976), 249
Sayre, Francis B., 222, 226, 318–19 (nn. 9, 10)
Scarves, screen-printed silk, 238
Schattschneider, Elmer, 34–35
Schatz, Arthur W., 322 (n. 49)
Schneebeli, Herman, 243
Schnittker, John, 194, 332 (n. 67), 333 (n. 73)
Schuker, Stephen, 137
Schumpeter, Joseph, xv
Schuyler, Eugene, 27
Schwartz, Anna, 115
Schwinn Company, 223
Scientific apparatus, 166
Scientific tariff. *See* Flexible tariff
Scissors and shears, 236–37
Scowcroft, Brent, 247
Screws. *See* Fasteners
Scrugham, James, 320 (n. 28)

Semiconductors, 206, 259, 260
Senate, U.S.: and high-tariff Republicans, 30–33; and low-tariff Democrats, 34–36; and nineteenth-century tariff battles, 37–42; rejects Zollverein treaty, 65–66; skeptical of Kennedy Round, 185–90. *See also* Congress, U.S.; Senate Commerce Committee; Senate Finance Committee; Senate Foreign Relations Committee
Senate Commerce Committee, U.S., 183–84
Senate Finance Committee, U.S., 67–70, 71, 76, 78–79, 117, 119, 308 (n. 88), 320 (n. 32); on 1958 RTAP renewal, 175–76, 328 (n. 10); on Kennedy Round, 192–94, 333 (n. 78); on antidumping, 199, 270, 332 (nn. 70, 71); on 1974 Trade Act, 215–16; on escape clause, 244–45, 340 (n. 76); on dumping and subsidies, 343 (n. 1). *See also* Aldrich, Nelson; Long, Russell; McCumber, Porter; Millikin, Eugene D.; Morrill, Justin; Sherman, John; Simmons, Furnifold; Smoot, Reed
Senate Foreign Relations Committee, U.S., 65, 76
Setser, Vernon, 6
Seward, William, 68–69
Sewing machines, 169
Shakes and shingles, 253, 255
Shatz, Howard, 286
Sheffield, Lord, 7
Sherman, John, 38, 71
Shipbuilding, 259
Shipping restrictions, 14, 296 (n. 39)
Shoes. *See* Footwear
Sholes, Walter, 129
Shortridge, Samuel, 31
Sidgwick, Henry, 286
Silk, 3, 63–64, 122
Simmons, Furnifold, 104
Simmons, Richard, 271–72
Simon, William, 247, 249, 273, 341 (n. 99)
Singapore, 56, 185
Slaughtering. *See* Dumping
Slichter, Sumner, 136
Slottje, Daniel J., 286
Smathers, George, 193
Smith, Adam, 2–4, 16–17, 141, 263; *Wealth*

of Nations, 2, 4, 16–17; and Ben Franklin, 293 (n. 4)

Smith, Alfred E., 44

Smith, Marshall, 173

Smith-Corona Marchant Company, 188

Smoot, Reed, 310 (n. 1); on America first, 31; and Smoot-Hawley Tariff, 100–139 passim; legislative workhorse, 105; defeat of, 135–36, 316 (n. 116)

Smoot-Hawley Tariff (1930), 23, 44, 95, 96, 99, 100–139, 143, 215, 281, 285; as metaphor for policy failure, xii, 100, 281; and popular wisdom, xviii, 101–3; in 1932 campaign, 45; or Hawley-Smoot, 103–5; as highest tariff, 106–9, 311 (n. 25); expands free list, 109, 311 (nn. 26, 27); and stock market crash, 109–12; and depression, 112–15; and retaliation, 115, 124–32, 281, 314 (nn. 72, 81); and foreign protests, 116–24, 281, 312 (nn. 47, 49, 50); and exports, 125–32; and automobiles, 129–30; and Ottawa Conference, 130; and Canada, 130–32, 315 (n. 99); and protest of economists, 132–34, 316 (n. 104); and 1932 politics, 135–36, 316 (n. 116); and political issue, 137–38, 317 (n. 123); bargaining down of, 160; Reagan on, 254; and countervailing duties, 263; votes on, 317 (n. 121)

Social dumping, 258

Soft drinks, 170

Solomon, Anthony, 194

Sorghum, 182

South Africa, 128

Soviet Union, xix, 56, 155–57, 176, 215, 230, 236–38, 280, 287

Soybeans, 172

Space amplifiers, 259–60

Spain, 7–8, 69, 73, 74, 76, 86, 91–93, 117, 119, 125–27; footwear, 246–48

Sparklers, xiv

Special trade representative, U.S., 190–91, 194–96, 210, 329 (n. 17)

Spirit of Commerce, 1–3

Sporting goods, 182, 340 (n. 75)

Spring-Rice, C., 85–86

Stans, Maurice, 212, 213

Stanwood, Edward, 15

State, U.S. Department of: and bargaining approach, 62–63; and reciprocity, 62–99 passim, 94–99; and Zollverein Treaty, 63–66; and Smoot-Hawley, 117–31; promotes imports, 136–37, 142–47, 149, 158–59, 165–67, 179, 283, 319 (nn. 11, 12), 320 (n. 36), 326 (n. 109); and RTAP, 141–43; and economic appeasement, 148–53; and Argentina, 154–55; accedes to unilateral concessions, 158, 165–67, 326 (n. 109); views trade surplus as problem, 158–59; and Geneva Round, 160–62; and Torquay, 162–63, 325 (nn. 81, 82); opposed to import restraints, 165–66, 176–77, 243; and Japan, 168–75, 327 (n. 121), 331 (n. 47); and Dillon Round, 180–83, 329 (nn. 14–17); and textile restraints, 183–85, 251, 329 (n. 20); post– Kennedy Round, 209; and escape clause administration, 221–44 passim; opposes vigorous unfair trade law administration, 264–71; Congress dissatisfied with, 329 (n. 17). *See also* Adams, John Quincy; Blaine, James G.; Calhoun, John C.; Everett, Edward; Fish, Hamilton; Foster, John W.; Frelinghuysen, Frederick; Hay, John; Hughes, Charles Evans; Hull, Cordell; Jefferson, Thomas; Kissinger, Henry; Knox, Philander Chase; Marcy, William; Rogers, William; Seward, William; Wheaton, Henry

Steagall, Jeffrey W., xiv

Steel, 34, 46, 55, 76, 157, 182, 201, 217, 231, 255, 259, 321 (n. 39); dumping, xiv, 260, 270–73; and Smoot-Hawley Tariff, 114, 130, 132–33; and Belgian reciprocity, 144–45, 221, 320 (n. 15); and escape clause, 221, 242, 252, 255, 340 (n. 75)

Steel, specialty, 128, 246, 249, 272, 340 (n. 75)

Stern, Paula, xiv, 251, 342 (n. 114)

Stevens, Raymond, 154, 222

Stevens, Robert, 175

Stewart, Andrew, 1, 25, 29

Stewart, Eugene, 242

Stewarts and Lloyds, 270

Stitt, Nelson, 187, 330 (n. 33)

Strange, Susan, 137

Strauss, Robert, 249–50

Stimson, Henry L., 118–20, 123

Strackbein, O. R., 267–68

Sturgeon, Leo D., 128

Subsidies, 219, 263, 273. *See also* Countervailing duties

Sugar, 3, 66, 71, 73, 74, 263; Hawaiian, 66,
69; Cuban, 79–81, 156, 307 (n. 70), 324
(n. 63); Philippine, 80–81; and Smoot-
Hawley Tariff, 108, 114, 125, 136; products
of, 174; Peruvian, 323 (n. 62)

Sulphite wrapping paper, 174

Suomela, John, 275

Surgical instruments, 169

Suzuki Company, 253

Swank, James M., 57, 62

Sweden, 7, 86, 117, 128–29, 174, 221, 232, 264,
268, 272

Switzerland, 20, 76, 117, 121–22, 125, 147–48,
221–23, 230–31, 265, 337 (n. 32)

Synthetic fibers, 170–71, 184, 251

Synthetic Organic Chemical Manufacturers Association, 210

Table damask, 170

Taft, Robert A., 337 (n. 12)

Taft, William H., 82–84

Taft-Hartley Act, 231

Taiwan, 185, 202, 247–49, 275

Talmadge, Herman, 194

Tanning extracts, 174

Tape recorders, 174

Tapioca, 222

Tarbell, Ida, 34, 300 (n. 19)

Tariff: as instrument of foreign policy,
4–13, 18–22, 27, 63–67, 68–78, 78–87,
90–93, 148–77, 282; and consumers, 16,
21–22, 31–33, 35–36, 38, 55, 88, 307 (n. 76);
first protective, 22; average duties on
all imports, 23, 42, 46–47, 52–55, 85, 88,
106–7, 112–13; and economic growth,
24, 50–56, 112–13; for revenue only,
24–25, 35–36; average duties on dutiable
imports, 28, 42, 46, 52–55, 88, 106–8,
112–13, 140; and percentage of imports
duty free, 42, 47, 107–9; and budget surplus, 46–47; comparative levels (1913),
52; multiple-schedule, 60–61, 82; bar-

gaining, 71, 74, 82–83, 85–89; unilateral
reduction in, 85; effects of changes in,
113–14, 311 (n. 35), 312 (nn. 36–38); scientific approach to, 134–35, 316 (n. 112);
protective effect of, 310 (n. 17); specific
vs. ad valorem duties in, 311 (n. 19); and
war debt payments, 312 (n. 42); flexible,
314 (n. 69); reduction in U.S., 317 (n. 1),
324 (n. 80)

Tariff Act of 1789, 13–14, 296 (n. 38)

Tariff Act of 1816, 22

Tariff Act of 1824, 22–23

Tariff Act of 1828. *See* Tariff of Abominations

Tariff Act of 1833, 23

Tariff Act of 1846. *See* Walker Tariff

Tariff Act of 1857, 25, 298 (n. 82)

Tariff Act of 1861. *See* Morrill Tariff

Tariff Act of 1890. *See* McKinley Tariff

Tariff Act of 1894. *See* Wilson-Gorman Tariff Act

Tariff Act of 1897. *See* Dingley Tariff Act

Tariff Act of 1909. *See* Payne-Aldrich Tariff

Tariff Act of 1913. *See* Underwood-
Simmons Act

Tariff Act of 1921 (emergency tariff), 88

Tariff Act of 1922. *See* Fordney-McCumber
Tariff

Tariff Act of 1930. *See* Smoot-Hawley Tariff

Tariff Commission, U.S. (TC), xiv, 142–43,
192, 199, 212; and Canadian reciprocity,
26, 67, 84; and 1932 campaign, 44; on
Kasson agreements, 76; on Cuban preferences, 80; on Payne Aldrich, 83; *Reciprocity and Commercial Treaties*, 87; and
flexible tariff, 89–90, 97; on reciprocity,
98; and impact of price decline on specific duties, 106–8; correlates higher
duties and import volumes, 114; and
flexible tariff, 119, 121–23, 134–35; and
trade discrimination, 127, 132, 203; on
U.K. agreement, 150–51; and velveteens,
170, 239, 340 (n. 66); on Japanese textiles, 175; on Kennedy Round results,
197, 204–5; Nixon appointments to, 212;
quotas on Swiss watches, 223, 230–31,
233–34; Congress prefers, 224; and
escape clause, 225; State Department

influence over, 226–27, 345 (n. 46); and garlic, 229–30; and brier pipes, 234–35, 338 (n. 46); and bicycles, 235–36; and safety pins, 240–41; and escape clause, 242; and Japanese dumping, 261; and antidumping, 269–74; and Japanese television, 271–72, 345 (n. 58)

Tariff of Abominations (1828), 23, 106

Taussig, Frank, 24, 87, 132, 289, 319 (n. 10)

Taylor, George, R., 24

Tea, 46, 73–75

Television, 158, 172, 188, 206, 246, 259, 271

Temin, Peter, 115, 137

Tetraethyl lead, 173

Textiles, 3, 25, 33, 55, 144, 149, 152, 157–58, 161, 163, 166, 221, 240, 255, 267, 322 (n. 50); dumping of, 21; and Smoot-Hawley Tariff, 121–22, 128, 133; and 1955 agreement with Japan, 169–76, 328 (nn. 130, 131); and Trade Expansion Act, 182–84; and Kennedy Round, 201, 205–6, 214–15, 217, 333 (n. 81); and escape clause, 206, 239, 242–43, 250–51

Thermometers, clinical, 175

Thomas, Elbert, 136

Thorp, Willard L., 319 (n. 11)

Thunberg, Penelope Hartland, 269

Thurmond, Strom, 189, 201

Thwaite, B. H.: *The American Invasion or England's Commercial Danger*, 60

Tile, 76, 174, 340 (n. 75)

Tires, 122, 127

Tobacco, xiv, 1, 9, 22, 24, 63–65, 79, 149–51, 160, 170, 183, 307 (n. 67), 322 (n. 42)

Tokyo Round (1979), 215–16, 249–50, 273–74

Tomatoes, 119, 123

Tomato paste, 173

Tonka, 75

Torquay Conference (1951), 162–63, 325 (n. 90)

Tourism, 123

Toyo cloth caps, 175

Toys, 169, 343 (n. 11)

Trade Act of 1974, 200–201, 215–16, 244–45

Trade Agreements Act of 1979, 262

Trade Agreements Extension Act (1951), 229–30

Trade balance, 144, 158, 177, 202–3, 218, 333 (n. 86), 335 (n. 123)

Trade Expansion Act of 1962, 184, 193, 199, 216; Kennedy on, 178; hearings, 187–88; approved, 188–90, 330 (nn. 38, 39)

Trade Expansion Act of 1968, 210

"Trade, not aid" policy, 158–59, 164–65, 230, 235, 309, 324

Trade Policy Committee, 182, 252

Trade Policy Staff Committee, 250

Trade representative, U.S., 249–50, 270

Trading interests, xix–xx, 282–89; and Jay-Gardoqui negotiations, 9; and Zollverein treaty, 63–66; pre–Civil War, 66–67; Republican resistance to, 67–70; and Blaine, 70–74; and Kasson treaties, 75–77; and State Department strategy for, 92–93, 98–99, 141–42; McKinley, T. Roosevelt and reciprocity without injury, 77–78; Taft and Canadian reciprocity, 82–84; and Committee on Trade Agreements, 143–44; and British agreement (1938), 152–53; reciprocity as tool of wartime diplomacy, 153–57; at Geneva (1947), 161–62, 325 (nn. 81, 82); at Torquay (1951), 162–63; and postwar trade discrimination, 164–65; in 1955 Japanese negotiations, 170–75, 327 (n. 121); and Dillon Round, 181–83; and textiles, 183–85, 250–51, 329 (n. 20); and Kennedy Round, 192–97, 211–14; in escape clause administration, 230–40, 243, 246–50; in unfair trade enforcement, 264–70; in 1953, 326 (n. 109)

Transformers, 272

Travertine stone, 119

Treadway, Allen, 318 (n. 6)

Treasury, U.S. Department of, xx, 185, 193, 234, 236, 250; and RTAP, 143; and 1921 antidumping act, 261–63; countervailing duties, 263–66; enforcement vagaries, 264–67; defers to State Department, 265, 268, 344 (nn. 32, 40); moves against Nazi Germany and Japan, 266; accused of star-chamber proceedings, 268–69, 343 (n. 19); antidumping record, 269; during Nixon years, 270; and steel industry, 270–72; and Japanese televisions, 271–72;

and William Simon, 273. *See also* Fowler, Henry; Humphrey, George; Morgenthau, Henry; Simon, William

Treaty of Amity and Commerce, Franco-American (1778), 5, 219, 294 (n. 17)

Treaty plan of 1776, 5–8, 294 (n. 14)

Trecker, Francis J., 187

Tropical products, 71, 73, 79

Trowbridge, Alexander, 194, 199

Trucks, 127

Truman, Harry S.: and Smoot-Hawley Tariff, 100, 102; on import competition, 158; offers no-injury pledge, 159, 166, 224; and Geneva Round (1947), 160–62; and Torquay Conference, 163; speech at Baylor University, 225; and escape clause, 225–34, 243; and antidumping, 264; on trade barriers, 324 (n. 69)

Tucker, John R., 35

Tuna fish, 155, 156, 171, 172, 232, 239

Turkey, 92–93, 128, 153–54

Turkeys, 174

Tuscany, 8

Twine, 222

Tyler, John, 63

Typewriters, 59, 120–21, 133, 165, 172, 188; ribbons for, 87

Umbrella frames, 175, 239

Underwood, Oscar, 35–36, 104

Underwood-Simmons Act (1913), 47, 48, 53, 85–86, 88, 104, 108, 112, 261, 308 (n. 88)

Unfair trade, xix, 254–55, 257–77. *See also* Antidumping; Countervailing duties

United Autoworkers, 218

United Kingdom, xiv, xix, 1, 14, 92–93, 146, 157, 166, 175, 183, 184, 282; and 1778 Treaty of Amity and Commerce, 5–6, 219; during Confederation, 7–9; and Jay Treaty, 12–13; and dumping, 18–19, 260, 269–70; promotes free trade in America, 25, 36, 164, 298 (n. 81), 300 (nn. 25, 29); reporting from Washington, 29; economic growth in, 50–52; declining share of world trade, 51; convention of 1815, 64, 66, 303 (n. 18); and Kasson treaties, 76; on Payne-Aldrich Tariff, 82; on

Underwood-Simmons Act, 85–86; and imperial preferences, 89, 92, 149–53, 160–65, 322 (n. 42), 325 (nn. 81, 82); and empire preferences, 89, 160–62, 322 (n. 42), 325 (nn. 81, 82); on Collier Tariff, 97; and Smoot-Hawley Tariff, 117–20, 124–25, 130, 132; and 1938 agreement, 148–53, 159, 322–23 (nn. 41–51); and 1947 agreement, 161–62, 325 (nn. 81, 82); and rubber, 162, 321 (n. 40), 325 (n. 82); and Torquay, 162–63; and free-trade propaganda, 164; opposes Japanese membership in GATT, 170; and EEC, 185–90; and Kennedy Round, 195; dollar crisis (1971), 215; and exports to U.S. (1941), 223; and escape clause cases, 225, 234–36, 248; and antidumping, 264–65, 270; tariff of, 322 (n. 41)

United Nations, 283

United Nations Conference on Trade and Development (UNCTAD), 191, 209, 287

United Press, 105

United Steelworkers, 218

United Textile Workers, 202

Uruguay, 127, 176, 323 (n. 57)

Uruguay Round (1994), 275–76, 281, 284–86, 347 (n. 19)

U.S.-Japan Trade Council, 187

Vacuum cleaners, 114

Valenti, Jack, 284

Valuation, customs, 23

Vandenberg, Arthur, 159, 166, 225, 324 (n. 72), 336 (n. 12)

Vanik, Charles, 250, 257, 270, 273

Vanilla, 75

Veblen, Thorstein, 346 (n. 4)

Vegetable oils, 183

Velveteens, cotton, 169, 170, 172, 175, 340 (n. 66)

Venezuela, 74, 154, 176

Vergennes, 7

Vermont, 67–68

Vietnam, 100, 185, 194

Viner, Jacob, 343 (n. 1)

Virgin Islands, 222

Vitamins, 165

Voluntary restraint agreements, 239, 242, 252, 255, 265

Voorhees, Daniel W., 69, 104

Walker, Robert J., 25, 36, 65–66, 104, 141, 298 (n. 80)

Walker Tariff (1846), 25, 30

Wallace, George, 211

Wallis, W. Allan, xvii

Wall Street Journal, 103, 105,

Walnuts, shelled, 169

Wanniski, Jude, 109

Warren, Francis, 76

Washington, George, 282; and "Farewell Address," 10–11, 27, 279, 295 (n. 27); favors domestic manufactures, 14–15, 296 (n. 41); first annual message, 15

Washington Post, xiii, 104, 109, 131

War of 1812, 18

Watches, 121, 147–48, 221, 223, 233–34, 259, 332 (n. 37), 338 (n. 43)

Watson, James E., 317 (n. 121)

Webster, Daniel, 23; and House of Barings, 298 (n. 73)

Weeks, Sinclair, 168, 170, 177, 240, 324 (n. 72), 326 (n. 107)

Welles, Sumner, 154

Wells, David A., 46

West Indies, 6, 9, 76, 80, 117

Westinghouse Corporation, 272

Wharton, Joseph, 34

Wheat, 67, 121, 130, 149, 182; flour, 144

Wheaton, Henry, 63–66, 92, 98

Wheeler, Leslie, 319 (n. 10)

Whigs, 22–23, 30, 65, 67–68

White, C. Thayer, 170–75

White, Eric Wyndham, 192

White, Harry Dexter, 319 (n. 10), 320 (n. 15)

Whittier Mills, 206

Wilcox, Clair, 132, 325 (n. 81)

Williams, Albert, 213

Williams, James D., 269

Williams Commission. *See* Commission on International Trade and Investment Policy, U.S.

Wilson, Harold, 196

Wilson, Hugh, 121–22

Wilson, William L., 38, 104

Wilson, Woodrow, 35, 43, 48, 85, 87, 99, 280; and antidumping, 261

Wilson-Gorman Tariff Act, 62, 74

Wine, 75, 127

Wire netting, 118

Witte, Sergei, 50

Wolff, Alan, 345 (n. 58)

Woll, Matthew, 133

Wood pulp, 128, 266

Wool, 154, 306 (n. 55)

Woolen goods, 149, 152, 163, 182–84, 251. *See also* Textiles

World Trade Organization, 284. *See also* General Agreement on Tariffs and Trade (GATT); International Trade Organization (ITO)

Yalta, 100

Yamaha Company, 253

Yarn, 114, 182

Yeutter, Clayton, 341 (n. 99)

Yoshida, Shigeru, 167

Zambia, 249

Zeiler, Thomas, 200

Zenith Radio Corporation, 272

Zinc, 176, 222–23, 237, 239

Zollverein, 63–66, 99, 303 (n. 16), 304 (n. 20)